It's All About
Muhammad

It's All About Muhammad

*A Biography of the World's
Most Notorious Prophet*

F. W. Burleigh

ZENGA
BOOKS

Publisher's Cataloging-in-Publication data

   Burleigh, F. W.
      It's all about Muhammad : a biography of the world's
   most notorious prophet / by F.W. Burleigh. – First
   edition.
      pages cm
      Includes bibliographical references and index.
      LCCN 2014939154
      ISBN 978-0-9960469-3-0

      1. Muhammad, Prophet, -632—Biography. 2. Islam—
   History.   I. Title.
   BP75.B87 2014   297.6'3092
                           QBI14-600072

Published in the United States of America by:

Zenga Books
Portland, Oregon

Author blog: www.ItsAllAboutMuhammad.com

Cover illustration licensed from Clipart.com
Manufactured in the United States of America

This work quotes from *The Life of Muhammad* by al-Waqidi, © 2011 Rizwi Faizer. Published by Routledge. Reproduced by permission of Taylor
& Francis Books UK.

In memory of
Theo van Gogh

TABLE OF CONTENTS

PART III: DARKNESS AT NOON

LIST OF ILLUSTRATIONS

Introduction

It's All About Muhammad is based almost entirely on the original literature of Islam: the biography by Ibn Ishaq, the history of Tabari, the collections of traditions of Bukhari, Muslim, and Abu Dawud, and the work of Waqidi and his student Ibn Sad—canonical sources one and all. Many other important sources were also referred to, among them the Koran commentary and the biography by the 14th century scholar Ibn Kathir. All these works are amply cited in the chapter notes.

In all, twenty thousand pages of material were given line-by-line scrutiny. If readers find the Muhammad of this biography disturbing, it is because what is written about him in the original literature is disturbing. He was beyond all doubt an extremely violent man, and stories about his violence are found throughout the literature. Indeed, more than two-thirds of the canonical biographical materials have to do with the violence he used to spread his religion.

What is interesting is that none of the original writers seem to have been disturbed by this. They were committed believers who swore by the first "pillar" of Islam, the primary declaration of faith: There is but one God, and Muhammad is his messenger. They were convinced Muhammad could do no wrong since all that he did was in furtherance of Allah's cause, so they faithfully reported all that he did no matter how chilling, no matter how cold-blooded. In so doing, they provided abundant evidence of crimes of assassination, mass murder, plunder, enslavement, torture, and more. If these historical records are as authentic as Muslims believe them to be, Muhammad committed almost every

9

crime listed by the International Criminal Court as constituting crimes against humanity.

Muslims are obligated by their faith to follow the decrees of Muhammad's Koran. Many of his verses were intended as incitements to violence against people who rejected him. Muslims are also obligated to follow his *sunna*, his practices in advancing "Allah's" cause. This covers a lot of ground, but it includes the example of his brutality against people who refused to accept him and his religion. Muslims are violent because Muhammad was violent, plainly and simply. This has been so since the beginning of what he created fourteen hundred years ago, and this will continue for as long as what he created is allowed to continue.

Muhammad's penchant for violence was abnormal and needs to be explained. As this book will show, it was likely the product of an epileptic temporal lobe that gave him feelings of communing with the divine joined with a pathological psychology. He believed God commanded him to do whatever he did, no matter how ungodly, and he was obedient to his Lord. The evidence that he suffered from epileptic seizures can be found in the literature: instances of dropping to the ground; visions of light that dazzled before him; objects that remained in his field of vision no matter which direction he turned. In one of these episodes the froth of saliva spotted his cheeks. These are classic symptoms of the falling sickness, as epilepsy has been called. Even his contemporaries thought he was devil possessed—the ancient explanation for epilepsy.

That his epileptic experiences led him to believe God talked to him is one of the important themes of this book. Another is that he was clearly a psychopath, the product of unfortunate early life circumstances that he did not choose, but were imposed on him. His early childhood is explored in the book. He is understandable. He was a victim, but then became a victimizer. There are precise, scientific terms for his psychological complexities, but psychopath is a useful catch-all that does the chore of conveying that there was something dangerously flawed about him. What word but psychopath applies to a man who once directed the beheading of as many as nine hundred men and boys—one per minute for a solid fifteen hours—because they refused to accept him as their prophet? Hands tied behind their backs, they were dragged to the edge of a trench, and two of Muhammad's first cousins chopped off their heads while he sat nearby and watched. He was a cold-blooded killer, cruel and heartless to people who rejected him. In short, a psychopath.

These themes intertwine. They are like conjoined twins that can never be separated. His epileptic experiences brought him to believe God talked to him; the psychopath in him led him to kill people who refused to believe it. The resulting terror he created was the key to his success in imposing his religion, which was the product of his epileptic delusions.

This book contains twenty-five illustrations, all of them scenes inspired by the original literature. Half of them are graphic renditions of atrocities Muhammad committed. Muslims have a ban against "depicting" their prophet, and it is easy to see why: The truth about him is horrific, and depicting him opens up a Pandora's Box. A lot of headless bodies are stuffed inside that box. If you have no prior knowledge of this subject, it is possible to get a good idea about Muhammad and what he created just by examining these illustrations and reading the captions. Better yet is to read the entire book, including the chapter notes. There is a great benefit in doing so.

A few observations about vocabulary:

Many words that are usually found in writings about Muhammad are omitted in this work. Take the word "revelation," for example. The standard wording—even in books and articles authored by people who should know better—is that God "revealed" the Koran to Muhammad; he received "revelations"; God "handed down" verses to him. The unqualified use of the word in a book or article about Muhammad establishes that the author believes or gives credibility to the idea that Muhammad was divinely inspired. This, of course, is nonsense. If there truly were a God capable of coming up with what is in the Koran and transmitting it to someone like Muhammad, all of creation would rise up in rebellion. The phraseology of this book is disciplined: Muhammad was the author the Koran. He "came up" with verses; he "composed" verses. The Koran was his handiwork, his composition. These are plain, simple, and true statements, and these are the words used in this book to express the straightforward truth.

There are other offender words that are omitted, the greatest being the words "Islam" and "Muslim." Other than in this introduction, in quotations, or in the titles of books in the bibliography and chapter notes, these words are scrupulously avoided. This is because they contain a false idea. The word "Islam" means submission to God's will. What is false about this is that Muslims do not worship God. This is a truth that is not generally understood. What they worship is a God concept and nothing more, a concept that was created by Muhammad. And who was Muhammad? An epileptic psychopath, a man who murdered nine hundred men and boys in cold blood, one of a great number of horrific crimes against humanity he committed. His God concept was a reflection of who he was. He was violent and intolerant; his Allah is violent and intolerant. He had a magma chamber of hatred burning inside of him; his Allah erupts with it. He projected himself onto the cosmic screen and proclaimed the image to be God.

The same problem arises with the word "Muslim." It means a person who submits to God's will. The spectacle can be seen everywhere of people bowing down and touching or even banging their heads on the ground. They have been conditioned to think they are praying to God, but they are deceived. They are worshipers of a God concept formulated by an epileptic psychopath, a deluded mass murderer.

This book has labored to avoid these words because their use gives an endorsement, however unwitting, to the false idea they contain. Muhammadan and Muhammadanism are old words that have fallen out of use, but they are honest words, like saying Christian and Christianity in connection with what Jesus brought about, or Buddhist and Buddhism for what the Buddha inspired, and so forth. In the end, this book settles on "what Muhammad created" as the most honest formulation.

Why should you read this book? Blood, that's why, eventually even yours or that of your descendants. Around the globe people who follow in the footsteps of their master continue to kill people who do not. By some estimates—made before the slaughter of Christians, Yazidis, and others began in Syria and Iraq—someone was getting murdered somewhere in the world every thirty minutes by people who have been brainwashed into believing that God talked to Muhammad and instructed him to kill people who refused to pronounce the words of the first pillar of Islam: There is but one God, and Muhammad is his messenger.

As the events of the Middle East portend, the slaughter will get worse over time, and after it gets worse, it will get even worse than before. It will threaten you and everything you believe in unless you do something about it. But how can you do anything about it unless you know what it is all about?

It's All About Muhammad is prescriptive. It is not its intention for readers merely to walk away shaking their heads and saying, "How awful. How terrible!" It gives a way out; it offers an avenue for doing something about it. What Muhammad created can be gotten rid of. It is an aberration. It is evil overturning good and claiming to be what is good. It was imposed by violence, for there was no other way for it to succeed; it continues through violence, because it has no other way to sustain itself. Muhammad was not born in the full light of history, as has been claimed. He was born shrouded in the fog of mythology, hidden in a mist of lies. Blow away the fog and the mist and expose him to the light of reason and common sense and what he created will die an overdue death. This is already happening to some extent, but it needs an accelerant. The accelerant is discussed in the Epilogue.

It's All About Muhammad is a book of revelation. It reveals what needs to be revealed about one of the most disruptive and sinister personalities in history, and it reveals what can be done about what he created.

If you have doubts about any of this, then all the more reason to read on.

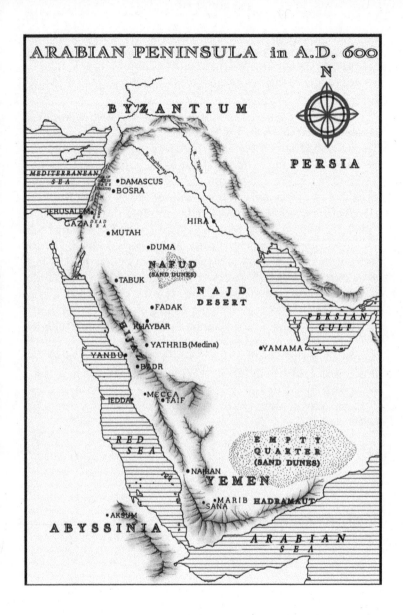

ARABIAN PENINSULA in A.D. 600

N

BYZANTIUM

PERSIA

MEDITERRANEAN SEA

• DAMASCUS
• BOSRA

JERUSALEM
GAZA • DEAD SEA
• MUTAH

HIRA •

• DUMA

NAFUD (SAND DUNES)

• TABUK

NAJD DESERT

• FADAK

KHAYBAR •

PERSIAN GULF

YANBU •

HIJAZ

• YATHRIB (Medina)

• BADR

• YAMAMA

JEDDA •
• MECCA
• TAIF

RED SEA

EMPTY QUARTER (SAND DUNES)

• NAJRAN

YEMEN

• MARIB HADRAMAUT
• SANA

• AKSUM

ABYSSINIA

ARABIAN SEA

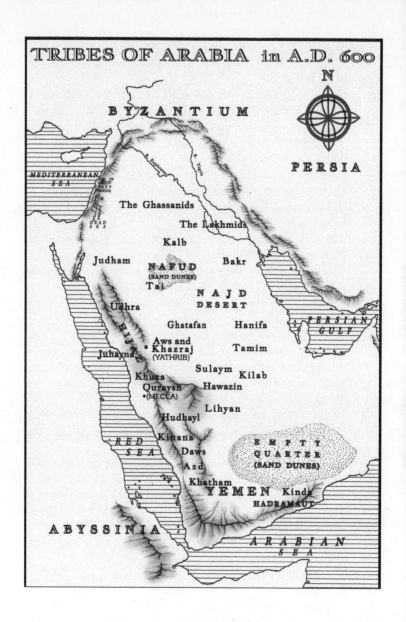

TRIBES OF ARABIA in A.D. 600

N

BYZANTIUM

PERSIA

MEDITERRANEAN SEA

The Ghassanids

The Lakhmids

Kalb

Judham

Bakr

NAFUD
(SAND DUNES)

Tai

NAJD
DESERT

Udhra

Ghatafan

Hanifa

PERSIAN
GULF

Aws and
Khazraj
(YATHRIB)

Tamim

Juhayna

Khuza

Sulaym

Kilab

Quraysh
(MECCA)

Hawazin

Lihyan

Hudhayl

RED
SEA

Kinana

EMPTY
QUARTER
(SAND DUNES)

Daws

Azd

Khatham

YEMEN

Kinda

HADRAMAUT

ABYSSINIA

ARABIAN
SEA

570   Birth in Mecca.

576   Orphaned, taken in by his grandfather, then an uncle.

595   Marries Khadija, a divorcee fifteen years older than him.

605   He helps reconstruct the moon temple of the Meccans into a cubic, roofed structure, from then on called the Kabah—the Cube—for its new shape.

610   Epileptic fits lead him to believe God talks to him.

613   He goes public with verses he claims come from God.

615   Religious conflict with the Meccans forces some of his followers to leave for Abyssinia.

616   The Meccans impose an economic and social boycott on Muhammad and his clan.

619   Khadija dies; he is betrothed to six-year-old Aisha; he goes public with the claim he was taken into heaven before the throne of God, who orders him and his followers to pray five times a day.

622   He declares war on all who refuse to accept him as "God's Messenger"; flees for his life to Yathrib (Medina) and builds a mosque—his *al-qaeda* for waging war on his enemies; marries Aisha, who is then nine years old.

623   He begins attacks on Meccan caravans.

624   Battle of Badr; assassination of poet-critics. The genocide of the Jews of Yathrib begins with the expulsion of the Qaynuqa Jews and the seizure of their property.

625   Battle of Uhud; expulsion of the Nadir Jews and the seizure of their property.

627   Battle of the Trench; mass murder of the Qurayza Jews.

628   Treaty of Hudaybiyya; conquest of the Jewish oasis of Khaybar.

629   Pilgrimage to Mecca where he rebrands the polytheist rituals of the moon temple as practices of Abraham.

630   Capitulation of Mecca; battle of Hunayn; seige of Taif; raid on Tabuk.

631   Capitulation of Taif.

632   Final pilgrimage to Mecca. He rebrands the sun worship practices of the polytheists at Arafat, Muzdalifa, and Mina as rituals of Abraham.

632   Death of Muhammad.

PART I

The Cave

CHAPTER I

Sanctuary

It began as a blaze in the night sky above the Hijaz, the land of the desert Arabs. It streaked downward like a sword slash and disappeared behind a mountain, gone in an instant.

The desert people saw it. They were always on the move in search of water and pasturage for their camels and goats, but at night they sat cross-legged around campfires and gazed at the heavens. They talked about the gods. The gods were everywhere, in rocks, in trees; even mountains had their lords, but the greatest were in the night sky: seven bright points that rotated against the blazing stillness. The moon was their ruler.

They had seen streaks of light before, but this one was brighter and burst into brilliance before it disappeared. The gods often hurled flaming darts to drive away the *jinn*, invisible beings that inhabited the desert and bedeviled humans, but this one seemed intended as a sign. At the first light of dawn the nomads, riding high on camels, drove their herds in the direction of the mountain where the flash had disappeared. They went up a gentle pass and down the other side into a valley covered with thorny trees so stunted from lack of water they were like bushes. While the women and children stopped to gather berries and watch the goats, the men nudged their camels farther down, following a dry riverbed that had been carved wide by occasional flash floods. Before long one of the youths shouted with excitement and the men rushed to look where he was pointing: Half buried in cratered dirt barely twenty paces from the riverbed was a round, blackened stone.

The only one who dared to touch it was the patriarch, a graybeard sheikh wearing a black turban and a flowing garment cinctured at the waist where he kept a dagger. After passing a trembling hand over the stone, he turned with a joyous look to his tribesmen and declared it to be a gift of the gods—a sure sign the valley was sacred. He ordered them to stack rocks into a pillar, and when it was shoulder high, he placed the blackened stone on top. He gathered his people and led them in solemn procession, orbiting the pillar seven times in imitation of the stars. It was what Arabs did with gifts from the heavens. With each turn the patriarch cried out, "We are here at your service, O Lord! We are here at your service!"

No one can say for sure when Muhammad's birthplace acquired its name, or even what it originally meant, though some speculate it was derived from a Yemeni word meaning sanctuary.[1] For with its blackened meteorite, that is what Mecca became—a sanctuary, a protectorate of the gods where violence was forbidden year round. Such sacred zones were a necessity in the Wild West of clannish Arabia, and fear of retaliation from the gods for any violation made them work. It is said that if a desperado fleeing tribal vengeance reached sacred territory, he could thumb his nose at his pursuers. The gods would pile misfortune on them if they attacked him within the boundaries, though outside the sacred place he was still fair game.

Such protected zones were the spiritual cousins of the holy months, the four months of the year—one in the spring and three consecutive months in the autumn—when people could travel without fear of retaliatory violence. In a land of endless blood feuds, these months offered the only opportunity for people to conduct commerce with distant lands, attend trade and cultural fairs, and perform pilgrimages to the shrines of beloved deities— all these shrines, like the shrine of the Black Stone of Mecca, protectorates of the gods.

It is also unclear when the valley of Mecca, narrow and dominated on all sides by mountains, became settled. The mythology has it that the Black Stone was a jewel God dropped into the valley from the heavens at the time of creation and that Adam was guided there after he was ejected from Paradise to build a temple. Muhammad imagined that Adam was at first so tall that his head penetrated Paradise so that he could see the throne of God, but by the time he built the first temple around the heavenly jewel he had been reduced in size to a mere sixty cubits. Later, the valley was peopled by the descendants of Abraham and Ishmael, or so goes the legend.[2]

The cold record of history, however, reveals that the valley was likely an uninhabited wilderness until the second century of the era after Jesus.[3] This is presumably when the Black Stone was discovered and the valley became a sanctuary. A mix of small drifter tribes gradually settled in. They built a primitive temple in the form of a low rectangular wall of stacked rocks. The original pillar that held the sacred stone formed one of the corners. As the fame of the sacred stone spread, worshippers from other regions began visiting during the pilgrimage season to perform the seven orbits, kiss the stone, and sacrifice animals.

In terms of pilgrimage clientele, Mecca became a rising star, but the fame of its Black Stone brought occasional trouble. The story is told of Yemeni raiders bent on carting off the sacred stone and its pillar in order to establish the temple in their own territory and draw the pilgrims to them, but they were blocked at the outskirts of Mecca by a coalition of local tribes and put to flight after a fierce battle.[4]

Also marking this early period were struggles for control over the valley. One tribe would force itself upon another and absorb it. Then a bigger tribe would come in and drive out or absorb the previous amalgamation. A river of ancestral tribal names flows through the histories: Azd, Qudah, Khuzayma, Kinana, Fihr, Mudar, Khuza, Bakr, Asad, Maadd, Lakhm, Dil, and many more. The only unifier was that they descended from peoples that had migrated out of an overpopulated Yemen. The exception seems to be the Jurhums, a mystery tribe some say was Christianized and had migrated from the top of the Persian Gulf to the Hijaz to escape Persian oppression. During their time in Mecca the Jurhums left the Black Stone standing for the pagans to worship. They were eventually driven out by the emerging Khuza tribe, and the Jurhums ended up four hundred miles south of Mecca in the Yemen town of Najran where they joined a growing Christian community.[5]

For Mecca, the Khuzas were important for their enhancement to the temple. It is said that Amr ibn Luhayy, the legendary father of the tribe, formally consecrated the humble shrine as a temple of moon worship by importing a humanlike statue of the Nabataean moon god Hubal from what is now southern Jordan. Carved out of red onyx and presenting a royal appearance, Hubal was the god of the manly virtues of valor in war and chivalry in victory. It was he who regulated time and kept the secrets of the future, symbolized by the divination arrows he held in one hand. For a fee and a temple offering, an oracle-priest would cast arrows to the ground in front of the statue and interpret what was to come from the way they fell. Amr placed Hubal on a pedestal inside the crude rectangle of walls, and it remained the central feature of the temple through subsequent upgrades until the time of Muhammad. If it had not been the belief before, it became the belief thereafter that the roundish Black Stone came from the moon, a gift of the moon god Hubal.

Of greater importance for the valley of Mecca was Qusay, the great-grandfather of Muhammad's grandfather. Qusay was a small-town man with big ideas and was wily and ruthless in bringing them to fruition. He ousted the Khuzas, turned Mecca into a bustling town with a city administration, and established the temple as its economic pillar. It is said that he was born in Mecca, but was raised by a tribe far north near Syria. His father Kilab had died before his birth, and by the time he was born his mother had remarried. The new husband took her and her newborn to his native territory in northern Arabia, a land belonging to the Qudahs, who, like the inhabitants of Mecca, traced their origin to Yemen. His mother evidently kept Qusay's background a secret from him, perhaps in the hope he would fit in with the tribe of his stepfather and half-brothers, but it did not work. One day when he was in his mid-teens, he won a bruising fight with one of the Qudah youth. The loser shouted, "Go back to your own place and people; you are not one of us."[6]

Qusay confronted his mother about it, and she had no choice then but to lay out his family history: His real father was Kilab, the son of Murra, the son of Kab, the son of Luway, the son of Ghalib, who was the son of Fihr. She kept naming ancestors going all the way back to the one who left the overcrowding of the Old Country—Yemen—to live the life of the Hijaz nomad. She pumped Qusay up that he was of noble lineage, whereas the youth of the Qudah tribe were of common stock, barely a level above the slave. Upon learning of his origin, Qusay was eager to go to

Mecca, but his mother cautioned him to wait until the safety of the holy months to travel with pilgrims. He would have enough time during the three months—Truce month, Pilgrimage month, and Forbidden month, the latter so named because it continued the prohibitions of the first two months—to undertake the long journey south and return home. But he never made it back. After reaching Mecca and paying pilgrim respect to the Black Stone and Hubal, he became enamored of the daughter of Hulayl, the Khuza ruler of Mecca, and married her.

Qusay was physically impressive, intelligent, and ambitious. A natural born leader, he got involved in the affairs of the valley and was a voice to be taken seriously in any and all tribal and religious matters. When his father-in-law died, Qusay took over. The literature reports two versions of the takeover. In the first, his father-in-law passed over his alcoholic son Abu Ghubshan and bequeathed power to Qusay—to the dismay of the Khuzas in general and Abu Ghubshan in particular. More likely is the story that Qusay staged a coup after rulership went to his wine-loving brother-in-law. Fondness for drink was not Abu Ghubshan's real problem; it was lack of authority. He was not taken seriously. When local tribes and visiting pilgrims skipped making the temple donations that used to be paid without fail to Hulayl, Qusay decided to take action. He got his brother-in-law drunk one night and talked him into selling him control over the valley and the temple for the equivalent of a song and a dance: a skin of wine, a lute, and a few camels. Both men woke up the next day with a headache: Abu Ghubshan with the job of explaining himself to his Khuza tribe, and Qusay with the task of quelling the stirrings of revolt among the Khuzas, who refused to recognize his authority. Qusay hatched a plot to crush resistance to his takeover. After marshaling support from the scattered clans that descended from his family line, he sent word to his half-brothers in northern Arabia that he needed their help. A battle was brewing and the Khuzas were numerically superior. In some versions of the story the half-brothers led three hundred warriors south to Mecca; other sources claim it was a thousand. Heavily armed, all the Qudah reinforcements went disguised as pilgrims.

The way it is related in the literature, Qusay planned first to infiltrate the sun pilgrimage, then launch an attack on the

Khuzas before they could organize a resistance. Back in those days, there were essentially two distinct pilgrimages, one involving moon worship at the Meccan shrine, the other involving sun worship. The sun pilgrimage began twelve miles east of the valley of Mecca at Arafat, a small mount in the middle of a wide valley where pilgrims stood until sunset in reverence of the sun and its mysteries. Once the sun disappeared below the horizon, the pilgrimage commanders would release the crowd to chase the sun. This was done by walking or riding camels in a westerly direction to another mount called Muzdalifa, a two hour journey on foot. The pilgrims remained overnight and broke into celebration when the sun reappeared in the morning. From there they were released to go farther west to Mina, a valley adjacent to the vale of Mecca where they stoned pillars of stacked rocks representing the devilish *jinn*. The throwing of stones was likely intended as the human equivalent of the flaming darts—meteorites—they believed the gods fired at the devils. Following the stoning was a three-day festival that began with the slaughter of sacrificial animals and the dedication of their life force to celestial objects or a favorite god. When the sacrificial slaughtering was finished, the sun pilgrimage officially came to an end. Some of the pilgrims would continue to Mecca to perform the rites of moon worship, others would stay to enjoy the revelry of the final days of the pilgrimage before packing their camels and returning home.

Qusay's coup began by stripping command of the sun pilgrimage from the tribe that had traditional control over it. This was a prestigious office that chiefly involved leadership of the rituals and the enforcement of the time of departure from each pilgrimage station. It had been the role of the Sufas, a small Bedouin tribe of obscure origin that lived east of Mecca. Dressed in the white garb of the pilgrim, Qusay's half-brothers and their three hundred or one thousand warriors participated in the pilgrimage as far as the valley of Mina. Prior to entering the valley through a pass called Aqaba, Qusay's Meccan supporters and his Qudah warrior-relatives unsheathed the swords they had concealed underneath their garments, and Qusay declared to the Sufa leaders that he was now in charge: "We have better title to (running the pilgrimage) than you."[7] When the Sufas insisted on retaining their traditional role, a battle broke out. Qusay was the victor. From there he moved his putsch to Mecca where he battled the Khuzas and their allies. They too were defeated.

Qusay had grossly violated the sacred months and the sacred territory of Mecca, but the wrath of the gods fell entirely upon his enemies. That the gods spared him legitimized his authority. He began his rule by purging the valley of the Khuzas and their allies, forcing them to move to the coastal area of the Red Sea. In their place he moved in the scattered clans that supported him and assigned them neighborhoods. They gave themselves the tribal name Quraysh, a word of obscure origin that some believe was derived from a word meaning joining, since Qusay joined together various distantly related peoples under his banner. Others believe it was derived from the word for shark, perhaps in recognition of Qusay's stealth tactics.

Mecca at that time was primarily a tent town. The Khuzas and other previous inhabitants were nomads slowly transitioning to a settled life. Most were content to live in leather tents, but they built chest-high walls around them to keep sand from blowing in. The relatively few permanent buildings were modest adobe structures built near the temple grounds on each side of the riverbed. Qusay laid out roads and streets and demolished anything that got in the way. He cut down the low thorn trees that crowded the valley, arguing that they were of better use as construction material—particularly for roofing. People at first balked at felling the trees. They were considered sacred, but Qusay led the way by removing the trees nearest the walls of the shrine. When thunderbolts and other divine punishments did not come down on him from the heavens, people followed his example. The branches and trunks of the stunted trees were too short for large structures, but they were adequate for narrow rooms, serving as beams to support a layer of hardened clay mixed with binders that kept the occasional rain out. Thus permanent buildings made of adobe bricks laid on a foundation of stone sprouted everywhere. Qusay built the largest for himself across from the shrine and added a front room big enough to serve as a meeting hall for the tribal sheikhs, prominent elders, and important visitors from other tribes. The main door opened toward the shrine.

The modest temple never got a roof. The walls covered an area too large to allow for one with the construction materials then available, but Qusay made improvements by thickening the walls and raising them higher. He added a door with a lock and gave himself exclusive authority to allow people inside for paid consultations with Hubal, the main source of revenue from the temple. Everyone else prayed and sacrificed animals outside the walls. He also made changes to the sun pilgrimage by ordering a bonfire atop Muzdalifa to serve as a beacon for pilgrims, who sometimes got lost in the darkness after leaving Arafat. More importantly, he required all sun worshippers to finish their pilgrimage in Mecca by performing the orbits of the moon shrine and kissing the Black Stone.

He also began the practice of inviting various tribes, both near and far, to set up their favored idols around the shrine, a motive for them to place Mecca on their annual pilgrimage itinerary. He continued the practice of previous rulers of supplying food and water to pilgrims. It was a sacred duty, but also a practical matter: People would keep coming back if they knew they would not go hungry and thirsty; many would spend money for consultations before Hubal. For water, he set up a network of leather cisterns that were filled with water drawn from various wells. As for food, he levied a tax on herds, meaning that all herd owners were required to turn over a portion of their livestock to the administration at the beginning of the pilgrimage season.

He could be called Good King Qusay. Despite the strong-arm beginning, his forty-year rule appears to have been benign, and he was said to be beloved by all, the exceptions being the diehard revanchists among the tribes he ousted. He knew how to govern. While keeping exclusive control of the moon temple revenues, providing food and water for pilgrims, and retaining the final word when it came to declaring war, he deftly delegated important responsibilities to associated tribes, as if handing out portfolios to cabinet members: One tribe handled armaments and military training, another was responsible for relations with distant tribes, a third mediated disputes. He even reinstated the Sufas in their role as commanders of the sun pilgrimage provided they recognized his authority over the pilgrimage and accept the changes he instituted. Until age enfeebled him, he presided over cross-legged meetings with the various tribal elders about community concerns, both great and minor.

It is not known to what extent Qusay developed the caravan trade, which would become a source of great wealth to many of his descendants, but the arrival and departure of strings of transport camels became a feature of Meccan life. The men of Qusay's time made money by hiring themselves and their camels out to caravans that originated from other parts of Arabia, and locals provided services to caravans passing through. Mecca did not have enough water to support agriculture so that food had to be imported: dates from the Jewish agricultural oases of Yathrib and Khaybar to the north, and fruits and vegetables from the walled town of Taif, a mountain agricultural region seventy miles east of Mecca. Money had to be made to pay for such imports, but other than selling leather goods and trinkets to pilgrims and travelers, the only way to make a living was through low-level employment in caravans.

All that changed with Qusay's descendants.

CHAPTER 2

Ancestors

The fifth and sixth centuries were great times for Meccan entrepreneurs. After centuries of decline, caravan commerce through the Hijaz—the western frontier of Arabia—was on the rebound. The camel transportation networks that had enriched the civilizations of Yemen and resulted in an exploding population, nearly collapsed in the early centuries of the new millennium, fueling a diaspora of impoverished southern dwellers to the rest of Arabia. This decline began in the second century after Rome secured the Red Sea from pirates and began shipping merchandise by sea. Sailors had learned to use seasonal winds so that they could sail from the top of the Red Sea to India and never have to step on land in between. In terms of transit, Arabia then became history. Many of the ancient caravan towns along the old routes through western Arabia and southern Syria that were at the crossroads of overland trade were abandoned and reclaimed by the piling sand. Adding to the declining fortunes of southern Arabia was the rise of Christianity. All the great civilizations—the Egyptian, Roman, Greek, and Persian—used to spend fortunes in gold for Yemeni frankincense, myrrh, and other aromatics to burn in religious ceremonies, all of it shipped north on the backs of camels. Early Christians, however, rejected their use, so that as Christianity spread, the market for aromatics declined. This took place at the same time the Romans opened up the sea lanes and took over international trade.

But then came a dramatic reversal in both geopolitics and Christian ritual. Roman power by the fifth and sixth centuries was in sharp decline. Pirates had reclaimed control of the seas, making it dangerous and costly to ship by sea. At the same time, Christians adopted the use of incense in their religious rites, creating a huge demand once again. Silk and other luxury goods were as much in demand as ever, but they now needed the backs of camels to get to market.

Seeing a future in transport, the Meccans stepped in. Their involvement began slowly with Qusay's children, but became big business with his numerous grandchildren. Unusual for Arabs of power, Qusay had only one wife and she bore him four sons and two daughters. The son who spawned the greatest of the Meccan merchant families was Mughira Abd al-Manaf ibn Qusay—Mughira, son of Qusay and devoted servant of the goddess Manaf, nicknamed Moonface because of his round, cheerful face. He had four sons: Hashim, Nawfal, Muttalib, and Abd Shams—Servant of the Sun.

It was these four men who brought Mecca into the mainstream of the caravan trade. Hoping to take advantage of the opportunities, the Meccans gave the sons of Moonface authority to negotiate safe passage and trade treaties with the surrounding powers. Hashim was dispatched to the Byzantine rulers of Syria and their Christianized Arab vassals; Nawfal secured treaties with the lords of Yemen; Muttalib returned to Mecca with the good news of a trade agreement with the Abyssinians; Abd Shams came back from a journey to the east with a treaty in hand that gave the Meccans a commercial entry into Persia.[1] At first the Meccans offered transport services for other people's merchandise, but eventually they became wealthy enough to buy merchandise on the cheap from distant producers that they resold for a handsome profit in foreign markets.

Hashim was Muhammad's great-grandfather, a celebrated Meccan whose clan would give rise to a dynasty of Muhammadan rulers. It was a nickname meaning in essence "provider of bread." His given name was Amr, but the nickname came into use after he saved Mecca from starvation. A drought had burned up the region. Food was scarce and people went hungry; some were dying. In desperation, Hashim went to Syria with sacks of his own money and bought tons of wheat and a convoy of transport camels. Back in Mecca, he distributed the wheat, and for a while the town survived on freshly baked bread dipped in stew made from the pack camels. It was enough to tide the town over, and the grateful community named him Hashim, the provider of bread—Breadman for short, which was how he was called from then on.

He eventually became the leader of Mecca, but only after a struggle with his numerous cousins over control. The conflict over power was largely Qusay's fault. He had bequeathed all his authority to only one of his four sons, Abd al-Dar—Servant of the House of Qusay. While the other sons accepted the arrangement out of respect for their father's wishes, their grandchildren wanted a share. Over time, two sides formed: one in support of the inherited right of the Abd al-Dar family, the other in support of dissidents from other families that demanded power. "We have a better right to it than you," was the dissident mantra. Led by Hashim, the dissenters called themselves the Perfumed Ones from a bowl of perfume a woman had placed in front of the temple for them to dip their hands into as a declaration of allegiance. The defender clan and their allies swore allegiance to their cause by dipping their hands into a bowl of blood and ended up being branded the Blood Lickers by the Perfumed Ones. The two sides were preparing to march to a field of battle outside of the borders of the sacred territory when cooler heads prevailed. There was nothing to be gained when cousins slaughtered cousins. A famed soothsayer was called in to mediate. In the end, Hashim was given control over providing food and water to pilgrims, which gave him the right to levy a tax on herds; the clan of Abd al-Dar maintained control of municipal affairs and leadership in war. They also retained doorkeeper control over the temple, meaning control over temple revenues.[2]

As the leader of the clan of Moonface, Hashim performed his pilgrimage duties with gusto. When the autumn holy months arrived, he rounded up livestock from herd owners—their annual temple tax. Once the pilgrims began to pour in, he oversaw the slaughtering and the cooking to provide food for thousands of people, meaning he had the logistical chore of lining up cooks, cooking pots, and firewood to make sure everyone was happily fed. Supplying water was also challenging, as crews needed to be assembled and supervised for the labor of drawing endless buckets of water from deep wells to fill leather cisterns set up wherever they were needed. These brigades were composed of the men of his clan.

Given his generosity and knack for leadership, Hashim soon acquired more control over municipal affairs than the hereditary leaders, but another conflict arose when one of his nephews challenged his leadership, claiming he had a better right to it than Hashim. This was Umayya, whose name would eventually be given to another dynasty of Muhammadan rulers. Umayya was the adopted son of Hashim's twin brother Abd Shams. Hashim and Abd Shams were born as conjoined twins, the fingers of Abd Shams right hand being attached to Hashim's head. It is said that their father used his sword as a knife to separate them, leading people to predict there would be bad blood between their descendants, a prediction that began to play out with Umayya and Hashim.

Umayya was fair-haired and blue-eyed. It is said that he was a slave of Byzantine origin adopted when he was young by Abd Shams. The story goes that the father of Abd Shams, fascinated by the boy's appearance, bought him from slave traders who were passing through Mecca with their captives. Though he initially intended to resell him in Yemen, he ended up giving him to his son Abd Shams, and Abd Shams, who was childless, adopted him and raised him as his son. With his family's support, Umayya was successful as a merchant, but he never truly fit in the Meccan world of brown men with black hair and dark eyes. Perhaps trying to compensate for his outsider appearance, he also sponsored acts of generosity during the famine that brought Hashim to prominence. Certain he had outshone his uncle in giving to the community, he challenged him to a contest before arbiters to make a determination as to who was the better man, a verdict of superiority.[3] Hashim agreed, but with the stipulation that the loser should go into exile for ten years and forfeit fifty camels. One version of the story holds that a soothsayer was appointed to make the decision, another that a panel of judges was selected. Such contests had rules: Each man was required to deliver an address at the meeting chamber touting his experience, personal qualities, accomplishments, and the merits of his family and their accomplishments. The opponent was given the opportunity for rebuttal. Witnesses were called to attest to the character of the contestants. It was like a political campaign except that the voters could be counted on one hand. The decision ended in favor of Hashim. Umayya suffered his banishment in Syria. Following his departure, Hashim threw a grand feast and distributed the flesh of the loser's camels among the poor of Mecca.

Hashim's most outstanding contribution to Mecca was to turn it into an export rather than just a transit town. Until then, if there were locally organized caravans, they were small, *ad hoc* affairs involving a limited number of people, and they traded regionally. Like his grandfather Qusay, Hashim was a visionary. After he and his brothers secured commercial agreements with the empires, he organized the entire community to gather all the locally produced goods that could turn a profit in order to ship them together in huge convoys, goods that included hides, silver ore, incense, perfume made from desert shrubs, weapons, livestock, and more. He either established, or his ideas later evolved into, an export cooperative in which resources to fund a caravan were pooled, and each investor obtained a return on the investment in proportion to the share. He continued the tradition of inviting tribes to bring their idols to Mecca to become part of the family of idols set up around or inside the temple. Establishing such ties enabled the Meccans to obtain advantageous agreements for their caravans to pass through tribal territories in security. Each idol brought to Mecca represented a diplomatic victory. They were like signatures on a treaty that bound distant tribes to Mecca spiritually and commercially.

When he was not attending to duties, Hashim was on the caravan trail, and it was on one of these trips that he fathered Muhammad's grandfather, Abdul Muttalib. This came about after his caravan stopped in Yathrib, a fertile agricultural oasis two hundred and thirty miles north of Mecca, and he became enamored of a comely Yathrib divorcée, Salma. It is said he spotted her at a market while she was giving instructions to a servant about purchases, and he made inquiries about her. She was of the Najjars, one of the clans of the Khazraj tribe, and had two children from a marriage that ended in divorce. She made it known that she would only remarry someone of rank provided she would be able to divorce him if she ended up disliking him. As Hashim was the renowned sheikh of the Meccans, a union with Salma was not difficult to arrange. Hashim's kinsmen from the caravan attended the wedding, with the bride's Najjar clan rounding out the guest list. She became pregnant before the caravan departed for Syria. The story goes that Hashim picked up his pregnant wife on the return trip, but brought her back to Yathrib on another caravan trip north so she would be with her family when she gave birth. He intended to pick up her and the child on the return trip to take them to Mecca, but he died during a stopover in Gaza.

As a boy, Muhammad's grandfather strongly resembled Hashim, and it was clear he would grow up with the same tall, commanding appearance. The mother called him Shayba, meaning old man, because he was born with streaks of gray in his hair. He spent the first decade of his life in Yathrib. Then one of Hashim's brothers, Muttalib, traveled to Yathrib to claim the child as a son of the Quraysh tribe. He pressured Salma to allow him to take him back to Mecca so that his character could be shaped in the Quraysh mold. He returned with the boy riding behind him on his camel. When the Quraysh saw them entering town, they assumed the boy was a slave Muttalib had purchased and called him Abdul Muttalib, the Slave or Servant of Muttalib, but he corrected them, "You speak rubbish! He is my nephew. He is Shayba, the son of Hashim, and I have brought him from Medina (Yathrib)."[4] Nevertheless, the name Slave of Muttalib stuck, as he became Muttalib's ward and was always with him.

When Hashim died, Muttalib succeeded him in his role of providing food and water to pilgrims, and he groomed his nephew for eventual succession by teaching him the duties. However, the uncle died while on a trade journey to Yemen when Abdul Muttalib was still too young to take his place, and it was not until he was an adult that he was able to assume the duties of the hereditary office, though not without a struggle. Following the death of Muttalib, another of Abdul Muttalib's paternal uncles, Nawfal, took over the pilgrimage duties and refused to relinquish them. He also made a grab of some properties that were due to his nephew from the estate of Hashim. When he came of age, Abdul Muttalib displayed an understanding of power: Unable to obtain Quraysh support to get his inheritance and take over the pilgrimage role that was rightfully his, he called on his maternal uncles in Yathrib for military assistance, perhaps recalling the history of his great-grandfather Qusay who enlisted the help of his Syrian half-brothers in his struggle for control over Mecca. A contingent of eighty armed horsemen under the leadership of one of Abdul Muttalib's maternal uncles arrived in Mecca. They cornered Nawfal in front of the temple and made it clear that they intended to make him pay with his blood if he did not give back to the son of Hashim what was rightfully his. Perhaps it was a bluff, as the killing of Nawfal within the sacred precinct would surely have sparked a tribal war, but Nawfal, with only the wall of the temple to back him up, blinked first. Abdul Muttalib got his properties and control of the pilgrimage duties that used to be performed by his father.[5] Once established in his role, he soon became one of the leading men of Mecca.

Abdul Muttalib, who was born in A.D. 497, lived during an era of geopolitical turmoil that nearly engulfed Mecca. The turmoil was centered in Yemen, which had suffered a succession of coups and military takeovers by foreign powers. This began with the overthrow of the hereditary ruler of Yemen by Dhu Nuwas, a convert to Judaism who sought to purge Yemen of a growing Christian presence, particularly in Najran where a large Christian community had taken root. Though the numbers are likely exaggerated, it is said that Dhu Nuwas slaughtered twenty thousand Najran Christians when they refused to convert to Judaism, an atrocity that led to the intervention of the Christian powers. The Byzantines, too distant to become directly involved, encouraged the Christian ruler of Abyssinia to take over Yemen and provided logistical support for a D-day invasion of seventy thousand Abyssinian troops across the Red Sea. Dhu Nuwas was either slain or committed suicide, and the Abyssinians took charge, but the African reign was also tumultuous. Commanders of the Abyssinian army fought amongst themselves for control, and the struggle was only resolved when two of the generals faced off in a duel to the death. A general named Abraha came out the winner, but with a deep gash across his face that earned him the nickname Splitface.[6]

Abraha was a forceful figure who was devoted to expanding both Christianity and Abyssinian power. He evidently formulated long-term plans to Christianize the tribal lands of Western Arabia and their spiritual center of Mecca, for he built a large cathedral in Sana and predicted the Christian cathedral would replace the pagan temple of Mecca as the pilgrim destination during the traditional holy months. But he found the Arab attachment to the Meccan temple and their pagan beliefs could not be easily severed. This became clear when someone who professed devotion to the Meccans temple stole into the cathedral one night and defecated in it—not in some discrete corner but right in front of the altar where the smear of excrement and its message of contempt would not go unnoticed. When he learned of the desecration, Abraha vowed to take over Mecca.

This he attempted first by crowning an influential Arab sheikh, a descendant of the Khuza tribe that Qusay ousted from Mecca, as king of Mecca and the surrounding tribal territories, but his viceroy was murdered by his own people the moment he returned to his land. In reprisal, Abraha led an army accompanied by armored elephants with the intention of destroying the heathen temple and occupying Mecca.[7]

The Meccans had no defense against such a force. When Abraha smashed through a feeble counterattack by tribes to the south of Mecca, Abdul Muttalib ordered his people to hide in the mountains. All that saved the temple from destruction and Mecca from an occupying army was an outbreak of smallpox among Abraha's troops. The spread of the disease was sudden, swift, and unsparing, and much of the army was destroyed. Abraha supposedly died from the pox not long after making it back to his palace in Sana with what was left of his army.[8] The Arabs saw the defeat as a sign that the gods favored their temple, and a legend arose that the Abyssinians were beaten by an enormous flocks of birds that dropped stones on them, causing bruises that resulted in the pustules of disease. Muhammad later made use of the failed attack as proof of God's power. It is among the earliest of his Koran compositions, and it is an example of his tendency to present myth as fact:

> Seest thou not how thy Lord dealt with
>   the people of the elephant?
> Did he not make their treacherous plan go astray?
> And he sent against them flights of birds,
> Striking them with stones of baked clay,
> Then did he make like an empty field of stalks and
> straw (of which the corn) has been eaten up.[9]

Abdul Muttalib had five wives who gave him ten sons and six daughters. Abdullah, Muhammad's father, was the youngest and was the favorite child. When he was about twenty-four years old, his father arranged for his marriage to Amina, the daughter of the sheik of an allied tribe, while Abdul Muttalib, then in his mid-seventies, married the last of his many wives, a woman from the same tribe as Amina. Some of the sources claim it was a double wedding and resulted in the birth of Muhammad to Abdullah, whereas the new wife of Abdul Muttalib bore Hamza and Safiya, an uncle and an aunt nearly the same age as Muhammad. Both would eventually rank among his most important early supporters.

There is little that can be factually said about Muhammad's father other than he died when he was around twenty-five years old, not long before Amina gave birth or soon after. Like many Meccans, Abdullah died while on a long-haul caravan trip, leaving his wife a widow and his child fatherless. In the build-up to the birth of Muhammad, the literature wraps Abdullah in the glowing legendry befitting the father of a prophet. Among the most interesting of the wraps is the story—a parallel to the Biblical account of Abraham's intended sacrifice of his son—in which Abdul Muttalib must slit Abdullah's throat as a sacrifice to the gods. God told Abraham to slay his son as a test of faith; Abdul brought it upon himself with a vow to sacrifice one of his sons if God granted his wish to have ten sons. He made the vow while digging a well near the temple to provide water for the pilgrims, one of his functions. At the time, he had only one son and the work was arduous. The Meccans refused to lend a hand due to the fact that Abdul Muttalib was in charge of providing water for the pilgrims, and whatever monetary benefit he derived from it went into his pocket, not theirs. At some point, while wiping the sweat from his brow, he looked up at the heavens and made the fateful vow. He ended up with ten sons, and the story goes that when they had grown to maturity he told them of his vow. They supposedly submitted to his desire to honor it and accepted to draw lots in the temple to determine which of the sons should be sacrificed. All his children, daughters included, assembled in front the statue of Hubal where ten arrow shafts had been prepared, each representing one of the sons. The priest-oracle conducted the casting ritual and drew the arrow that corresponded to Abdullah.[10] Like Abraham on Mount Moriah, Abdul Muttalib reluctantly took out a knife, but serving as the angel of the Bible story, the daughters restrained his hand by weeping and begging him not to go through with it. Ultimately, a compromise with the gods was reached whereby Abdul Muttalib had to sacrifice a hundred camels, the number determined by the casting of additional arrows.[11]

In another legend, this one having to do with the conception of Muhammad, Abdullah was propositioned by a woman who offered him a hundred camels to sleep with him. Various versions can be found, but with a common story line: He was with his father on their way to the tribe of his future wife and the double marriage of him and his father to the tribal women, both cousins. Though interested, Abdullah had to brush the lady off, saying, "I am with my father, and I cannot leave him." He married Amina, got her pregnant, then shortly after he ran into the woman again and offered to take her up on her proposition, but she dumped cold water on him: "I am not an immoral woman," she protested. She had only wanted to sleep with him because of a glowing white light she had seen between his eyes that told her he would be the father of a prophet. She wanted to be the mother, but now the light was gone from him. He had already gotten another woman pregnant and accomplished what the glow signified as his purpose.[12]

Not long after, Abdullah signed on with a caravan traveling to Syria, but he fell ill, and the caravan left him behind in Yathrib so that he could be in the care of his Najjar relatives. When news reached Abdul Muttalib that his youngest son was ill, he sent his eldest son al-Harith to Yathrib to check up on him, but by the time he arrived Abdullah had been dead for a month and was buried in the courtyard of a relative. Abdullah left Amina his earthly possessions: an Abyssinian slave girl, five camels, and a flock of goats.

Muhammad was born several months later. After she gave birth, Amina sent word to Abdul Muttalib to come to her. He went to her modest room, picked up the swathed infant, and carried him into the temple where he gave thanks to the gods before the statue of Hubal.

Muhammad's birth was in A.D. 570, the Year of the Elephant, the year a scar-faced Christian warlord marched on Mecca to destroy the moon temple, but was driven away by flocks of birds dropping stones of baked clay.

CHAPTER 3

Fits

There are two Muhammads: the Muhammad of fact and the Muhammad of fiction—the mythologized Muhammad. The former could never have attained longevity without the latter.

Other than the details of time and place, Muhammad's coming into the world was no different from that of anyone else. He was delivered while Amina labored on a crude leather mattress on the dirt floor of an adobe hovel with women of her tribe helping her through the ordeal. The umbilical cord was cut and the infant was cleaned up, swaddled in a soft wrap, and handed to the waiting arms of his mother.

In the mythologized version, Muhammad's birth was accompanied by klieg lights of prophesy: The pregnant Amina dreamed that a light came out of her body that allowed her to see "the fortresses of Busra in the land of Syria," a foreshadowing of Muhammad's conquests. Upon giving birth, Amina saw the world lighting up and the "stars drawing near me to such a point that I can say that they are falling on top of me."[1] Muhammad was born as clean as if bathed, with the umbilical cord already cut. His first act upon entering the world was not to squeal or cry, but to fall on his hands and knees in prostration to God.[2]

Some of the details surrounding his birth as found in the early Muhammadan literature—the exclusive source of information about Muhammad—have more of the timbre of truth, as they tell a story of maternal rejection and emotional deprivation. A few days after he was born, the infant was sent off with a nurse for hire to a faraway land and was not reunited with his mother until four or five years later. The literature holds that Meccan women had the custom of farming out their infants to out-of-town wet nurses in order to get them away from the danger of plague that caused a higher mortality rate among the children of the cramped town than among the offspring of hardier desert people. Children were kept from their natural mothers for years before being returned, physically robust and with clear minds. Such is the claim, at any rate, though it would have been as unnatural then as it would be now for a mother to give away her infant to another woman, particularly to a stranger, for early rearing. Such a practice would be harmful to the development of a child, who would end up with confused attachments and deep emotional trauma when eventually returned to the biological mother.

It is likely this fate only befell children of parents who were unable or unwilling to care for them. There is no evidence that Hamza and Safiya, the youngest children of Abdul Muttalib by his last wife, both close to Muhammad in age, were similarly treated; nor were any other members of the Abdul Muttalib family. It can be concluded that Amina was not able to care for her newborn, or possibly she did not want to. If there is any basis to the legends of the visions that are attributed to Amina, they could be explained as products of the same epileptic disorder from which Muhammad evidently suffered, a neurological ailment that shaped his destiny.[3]

The literature relates that Muhammad's grandfather immediately set about to find a foster mother for him. A slave girl belonging to Abu Lahab, one of Muhammad's uncles and later a bitter enemy, filled the role of wet nurse for several days until a permanent nurse could be found. This turned out to be a Bedouin named Halima whose nomadic tribe camped in the foothills of Taif, a three-day journey to the southeast of Mecca.[4] It is said that she and other women from the tribe supplemented their meager pastoral livelihood by offering themselves as substitute mothers to women from the towns.

As a wet nurse, Halima was less than ideal: She was emaciated and unable to nurse even her own infant. In the first-person narrative attributed to her, she said she arrived in Mecca during a time of famine with ten other women from her tribe, all searching for gigs as long-term foster mothers. She was riding a gray-white female donkey and brought her infant with her as well as her husband, whose mount was a dried-up she-camel. They brought their herd of goats with them too. Because she had little food to nourish herself, Halima did not have much breast milk. The camel, the donkey, and the goats were not producing milk either.

Amina offered Muhammad to each of the women, but all of them turned her down. They feared they would not receive sufficient money from a widow, particularly one who did not appear to be much better off than they were. Unable to find any other child to nurse, Halima ended up accepting Muhammad rather than deal with the shame of being the only woman to return to her people without a foster child.

The mythmeisters jazz up the story from here: On the way to Mecca, they write, Halima and her entourage of husband, child, and animals had been so pitifully weak they trailed far behind the other mothers-for-hire and were a nuisance. On the return trip, however, her animals were inexplicably peppy and pulled way ahead of the others so that the women scolded her: "Confound you, Halima, stop and wait for us!" Halima's animals mysteriously swelled with milk, as did her breasts so that she was able to nurse both Muhammad and her own son, and that made the other women jealous. Her husband drew the appropriate conclusion: Their new charge was responsible for their good fortune. "Do you know, Halima, you have taken a blessed creature?" To which she replied, "By God, I hope so!"[5]

The legends have it that the good fortune the foster parents experienced from having a child so clearly favored by God continued for the next two years. Halima's animals stayed fat while the animals of other members of the tribe were thin and sickly. Hoping to benefit from whatever it was that allowed Halima's animals to thrive, herdsmen drove their animals to the same pastures where her animals grazed, but to no avail. Only Halima's animals flourished. She weaned Muhammad after two years and took him back to Mecca. She was reluctant to give the boy back because it would end their good fortune, but Muhammad ended up staying in her care. One source claims Halima and her husband persuaded Amina to let them keep the boy longer by warning her of an outbreak of plague in Mecca. Another affirms it was Amina's idea. She was the one concerned about the plague and sent the child off again with them.

Some time after the return to the nomad encampment, Muhammad suffered his first epileptic fit, a deeply traumatic physical and visual experience that he misunderstood and never forgot.[6] He later told his followers that three angels came to him while he was playing with other children. One of them laid him on the ground, slit open his belly, and ran his hand inside his body in search of something and finished up cleansing him with water. In his frequent retelling of the story, Muhammad said the angels weighed him against ten people and found that he outweighed them—meaning he was better than all ten combined. Then they weighed him against a hundred and finally a thousand people with the same result. "Even if you were to weigh him against the whole of his community, he would outweigh them all!" the angels said.[7] Children who were playing with him when the fit started ran to alert Halima and her husband that something was wrong with the boy. By the time the foster parents got to him, Muhammad was on his feet, but his face was pallid. When he told them what he believed had happened to him, Halima's husband realized he had suffered a fit and became frightened. In the ancient world, epilepsy was thought to be the result of devil possession. How else to account for the convulsions, the frothing at the mouth, the strange talk? Maybe they were not so fortunate after all, the husband told his wife. Better to take him back to his mother before something worse happened.

They returned to Mecca intending to hand Muhammad over to his mother and leave without any further ado, but surprised at their change of heart Amina pressed them for an explanation. When they described what happened and said they feared "something untoward may afflict him," Amina asked if they were afraid a demon had possessed him.[8] Her response suggests that she was familiar with the experience. She convinced them to take the boy back to the desert.[9]

The religion accepts only a spiritual explanation for Muhammad's experience, that it was either a visitation by divine beings, an objective, external event, or that it was a deeply internal religious experience. Yet the details provided in the official accounts along with the reaction of participants allow for a prosaic medical explanation: Muhammad had the misfortune of being saddled with a neurological disease that he possibly inherited from his mother.

According to Muhammad's lengthy personal account of that event, Halima took him to a *kahin*—a soothsayer—to have him examined and cured. Here we are subjected to a further dose of mythology: After listening to the little boy tell of his experience, the *kahin* threw his arms around him and shouted, "O Arabs, O Arabs, forward! Kill this lad, and kill me with him, for by al-Lat and al-Uzza, if you let him be and he reaches the age of puberty, he will most certainly subvert your religion, declare your minds and those of your forefathers to be deluded, oppose your way of life, and bring forward for you a religion of whose like you have never heard."[10]

He stayed with Halima until his fifth year, but because of his malady, she kept him close to her—that is, until the day she saw a cloud shadowing him. "It stopped when he stopped and moved when he moved," the account goes. This frightened her to the point that she and her husband were determined to return him to his mother.[11]

The return did not go smoothly. Muhammad must have been told that he was going back to his real mother, that she had given him into the care of Halima after he was born, and now it was time to return him to her. His emotional confusion would have been devastating: Wasn't Halima his real mother? She was the only mother he had ever known. He didn't want to go to this stranger; he wanted to stay where he belonged, near Taif in the land of Halima's tribe. When they reached Mecca, he broke free of his foster parents and ran away. A search party went out. He was found by Waraqa, a Meccan who would later embrace a sect of Christianity and translate parts of the New Testament into Arabic. He located Muhammad in upper Mecca, a logical place to search for him because the road to Taif started there. Was the boy in tears? Was he walking defiantly in the direction of Taif? Did he struggle with Waraqa, or did he allow himself to be led away? We are not told.

Waraqa brought the child to his grandfather at the temple. Abdul Muttalib lifted him onto his shoulders and performed orbits, saying prayers to the gods for Muhammad's well being. Finally he was brought to Amina.

A year later, Muhammad suffered another emotional trauma when Amina died. This occurred after they visited his maternal uncles of the Najjar clan of his grandmother Salma in Yathrib, a

ten-day journey north. They had departed with her Abyssinian slave girl Baraka on two camels and stayed with relatives
for a month. Muhammad later told how he played with local
children, flew pigeons with them, and learned to swim in a
pond belonging to the tribe. He was also shown the grave of
his father Abdullah. On the return trip, Amina fell ill at the
village of al-Abwa south of Yathrib and died. We are not given
details other than the fact she was buried there. The slave girl
brought the orphaned child back to Mecca where he became the
ward of his grandfather. We are not told if Muhammad was at his
mother's side when she died. Certainly he was present when her
body, wrapped in a shroud, was lowered into the ground and dirt
was shoveled over her. One can imagine his grief and confusion,
his life again ripped apart by a start-stop primal relationship.

His grandfather was eighty years old when Muhammad came
into his care and lived for only two more years. He was fond
of the boy to the point of favoring him over his own children,
perhaps in compensation for the emotional deprivations of his
grandson's first six years. He referred to him as "my son." As
the grandfather's strength faded, his children set out a mattress
for him in the shade of the temple so that he could rest during the day. His sons used to sit next to the bed until he came
out to it, but none except Muhammad dared sit on it. Feeling
privileged, he would hop onto it only to be driven off it by his
jealous uncles. When Abdul Muttalib saw this, he would stop
them and have Muhammad sit beside him and affectionately
stroke his back.

As a temple official and knowledgeable about its history and
lore, Abdul Muttalib would have taught Muhammad about the
importance of the temple and spoken to him about the gods
whose stone and wooden representations were set up inside and
outside and served as sacrificial altars. It is also likely Abdul
Muttalib took Muhammad with him during the performance
of his temple duties. Due to his advanced age, his role by
then may have been mainly administrative, such as appointing
people to ensure pilgrims had adequate food and water during
the pilgrimage season. His may have had a priestly role as well,
taking the lead in important rituals such as the orbiting of the
temple. He may have delivered homilies in praise of ancestors
and the customs and beliefs they had passed down. What is

certain is that while Abdul Muttalib was alive, Muhammad was at the center of the hustle and bustle of the annual rituals, not to mention the daily activities of the temple, and these experiences left a deep impression on him.

When his grandfather died, Muhammad was eight years old. Because of his importance as a religious leader, Abdul Muttalib was given the equivalent of a state funeral that was attended by the important people of the town. Each of his six daughters composed eulogies that were recited to him before his death, bringing him to tears, and they were recited again after he was laid into the ground. Muhammad wept while standing behind the bier, grieved by yet another precocious experience of the transience and suffering of life.

Though Abdul Muttalib had great influence and prestige, he did not leave much of an inheritance to his numerous offspring and as a consequence Muhammad ended in impoverished circumstances. The economic and social structure of Mecca had changed since the days of Qusay when all power, religious and secular, centered in one leader. Over the course of several generations, the commercial success of the Meccan merchants who descended from Qusay's grandson Abd Shams and his adopted son Umayya brought them wealth and power, whereas those families carrying out the various religious duties of the temple—the descendants of Hashim—saw their incomes and influence diminish. Important positions involving city administration and military leadership were in the hands of the better-off merchant families. The priestly income derived from tending to the needs of pilgrims was paltry compared to the sacks of coin and the valuable merchandise the caravans brought back from abroad. Abdul Muttalib had a prominent place in the Quraysh council chamber across from the temple, but his was only one voice among much wealthier ones.

Before he died, Abdul Muttalib gave custody of Muhammad to one of his older sons, Abu Talib, who briefly took over his father's temple duties before relinquishing them to Abbas, a younger brother. In the literature, Abu Talib and his wife Fatima are presented as good hearted, and it is said they lavished attention on Muhammad. Perhaps they understood better than anyone the emotional privations he had experienced and felt pity for him. It is likely they had witnessed his fits, and as an expression of their kindness they wrapped their arms around him to protect him from evil tongues that he was devil possessed. Fatima became like a mother to him. Muhammad would later remember her with warmth.

The boy, marked by early traumatic experience and saddled with an apparently inherited neurological disorder, developed a reserved personality and was excessively shy and modest to the point of prudishness. He spent much of his time alone on the slopes of mountains herding goats, first for his uncle and later for hire. Grazing animals was the humblest of occupations, one reserved for people at the low end of the Meccan economic scale. He was paid a pittance, sometimes in tamarisk seeds, and had to supplement his diet with black fruit picked from desert shrubs. When he gazed down at the bustle of the town below, with its roofless temple in the center, the multi-story stone and adobe homes of the well to do on each side of the wide riverbed, and the more humble abodes of the neighborhoods that climbed into the ravines of the foothills, he must have wondered if he would ever rise above such a lowly station. He later saved face with his followers by saying that there had never been a prophet who had not grazed goats.[12]

The literature reveals two more likely epileptic episodes Muhammad suffered as a youth. In one of these, he left his goats late one night in the care of another herdsman and headed for the bawdy quarter of Mecca to have some fun at the wine taverns. But when he reached the outskirts he heard music. He sat down to listen and suddenly lost consciousness only to regain his senses the next morning when the sun was burning his face. This happened on a second occasion when, as soon as he entered town, he heard similar music and again passed out.[13] Muhammad explained his loss of consciousness as divine intervention to keep him from falling into the "vileness" of heathenism.[14] Dede Korkut, a Turkish-born neuropsychologist, believes a more likely explanation for these experiences is that he suffered an auditory seizure prior to blacking out, one of the symptoms found in temporal lobe epilepsy.[15]

While still young, Muhammad went on at least one major caravan trip. Some sources claim he was twelve years old, others younger, when he joined his uncle on a trade expedition to the city of Bosra in southern Syria with a large group of Meccan merchants. He had not been included in the trip, but when Abu Talib was about to set out with the caravan Muhammad clung to his leg and begged to be taken along. It was not so much that he wanted to go on the adventure of a trip abroad: He could not bear to be separated from his uncle for three months. Abu Talib relented, and Muhammad, mounted behind his uncle in the high camel saddle, plodded north with the caravan.

The journey served as an opening for later writers to insert a prediction about Muhammad's future greatness as prophet of God, this coming from the mouth of a learned Christian monk named Bahira. It so happened that the caravan stopped near his monastic cell. Spotting Muhammad amid the Meccan cameleers, Bahira rushed out to inquire about him. The story goes that the monk was in possession of a sacred book handed down from previous generations of monks that supposedly contained a description of a coming prophet. And here was this foretold prophet right in front of him! "This is the Chief of the Worlds," Bahira gushed. "This is the Messenger of the Lord of the Worlds. This person has been sent by God as a mercy to the Worlds." Bahira explained to the startled Meccans that he was certain Muhammad was the foretold prophet the moment he saw their caravan clear the top of the mountain pass. "There was not a tree or a stone that did not prostrate itself in worship, and they only prostrate themselves to a prophet." Bahira then cautioned against the Jews. He warned Abu Talib to get the boy home as quickly as possible before the Jews could get their hands on him. "If they see him and know about him what I know about him, they will do him evil." Just then, heavily armed men, as evil in appearance as the dark horsemen of *The Lord of the Rings*, were seen galloping up the road. They had been told of a boy prophet and intended to slay him, but Bahira was able to persuade them to leave in peace.[16] In one version of the story, the monk then died.

Mythology aside, the trip had to have been an important formative experience for Muhammad. The journey north would have taken him along the Dead Sea and through abandoned caravan towns and tumbled Roman ruins, inglorious testimonies to the transience of man and his mortal efforts. It was a learning experience every step of the way, for after the Meccan traders circled their camels for the night in defensive formation, perhaps within sight of the ancient tombs carved into the rocks of Petra or the abandoned Roman amphitheater of Jerash, the older, well-traveled merchants and cameleers would have shared their knowledge of these places. What else was there to do at night while sitting around campfires or reclined on leather cushions inside their tents but talk about what they knew of such places? When they finally reached Bosra Muhammad would have marveled at the sight of the Christian culture that had flourished there for centuries, yet the inhabitants were as Arab as the Meccans. He saw magnificent churches, heard the peal of church bells (possibly by then a neurologically unsettling sound for him), observed monks and nuns in black garb, and saw the worship of the congregations. Was he told scriptural stories? Did he hear legends of the Jewish prophets? Did he learn about Jesus? Historian William Muir observed that Muhammad's impressions "would be rendered all the more practical and lasting by the sight of whole tribes, Arabs like himself, belonging to the same faith and practicing the same observances."[17]

About the time Muhammad returned to Mecca, a series of regional tribal fights later tagged the Sacrilegious Wars broke out, upsetting the peace in southwestern Arabia for half a decade. The initial spark began at the Ukaz Fair, some forty miles east of Mecca. This was an annual autumn commercial and cultural event that attracted Arabs from throughout Arabia. It was held during the first three weeks of Truce Month and preceded the pilgrimage to Mecca and other holy sites such as the temple of al-Lat in Taif. Horse and camel races along with poetry contests were part of the program, as were performances by musicians, jugglers, dancers, and acrobats. Anything and everything could be bought or sold there, including slaves. Christian preachers mingled with the crowds and talked about Jesus to whoever would listen. It is believed Muhammad once heard a sermon there by a famed Christian bishop from Najran. This particular fair happened to attract a hothead who was owed money by someone from a different tribe, and he had not been paid. The hothead had with him a monkey, and after being rebuffed again for what was owed, he shouted, "Who will exchange this monkey for the monkey who owes me money?" or something to that effect, and he cursed the debtor and the debtor's forefathers going back ten generations. He kept it up until someone drew a sword and lopped off the monkey's head. Swords were unsheathed, and a deadly melee broke out.[18]

Though this outbreak was contained, other incidents of violence occurred, either that same year or in subsequent years, that pitted various tribes against one another, each a violation of the sanctity of the holy months. One began when a loudmouthed and possibly drunken poet insulted other tribes by boasting his tribe was the most respected among all the tribes of Arabia. Someone from one of the insulted tribes ran him through with a sword, again sparking a deadly fight. A further violation occurred after a comely young woman was insulted by a pack of youths from a different tribe than hers. The story goes that she rudely ignored their amorous advances and their demands to lower her veil so that they could see her face. In reprisal one of them pinned her skirt behind her without her knowing it so that when she stood up her bare bottom was exposed. The youths laughed and said, "You prevented us from seeing your front, but you granted us a view of your rear."[19] Swords drawn, her clansmen rushed in to deal with the disrespectful youths.

In each instance, tribal leaders stepped in to put a halt to the bloodshed, and blood money was paid in recompense for loss of life and limb. These outbreaks were serious violations of the sacred months, yet were containable since they were spontaneous rather than premeditated. Everyone had a commercial and cultural stake in Ukaz, but order had to be maintained for it to work. The leaders eventually decided that all future Ukaz attendees had to leave their weapons in their camps or hand them over to the fair organizers before being allowed entrance.

This new rule, however, did not prevent the fourth and more serious desecration of the sacred months, which began with a premeditated murder and led to combat between the military forces of two major tribal groups, a fight that swept a young Muhammad into the conflict. What precipitated the murder was vengeance: A man of the Kinana tribe, an ally of the Quraysh and close friend of its leaders, murdered a caravan master who had beaten him out of a lucrative contract with the king of Hira to transport merchandise to the Ukaz fair. For reasons that are not explained, the Kinana tribesman was passed over for the job and felt slighted. He had offered his services to the king, but was rebuffed in a manner that affected his dignity. Presumably with a crew of accomplices, he ended up falling upon his hapless rival, a member of one of the clans the Hawazin tribe, while the latter was en route to the fair, slaying him and everyone with him who resisted. He made off with the merchandise and fled to Khaybar, but sent word of what had happened to the Kinana and Quraysh leaders camped out at Ukaz. These men immediately understood the implications: In tribal life, it was all for one and one for all. Though they had no hand in it, the vile murder during the sacred months drew them into a conflict with the powerful Hawazins. The killer was of the Kinana tribe; the Quraysh were allies of the Kinanas, but not of the Hawazins, so they were obligated to back the Kinanas. Unprepared for conflict, both tribes hurriedly packed their merchandise, tents, and families onto camels and made a dash for the sacred territory of Mecca with Hawazin warriors in hot pursuit.

Once inside the sacred territory, the Meccans and their Kinana allies taunted their pursuers, knowing they would not dare cross the line to get at them, but the two sides agreed to fight the following year on neutral ground. The Ukaz fair was suspended as both sides prepared for war. Skirmishes and pitched battles were waged over the next four or five years, with a final major battle taking place between two large forces of cavalry and foot soldiers. Muhammad, who had acquired skill as a bowman, shot arrows at the enemy. The leaders decided to put an end to the conflict after large numbers of warriors from each faction lay dead on the battlefield. When the slain from both sides were counted, the Quraysh turned out to be the nominal victors, and they agreed to pay blood money for the number of enemy dead in excess of their own.[20]

It is likely that Muhammad, who later showed skillful military leadership as he spread his religion by the sword, absorbed much about warfare by paying attention to the military actions as they unfolded and later by listening to combatants, who, like veterans of any war, would have talked about their experiences and critiqued the strategies and tactics of the battles.

This final battle of the Sacrilegious Wars took place twenty years after the Year of the Elephant, the year Abraha and his Abyssinian army marched on Mecca. Muhammad was therefore twenty years old, one of dozens of grandchildren of Abdul

Muttalib. But he was an orphan and a ward of an impoverished family of the Hashimite clan to which Abdul Muttalib's
descendants belonged, and he was therefore a nobody in the
Meccan scheme of things.

Marriage to a wealthy woman would eventually change that.

CHAPTER 4

Protectress

A bu Talib was a merry old man with a house full of kids that he could not feed, or so the story goes. This was likely the case on occasion, as droughts sometimes drastically drew down food supplies in Mecca and people went hungry. But just as Halima noted after she took charge of Muhammad, Abu Talib learned that curious things occurred when he was present. Whenever he was absent at mealtime, the portions sometimes had to be doled out, and everyone went away still hungry. Bring in Muhammad and the meager rations grew to the point where everyone left the dinner mat rubbing their bellies and burping with satisfaction. There was even food left over, more than had been in the pot at the beginning of the meal!

Abu Talib was not rich, but it is unlikely that he was in such dire circumstances that he needed divine intervention to feed his family. As one of the eldest and most prominent of the surviving sons of Abdul Muttalib, he was head of the Hashimite clan and was one of the important religious officers of the temple. At some point he relinquished the latter role to a younger brother to devote his time to trade. His position among the Hashimites assured him commercial opportunities, though given his personality it is not likely he cut much of a figure in business. He was of a kindly disposition, more likely to give than to take; in striking deals, he was a weaker negotiator than many of his sharp-eyed compatriots or hard-nosed trading partners. In short, he was a pushover. Yet there is no reason to suspect he was incapable at that time of providing for his growing family and the extra burden brought on by Muhammad.

Muhammad shared the modest home near the temple with Abu Talib's many sons and daughters. Talib, the eldest son, was about Muhammad's age; brothers Aqil and Jafar were much younger; Ali, who would later become a key member of Muhammad's religion and a future caliph, was not yet born. In the household were several daughters: Jumana, Tayta, and Fakhita. The latter also went by her mother's name, Fatima, and eventually became known as Umm Hani—the mother of Hani. When he was in his teens, Muhammad fell in love with her and asked his uncle for permission to marry her. First cousin marriages were not uncommon among Arabs, so the close blood relationship would not have been an obstacle. But his uncle opposed it, very likely because Muhammad was not able to stand on his own feet financially. Moreover, Abu Talib was arranging her marriage with a well-to-do member of the Makhzums, one of the successful merchant clans that descended from Qusay. Abu Talib's mother was from that clan, and the groom was one of Abu Talib's first cousins. Fakhita ended up marrying the Makhzumite, and Muhammad was left with a broken heart.

We do not learn much from the literature about Muhammad's employment during this period. He may have had a more active role in the caravan trade than is revealed, but only a single caravan expedition is reported, a trip that paved the way for his marriage to Khadija, a Meccan businesswoman, when he was twenty-five years old. The Muhammadan historian Ibn Sad suggests Muhammad did not actively seek out work, as his uncle once obliquely upbraided him, like a parent who has decided it was time his layabout offspring earned his keep. He informed Muhammad of a business opportunity and urged him to take advantage of it. "I am a man without wealth, and we are passing through hard days; here is a caravan for your people going to Syria. Khadijah bint Khuwaylid sends men from among your people with her commodities; if you go and offer your services to her, she will readily accept."[1] Abu Talib had already prepared the way. Upon learning she was looking for a trade representative, he had gone to her hillside home to pitch his nephew as dependable and worth considering.

By all accounts Khadija was an exceptional woman who stood out for her intelligence, looks, and wealth. She was the daughter of the Meccan merchant Khuwaylid who, according to some accounts, was killed during the Sacrilegious Wars, while other reports claim he was still alive at the time of Muhammad's marriage to Khadija. She learned the caravan business from him and financed merchandise that went out with the major commercial missions to Syria and Yemen. It is likely she also engaged in trade with towns and agricultural centers that dotted Western Arabia such as Taif and Yathrib, as regional trade was as much a part of the commercial activity of the Meccans as international trade.[2] It is not known what merchandise she dealt in. Meccan trade by that time had become specialized, with some merchants dealing in finished leather goods or tanned hides, others in mining products, while others sold camels, horses, and donkeys. A merchant named Judan specialized in slaves. They came back from trade missions with their profits and their camels laden with whatever could be sold in Mecca, from textiles to lumber, perfumes to food; or they packed in merchandise that had to be warehoused until the next caravan went out. It is said that Khadija, who at that time was forty years old, had two or three children from previous marriages, one that ended with the death of her husband, the other in divorce. She was sought after by wealthy Meccans, but turned down offers of marriage.

At twenty-five, Muhammad was neither handsome nor unattractive, average in height with broad shoulders, a large head, a roundish face, and a full beard. He wore a black or white turban wrapped in the style of the day, which left a long tail that could be pulled around his face in the event of a dust storm, but was usually tossed over his shoulder and dangled down his back. His eyes were always bloodshot, though not from drinking, and he walked with a lurching motion. He is styled as more of a dreamer than a practical man, with a reserved, guarded personality. He was more inclined to listen to conversations than to participate. He rarely looked directly into the eyes of the person he spoke to, but rather glanced to one side. He had a tendency toward melancholy, and underlying this condition was likely the neurological problem that caused his fits, a malady that would plague him throughout his life. What was appealing about him was his lucid mind along with a certain charm in his manners and a reputation for honesty. He was eloquent and spoke in the pleasing cadences of the Arabic he learned during his formative years with Halima's Bedouin tribe.[3]

It is certain Muhammad and Khadija were already acquainted, if only from a distance, through family ties. Muhammad's aunt Safiya had recently married Awwam, one of Khadija's many brothers, and they had already produced a child. Following Abu Talib's visit, Khadija sent for Muhammad and was impressed enough to hire him as her agent. He went off with the caravan astride a she-camel and was accompanied by one of her slaves whom she sent to attend to his needs. Except to note that Muhammad acquitted himself admirably, doubling Khadija's investment through shrewd bargaining at Syrian markets, the literature is remarkably lacking in credible details about the journey. Muir speculates that Muhammad may have traveled as far as the Mediterranean port of Gaza, a frequent destination for Meccan merchants, for a verse in the Koran speaks of ships "like mountains riding furious seas," a description that Muhammad could only have composed if he had personally seen a storming Mediterranean and observed its maritime activity.[4]

Instead of believable details about the trip, we are given further predictions of Muhammad's future as a prophet. When the caravan reached Syria, for instance, it made a stage stop that happened to be near the cell of yet another Christian hermit monk, a Yoda-like character named Nastur who happened to be in possession of yet another set of Christian scriptures that predicted the coming of a prophet and gave a description that remarkably resembled Muhammad. This future prophet caught the monk's attention after he dismounted from his camel and sat in the shade of a nearby tree. In one version of the story, the monk excitedly asked Khadija's slave about him. "He is of the Quraysh, one of the people of the sacred precinct," the slave said. Nastur replied, "No one has ever halted beneath this tree but a prophet." The hermit monk then asked, "Is there redness in his eyes?" The slave answered, "Yes! It never vanishes." In another version, the monk proclaimed that Muhammad was not only a prophet, but he was "the last of them" and enumerated the traits of this chosen one that were supposedly found in sacred Christian writings. Further pumping up the mythologized account of the journey, the literature reports that the slave observed two angels hovering over Muhammad to shade him from the desert heat.[5]

The early writers used the angel tale as the set up for the marriage of Muhammad and Khadija. An advance guard had already alerted Mecca that the caravan was about to return from Syria, and the entire town poured out to greet it. Khadija waited with several women in an upper room of her hillside home, which had a clear view of the temple and the meeting hall across from it. The weary caravan leaders—along with camel drivers, armed guards, and the endless line of pack camels—plodded into the valley in the afternoon and stopped in front of the town hall where a crowd assembled. Muhammad could be seen breaking away from the pack and riding his camel up the hill toward Khadija's residence. As he approached, Khadija spotted two angels casting a shadow over him. She pointed this out to the other women, and they were "wonderstruck."[6] The slave who had accompanied Muhammad rushed ahead to give her glad tidings of the journey, reporting what the hermit monk said and that he had witnessed angels hovering over Muhammad during the return trip. Khadija, of course, was smitten. She had heard of a coming prophet; indeed, all Arabia was awash in talk of a Chosen One who would bring a new religion, or so says the literature. And here was the very one who had been chosen riding up to her residence with the profits of the trade mission!

She paid Muhammad twice what she had agreed upon: eight camels instead of four, then plotted how to make a discreet proposal to avoid embarrassment if she was turned down, certainly a possibility given the difference in their age. She sent her friend Nafisa, one of the women with her when Muhammad returned from the journey, to speak to him on her behalf. After engaging him in small talk, Nafisa brought up the subject of his age and why, at twenty-five, he was not yet married. "I have no means to marry," he replied. "If you get enough means, and you get a proposal from a lady of beauty, wealth, dignity, and equal status, will you accept?" When he learned she was referring to Khadija, he asked how it would be possible. "Don't worry about it. I'll arrange it," she said.[7]

Muhammad told his uncle about the proposal. Marriages were a tribal affair and customs needed to be followed. In one version of the story in which Khadija's father was no longer alive, Abu Talib, accompanied by his brothers Hamza and Abbas, paid a visit to Khadija's uncle Amr to discuss the matter. They agree on a dowry of twenty young she-camels, the equivalent of five hundred silver dirhams, half to be paid up front. Details of the ceremony are lacking, but it is likely a large number of people from Muhammad's Hashimite clan and Khadija's Asad clan attended. Khadija's uncle gave a speech and married the couple, then the wedding was celebrated with a feast in which a camel and a goat or two were slaughtered.

In another version, the wedding did not go so smoothly. In this account, Khadija's father Khuwaylid was still alive and flatly opposed the marriage because Muhammad did not have any standing in Mecca. He had little if any money, his immediate family was not well off, and there were so many better choices, although in truth Khuwaylid had disapproved of other requests for his daughter's hand even though they were from Meccans with money and solid reputation. The story goes that Khadija got around her father's opposition by getting him drunk. Once he was sufficiently deprived of his senses, she dressed him in his finest striped robe, sprinkled perfume on him, then got him to give her away in a tipsy ceremony. He snored through the rest. When he sobered up, he looked at his clothing and at what was left over from the wedding feast and said, "What is this meat, this perfume, this garment?" She replied, "You have married me to Muhammad, the son of Abdullah." "I have not done so," he said. "Would I do this when the greatest men of Mecca have asked for you and I have not agreed?"[8] In yet another version, Khadija and Muhammad both conspired to get Khuwaylid drunk, then dressed him up in a fine robe and got him to pronounce the marriage. When the sobered-up father realized what had been done to him, he went to get his sword, but so did Muhammad's kinfolk, leading to a standoff and ultimately to the father's acceptance of the arrangement.[9]

From a psychological point of view the marriage is revealing. Khadija filled an emotional need in Muhammad created by his early experience of rejection and abandonment by his birth mother, then by his foster mother, and finally by the premature death of his biological mother a year after he was returned to her. Khadija became his mother-wife. What else would explain her attraction to him, angels aside, but her own need to fill the rôle? Muhammad must have calculated that the union would be an excellent deal for him. Given her wealth, he would no longer have to rely on his uncle for support; he would now be a man with a pile of gold dinars and silver dirhams backing him up. Her social status, to the extent that it was transferable to him, would certainly act as a cure for his lowly status.

Over the course of their long marriage, which began in A.D. 595 and lasted twenty-five years, Khadija bore him four daughters and two or three sons. There is disagreement about the number of sons, but not about the fact that the male offspring died young. Qasim, a boy, was the first child, and Muhammad became known as Abu al-Qasim—father of Qasim—following the Arab custom for a father to assume a nickname derived from the name of the firstborn son. But life again inflicted a cruelty on Muhammad when Qasim died before reaching his second birthday. The Muhammad biographies, from the earliest versions of the Muhammadan scholars to later Western attempts, merely make a note of this fact without commentary, but it had to have been a shattering experience. Already of a morose nature, Muhammad would have been dragged even further into melancholy and brooding. It cannot be ruled out that Qasim's death was the spark that pushed him into musing about the fundamental questions of life and led him eventually to doubt the religious beliefs of his day and age.

Another son, the last child, died as well, but all four daughters survived: Zaynab, Ruqaya, Umm Kulthum, and Fatima.[10] Khadija was constantly pregnant, giving birth to one child a year. Salma, a freed slave of Muhammad's aunt Safiya, served as the midwife in each of the deliveries. Following tradition, Khadija sacrificed two goats at the birth of each male child and one goat for each of her daughters. Prior to the births, Khadija engaged wet nurses, but there is no indication that these were women like Halima, nomads living in a far-off tent with their charges cut off from their biological mother for years. More than likely these were women who lived nearby or were employees or even slaves residing in the Khadija-Muhammad household.

Aside from the presence of slaves and differences in architecture and furnishings, the scene at the home would be familiar to people of any day and age: children chasing one another through corridors and up and down stairs, rug rats crawling along the floor, frazzled parents trying to maintain order. Because of her wealth, Khadija's home would have been the center of gravity for a large number of in-laws and friends, meaning a flow of people in and out. The home would have served as Khadija's business office as well, a place where investment plans were made and deals struck. The literature does not speak of further caravan trips that Muhammad took part in, but it is logical to assume he had a role in the business.

For Muhammad, the marriage gave him a boost up the ladder of Meccan affairs. He was now someone whose friendship was worth cultivating if only as a means of gaining influence with Khadija. That he remained dependent on her becomes clear when he got a visit from his aging foster mother Halima. The region was suffering from drought and Halima's Bedouin tribe, which lived off their livestock, was suffering. Many of her animals had perished, and she appealed to Muhammad for help. Muhammad, in turn, discussed the matter with Khadija, who ended up giving the woman forty head of sheep and a camel packed high with provisions. If Muhammad had owned livestock, he would have been able to give from his own herd without the need for Khadija's approval, but he evidently did not have anything of his own to give away.[11]

In addition to his children, Muhammad also had a hand in raising several boys who would later become key players in the expansion of his religion. Foremost among them was Ali, the youngest son of Abu Talib and a future caliph whose birth took place several years after the marriage of Muhammad and Khadija. The mythology has it that Ali was born inside the then-roofless temple in A.D. 598, but he did not open his eyes until days later when Muhammad and Khadija paid a visit to Abu Talib's residence to see the child and congratulate the parents. The story goes that the infant opened his eyes only after he was placed in Muhammad's lap. The parents wanted to name him Zayd or Asad, but Muhammad suggested calling him Ali, a name derived from Allah, the high god of the Meccans to whom all other gods were subordinate, because his mother had given birth inside the temple. Ali remained with his parents for the next five or six years but then became the ward of Muhammad. This occurred because of a period of drought and famine, possibly during the time that Halima went to Muhammad for help. Abu Talib's ability to feed his large family was severely strained to the point that he beseeched Muhammad to take in Ali. Another well-to-do relative, Abu Talib's younger brother Abbas, took in Ali's older brother Jafar, who was at that time fifteen years old.[12]

Another member of Muhammad's household was the slave boy Zayd. He was from a Christian tribe from Yemen and had been captured at the age of eight when marauders attacked a caravan he was traveling with. He was said to have been of mixed race, half Abyssinian, half Arab, with African features predominating. He was put up for sale at the slave market of Ukaz where he caught the attention of Khadija's nephew Hakim. Hakim purchased the boy and gave him to Khadija as a present. Following his marriage to Khadija, Muhammad took an interest in the boy because of his diligent attention to the tasks he was given, his graceful manners, and also because of his Abyssinian-Christian background. He knew something of the religion and spoke to Muhammad about it. Khadija ended up giving him to Muhammad, who treated him like a son.

That there was a real affection between them became evident when Zayd's father Haritha learned of his whereabouts and showed up in Mecca with money to buy his son back. By then, Zayd had been missing for seven years. His father was overjoyed at finding him. Muhammad declined the ransom money and offered to return Zayd to his rightful father, but left the decision to Zayd. By then, the boy had formed a deep bond with Muhammad, who had treated him well despite his slave status, whereas his father was now almost a stranger. Zayd therefore chose to stay with Muhammad. In response, Muhammad took the boy to the temple and publicly announced that he was adopting Zayd; thenceforth he would be known as Zayd ibn Muhammad—Zayd the son of Muhammad.[13]

And then there was Zubayr, the son of Muhammad's aunt Safiya and Khadija's brother Awwam, who was born the year before Muhammad married Khadija. Zubayr was a frequent and often long-term presence at Khadija's home as his father died when he was young and his mother grossly mistreated him. Safiya was a hot-tempered disciplinarian and frequently beat him, sometimes savagely. An uncle named Nawfal once witnessed her maltreatment and complained to the clan elders about it. Safiya insisted she was doing it for his own good: "Whoever thinks that I beat Zubayr with ill intention, he is mistaken. I beat him so that he may become wise and brave and defeat the army of the enemies and capture booty." As a result of the thrashings, Zubayr developed a violent streak. The story is told of a fistfight he got into with an adult. Zubayr punched the man so hard that he broke his hand. He must have been the one who started the fight, because people complained to Safiya about it. She was proud of him. She responded, "How did you find Zubayr, brave or cowardly?"[14] All three of the youths—Ali, Zayd, and Zubayr—would eventually become key members of Muhammad's inner circle and would count among the most ferocious of his fighters.

Also part of the household was Baraka, the Abyssinian slave girl who had belonged to Muhammad's father and was with the six-year old Muhammad when his mother died. She became his property and remained with him the entire time he lived with Abu Talib. Muhammad was fond of her, often calling her Mommy. He freed her following his marriage to Khadija, and she moved to Yathrib after marrying a man from there. She bore him a son they named Ayman. When her husband died shortly after the birth, she went back to Mecca with Ayman and stayed with her former master. Muhammad later persuaded Zayd to marry Baraka even though she was twice his age, and she bore him a son, Osama, who would eventually become one of the most fearsome of Muhammad's followers.

In A.D. 605, when Muhammad was thirty-five years old, the venerable moon temple underwent a major upgrade as a result of flood damage. Heavy rainfall was rare in Mecca, but occasionally it poured sufficiently to cause flash floods to course down the usually dry riverbed that cut through the center of the valley. The temple was prone to damage from such floods, as it sat near one side of the riverbed. It had seen improvements since the days of Qusay, but it still remained a roofless, rectangular wall about the height of a one-story building. After one of the walls was breached in a flash flood that year, the powerful of Mecca decided it needed to be rebuilt from the ground up and turned into a real temple, one reflecting the commercial and religious status of the town. That meant a temple with a roof.[15]

The reconstruction project was an ambitious undertaking, and the scope of it was determined by the shipwreck of a Byzantine merchant vessel near Jedda, a fishing hamlet and minor port of call on the Red Sea some forty miles west of Mecca. The Meccans purchased the wreck, dismantled it board by board, and transported the salvage to Mecca. Wood for construction was in short supply in Mecca, and so were the skills and tools needed to work with it. It turned out the ship's captain, a Coptic Christian named Baqum, was a skilled carpenter and mason. The Meccans hired him to help with the reconstruction.

Obtaining building materials was one thing; overcoming fear of offending the gods another. The Meccans worried about angering the gods if they tore down the old temple, and they prayed for the gods to recognize the rebuilding as an act of piety. Walid, the chief of the Makhzum clan and one of the leading Meccans, took up a pickaxe, said a prayer assuring the gods that nothing but good was intended, and proceeded to break down a section of the old wall. Fearing a lightning bolt from the sky—Hubal was believed to flash his anger that way—none of the Meccans dared join Walid until the next morning when he showed up for work alive and well.[16]

All the Quraysh clans participated in the project by providing money and manpower. Muhammad took part in the work by carrying rocks from nearby hills to the worksite. With Baqum's guidance, large stones were chiseled into tight-fitting blocks. A stone platform rising eight feet above the ground as a rampart against future floods was constructed first. The walls were more than a yard thick at the base, and in the completed structure they rose to about forty feet above the platform.

While constructing the platform, the Meccans fell into a dispute over the placement of the Black Stone. The sacred object had been carefully removed during the demolition, and it needed to be reinserted into a corner of the new wall. A niche had been prepared for it about five feet off the ground, but the Meccans could not agree about which of the clans should have the honor of putting it into place. It was a serious matter because it involved status, and the Meccans nearly came to blows. They finally decided on arbitration: Let the first person who came walking out of the Hashimite neighborhood decide how the matter should be handled. It happened Muhammad was that person, and he came up with an equitable solution: He placed his mantle on the ground, told them to put the stone in the middle, then each group took hold of one corner. Together they lifted the stone so it could be inserted into the niche. Muhammad was given the honor of pushing it into place. As for the roof, the salvaged wood provided beams and planks, and pillars cut from the masts of the wrecked ship supported the beams.[17] As a final touch, a narrow stone staircase without side rails was built leading up to a thick wooden door, the sole entrance to the building. When completed, the temple was nearly cubic in form, causing the Meccans to call it the Kabah, the Arabic word for cube, certainly the first use of the word in connection with the Meccan temple.

The new temple included a semicircular stone platform built next to the northwest wall. It had the same elevation as the platform the temple was built on. The Meccans had at first intended to incorporate it into the building, which would have made it resemble an early Christian church. Muhammad would later comment that the section was left out because the Meccans ran out of money and construction material.[18] Instead, a low stone wall was built atop the platform and it became an outdoor meeting site for the important people of the town. During the hot summer months it was shaded with an awning.

During the construction, Muhammad suffered another epileptic seizure. This occurred after he was pressured by his fellow workers to strip naked, the practice among construction workers at the time. In order to protect their shoulders while carrying heavy rocks, workers would wrap their waist cloths into a thick cushion and use it as padding over the shoulder and neck area where the heavy rock was carried. Morbidly modest, Muhammad was reluctant to disrobe, but his uncles Abu Talib and Abbas pestered him to do like everyone else. This triggered what appeared to be an epileptic fit, for as soon as he took off his garment he fell to the ground unconscious. It is not known how long he remained unconscious, but when he came to his senses, he cried, "My waist sheet! My waist sheet!" and quickly reattached the cloth. In the literature, this is made out to be a divine event in which Muhammad was imparted a lesson in modesty, for he was said to hear a voice out of nowhere that warned: "Beware of your nakedness!"[19]

If it is true that he believed he heard a voice—the first of many that he would claim to hear—it provides evidence of an epileptic attack, as auditory hallucinations often occur during seizures. To save face, Muhammad claimed he had slipped, but the men who had seen his face while he was unconscious knew it was something other than a slip-and-fall accident. He never again showed his body to anyone. Indeed, one of his wives would later note that in all the time they were together, she never once saw his private parts.[20]

That Muhammad was deeply ashamed of his body and body functions comes through in a number of anecdotes about defecation. Rich or poor, nobody in Mecca had sanitary facilities in their homes, and most people made do in the bush. It is possible the Meccans developed a network of communal latrines, but they would have lacked privacy. The literature reveals the lengths Muhammad would go through to "ease" himself in private. It did not take long to be outside of Mecca, but he would hike out far beyond the last abode in order not to be seen. One of the stories that is intended to underscore Muhammad's modesty ends up giving a humorous take on it: On the way to finding a place secure from eyes he heard voices everywhere greeting him: "O Apostle of Allah! May peace be upon you!" This caused Muhammad to look around nervously to see who was there.[21]

Even more humorous was the power the literature gave Muhammad over nature to help him secure privacy while defecating. In one instance when no hiding place was to be found, he pointed to a couple of trees to one of the believers who accompanied him, the shepherd boy Masud, and said, "Go and stand between them and say to them, 'Verily, the Apostle of Allah has sent me to you to come closer till he eases himself behind you.'" Masud did as instructed, the trees closed ranks to form a protective shield, and Muhammad took care of business in private. The story goes that when he was done, the trees slid back to their former position.[22]

The official record of Muhammad's early years is heavily mixed with the mythical, and it is therefore difficult to develop a rounded portrait of him in his early and mid-adult life. Among other things, we do not know much about his employment. Did he contribute to the marital community, or did he live off of his wife's wealth? The literature presents a picture of a man of saintly forbearance, but the image does not square with the later Muhammad, a man whose story becomes one of barbaric crimes and cruel atrocities against anyone who opposed his belief in himself as a prophet of God. If the child is the father of the man, this child cannot be clearly discerned in the literature.

One of the ideas that can be comfortably extracted from the canonical literature is that during their time together and to the end of her life, Khadija remained Muhammad's friend, supporter, cheerleader, financier, and protectress. He was a man with a shaky emotional foundation who needed the prop of a strong woman. Without her, it is possible his religion would never have gone beyond the narrow confines of the vale of Mecca.

CHAPTER 5

Cave Dwellers

Muhammad was raised within the homogenous culture of polytheism that existed in Mecca at the time and took part in the rites and rituals well into the fourth decade of his life. Even he acknowledged having sacrificed animals to the gods. It was a way of life that had been handed down for generations, and it had a history in Arabia going back at least fifteen hundred years, with only minor variations in substance to be found in the pagan kingdoms of south and north Arabia that had risen and fallen long before Muhammad's time. This culture now had a sturdy foothold in Mecca because of the centrality of its temple in the rituals of the pilgrimage that had a later development in western Arabia. Though as accustomed as any other Meccan to this way of life, at some point he began to question the validity of what he was raised to think of as true.

The literature, which holds that Muhammad's first act upon coming into the world was to get down on his hands and knees in the prayer style he later developed, is hardly a reliable guide to understand when this process began. One has to search between the lines to find emotional and intellectual triggers. An important trigger may have been the death of his firstborn son Qasim. The literature does not indicate a cause of death, but only notes that the child died before reaching his second birthday. Given the emotional devastation of such an experience, it cannot be ruled out that this shattering loss brought about the first fissure in Muhammad's beliefs. It is easy to imagine the suffering of Muhammad and Khadija as they watched their ailing toddler struggle to hold onto life: The child, cradled in their arms, screams for life, but loses the battle and within a day the enshrouded body is laid into the ground amid a crowd of mourners. Following the burial, the grieving parents are in their home, now empty of the child, and they weep. In this reconstruction one must also imagine the presence of a stone idol in a corner of the room, a rectangular or rounded stone with eyes, a nose, and a mouth carved in relief. It is enthroned on a pedestal and seems to stare down at them. Does Muhammad, his eyes blurred by tears, return the stare? Does a curse rise in his throat?

Most Meccan homes, even the most humble, contained idols, one representing a major deity while others were tribal or personal. Khadija's home was no exception. She was known to be a devotee of the goddess al-Uzza. There is reason to believe she even named the child Abd al-Uzza, the Servant of al-Uzza.[1] Qasim was more of a nickname, as it meant "one who shares with his people." Following the birth, she and Muhammad sacrificed two animals to the goddess, very likely at an altar on the grounds outside the Meccan temple. Al-Uzza was a mother-goddess. To worship her was to worship the energy that animates all life. She was held with the same devotional love that many Christians have for the mother of Jesus. Her sanctuary at Nakhla, a day's journey to the east of Mecca, was a modest temple erected on a hillside amid a cluster of acacia trees. The ritual of supplication through blood sacrifice was the means of approaching and petitioning deity. To give was to get. While Khadija held the swaddled infant, Muhammad would therefore have undertaken the task of slitting the throats of the sacrificial animals. As the blood flowed on the altar and spilled to the ground, he and Khadija and whoever else accompanied them offered prayers of gratitude for the gift of the child and beseeched the mother goddess to accept the offering of the animals. They dedicated their infant to her as a means of obtaining her protection over the child and her intercession with Allah, the High God of the Meccans, for the child's good fortune in life. Following the custom, Muhammad smeared the blood on the stone face of the statue in order for the goddess to share in the vital energy.

But now this fresh babe of al-Uzza was lying beneath the ground. They had beseeched her protection, but the child died. What was the power of this goddess if their child died? Were

THE KABAH IS THE NAME used for the temple of Mecca. It means Cube, a nickname it acquired in A.D. 605 after it was rebuilt because of flood damage. Muhammad, who was at that time thirty-five years old, was part of the work crew. Prior to the reconstruction, the temple consisted of a one-story rectangular wall without a roof. The original temple, which was devoted to moon worship, began several centuries earlier as a low-wall enclosure of stacked rocks with the Black Stone meteorite inserted in one corner.

they deceived? One can feel Muhammad's emerging rage and imagine him questioning al-Uzza about why she did not protect his beloved son. But the mother goddess does not give him an answer, and Muhammad becomes angry. He paces back and forth as he remembers the lonely hurt when his mother died and he watched the dirt being shoveled over her at al-Abwa, and then his grandfather's burial in Mecca. He remembers the pain of being cast off as an orphan and the sting of poverty and lowly status that resulted from this misfortune. He shouts more questions: "Where were you and where were the other gods during all of this? Why is there all this suffering? What is the meaning of this? Speak to me!"

But there was only silence.

There were intellectual triggers, possibly beginning as early as his trip to Syria with his uncle Abu Talib when he was first exposed to a foreign culture and a different religion. The impressions of this trip would have lodged in his mind to await further links and associations before acquiring importance. Assuming no other ventures that far north, his second exposure to a foreign religion would have occurred during his trip to Syria on behalf of Khadija. By then, he would have been better prepared to understand what he observed. Intelligent and inquisitive, he would have asked questions of everyone he came in contact with. Why do they say this? Why do they think that? Yet he returned to Mecca still a polytheist, as seen in his sacrifices to the gods following the birth of his son and later children.

Possibly the greatest trigger came indirectly as the result of his marriage to Khadija. She brought him into contact with a small group of religious dissenters, pagan apostates who had come to the conclusion that the rituals and beliefs of their society were meaningless. Among them was Waraqa, her aging uncle, the man who found the five-year-old Muhammad on the road to Taif after he ran away from his foster parents. Waraqa was literate and learned. He had studied Judaism and one of the sects of Christianity. He had adopted this version of Christianity as his own. It was said that he translated portions of the New Testament into Arabic. It is difficult to believe that he did not hold discussions about his knowledge with Muhammad and Khadija, perhaps in the main room of their residence as they reclined on leather cushions with slaves in attendance. Khadija was said to have at some point embraced the Christian faith, though Muhammad remained less convinced. Nevertheless, that he acquired an admiration for Jesus is shown in his early Koranic compositions. There were other members of this small group of seekers, including one of Muhammad's cousins. All but one ended up embracing Christianity. With their rejection of paganism, these religious inquirers would have helped to push Muhammad into reflection about his inherited beliefs.

The religious seeker who had the greatest influence on Muhammad was Zayd ibn Amr, a crusty, in-your-face contrarian who at some point ran afoul of the Meccans for his open disdain of their religious practices. Zayd was about the same age as Waraqa, meaning he was thirty years older than Muhammad. Just as the other seekers, Zayd had lost his polytheist faith and was searching for a new religion. Like Waraqa, he made an effort to study the beliefs of the Christians and Jews, but among these seekers he was the only one to reject them. "I smelt Christianity and Judaism, but I disliked them," he would say.[2]

Zayd traveled to Christianized Syria in search of true religion. Priests, monks, rabbis, even magis—he did not spare anyone his questioning: What do you believe? Why do you believe what you believe? What he learned during his travels is a matter of conjecture, but he would certainly have heard about the diverse interpretations of the nature of Jesus and the Christian sects that formed around these interpretations, perhaps leading to his distaste for Christianity: The believers were so fractured and fractious. Predictably, the literature has him encounter yet another hermit monk—and also a couple of rabbis—who told him of a coming prophet. As for the Jews, Zayd never entered deeply into their beliefs. He found that theirs was more a way of life than a religion. They had the Torah, their sacred book that formed the basis of the laws they lived by. What interested Zayd most about the Jews was their claim of descent from Abraham, certainly a prophet after Zayd's own heart. Abraham was an iconoclast who, according to Jewish legend, destroyed the idols of his father and preached the worship of a singular god. Prior to his trip north, Zayd became obsessed with the idea that there existed a pure form of monotheism that antedated both Christianity and Judaism—the religion of Abraham, as he called it. It was a religion of a man so firm in his belief in the one God that he was willing to sacrifice his son to prove it.

Western scholars generally accept that the stories of Abraham and other Jewish prophets were known in Arabia long before the birth of Muhammad, though they question the extent and depth of the knowledge. Colonies of Jews had thrived in the oases of western Arabia for nearly a thousand years so that the stories of Abraham had to have been common knowledge among their polytheist neighbors. Christian missionaries in Yemen spread the idea that Arabs were part of the family of Abraham because of their supposed descent through one of his sons. Such stories had only superficial penetration in Mecca and other towns and villages of the Hijaz, but they were certainly known. Of greatest interest to Zayd were the Biblical stories of the two major lines of descent from Abraham: one through Isaac, the son of Sarah, and another through Ishmael, the son of Hagar. Each had twelve sons whose descendants founded great tribes. One of the reasons Zayd dismissed Judaism was his belief that the progeny of Isaac had strayed from the original religion of Abraham. The Ishmaelites, however, had developed separately and they therefore must have practiced the original and uncorrupted monotheism of Abraham, or so Zayd believed.

If he had gone in search of practitioners of this pure form of the religion of Abraham, he returned to Mecca empty handed. Not only did it no longer exist, the supposed monotheistic purity of Ishmael's line had been compromised early. Historians have shown that the descendants of Ishmael, who lived as nomads along the east-west caravan routes of the northern deserts, adopted the pagan practices of surrounding tribes.[3] Later, they became involved in the caravan trade, first as armed guards and guides, then as merchants. A powerful confederation of pagan Ishmaelite tribes flourished, but these groupings were later crushed by the Assyrians and Babylonians. Remnants of the paganized Ishmaelites were eventually absorbed into the Nabataean kingdom that was noted for its control over the caravan trade from Yemen to Syria and for the haunting mausoleums it carved into sandstone cliffs outside its capital city of Petra. But Nabataean control over trade ended when Rome acquired it as a province in A.D. 106. An earthquake in the fourth century demolished its temples, including those that were dedicated to the same gods worshipped by the Meccans. By Zayd's time, Petra was a ruined ghost town, and the descendants of the Nabataeans had turned to Christianity. Thenceforward, the Ishmaelites lived on only in place names such as Tayma and Duma. One of the monks Zayd encountered told him flatly that what he was seeking no longer existed.[4] There may have been isolated Ishmaelite tribes who retained their Abrahamic faith, but the fifth-century ecclesiastical historian Sozomen notes they eventually came in contact with their long-lost Judaic brethren and adopted the rites and practices of the Jews. By Zayd's time they too had lost their Ishmaelite identity.[5]

Upon his return to Mecca, Zayd became a champion of the mythical religion of Abraham, though without being able to say of what such a faith consisted. Zaydism, as it can be called, was the simple belief in the uniqueness and singularity of God and in the need to follow Abraham's example of total submission to His will. He despaired over his inability to add more to it, and would cry out: "O God, if I knew which manner is most pleasing to Thee, I should worship Thee in it; but I know it not."[6]

Like the Biblical prophet who inspired him, Zayd railed against the Meccans for their idolatry and also attacked the injustices of the day. He particularly fulminated against a practice, however rare, of burying female infants alive. The literature never cites any specific instances, so it was likely an infrequent though real occurrence. Muhammad later decried female infanticide in one of his Koran verses, but linked it to desperation arising from famine.[7] It is said that Zayd, if he heard of someone contemplating such a drastic action, would go to the parents and offer to raise the child himself. He also found it an abomination that the Meccans sacrificed animals to their gods and goddesses instead of the one true God. The God of Abraham not only created animals, but also the rain that caused the grass to grow that they fed on, "Yet you slaughter it in other than the name of Allah."[8] He also ridiculed the practice of kissing the Black Stone. It was senseless. The Black Stone was nothing more than a stone. Maybe it had fallen from the heavens like they believed, but it was still just a stone and could not have any effect in any way whatsoever—not any more than the stone and wood idols the Meccans worshipped. While it was still safe for him in Mecca, Zayd was once spotted with his back against the temple hectoring the Meccans: "O people of the Quraysh! By Allah! None amongst you is on the religion of Abraham except me."[9]

Given his crustiness and zeal, Zayd made enemies even among his own family. His half-brother Khattab made his life miserable. Khattab was known for his temper. Like Muhammad's aunt Safiya who used to beat her son Zubayr, Khattab was merciless with his son Umar, an eventual Muhammad insider and a future caliph.[10] At some point, Khattab turned his heavy fist on Zayd and took it upon himself to persecute him as an apostate. Fearful that Zayd would influence others to abandon their religious heritage, he incited other Meccans against him. There may have been some family issues behind the hostility, as the literature does not single out other relentless persecutors. Zayd and Khattab shared the same mother, but Zayd's father was the son of Khattab's father, making Khattab simultaneously his brother and his uncle.[11] Khattab eventually drove Zayd out of Mecca, and he took up living in a cave on Mount Hira, a rocky mountain in the shape of a butte just north of town. He would only venture into Mecca at night. One can conjecture that he would go to the home of Khadija under cover of darkness for secret meetings with Muhammad, Khadija, Waraqa, and others of this small group of religious seekers. At some point even these visits became risky, as Khattab learned he was entering Mecca during the night and alerted Meccans to watch for him. He remained an outcast, but sympathizers, among them Muhammad, brought him food and listened to him fume against polytheism and discourse on the God of Abraham.

That Muhammad was among Zayd's supporters becomes evident in a tradition indicating he had once brought the banished Zayd a dish of meat, but was rebuked. Zayd refused to touch it when he learned it was from an animal that had been sacrificed to one of the pagan gods, presumably by Muhammad. "I never eat what you sacrifice before your idols. I eat only that which the name of God has been mentioned."[12]

Zayd composed poems to articulate his views. A poem attributed to him contains many of the themes that Muhammad would later elaborate in a distinctly different poetic style:

> Am I to worship one lord or a thousand?
> If there are as many as you claim,
> I renounce al-Lat and al-Uzza both of them
> As any strong-minded person would.
> I will not worship al-Uzza and her two daughters,[13]
> Nor will I visit the two images of the Banu Amr.
> I will not worship Hubal though he was our lord
> In the days when I had little sense.
> I wondered (for in the night much is strange
> Which in daylight is plain to the discerning),
> That God had annihilated many men
> Whose deeds were thoroughly evil
> And spared others through the piety of a people
> So that a little child could grow in manhood.

A man may languish for a time and then recover
As the branch of a tree revives after the rain.
I serve my Lord the compassionate
That the forgiving Lord may pardon my sin,
So keep to the fear of God your Lord;
While you hold to that you will not perish.
You will see the pious living in gardens,
While for the infidels hell fire is burning.
Shamed in life, when they die
Their breasts will contract in anguish.[14]

There is no telling Zayd's age when he died, but it is known that his death occurred some time after the reconstruction of the temple. In one version, he was murdered in southern Iraq while on a return trip from Syria, with no suspects or motives mentioned. A second version does not give a cause of death, but indicates he was buried on Mount Hira. Waraqa composed an elegy in his memory, and Muhammad later eulogized him.

It is possible that the suffering Muhammad experienced at the death of his sons, particularly of his first born, was the key experience that first attracted him to Zaydism. Because of his loss and the anguish that came from it, Muhammad could identify with the suffering that Abraham would have brought upon himself by cutting the throat of his own son had the angel not stayed his hand at the last minute. That Abraham was obeying God's command as a demonstration of faith would not have lessened the horror of taking the life of his beloved son nor the depth of pain that he would have experienced afterward. Abraham's submission to God's will was total and unwavering regardless of the cost.

About the time of Zayd's death, Muhammad entered into a period of intellectual and emotional instability. The alternate religious ideas coming from Zayd and other sources were like hammer blows raining down on his inherited world view, which was by now nearing complete demolition. At the same time, he was a bundle of neurological and emotional problems and was heading toward collapse. The humiliation of his epileptic fit during the rebuilding of the temple had to have weighed heavily on him, particularly if it was the first public display of his falling sickness. Many Meccans would have cooled to him at that point:

Epilepsy and devil possession went hand in hand, they believed. At a minimum, they would have now viewed him as a peculiar fellow. Hypersensitive, he then kept from people to avoid the sting of their reproving eyes. The public display of his illness could not have helped his self esteem, for deep within him was still the wounded little boy who had to be reassured he weighed in importance not just more than ten, or a hundred, or a thousand people, but more than everybody combined.

In addition to epilepsy, he also appears to have suffered from an acute anxiety condition that may have been linked to epilepsy, but more likely was a separate emotional illness stemming from early life trauma. He needed to be medicated, but there were not any pharmaceuticals to deal with such a disorder, nor were there therapists and therapeutic couches to delve into the cause. He would eventually gain control over anxiety by elaborating and practicing a complex prayer ritual marked by repetition and precise, time-consuming body movements.

Influenced by Zayd and other dissenters, he became obsessed with religious questions. His spiritual longings had to have been genuine since they were driven by legitimate doubts about his religious heritage, but they were raised to the level of obsession thanks to his neurological disorder. The neurological power that magnified his legitimate preoccupations could only have worsened his anxiety, for they would have stripped away his old beliefs without replacing them—as yet—with the security of something new, leaving him trapped in what today would be called an existential crisis.[15]

Always standoffish, Muhammad began to isolate himself. It is said that he spent days alone meditating in a cave near the summit of Mount Hira, possibly the same cave that Zayd had lived in. From the cave entrance was a lofty view of Mecca below and the brown mountains and dry valleys beyond. Some accounts state that he went to Mount Hira to undertake the practice of fasting during the month of Ramadan, but this was unlikely since the Ramadan fast was a later invention. Other entries indicate that he returned home every few days to stock up on supplies, showing he was not engaged in a fast but had chosen to spend time alone.

It had to have been a mentally anguishing time for him. Every question he posed to himself led to more questions: How do you explain the fact of existence and all the experiences contained therein, the good and the bad included? How can the moon explain it, or the sun—both objects of worship of the Meccans? Did they cause you to be? If the answer cannot be found in the gods and goddesses and objects of worship of the ancestors, then was it to be found in the God of Abraham? What was the nature of this God? What was his relationship to man? It was an exercise in futility, like grabbing at the air in the hope of coming up with something solid. He was pondering questions with no sure answers except in faith, but faith in what? A God who is the creator of all things including the sun and the moon? A God of reward and punishment, of Heaven and Hell? Is there a hereafter, and is it the garden of Zayd's poem? A material heaven? If so, then is there also a material Hell, a place of fire and burning flesh? Isn't the misery and suffering of this world enough? The more he anguished over not knowing, the more he pushed himself to understand. The more he realized he could not find answers, the more desperate he was for answers. He became like the anguished figure of the Edvard Munch painting. He had to arrive at the stable ground of certainty or he would surely turn into the madman that many people already thought he was.

It was during this period of emotional and intellectual upheaval that his overcharged brain, wracked by doubts and suffering, came to his rescue in the form of a series of spectacular hallucinatory experiences that convinced him he was unique and had been singled out by God for a special purpose. This took place in A.D. 610 when Muhammad was forty years old. These began as vivid dreams of light that "came like the bright light of dawn." He continued secluding himself in the cave of Mount Hira, sometimes spending days there until food ran out. At some point he had a vivid dream of an angel that came to him at the break of dawn and showed him a brocaded cloth on which there was writing. The angel said, "Recite," commanding him to read what was written, but Muhammad said, "I cannot recite," meaning that he did not know how to read. The angel squeezed him to the point he could no longer bear the pain, but released him and told him again to recite what was on the cloth. When he protested that he could not read, the angel squeezed him so hard he thought he was going to die. To free himself, he finally said, "What shall I recite?" The angel recited some verses, and he repeated them. At that, the angel disappeared and Muhammad woke up terrified, believing he had become devil-possessed or had lost his mind. He rushed out of the cave intending on throwing himself off a cliff. There was nothing worse in this world than being a madman. By taking his own life, he would escape being branded as such by the Meccans. As he was climbing towards a convenient crag, however, he heard a voice: "O Muhammad, I am Gabriel and you are the prophet of God." On the horizon was a huge figure that filled the sky. Muhammad felt stuck, as if he was glued in place, but he could still turn his head. No matter which direction he looked, there was the angel filling the sky with six hundred wings on each side. One version relates that Muhammad first saw the angel in human form close up, so close it could almost be touched. The angel only assumed its majestic size at Muhammad's request, but when he saw him in his true form looming over the entire horizon, Muhammad was knocked unconscious.[16] Gabriel then shrank back down to human size, revived Muhammad, and "wiped the saliva off his cheeks."[17]

The stories continue with Muhammad rushing home in the grip of a panic attack. He jumped under the bed covers like Scrooge after seeing Marley's ghost and cried to his wife, "Wrap me up! Wrap me up!" Shivering with fear, he told her what happened, that he believed he had seen a demon or a *jinn*. "Khadija, I think I have gone mad!" and, "I think my life is in danger." He may have already had several such experiences, because she asked him to tell her "when this companion of yours" comes again. The next time it occurred, she was with him and conducted an experiment to get to the bottom of it: She had him sit on her left thigh, then inquired if he still saw the figure. When he said he did, she had him sit on her other thigh—to no avail as he continued seeing it. Then she stripped off her upper garments and asked him again if he saw it. It turned out he no longer saw it, leading her to conclude it was an angel rather than a demon, since an angel would respect a woman's modesty whereas a demon would not. "Rejoice, cousin, and stand firm," she said. "By Him in whose hand is Khadija's soul, I hope that you may be the prophet of this community." Not yet completely convinced, she sought out a second opinion from her uncle Waraqa. Now aging and blind, Waraqa affirmed that Muhammad was indeed a prophet because if what he said was true, he had been visited by the same angel that appeared to Moses.

With the encouragement of his wife, Muhammad came to believe he was "commissioned" during his cave experience as a prophet of the one God, the God of Abraham. The power of his neurological experiences was such that he truly believed he experienced angelic visitations. His belief became unshakable and later became the unshakable belief of his followers even though the disturbed content of much of the Koran and his later ruthless behavior as "God's Messenger"—the massacres, murders, torture, banditry, pillage, rape, the enslavement of men, women, and children, and other atrocities he perpetrated—make such a belief beyond ludicrous.

The neurological explanation for Muhammad's cave experience, while less dramatic than the spiritual, occupies the high ground of credibility. That he suffered from epilepsy has been noted in Western literature ever since the eighth century when Byzantine historian Theophanes made a scathing claim that Khadija had whined about being married to an epileptic.[18] Western historians and religious scholars have debated the matter ever since. Today, the question of Muhammad's epilepsy has shifted from academia to neuroscience. Books about epilepsy include him among case studies of famous people afflicted with the disease, and his symptoms, as described in the canonical literature, have become the object of clinical scrutiny. In 1976, neurologist F. R. Freeman offered a tentative conclusion that the "most tenable diagnosis" would be that Muhammad suffered from the type of seizures found in temporal lobe epilepsy.[19]

More recently, Dede Korkut, the neuropsychologist who authored a book that examines evidence of Muhammad's neurological disorders, also described these seizures as exhibiting the characteristics of temporal lobe epilepsy, a condition that he believes Muhammad inherited from his mother.[20] Such seizures occur when abnormal bursts of electrical impulses surge in the temporal lobe, creating an uncontrolled release of electrical activity throughout the temporal lobe and in adjoining regions, like flashes of lightening in thunderclouds. The temporal lobe plays an important role in vision and hearing, so that such seizures can result in visual and auditory and even olfactory hallucinations, the contents of which are as determined by the mental life of the victim as are dreams. Korkut concludes that Muhammad's "religious and theological views were derived from his illness, including the self-deceptive view that he was a prophet."[21]

The cave can be seen as symbolic. The cave was a womb and a new Muhammad was born from it. He had molted from his old self, and now he looked down without sorrow at the shriveled fluff of his former being. Gone was the poor orphan, the goat herder, the man whose status in Mecca depended on his marriage to a wealthy woman. God had weighed him against ten of his own people and found he outweighed them, and he weighed him against a hundred and found that he outweighed them, and then he weighed him against a thousand people with the same result. Verily, Muhammad outweighed them all combined. He had grown in size and he was now taller than the tallest mountain—tall like Adam who had such height that his head thrust into Heaven and he could hear the angels talking among themselves and could even perceive the throne of God.

His naked wife cooed: "You are a prophet, Muhammad."

CHAPTER 6

The Amalgamated Monotheism of Mecca

If you are going to be a prophet, you need to have something to say.

Muhammad's powerful neurological experiences and his subsequent conviction that God had commissioned him as a prophet caught him short of material, and it took him several years to work out the general lines of his religion. This process of acquiring content, of course, had an earlier start through his exposure to Christianity, Judaism, and other religions as a result of his contacts with foreigners of those faiths and through his friendship with those few people of Mecca who, like Zayd and Waraqa, had studied them. His education now continued through informal contacts with people who gave him broader knowledge of the monotheistic religions, some of it heretical judging from the Koranic versions he later produced. These influences gave Muhammad a jumble of ideas. He was already a believer in Zaydism. Now, powered by the conviction God had chosen him for a special purpose, he set about to arrange all these elements into something that made sense to him.

Zayd had simplified his task by providing him with a framework centered in his belief in the existence of a pure religion of Abraham, a monotheistic path which held that Christianity and Judaism had deviated, each in its own way, from the original message of Abraham. There was but one God, the God that Abraham worshipped. He was the starter and controller of all creation, and the example of Abraham's unswerving faith under the severest of tests showed the way to live a virtuous life through complete submission to the will of this God. Zayd was unable to advance his belief much beyond this primary idea so that it remained an empty vessel in need of filling.

As elaborations of Zaydism, the earliest concepts Muhammad made use of were an amalgamation of the Judaic and Christian beliefs Zayd alluded to in his poetry. These were essentially twofold: the belief in the existence of sin as an offense against an almighty, all-seeing, all-knowing Creator and the belief in a hereafter in which reward in Heaven or punishment in Hell is dispensed. Muhammad also embraced the corollary ideas of the resurrection of the dead and a day of reckoning in which the creatures of God are made to stand before their Creator, who then makes the determination of reward or punishment based upon their obedience or disobedience to the divine will. In Muhammad's dogma, the greatest offense against this God concept was to worship false gods in the place of the real God. Muhammad also arrived at the conclusion that the resurrected body had to be physical. If not, how could the punishments of Hell be inflicted or the rewards of Heaven enjoyed? If the God of his imaginings was able to create his material creatures, he certainly had the power to reassemble them in their physical form even after death.

What was original about these ideas was Muhammad's claim they were original, that they were unambiguous communiqués to him and to him alone from the Creator, transmitted in the clear tongue of Arabia.

Muhammad's polytheist contemporaries had different ideas about sin and the afterlife. For the Arab pagans, to sin was to violate tribal custom, very much a here and now affair with consequences in the here and now. One could certainly anger the gods, but the consequences were also temporal. The gods of their pantheon lived in some invisible realm and had a mysterious influence over the affairs of man; they were beloved but feared meddlers. Earn their wrath and there was certainly hell to pay—but in this life. Propitiating the gods and earning their goodwill was therefore part of the pagan motive for worship and blood sacrifice. As for the hereafter, pagan Arabs believed in its existence, but not in reward or punishment therein. It was an indefinable state of being. That they held an afterlife belief can be seen from the olden practice of tying a favorite camel to the grave of its owner. Once the camel died from thirst, the deceased owner would have a mount in the hereafter. If pagan Arabs sought immortality, it was the immortality of poetry celebrating their deeds in life so that they lived on in the minds and hearts of their descendants. They sought the immortality of enduring fame.

Muhammad's first order of business following his hallucinatory experiences was to deal with a severe anxiety condition, and he found relief through the creation of exhausting cleansing and prayer routines that became hallmarks of his religion. It so happened that the Angel Gabriel gave him an assist with these formulations by appearing in human form while he was out and about in the foothills of Mount Hira. The story goes that the angel dug his heel into the ground, causing a spring to gush forth. Using this water, the angel taught Muhammad the ins and outs of the ritual purification that God required before prayer could be addressed to Him, then demonstrated the form prayer had to take in order to be accepted by the Almighty.[1]

The ablution—ritual cleansing—begins with the rinsing the hands and mouth, cleaning the nostrils by breathing in water and blowing it out, washing the face, scrubbing the right arm up to the elbow and then the left arm—each step of this routine performed three times. The ritual continues with wiping the head, ears, and neck with wet hands. The cleansing is finalized by washing both feet up to the ankles, also performed three times, beginning with the right foot. The prayer routine, equally elaborate, is characterized by precise motions of the body and the arms, with exactness in placing the palms of the hands and toes of the feet while the body flexes forward and the forehead touches the ground. The prayer prostrations are preceded by ritual motions one performs while standing and are followed by exacting posture while sitting on one's knees, camel-like. Muhammad was soon washing and praying like this five times a day, seven days a week. He would also frequently spend much of the night standing until his feet were swollen in what he termed voluntary prayer, which were in addition to the eventual five obligatory daily prayer sessions he imposed on himself and his followers. Failure to properly perform the ritual cleansing and prayer routine would invalidate them in the eyes of God, Muhammad declared.[2]

The amount of time Muhammad spent in ritual purification and in prayer "performance"—the word always used in connection with the carrying out of these rituals—is an indication that more was going on with him than merely giving praise to his idea of God. What these rituals suggest is that he was suffering from a severe obsessive-compulsive disorder, an infirmity that has its roots in debilitating anxiety. His rituals were so consuming that he could be considered an extreme example of the condition. It is defined as an "anxiety disorder characterized by intrusive thoughts that produce uneasiness, apprehension, fear, or worry, and by repetitive behaviors aimed at reducing the associated anxiety, or by a combination of such obsessions and compulsion."[3] The rituals of the obsessive-compulsive serve to put a lid on anxiety, which returns with a vengeance if the victim of the disorder is prevented from performing the anti-anxiety routine.

It is likely that underlying Muhammad's anxiety were feelings of inferiority, guilt, and shame, and a set of memories of negative life experiences that gave his screaming inner voice inexhaustible resources to dish up intrusive, self-whipping thoughts. That he was in the grip of such a powerfully negative self-image is suggested in the source materials, wherein Muhammad constantly begs God to forgive him for his abysmalness—in essence desperate appeals for relief from his mental demons.[4] The literature of neurology ties a tendency towards such merciless self-recrimination to the epileptic experience, a feature, along with hyper-religiosity and hyper-moralism, of what neurologists call the epileptic character. If so, it would help to explain Muhammad's attraction to the Judeo-Christian concept of a judgmental God: God was the inner voice screaming at him. He must find a way to please this God; he must obey its will. But what was the divine will that must be obeyed?

Now that he was the prophet of God—and soon elevated to messenger—he set about to explain to himself and the world just what this screaming God wanted. For the next twenty-three years, he conveyed his ideas in rhyming prose, at first in short, focused poems and later in long, convoluted compositions. He attributed the words to God. The listener was to believe that God was the composer of an original tablet containing the Koran, which means Recital, and that God transmitted such verses piecemeal over the years to the Angel Gabriel, who then handed them down to him either in person or through paranormal means. These "revelations" sometimes occurred during an epileptic seizure, usually real though at times clearly faked, during which he would wrap himself in a blanket and hunker down until it was over. Then out came new verse, material he had been cogitating on for some time that took final form at or about the time of an epileptic episode—real or faked. Overall, the style of the Koran suggests the work of someone who knew what he was doing.

One of his earliest compositions, a brief set of verses that serves as the preamble to the standard version of Muhammad's Recital, reveals his struggle with a harsh inner voice:

> Praise be to God, Lord of the worlds!
> The compassionate, the merciful!
> King on the day of reckoning!
> Thee only do we worship, and to Thee do we cry for help.
> Guide Thou us on the straight path,
> The path of those to whom Thou hast been gracious;—
>   with whom
> Thou art not angry, and who go not astray.[5,6]

The use of the often obscure verses of the Koran to convey divine will does not seem a likely medium for the Creator of all Things, but it was the vehicle of choice for a verbally gifted Arab who set about to create an idea about the Creator of all Things. As previously noted, poetry was a cultural passion among the Arabs. Famous poets were the stage stars of the age, lionized by the people and imitated by lesser talent. Their poetic genius celebrated tribal life and reaffirmed tribal values, but poetry was also an all-purpose tool that was used by lesser talent to praise one's own tribe, put down others, record brave deeds, eulogize the dead, capture the longings of the heart, and comment on the news.

Like Zayd, Muhammad made use of poetry to convey his ideas, but Muhammad's verse was original in both form and content. His work broke through the constraints of traditional Arab poetic forms. Some of it was ingenious and experimental, as is evident in "The Merciful,"[7] an early composition whose theme is divine reward and punishment. In this composition Muhammad attempted a quickening tempo by inserting a refrain after the introductory verses. As the poem continues, the refrain is repeated every other line. The effect is to build up dizzying excitement until the seemingly orgasmic release of the concluding lines, which promise the faithful infinite sex in Paradise with dark-eyed virgins.

In addition to being a cleverer wordsmith than Zayd, he was a better tactician. He understood that his words needed the voice of authority that Zayd's lacked. Zayd offered opinion, and he used the point of view of a perplexed mortal. Muhammad gave his productions a loftier and authoritative point of view. It was therefore God Almighty speaking in verse through the Angel Gabriel, not Muhammad. He pushed himself into the background by making use of the rhetorical "We" or "Us" or "Our" when using the God voice.[8] Muhammad's voice only emerges when he allows God, through the Angel Gabriel, to order him to repeat certain verses in his own merely human voice. This down-stepping of the missive was accomplished through the use of the word "Say." Whenever Muhammad pronounced the word "Say" in his verse, the listener was to understand that God was ceding the microphone to him. Through these devices, the Koran attained the sound of high authority. To the simpler minds of the age and of later ages, it had the appearance of a voice thundering down to their world from the heavens above.

Though Muhammad displayed a remarkable verbal talent, there is nothing in the literature to show he was an early entrant into the literary field. This may be due to the possibility evidence was suppressed by early believers in order to enhance the claim that Muhammad's work came from God. Historian Muir speculates that Muhammad began his poetic life before the hallucinatory cave experience by composing "wild and impassioned poetry" and "soliloquies full of melancholy for the state and prospects of mankind." During this product-development phase, Muhammad would have shared his work with his immediate family, but much of this early output was lost because it did not fit into the later God-voice mold. Fragments that survived this apprenticeship, Muir believes, were incorporated into later Koranic compositions either by Muhammad or by his followers.[9]

Muhammad's first recruit to his religion was his wife. The literature has a breathless Muhammad rushing home to Khadija after the Angel Gabriel showed him how to wash and pray, and he taught these routines to her. She then joined him in prayer, repeating verses he had composed. Two more family members soon came on board. The first was Ali, the son of Abu Talib whom Muhammad had taken into his home four years earlier. Now a chubby ten year old, Ali happened to walk in on Muhammad and

Khadija while they were engaged in prayer and asked them what they were doing. When Muhammad explained and invited him to join them, the boy balked and said he would have to talk it over with his father first. Muhammad, however, cautioned him not to reveal anything to Abu Talib or to anyone else. He had seen the treatment given to Zayd, and he wanted to keep it secret. Besides, he was not yet ready to go public. What he was planning was radical: It was not merely a denunciation of the polytheism of his contemporaries as Zayd had done, but the offering of an indigenous monotheistic alternative to the religion of the Meccans. It still needed more thought, more "revelation," to round it out.

A day later or a month later—the sources are not clear on the timeframe—Ali asked Muhammad what he needed to do to join the new religion. "Bear witness that there is no god but Allah, alone and without associate; disavow al-Lat and al-Uzza, and renounce rivals." Some time after Ali's conversion, Zayd, the former Christian slave whom Muhammad had adopted, also declared belief that Muhammad was divinely inspired and joined in the rituals.

It is said that prior to Zayd's conversion, Muhammad and Ali used to go outside of town in the late afternoon to perform the prayer rituals, hiding in a glen where they felt secure from prying eyes. On one occasion, however, Abu Talib came upon them and asked, "What is this religion I see you practicing?" Muhammad explained and said, "God has sent me as an apostle to mankind, and you, my uncle, most deserve that I should teach you the truth and call you to guidance." Abu Talib declined, saying he could not reject the religion of his fathers. However, he did not object to his son's allegiance and offered them the protection of the Hashimite clan.[10]

Despite these early successes, there was resistance within Muhammad's immediate family, for the literature does not include his four daughters—Fatima, Zaynab, Ruqaya, and Umm Kulthum—as converts. Fatima was indisputably a holdout, as one of the traditions states Muhammad made a public appeal to her after he came out of the closet and began to preach his religion to the Meccans.

Muhammad's first convert outside of his fractured family was a close friend, Abu Bakr, a well-to-do cloth merchant who would become the first ruler of the faithful after Muhammad's death. They had likely been acquainted for several decades, as some of the literature states that Abu Bakr was a member of the same caravan that Muhammad went on with Abu Talib. Both men participated in the Sacrilegious Wars and may have become closer shortly thereafter when several Meccan clans formed a goodwill association to help prevent the swindling of foreigners by unscrupulous Meccan traders. Muhammad had taken part in a group pledge to uphold ethical commercial behavior with outsiders, and it is presumed Abu Bakr was also present, as his Taym clan was one of the founders and promoters of the association.

Physically, Abu Bakr stood out. Unlike the generally swarthy Meccans, he had fair skin. He was thin to the point of emacia-tion and had a sparse beard and a slightly hunched frame. His eyes were seemingly sunken by a prominent forehead—the head of a mathematician. He had a passion for genealogy and knew the lineage of practically everyone of importance in Mecca going back to Qusay and even beyond. That knowledge plus a gift for interpreting dreams made him sought after. Historian Aloys Sprenger sees him as a man devoid of original ideas, yet an ideal ally for someone like Muhammad, as he "was staunch as a friend, and made by nature to work out the ideas of others."[11] He had a house, fancy by Meccan standards, in the same part of town as Khadija, so that when Muhammad moved in with his well-off wife, he and Abu Bakr became neighbors.

What may have also brought them close was a shared interest in poetry. Abu Bakr was said to have been a contestant in the literary tournaments at the annual Ukaz fair. He could remember entire poems after hearing them recited only once, an ability Muhammad also supposedly possessed. Adding to their affinity was the fact that Abu Bakr had become disenchanted with polytheism after realizing his supplications to the idols had gone unanswered. It is likely the subject of religion was part of an on-going conver-sation between them, a meeting of the minds of two men who had distanced themselves emotionally and intellectually from the religious practices of the Meccans.

When Muhammad began experiencing his neurological epiphanies on Mount Hira, Abu Bakr was on a commercial trip to Yemen. By the time he returned, word had seeped out that Mu-hammad was proposing a new religion. When Abu Bakr learned of this, he paid a visit to his friend, and it is certain Muhammad explained to him in detail what he had experienced and what he believed about his experiences. Perhaps out of sensitivity to criticism, Muhammad had never shared his earlier poetic work with anyone outside his immediate family. But now, convinced of his divine mission and that his words sprang from God and were therefore perfect, he recited his latest compositions to his friend, then gave a performance of his prayer routine. He was now God's recruiter; it was his role to shepherd people like Abu Bakr into God's fold of submission.

Given his personality, Abu Bakr was an easy touch. Like Muhammad, he was prudish and avoided the drinking, womanizing, and gambling that characterized the Meccan milieu. He was said to be an upright man, a straight shooter in business and all other affairs of his life. He was emotional to the point of wearing his heart on his sleeve: When he hurt, he cried; when joyful he laughed; when angry he lashed out. Devoid of deviousness and duplicity, he was prone to gullibility, and Muhammad's eloquent pitch hit his credulity nerve. Moreover, the poetry Muhammad recited had a quality to it that made it different from anything else he had ever heard. It was idea poetry, verse that appealed as much to the mind as to the heart. What he heard made Abu Bakr weep, and because it created such a profound response in him, he believed it had to be the truth. The literature holds that Abu Bakr converted on the spot. Muhammad's conviction about himself was so powerful that it became his friend's conviction in him.

Abu Bakr turned into a one-man recruiting agency. Within a short time, he influenced a dozen people to adopt the religion, including several of Muhammad's close relatives such as Safiya's son, the oft-thrashed Zubayr, who had kept a skeptical distance. Muhammad wanted to keep things quiet, but Abu Bakr ended up talking about him to people with whom he had done business or had family or social ties in an attempt to convert them. They, of course, talked to others. It was hard to keep a secret in a small town like Mecca.

As can be expected, the literature holds that prophesy, miracles, and dreams also played a recruitment role, as occurred with Talha, a cousin of Abu Bakr who would eventually become one of the richest men of the religion thanks to plunder, and Abdullah Masud, a lowly shepherd boy who would later gain fame as a

Koran reciter and jurist. Then about twenty years old, Talha was supposedly influenced by a prophesy: He happened to be passing through Bosra on the return from a caravan journey to Syria when yet another Christian monk came rushing forward, this one to tell not just of the coming of a prophet, but to announce that he was at that very moment arriving! With breathless enthusiasm, the monk urged Talha to hasten back to Mecca and harken to a man named Ahmad, the grandson of Abdul Muttalib and the son of Abdullah, for he was about to declare his prophethood. "This is the month during which he will appear. He is the last of the prophets."[12] The story goes that as soon as he got back to Mecca, Talha learned from Abu Bakr that Muhammad was the man of the prophesy. He instructed him about the basics of the new religion and took him to Muhammad. Talha, who would one day lead Muhammadan armies, immediately signed on.

As for the shepherd boy Masud, the literature relates that his conversion happened as a result of a miracle Muhammad performed. This came about while Muhammad and Abu Bakr were walking in the foothills of Mecca where Masud, then a teenager, was grazing a flock of goats. Thirsty from the hike, Muhammad asked the boy for milk from one of the goats. When the shepherd told them he could not do so without the permission of the owner, Muhammad asked him to bring him a goat that was still too young to give milk. Muhammad touched the goat on the udder, which became swollen with milk. After milking the animal and satisfying their thirst, Muhammad said, "Shrink!" and the udder shrank back to the way it was before. The story goes that Masud, dazzled by Muhammad's command over nature, converted a few days later.[13]

A dream supposedly brought the conversion of Uthman, the son of Affan, another future caliph. Described in the literature as wealthy and handsome yet modest, Uthman, then thirty-four years old, was returning from a commercial trip to Syria when he had a dream of a voice that said, "O you who are asleep, wake up, for in Mecca the Prophet Ahmad has appeared!"[14] Like Talha, Uthman had a long-standing friendship with Abu Bakr so that once back in Mecca he told him about the dream. Interpreting this one was a piece of cake for Abu Bakr, who explained to him about the new religion and that Ahmad was none other than Muhammad—the "Apostle of Truth." He had been honored with visitations from an angelic being who transmitted God's word to him. Abu Bakr converted Uthman and then brought him to Muhammad to seal the deal.

While having a well-connected ally like Abu Bakr was an enormous help in bringing about conversions, historians such as Sprenger believe Muhammad's recruitment success lay primarily in the fact that he was a product of the monotheistic "spirit of the time"[15]and had arrived on the scene at an opportune moment. It is said that if he had appeared a century earlier, he would have gotten nowhere; a century later, he would have been irrelevant. At that time, however, monotheism was in rapid advance in the larger world. Mecca was an isolated isle of polytheism surrounded by a sea of one-God worship.

In its Judaic and Christian forms, monotheism had largely colonized regions to the north, south, east, and west of the Hijaz. Yemen had in turn been ruled by Jews, Christians, and Zoroastrians. Najran, a large town ten days journey to the south of Mecca, had an important Christian presence. Western Arabian oasis-towns such as Yathrib, Khaybar, and Fadak had been either significantly or entirely Jewish for nearly a millennium. Across the Red Sea was the Christian empire of the Abyssinians. To the north, Syria and the entire fringe of the Mediterranean including Egypt had been Christianized. The Arab kingdoms of the Ghassanids and Lakhmids—the Christian vassals of the Byzantine and Persian empires—ruled large areas that touched on northern Arabia. The belief in the existence of a multiplicity of gods, faith in the influence of astral bodies, and the worship before idols representing these deities and forces was in decline everywhere. Given several generations of normal change, the Meccans would likely have embraced one of the several influential Christian sects; the cubic temple would have been transformed into a church. What was at stake was not the outcome, but the content of it.

Many of the early converts were intelligent young Meccans who had been exposed to monotheistic tenets through their travels abroad; they had already begun questioning the validity of their religion and were therefore ripe for new ideas. They were open to being persuaded that more lay beyond the grave than the prospect of having the spirit of a dead camel for a mount. Other early converts were Christian slaves. Muhammad's religion seemingly was little different from theirs, and his appeal was heightened when some the moneyed believers offered to buy their freedom provided they embrace Muhammad's religion.

Muhammad's production of verse during this period was minimal—at most a meager dozen compositions. Most of them were under ten lines, but several were of moderate length. Scholars believe this dry period, or "intermission" as it is called, lasted three years. Despite their brevity, the verses of the period contain the core tenets of the faith: a day of doom leading to physical resurrection, judgment of all mankind before God, reward in Paradise or punishment in Hell, and the need for submission to God's will to attain Paradise and avoid Hell.

Muhammad's fixation on doomsday was immediate. He did not work into the subject slowly, a verse here and a verse there. He jumped into the thick of it. In a chapter entitled "The Enfolded," he says of the end of time, which he was certain was approaching: "The day cometh when the earth and the mountains shall be shaken; and the mountains shall become a loose sand heap."[16] He has God rubbing his hands in anticipation of squeezing divine fingers around the necks of resurrected disbelievers, particularly the necks belonging to the rich folk of Mecca: "And let me alone with the gainsayers, rich in the pleasures of this life; and bear thou with them a little while; for with Us are strong fetters, and a flaming fire, and food that choketh, and a sore torment."[17] Muhammad has God grabbing people by the hair—by "the lying sinful forelock!"[18]—and summoning the guards of Hell to come for them.

From the start, his Hell imagery is sadistic. In another chapter of this period entitled "Enwrapped," apparently inspired by the frightening hallucination that sent him running to the lap of his wife, he instructs himself to come out from under the blanket and warn people of the dreadful things that are coming to those who merit God's anger. In his God voice, Muhammad declares: "And who will teach thee what hellfire is? It leaveth not, it spareth not, blackening the skin."[19]

More than anything, such verses reveal the mind of an extremely angry man, someone with a seething inner life that was building in pressure like magma before an eruption. Without a doubt, he had much to be angry about: More than a share of abuse had been his lot, very likely to a greater degree than has been revealed in the literature. Additionally, and to some extent provoking the abuse, was the fact that he was saddled with a disease he had not asked for or deserved, but was imposed on him by genetic misfortune. Now that this disease had convinced him of a divine mission, he was setting himself up for even greater abuse and therefore for even more anger. His anger was at first a diffuse but powerful emotion; it was probing for a real outlet. Sooner or later somebody was going to pay.

The limited poetic output during this period is an indication that Muhammad was suffering from a bad case of writer's block, and it brought him to the point of despair. In his home was a small room that he used for prayer and meditation, essentially a home office where the mental composition of many of the early Koran verses took place. The dry period coincided with a cessation of fits. Since he linked inspiration with the blissful moments of epileptic ecstasy, he eagerly sought more such experiences in his prayer room in order to stoke his creativity, but they were not forthcoming. He had become an ecstasy junky. He needed another fix to further his need for self-expression, but his brain was not cooperating. He fell into a deep depression. The literature has him again climbing the surrounding hills in search of a place to kill himself.

Russian novelist Fydor Dostoevsky, who also suffered from epilepsy, once commented that if Muhammad's experience of the disease was anything like his own, then during such episodes of neural fireworks Muhammad "had veritably been in Paradise."[20] Dostoevsky described the experience as a "feeling of happiness which I never experienced in my normal state and which one cannot imagine. It is a complete harmony in myself and in the wide world and this feeling is so sweet, so strong, that, I assure you, for a few seconds of this felicity one could give ten years of his life, indeed his entire life."[21]

Muhammad was saved from suicide by a snippy comment variously attributed to a friend, an enemy, or to his wife. If the circumstances were truthfully reported, it reads like Jewish humor: After months without coming up with anything new, Muhammad had apparently lamented his lack of inspirational moments to the friend, enemy, or wife, who then said, very likely with a sarcastic edge: "So your spirit soon abandoned you then!"[22] That was all he needed! Even Allah must have had his hackles raised. An electrical storm broke out in Muhammad's temporal lobe; intimations of eternity flooded his head; feelings of merging with the godhead enveloped him; and at last inspired words came in the form of a rebuttal: "Thy Lord hath not forsaken thee, nor hath he been displeased. And surely the future shall be better for thee than the past. And in the end shall thy Lord be bounteous to thee and thou be satisfied."[23] As the verses continue, Muhammad reminds himself in his Allah voice how God had found him as an orphan and had given him a home and had eventually enriched him through marriage to a wealthy woman. He had a lot to be thankful for.

With this neural tonic, the intermission ended. Muhammad regained his certainty that the Lord was with him. He was soon composing further verses in which he instructed himself via the Allah-Angel Gabriel circuitry to go public with his faith in the one God of Abraham and his role as prophet.

CHAPTER 7

Fire and Brimstone

For Muhammad, going public was merely a formality. Rumors of his claim that God talked to him through an angel had already spread around Mecca. Some of the leading Meccans now considered him an oddball and were not above making cutting remarks. He could not avoid their taunts. He had retained the habit of orbiting the temple—for him it was now the House of God—and the roundabouts encompassed the semicircular stone platform where the notables of town gathered. Each time he came around the platform, one of them would remark loudly enough for him to hear: "Hey, there's that Hashimite fellow who talks to God!" or taunt him: "And what has God said to you of late, Muhammad?"

His claims about himself were even less a secret among his own family members. Apart from Khadija, Ali, Zayd, and Zubayr, the other members of the extended family remained devoutly polytheistic and were antagonistic toward Muhammad. On one occasion while visiting the home of Abu Talib, he got into a heated argument with *everyone* regarding an upcoming minor pilgrimage to the sanctuary of one of the goddesses revered by the Meccans. Abu Talib was organizing his clan for the journey, which would keep them on the road for several days. They had to fetch camels and sacrificial animals from grazing lands, load the baggage camels with tents and provisions, and coordinate among themselves so that they all left together. Previously, Muhammad and his wife and children would have gone with them, but this time he refused, causing a great commotion. He informed them he had made a complete break with polytheism, and there was no turning back. It is likely he attempted to turn this situation into an opportunity to condemn the worship of idols and preach to them about his one God idea. Everyone—aunts, uncles, cousins, and even the usually even-tempered and supportive Abu Talib—blew up at him, showing him "the utmost anger," recalled Baraka, his freed Abyssinian slave.[1]

But confident that he now had the support of a small corps of committed followers—at that time no more than two dozen men and women—Muhammad finally made a public proclamation of his religion. Several accounts of how he carried this out are given. In the mythologized version he ordered Ali, by then a barrel-chested thirteen-year-old with spindly legs, to organize a dinner for his clansmen, telling him that the Angel Gabriel had come to him with a warning that if he did not go public "the Lord would punish me."[2] Forty men including all the surviving sons of Abdul Muttalib and many of Muhammad's first cousins duly showed up. Ali had only been able to round up a cut of mutton and some milk, barely enough for a single person, but this meager fare kept multiplying before the very eyes of the guests so that all the men end up sated. The intended effect of the food miracle fell through, however, when Abu Lahab, one of Muhammad's paternal uncles, pointed his finger at Muhammad and charged that what they had witnessed was the work of a sorcerer. Following Abu Lahab, everyone bolted before Muhammad had the chance to make the announcement of his prophethood and call them to his religion.

Undeterred, Muhammad threw another dinner, but this time the story is told without the food multiplication miracle, and he was able to get in a few words: "O sons of Abdul Muttalib, I know of no young man among the Arabs who brought his people something better than what I have brought you. I bring you the best of this world and the next, for God has commanded me to summon you to him. Which of you will aid me in this matter?"

His uncles and cousins, sitting cross-legged before a leather mat that served as table and table cloth, rolled their eyes or smirked, but remained silent. Ali finally jumped to his feet. "O Prophet of Allah, I will be your helper in this." Muhammad put his arm around his shoulder and said, "This is my brother so listen to him and obey him." Muhammad's endorsement of his enthusiastic cousin provoked laughter, and his clansmen got up to leave, some shaking their heads. Several of them elbowed Abu Talib and said in effect, "Can you believe it? He has ordered you to obey your own son."[3]

The most credible of the coming-out stories involves a general call to the various Quraysh clans to meet him at Mount Safa to hear an important announcement. Safa was one of two low granite hills not more than fifty feet at their highest elevation that stood near the temple. The other was Mount Marwa on the other side of the riverbed. Both were holy sites, and Safa had the distinction of being the place to raise a general alarm in the event of an approaching disaster. This was done by someone climbing to the top of the mount and shouting "Calamity!" loud enough for the entire valley to hear. Muhammad therefore climbed to the top of Safa to give his shout of warning. He also sent Ali to make the rounds of the Hashimite neighborhood to call the people to the sacred mount. It appears that a significant number heeded the call, though more out of curiosity than concern. Once the crowd assembled, Muhammad said, "O tribe of Abdul Muttalib, O tribe of Fihr, O tribe of Kab," continuing through the roster of clans and subclans. "If I were to tell you that there are horsemen on the heights of yon mountain who are planning on attacking you, would you believe me?" Someone shouted out, "Yes, we know you to be a truthful man, O Muhammad." "Well then," continued Muhammad, "I have come to warn you of a terrible punishment." Before he could continue with a sermon about doomsday and the torments of Hell, Abu Lahab jumped to his feet and shouted, "Damn you! May you perish all day long! You called us out here for this?"[4]

Muhammad soldiered on, giving warnings of hellfire for those who rejected the guidance of God's prophet. He proclaimed that he knew the reality of what lay beyond the grave because God had informed him about it and ordered him to reveal these truths to his people. "O Quraysh, save yourselves from the hellfire! O tribe of Banu Kalb, save yourselves from hellfire!" He named holdouts, including his youngest daughter and his aunt Safiya, evidence that they had rejected his religion. "O Fatima, daughter of Muhammad, save yourself from hellfire! For I swear by God I have nothing to protect you from Allah, except the fact that you have kinship with me."[5]

Apart from the scoffing of Abu Lahab, it can only be guessed at what followed, but it is likely the event degenerated into a shouting match between Muhammad and his detractors. In the words of J. C. V. Bodley, Muhammad did not have "highly developed ideals about turning the other cheek,"[6] and he likely flamed Abu Lahab then and there with predictions of the tortures awaiting him.

The list of Muhammad's Meccan enemies would soon grow long, and at the top of it was his paternal uncle. It happened that Abu Lahab and his wife Umm Jamil lived across the lane from Khadija's house. In earlier days they were on friendly terms, so much so that Muhammad allowed two of his daughters to become betrothed to sons of Abu Lahab. Muhammad's close relationship with his uncle went back a long time, as it was Abu Lahab's slave Thuwaiba who had first nursed Muhammad before he was sent off with Halima, but their relationship cooled after Muhammad's cave experience and his not-so-secret conviction he had seen an angel of the Lord. In his youth, the uncle had been dashingly handsome. His real name was Abd al-Uzza, servant of al-Uzza, and he had acquired the nickname of Abu Lahab, meaning "father of radiance" because of his appealing looks. But small pox had left deep scars on his face, and age had shriveled his body and thinned his face. Following the coming-out tiff with his uncle, Muhammad composed a few lines that have immortalized his anger over his uncle's rejection, verses that form one of the earliest and shortest chapters of the Koran:

> Let the hands of Abu Lahab perish, and let
> himself perish!
> His wealth and his gains shall avail him not.
> Burned shall he be at the fiery flame,
> And his wife laden with fire wood,—
> On her neck a rope of palm fiber.[7]

Abu Lahab's wife Umm Jamil was not mentioned by name, but the last two lines consign her to Hell along with her husband with an implied task of piling firewood on him to enhance his torture. The verses quickly spread around town. When she and Abu Lahab learned of them, the uncle hissed at Muhammad from the confines of his home, but Umm Jamil grabbed a rock and went looking for him. It so happened that Muhammad was at the temple with Abu Bakr. The literature has God protecting him from Umm Jamil's fury by wrapping him in an invisibility cloak so that she could not see him, but he could see her and hear her berate him. What is rather more likely is that he saw her coming and left his loyal friend to deal with her. After venting her anger on Abu Bakr, Umm Jamil kissed the Black Stone and performed seven circuits around the temple as defiant affirmations of her belief in Hubal, al-Uzza, al-Lat, and the other deities of the Meccan pantheon. Half blind and in a foul mood, she kept stumbling over the hem of her dress, cursing Muhammad as she did the orbits.[8]

Muhammad and Khadija lived in the exclusive Umayyad section of town, which had houses that would be considered upper middle class to upper class by Meccan standards. It was so named because it was the neighborhood of wealthy merchants who descended from Umayya, the man who had challenged Muhammad's great-grandfather Hashim over control of Mecca. The forty thousand silver coins that Abu Bakr was reputed to possess—his profits as a cloth merchant—gives an idea of the wealth of the residents. Khadija's house, barely two hundred yards from the temple, was at the edge of the neighborhood. Next door to Khadija lived an Umayyad merchant named Abu Sufyan,[9] a grandson of Umayya and an up-and-coming leader in Meccan commercial and civic affairs. Though a Hashimite, Abu Lahab found a niche there due to the fact that his wife was the sister of Abu Sufyan.

It had been a peaceful neighborhood, but following Muhammad's formal announcement that he was bringing forth a new religion, it became for him enemy territory. On more than one occasion, he found excrement dumped at his door, or dead animals turned up in the cooking pot in the courtyard, which served as kitchen and patio. He was also ambushed occasionally when returning home by people throwing stones, and he had to duck into his house to avoid getting hit. "Is this the courtesy of a neighbor?" he would shout loud enough for the entire street to hear.[10] Adding to the insults, Abu Lahab forced his sons to renounce their betrothals to Muhammad's daughters.

To a large extent, Muhammad brought the hostility on himself, a fact acknowledged though rationalized in the literature.[11] Like Zayd before him, he openly reviled the religion of the Meccans;

he ridiculed their idols and statues; he condemned each and every polytheist to the fires of Hell. He also condemned their ancestors to eternal torment for dying in the state of false belief. For him, it was a matter of simple, inflexible logic. There was only one God; polytheists worshipped false gods in the place of the true God; to do so was an unpardonable sin; worship the one God or fry in Hell. The narrowness of his ideas was offensive to the Meccans, who were traditionally tolerant of everyone's God concept. They tolerated everything except intolerance. That is what had gotten Zayd in trouble with the Meccans, and now Muhammad had become another Zayd. Armed with his inflexible message, Muhammad began attending the tribal councils, from local clan gatherings to the more important councils of the elders in the administrative building across from the temple, to preach his ideas and give warnings. He also crashed private gatherings with the same message.[12]

The more resistance Muhammad met, the more his Koran verses became aggressive. Many were descriptions of the torments of Hell, a warning of what awaited people who refused to listen to him: "Hell shall truly be a place of snares, the home of transgressors, to abide therein ages; no coolness shall they taste therein nor drink, save boiling water and running sores."[13] He also ventured into his first descriptions of Paradise as a place of sensual reward, though he did not yet link it as a reward for fighting and dying for his cause: "But, for the god-fearing is a blissful abode, enclosed gardens and vineyards; and damsels with swelling breasts, their peers in age."[14]

For a people who cherished their ancestry and glorified their forefathers in poetry, Muhammad's condemnation was the last straw. Within a year of his coming out, the Meccans decided they had to do something about him to protect their society. If they could not silence him, their only recourse would be to kill him. Killing someone in a tribal society, however, was a delicate matter. Muhammad's clansmen were bound by honor and custom to protect him even if they did not agree with him. Most did not, yet they would still fight to the death to uphold the tribal value. The only way to avoid a war between the clans was to obtain permission from the Hashimite leader, Muhammad's uncle Abu Talib, to kill him. If he agreed to withdraw the clan's protection, the Meccans could then proceed to get rid of him.

The Meccan leaders sent a delegation to Abu Talib to argue that Muhammad was a deranged troublemaker who was turning people against one another and that he had to be dealt with in order to preserve the unity of the community. Abu Talib's visitors were the leaders of Mecca at that time: Utba and Shayba Rabia, both wealthy merchants who owned orchards and wells in Taif; Abu Sufyan, Muhammad's next door neighbor who was married to Utba's daughter Hind; Amr ibn Hisham, whom the Meccans referred to as Abul Hakam—Man of Wise Counsel, but whom Muhammad branded as Abu Jahl—the Spawner of Madness; Walid Mughira, an uncle of Abul Hakam and the man who had led the reconstruction of the temple; and several other prominent men.

It is not reported which of the visitors addressed Abu Talib, only what was said: "O Abu Talib, your nephew has cursed our gods, insulted our religion, mocked our way of life and accused our forefathers of error; either you must stop him or you must let us get at him and we will rid you of him."[15] Muhammad's uncle allowed them to continue their pitch. He understood their point of view. He had watched the problem that his nephew posed unfold for years. His own son Ali had joined the religion. Abu Talib upheld Meccan beliefs, not Muhammad's, but he was trapped by his affection for his nephew. His reply was conciliatory. He told them he would see what he could do about him, but to the dismay of the Meccans nothing changed. Muhammad continued as before, and as the months progressed he continued to acquire converts from among Meccan youth. The Meccans again sent leaders to Abu Talib, but this time they threatened war if the Muhammad problem was not resolved. "By God, we cannot endure that our fathers should be reviled, our customs mocked, and our gods insulted. Until you rid us of him we will fight the pair of you until one side perishes."[16]

The literature reports that a dispirited Abu Talib summoned Muhammad before him and begged him not to put on him a burden greater than he could bear. Muhammad interpreted this as meaning that his uncle intended to withdraw Hashimite protection—a death sentence. But Muhammad, whose certainty that God talked to him was unshakeable, said that he had no choice but to continue as before no matter what the consequences. "O my uncle, by God, if they put the sun in my right hand and the moon in my left on condition that I abandon this course . . . I would not abandon it." He would either be victorious in bringing out his religion, or he would perish trying.

During this meeting, Muhammad was sitting cross-legged with Abu Talib opposite him. Once he had made his position clear, he burst into tears and got to his feet. Abu Talib was nothing if not a sucker for tears. Muhammad had just about gone out the door when his uncle called him back and said, "Go and say what you please, for by God, I will never give you up on any account."[17]

The literature reports a third delegation. This time the Meccan leaders offered Abu Talib a bribe. They brought with them Umara, one of Walid's sons, and proposed to exchange him for Muhammad. "Adopt him as a son and give up to us this nephew of yours." It had to have been difficult for Walid to agree to sacrifice a son like Umara. Any of the Meccan families would have been proud to claim him as their own. He was tall, handsome, athletic in build, and recognized in Mecca for his poetic skills. He would be a sure support for a father who was aging and in need of a productive son, but Abu Talib was incensed and called the offer evil. He said in effect, "I'm supposed to take your son and feed him for you and in exchange you take mine and kill him? By God, this shall never be."[18]

The quarrel spread beyond the meeting room and became the talk of the town. Abu Talib composed poetry ridiculing the Meccan offer and threatened a civil war. He called on his Hashimite clan to make a determined stand behind Muhammad. The entire clan was now at odds with the rest of Mecca over Muhammad, an irony in that the Hashimites held the hereditary office of supplying food and water during the pilgrimage season to people who were worshippers of a pantheon of gods and goddesses that Muhammad reviled. Most of the Hashimites continued to worship the various gods, but now they were forced by their tribal ways to rally behind a man who condemned them to Hell for believing in those very gods.

When the offer of Walid's son was spurned, the Meccan leaders convened to discuss their options. The annual fairs of the sacred months had begun, and they would end with thousands of pilgrims converging on Mecca. They learned that Muhammad had taken his preaching on the road and was attending fairs to pitch his religion to anyone who would listen. He had become pushy to the point of following people into their tents, presumably to be thrown out by the ones who did not want to listen to him. Walid suggested their best defense against Muhammad was to launch a smear campaign in order to shape opinion about him among the pilgrims. They were going to hear about him anyway, better they hear the truth. Brand him as a *kahin*, or a poet, or a sorcerer, Walid proposed. The Meccan leaders discussed each tag, but ruled out *kahin* and poet. *Kahins* were soothsayers, oracles who spoke contrived gibberish in rhyme, but Muhammad had a honey tongue and spoke in complete sentences. Calling him a poet, a man inspired by the *jinn*, would not work either, for his productions generally did not match the content or poetic forms familiar to the Arabs. What he possessed was a brilliance for words that turned people against one another. He could therefore justly be called a sorcerer.

When the pilgrimage began, the Meccan leaders sent people to set up checkpoints along the many routes leading to Mecca where people who had attended the fairs would pass through before donning pilgrim clothing. They warned everyone of the sorcerer Muhammad, a man who would try to beguile and bewitch them with a false religion.

When Muhammad learned of this, he drew down the firepower of Heaven and had God blast the instigators. These verses represent a rare instance of Muhammad having God speak in the first person singular. Though Walid Mughira, whose son had been offered to Abu Talib in exchange for Muhammad, is not named, these lines are said to refer to him:

> Leave me alone to deal with him whom I have created,
> And on whom I have bestowed vast riches,
> And sons dwelling before him,
> And for whom I have smoothed things
>   smoothingly down;—
> Yet desireth he that I should add more![19]

Muhammad has God threaten to lay "grievous woes" on Walid for his ingratitude to God and for his aggressions against his prophet. These verses, intended to be recited in a seething voice, continue:

For he plotted and he planned!
May he be cursed! How he planned!
Again, may he be cursed! How he planned!
Then looked he around him,
Then frowned and scowled,
Then turned his back and swelled with disdain,
And said, "This is merely magic that will be wrought;
It is merely the words of a mortal."[20]

Increasingly, Muhammad turned the Koran into a debate platform. The Meccans undoubtedly riposted with their own poetry, but none from this period has survived. His compositions, nevertheless, open a window for understanding the accusations made against him and the behavior toward him that added to the hatred building up in him. Typical of these entries:

... your compatriot is not one possessed by *jinn*;
For he saw him in the clear horizon:
Nor doth he grapple with heaven's secrets,
Nor doth he teach the doctrine of a cursed Satan.[21]

And:

The sinners indeed laugh the faithful to scorn:
And when they pass by them they wink at one another,
And when they return to their people they return jesting,
And when they see them they say, "These are
    the erring ones."[22]

While the Meccans plotted their plots, Muhammad scored an occasional new convert—an average of about one a month during the several years following his move to public preaching. More often than not, these conversions came about as a result of Abu Bakr's efforts. As the hostility toward him built up, Muhammad quietly moved into a house belonging to a young convert named Arqam and held secret meetings of the faithful there. The house was at the foot of Mount Safa near the Hashimite neighborhood. To avoid detection, people came and went after dark, tapping on the door in code before being allowed in. Abu Bakr would bring promising people to hear Muhammad preach.

Many of the early converts were still in their teens, and families with children who had gone over to Muhammad dealt with these apostates on their own. One of the young men Abu Bakr brought into the fold was Khalid Said, whose family could be considered middle class. Khalid supposedly had a nightmare in which he was being pushed toward a blazing fire, but he was grabbed from behind and saved at the last moment. He went to see Abu Bakr about it, as he was famed as a dream interpreter. For Abu Bakr, this dream was hardly a challenge: It was none other than Muhammad rescuing Khalid from the flames of Hell, and the dream was calling Khalid to the religion of submission to God's will. After listening to Muhammad preach at the house of Arqam, Khalid made the declaration of faith, learned the ablution and prayer techniques, and memorized verse. He attempted to keep his conversion secret, but word got out. When his father found out, he hit Khalid over the head with a club and threatened to starve him to death if he did not return to the faith of his ancestors. Khalid ran away and ended up staying with Muhammad at the house of Arqam.[23]

Another whose conversion brought grief to his family was Musab, the son of Umayr. He was from a wealthy family and always sported the latest fashionable clothes. He did not have a worry in the world except for his mother, who was influential in Meccan society and had an overbearing personality. Musab was another Abu Bakr success story. He learned about Muhammad's religion from Abu Bakr and accompanied him one day to the house of Arqam to hear what Muhammad had to say. He soon declared belief. Like Khalid, Musab tried to keep it secret, but his mother found out after he was spotted praying in the Muhammad style. She ordered her servants to tie him up, tether him in the corner of a room, and keep guard over him. He became a prisoner in his own house. He eventually escaped and fled with other Submitters across the Red Sea to Abyssinia, but returned several years later. When his mother again threatened to imprison him, he swore he would kill anyone who helped her. He tried to persuade her to join. She declined, telling him that her brain could shrivel up but she would still have too much intelligence left to convert to Muhammad's religion. With this, she threw Musab out and disowned him. He eventually became involved in Muhammad's wars and died in battle.[25]

MUHAMMAD IMAGINED SADISTIC TORTURES awaiting people in hell if they did not believe in him as God's messenger and obey him. His Koran is full of descriptions of horrific torture: people burning in lakes of fire; boiling water or molten metal poured down their throats; women suspended over fire with a hook through their tongues. His imagery worked its way into Christianity via Dante, whose hell scenes in the *Divine Comedy* were inspired by Muhammad's cruel imagination.[24]

Another family torn apart by the new religion was that of Sad, the son of Abu Waqqas of the Zuhra tribe. It was the tribe of Muhammad's mother that had descended from Zuhra, a brother of Qusay. Though he was younger than Muhammad, Sad was one of Muhammad's maternal uncles. When his mother learned about his conversion, she took a different approach to dealing with him: She threatened to starve herself to death and carried out the threat to the point of emaciation. Sad brought her back to reality by informing her that she could die a thousand deaths, but it would not make him change his mind.

Sad gained lasting fame by being the first to draw blood in Muhammad's cause. This occurred when he and a small group of believers hiked to a ravine outside of Mecca to do their ablution and prayer rituals. They thought they were out of sight, but a group of Meccans happened to come upon them. When they began to scold and ridicule them, Sad and his group attacked them. No one was carrying a sword since they were still within the borders of the sanctuary where blood violence was forbidden. It turned into a brawl and became bloody when Sad picked up the jawbone of a camel and whacked the head of one of the Meccans with it, causing a deep gash.[26] Sad, who would eventually fight in numerous battles and lead Muhammadan armies, was proud of the bloodletting and boasted about it for the rest of his life.

What started as a trickle of blood would one day turn into a river.

CHAPTER 8

I Will Bring You Slaughter

Somewhere around this time—no one can say for sure, but it was likely during the first year or two of his going public—Muhammad gave himself a promotion by elevating himself to the rank of messenger of God. Following his cave experience, he first saw himself as a mere prophet whose job was to sound the alarm, to warn his own people of painful things to come in the afterlife if they continued their evil ways. "Warn thou then; for thou art a warner only," he said of this limited role.[1]

But very quickly the title wore thin. Through his contacts with Jews, Christians, and people of other religions, he was learning ever more about prophets. It was part of an ongoing education that fed his imagination, and he came to understand that he was under-reaching: Prophets were a dime a dozen. Throughout time, all the peoples of the world had their prophets, surely tens of thousands throughout the ages. But of those, God had commissioned only a select few to serve a more important role, that of messenger. Noah was the first of the messengers, then Abraham, followed by Moses and Jesus. This was the highest honor God could bestow upon a mortal, Muhammad became convinced, because the role of a messenger was more than to sound warnings; it was to convey the idea of God's reality, and not only to some assortment of tribes whose traces would eventually be swallowed by the shifting sands, but to all mankind and for as long as time lasted. Messengers were the transmitters of God's will; they provided a code for people to follow in order to stay in the good graces of God and have hope of a favorable outcome in the afterlife.

It was sufficient for Muhammad to think something for it to become the truth. He was convinced that whatever came into his head came from God. Thus when the idea that he was more than just a prophet solidified in his mind, he humbly informed his people of the elevation God had granted him. This honor was doubled, he told them, because God had also given him the unique privilege of being the last and final of the messengers. The logic of this assertion was straightforward: He was certain the end of the world was at hand; the Day of Resurrection and the Day of Judgment were imminent; there would not be a need for God to commission any more messengers. He was the final brick of the revelational edifice.[2]

At some point, therefore, he began to call himself "Messenger of God," and in due course his followers addressed him as such. When they spoke to him, they would begin by saying: "O Messenger of God." It was a title, like saying "Your Highness" to a king. It also became part of the declaration of faith—the first pillar of his religion of submission to God's will, which he and he alone as messenger was able define. Prior to his elevation to messenger, all one had to do to become a Submitter, a member of Muhammad's religion, was to declare faith in the one God. The procedure called for the convert to clasp Muhammad's hands while pronouncing a simple statement of belief: "I declare there is no god but God."

Following Muhammad's elevation of himself to the status of messenger of God, the statement now contained an affirmation of belief in his special role. From then on he required new converts to say, "There is but one God, and Muhammad is his messenger."[3]

As far as the Meccans were concerned, this warner-prophet-messenger was an increasingly dangerous agitator and subversive. They worried over the fact that he continued to mesmerize some of their young people to the point that they became hostile to their own families. Some of them returned home after their conversion to tell their parents they could no longer have anything to do with them because of their idol worship; to worship anything but the one true God was the greatest of sins. Muhammad had instructed them it was God's command they should not associate with such people—regardless of ties of kinship.

Unable to kill Muhammad, the Meccans persecuted his followers, and the ones without the formal protection of a clan or a well-connected tribesman became fair game for public furor. Abdullah Masud, the shepherd boy, was publicly beaten after he dared to recite Koran verses outside the temple. At the time, he was living at the house of Arqam with a number of other young converts. One of them came up with a suggestion that their lot would improve if only someone had the courage to go to the temple to recite one of the Koran chapters. The Meccans would surely be as mesmerized by the words God had transmitted to Muhammad through the angel as they were, but the person to do the recital should be someone who had reliable protection, someone from a noted family. When nobody took up the challenge, Masud volunteered. His friends tried to talk him out of it. He was the son of a slave woman, a nobody, and would likely be attacked. This proved to be the case. Itinerant poets often worked the crowds in Mecca for money so that the sight of someone reciting poetry in front of the temple was not unusual. However, as soon as the Meccans realized he was one of Muhammad's people and that he was reciting Muhammad's verses, a flash mob formed. Masud was beaten and left with a bloody nose. He returned to the house of Arqam proud of his bruises.[4]

Even some of the well-born converts were not spared the rod of public ire. Both Abu Bakr and Talha Ubaydullah, his young merchant cousin, were once tied together and beaten in the streets.[5] Talha's mother had tried persuasion to get her son to renounce Muhammad, but when that failed she encouraged Meccans to teach him a lesson. The story is told that Nawfal Khuwaylid,[6] one of Khadija's brothers and a relentless opponent of Muhammad, roped Talha and Abu Bakr together and pushed them through the streets of Mecca where taunting crowds pummeled them and pulled them by their beards. Carrying a lash, Talha's mother set the example by repeatedly whipping and cursing her son for being a follower of that "man from the Hashim clan."[7] After being paraded through Mecca like war captives, they were dumped on a road outside of town.

If they could not be physically punished due to family ties, they could be singled out for public contempt. Whenever Abul Hakam, one of the Meccan leaders who had sought Abu Talib's permission to kill Muhammad, learned that someone of high lineage had taken up with Muhammad, he would confront him publicly and upbraid him for abandoning the religion of his forefathers. "We will declare you a blockhead and brand you as a fool and destroy your reputation." If the turncoat was a merchant, Abul Hakam would threaten a boycott to reduce him to begging in the streets. For the lower classes of freemen and slaves, he would have them beaten.[8]

With each new defection, the level of anger against Muhammad increased. He was undermining Meccan unity. Abul Hakam, who was famed among his contemporaries for his generosity, bravery in war, and success as a merchant, became so obsessed with the fact that Muhammad was getting away with harming their culture that at one point he threatened to step on his head the next time he saw him praying in front of the temple. In one version of the story, he also threatened to smash Muhammad's head open with a rock. When Muhammad learned about the threat, he flew into a rage and rushed to the temple so blinded by anger that he bumped into things along the way. Once at the temple, however, he cooled down. Violence was no more in his interest than it was for his opponents, as any violence on his part could undermine his Hashimite support and justify retaliation by his enemies. He limited himself to reciting verse in front of the temple loudly enough to irritate Abul Hakam and other leaders, who were lounging within earshot on the temple's semicircular platform.[9]

Muhammad enjoyed getting under their skin. He could not at that time get away with the overt aggression and the extraordinary violence that would come later, but he had a passive-aggressive way of needling that infuriated them. This consisted in performing his ablutions and prayers in full view of them with total concentration on the minutest details of his obsessive-compulsive routines while at the same time displaying utter indifference to his audience, though he well knew they were watching him. He would come to the temple in the late morning accompanied by Masud, now his devoted valet. This was the time of the day Meccan notables generally got together on the platform, weather permitting, to discuss affairs and relax. While the former shepherd boy held a jug of water, Muhammad would begin with the ritual cleansing that included breathing water into his nostrils three times and then snorting it out one nostril at a time, followed by rinsing his mouth by swirling water in one cheek and then the other before spitting it to the ground, again three times. He would go through the entire checklist with utmost attention to the forms until all the ablution requirements were completed. Then he would initiate the prayers by reciting some of his compositions while in the standing position, and finally proceed to the bowing, kneeling, and prostration phase, with more recitations as his head touched the ground.

From the platform the Meccans would observe this with a mixture of revulsion and indignation. What helped stoke their anger was the fact that Muhammad was doing these insulting routines in front of the greatest symbol of their way of life. The temple was a testimony not only to their beliefs, but to their traditions going back centuries. Decade after decade, generation after generation, pilgrims had come to this sacred ground to show reverence to their many gods and petition them to intercede on their behalf with a distant and unknowable supreme deity. The sacred precinct had always housed hundreds of idols, showing the unity of their tolerance. This holier-than-thou show-off was now perverting its meaning by performing the rituals of his intolerant belief in front of their holy edifice.

One day, indignation and revulsion got the better of Abul Hakam. He was sitting with other important Meccans on the stone benches of the platform. With him were Uqbah Muayt, one of Muhammad's neighbors of the Umayyad district and likely one of the people who had dumped excrement at his door and taken part in stone-throwing ambushes, causing Muhammad to hide out in the house of Arqam; Umayya Khalaf, an important merchant of enormous girth and a haughty attitude; the Rabia brothers Utba and Shayba; and several other Meccan notables. Muhammad had come to the temple that morning with his manservant Masud and his daughter Fatima, who was then about ten years old. After watching Muhammad run through his cleansing ritual, Abul Hakam sent Uqbah to fetch the entrails of a recently slaughtered camel. As soon as Muhammad launched into a prayer prostration, the men came down from the platform and watched Uqbah dump the entrails onto his back. Everyone burst out laughing, doubling up or falling against one another. The former shepherd boy could do nothing to help. He was too young and too slight of build. He used to tend Uqbah Muayt's flocks and was afraid of him.

Muhammad's daughter, however, became enraged. She threw the entrails from her father's back and cursed the men for their cruel prank. Muhammad continued with his prayers. For him, precision in performance was everything, and he needed to complete what he had started for it to have any value in the eyes of God. What was more, he did not want to give them the satisfaction of getting a rise out of him. Nevertheless, his magma was pushing to the surface. It is clear from the literature that he had a black temper. A vein in the middle of his forehead would swell up whenever he became extremely angry, and it was now throbbing. When he was finished with his prayers, he stood up. Looking toward the temple, he raised his arms to the heavens and cried out, "O Allah, destroy the Quraysh!" He went on with the same supplication for each of the men: "O Allah, destroy Abu Jahl (Abul Hakam)! O Allah, destroy Uqbah Muayt! O Allah, destroy Umayya Khalaf! O Allah, destroy Utba Rabia!"[10] He continued until he had named each of the men. He followed up by saying, "Great is the wrath of Allah upon a people who have done this to his Messenger."

The Meccans leaders did not let up. Not long after, Muhammad was again at the temple, this time performing the counterclockwise orbits after kissing the Black Stone. With each turn he had to go around the platform where the Meccan notables were gathered. As had happened in the past, each time he came near the platform, one of the men would make insulting comments about him loud enough for him to hear. At the end of one of the circuits, Muhammad stopped in front of them and said, "Are you listening to me, O Quraysh? By him who holds my life in his hands, I will bring you slaughter." He made the threat with such icy hatred that the men were shocked into silence. One of them finally struck up a conciliatory tone. "Why don't you be sensible and leave, Abu al-Qasim? You've never acted foolishly."[11]

After he left, the Meccans discussed his threat and ended up more furious with him than before. He had no reason to threaten them. Their words and actions toward him were not the problem. He was the problem. It was he who had rejected the gods of the temple; it was he who mocked their way of life; it was he who had insulted their intelligence with threats of hellfire if they did not adopt his religion. And now he threatened to slaughter them because they did not like what he preached nor the damage he had already done to their society? When Muhammad showed up the next day to perform the usual prayers, the Meccan leaders surrounded him. One of them grabbed him by his robe and choked him, and it appeared the men were about to harm him when Abu Bakr stepped between them. He had been alerted that Muhammad was in danger and rushed to the scene. He broke into tears and said, "Would you kill a man for saying Allah is my Lord?" He later acknowledged that this was the worst treatment that Muhammad had ever gotten from the Meccans.[12]

The mounting tension worked in Muhammad's favor when another incident caused Hamza, one of his standoffish uncles, to join the religion. The story goes that Abul Hakam was walking along a path that went around the foot of Mount Safa when he ran into Muhammad, who was either sitting on a rock or was coming from the other direction. Abul Hakam blew up at him, cursing him loudly enough to grab the attention of people living in the neighborhood. When he was done venting his anger, Abul Hakam went to the temple and took a seat among other notables on the platform. Shortly after this encounter, Muhammad's uncle Hamza rode into town from a hunt, his bow slung over his shoulder. He was a famed hunter who split his time between catching game and partying in Meccan wine taverns. He was a man of great strength and had a quick temper. Normally when he returned from the hunt with a camel in tow carrying his latest catch, he would hitch his horse and hobble the camel outside the temple area, then kiss the Black Stone and perform the seven orbits to thank the deities for his good fortune in the hunt. On this occasion, however, a slave woman who heard the insults stopped him before he got to the temple and told him what Abul Hakam said to Muhammad. Hamza flew into a rage. He galloped to the temple, leaped onto the platform, and whacked Abul Hakam over the head with his bow. He shouted, "Will you insult him when I follow his religion and say what he says? Hit me back if you can!" Several people of Abul Hakam's Makhzum clan were on the platform. They jumped to their feet, but Abul Hakam stayed them. "Let him alone, for, by God, I insulted his nephew deeply." Hamza, who had previously been indifferent to Muhammad's religion, went to his nephew to declare his faith. With the conversion of his uncle, Muhammad gained a fearsome ally.[13]

Following this incident, the Meccan leaders took a softer approach to dealing with Muhammad. Not long after, Utba Rabia struck up a conversation with him in a calm and reasoning voice in an attempt to persuade him to change his divisive behavior. To do so, Utba had to swallow his anger, for one his sons, Abu Hudhaifa, had joined Muhammad, denounced his father's beliefs, and refused to have anything more to do with him. Muhammad was spotted sitting alone with his back to the temple. Utba came down from the platform where he was socializing with other Meccan leaders and sat next to him. He opened the conversation by praising Muhammad as holding a worthy place in Quraysh ancestry, but pointed out that he was dividing the community. This concerned and distressed his fellow Meccans, Utba said. The literature states that Utba proposed a deal: If Muhammad so desired, and if he would cease cursing the Meccan gods, the leaders were prepared to round up a large sum of money for him. He could get in on lucrative investment opportunities. If he wanted leadership, they could make him a prince or even set him up as king over the Meccans.

Most Western scholars dismiss these offers as unlikely. At the time, Muhammad was more than a nuisance but less than an existential threat. Utba went on to present another and more likely offer: They would pay all the medical expenses needed to cure him of his delusions. The Meccans had come to the conclusion that he was doing what he was doing because he was possessed by a malicious *jinn*. Some of them had formed this idea ever since they saw him fall unconscious and foam at the mouth back when they were rebuilding the temple. The *jinn* were invisible entities that coexisted with mankind. They could be helpful to people but more often than not they were malicious and could mess with people's lives, particularly if they were able to gain possession of someone's mind. And with Muhammad it looked like a sure case of *jinn* possession. "If this ghost which comes to you, which you see, is such that you cannot get rid of him, we will find a physician for you, and exhaust our means in getting you cured, for often a familiar spirit gets possession of a man until he can be cured of it." The Meccans were willing to scour the land to find the best *kahin* around to chase this *jinn* from him. They would travel to Syria, to Yemen, to Abyssinia, wherever necessary to find someone to cure him.[14]

Muhammad listened patiently. When Utba was done, he said, "Will you listen now to me?" He then recited one of his most recent compositions, which began with praise for his previous compositions: "The Koran," Muhammad intoned, is "a revelation from the Compassionate, the Merciful. A book whose verses are made plain, an Arabic Koran for men of knowledge; Announcer of glad tidings and charged with warnings!"[15] Muhammad then gave himself the down-stepping command that allowed him to speak a few lines in his own voice. He turned to Utba and said, "SAY: I am only a man like you. It is revealed to me that your God is one God: go straight to him then, and implore his pardon. And woe to those who join gods with God."[16] He then returned to the God-voice mode and repeated a theme that ran throughout his work: that the Meccans worshipped things that God created, not God Himself. "Bend not in adoration to the sun or the moon, but bend in adoration before God who created them both."[17]

Utba was taken aback. He had sat down next to Muhammad to engage him in a polite discussion about the problem he was causing Meccan society, but instead got an earful of poetry recited to him that precluded any further discussion. The literature wraps up the episode by stating Utba was so mesmerized by what he heard that his colleagues had to snap him out of it. "He has bewitched you by his tongue," they said when he returned to the platform.[18]

The Meccans remained unmoved by Muhammad's theology. For one, none of them disputed the existence of a supreme deity. They believed in a supreme Lord, but he was remote and unknowable, and it was only through supplications to his daughters or other deities such as Hubal that he was approachable. The word "Allah" was part of their religious culture. Indeed, many polytheists named their children Abdullah, meaning Servant or Slave of Allah. What was different with Muhammad was his repudiation of all the other deities the Meccans worshipped in addition to the supreme Allah. They were infuriated by his mischaracterization of their beliefs. He branded them as idol worshippers, as if they believed lowly objects had sacred powers. Certainly, there were people who had such fetishes, but most Meccans of intelligence understood that stone and wooden idols were only representations of higher powers, not the powers themselves. To pray before a stone idol of al-Uzza and to offer sacrifices before it was not to pray to the stone and seek benefits from the stone but from that which the stone represented. How could Allah find any offense in praying to al-Uzza, whom he created as the giver of the life force that enabled them have their being? And to see and feel and think? How could Allah be angered if one prayed to al-Lat, the goddess of love who caused all things, from plants and animals to man himself, to reproduce? Or to Hubal, the manly Lord of the Sacred Precinct who gave them strength and courage when they most needed it, as in battle, and who gave them guidance whenever they sought it before his stone representation inside the temple? Was Hubal not like a son of Allah? Would a father be offended if someone said words of praise and offered gifts to any of his children?

Still hoping to bring Muhammad to his senses and restore Mecca to peace, the Meccans repeated Utba's offers. More than a dozen of the leading people sent word to him that they wished to converse with him peacefully. He showed up at the platform and took a seat among them. They calmly repeated their frequent charge that no Arab had ever treated his own kin as he had, and they offered him money and power if he agreed to desist. They again offered medical care to free him from his demons.

Muhammad again dismissed their offers, calling them misguided. He was not demon-possessed, he told them. God had sent him revelations that gave good advice for their spiritual welfare. If they listened to God's words, a good outcome for them would be assured in the next life. Even in this life they would be beneficiaries. All they had to do was listen and follow the lead of God's messenger.

The Meccans countered with a demand for proofs. All they had to go on that God spoke to him through an angel was his claim that it was so, and they did not find the words he attributed to God very convincing. "We do not consider you as a liar, but we consider what you preach as a lie," said Abul Hakam.[19] One of them proposed that Muhammad give them proof by having God clear away the mountains that hemmed in Mecca and create rivers so they could engage in agriculture; or since Muhammad insisted that resurrection of the dead would happen, then he should have God resurrect their mutual ancestor

Qusay and restore him as leader of Mecca. Perhaps God would not object to a request to build a castle for Muhammad and fill it with gardens and gold. If such things were too great a demand to place on the Creator, Muhammad could at least have his angel appear to them so that they might also believe. Failing that, then "let the heavens be dropped on us in pieces as you assert your Lord could do if he wished."[20]

Muhammad begged off. He had not been sent to them to call on God to work miracles, he told them, but to convey God's message, and they "could either accept it with advantage, or reject it and await God's judgment."[21] If they were truly looking for a miracle, then he advised them to listen to the Koran, for it was the miracle they sought.

One of Muhammad's first cousins was present, Abdullah, the son of Muhammad's paternal aunt Atika. He expressed the general opinion: "By God, I will never believe in you until you get a ladder to the sky, and mount it . . . while I am looking on, and until four angels come with you testifying that you are speaking the truth, and by God, even if you did that I do not think I would believe you."[22]

Frustrated by Muhammad's inflexibility, the Meccans attempted to discredit him by consulting Jewish rabbis regarding his claim to prophethood. They knew nothing about prophets, but the Jews did. They sent Nader al-Harith and Muhammad's unruly neighbor Uqbah Muayt to Yathrib to question the Jewish religious scholars about their prophets and ask for help in dealing with Muhammad. Yathrib, an agricultural oasis two hundred and thirty miles north of Mecca, had been an important Jewish center for nearly a thousand years and was the home of three major Jewish tribes, each with its own rabbis. The Meccans told the rabbis about Muhammad's claim to be a prophet, that he spoke of Jewish prophets in verse he claimed came from God, yet he was not Jewish. Was there a way to test him? The rabbis replied that the man had to be a fraud if he claimed to be one of their prophets. They had three questions that would trip him up since none had anything to do with Jewish prophets, but he would think they did if he was told they came from rabbis and would make wild guesses or invent. They instructed the Meccans to ask him first, "What happened to the young men

MUHAMMAD HUMILIATED. The Meccans despised Muhammad for his intolerance of their polytheistic beliefs, his demands they convert to his religion, and his threats of hellfire if they refused to accept his Koran as the word of God and him as the messenger of God. Here, one of the leading Meccan merchants drops camel entrails onto Muhammad's back while he performs his prayer ritual, to the amusement of other merchants.

who disappeared in ancient days." This question had to do with the Christian legend of the Seven Sleepers, seven young Ephesian Christians who hid in a cave to escape persecution by the Roman emperor Decius. They fell asleep and awoke two centuries later during the reign of Theodocius, a Christian king. The second question concerned the identity of a "mighty traveler who had reached the confines of both the East and the West." This was Alexander the Great, who was known in Arabia as Dhul Qarnayn. He had conquered much of the world from Egypt in the west to India in the east. The final question concerned the nature of spirit. "Ask him what the spirit is. If he can answer, then follow him."[23]

The Meccans posed these questions to Muhammad and challenged him to give the answers, telling him the questions were from the Jews who said if he were truly a prophet he would know the answers. Unable to respond at the moment, Muhammad told them he would get back with them the next day, but day after day went by and still they did not hear from him. Muhammad's enemies gloated that they had finally nailed him as a fraud, but fifteen days later he emerged with a lengthy chapter called "The Cave" that showed off knowledge of both the sleeper tale and Dhul Qarnayn.[24] He may have tapped Christian and Jewish sources in Mecca for the answers, or he may have sent someone to Yathrib to trick the rabbis into revealing them. What is most probable is that a sympathetic insider learned the answers and reported them to him. Regarding the query about spirit, Muhammad dodged the question with a clever non-answer: "They will ask you about the Spirit. SAY: The Spirit is a matter for my Lord, and you have only a little knowledge of it."[25] This response passed muster. The rabbis of Yathrib did not provide an explanation either.

Failing in their attempts to discredit Muhammad, the Meccans stepped up the persecution of his followers. By this time, he had acquired about fifty committed followers, a third of them slaves or freed slaves who occupied the bottom level of the social scale. The literature claims that slaves who were found to sympathize with Muhammad were beaten, imprisoned, and deprived of food and water. Some were staked to the ground in the hot sun or dragged on their faces through the streets, leading some of them to recant and denounce Muhammad. Ammar, a freed slave whose mother Somaya was said to have died from torture, was forced to recant, but later he went in tears to Muhammad to confess and reaffirm his faith in him. "They would not let me go until I had abused you and spoken well of their gods." As a result of such forced recantations, Muhammad came up with a situational verse allowing believers in such circumstances to fake apostasy without incurring the wrath of God.[26]

The literature relates that Abu Bakr, whose stash of silver coins subsidized Muhammad and the converts staying at the house of Arqam, spent money to free slaves who had been subjected to severe abuse after converting. If he learned of a slave being mistreated, he would go to the owner with an offer to buy him. One of the slaves he freed was Bilal, who was born in Mecca to slaves of Abyssinian origin and was the property of Umayya Khalaf. Bilal had been defiant about his conversion and refused to recant despite beatings Khalaf subjected him to. Khalaf stepped up the pressure one day by staking Bilal to the ground under the hot sun. He placed a heavy rock on his chest and threatened to leave him there until he died. It so happened that Abu Bakr passed by at that moment and offered to exchange Bilal for one of his own slaves, a reliable worker of sturdy build who had chosen to remain a heathen. Khalaf accepted. Set free, Bilal joined the other converts at the house of Arqam.

Such pressures, however, wore on the Submitters and they complained to Muhammad about it. One of them went to him one day while he was resting at the temple, his back against the wall, and begged him to plead to God to strike down their enemies, to do something—anything—to spare them mistreatment. Muhammad became furious and lectured him. In past ages, people had their skin scraped down to the bone or their heads sawed in two because of their beliefs, but they persisted in their faith. He told him to be patient because the day would come when the religion of submission to God's will would be everywhere, and people would not have to fear anything any longer except for God.[27]

However, concerned about the resilience of his followers, he finally gave them permission to emigrate to Abyssinia, whose Christian ruler had a reputation for tolerance. His valet Masud was among those who left, as were Muhammad's daughter Ruqaya and her husband Uthman, a future caliph. Muhammad's cousin Zubayr and about a dozen other converts also emigrated. They left in a group, but did so secretly out of fear of being detained by the Meccans if they caught on to their plans. They made their way to a port near modern day Jedda and paid half a dinar each for safe passage across the Red Sea to an African port that led to Akzum, the capital of Abyssinia.

Despite the precautions, the Meccans caught wind of their flight and rushed to the Red Sea to capture them, but they had already departed aboard merchant vessels.

CHAPTER 9

Obey Me!

Prophets, prophets, and more prophets, the world was awash in prophets! One hundred and twenty-four thousand was the number Muhammad came up with. They had been sent to their people with warnings of God's wrath if they did not shape up. But the people did not listen to them, just as the Meccans were not listening to Muhammad. They did not obey God's spokesmen, therefore they were destroyed. Muhammad brought in God to tell some of these woeful tales: "Hath the story of Moses reached thee yet?"[1] And of Noah, and Jonah, and Abraham, and Lot, and Joseph, among others.

In his earliest Koran compositions, Muhammad mentioned Biblical figures, but provided spare detail. About the time his followers began emigrating to Abyssinia, he launched into more detailed versions, purloining the legends of the major heroes of Jewish scripture and retelling them as if they were freshly handed down to him from the heavens.

Most of the prophet stories of the Koran show that Muhammad was more acquainted with the Jewish prophet legends than with the Biblical accounts. These legends—Jewish folk versions of the Bible stories that later became an inspiration for the learned homilies of the rabbis—were in wide circulation among Jews by Muhammad's time. Their influence on Muhammad can be clearly seen in his rendering of the Abraham story. In the Jewish legend Abraham is depicted as an anti-pagan agitator. In his youth, he destroys the idols of the god-king Nimrod, and as punishment he is to be thrown into a blazing bonfire, but he is saved when God transforms the fire into a garden. Picking up on Abraham's iconoclasm, Muhammad has God narrate these lines:

> So he broke them all in pieces, except the chief
>   of them, that to it they might return, inquiring.
> They said, "Who hath done this to our gods?
>   Verily he is one of the unjust."
> They said, "We heard a youth make mention of them:
>   they call him Abraham."
> They said, "Then bring him before the people's eyes,
>   that they may witness against him."[2]

As in the Jewish legend, Muhammad's Abraham is condemned to be burned to death: "They said, 'Build him a furnace, and throw him into the blazing fire!'"[3] This episode does not appear in Genesis, however, only in the Jewish legend, and it is but one example of Muhammad's use of the legends. This suggests that Muhammad's sources were more familiar with Jewish prophet folk tales than with the Biblical accounts. The influence of these Jewish legends on the Koran is so extensive that it led historian W. St. Clair Tisdall to remark that Muhammad "seems to have been ignorant of the true history of the prophets as related in the canonical books of the Old Testament."[4] Yet when he was later confronted with these discrepancies, Muhammad brazenly insisted that his versions were the correct ones because they were dictated to him by an angel of the Lord. The others were corruptions of the word of the God.

Religions have always influenced one another, but the process of absorption of foreign religious ideas and practices generally takes place over time and involves entire cultures. With Muhammad this absorption—"borrowing" is the word historians use—was so swift and blatant that it was more like a heist. The Jews had something of value. He wanted it, and so he took it. He needed the Jewish stories to shore up his own concept of himself as a prophet. In his remodeled versions, therefore, the prophets experience the same rejection from their people as he experienced from his, making the fact of his rejection by the Meccans proof that he was who he proclaimed himself to be.

The religious debate between Muhammad and the Meccans continued, but it lost, at least temporarily, some of its edge. This came about when Muhammad, worn down by the hostility that led to the emigration of many of his earliest converts, adopted a more conciliatory approach. He dropped direct attacks on the Meccan gods and instead focused his efforts on expounding and defending his doctrines. To the Meccans, Muhammad was still the deluded Hashimite reprobate who set cousin against cousin and son against father, but this new persona of patient preacher was a welcome relief.

He was now allowed to sit among the leaders and opinion makers when they gathered under the canopy of the semicircular temple platform or assembled in the meeting room of the municipal hall across from the temple. And he attended the smaller clan meetings held around town. At such gatherings, everyone sat cross-legged unless they were addressing the assembly, in which case they would stand. When he was given the floor, Muhammad talked his talk; the Meccans listened and politely debated with him.

Whenever he had such an audience, Muhammad would launch into prophet stories. That the prophets were sent with warnings but were not listened to was a recurring theme. And so were the stories of what happened to the people for not listening. Look at the fate of the Thamudites to whom the Arab prophet Saleh was sent, Muhammad would say in one of his invented prophet stories. The Thamudites did not obey Saleh when he told them they must submit to God's will if they desired salvation. If they did not follow his guidance, they would face the punishment of the fire in the next life; they would be stung by God's wrath in this life as well. Muhammad conjured up the images of the ruined stone city of Madain Saleh. It was evidence of the retribution they suffered for not obeying God's prophet.

The Meccans listened, but were not impressed. In their travels, many of them had visited the abandoned tombs and temples that the Thamudites, a branch of the Nabataeans of Petra, had carved into sandstone mountains. They knew history. Madain Saleh had been a flourishing commercial center when the caravan trade was booming through Western Arabia centuries before, but the Romans had taken away much of the Arab business after they learned how to sail directly to and from India from the Red Sea. It was commercial competition that ruined caravan cities such as Madain Saleh, not God. Caravan commerce was now back in importance, bringing wealth to Mecca. If Mecca ever suffered the fate of the Thamudites, it would be the result of someone else taking over their business, not because of the wrath of Muhammad's fire-breathing Allah.

Nader al-Harith, one of the men who had brought back the trick questions from the Jewish scholars of Yathrib, often tailed Muhammad to these meetings. Nader would either interrupt him, only to be put in his place by the tribal elders, or he would wait until Muhammad finished to announce that he had better stories to tell, authentic Persian stories of kings and heroes. He charged that Muhammad's prophet stories were nothing more than fables of the ancients that he had learned from various people. Nader was learned, well-traveled, and was a gifted raconteur. He had spent time in the court of the Lakhmids, a vassal kingdom of the Persians at the top of the Persian Gulf, where he heard these tales. He brought back Persian books and manuscripts and presumably knew how to read them. People eagerly listened to him, leading Muhammad to slam him in the Koran: "And they say, stories of the ancients which he has copied down, and they are read to him morning and night. SAY: He who knows the secrets of Heaven and earth has sent it down. Verily, He is merciful, forgiving."[5]

Nader became a persistent pain for Muhammad, and he once lost his temper with him while talking with Walid Mughira, Abul Hakam, and other Meccan notables on the shaded temple platform. Nader had arrived while Muhammad was holding forth about the prophets, and he interrupted, as usual, with an offer to tell Persian stories. Muhammad raised his voice and drowned Nader out until he shut up, then recited a verse that threatened hellfire: "Verily ye and what ye worship beside God shall be fuel for Hell: Ye shall go down into it."[6]

This idea of hellfire made no sense to the Meccans, and Abul Hakam joked that Muhammad was trying to spook them into obeying him with sadistic descriptions of an afterlife of punishment, like the Zaqqum tree he talked about that was supposed to grow in Hell and would provide flaming food for the damned. Muhammad had recited verses to them about the fruit of the Zaqqum tree: "Like dregs of oil shall it boil up in their bellies, like the boiling of scalding water."[7] Muhammad got the idea of the Hell tree from the Jews, Abul Hakam claimed. "Do you know what this *al-zaqqum* is? It is dates mashed in butter. Bring it along, we'll enjoy it!"[8]

To the Meccans, Muhammad's preachments about the resurrection of the body was as absurd as his talk about Hell. Once dead, the body putrefies and in time there is nothing left but dust. Yet Muhammad declared the physical body will be resurrected on this Day of Judgment that he kept talking about. To prove to Muhammad the ridiculousness of his claim, Ubayy Khalaf, a brother of the big-girthed merchant Umayya, once held up a decayed bone and said, "Muhammad, do you allege that God can revivify this after it has decayed?" Ubayy crushed the bone into dust and blew it into Muhammad's face. Muhammad's reply was the warning of torment: "Yes, I do say that. God will raise it and you, after you have become like this. Then He will place you in the fire."[9]

At some point the debate between Muhammad and the Meccans turned on Christianity, but on this subject it was the blind leading the blind. The Meccans held a vague idea that Christians practiced a form of polytheism because of the position they assigned to Jesus as the son of God and to Mary as the mother of the son of God. Christians prayed to both of them just as the Meccans prayed to al-Uzza, al-Lat, Manat, Hubal and others of their pantheon. To them, Mary was like al-Uzza, the mother-goddess beloved by the Meccans; they could identify with the Christian devotional love for Mary. Therefore, on one occasion when Muhammad held Jesus up as an example of a prophet with a message about the one God who had been spurned by his own people, the Meccans broke out in knee-slapping laughter. By citing Jesus, was he not endorsing belief in a polytheistic religion little different from theirs?

Muhammad's idea of Jesus was dictated by his idea about himself. Though he believed Jesus was divinely inspired, he cast him as merely mortal, not the divine Son of God of the Christians.[10] Muhammad embraced this view out of necessity. His grandiose concept of himself as last and final messenger of God could not support the idea of being second to anybody. If Jesus were indeed divine, then he, Muhammad, would be of little importance. He set the Meccans straight: Christians perverted the religion of Jesus by elevating him as son of God. It was the Christians who turned the religion of Jesus into a religion of polytheism, not Jesus. They worshipped Jesus and Mary instead of the one true God.[11]

This period of a more civil dialog with Muhammad led the Meccans to make him another offer. One day while Muhammad was walking around the temple, Walid Mughira, Umayya Khalaf, and a third man stopped him and said, "'Muhammad, come let us worship what you worship, and you worship what we worship. You and we will combine in the matter. If what you worship is better than what we worship we will take a share of it, and if what we worship is better than what you worship, you can take a share of that."[12]

It was a reasonable approach to a thorny problem by reasonable men who were accustomed to accommodating other religious expressions to their way of life. They wanted to put an end to the strains Muhammad had caused and heal their community. Muhammad at first refused any accommodation by saying that they had their religion and that he had his; there was no way to join the two. However, not long after the Meccan offer, he recited what came to be known as the Satanic Verses. This happened while he discoursed with the Meccan leaders on the temple platform. He had recited the beginnings of a new chapter that contained standard fare, but then added lines which accepted the three goddesses of the Meccans as intercessors with God: "Do you see Al-Lat and Al-Uzza, and Manat the third idol besides? They are the Sublime Birds, and their intercession is desirable indeed!"[13]

The Meccans were stunned. Had Muhammad finally come to his senses? Were all the problems of recent years now at an end? He had just recognized the validity of their three goddesses and their practice of praying to them to intercede for them with God! They were so overjoyed that when Muhammad invited them to follow him in prayer, they trooped down from the platform to an area near the temple entrance. Awkwardly, they imitated his prayer routines, ending with their foreheads touching the ground. The white-bearded Walid, his bones too creaky for such calisthenics, sat cross-legged amid the group and contented himself with grabbing a handful of dirt and touching it to his forehead.

What prompted such a concession by a man as inflexible as Muhammad is a matter of conjecture. Possibly it was a calculated move to pull them into his orbit by making a tactical concession. It is also possible he was as weary of conflict as were the Meccans. In one account, Muhammad expressed regret that he had stirred up so much trouble. He is reported to have said, "I wish Allah had not revealed to me anything distasteful to them."[14] Their recent offer of compromise had been respectful and from the heart. Should he not respond in kind?

While the Meccans were thrilled, Muhammad's followers were appalled. Their own spiritual leader had apostatized by renouncing his fundamental teachings, that there is but one God and that it is the worst of sins to join other gods to the one God. It is said that some of his followers abandoned him, while others pressured him to recant and reassert his faith. The literature holds that the Angel Gabriel gave him a tongue lashing as well. Within a few days, Muhammad revised the composition and spread the word among his followers that Satan, the evil deceiver, was at fault. Satan had put these vile words into his mind, and he confused them with the godly promptings of the Angel Gabriel.[15]

The détente was over. When the Meccans learned of the revision, they were infuriated. They renewed their hostility toward Muhammad and stepped up harassment of his followers. Muhammad, in turn, renewed his attacks on their beliefs and threatened them again with hellfire. "Obey me if you want salvation!" was his message.

Across the Red Sea, Muhammad's followers, who had been in Abyssinia for about four months, heard news that the Meccans had embraced Muhammad's religion, but did not learn of the upshot. Eagerly packing their belongings, they headed back to Arabia, but before they reached Mecca, a horseman coming from Mecca told them of the renewed friction. The expatriates had intended to march triumphantly into Mecca, expecting to be welcomed with open arms, but they ended up having to sneak into town under the cover of darkness and seek guarantees of protection before showing their faces in public. They found the situation was exactly as it was before they left: Their families were hostile to them, and converts among slaves and former slaves continued to be mistreated.

One of the returnees was Uthman Mazun, a nephew of Walid. He beseeched his uncle for protection, but later renounced it when he saw some of the unprotected converts being pushed around and insulted. To show his solidarity with them, he decided to dispense with the protection of his polytheist uncle and from then on put his trust in God. The uncle made a public announcement at the temple to confirm the withdrawal of his support. As it turned out, God proved less reliable than Walid. Not long after, Uthman attended a poetry reading given by the famous Arabian poet Labid. During the recital, Uthman's Muhammadan sensitivities became offended by the pagan philosophy of some of Labid's verses. He interrupted with accusations Labid was lying and launched into a Muhammad-inspired rant. Aghast, the famous poet said that no one had ever been insulted by his poetry before, so how had this come about? "This is just one of those fools allied with Muhammad; they have abandoned our faith. Don't take to heart what he says," said one man. Uthman kept it up until another member of the audience punched him in the face, giving him a black eye. Walid happened to be there and quipped, "Well, nephew, your eye didn't need to suffer so. Earlier you were fully protected!"[16]

It was not long before Muhammad again gave permission to his followers to emigrate to Abyssinia, and this time nearly a hundred men, women, and children left, including most of the people who had returned from the previous emigration. They left in small groups at night and started a community in Abyssinia. They awaited word from Muhammad to rejoin him. He told them in parting that he might have to emigrate as well, but he would await God's command before doing so.

Abu Bakr, Muhammad's enthusiastic recruiter, also wanted to emigrate, but like the other believers, he first obtained Muhammad's permission, an expression of his blind faith that Muhammad was in contact with God Almighty. If Muhammad gave him permission to leave, it meant it was in line with God's will. But the divine will evidently had other plans for Abu Bakr, Muhammad's permission notwithstanding. Just before reaching the Red Sea port, he happened to cross paths with Ibn Daghina, a tribal chieftain Abu Bakr had known for some time. He complained to the sheikh about the ill treatment he had received at the hands of Meccans. Daghina offered him protection. Though not of the Quraysh, he had a power base of his own with an outlying tribe, and his guarantee of protection would be respected. He accompanied Abu Bakr to Mecca and made courtesy calls on all the important sheikhs to inform them of his decision before making a public announcement at the temple. At the temple he said, "O Quraysh, I have placed the son of Abu Quhafa under my protection. Let no man do anything but good to him."[17]

However, Daghina soon found it necessary to withdraw his protection. This came about after Abu Bakr set up a prayer area in the courtyard of his house and his praying became a public nuisance. His loud recitation of verses five times a day bothered his neighbors, especially at dawn. His tendency to weep when reciting certain verses also riled people. He was making a spectacle of himself, and his neighbors, knowing he recruited people for Muhammad, were afraid he would be a bad influence on their women, children, and slaves. They complained about it around town, and word of this soon reached his protector. Daghina paid him a visit and told him to he had to take his praying inside the house. There he could do whatever he wanted, but when Abu Bakr refused, Daghina went to the temple to proclaim he had withdrawn his support. "Do with him whatever you wish," he said to the people who had gathered to listen.[18] The worst that happened to Abu Bakr after this loss of protection occurred one day when someone threw dirt on his head as he was walking to the temple. Brushing the dirt out of his hair, he complained about the perpetrator to Walid. The aging leader showed him no sympathy: "You brought this on yourself," he said.[19]

That so many of their youth fled across the Red Sea disturbed the Meccans. They wanted them back in Mecca to continue pressuring them to renounce Muhammad. The fact that some of his followers repudiated him after he pronounced the Satanic Verses made them believe his grip on them could be broken. They also wanted them back because of a historical concern about the imperial reach of Abyssinia. The Abyssinians controlled Yemen for much of the previous century before being pushed out by the Persians, and less than five decades before, within memory of many people still alive in Mecca, an Abyssinian army under the command of Abraha marched on Mecca, ostensibly to eliminate its temple but more likely with the aim of expanding its empire. The defection of so many of their own to Abyssinia made Mecca look weak and divided. It was in the interest of the Meccans to appear in control of their own people.

They therefore sent two envoys to Abyssinia to seek the expulsion of Muhammad's followers. The envoys brought presents for the Christian king and his advisers, a large quantity of fine red leather—Moroccan leather as it is called today. In the traditional accounts, they first bribed the advisers to obtain support for the repatriation of the apostates. The Meccan envoys were brought before the king to make their case. One of them was Amr al-As, an articulate and successful merchant with high standing among the Meccans. He argued that the renegades had brought with them an invented religion that had nothing to do with the religion of the Abyssinians nor with that of the Meccans. "They have forsaken our religion and they have not adopted yours," he said.[20] He beseeched the Negus, as the king was called, for their return so that their families could deal with them.

Despite the backing of the bribed counselors, who urged the king to honor the request, the Negus refused without first hearing from the Meccan refugees. Two of Muhammad's people were brought before him, one of them Jafar, a son of Abu Talib. He gave a synopsis of the dogma and their belief that Muhammad was in receipt of divine revelation that came to him in the form of verse. When the Negus demanded to know what they believed about "Jesus son of Mary and His mother," Jafar played the Christian card to perfection by reciting verses that repeated the story of the virgin birth. He stopped short of revealing any of Muhammad's heretical beliefs about Jesus. "We say as God did: He is His word and His spirit which He cast in the Virgin whom no man had touched and no child had been inside."[21,22]

The Meccan envoys were anything but theologians and were unable to provide a credible rebuttal. Muhammad's followers played their hand well, for the Negus deemed them to be a Christian sect that suffered persecution at the hands of pagans. He allowed Muhammad's people to stay in Abyssinia under his royal protection. He returned the leather gifts to the Meccans and ordered them to leave his kingdom.

Thus shamed, the envoys returned to Mecca to report their failure.

CHAPTER 10

Obey You? YOU?

Though a large number of Muhammad's followers had forsaken Mecca for Abyssinia, about forty committed believers
including Muhammad's uncle Hamza still remained. They congre-
gated at the house of Arqam and rarely went out. Fearing attack,
they kept the doors locked, and only people who knew the secret
code were let in. Their fears were soon lifted, however, with the
conversion of Umar Khattab, until then one of Muhammad's
most forceful enemies.

Umar, who would eventually orchestrate the conquest of Persia
and much of the Levant, was a nephew of Abul Hakam, the brother
of Umar's mother. Umar was unusually tall and strapping and was
known for explosive anger. He is described in the literature as a
complex man shaped by physical and emotional abuse when he
was young. Subjected to severe beatings from his father, he had
developed a bullying personality and relished getting into fights.
With the encouragement of Abul Hakam, he often participated in the beating of some of Muhammad's unprotected
followers. He was said to have once savagely whipped a converted slave woman, only stopping when he became exhausted.
Even polytheist Meccans feared him. At the same time, he was
intelligent, literate, and articulate, and was sought after to arbitrate quarrels among Meccans and represent them in disputes
with outside tribes.

The way the conversion story is told, Umar, inflamed by his
uncle and other Meccan leaders, decided to take it upon himself
to get rid of the source of the problem that was dividing Mecca by

killing Muhammad, the consequences be damned. Someone informed him that Muhammad was at the house of Arqam. His sword strapped on, he pumped himself up for the kill while marching in the direction of the house. Before getting there, however, he came across a secret Muhammad sympathizer who asked him where he was going wearing his sword. Known for his blunt truthfulness, Umar told him he was going to the house of Arqam to slay Muhammad. The secret sympathizer hid his alarm and suggested that Umar should think twice before taking on Muhammad, because if he killed him he would not have much time left to live: Muhammad's Hashimite clan would surely seek swift vengeance. Umar, he suggested, should first put his own house in order because some of his family members, including his sister and brother-in-law, had gone over to Muhammad's religion.

While the sympathizer slinked off to warn Muhammad, Umar did an about face and stormed toward the home of his sister Fatima. She was married to Said, the son of the religion-of-Abraham seeker Zayd who had influenced Muhammad with his ideal of a pure Abrahamic monotheism. Fatima and Said had recently converted, but kept it from Umar. When he got to the door, Umar heard what sounded like someone reading out loud. His sister and brother-in-law were in the company of Khabbab, a literate slave and one of the earliest of the converts, who was reading aloud Muhammad's verses about Moses. When Umar banged on the door, Fatima hid the manuscript. Once inside, Umar accused them of joining Muhammad's religion. When they denied it, he grabbed his brother-in-law by the throat and punched his sister in the face when she jumped to his defense, giving her a bloody nose. At the sight of the blood, Umar cooled down and apologized. He asked to see what they had been read-ing and read the first two dozen verses. A poet in his own right, he was taken by the clever expressions and was stunned by the lofty God voice. He had never seen anything like it before. He told them he did not think the contents of what he read justified the animosity that had grown around Muhammad.

The way the story goes, he was an instant convert and went to the house of Arqam to declare his belief to Muhammad. But forewarned of his earlier intention, Muhammad and his followers were prepared for a fight. "If he has ill intentions, we'll disarm him and kill him with his own sword," said Muhammad's uncle Hamza. They laid a trap. After he was let in, Muhammad grabbed Umar by the waistband and dragged him violently into the middle of the room, presumably so that Hamza and others could get behind him. Muhammad warned Umar that if he was looking for trouble he was about to get it. But then Umar said the magic words: "O Apostle of God, I have come to you to believe in God and His apostle and what he has brought from God."[1] Muhammad was so thrilled he let out a cry of "*Allahu Akbar!*"

Throughout his life, Umar was driven by fanatical energy; all he needed was a cause to give it direction. Previously, he had used his fierce enthusiasm in the defense of the traditions of the Meccans. Now he channeled it in the cause of Muhammad's religion. After undergoing indoctrination and training at the house of Arqam, he declared that Muhammad's religion needed to be preached openly, not kept hidden in darkened rooms, but Muhammad cautioned him. "We are but few, and you saw what happened to us." Umar had his own ideas. His first action was to go to the homes of the notables, including that of his uncle Abul Hakam, to announce his new faith. In each instance, he got the door slammed in his face. Umar then went to the temple to announce his conversion, but before he could do so one of the Meccans ran to the top of the temple stairs and cried, "O Quraysh, Umar has become a Sabian!"[2] A crowd surrounded him. Some threw punches, but Umar grabbed an old man and held him in front of him as a human shield, thrusting him toward anyone who got close. Undeterred by the hostility, he went to clan and tribal meetings to declare his new belief and challenged anybody that wanted to do something about it to give it a try. After a number of bruising fistfights, the Meccans left him alone.

Umar's ferocity gave other believers confidence, and soon groups of people were soon doing showy prayer routines and reciting Koran verse in front of the temple, to the consternation of the Meccans. Following his conversion, some of the fence sitters declared their belief and joined in the public prayers. While the number of converts was still small compared to the population of Mecca, the Meccans saw the new conversions as a disturbing trend. Adding to their worries was the fact that word about Muhammad's religion had spread beyond the valley, and outsiders were now showing up asking to be directed to him. Muhammad welcomed them and happily explained his religion of submission and its requirements. Some joined and were soon memorizing Koran verses and learning the ablution and prayer routines. Muhammad sent them back to their tribes to spread the religion among their people.

Frightened by these developments, the Meccans took the extreme measure of punishing Muhammad's entire Hashimite clan, blaming them for protecting him. While most of the Hashimites rejected Muhammad's religion, they had closed ranks behind Abu Talib as a show of clan loyalty. The Meccans reasoned that if they could break the will of the Hashimites and bring them to renounce their support for Muhammad, they could then deal with him without fear of civil war. His death would bring an end to his religion and the problems he caused to their way of life. To bring this about, the leadership agreed on a citywide social and economic boycott of the Hashimites. Muhammad and his clansmen were declared outlaws, and it was forbidden for Meccans to have anything to do with them. The Quraysh were barred from marrying them, and they were prohibited from doing business with them, either buying or selling. The Meccan leaders wrote up a boycott decree that was posted inside the temple after representatives of the various Quraysh clans and their allies signed it or put their marks on it. The decree contained a list of accusations against Muhammad: He had broken the bonds of kinship of many Meccan families, he had reviled Meccan beliefs and traditions, and he had corrupted their youth with a fabricated religion.

The Hashimites were shunned. People turned their backs on them if they attempted to strike up a conversation. They would no longer allow even old Hashimite friends into their homes. Whenever Muhammad and his followers recited prayers in front of the temple, people would make a show of plugging their ears and would run away. Eventually, fearful the animosity could result in harm, the Hashimites sealed themselves into their own section of town, a neighborhood that began at the mouth of a ravine. Their houses were built up the hillsides and were accessed through a network of narrow and often steep alleys. The only Hashimite who did not join them was Muhammad's uncle Abu Lahab.

Muhammad moved his family from the hostile neighborhood of the Umayyads into the Hashimite quarter. For their own safety, some of Muhammad's non-Hashimite followers also took up residence in the ravine. Umar's ferocity notwithstanding, the group prayers in front of the temple became less frequent and eventually came to an end. The only time the Hashimites ventured out of their neighborhood was during the sacred months, but even then they were shunned. The boycott lasted more than two years and had severe consequences on Muhammad's clansmen as their food supplies were eventually exhausted and people went hungry. Some of the Meccans felt sorry for their plight, particularly for the children who on occasion could be heard wailing from hunger, and they smuggled food in. The sympathetic would load up a camel with provisions, lead it late at night to the entrance of the neighborhood, then slap it on the flank so that it would run into the Hashimite quarter. The camels were intended for consumption as well. The smuggling of supplies also occurred through the back trails of the ravines and was the lifeline that kept the Hashimites from starvation. But smugglers charged inflated fees for their goods and services, and the Hashimites who used to engage in caravan commerce found themselves spending their capital for smuggled food without the possibility of replenishing their money through trade. Khadija had already spent much of her wealth supporting Muhammad; the boycott took what was left. By the end of it she was ruined and in poor health. Despite the hardships, the Hashimites stood firm.

The boycott came to an end after support for it weakened among the Meccans. Over time, the leaders split into conservative and liberal camps. The conservatives, led by Abul Hakam, insisted that Muhammad was dangerous, and they needed to continue the boycott until he was turned over to them. The liberals, led by four or five influential merchants, became alarmed about the impact of the boycott. They recognized that Muhammad was a problem, but they did not believe his clansmen should be punished any longer because of him. Besides, the boycott was not working as people were increasingly flouting it and were sending the Hashimites supplies. Whenever the subject of terminating the boycott came up, an enraged Abul Hakam would jump to his feet and shout, "This matter is not revocable!"[3] Mecca, however, was ruled by consensus, and the liberal sentiment eventually won over the majority of the leaders. The boycott decree was torn up, the Hashimites resumed a normal life, and Muhammad and his followers went about as before.

This was a short-lived victory for Muhammad, however, as both Khadija and Abu Talib died soon after the boycott ended, and he found himself dangerously exposed. Abu Talib was the first to die. Perhaps because of the privations of the boycott, he fell ill, and when it was clear he would not recover, Meccan leaders came to him about Muhammad while they still had the chance. Eager for some solution, they asked the dying man to influence Muhammad to work out a live-and-let-live arrangement. "Would you now call him and reach a compromise by which he will do us no harm nor we to him; let him tolerate our religion and we will tolerate his."[4] Abu Talib sent for Muhammad, and when he joined the gathering Abu Talib pointed to the men and told him of their desire for a compromise, but Muhammad refused. All he would accept from them was a declaration that there is but one God and a repudiation of their pagan deities. His intransigence angered the Meccans. What he wanted was obedience to him, and he was not someone they intended to obey. One of the Meccan leaders said, "This man is not going to give us any part of what we want. We should leave and continue in the religion of our fathers until God decides between us and him."[5]

Despite Muhammad's efforts to convert him, Abu Talib died holding the beliefs of his forefathers. Muhammad was convinced his kindly uncle was hell bound unless he said the magic words of belief, but Abu Talib declined, saying that if he were to make such a declaration it would only be to please Muhammad, not out of sincerity. According to some of the traditions, Muhammad refused to attend the funeral, whereas other accounts maintain he was present, but stood far back from the grave to keep from becoming contaminated by someone destined for the flames.[6]

Khadija died about a month later. She was sixty-five years old, and as with Abu Talib, her death was likely due to the hardships created by the boycott. What was left of her money had been used up during the boycott so that her burial was a simple affair. Her body was wrapped in Muhammad's cloak instead of the usual white shroud, and she was buried in a simple grave in a cemetery in upper Mecca. Before she died, Muhammad told her that the

Angel Gabriel had given him greetings for her and an assurance that she would reside in Paradise in a house "made of pearl shell and where there is neither noise nor trouble."[7]

Now that he was without the protection Abu Talib had given him, Muhammad had reasons to be concerned for his safety. He was reminded of this when someone dumped some dirt on his head while he was praying in front of the temple. The harassment continued until the day his uncle Abu Lahab paid him a surprise visit. He was now chieftain of the Hashimites. He had heard about the harassment and told Muhammad it was incumbent on him to renew the clan's protection. "Do whatever you did when Abu Talib was alive. By al-Lat, I swear no harm will befall you before I die." Though previously one of his most persistent enemies, Abu Lahab made a public announcement of his protection and showed that he meant it when he lashed out at a man who had insulted Muhammad. The man ran off shouting that he had become "a Sabian," a religious turncoat, but Abu Lahab assured the Meccans that this was not so. "I have not left the faith of Abdul Muttalib. But I will prevent my nephew from being harmed and ensure his own freedom of action."[8]

Abu Lahab's protection did not last long, however. Two of Muhammad's enemies, Abul Hakam and Uqbah Muayt, conspired to undermine it by repeating a rumor to Abu Lahab that Muhammad had condemned Abdul Muttalib—Abu Lahab's father and Muhammad's grandfather—to burn in Hell. When Abu Lahab confronted him about it, Muhammad first tried to dance around the subject by saying that Abdul Muttalib was "with his people." But when his uncle persisted in questioning him, Muhammad laid out the dogma: "Whoever dies in the state Abdul Muttalib was in does go into hellfire." Abu Lahab blew up at him. "By God, I shall always be your enemy for your claiming that Abdul Muttalib is in the fire!" In a public announcement outside the temple, Abu Lahab withdrew his support.[9]

Fearing he would be killed if he remained in Mecca, Muhammad fled to Taif, a walled mountain city a three-day journey to the east, to seek protection and push his religion.[10] Taif was an agricultural town that received more rainfall than the rest of the frontier region. The Thaqifs were the principal tribe and ruled over a thriving domain of vineyards, fruit groves, and pastures. They maintained close trade relations with the Meccans, and many of the wealthy Meccans owned vineyards there. The chief deity was the fertility goddess al-Lat whose temple stood in the center of town and drew pilgrims during the holy months.

Muhammad hoped to obtain their protection, but he had little to offer that would interest people who worshipped the liberality of nature. The leaders of Taif, three brothers, invited him to their meeting place where they sat crossed-legged on imported cushions and carpets amid bowls of fruit that slaves brought in. Because of the proximity of Taif to Mecca, it is likely they had heard something about Muhammad, but they were open-minded and willing to listen to him. He explained his presence: He had been treated unjustly by his tribe because he brought God's word to them. God entrusted him with a message for their salvation. He recited Koran verses and explained the doctrines. He invited them to join his religion and asked them to protect him from his Meccan persecutors. At first, the brothers listened politely, but they soon turned scornful. One of the brothers said, "Could not God have found someone better than you to send?" Another said, "By God, don't let me ever speak to you. If you are an apostle from God as you say you are, you are far too important for me to reply to, and if you are lying against God it is not right that I should speak to you."[11]

Granting tribal protection to an outsider was something that was never to be taken lightly. There had to be some benefit, but as far as the brothers were concerned, there was no benefit here: Muhammad was an outcast, clearly a troublemaker, and very likely insane. Were they to bring him under their wing, they would be obligated to defend him against the Quraysh, who were friends and trading partners. Sooner or later, it would result in conflict.

Muhammad was shaken by their scorn. He could not understand that they were not taken by words he believed came from God. Not only were they not mesmerized, they were furious. When he asked them to keep quiet about the meeting, they threw him out. They stirred up street urchins and loafers to pelt him with stones. The crowd chased him through the main gate and followed him into the countryside. He finally shook them off by ducking into an orchard.[12]

It happened that the orchard belonged to Utba and Shayba Rabia, two of Muhammad's staunchest detractors who were among the people he had once threatened with slaughter. They happened to be tending to their trees and vines and saw Muhammad being run out of Taif. They took pity on him and told one of their slaves, a young Christian named Addas, to take a plate of grapes to him. Though down on his luck, Muhammad could not refrain from proselytizing. He got into a conversation with the slave about prophets and impressed him by his knowledge of Jonah, who was famed for his connection to the slave's home town of Ninevah. Pleased that he had finally found someone who listened to him, Muhammad said, "He (Jonas) was a prophet, and I am a prophet." Utba and Shayba overheard the conversation and said to the slave, "Don't let him seduce you from your religion, for yours is better than his."[13] Though the brothers had reasons to despise Muhammad, they assisted him by recovering his mount and giving him provisions.

Muhammad was demoralized by the humiliating expulsion. On the return trip he was dazed, depressed, and fearful of the future. Word of his visit to Taif would surely get to the Meccans, who would see it as treason—one more reason for him to be killed. An indication of how deeply the humiliation affected him can be seen in his experience when he reached Nakhla—Palm Valley— a day's journey from Taif and the location of the sanctuary of Al-Uzza. The literature relates that he attempted to deal with his distraught emotional state by engaging in prayers deep into the night, but he must have suffered an epileptic fit because he imagined the Angel Gabriel informing him that a troop of friendly *jinn* had gathered around him to listen to him pray. He spent the remainder of the night composing a short chapter that came to be known as "The *Jinn*." In it he imagines he has converted the *jinn*, and he attributes dialogue to them that restates some of the tenets of his religion. The chapter ends as a masterful piece of denial: The people of Taif did not reject him because he was a troublemaker and a traitor to his own people, but because he was the bearer of God's guidance; they rejected guidance, and for this they would face God's punishment. "For any that disobey God and his messenger, for them is Hell; they shall dwell therein for eternity."[14]

Having regained his emotional balance by imagining the people of Taif burning forever, Muhammad proceeded to Mecca. Still fearful for his life, he hid out on Mount Hira, possibly in the cave where he had first had the hallucinatory experiences that led

CHASED OUT OF TAIF. Muhammad fled to neighboring Taif when it became unsafe for him in Mecca. He attempted to convert the people and convince them to take up his cause. The leaders at first listened politely, but when they understood he wanted to involve them in his conflict with the Meccans they ran him out of town.

him to believe he was in contact with God. He did not dare to venture farther without a protection arrangement. Before reaching Mecca, he had chanced upon a man from the Khuza tribe who agreed to take a message on his behalf to various Meccan leaders asking for their help, but these requests were turned down. His luck turned for the better when he made his pitch to Mutim Adi, one of the liberal Meccans who led the push to end the boycott. The aging Mutim, widely respected for his military leadership during the Sacrilegious Wars, accepted. He instructed his sons to put on their armor and weapons. Mounted on war horses, they accompanied Muhammad to the temple where Mutim, standing in his stirrups, proclaimed, "O Quraysh! I have taken Muhammad in my protection, so none should attack him." Muhammad then stepped forward, kissed the Black Stone, performed two sets of prayer prostrations, and commenced the seven circuits around the temple.[15] When he was finished he returned to the house of Khadija accompanied by Mutim's mounted clansmen.

Muhammad took advantage of this newfound security to remarry. Within two months of the death of Khadija, he contracted marriage with Sauda, a tall, stout, good-natured widow of one of his followers who died after emigrating to Abyssinia. About the same time, he became betrothed to Aisha, the six-year-old daughter of Abu Bakr.

The story goes that Muhammad played a passive role in arranging the marriages. The wife of one of his early followers suggested both unions to him, Sauda because she was a believer and Aisha because she was a virgin. When Muhammad expressed his interest, the woman served as the intermediary to pitch the idea to the respective families. Sauda was thrilled that Muhammad would consider her for a wife and readily accepted, as did her aging father with whom she lived with her children. She promised Muhammad she would not allow her children to bother him. Though her brother opposed the marriage and dowsed himself with dirt in protest, her father married Sauda to Muhammad. She moved into the house of Khadija and took charge.

The passive role given to Muhammad with respect to the marriage proposal to Sauda is believable, but less so with Abu Bakr's daughter. As a frequent visitor to the home of Abu Bakr, Muhammad had an avuncular relationship with Aisha ever since she was born. He had watched her grow from infant to toddler to a sprite little girl with a collection of rag dolls. He confessed to dreams about her: God had "shown" her to him twice in dreams wearing a silken garment or wrapped in silk that covered her face. He heard a voice that said, "This is your wife, so unveil her." He pulled back the silk veil and beheld the small sweet face and bright eyes of little Aisha.[16] The idea of marrying her therefore had to have been his, and the woman who arranged the marriage of Muhammad to Sauda served as facilitator with Abu Bakr. Abu Bakr did not object when he learned of Muhammad's interest, but there was a complication: He had already agreed to marry Aisha to one of the sons of Mutim Adi, the man who was now Muhammad's protector. An able diplomat, Abu Bakr extricated himself from this arrangement without undermining the protection Mutim had given Muhammad.

It is generally accepted that Aisha remained at the paternal home until three years later when Muhammad "consummated" their marriage, as the literature phrases it. There is reason to believe that Abu Bakr agreed to the marriage because he was hoping for a *quid pro quo* from Muhammad: He wanted to marry Muhammad's youngest daughter Fatima, then about fourteen years old. But Muhammad kept stalling him, telling him that he was "waiting for a revelation" from God about the matter.[17]

God never came through, and Muhammad eventually married Fatima to his cousin Ali.

CHAPTER 11

Winging It

Muhammad's temporal lobe exploded one night while he was staying at the home of Abu Talib's daughter Umm Hani, resulting in an epileptic hallucination or lucid dream that he was taken into Heaven by the Angel Gabriel. It became known as the "Night Journey," and during this experience he believed he was introduced to the heroes of the Jewish legends and brought before the throne of God.

Muhammad's imagination transformed this neural event into a convoluted and richly entertaining tale worthy of *One Thousand and One Nights*. The basic story is straightforward: As in an alien abduction scenario, entities extracted him from Umm Hani's house through a dissolving roof and brought him to a well next to the temple where he was handed over to the Angel Gabriel. The angel of the Lord sliced him open from throat to groin, cleansed his intestines and heart with water and stitched him back up—a repeat of his experience while in Halima's care. This time it was a special cleansing, the ultimate ablution, for he was about to be brought before God Almighty via Jerusalem. He was flown on the back of a winged animal a thousand miles over mountains, valleys, and wind-whipped desert to the Temple Mount of Jerusalem. From there he ascended with Gabriel to the various levels of Heaven, each level being the abode of one of the prophets. Reaching the top of the heavens, he was brought before the throne of God. At the end of the experience, Muhammad was back in bed at the house of Umm Hani.[1]

When he told her what happened to him, she begged him not to tell anyone about it, but convinced he had actually gone to

Jerusalem and had been summoned before God, he was unable to keep his mouth shut. It is said that she grabbed his garment in an attempt to keep him from going out the door, but he pulled away from her. Predictably, the Meccans scoffed and made fun of him. Some of his followers abandoned him. Most, however, remained loyal and agreed with Abu Bakr, who declared, "If he said it, he spoke the truth."[2]

As word spread that Muhammad had been brought before the throne of God, the true believers were ecstatic and were dying to hear about it. Muhammad gathered them at the house of Arqam. His listeners were horse and camel *aficionados*, and they wanted to hear first about the fabulous winged mount that had taken him to Jerusalem. Muhammad was a master of magical realism and was perhaps its first practitioner: Buraq was its name, he told them, white was its color—a magnificent animal! In size it was between a mule and a donkey and had enormous wings and a human face; its ears were like those of an elephant; it could travel as far as one could see in a single bound. It was the official mount of the prophets. At one time or another, all his predecessors in the office of Messenger of God had made use of its transport services. Abraham flew across the endless tracts of desert to pay visits to Ishmael in Mecca, and Ishmael had benefited from its swiftness to attend his father's funeral in the land of the northern sun.

Now it was Muhammad's turn to ride Buraq. The heavenly steed appeared before him saddled and ready to ride, but it was highly spirited and in a rebellious mood. Its services had not been needed since the time of Jesus, and it bucked when Muhammad approached, earning a stern rebuke from Gabriel who was holding the reins. "Now Buraq, aren't you ashamed to do that? I swear, no servant of God more noble than Muhammad has ever ridden you."[3] Muhammad mounted it, and off they streaked to the famed Temple Mount where he tethered Buraq to a hitching post reserved for the prophets.[4] After Muhammad performed two sets of prayer prostrations, Gabriel brought him refreshments to choose from: wine, honey, and milk. Muhammad chose the milk, earning Gabriel's praise. It was a test. If he had chosen wine, it meant he would lead his followers astray; if he had chosen honey, they would have been seduced by the pleasures of the world. The fact that he chose milk showed that under his tutelage as prophet his followers would be rightly guided, set on the narrow but sure path to Paradise.

Like any gifted storyteller, Muhammad could read his audience, and the faces of his listeners showed he had them. They were grown men with full beards and tightly wrapped turbans. Within a few years they would become assassins, mass murderers, plunderers, highwaymen, rapists, enslavers, and destroyers of civilizations as they spread his religion. Yet they sat before him like a group of wide-eyed children listening to fairy tales. He could get away with telling them anything so firmly did they believe in him. They were dazzled by the belief that the man standing in front of them had just come back to Mecca after an audience with God Almighty. They believed his stories because he believed them himself.

Muhammad continued the tale, now with the account of his ascension into Heaven. In one version, he climbed a ladder; in another, Gabriel took him by the hand, and they ascended to the first and lowest level of Heaven where the angel asked permission to enter.[5]

A voice was heard from behind the pearly gate. "Who are you?"

"Gabriel."

"Who is with you?"

"Muhammad."

"Has his mission started?"

"His mission has started."[6]

Following in the footsteps of Gabriel, Muhammad entered Heaven and saw a man seated with a multitude of people on his right and another multitude on his left. When the man looked to his right, he laughed and when he looked to his left, he wept. He had warm words of greeting for Muhammad: "Welcome to the righteous apostle and the righteous son!" Muhammad asked Gabriel who he was, and he replied, "He is Adam and these parties on his right and on his left are the souls of his descendants. Those of them on his right are the inmates of Paradise and the parties which are on his left side are the inmates of Hell."

Armies of angels were bivouacked everywhere. Muhammad learned the identity of their commander: His name was Ismail, and under him were twelve thousand angels, each of whom commanded another twelve thousand angels. All the angels he encountered smiled at him with one exception. This was Malik, the keeper of Hell. When he learned of Malik's role, Muhammad asked permission to see the place of eternal torment. Reluctantly, Gabriel commanded the grim keeper to show him, whereupon Malik pulled away the covers of Hell and flames blazed high into the air.

Looking sternly at the men seated in front of him, Muhammad held back a beat before telling them what he saw. God had allowed him to see Hell with his own eyes so that he could warn them of what was in store for them if they disobeyed God and his messenger. Were they ready to know the truth? When he saw the fearful nods, Muhammad described the horrors he had witnessed, the torments awaiting the sinful. The torment depends on the sin. With great relish, he described how the fingernails of backbiters and slanderers had been transformed into copper for them to gouge their faces and chests. Thus they were made to suffer as they had made others suffer. "I saw men with lips like camels. In their hands were pieces of fire like stones, which they thrust into their mouths and they would come out of their posteriors. I was told that these were those who sinfully devoured the wealth of orphans."[7] He had seen the fate of usurers and adulterers and sinners of all stripes and described the tortures specific to their offenses. He had witnessed so much! Would there ever be time enough to tell them the whole of it?

Muhammad was a masterful speaker, knowing when to raise his voice to a thunder or drop it to a whisper. His eyes would flash with indignation or melt with angelic kindness. Sensing their distress at these hellish descriptions, he deftly brought them back to the heavenly ascent, changing their despair over the possibility of damnation for their wretched sins into hope for their future life—provided, of course, they followed the right guidance of their prophet. If they did, Heaven was theirs for the taking. All they had to do was obey!

Muhammad described how at each level of the heavenly realm the Angel Gabriel asked permission to gain entry. In the second Heaven, he met Jesus and John the Baptist; in the third he was introduced to Joseph. The fourth level was the abode of Enoch. Occupying the fifth level was Aaron, and in the sixth was Moses. After being admitted to their abodes, Muhammad would greet them, and they would reply, "Welcome, O pious brother and pious prophet!" Muhammad described the prophets: Jesus was of medium stature, with a red complexion as if he had just rubbed himself dry after a bath. Joseph had a face that shone like the full moon. Aaron was a dignified man with a flowing white beard. Moses had a white beard too, but he had the athletic build of a young man and had curly hair and a hooked nose. Never above flattery, Muhammad compared the appearance of one his followers to Jesus, eliciting smiles and nods from his audience. Abraham was the easiest to describe because it was like looking into a mirror: "Among his children I have the greatest resemblance with him," Muhammad declared.

He encountered his hero Abraham in the seventh Heaven. The patriarch was leaning against the temple of God. Again the greeting: "Welcome, O pious brother and pious prophet!" From there, Gabriel escorted him beyond the heavenly temple to the farthest reaches of Paradise, demarked by an enormous tree. At some point he heard the squeaking of pens, and when he asked about it, he was told the noise was caused by angelic scribes recording the decrees of God. And then he found himself in the presence of the Creator. God had a command for him: Muhammad and his people were to worship him fifty times a day.

Muhammad's listeners were stunned. Fifty times! But how would that be possible? They would have to spend the entire day and night in prayer. There was a punch line, and Muhammad withheld it to build up tension. He could not dispute the command of God, he told his audience. Who can argue with the Creator? If God said fifty times, he meant fifty times. Instead of arguing with God, he humbly went back the way he came, but he crossed paths with Moses.

Moses asked him, "What orders were you given?"

"I was ordered to pray fifty times each day," Muhammad replied.

Moses scoffed. "Your nation can't manage fifty prayers a day. I swear, I put people to the test before your time. I made some very severe requirements of the people of Israel, but they couldn't handle it. Return to your Lord and ask him for some relief for your nation."

Muhammad did as Moses recommended. It ended up as a series of back-and-forth negotiations with God over the frequency of prayer. Muhammad and God finally came to an agreement.

Prayers would only be obligatory five times a day, broken down as follows: The faithful were to perform two sets of prostrations at the crack of dawn, four sets during the midday, afternoon, and late night prayer sessions; three sets would suffice for the sunset prayers. But in each and every one of these obligatory prayer sessions, Koran verses—those eternally existing words transmitted to Muhammad via the Angel Gabriel—were to be recited out loud during the first two sets. One can sense the relief among Muhammad's faithful listeners. God had upped the cost of salvation for them, but Muhammad had reduced it through his superb negotiating skills.

The audience then learned that as a sign of Muhammad's importance in the divine scheme of things, God granted him the highest of honors by permitting him to lead the other prophets in prayer. This distinction was accorded to him to signify that he was not only last of the prophets, but the best of them. Muhammad snapped his finger to show how he was instantly transported back to the Temple Mount. The prophets of fame appeared there too and lined up in prayer formation. Muhammad was in the lead position. Jesus, John the Baptist, Moses, Aaron, Enoch, Joseph, and Abraham formed rows behind him. The prophets did not need to be taught anything other than their place as they already had plenty of time to perfect the same prayer routines that Muhammad had learned only a decade earlier from the Angel Gabriel. Jesus had been at it for six hundred years, whereas Abraham already had more than two thousand years of practice. Yet none of them could match Muhammad in perfection of performance. None could rival the way he cupped his hands to his ears and knelt in the camel position with his hands placed precisely on his thighs; none could match the precision of his elbows that arched outward after he placed the palms of his hands forward for support and touched his forehead to the ground. He was inimitable. He was the matchless Submitter, the archetype of worship. By allowing Muhammad the lead, God ensured that everyone knew of his superiority and set him as the model for everyone to emulate.

Prayers over, it was time for Muhammad to go home. His place was in Mecca among his people, among the believers who were now seated or kneeling before him in the house of Arqam. He told them how, wings flapping, Buraq flew him back to Mecca in time for dawn prayer. But on the way back, he had another adventure when he became thirsty. As they streaked through the air—he aboard Buraq and the Angel Gabriel flying alongside—Muhammad spotted a caravan that had stopped for the night less than a day's journey from Mecca. The men of the caravan had bedded down for the night, but they left a jar of water out in the open. Buraq made a quick landing; Muhammad jumped off, drank the water, then hopped back on the saddle for the last leg of the flight back to Mecca.

Muhammad's audience was dazzled. He wrapped up the session by answering questions. The most interesting was posed by Abu Dharr, a leader of the Daws, a coastal tribe with a reputation for banditry. He said, "O Messenger of Allah, did you see Allah?" "I saw a light," was Muhammad's response. He added that he could not see God directly because the Almighty Lord was veiled by light that emanated from him.[8]

Later that day, Muhammad trooped his followers out to the temple where they engaged in group prayer, the Meccans be damned. As prayer leader, Muhammad was in front and the faithful were behind him in several straight rows. He cupped his hands to his head, bowed, knelt, and leaned forward for the prostration, demonstrating the perfection of his arching elbows and the placement of the palms of his hands. Following Muhammad's lead, the believers performed four sets of prostrations, repeating the Koran verses that he recited.

When these prayers were over the faithful were startled to learn that, contrary to appearances, Muhammad had not been in the lead. He informed them that the Angel Gabriel had appeared and had assumed the role of prayer leader. If they had but eyes to see, they would have seen the great angel in front of them.

But they did not have the eyes to see. God had granted that ability exclusively to his messenger.

CHAPTER 12

War on the World

Despite Mutim's protection, Muhammad had reasons to worry about the future. Mutim was old; he could die at any time. Some of his sons and grandsons were hostile to Muhammad, and it was unlikely the clan would continue giving him protection. The Meccans, meanwhile, were not waiting for Mutim to die, but were building a dossier of accusations to persuade him to turn against Muhammad. In addition to the usual charges of undermining the unity of their community and corrupting their youth with a fabricated religion, they now added treason. The Rabia brothers and others had brought back news of Muhammad's trip to Taif and reports he had tried to stir the people of Taif against them. Now, with Muhammad's claim that a winged mule had flown to Jerusalem and that he had been taken up into Heaven, they had yet another argument to turn his supporter against him: clear evidence that he was insane.

Muhammad had informed none other than Abul Hakam about his experience. After leaving Umm Hani's house in a state of exaltation, he had gone to the temple, but by the time he got there he had fallen into a depression. Abul Hakam asked him what was going on with him, and Muhammad told him about his Jerusalem experience. Always in search of ways to discredit Muhammad, Abul Hakam said coolly, "If I were to call your people over to you for you to tell them, would you say to them what you said to me?" "Yes, I would," Muhammad replied. All the important Meccans, presumably including Mutim, were summoned to the temple platform, and Muhammad repeated what he had told Abul Hakam.[1]

Mutim held firm, but seeing that his time was running out, Muhammad renewed his search for a new home. When the holy months began, he went on the road to pitch his religion and seek a protector from one of the Bedouin tribes. Surrounding himself with his closest people—Abu Bakr, Ali, Umar, and others—he visited tribal encampments at the various fairs that were held simultaneously with the pilgrimage. Before departing Mecca, he warned Abul Hakam and other Meccan enemies of "a great blow of fate" that would soon befall them wherein they would "laugh little and weep much."[2]

He started with the major trade and cultural fair at Ukaz, a two-day journey from Mecca, and ended at the fairs of Majanna and Dhu al-Majaz, two smaller fairs closer to Mecca. At the surrounding encampments, one of Muhammad's people would play pitchman, laying the ground for Muhammad's entrance. His advance man would trot his camel into a camp, inquire about the tribe's place of origin and the names of its leaders, then follow up with a question: "Would you like to achieve good?" "How would that be?" they would ask. "You would bear witness that there is no god but God, and would engage in prayer and believe in God's message."[3]

If there was interest Muhammad would arrive on the scene and join the sheikhs in their main tent or sit around a campfire with them. Many of these groups were of simple means and possessed modest tents. Others were tribes of regional importance and brought capacious tents full of carpets and cushions. Their sheikhs wore fine robes and offered abundant food and drink to visitors. Since they wielded more power than lesser tribes and clans, Muhammad eagerly sought them out. When invited before such leaders, Muhammad would take a seat among them dressed in his finest. The pitchman, usually the eloquent Abu Bakr, would give a short speech to introduce him. At that point, Muhammad would find something flattering to say about the tribal leaders and their ancestors, following which he would launch into the heart of the matter. Depending on his audience, he might skip the theology until the last and instead play up the idea of injustice. Arabs hated injustice, he would remind them. Sword in hand, they were the first to jump to the defense of the defenseless, the first to come to the aid of victims of mean-spirited and cruel injustice. It was an Arab thing to do so, and the best poetry celebrated such deeds. He was such a victim, he informed them. He had only sought the benefit of his people by bringing the word of the one true God to them, and for this he was persecuted. Was that just? After making his case, he would petition them to come under their protective wing: "I don't wish to force any one of you to do anything. Any of you who agree to what I ask may do so, but I would not compel anyone not so wishing. All I want is to guard myself against those wanting to kill me so that I may fulfill my Lord's mission and carry out whatever decree he wishes regarding myself and those who support me."[4]

As always, he was masterful at reading his audience. If people looked receptive, he would enter into the thick of his theology by reciting verses from his Koran and summarizing the tenets. He would explain that the authority behind the words of this "marvelous book," as he termed the Koran, was God Almighty who transmitted his eternal words through his humble messenger via one of his angels. "I am the Messenger of God to you. I tell you to worship God and to associate no other with him and to abandon those others you revere; and you should have faith and belief in me and protect me so that I make evident that with which God sent me."[5]

For the Arabs, Muhammad's theology was one thing, reality another. His request for protection had a clear implication: Taking up him and cause would lead to strife with other tribes, particularly with the Quraysh who were the guardians of the sacred territory and its eclectic temple. This killed interest, but the rejection was usually wrapped in polite, noncommittal language. Some of the tribes told Muhammad it was not possible to respond to him immediately, as they needed to discuss the matter in tribal councils. He never heard back from them. Others wiggled out by expressing fear he would drop them and leave "their necks" exposed to reprisals if he was victorious over his opponents. Asked what was in it for them, he told one group, "Paradise!" That was also a deal breaker.

Sometimes the rejection was blunt. One of the Yemeni tribes said to him, "You have come to us to keep us from our gods and you would have us go to war with the Arabs? Remain with your people. We have no need of you!"[6] At times he was recognized when he entered encampments. People would point a finger at him and tell their friends and relatives: "Watch out that that man of the Quraysh doesn't corrupt you!"[7]

His efforts finally appeared to bear fruit when a clan of the northern Amir tribe, though remaining uncommitted to his religion, invited him to return with them to their territory once the fairs and pilgrimages were over. "We will protect you until you fulfill your Lord's mission," said one of their leaders. Muhammad's entry with them came through one of their women who had joined his religion in Mecca. Eager to convert them, Muhammad moved in then and there at the fairgrounds and began the labor of proselytizing. But this arrangement had a short life. When one of the senior tribal leaders discovered he was staying with one of the clans, he lashed out at the family and ordered Muhammad to leave. "His people know him very well. If they had perceived good in him, they would have been most delighted with him. Will you support a man cast out and denied by his own people and give him shelter and aid?" He thundered at Muhammad: "Get up and join your own people. I swear if you weren't here among my kin, I would strike you down!"

Shaken by this turn of events, Muhammad mounted his camel to leave, but was thrown off when the sheikh jabbed its flank with a spear, causing the camel to bolt. The woman convert who arranged his stay became furious. "Could this really happen to the Messenger of God, right here among you without any one of you protecting him?" At this, some of her menfolk assaulted the sheikh, who was accompanied by several of his own men, resulting in a scuffle. The sheikh ended up pinned to the ground, with one of the woman's kinsmen slapping his face while kneeling on his chest. Delighted by the energy that had been stirred up in his favor, Muhammad said, "May God bless these men and damn the others!"[8]

In the face of such consistent rejection and setbacks, Muhammad displayed remarkable perseverance. His tenacity eventually paid off when he gained the confidence of members of two Arab tribes from Yathrib, the agricultural oasis north of Mecca. These were the Khazraj and the Aws, two fractious polytheist tribes that frequently waged war against one another or against the Jewish tribes with whom they shared the oasis. Several years earlier, Muhammad made a religious pitch to a delegation of Aws tribesmen that had come to Mecca to seek an alliance with the Quraysh against the Khazraj, but he was rebuffed when one of the men said, "This is not what we came here for." On this occasion men of both of these tribes were camped at Mina outside of Mecca during the final phase of the sun pilgrimage, and Muhammad came upon them while they were shaving their heads, the act signifying completion of the pilgrimage. Muhammad struck up a conversation using his ancestry as an opening. His great-grandmother Salma, the mother of his grandfather Abdul Muttalib, belonged to one of the Khazraj clans. His talk was the usual fare: He was the messenger of God, commissioned to bring divine truth of the one God, but he was being persecuted for it and required protection in order to complete his mission.

His claim to prophethood struck a chord with them. They had heard prophecies about a coming Messiah from the Jews of Yathrib, usually hurled at them as a deterrent against aggression. The Aws and Khazraj were often bad neighbors. They had migrated as a single tribe to Yathrib more than a century before from Yemen, and their numbers rapidly expanded. As their numbers grew, they split into the Aws and Khazraj tribes. Though Yathrib was a huge oasis, their population growth led them into conflict with the Jews and each other over land and water. The Jews, who were ultimately pushed into the eastern highlands of Yathrib, had often threatened them with the bogeyman of a coming Messiah who would be the political leader of the Jews against their enemies. "A prophet will be sent soon. His day is at hand. We shall follow him and kill you by his aid," they warned.[9]

Muhammad, who by then had completed his absorption of the major Jewish prophets into his religion, knew the Jews still believed in a coming Messiah and exploited it to his advantage: *He* was the prophet of whom they spoke, he told the small group of Yathrib pilgrims, but he had not been raised to prophethood to lead the Jews against their enemies. Rather, his role was to bring the truth of the one God to all mankind. This had been the mission of the Jews, but they defaulted. This mission was now being taken up by an Arab prophet, by Muhammad, the grandson of Abdul Muttalib, who was the son of Salma, who was born of the Najjar, a clan of the Khazraj!

Six men in this group were of the Khazraj, and some of the sources say there were also two men of the Aws. What Muhammad had to say interested them, but they were not able to offer the protection he sought. They did not have the authority, and if he were to go to Yathrib without it, he would step unprotected into the middle of political turmoil that had resulted from intertribal fighting. Several years earlier the Khazraj and Aws had fought a bloody pitched battle, the culmination of previous conflicts, bringing about the deaths of many of their noblemen. The Jews had been drawn into the battle due to alliances with the polytheists. Yathrib was now looking for a leader from their midst to unify all the tribes of the valley, polytheists and Jews alike, but this had not yet come about. Impressed by Muhammad's family connection to Yathrib and eager to have this self-declared prophet live among them, the men promised to talk about his religion to their clansmen and return during the next pilgrimage to discuss the matter further with him.

The following year, a group of twelve men—ten of them of the Khazraj and two of the Aws—visited Muhammad and formally embraced his religion. This meeting took place in a ravine at Aqaba, the mountain pass that led to the pilgrimage station of Mina and its animal sacrifice and pillars for stoning. These men, some of them the same men Muhammad had spoken to the previous year, were still not in a position to extend protection to him, but they pledged to abide by the tenets of his religion and obey him. Though they were few in number, their conversion gave Muhammad a foothold in Yathrib that would soon turn into a safe haven. After the new recruits departed, Muhammad sent Musab Umayr, the early convert who had once threatened to kill anyone who tried to keep him from Muhammad's religion, to proselytize and teach the Koran and the ablution and prayer routines.

Muhammad's situation in Mecca, meanwhile, was deteriorating. Mutim was in declining health, and Muhammad was certain that when he died the Meccans would not hesitate to move against him. The Meccans were keeping him and his people under constant surveillance. Muhammad had his own informants, sympathizers or secret followers who brought him the talk of the town and anything relating to him that was discussed in tribal and clan meetings. He would thereby learn of dangerous developments, but he still needed to establish a safe haven if it became necessary to flee.

IT'S ALL ABOUT MUHAMMAD

In Yathrib, developments were encouraging. An aggressive and smooth-talking proselytizer, Musab made more converts in the short time he was there than Muhammad had made during more than a decade of preaching in Mecca. Among his converts were two important leaders of the Aws who in turn influenced their clansmen to join the religion. It is believed these successes were due to a number of factors. For one, polytheism was weaker in Yathrib than in Mecca. Unlike Mecca with its homogeneous religious culture centered in the sacred temple, Yathrib was without a unifying temple or communal rituals. The Yathrib polytheists were devotees of Manat, the goddess of fate, the third of the three daughters of Allah, but her sanctuary was located a two day's journey to the west near the Red Sea. The polytheists also prayed to an assortment of tribal and family deities along with Manat, the idols of which were kept in their homes. Another important factor lay in their proximity to the monotheistic religion of the Jews. They were neighbors and often business partners, so the polytheists knew something of the Jewish faith. For the most part they kept their distance from it: It was brought from a foreign land, but they were ready to accept the Arabic monotheism that Muhammad preached.

Using go-betweens such as Musab, Muhammad negotiated with his growing base of Yathrib supporters about a protection arrangement. He was eager to make his move, but it had to be on his terms. He needed an ironclad guarantee of security, but even more, he needed to lock them into an agreement that they would assist him in war. His hatred for his enemies had grown to the point that he wanted to carry out his earlier threats to bring them slaughter for humiliating him and refusing to accept his religion. He had meant what he said, but at the time he made the threat he was not capable of carrying it out. He needed people to do it for him. In his search for allies, he had not yet explicitly asked for anyone to fight on his behalf. It was merely implicit in the alliances he sought, and the tribes and clans he had pitched for protection understood this and therefore rejected him. Now he openly pushed the idea. He instructed Musab to get the new converts to accept the idea of fighting, and when Musab confirmed their acceptance, Muhammad announced to Abu Bakr that he had just received a new directive from God: "I have been given the command to fight!" To give it the stamp of the heavens, he

quickly spiffed it up for the Koran: "Permission is given to those
fought against, because they have been wronged; and surely, Allah
is able to give them victory."[10]

Muhammad asked for a formal and binding pledge. During
the next pilgrimage season, seventy-five of the new converts—
seventy-three men and two women—went to Mecca disguised as
pilgrims to give their pledges of allegiance in person. To avoid
arousing suspicion, they performed the pilgrim rituals with
the Yathrib polytheists, who were unaware of their intentions.
The arrangement, worked out ahead of time with Musab, was
for them to join Muhammad during the night following the
day of the slaughter of the sacrificial animals. This was an ideal
time. The three days following the slaughter were devoted to
eating, drinking, and catching up on the sex the pilgrims had
denied themselves during the pilgrimage, and so they tended
to bed down for the night in a state of complete exhaustion.
Thus in the middle of the night, while everyone else was in deep
sleep, the conspirators arose from their camps and went singly
or in small groups to the Aqaba ravine, the same ravine where
Muhammad met the twelve Yathrib converts the year before.

With Muhammad was Abbas, one of his uncles. Though not
yet a convert, Abbas spent a great deal of time with him and
was one of his trusted advisers. He was also one of Muhammad's best informants due to his business ties to Muhammad's
enemies, who accepted him as one of their own. Fearing leaks or
that his people could be followed, Muhammad had not revealed
the meeting to anyone else, not even to Abu Bakr or Ali. After the
Yathrib converts assembled, Abbas stood atop a boulder and made
a brief speech that stated the reason for the gathering: to pledge
loyalty to Muhammad to the point of going to war on his behalf
if necessary. "If you think that you can be faithful to what you
have promised him and protect him from his opponents,
then assume the burden you have undertaken. But if you think
that you will betray and abandon him after he has gone out with
you, then leave him now. For he is safe where he is."[11]

Someone shouted for Muhammad to speak. He stepped forward, made a few prefatory remarks, recited Koran verses, and
said, "I invite your allegiance on the basis that you protect me
as you would your women and children." One of the Khazraj
chieftains stood up and declared that the converts from his

tribe accepted Muhammad's terms. "We give our allegiance, and we are men of war possessing arms which have been passed on from father to son." One of Aws leaders, however, advised caution: They should remember that they had longstanding alliances with the three Jewish tribes of the oasis. If they followed Muhammad, they might have to break off such ties, fight their former allies, and suffer unforeseen consequences. He wanted a guarantee Muhammad would not abandon them once "God" had given him victory over his enemies. "Will you return to your people and leave us?" he asked.

Bathing them with a reassuring smile, Muhammad said, "I am of you and you are of me. I will war against them that war against you and be at peace with those at peace with you."[12]

Another man warned the group that they should have no illusions about what they were getting themselves into: "O men of Khazraj, do you realize what you are committing yourselves to in pledging your support to this man? It is to war against all and sundry," meaning endless warfare, warfare against all mankind until the entire world was subjected.[13]

Muhammad promised they would be awarded a place in Paradise for fighting his enemies. At this, one of the converts became so enthusiastic that he suggested they slaughter the pilgrims encamped at nearby Mina first thing in the morning. Muhammad, however, cooled his ardor by saying that God had not instructed them to do so.

The promise of Paradise sealed the deal. One by one they stepped forward to clasp Muhammad's hand and pledge to protect him, wage war on his behalf and in furtherance of his religion, follow the dictates of his religion, and obey him in all things. He allowed each of the men to grip his hand as they made their pledge, but he refrained from touching the women. When the ceremony was finished, Muhammad issued his first command. They were to select twelve leaders. These leaders would be like the twelve disciples of Jesus or the twelve tribes of the Jews, he told them. Just as the apostles were answerable to Jesus and the twelve tribes to Moses, so would the twelve leaders be answerable to Muhammad. After they were selected, Muhammad ordered the pledgers to return to Yathrib and await further instructions.

Despite the precautions, the Meccans learned of the meeting, and that morning a group of their leaders, mounted on warhorses, galloped into the Khazraj camp to demand an explanation. "O people of al-Khazraj, information has reached us that you met our man last night and have promised him on oath to fight against us."[14] Most of the Khazraj pilgrims knew nothing about it and were perplexed by the accusation. The ones who knew the truth kept their mouths shut. The Meccans backed off, but they were certain a conspiracy was afoot and continued investigating the matter with other clans and tribes. They concluded there had indeed been a pact sworn against them, even if only in general terms.

The main body of the Yathrib pilgrims was still camped at Mina, but the Khazraj and Aws conspirators who infiltrated the pilgrimage had already skipped town. When they learned of this, the Meccans went in pursuit. They captured two of the conspirators: Sad Ubada, a Yathrib merchant and an important leader of the Khazraj, and another man named Mundhir Amr, who was able to escape. The Meccans dragged Sad back to Mecca with his hands tied behind his neck, intending to interrogate him, but he claimed he was untouchable due to bonds of protection he had forged with Jubayr Mutim, one of the sons of Muhammad's protector Mutim Adi, and with a close relative of Abu Sufyan named Harith. They owed him their protection because he assured their security whenever they were in Yathrib on business. The two Meccans confirmed Sad's claim, and Sad was released just in time to keep his companions from raiding Mecca. They had learned about what happened to him from Mundhir and were preparing to circle back to rescue him.[15]

Encouraged by the allegiance of the Yathrib converts, Muhammad ordered his Meccan followers to emigrate, wrapping the command in revelatory terms: "I have been shown the place of your migration; I have been shown a salty, swampy plain with palm-groves between two tracts of rocks," he said, referring to the ancient lava beds that hemmed Yathrib to the east and to the west.[16] Thus a second exodus from Mecca began, and the believers used the same stratagem of the previous émigrés by leaving in small groups in the dead of night. Once in Yathrib, they moved in with the "Helpers," as Muhammad now called his new allies and converts. Many of the émigrés had memorized all or part of what Muhammad had composed so far of the Koran and taught what they knew to the Helpers and their clans. Over the next two months, somewhere between seventy and one hundred Meccans migrated north. Muhammad also sent word to his followers in Abyssinia that they now had the "permission of Allah" to go to Yathrib. Before long, some of the Abyssinian émigrés began showing up in Yathrib. Muhammad gave his Meccan followers a name to distinguish them from the fervent Yathrib Helpers: They were now known as the Emigrants.

The emigration did not go smoothly for everyone. When the Meccans discovered that Sohayb, a freed slave and early convert nicknamed "the Roman," was plotting to depart, they accused him of ingratitude for everything they had done for him and imprisoned him. Captured as a child somewhere in Byzantium, he had been brought to Mecca as a slave, but was later given his freedom and prospered under the protection of his former owner. The Meccans only allowed him to leave after he offered to turn over the money he had accumulated to them.[17] Ayyash, another early convert and a close relative of Abul Hakam, left in secrecy for Yathrib with Umar, but he was kidnapped by agents of Abul Hakam and brought back to Mecca where he was kept imprisoned until he denounced Muhammad and his religion. "Deal with your fools as we have dealt with this fool of ours," Abul Hakam advised the Meccans.[18] Ayyash later fled to Yathrib, but he was terrified he had earned a place in the fires of Hell for denouncing Muhammad, even if it was under coercion. Muhammad told him not to worry about it; faking apostasy under duress was allowed. God knew and approved.

After the Aqaba meeting, Muhammad remained in Mecca for three months, in part to wrap up whatever personal affairs that needed to be wrapped up, but primarily to oversee the departure of the faithful. He told his followers that God had not yet commanded him to leave. At the end of the three months, Mecca was nearly clear of his followers. Only he, Abu Bakr, Ali, and their families and servants remained, along with a handful of believers who were either incarcerated or too infirm to leave.

During that time, Muhammad's security collapsed. Mutim died, and, as he had anticipated, his sons withdrew their protection. Yet even though he was now exposed, the Meccans still dragged their feet about killing him. Some of the leaders still argued against it out of fear of civil war and the cycles of

THE PLEDGE OF AQABA. Muhammad obtained a promise of security from Yathrib (Medina) supporters when six dozen people came to him in Mecca disguised as pilgrims to pledge to fight "all and sundry" who opposed him. The pledge was essentially a declaration of war against mankind that would last until all people of the world adopted his religion and believed in him as God's messenger.

vengeance that would result, but for many the reality of their situation was beginning to sink in. Under the umbrella of their inaction over the years, Muhammad had now created a nucleus of hostility against them in Yathrib, which could lead them into conflict against tribes with a warlike reputation. They could end up being attacked and their commerce endangered. Their caravans to Syria went either through or around Yathrib. No matter which route they took, they would be within striking distance of Yathrib. This realization sent shudders down their spines. Their very existence depended on trade. With the exception of meat and milk from their herds, all their food had to be imported. That meant it had to be paid for. Aside from temple and pilgrimage revenues, their money came from trade, the greater part of it with Syria. If that avenue of commerce were lost, the town would die a slow death. They had to do something about Muhammad before it was too late.

The Meccans called for an emergency meeting. The Rabia brothers, Abu Sufyan, Abul Hakam, Nader al-Harith, Umayya Khalaf, Uqbah Muayt, and a dozen other people of importance attended, including a son and a brother of Mutim Adi. Their anger about Muhammad surfaced when they recalled all the disruptions he had caused over the previous decade. They knew they had to act, but they could not agree on what to do. Someone suggested locking him up and throwing away the key. They had taken care of other troublemakers that way, but that idea was quickly shot down: His followers would likely attack Mecca in order to free him. Then exile him, someone else suggested. "So long as he is gone, we'll be rid of him and we'll be able to restore our affairs as they were before."[19] That idea was dismissed as well. That would give him free reign to stir up trouble against Mecca, and from the looks of it, he intended to do just that in Yathrib.

Abul Hakam argued that killing Muhammad was the only option, but they should spread the responsibility around. Select a man from each clan—young, physically strong men. Together they would plunge their swords into him. That way all the Meccan clans with the exception of the Hashimites would be responsible for Muhammad's blood. Would the descendants of Abdul Muttalib dare to rise up against everyone? They would have no choice but to accept blood money, and all the participating clans would contribute to pay the amount. With that the discussion came to an end. The Meccans agreed to kill Muhammad in the manner Abul Hakam suggested and set about to organize the assassination.

It was hard to keep a secret in Mecca. Muhammad, who was staying at the house of Khadija, learned of the plot and planned his escape. He believed the assassins would likely break into the house at night and attack him while he slept. He ordered Ali to lie in his bed under his leather blanket. Either Muhammad saw his cousin as expendable in the cause of his religion, or he was confident the Meccans would not thrust their swords into a lump underneath a blanket. They would pull the blanket back to ensure they had the right man. In the meantime, Muhammad, possibly disguised in women's clothes and wearing a veil, slipped by the men the Meccans had posted near his home and made his way to the house of Abu Bakr.

Presumably with a straight face, Muhammad informed his friend that God had just given him the order to emigrate to Yathrib, and Abu Bakr was to be his companion in flight. When Muhammad told him that God had mentioned him by name, Abu Bakr was so overwhelmed that he was unable to speak and broke into tears.

They did not have any time to waste. As soon as the Meccans discovered the ruse, they would launch a manhunt. Muhammad had thought it through: His enemies knew he was heading for Yathrib, so they would first search the north part of the valley and the roads leading to Yathrib. Muhammad and Abu Bakr therefore headed south on foot and hid in a mountain cave about five miles out of town. Only Abu Bakr's teenage daughter Asma, his son Abdullah, and his personal servant Amir Fuhayra, knew of the location. Before leaving for the hideout, Abu Bakr hired a Bedouin guide who was to come to them at the appropriate time with two riding camels, and the Bedouin would lead them through the mountains and valleys of the back country to the safety of Yathrib.

As soon as the Meccans realized they had been tricked, they put a price on Muhammad's head: one hundred camels to anyone who brought him in. They searched square miles of the sunbaked desolation surrounding Mecca. They grilled everyone who might know something. The day after Muhammad and Abu

MUHAMMAD FLEES TO YATHRIB. Concerned about Muhammad's efforts to subvert their way of life, the Meccan leaders decided to kill him. He learned of their plot and escaped from Mecca in the company of Abu Bakr, his most trusted friend. They hid for three days in a cave and fled through the desert on camels, traveling at night to escape detection. After a journey of two weeks, they reached Yathrib, Muhammad's home for the next ten years.

Bakr set out for the cave, Abul Hakam turned up at Abu Bakr's home and demanded to know his whereabouts from Asma. When she told him she did not know, he hit her on the side of the head, but to no avail. She would not talk.

Muhammad and Abu Bakr stayed in the cave for three days. Asma brought them food and water along with provisions for the journey north, covering her tracks to and from the cave by walking ahead of a herd of goats led by a shepherd who was in on the escape. In Mecca, Abu Bakr's son Abdullah mingled with the townspeople to find out what he could and reported every night to Muhammad. At one point, a search team came close to the cave, but kept on going after overlooking the entrance.

On the third day, when the searchers had all but given up, the Bedouin guide and Abu Bakr's servant Amir Fuhayra arrived with the mounts, and the four men set out for Yathrib. The guide first took them farther south and then cut west. They went half way to the Red Sea before turning north. They traveled for nearly two weeks, zigzagging the entire way, trekking chiefly through uninhabited lands to avoid detection. They finally arrived in Yathrib, weary but out of danger.

Abu Bakr brought with him all that was left of his wealth. Paying for the expenses of Muhammad's religion over the years had brought his fortune of forty thousand dirhams down to about six thousand, roughly fifty pounds of silver coins that he bagged onto his camel along with water skins and leather-wrapped provisions. Muhammad, who nourished his Koran with the events of his life, later exulted in verse about the escape. Using his God voice, he said: "And when the disbelievers plotted against you to imprison you, or to kill you, or to exile you; they were plotting and Allah too was plotting, and Allah is the best of those who plot."[20]

Thirteen years had gone by since his cave experience on Mount Hira. During those years he saw more effulgences and bright shapes and heard more strange sounds,[21] and he drew all the wrong conclusions about their meaning. More than half of what would later be bound together as the Koran was composed during those years of conflict, and with these verses he laid the foundation of his religion with its incitements to violence against all who opposed it.

A magma chamber had formed in him, and it was filled with molten hatred. It was pressuring to the surface, preparing for eruption. Even before he left his home of fifty-three years, his magma was palpable in the curses he called down upon the Meccans from the heavens. Standing with hands cupped to his ears, kneeling in the camel position, bending his torso forward with elbows outward and touching his forehead to the ground, he prayed for their deaths or the deaths of their firstborn sons; he prayed for the punishment of plagues and pustules and disasters to be visited upon them. "O God, bring down on the Quraysh for me the seven years like those of Joseph."[22]

It was year 622 of the Christian era, but Muhammad's followers would eventually begin their calendar from the time he escaped to Yathrib. They call it the Year of the Flight. This was Year One for the religion of submission to Muhammad's God concept. It was the year Muhammad declared war on all and sundry who refused to bow down to his idea of God—the year he declared war on the world.

PART II

The Twilight Zone

CHAPTER 13

Al-Qaeda

After the arduous journey of hiding by day and traveling by night, Muhammad and his companions finally reached a narrow mountain pass leading to the southeast region of the oasis of Yathrib. It was late September and below them was a vast garden, roughly twenty-five square miles of arable land squeezed between mountains and the blackish remains of ancient lava flows.

Muhammad first gazed upon the sprawling valley when his mother brought him there to visit relatives of the Najjar clan and the grave of his father Abdullah. It is likely he also visited Yathrib on the two caravan journeys he was known to have made to Syria, first with his uncle Abu Talib and later as commercial agent for Khadija, as the valley was along one of the two major northern caravan routes.

He therefore knew the lay of the land and something of the tribal complexities: Behind the bucolic façade was a highly Balkanized oasis that was divided into numerous autonomous mini-territories all bound together in the intrigue, shifting loyalty, and treachery of complex tribal alliances. In the highlands of the southeast were the territories of the major Jewish tribes and smaller polytheistic clans that were generally friendly to the Jews. Upper Yathrib, as the highlands were called, held the most fertile soil and the largest fortresses. To the west and north were the lowlands controlled by the major groups of the Aws and Khazraj, whose fields and groves were subject to occasional flooding during the rainy season when water coursed down from highland arroyos. Throughout Yathrib were the fortresses of the major tribes and the blockhouse habitations of subgroups, all of them separated from one another by palm groves and cropland. Surrounding many of the larger fortresses were villages.[1] Though decentralized, the population of the valley was the most concentrated in the Najjar territory, which was situated in the middle of the valley near a bridge over one of the major riverbeds. If there was a center to Yathrib, it was the territory of the tribe of Muhammad's great-grandmother.

At the time Muhammad gazed down upon the valley from the highland mountain pass, Yathrib was on the cusp of political change. Two centuries before, the oasis had been overwhelmingly Jewish. Their presence in the valley can be traced to the days of the Babylonian empire, but their predominance began to erode with the arrival of Arab refugees from Yemen who migrated to Yathrib near the end of the fifth century following the collapse of the fabled dam of Marib. As Arab numbers grew, so did disputes with the Jews over the control of land and water. The Arabs, who split into the two major tribes of the Aws and the Khazraj, also fought among themselves, at times feuding over land, but anything could spark a fight. One war broke out over a rigged horse race, while others resulted from murders that led to cycles of blood vengeance. The Jewish tribes were sometimes drawn into fighting one another due to the tangle of alliances that grew out of the Arab presence. Over time their territories shrank and now consisted of enclaves in the highlands. At the time of Muhammad's arrival, a half-century of on-and-off fighting had drained the valley of the desire for war, and tribal chieftains were searching for a leader to unite the entire valley under his rule. Emerging for the role was the Khazraj sheikh Abdullah Ubayy, a tall burly man with a patriarchal gray beard who possessed the most impressive of the Khazraj fortresses along with surrounding date plantations and cropland. He had played a major role in bringing about peace between rivals after a ferocious battle that had occurred at a highland region called Buath. The tribes were so eager for peace they were prepared to crown Abdullah Ubayy king and had fashioned a jeweled diadem for him. It is likely the Jews would have also accepted his authority, as he was allied with the Qaynuqa Jews, one of three major Jewish tribes of Yathrib, and was respected by the others. But then Muhammad arrived and upset the political balance of Yathrib, collapsing support for a king.

Muhammad descended into the valley on a scorching day in late September of A.D. 622. His followers learned he had fled Mecca with Abu Bakr, but they grew anxious as each day passed without sight of him. Knowing he would travel the mountain road that descended into the highlands, believers went out in small groups every morning in the hope of being the first to greet him, but returned home when the heat became unbearable. The first to spot him was a Jew on the roof of a blockhouse near Quba, the southernmost village of the highlands. "O Arabs," he cried, "here's your great man you've been awaiting!"[2]

Through the shimmering heat, the figures of four men atop camels became increasingly distinct. When the riders finally plodded into the village, the believers shouted, *"Allahu Akbar!"* and showered the men with greetings and invitations to stay with them. None of them had ever seen Muhammad and only understood who was who when the men alighted from their camels and Abu Bakr scurried to shield Muhammad from the sun with a makeshift parasol. Muhammad ended up staying at the home of an older convert named Kulthum, a member of an Aws clan. Abu Bakr, meanwhile, accepted an invitation from a highland Khazraj family.

Kulthum's home had become a reception center for the émigrés, having previously housed Umar and other Meccan transplants. It was the first stop for Muhammad before moving on towards the center of the oasis, a distance of four miles along a road that cut through villages, palm groves, fields, and orchards. During the brief time he stayed in Quba,[3] Muhammad led his faithful in prayer sessions, preached and recited verse, received visits from supporters, and accepted oaths of allegiance from new converts. He also traced out the foundation of a mosque for Quba.

It was his intention to establish himself in the territory of the Najjar tribe of his great-grandmother, and he and his followers planned a formal entry, publicizing it ahead of time to attract crowds along the way. On the scheduled day, Muhammad mounted his camel and made the journey surrounded by a retinue of prominent followers. Accompanying the procession was an armed guard of Najjar horsemen.

It was not every day that people got to see a man who claimed to have been taken up into Heaven. Everyone in Yathrib had heard the stories about him: He saw things no one else could see and heard things no one else could hear; an angel transmitted the words of God to him; he was a humble, illiterate holy man who had been summoned before the Lord to receive the divine command to pray five times a day and follow a narrow path through life that led to Paradise. Crowds jammed the road and many people climbed onto roofs to get a look at him. Some shouted, "Muhammad has come!" Others cried, "*Allahu Akbar*, the Messenger of God has arrived!" Along the route, people ran alongside his camel. Some shouted invitations for him to stay with them, but he politely declined by saying his camel was guided by God and would make the decision about where to stop. Before reaching his destination, he went by the fortress of Abdullah Ubayy, perhaps fishing for an invitation to lodge with the would-be king of Yathrib. But the Khazraj chieftain, glaring down at him from the battlement, told him to move on. "Look to those who invited you. Stay with them."[4]

While the converts were joyful, many in Yathrib smelled trouble. His followers were still a small minority and were made up largely of young people. Out of the twenty thousand people living in the oasis—half of them Jewish—Muhammad could count between three hundred to five hundred core believers, including the Meccan émigrés.[5] Though small in number, they were militant and had gone on idol-smashing rampages prior to Muhammad's arrival, breaking into homes to destroy or steal the idols of the heathens, an activity that was ongoing at the time of Muhammad's arrival. Such aggressiveness was especially apparent in young converts whose parents remained pagan. The story is told of the son of a sheikh who replaced an idol belonging to his father with a dead dog and threw the idol—a statue of the goddess Manat—into a cesspool.[6] In light of such aggressive behavior, many of the older generation viewed Muhammad's arrival with concern.

Once in Najjar territory, Muhammad made a point of traveling through the village of the descendants of his great-grandmother, but turned down invitations to stay there. Instead, he allowed his camel to wander farther down the road until it stopped in front of the two-story blockhouse of Abu Ayyub, one of the Aqaba pledgers. It is likely that this was prearranged, because Abu Ayyub rushed out of his house to remove the saddle and baggage from

Muhammad's camel and lug everything inside. Still surrounded by adoring crowds who continued to shout invitations for him to stay with them, Muhammad waved them off saying, "A man must go where his saddle goes." But he was so moved by the adoration that after arranging his belongings inside the house he came out to speak to the crowd. He asked, "Do you love me?" When people shouted, "Oh, yes, Messenger of God," Muhammad could barely restrain the tears. He said, "And I, by God, love you all! By God, I love you all!"[7]

Once settled into the house of Abu Ayyub, Muhammad was faced with the pressing task of building a permanent residence, and he envisioned a combination abode and mosque. To this end, he purchased open land across from Abu Ayyub's house with money Abu Bakr provided. Except for a small cemetery at one end, a few date palms, and a shed, the property was empty. Over the next seven months, the Yathrib converts and the Meccan émigrés pitched in to build the complex, using stone and adobe as the basic construction materials. The completed structure was a compound surrounded by walls ten feet high and about one hundred and fifty feet in length on each side. Additionally, a string of apartments with entrances to the courtyard were built along one side. A prayer area was set up in a corner using the trunks of palm trees as pillars to support a roof of palm branches. A preacher platform was built, and mats of woven palm fibers were laid over the prayer area.

The completed structure was intended to serve multiple functions: It was a residence for Muhammad and his family, a prayer area for the faithful, a center for the indoctrination of newcomers, and a seminary for the training of preachers. And it would soon be Muhammad's base for waging war against his enemies, his *al-qaeda*.

During the construction, he used the living quarters on the lower floor of Abu Ayyub's house as his headquarters. A stream of people visited him, many of them to educate him on the Who's Who of the valley and the complexities of Yathrib's tribal alliances. Believers came to him for instruction and also sought him out to arbitrate disputes. Within months of his arrival he took over formal leadership of the Najjar clan following the death of the chieftain, a descendant of Muhammad's great grandmother. The Najjar clan leaders came to Muhammad to ask him to appoint a new sheikh, and he ended up appointing himself. This role gave him an important seat at the tribal council of the various Khazraj clans.

During these early months he had to resolve a multitude of problems. Among them was the fact that the Meccan émigrés were scattered throughout the various autonomous territories of Yathrib, and most of the Yathribites considered them foreigners. In part to give them protection, in part to mitigate the poverty many of them had fallen into after leaving everything they owned in Mecca, Muhammad initiated a program of pairing Meccan emigrants with Yathrib converts, calling it "brothering." Abu Bakr was paired with the head of the highland Khazraj family he moved in with upon arriving in Yathrib. He became so tight with his new brother that he married one of his young daughters. One of the Yathrib converts took the bond of brotherhood to an extreme by cheerfully offering one of his wives to his new Meccan partner. "I have two wives. Look and see which of them you prefer, and I'll divorce her!"[8]

Also to ensure their protection and at the same time assert his authority, Muhammad issued an edict declaring that his believers constituted an independent and distinct tribal entity among the diverse groups of Yathrib, with himself as leader of the new community. Though scattered throughout Yathrib, believers were thenceforward exclusively under his authority. All conflicts involving his followers were to be brought before him for resolution even if one of the parties was a nonbeliever. He endowed this new community with the ethos of the typical tribal group: An attack on one was an attack on them all. While carving out this new community, Muhammad astutely avoided alienating Yathrib's polytheist tribes, as the edict also bound his new Yathrib followers to respect the customs of their birth tribes regarding blood money and the demands of their political alliances provided these did not conflict with the new entity. He also opened the door to the Jews. It was his ardent desire for them to join his religion, and in the beginning he attempted to bring them into his fold by offering a promise of tolerance. Over time, the organizational edict went through revisions and updates and eventually consisted of forty-seven articles. The final version, generally called the "Constitution of Medina," laid the foundation for a theocracy.[9]

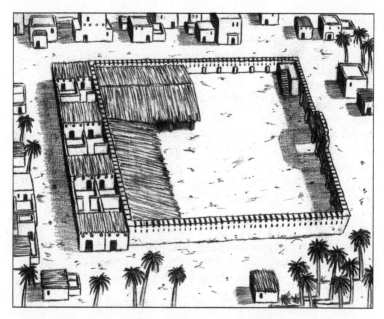

MUHAMMAD'S MOSQUE WAS HIS *AL-QAEDA*, meaning his base of operations. It was built after he arrived in Yathrib and served as a prayer area, residence, indoctrination center, and headquarters for the war he initiated first against his Meccan enemies and later against the Jews of Yathrib after they refused to accept him as their prophet.

The mosque complex opened seven months after Muhammad arrived in Yathrib. He allotted space to his family in the residential wing. His cousin Ali was given one of the apartments while Muhammad's daughters occupied other rooms. The matronly Sauda was given yet another.

One of Muhammad's first acts upon finishing the complex was to have Aisha, now nine years old, turned over to him. They were betrothed three years earlier with Abu Bakr's blessing; Muhammad now claimed her as a wife. She was living with her parents at the house of the highland Khazraj convert with whom Abu Bakr had brothered. On the appointed day, Muhammad visited the home. While he prepared himself inside Abu Bakr's home to "consummate" the marriage, as the phraseology of the literature puts it, Aisha's mother called for her. She was in the courtyard playing with friends and was out of breath when she reached the house. Her mother made her sit down at the door to calm her. Aisha later recalled the event: "She took some water and, having wiped my face and head, led me into the house. Then she took me in and there was the Messenger of God, peace be upon him, seated on a bed inside our house, in the company of a group of the Ansar (Helpers), both men and women. She sat me down in his lap and said, 'These are your family; may God bless you by them and they by you.' The men and women then jumped up and left. The Messenger of God, peace be upon him, consummated our marriage there in our house."[10]

Like Sauda, Aisha had her own space at the mosque. It was a room built for Muhammad directly behind the preacher platform. An opening that served as a door and window gave Muhammad easy access to the platform. The only separation between the platform and the room was a curtain. Aisha brought with her a collection of dolls, and Muhammad sometimes played doll games with her and the playmates he allowed to visit her.

With the opening of the mosque came organizational problems, particularly the matter of getting people to show up on time for the mandatory prayer performances. Laggards were a nuisance, especially at dawn prayers. By then, Muhammad had begun the routine of lining people up in rows for prayer, in part to instill discipline, but also, as he informed his congregation, to imitate the practice of the angels when they prayed to God. People would straggle in and disrupt the tightly scripted performances by squeezing themselves into the prostrating ranks. Muhammad did not wait for guidance from above, but consulted his closest advisers. The reason for the tardiness was simple: People were on their own guessing the time. To solve the problem, someone suggested ringing a bell to announce prayer time, but Muhammad ruled that out. It was too much like the Christian practice, and he loathed the sound. Another suggested sounding a trumpet, but Muhammad disliked that idea as well because it reminded him of the Jews. Others thought of lighting a fire, others of clapping wood together. Finally someone suggested having a caller announce prayer time from the rooftops.

Muhammad liked the idea. Wording for the prayer call was hammered out: "God is the greatest, God is the greatest. I bear witness that there is no god but God. I bear witness that Muhammad is the messenger of God. Come to prayer. Come to salvation.

God is the greatest. There is no god but God." This was to be repeated twice to announce prayer time, and then a third time after everyone had assembled to mark the beginning of prayer. Because of his strong voice, Bilal, the former black slave who had belonged to Umayya Khalaf, was given the role of prayer announcer. Until a tower was built, he would climb on the roof of a neighboring building each morning and wait until the first light to make the call and would repeat it for the other mandatory prayer sessions.

The call to prayer solved the tardiness problem. Additionally, it provided Muhammad with a steady stream of free publicity. Thenceforth, his brand name of "Messenger of God" would be loudly repeated three times for each prayer session, or fifteen times per day. Everyone within a good distance from the mosque would hear it whether they wanted to or not. It was an advertiser's dream of continuous and free repetition.

As soon as his *al-qaeda* was firmly established and his political position in Yathrib secure, Muhammad formally launched the war on "all and sundry" that he had declared only seven months before at Aqaba. At this point this meant the Meccans, and he began with a series of raids, for the most part unsuccessful, against their caravans. The first took place in March of A.D. 623 after he learned that a huge caravan under the leadership of Abul Hakam was returning from Syria along the Red Sea. It was one of the major annual caravans, this one with three hundred merchants, guards, and camel drivers carrying profits of gold and silver and hundreds of tons of merchandise strapped on the backs of two thousand camels.[11]

Selecting a crew of thirty Meccan expatriates, Muhammad put them under the command of his uncle Hamza and gave him orders to attack the caravan, kill anyone who resisted, and return to Yathrib with the caravan. If successful, it would deal a crippling blow to the Meccans, and it would provide Muhammad with funds to further his activities and free the Yathrib converts of the burden of supporting the Meccan émigrés.

Hamza and his warriors hastened out of Yathrib on swift camels and intercepted the caravan at the Red Sea in the territory of the Juhayna tribe, but the raid turned out a failure. The Meccans had enough time to circle the caravan in a defensive formation. It turned into a standoff that ended when the Juhayna chieftain, who collected a tax from the Meccans for the right to travel through his territory, stood between the opposing forces and persuaded them not to fight. Hamza returned to Yathrib empty-handed, and Abul Hakam's caravan continued south.

Over the next few months, Muhammad sent out more raiding parties against Meccan caravans, also without success. During one of these raids, Muhammad's maternal cousin Sad Waqqas, who ten years earlier split open the head of a Meccan by whacking him with a camel jaw, again gained notoriety by getting close enough to a caravan led by Abu Sufyan to shoot arrows. But heavily out-numbered, Waqqas and his fellow marauders backed away. Other raids failed because the caravans had already gotten through the danger zone and were out of reach.

Frustrated by the lack of success, Muhammad led several raids, but these also failed. On one occasion he led two hundred men to attack a caravan headed by Umayya Khalaf near al-Abwa, the village south of Yathrib where his mother was buried, but by the time he arrived Khalaf had eluded him. The trip, however, was not wasted. On the return swing, Muhammad, backed up by his fighters, secured a nonaggression treaty with one of the Bedouin tribes of the region.

The only attack that brought in booty—and some blowback for Muhammad—came from a small raid he launched against an equally small caravan traveling from Taif to Mecca with a cargo of raisins, wine, and leather goods. When Muhammad learned the date of departure, he appointed Abdullah Jahsh, a close cousin, as commander to lead eight other Meccan expatriates against the caravan. But so fearful was Muhammad of a leak that he gave Jahsh sealed instructions with an order not to open it until two days after their departure. It was only when he unsealed the letter that Jahsh learned they were to proceed to Nakhla, the site of the sanctuary of al-Uzza where the road descended south to Taif, and wait to ambush the caravan. Before getting there, Jahsh lost two of his men, one of them Sad Waqqas, when the camel they shared ran off, and they had to stay behind to recover it. The caravan was easy pickings: four young riders leading a dozen pack animals. Jahsh killed one of the men with an arrow, captured two others, while the fourth man escaped. The raiders returned to Yathrib with the pack animals and prisoners.[12]

This killing happened to take place on the last day of the holy month of Rajab when the Meccans still had an expectation of security. Though Muhammad did not have any use for the practice, his Meccan enemies and his Yathrib opponents used the violation to stir people against him. Many of the Yathrib converts, not far removed from their polytheistic roots, were also upset and criticized Jahsh and his men. Muhammad finally settled the controversy by composing a Koran verse that projected the blame on the Meccans: They had refused to listen to the words of God that had been transmitted to them through his messenger, and they had offended God by driving him and his followers out of Mecca; therefore they were fair game for God's vengeance even during the sacred months.[13]

The Meccans sent money to ransom the captives, but Muhammad at first refused to accept it because Waqqas and his riding companion were still missing. He warned the Meccans that if it turned out his men had been captured and killed, he would slay the two hapless captives in reprisal. Umar, always quick with his sword, offered "to send them immediately to Hell." One of the captives was so traumatized by all the talk of cutting his head off that he made a frantic declaration of faith: "There is but one God and Muhammad is his messenger!" The two missing men eventually straggled back to Yathrib, dehydrated and famished. They had failed to recover their camel and had to make their way back to Yathrib on foot. The remaining captive, the one who had not converted, was set free, and he returned to Mecca.

The final act of the episode occurred when Muhammad divided the stolen merchandise among the raiders, keeping one fifth for himself. This was the first instance of what came to be called the *khumus*—Muhammad's twenty percent take of the booty. Over time, the cumulative plunder from raids and battles would amount to an emperor's fortune, making Muhammad and many of his followers rich beyond their wildest dreams.

CHAPTER 14

The Jewish Question

When he arrived in Yathrib, Muhammad had great hopes for living in harmony with the "People of the Book," as he called the Jews. In his mind, his religion was their religion, but in purified form, and he anticipated they would recognize this and welcome him with open arms. It would be like a joyful reunion of long-separated brothers.

For their part, the Jews were curious about him. He had been news throughout Arabia before he arrived in their valley. Much of what they had heard about him came from their Meccan contacts. It was anything but flattering, but that was understandable given that he denounced their beliefs. The Jews were determined to make up their own minds about him.

While he was still living at the house of Abu Ayyub, rabbis from the major Jewish tribes paid him cordial visits and listened to him politely. Muhammad returned the courtesy and went to great lengths to show goodwill. It was not his intention at first to force them to convert, only to bring them alongside like two caravans traveling together to reach the same destination. To this end, he ordered his followers to pray in the direction of Jerusalem. Though choosing Friday as his day of rest rather than the Saturday of the Jews, he adopted some of Jewish rites, such as fasting on the Day of Atonement, the most important of the Jewish holy days. He also ordered his followers to observe Jewish kosher laws. In the so-called Constitution of Medina, which gathered his followers into a new tribe, he declared the Jews were free to follow their own religion.

The curiosity of the Jews quickly faded, however, and was replaced first by amusement and then indignation when Muhammad claimed he was their prophet, the Messiah they had long prayed for. Not only had he been foretold in their holy book, Muhammad declared, but the Jews of Yathrib themselves had also foretold his coming. He reminded them of the threats they used to make against the Aws and the Khazraj of a coming Messiah who would restore Jews to their land—not only to Israel but also the lowland plantations of Yathrib that the Aws and Khazraj had seized from them over the course of the last century. The Jews were stunned that he would make such a claim. He was an Arab whose lineage could be traced back to Yemen, the same as the Aws and the Khazraj. The prophet foretold in their scriptures—the Messiah—would have to descend from Aaron. He would have to be a Jew. How could he not know that? Yet Muhammad insisted he was the prophet foretold in their scriptures. Even his name was mentioned in the Torah; his physical description was given as well. To show his error, the rabbis took pains to translate into Arabic the Torah verses that Muhammad claimed contained references to him. When the translations were read to him, Muhammad accused the Jews of falsifying them.[1]

The rabbis also questioned his versions of their prophet stories. They were Torah scholars and were also versed in the legends of the prophets, the embellished popular versions of the Biblical stories that had evolved over the centuries. The legends were morality tales, and the rabbis made use of them in their homilies. The more they knew about Muhammad's prophet stories, the more they could see that they were not based on the Torah, but on the legends. Even then there were significant errors and discrepancies.[2] Could it be that God had revealed the books of the Torah to the Jews, yet to Muhammad he revealed a skewed version of the derivative folk tales? Or was it more likely Muhammad had heard the legends from people whose knowledge of them was inaccurate? Or perhaps he had heard the correct versions, but changed them to suit his fancy. Sallam Mishkam, a leading rabbi of the Nadir tribe, rendered the verdict: "He has not brought us anything we recognize."[3]

As had occurred when the Meccans doubted him, Muhammad became infuriated. He went on the offensive with Koran verses critical of the Jews and recited them to the rabbis. He offered them as proof that not only did God talk to him, but that God was using him to indict the Jews for perverting the truth that had been revealed to them and to call them back to the right path. In one verse Muhammad said, "There came to you Moses with clear (Signs); yet ye worshipped the calf (Even) after that, and ye did behave wrongfully."[4] In another, he said their rejection of him was part of the old pattern of the Jews rejecting their prophets: "Then if they reject thee, so were rejected messengers before thee, who came with Clear Signs, Books of dark prophecies, and the Book of Enlightenment."[5]

Muhammad threw out a challenge to the rabbis: Produce something as marvelous as the Koran or even close to it, but the rabbis passed on it. They had heard enough of his work to conclude his claim to revelation was bogus. They haughtily turned the tables on him: Cause a book to come down from Heaven, just as the Torah was sent down to Moses, but it should be sent down to one of their rabbis testifying that Muhammad was indeed a prophet. Then they would believe. Muhammad responded with a Koran verse that again accused them of chronic disbelief: "The people of the Scripture (Jews) ask you to cause a book to descend upon them from Heaven. Indeed they asked Musa (Moses) for even greater than that, when they said: 'Show us Allah in public,' but they were struck with thunderclap and lightning for their wickedness. Then they worshipped the calf even after clear proofs, evidence, and signs had come to them. (Even) so We forgave them. And We gave Musa (Moses) a clear proof of authority."[6]

Muhammad claimed he had come to reform Judaism and Christianity. Jews and Christians had deviated from the revelations that had been made to them. To advance his case, Muhammad once hosted a meeting between rabbis and Christians.[7] He goaded them into an argument and used their hostility to one another as evidence they had lost their way and were in need of his guidance. To Muhammad's delight, the Jews accused the Christians of falsifying their religion; the Christians accused the Jews of murdering their Messiah. The Jews said there was no place for Christians in Paradise because they followed a false prophet, whereas the Christians claimed the path to the hereafter lay exclusively through belief in Jesus as redeemer. When they were done arguing, Muhammad pointed out that they both claimed revelation, yet they could not agree on anything, therefore they were both wrong. Jews had perverted God's word, he said, but Christians were in error because they falsely attributed a divine nature to Jesus; they could not even come to an agreement among themselves as to the nature of the divine nature. They fractured into various sects, each proclaiming to know the truth about the matter. Even worse, they committed the sin of polytheism by claiming that Jesus was the son of God.[8] Jews and Christians had corrupted the message of God and he, Muhammad, had been sent to the world as the last and final prophet to reveal the truth and guide people to the right path.

To the astonishment of both the Jews and Christians, Muhammad exonerated the Jews of the death of Jesus. They had not crucified Jesus, Muhammad informed them, but a substitute. At the time of the Last Supper, when his enemies were plotting his death, Jesus asked for a volunteer from among his disciples to die in his place, promising him a special place in Paradise. God changed the appearance of the volunteer to resemble Jesus. It was the volunteer who was tortured and put to death on the cross. Before the volunteer was dragged away, God caused Jesus to fall asleep, opened up a hole in the roof of the building where the Last Supper took place, and Jesus was taken up into Heaven. The disciples who witnessed his ascension kept quiet about it. Even the mother of Jesus was fooled by the substitution.[9,10]

Within in a year of Muhammad's arrival in Yathrib, the Jews quit talking to him. As far as they were concerned, he was inflexible and strange. His accusations against them were made up of half-truths, distortions, outright lies, or weird inventions, such as his Jesus story. What use was it to talk to someone like him? He was always right, they were always wrong, and no amount of arguing was ever going to convince him otherwise. Just as the Meccans had done, they began openly to mock him. One of the Jewish poets, a prominent Nadir merchant named Kab Ashraf, skewered Muhammad with satirical poems. He was joined by other Jewish poets. Whenever they encountered Muhammad or any of his people, the Jews would alter the wording of the usual greeting of peace by using a near homonym for "peace" meaning "death," so that the greeting expressed the opposite sentiment: "May death be upon you."

When it was clear the Jews would not accept him, Muhammad became aggressive. His epileptic experiences had convinced him God talked to him so that by now he believed that everything that came into his head came from God, and God did not lie. Were the Jews calling God a liar? How could they not grasp that he had brought the truth to them? At one point, he and a contingent of his closest people barged into one of the synagogues during a holy day service and gave the Jews what amounted to an ultimatum: "O ye Jews, show me twelve men among the Jews who believe that there is no god but God and that Mohammad is his messenger, and God will spare all the Jews under Heaven his wrath." He repeated it twice more, but the Jews remained silent. He said, "You refuse! By God, I am the last Prophet and I am the final Prophet and I am the chosen Prophet; whether you believe or not."[11]

To distinguish his followers from the Jews who kept their beards trim and their mustaches bushy, he ordered the believers to grow their beards long and trim their mustaches. At the mosque, he cursed the Jews during congregational prayers and in sermons, following the pattern of the hate prayers he had formulated in Mecca that called on God to inflict suffering on his opponents: "O God, punish them in this life and in the hereafter because of their disbelief and errors. Verily, they are the wrongdoers." Often, the prayers were Koran verses, many of which were elaborate curses. His followers parroted him. He had indoctrinated them with the idea that his behavior was invariably a reflection of the will of God so that to imitate him was to follow the straight and narrow path that led to Paradise. In their prayers, therefore, the faithful repeated his curses against the Jews; they memorized the Koran verses that condemned them. Muhammad's hatred became their hatred; his enemies became their enemies.

Once Muhammad began demonizing the Jews, he never stopped. He mounted an aggressive smear campaign. During the height of it, he latched onto a Jewish legend that God had once transformed some Jewish fishermen into apes because they defied his commandment to rest on the Sabbath. They had devised a clever way to passively trap fish on Saturday and collect them on Sunday, and for this enterprising subterfuge the men and women were transformed into apes. Muhammad turned the tale on the

Jews and began calling them "apes." He added his version of the story to the Koran: "And you knew well those amongst you who transgressed in the matter of the Sabbath. We said to them, 'Be you apes, despised and rejected.'"[12]

For all the aggressive rhetoric, Muhammad was kept in check by the military might of the Jews and limited himself to invective. Each of the three Jewish tribes could field seven hundred warriors. One of the tribes was an ally of Abdullah Ubayy, the Khazraj chieftain who had not yet given up hope of leadership over the entire valley. Though many of the Aws and Khazraj had gone over to Muhammad, Abdullah could still raise warriors by the hundreds. The regional balance of power did not favor Muhammad either. The Jews were on friendly terms with the Meccans and with important Bedouin tribes to the northeast and southeast of Yathrib. Additionally, they were related by religion and family ties to the tribes of the prosperous Khaybar oasis ninety miles north of Yathrib. The only advantage Muhammad had was the fact that the Jews of Yathrib were not united. Because of alliances with polytheist tribes, they had fought one another in the recent intertribal wars and bitter feelings persisted. But he feared that if he provoked them they could coalesce into a powerful force and crush him.

For their part, the Jews grew increasingly concerned about Muhammad. He had already shown disturbing signs of violence, first with the idol-smashing rampages of his followers that could only have occurred at his instigation. More recently, he had undertaken raids against Meccan caravans—against his own kith and kin. These raids had started small, but lately he had been able to send out one or two hundred warriors. His power was clearly on the rise.

Suspicious of Muhammad's intentions, the Jews spied on him, though ineptly. The story is told of a half-dozen Jews who feigned conversion in order to attend the mosque. They were thus able to listen to Muhammad's sermons and pick up on gossip, which they reported to the rabbis. Muhammad was pleased when they converted, believing that his proselytizing among the Jews was at last paying off, but before long he doubted their sincerity. When they stood at the initiation of the prayer performances, they slouched, scratched themselves, and wiped their noses. They mumbled Koran verses. When it got down to prostrations, they were out of sync with the other worshippers. Even more upsetting, they stuck together in the back rows and talked among themselves. On one occasion while he was giving a sermon, Muhammad exploded when he heard them snickering. He accused them of being hypocrites, insincere believers, and ordered them thrown out of the mosque. The congregation jumped them, beat them to the ground, and dragged them into the street. One of the men was dragged by his hair, another by his beard. "Don't come near the Apostle's mosque again," one of the faithful shouted once they were pushed out into the street, "for you are unclean!"[13]

It can be deduced from its position in the Koran that Muhammad invented his version of the story of Abraham, Ishmael, and Hagar around this time. Despairing of ever obtaining acceptance by the Jews, he got vengeance by relocating the Biblical Abraham and his firstborn son Ishmael to Mecca. Whereas in the Bible the family drama of Abraham, Sarah, Ishmael, and Hagar plays out exclusively in the Levant, Muhammad now developed a storyline whereby Abraham leads Ishmael and his mother to the vale of Mecca and abandons them. There, Ishmael begets a line of descendants that ends up with Muhammad. Under this new scenario, Muhammad was now a direct descendant of Abraham, who was neither Jew nor Christian, but was the first believer in the one God. And as his direct descendant Muhammad was commissioned by God to restore the true faith of "our father Abraham," as Muhammad called him. Thus he became the hero of his own epic script.[14,15]

The new version comes to life in Koran verse: Ishmael and his mother are left to fend for themselves in a desolate valley without water. When they grow weak from thirst Hagar runs in panic between the two low stone mounts of Safa and Marwa in search of water; Ishmael strikes the ground and out comes a gush of life-saving water. Abraham eventually returns, and he and Ishmael build the temple. As the height of the walls grows, Abraham stands on a large stone block, which Muhammad later called "The Station of Abraham," to hand up construction rocks to Ishmael.

Once Muhammad completed the script, he ordered his followers to change the *qibla*—the direction of prayer—from Jerusalem to Mecca. The literature tells the mythologized version of this turnabout: During the course of a congregational prayer session at one of the satellite mosques, while everyone was in prostration mode, God "instructed" Muhammad to change direction. Always in front of the rows of worshippers, Muhammad suddenly made an about face, from due north to due south, and he ordered the congregation to do the same, informing them that he had just received a command from God to do so. From then on they were to pray toward Mecca and its temple, the "House of God" that Abraham and Ishmael built.

Changing the direction of prayer was symbolic of Muhammad's repudiation of the Jews, and it would have serious consequences for them. Over the next few years he would purge Yathrib of its Jewish population. He would drive two of the major tribes from the valley and seize their ancestral properties. The third tribe would suffer an even worse fate.

Evidence that Muhammad devised the Abraham-Mecca storyline after his arrival in Yathrib can be found in the literature. In his Koran commentary, the 14th century scholar Ibn Kathir notes that during one of the pilgrimages to Mecca that Muhammad undertook years after his escape to Yathrib, Umar pointed to a large, square stone next to the temple and asked Muhammad if it was the stone that "our father Abraham" had used to hand up rocks to Ishmael when building the temple. Muhammad said, "Yes."[16] Umar's question is a smoking gun, a marker that shows Muhammad invented the story after fleeing Mecca as a fanciful addition to the Abraham-in-Mecca tale. Had the stone been part of the lore of Mecca, Umar would have known about it because he was born and raised in Mecca. But the lore of Mecca was exclusively about the migration of its forefathers from Yemen ten generations before Muhammad came on the scene. More importantly, if Muhammad had invented the story while he was still in Mecca, Umar would have been among the first to be informed about it. The fact that he had to ask suggests the entire Abraham-Mecca storyline was invented after Muhammad fled to Yathrib, but prior to pilgrimages he later made to Mecca. Umar could only have asked his revealing question during one of those pilgrimages.

At that time, Umar also asked, "Should we make it a place of prayer?" God must have been listening, because Muhammad quickly came up with a verse authorizing it: "And We made the House a place of gathering for humanity, and security. And take the Station of Abraham as a place of prayer."[17]

The stone has a story, but not the one Muhammad invented. It was a hewn block half-sunk into the ground near the entrance to the Meccan temple, a stone that was possibly dragged there during the temple reconstruction in A.D. 605. This was the year the temple first acquired its cubic shape with the help of Muhammad, who suffered an epileptic seizure when he was pressured to strip off his clothes. Was it used as a stepping stone during the construction? Did Muhammad himself stand on it to hand up rocks to fellow workers before or after his embarrassing falling experience? Whatever its purpose during the reconstruction, the stone was left behind and became a stump that people sat on in the shade on hot summer days. Everybody in Mecca knew about it and used to sit on it when the temple cast a cooling shadow. Even Muhammad must have sat on it. With the same flair he had used to create the story of Abraham in Mecca, Muhammad transformed a lowly block into the stepping stone of the Patriarch.

And with his guileless questions, Umar leaves us with evidence of the fictional origin of both.

CHAPTER 15

I Bring You Slaughter

Outside of Yathrib Muhammad and his zealots were earning a reputation for brigandage. Muhammad looked for every opportunity to attack Meccan caravans, both to cause Mecca economic harm and to bring in money to pay his people and finance the growth of his movement. Many of the Meccan expatriates were impecunious and lived from day to day by hiring themselves out as laborers. The brothering with Yathrib converts relieved some of their stress, but it transferred their money problems to the Yathrib converts. His followers needed more than promises they would be spared eternal hellfire by believing in him. They needed hard money—and soon.

An opportunity to score big came about sixteen months after Muhammad arrived in Yathrib when he learned that his former next-door neighbor Abu Sufyan was in charge of a major caravan that was on its way to Syria. He sent out a force to intercept it, but his information was several days old, and the caravan slipped through along the coast above Yanbu. However, what went north had to come south again. Calculating the likely return time, Muhammad sent Talha, the man the Meccans had once roped together with Abu Bakr, and Said, the son of the first religion-of-Abraham seeker Zayd, to locate the returning caravan. They spotted it coming down the Red Sea route. Rushing back to Yathrib, they reported to Muhammad with a count of the men, the number of camels, and a guess as to the merchandise from the way it was bundled on the camels. Muhammad asked for volunteers and as an incentive offered the prospect of booty: "This caravan holds the wealth of the Meccans, and perhaps God will grant it to you as plunder!"[1] This raid, he informed his followers, was warfare for the sake of God—*jihad*—so that anyone killed would be granted God's reward of Paradise while those who survived were assured a share of the plunder.

To overpower such a large caravan, Muhammad needed more manpower than he could muster from among the Meccan emigrants alone, so he encouraged Yathrib converts to join him on the expedition. With promises of booty or Paradise, he quickly assembled three hundred men, three-quarters of whom were Yathrib converts, but among them they possessed only seventy camels and two horses. They brought with them whatever weapons and gear they owned: swords, bows, quivers of arrows, spears, shields, and sidearms like daggers and slings. Some of them owned helmets and coats of mail. It is said that Muhammad's closest advisers objected to him going as it could endanger the life of the man whom God had commissioned for a unique spiritualizing mission to mankind, but he overruled them.

With Muhammad in the lead, the small army marched toward the caravan stop of Badr, an oasis about eighty miles to the southwest of Yathrib that was popular with caravans due to the abundant water of its springs and the cooling shade of its palm trees. Since it was situated at the junction of roads to Syria, Yathrib, and Mecca, Muhammad believed it to be the likely destination of Abu Sufyan's caravan. His guess was confirmed when two spies he sent to the oasis, ostensibly to water their camels, overheard slave girls chatting about the arrival of the Meccan convoy in the next day or two.

Abu Sufyan, meanwhile, was on the alert for an attack. Before leaving Syria, he learned that Muhammad had stalked his caravan during the northward trek and was warned that he planned to hijack it on the return trip. He dispatched a fast rider to Mecca to sound the alarm. It did not take much to rally the Meccans. The returning caravan was hauling merchandise and profits said to be worth fifty thousand gold dinars, a fortune even today, with many investors big and small having a stake. In three days the Meccans assembled an army of nine hundred and fifty men and marched north under the command of Abul Hakam. "Does Muhammad think that he can take from us what his companions took at Nakhla?" he said as they readied their camels and war horses. "He will know whether we protect our caravan or not!"[2] Far to the north, meanwhile, Abu Sufyan halted the caravan at a safe distance to await the Meccan army and sent scouts to locate Muhammad's force. He himself paid a visit to Badr late at night and learned about Muhammad's spies. He became certain they were from Yathrib after finding date pits in dung left by their camels that bore the peculiar patterns of a date variety grown only in Yathrib. Instead of heading for the Badr oasis, therefore, he rushed the caravan over a mountain pass to the Red Sea and followed the coast south. After two days of forced marching, he had put an insurmountable distance between him and Muhammad. Once he was certain the caravan was safe, he sent word to Abul Hakam that they were out of danger and that he should return with his army to Mecca.

When he learned of this development, however, Abul Hakam refused to back down. Were they to return to Mecca, they would appear weak, and Muhammad would seek to block Meccan commerce with further raids. Nothing would be gained by returning empty handed, but everything could be lost. He vowed to kill or capture Muhammad, and if they took him alive to bring him back to Mecca in chains for punishment. If it turned out that Muhammad ran from a fight, they would spend three days at Badr feasting and celebrating victory by default.

Not all the Meccan leaders were as eager for battle as he. Important merchants such as the Rabia brothers thought it better to return to Mecca. They had set out to protect the caravan, Utba Rabia argued. Now that the caravan was safe he saw no reason to proceed. If Muhammad was the liar and fraud they believed him to be, other Arabs would soon rise up against him and kill him. Abul Hakam accused Utba of cowardice. The only reason he did not want to fight was because his son Abu Hudhayfa had joined with Muhammad, and he feared his son would be killed. Abul Hakam offered a compromise: They would not seek to kill any of these traitors, only to capture them and bring them back to Mecca. Perhaps they could still be rehabilitated and returned to the religion of their fathers. The Rabia brothers, however, continued to argue for abandoning the march. They were certain no good would come of it.

It turned into a shouting match. That night, two small tribes abandoned the army, taking a hundred warriors with them. In the end Abul Hakam, backed up by Umayya Khalaf and other leaders, won over the Rabias and their clansmen, and what was left of the army moved on toward Badr.

Muhammad learned of the Meccan army when he was only a day from Badr. This presented him with a dilemma: They had set out to plunder Meccan wealth, but now they were faced with Meccan steel. Perhaps looking for a way to back out without losing face, he held a tent meeting and asked for advice from his top people. Abu Bakr and Umar argued against confronting an overwhelming Meccan force, but two of the leading Yathrib believers, Sad Muadh and Miqdad, jumped to their feet in support of war. In an emotional speech, Sad argued that Muhammad was guided by God and could do no wrong. If Muhammad told them to fight, it was because God told Muhammad to fight. "We believe in you," Sad said. "We declare your truth, and we witness that what you have brought is the truth, and we have given you our word and agreement to hear and obey; so go where you wish, we are with you; and by God, if you were to ask us to cross this sea and you plunged into it, we would plunge into it with you; not a man would stay behind. We do not dislike the idea of meeting your enemy tomorrow. We are experienced in war, trustworthy in combat."[3]

With that, Muhammad decided to fight and threw himself into it with determination. Posing as travelers from Iraq, he and several of his companions rode into the valley and stopped people along the way to gather news about the Meccan army.[4] He learned the Meccans were encamped behind a stretch of huge sand dunes. Returning to his forces, he dispatched his cousins Ali, Zubayr, Sad Waqqas, and others for water and to gather further intelligence. He wanted to know the size and makeup of the Meccan army, but he was also eager to learn the whereabouts of the caravan, thinking there might still be a chance to attack it before the Meccan army could intervene.

At one of the numerous Badr wells, Muhammad's cousins captured water boys the Meccans sent to fill leather water bags. They brought them to their camp and beat them while Muhammad performed prayer prostrations nearby. The beating loosened their tongues. They did not know the exact number of Meccans, only that the army slaughtered between nine and ten camels each day for food. From that, Muhammad deduced the size of the force at somewhere between nine hundred and one thousand men. The boys knew nothing about the caravan as they were attached to the Meccan army. When they recited the names of the leaders, Muhammad rejoiced. Every one of them was on his vengeance list. "Mecca has thrown you slices of its very liver!" he said to his cousins.[5]

Taking the advice of a Yathrib convert who knew the Badr valley, Muhammad pitched camp at a spring that was the closest to the Meccan position. This was an astute move because it blocked the Meccans from the oasis where the main Badr springs were located. His men erected a leather cistern to hold water sufficient for their needs. The location was also a clever choice because the terrain was strewn with rocks large enough to prevent the Meccans from mounting a cavalry attack. Additionally, Muhammad positioned his camp so that the morning sun would be in the eyes of the advancing Meccans. To give himself an overview of the battlefield and to keep out of range of arrows, he had a command hut built on a low rise nearby.

Despite the warrior bravado and his preacher talk about the rewards of Paradise, Muhammad was running scared. The Meccans outnumbered them three to one and were better armed. He now faced the possibility that he could die, and if he died his religion would likely perish too. It is said he spent much of the night in prayer, frequently weeping and cursing the Meccans and calling on God to destroy them for rejecting him.

That night it drizzled, and Muhammad's men sheltered themselves under their shields. At the crack of dawn, he called them out for the usual prayers, and they performed them on the wet ground. When it was light out, he lined them in tight formation. Though they were a mix of rough people from oft-feuding tribes, the physically demanding rituals of prayer had served almost as boot camp for them, instilling discipline. Muhammad had always insisted on straight prayers rows because that was the way he believed the angels prayed. He had also insisted they do their prayer routines in unison so that lining up in military formation now came almost naturally. Like a drill sergeant, he went up and down the rows and jabbed anyone who stood out with the razor tip of an arrow. A man named Sawwad became angry when his blood was drawn and insisted on the right to retaliate, blood for blood. Muhammad handed him the arrow. He pulled open his shirt, exposing his belly, and said in essence, "Go ahead, stick me with it!" Instead of retaliating, the man threw his arms around his neck, sank to his knees, and kissed Muhammad's bare belly. When Muhammad asked him why he did that, he said, "O Messenger of God, you can see what is about to happen. I wanted my last contact with you to be my skin touching yours." Muhammad thanked him for his vote of confidence in the outcome and said a prayer for him.[6]

By then the Meccans, their banners flapping in the breeze and their idols of Hubal, al-Uzza, and al-Lat held high on poles, were pouring down the sand dunes on horse and on foot. They soon formed their own lines opposite Muhammad's, staying out of the range of arrows. It turned out that many of them were thirsty, some to the point of desperation. The night before, Muhammad's men had deprived them not only of their water boys but also their water camels and water bags. The location of his camp had cut them off from the valley's water sources. That this shortage had a serious impact on the Meccans became evident when a group of them broke from their ranks and ran to the leather cistern Muhammad's people had erected, which was on his side of the battlefield. Muhammad gave orders to let them drink, mainly because one of them was Khadija's nephew Hakim Hizam, the man who purchased Zayd Haritha at a slave market and gave him to her as a present. After they returned to their ranks, a man named Aswad of Abul Hakam's Makhzum clan ran to the cistern, but he was on Muhammad's vengeance list and was not shown mercy. Muhammad signaled to Hamza to deal with him. Hamza cut off one of Aswad's legs before he could get to the water and followed him as he dragged himself into the cistern in one last effort to get water. Hamza plunged his sword into his back and left him floating facedown.

Just before the two sides came together in battle, Muhammad suffered an epileptic fit. The stresses of the moment were too great for his neural wiring, which began misfiring when he was lining up his men for battle. He knew the symptoms: the cold sweats, the leaden feeling inside his head, the sound of bells tinkling, and the breakout of diffuse, throat-choking panic. He rushed for the hut, an alarmed Abu Bakr following behind, and fell into feverish prayer in an attempt to keep the fit at bay. He kept praying to the point that even the usually obsequious Abu Bakr became exasperated. "That is enough, O Messenger of God! You are pestering your Lord."[7]

Before he sank into the fit, Muhammad gasped out orders to Abu Bakr: "Do not fight until I command you. If they draw near, aim at them with arrows but do not draw your swords until they overpower you." As the seizure progressed, Muhammad's face turned red and his lips made bizarre contortions. Abu Bakr stood guard over him with his sword drawn and would not let anyone get close, not even Umar or any of the other lieutenants who rushed to the hut for instructions. They invariably got Abu Bakr's sword pointed at them and a repeat of Muhammad's orders.

When he finally came out of it, Muhammad was in a state of exaltation. His temporal lobe had dished up feelings of ecstasy and the visions he so needed: He had seen the Angel Gabriel mounted on a horse somewhere between Heaven and earth, and his horse was pawing the firmament in eagerness for battle. Other important angels such as Michael, the enemy of disbelievers, and Israfil, the angel of the trumpet, were in command of legions of angelic forms dressed in glimmering white and mounted on pie-bald steeds. Down they were coming, swords held high, to fight on the side of the believers—Michael with a thousand angels to the right of their lines, Israfil with another thousand on the left, and Gabriel with a thousand of his own.[8]

In the grip of his delusions, Muhammad rushed out of the hut to shout the joyful news of the Lord's help to his people. Word of the angelic reinforcements quickly spread and injected much needed courage into the rank and file of the outnumbered army. Muhammad backed up the effects of the glad tidings with promises of booty for the survivors and Paradise for the ones who died fighting for God and his messenger. The believers already knew of these rewards; that was why they had volunteered for the expedition, but hearing it again from their hyped-up prophet supercharged their morale.

The Meccan line appeared as a formidable wall of helmeted warriors on horseback and on foot. The ground troops, many of them Abyssinian mercenaries, brandished swords and spears while archers notched arrows into their bows. The unity of the Meccan battle formation, however, hid the divisions within. Even as they formed their lines, the Meccan leaders continued the bickering of the night before. Abul Hakam, seated on a warhorse and dressed in a coat of chain mail that reeked of the perfume he had doused himself with while putting on his armor, could not resist taking a dig at Utba Rabia about his courage. "Your lungs have filled your belly with fear!" he said. Enraged, Utba slashed the foreleg of Abul Hakam's horse, severing the tendons and causing the animal to drop. He snarled at Abul Hakam to fight on his feet like everyone else.[9]

To prove his bravery, Utba stepped out in front of the Meccan lines along with his son Walid and his brother Shayba and challenged the enemy to a duel. Three young Yathrib converts stepped out of the ranks, but Utba complained they were not their equals. A herald from the Meccan side demanded warriors of rank. By then, Muhammad had come out of his epileptic fit and was running up and down his lines shouting to everybody of the angelic reinforcements. He ordered Hamza, Ali, and Ubayda Harith, another close relative who had commanded one of the caravan raids the previous year, to take them on. They stepped out wearing helmets with face plates that disguised them and only identified themselves when Utba demanded to know who they were. It was an uneven match. Utba and Shayba were older men, valiant but out of shape. Hamza, famed for his hunting skills and hot temper, was pushing sixty, but he was still physically powerful. With ferocious slashes, he quickly killed Utba, while Ali, short but with muscular arms and torso, slew Utba's son Walid. Shayba was able to get the better of Ubayda, severing one of his legs, but Hamza and Ali then hacked Shayba to death.

Each side dragged their slain or wounded from the battlefield. Ubayda was carried to Muhammad's hut and was laid before him, blood gushing from his amputated leg. Muhammad allowed him to rest his head on his foot so that he would have the honor of dying while touching the messenger of God. "I bear witness that you are a martyr," Muhammad declared when Ubayda died from loss of blood.[10]

At that point, the battle began in earnest. Arrows flew in each direction as the two sides moved forward. With their tighter lines, Muhammad's fighters were better protected behind their shields against the barrage of arrows. Very quickly, the two lines clashed and the battle turned into a melee of hand-to-hand combat. Swords rose everywhere and slashed down on helmets and armor. Spears thrust through face plates and into skulls.

It was the battlefield of the gods: Al-Uzza, the divine mother; al-Lat, the goddess of the reproductive force; and Hubal, the god of manly virtue clashing with the vengeful one God of Muhammad, the dispenser of eternal torment to those who refused to believe in Muhammad.

Though outnumbered, Muhammad's people had the advantage of zealotry. They were whipped to a frenzy with the promise of booty or Paradise. Ali, excited by the blood and the efficiency of his sword, stormed across the battlefield, slaying one man after another. He slew Hajiz, Nubayy, Amir, Zayd, Umayr, Masud, Abdullah, Yazid, Amwas, and many more. Several of his kills were Meccans of note, such as Hanzala, one of the sons of Abu Sufyan. After the battle was over, Ali also slew one of the important captives: Nawfal, the son of Khuwaylid and a half-brother of Khadija who had once rescued Zubayr from the beatings of his mother Safiya. His brother-in-law had been such a persistent enemy that when Muhammad learned Ali had killed him, he shouted, "*Allahu Akbar!* Praise be to Allah who answered my prayer concerning him."[11]

The battle pitted brother against brother, cousin against cousin, father against son. The story is told of a zealot named Abu Ubayda who slew his father Abdullah. Loathing his son for abandoning the religion of Mecca and joining with the likes of Muhammad, Abdullah stalked him during the battle. Abu Ubayda was able to avoid him until his father blocked his path. After a brief duel, the son drove his sword into his father. It is also said that Abu Bakr stalked one of his sons during the battle, intending to kill him for refusing Muhammad's religion, but the son stayed out of his reach.

Muhammad had a genius for getting people to die for him. During the thick of the fight, one of the young believers ran up to his command post to ask him what Submitters should do that would best please God. When Muhammad said, "For them to charge into the enemy unprotected by helmet or chain-mail," the young man stripped off his chain mail and rushed into the fight and was soon killed.[12] Another young man who had been holding back from fighting overheard Muhammad cry out, "Every man who fights them bravely and advances without retreating will have God give him entry into Heaven." After hearing this, the man shouted, "Great! Great! Is all that stands between me and Paradise is to have them kill me?" He rushed into the fray and fought until he was killed.[13]

At the top of Muhammad's kill list was Abul Hakam. All Muhammad's fighters knew he was a prime target. After the battle started, his clansmen shielded him from fanatical rushes, but Muhammad's people were determined to get him. When they saw a break in the ranks, three of them made a dash for him. Abul Hakam fought as valiantly as an older man could against young opponents. His son Ikrima fought by his side, protecting his father, but one of the attackers dealt Abul Hakam a fatal blow by cutting off one of his legs mid-thigh. Ikrima slashed the arm of the attacker, leaving it dangling on a thin strap of flesh. It is said that the wounded man tore his arm off and stayed in the fight until pain and loss of blood forced him from the battlefield.

Muhammad watched the bodies pile up from the elevated observation post. He was like the sorcerer's apprentice who had unleashed powerful energies. The savage spectacle excited him, but he was not taking any chances that these energies could turn against him. Surrounding him as guards were his top people: Umar, Abu Bakr, Sad Muadh, Miqdad, and others. The only two horses of the expedition were hitched outside the hut. If the valley filled with blood and if the blood kept rising and threatened to engulf him, he and Abu Bakr were prepared to hop on those steeds and make a fast getaway.

It is not recorded how long the battle lasted, but it ended as an overwhelming victory for Muhammad. His followers, so certain they would end up in Paradise if they were killed, beat back the superior force, and the bulk of the Meccan army fled. Left on the battlefield were the bodies of seventy Meccans, including most of the Meccan leaders. Another seventy Meccans were captured. Only fourteen of Muhammad's men were killed.

When the fighting ended, Muhammad sent his trusted servant Abdullah Masud, the former shepherd boy, to find Abul Hakam's body. Muhammad instructed Masud that if he had trouble identifying him, he was to look for a scar on his knee. When they were boys, Muhammad had once shoved Abul Hakam off a bench during a banquet to make room for himself, and he had gashed his knee on the stone floor, leaving a permanent scar. The Meccan leader was still alive when Masud found him. He was lying on his back in a thicket of thorn bushes, too weak from loss of blood to lift his sword to defend himself. Masud had a personal hatred for him, for he was among the Meccans who had once beat him for reciting Muhammad's verses in front of the temple. Abul Hakam recognized him and said, "You've risen up in the world, little shepherd boy." Masud ripped off his helmet and cut off his head. He took the head to Muhammad and placed it at his feet. Muhammad was so pleased that he raised his hands heavenward and gave praise to God, saying the death of Abul Hakam was a better present to him than "the best camels of Arabia." He then performed two sets of prayer prostrations and gave Masud Abul Hakam's sword to keep, a showpiece weapon with a silver-inlaid hilt that remained a family heirloom for generations.[14]

Umayya Khalaf, one of the merchants who had often looked down on Muhammad with seigniorial scorn from the meeting platform of Mecca's temple, was killed after surrendering. It so happened that Bilal, his former slave, spotted him and his son among the captives. Umayya had once staked Bilal to the scorching ground and placed a heavy stone on his chest to get him to renounce Muhammad's religion. When he saw Khalaf in custody, Bilal cried out, "Hey, there's that polytheist-in-chief Umayya Khalaf. I'll not live on if he does!"[15] Umayya and his son were quickly surrounded. His captor tried to protect them, but he was pushed aside and Umayya and his son were hacked to death.

Muhammad celebrated the smashing victory in a way that only Muhammad would celebrate it: He prayed, after which he prayed more. Following the prayers, he ordered captured camels to be slaughtered for his men to feast on. In between praying and feasting he organized the burial of the "martyrs" of his cause as well as the rank and file of the Meccan dead. For the ones who were on his vengeance list, he arranged a special funeral. Their bodies were thrown into an abandoned well the locals used as a dump for their refuse.

That burial took place three days after the battle and the bodies had begun to bloat and putrefy under the intense sun. Seated on his camel, Muhammad presided over the event. Abu Bakr called out the names of the dead one at a time. The corpses were picked up by the arms and legs and swung into the pit. Abu Hudhayfa, the son of Utba Rabia, was present when Abu

Bakr called out the name of his father. Before the body was tossed into the pit, Muhammad asked him if he was saddened by the death of his father. Hudhayfa insisted he was not. He remembered his father as wise, cultured, and virtuous, but he had refused to believe in God and his messenger and therefore brought about his own destruction. "I hoped that God would guide him to Islam. And when that eluded him and I saw he did not take it, it irritated me."[16]

The only Meccan who was not thrown into the pit was Umayya Khalaf, and that was because he was so obese that his limbs pulled off when they tried to lift his body. They ended up piling dirt and stones on him for a grave.

When the last of the bodies was tossed into the pit, Muhammad taunted the dead, shouting down at their grave from atop his camel: "Don't you wish you had obeyed Allah and his messenger?" When Umar pointed out that he was talking to the dead, Muhammad replied that even though they were down in the grave, they could hear him. They could hear him just as surely as Umar heard him.[17]

His hatred for his enemies kept burning in him. Late into the night people heard him raving, "O Utba, O Shayba, O Umayya, O Abu Jahl. I have found that which my Lord promised me is true. Have you found what your gods promised you is true?"[18]

Muhammad had more than bodies to dispose of. The fate of the prisoners now had to be decided and the profits of war distributed. What they got from the battle was little compared to what they would have scored had they been able to capture the caravan, but "Allah's bounty," as Muhammad phrased it, was still in evidence: In addition to the weapons and battle gear, the spoils included a hundred and fifty pack camels, ten horses, and the tents, clothing, and miscellaneous personal belongings the Meccans had abandoned at their camp on the other side of the sand dunes.

Distributing the booty turned out to be a nightmare. Three hundred men made claims and counterclaims. Muhammad was responsible for the confusion. When the battle was underway, he sent out a herald to whip up fervor by crying, "Whoever kills a man, to him belongs his booty; whoever takes a prisoner, keeps him." The warriors who scored kills or took prisoners were the primary beneficiaries, but not everyone had been able to score

MUHAMMAD REJOICES WHEN THE HEAD of his chief Meccan adversary is brought to him. The Meccans nicknamed him Abul Hakam, meaning "Man of Wise Counsel," but Muhammad called him Abu Jahl, the "Spawner of Madness." He was mortally wounded in a battle defending a Meccan caravan from an attack by Muhammad. Muhammad sent one of his servants to find Abul Hakam's body after it was reported he had been killed in the fighting. When the servant found him still alive, he cut off his head and brought it to Muhammad, who gave thanks to God for answering his prayers for the death of the Meccan leader.

a kill or capture an enemy, such as the people who guarded Muhammad at his command post. Should they get nothing? There were other issues: Many of the men were furious that some of their prisoners had been wantonly killed, such as Umayya Khalaf and his son, who were slain at Bilal's instigation. Ali and Umar caused trouble too because they had grabbed some of the hated prisoners from their captors and decapitated them. Technically speaking, Ali and Umar could therefore claim credit for these kills, not their captors, and be awarded plunder. Adding to the complications was the fact that the rightful captors would be deprived of the ransom value of their slain prisoners. Dead men were worth nothing. Then there was the problem of the angels. Who was going to benefit from their kills? Some of Muhammad's fighters swore they had seen angels on the battlefield. One man brought Muhammad the heads of three Meccans to validate his booty claims, but admitted to cutting off the heads of only two of them. "As for the third, I saw a tall white man strike off his head and it rolled before him, and I picked it up." Muhammad said, "That was one of the angels."[19]

Muhammad got so fed up with all the bickering that he ordered *everything* to be turned over to him—booty and captives alike. He warned his people that God knew everything so that if they withheld anything, even a thread from a worn saddle blanket, they would be answerable to God in the next life—and to Muhammad in this life if they were discovered. He must have spent the better part of two days, in between the five daily prayer sessions and all his extracurricular praying, figuring out who got what. In the end he displayed the wisdom of Solomon: He kept one fifth of the booty for himself, and everyone else got an equitable portion of the remainder. The two men who had brought horses were each awarded an extra share because of the value of their horses to the enterprise and the cost of their maintenance.

The prisoners were the thorniest problem. Muhammad at first agreed with Umar that they should all have their heads struck off. A problem arose, however, when the captives were assembled and Muhammad saw among them close relatives: His uncle Abbas, always a sympathizer but a fence-sitter, was among the prisoners, as was Muhammad's son-in-law, Abu al-As, the son of Khadija's sister and the husband of Muhammad's daughter Zaynab, who remained with her husband in Mecca after Muhammad escaped to Yathrib. Aqil, one of Ali's older brothers, was also among the captives. Even though Aqil rejected Muhammad's claim to prophethood and remained a polytheist, Muhammad had grown up with him in the house of Abu Talib, and Aqil was still like a brother. Should Muhammad put everyone to the sword but spare his close relatives?

Muhammad called his top people for advice. Umar, Sad Muadh, and Miqdad were the hardliners: Cut off their heads was their advice. To a man, they argued, the captives were enemies of God and his messenger, so none should be spared. Umar went so far as to offer to serve as an example by cutting off the heads of his close relatives who were among the prisoners, and he was certain Ali would be pleased to chop off the head of his brother Aqil. Abdullah Rawaha, one of the Aqaba pledgers, suggested an alternative to beheading: Tie all the prisoners to trees in a forest and set the forest ablaze. But Abu Bakr, tears welling in his eyes, appealed for mercy and pointed out the captives were worth more alive than dead since the Meccans would pay handsomely for their return. The young Abdullah Masud, a man of slight build who had earned a place among these bearded and burly leaders for his beheading of Abul Hakam, was also a softie. He chirped in with a supportive word for a captive named Suhayl, a merchant who used to treat him well.

After listening to his advisers, Muhammad withdrew to his tent and let his mental life take over the decision making. He had constructed a fantasy world peopled with prophets and angels, and he lived inside his head with them as his most intimate companions.[20] They were as real if not more so than his flesh-and-blood companions. The stories of the prophets, or at least his version of their stories, had become points of reference for him and served as a framework for his thinking. He often made use of these revamped stories to explain the outside world and make important decisions.

When he finally emerged from his tent, Muhammad had flattering words for both Abu Bakr and Umar. They had given excellent advice, he told them. They were like the ancient prophets and were practically brothers of the greatest of the angels. Abu Bakr, in fact, had much in common with the Angel Michael, whose function was to reveal the satisfaction of the Lord for his people and his forgiveness of them. And he was also much like Abraham, a prophet who was sweeter than honey with people even though they had once thrown him into a furnace. And certainly he was also like the gentle Jesus, who praised the forgiveness of God as proof the Lord was mighty in wisdom. Umar, on the other hand, was more like the Angel Gabriel, whose function was to reveal God's displeasure and ensure vengeance against those who transgressed the limits established by God. Umar was also like Noah, a prophet who was as hard as stone against his own people when they departed from the path of God. Umar also bore striking similarities to Moses, who was also a hardliner. Muhammad repeated the words he had put into the mouth of

Moses: "O Lord, destroy their wealth and harden their hearts for they will not believe until they see grievous pain."[21]

After praising them in this manner, Muhammad rendered the decision of God. It was a mix of the wisdom of both Abu Bakr and Umar: Forgiveness through ransom for the many, but death for those who had transgressed God and his messenger beyond the limits. The traditional sources state that seventy prisoners were taken at Badr, but only forty-nine made it to Yathrib. We know of two people who were executed during the return trip to Yathrib: Nader al-Harith and Uqbah Muayt. Both were top-of-the-list offenders. Nader was hated for ridiculing Muhammad's prophet stories as fables of the ancients and offering to tell more interesting stories about Persian kings and heroes. This had irritated Muhammad so much that he ended up belittling the phrase several times in the Koran. Uqbah Muayt was the Meccan who slopped camel entrails on Muhammad's back while he was praying in front of the temple, provoking hearty laughter among other Meccan leaders and bringing Muhammad to call upon God to destroy them all.

At the first stage stop on the return trip, Muhammad ordered Ali to cut off Nader's head, this over the objection of Miqdad, his captor who would lose Nader's ransom. Miqdad said in essence, "Hey, don't do that, he's my prisoner!" Nader, his hands tied behind his back, was forced to kneel, and Ali swung his sword down on his neck. The decapitation was so swift that Nader's head hit the ground before his body slumped over. Muhammad soothed Miqdad for his loss by promising him God's reward in the afterlife. Uqbah Muayt was beheaded at the next stage stop. When Muhammad ordered him to be killed, Uqbah begged for his life, saying, "But who will look after my children?" Muhammad roared, "Hellfire!" and signaled to a convert named Asim Thabit to do the decapitation.

Muhammad composed an entire chapter about the battle, the first of the Koran war verses. Among the militant verses: "And fight them until there is no more tumult or oppression, and religion becomes Allah's in its entirety."[22] And: "Against them make ready your strength to the utmost of your power, including steeds of war, to strike terror into the hearts of the enemies."[23]

With this chapter, entitled "The Spoils of War," Muhammad transformed his religion into an organized criminal enterprise

MUHAMMAD NEVER FORGOT INSULTS. Here, Muhammad's first cousin Ali beheads one of the Badr captives, Nader al-Harith, a man who had frequently mocked Muhammad in Mecca over his claims that God talked to him. Nader used to follow him around and offer to recite the epic tales of the Persians to the people Muhammad had addressed in assemblies, telling them the Persian tales were more interesting than Muhammad's prophet stories.

for its approval of plunder. He also announced in these verses his general policy for the distribution of plunder: He would get a fifth of all future takes, the rest going to participating believers. "Enjoy" what you take in war," he tells the faithful, for it is "lawful and good."[24]

The Meccans lost the battle at Badr for a number of reasons. The most obvious noted by historians is that their leaders were bickering, inept old merchants who were overconfident because of their numerical strength. If they had been astute, the leaders would have seen the terrain advantages Muhammad had given himself and would have devised a strategy to dislodge and destroy him. If they had been wily and ruthless, they would have taken advantage of the fact their enemy prayed *en masse* at the crack of dawn and would have launched a devastating stealth attack when

Muhammad and his people were in vulnerable prayer formations. But the Meccan leaders were old men who played by the old rules of tribal warfare: Attack and fight bravely, then withdraw to see if the enemy desired to settle, and if they did, then even out the score with blood money.

The Meccans also lost for a reason that is not obvious: They failed to understand what they were up against. They had never before dealt with an epileptic psychopath. They had the experience in their society of both elements separately, but never both combined in one person. They knew about epilepsy. It was as common a malady then as it is today, but in their day epilepsy was given a different explanation: It was due to possession by the mischievous *jinn*—demon possession—just as Halima suspected about Muhammad when he had his first epileptic attack while in her care. Epileptics in such a society often grew up to be diviners and soothsayers, scorned and feared, yet with an accepted role. Meccans also had the experience of psychopathic personalities. How could they not in a society where Muhammad's aunt Safiya savagely beat her son Zubayr to prepare him for the world, or where Khattab ruthlessly beat his son Umar for every infraction of the paternal will? Such products of Arab society were often the cause of blood feuds that turned clans and tribes against one another. Both of these elements were fused together in the person of Muhammad. His epilepsy led him to believe that God talked to him; his psychopathic side led him to kill people who refused believe him.

Yet a third element was his gift of eloquence. He was able to spin a web of words that ensnared the ignorant into believing his delusions. He drew them inside his mental world and made it more real than the real world. Incited by their belief in this fictional world, Muhammad's followers brought the slaughter to the Meccans at Badr that he had so often prayed for.

While he was in Mecca, Muhammad had never gone beyond threats of violence because he did not then have the power to get away with it. Now he had the power.

CHAPTER 16

Murder, Inc.

When Muhammad left Yathrib to attack the Meccan caravan, the Jews and polytheists were nervous. When he returned victorious over the Meccan army, they were terrified.

The day of the beheading of Uqbah Muayt, Muhammad dispatched two heralds to Yathrib to announce his victory. Arriving in the heat of the late morning on Muhammad's personal camel, his adopted son Zayd spread the news in Lower Yathrib, while Abdullah Rawaha, the man who urged Muhammad to incinerate all the Badr captives in a forest fire, brought the news to Upper Yathrib. Riding his mount into the courtyard of the mosque, Zayd proclaimed the victory from atop the camel. "O Helpers, rejoice at the safety of the Messenger of God and at the killing and capture of the polytheists!" When he named the dead Meccans, the believers broke into cries of *Allahu Akbar*! Children ran through the streets and alleys crying, "The evil Abu Jahl is dead!"—repeating Muhammad's nickname for Abul Hakam.[1]

The Jews and polytheist Arabs were in a state of shock and at first refused to believe it. They turned the fact that Zayd was riding Muhammad's camel into evidence that he had in fact been slain and his army defeated. It was a trick of some kind. One of the polytheists boasted to Osama, the nine-year-old son of Zayd, "Your master has been killed, and all those with him!" The boy ran to his father to ask about it. Zayd told him it was untrue. Muhammad had indeed been victorious, and he, his army, and their prisoners would arrive in Yathrib in the next day or two. The youngster ran back to the polytheist and accused him of spreading lies.

"We're going to have you up before the Messenger of God, and he will execute you!"[2] The rumor of Muhammad's death took on a life of its own and was not contained until enraged followers poured into the streets and frightened nonbelievers with threats of violence.

Muhammad arrived the next morning, a day ahead of his triumphant warriors and their dejected captives. When he entered Najjar territory, he lifted the skinny Osama onto the camel to ride with him the rest of the way. Once he was back at his mosque, powerful clan leaders who had kept their distance from him found it prudent to drop in to congratulate him for his victory.

Muhammad had brought one of the captives, Suhayl Amr, with him and turned Sauda's room into a holding cell. An important Meccan leader, Suhayl was a former brother-in-law of Sauda and was the man Muhammad had first appealed to for protection after he was run out of Taif four years earlier. While Suhayl had kept a polite distance from Muhammad's religion, his brother Sakran had joined it as had his wife Sauda, and they were among the second wave of émigrés to Abyssinia. Sakran later died there. Suhayl was captured at Badr, but escaped during the forced march to Yathrib. Muhammad ordered that whoever found him should kill him, but after he was discovered hiding in a clutch of trees, Muhammad tethered him to his camel and forced him walk to Yathrib with his hands tied behind his neck. Muhammad apparently did not have the opportunity to inform Sauda about the guest arrangement. When he arrived at the mosque with his captive in tow, she was out visiting the family of two young men who had been killed at Badr. Upon returning home she was startled to find her former brother-in-law on his knees in the corner of her room, his hands still roped behind his neck. "O Abu Yazid," she said, calling him by his nickname. "You gave yourself up then! Couldn't you have died a noble death?"[3]

Muhammad spent much of the next month working out ransom deals. The high-value prisoners ended up paying four thousand dirhams for their release, representing about thirty pounds of pure silver. As one of the important captives, Suhayl was made to pay the full amount. A Meccan who went to Yathrib to negotiate his release traded places with him and was kept as a hostage until Suhayl sent the ransom money from Mecca. Some of the indigent captives who were literate were offered their freedom in exchange for teaching reading and writing to the children of the Yathrib converts.

Muhammad's uncle Abbas paid the most for his freedom. As a major investor in all the caravans going out of Mecca, Abbas was well off and was known for his fondness for gold. At that time he owned forty slaves whom he employed in his various import-export enterprises. The literature states he was made to pay forty *awqiyyas* in gold dinars, equivalent to one hundred and seventy-five ounces of gold,[4] to secure his release and that of several of his nephews and confederates. As with the war booty, Muhammad kept one fifth of the ransom amounts, the balance distributed to the captors.

The thorniest ransom involved his son in law, Abu al-As, the son of Khadija's sister Hala. Muhammad had married his eldest daughter Zaynab to him a year or so before the epileptic experience on Mount Hira. Though she accepted her father's religion, she remained in Mecca with her disbelieving husband after Muhammad fled for his life to Yathrib. By all accounts they deeply loved one another. When news of her husband's capture reached her, she sent ransom money and an onyx necklace Khadija had given her as a wedding present. Muhammad let his son-in-law go after he agreed to send Zaynab to Yathrib and to recognize that they were no longer married due to the fact he refused to join the religion. Once back in Mecca, Abu al-As told his wife they had no choice but to separate and arranged for his brother to escort her to Yathrib.

The Meccans, however, intervened when she was already on the road, having learned about her departure at the last minute. They saw her leaving as an insult. Her father had slaughtered dozens of their people and was holding many more for ransom, so they forced her to return as a hostage. She was pregnant at the time, and the tussling caused her to fall from her camel. As a result she miscarried. Abu Sufyan, who was now the most powerful man of Mecca, finally allowed her to leave. He wanted revenge against Muhammad, but he did not believe that withholding a daughter from her father was the right thing to do. Muhammad later sent a raiding party with orders to burn to death the men who had forced her back to Mecca, bringing about the miscarriage, but a day after the raiders left, he sent word he had changed his mind about roasting them alive. "Just kill them," he told them. "No one has the right to punish by fire save God."[5]

In Mecca, the news of the Badr defeat shattered the town. Everyone was related to everyone, and everyone therefore had lost a son, brother, father, cousin, or uncle. Even though he himself had lost a son and many close relatives, Abu Sufyan suppressed his grief and advised the people against mourning because it would drain too much of their sorrow. That would take away the energy needed for vengeance. Hearing this, a blind man who lost three sons had a slave lead him to a mountain retreat overlooking the town so that he could grieve in private. He brought wine with him, and after getting drunk he wept inconsolably and poured sand over his head. While he was grieving, a wave of wailing broke out in the valley, and the sound reached him. The Meccans ignored Abu Sufyan's advice, and their sorrow broke out all across town. The blind man sent the slave to investigate. The slave returned and lied about it, telling his master that it was only a woman weeping over a lost camel.

Instead of refraining from mourning, the women of Mecca cut their hair and put up curtains in the alleys and roads to mark places for people to gather to grieve for their beloved. A favorite camel or horse of the slain would be brought and they would stand around it with their heads bowed and one hand placed gently on the creature as if to connect with the spirit of the dead through the animal.

One of the few who refused to mourn was Abu Sufyan's wife Hind, a strong-willed woman who burned with desire for vengeance against Muhammad for killing her son Hanzala, her father Utba Rabia, her brother Walid, and her uncle Shayba. When a woman asked her, "Will you not cry over the people of your house?" she replied, "May God afflict your throat! Shall I cry over them so it will reach Muhammad and his companions and the women of the Khazraj, so they will rejoice over our misfortune? No, by God, not until I am revenged of Muhammad and his companions."[6]

Hind refused to sleep with her husband until he struck back at Muhammad, and Abu Sufyan himself publicly renounced the pleasures of life until he made a display of Meccan backbone. As soon as all the ransom money had been paid and the captured

Meccans returned, he organized a raiding party of two hundred men and led them north to Yathrib. They waited until late at night to enter through the rugged southeast mountain pass into the highlands where the Jewish fortresses were located. Abu Sufyan first banged on the heavy gate of the fortress of Huyayy Akhtab, one of the leaders of the Nadir tribe, to request entry for himself and his men, but was refused. He led his men to the nearby fortress of Sallam Mishkam, the chief rabbi of the Nadirs, who swung the doors open and regaled them with food and wine. Sallam, one of the rabbis who had debated theology with Muhammad and later ridiculed him, shared what intelligence he had about him. Abu Sufyan wanted to kill Muhammad, but the only way to do so would be to attack him at his mosque in the center of Najjar territory. Under cover of darkness, he and his small force could reach the mosque before being detected, but Sallam warned him that even if they were able to kill Muhammad it was not likely many of them would get out of Yathrib alive. It would be a suicide mission.

Abu Sufyan needed something to show for the raid. Sallam pointed out an easy target—a farm owned by one of Muhammad's followers located in the southeast corner of the highlands. That morning, the Meccans struck the farm, killing the owner and a slave. They set fire to the houses, barley fields, and palm groves and were gone before Muhammad could muster a force against them. Muhammad chased the raiding party for several days, but Abu Sufyan slipped away through the desert.

The victory at Badr gave Muhammad the confidence to take on his Yathrib enemies. Immediately following his return from Badr, he orchestrated the assassination of poets who had mocked or criticized him. Their influence worried him. News spread by gossip, but the attitude toward the news was shaped by poetry—the editorials of the day. Jewish poets and pagan poets friendly to the Jews were whipping up opposition to him with their verses, branding him an outsider and questioning the wisdom of letting him acquire power in Yathrib. Muhammad decided that murder was the best way to deal with them.

The first of the poets to die was an elderly sheikh named Abu Afak who had irked Muhammad even before Badr with satirical verses. After Muhammad returned victorious, the sheikh composed

"WHO WILL RID ME OF OF . . . ?" Whenever he wanted someone dead, Muhammad would recruit an assassin at the mosque. When the killer returned to report the murder was successfully carried out, Muhammad would praise him in front of the congregation for his good work in "the cause of Allah."

a strident poem that obliquely called for Muhammad's ouster by heaping praise on Yathrib's ancestors who had repulsed foreign invasions. When Muhammad heard of the poem, he solicited a killer at one of the mosque assemblies: "Who will deal with this rascal for me?"[7] A convert of the Najjar tribe who had fought at Badr took up the challenge. He plunged his sword into the sheikh while he was asleep in the courtyard of his home.

Equally ruthless was the murder of Asma, the daughter of Marwan, who was noted for her strong opinions and sharp tongue. The details of her background are sketchy, but she may have been a Jewish convert or belonged to a clan on friendly terms with the Jews because she lived in the shadow of one of the Jewish fortresses. Instead of being intimidated by the murder of Abu Afak, she composed forceful verses blasting the tribes of Yathrib for allowing an outsider the run of their valley. "Screw the men of Malik and Nabit and Aws and Khazraj! You obey a stranger who does not belong among you."[8] The poem went on to criticize her people for letting Muhammad get away with the murder of their leaders, an allusion to the killing of Abu Afak, and she called for a manly man to take it upon himself to slay him.

Muhammad reacted to these words the same way he reacted to Abu Afak's verses. At a mosque assembly, he fumed that the woman had harmed God and his messenger and therefore deserved to die. "Who will rid me of Marwan's daughter?" he bellowed.[9] A member of the tribe of Asma's husband jumped to his feet. He was partly blind, but he could see sufficiently to make his way to her home late that same night. It is said that when the assassin broke into her home, Asma was asleep with her young children and had a swaddled newborn in her arms. The killer moved the infant to one side and plunged his sword into her. At dawn prayers, he went to the mosque to report his success to Muhammad. When Muhammad saw him enter, he motioned for him to come to him and said, "Did you kill the daughter of Marwan?" The assassin replied, "Yes, for you are dearer to me than my father, O Messenger of God." The killer, however, worried that his action might have angered God, but Muhammad told him not to lose any sleep over it: "Two goats won't butt their heads together over her."[10] Turning to his congregation, Muhammad gave an account of the deed and praised the killer as a man who had greatly helped God and his messenger.

By chance or by design, the assassin walked through the cemetery during Asma's burial. One the grieving family members pointed him out as her killer. He boasted about it to them and challenged them to do something about it. He warned them that the same fate would befall them if they insulted Muhammad.

The affair came to an end with another poem. Around that time, Muhammad began using the public relations talent of Hassan Thabit, a Yathrib poet who would serve from then on as one of his spokesmen. One of Thabit's first compositions praised Asma's killer:

> She stirred up a man of glorious origin,
> Noble in his coming in and his going out.

He colored her in the redness of blood
Shortly before dawn, and he felt no guilt.[11]

In addition to murdering his critics, Muhammad also launched the first phase of an unprecedented program of religious cleansing and genocide against the Jews of Yathrib, beginning with his closest Jewish neighbors, the Qaynuqas. With the change of prayer direction to Mecca and the invention of a new Abraham storyline, Muhammad signaled that he had severed his links to their religion for good. But merely turning his back on them was not enough. A few weeks after the battle of Badr, he stood before the gate of their fortress and gave the entire tribe an ultimatum: Join his religion, or God would bring down his vengeance on them just as he had done to the Meccans for rejecting him as the bearer of truth. "You know that I am a prophet who has been sent—you will find that in your scriptures and God's covenant with you."[12]

The Qaynuqa fortress, less than two miles from Muhammad's mosque, was an imposing four-story castle built at the top of the slope leading to Upper Yathrib and was near a strategic bridge over one of the major riverbeds that had been gouged deep by torrential runoff. Unlike the Nadir and Qurayza Jews who owed their wealth to agriculture, the Qaynuqas made their money as goldsmiths, artisans, arms manufacturers, and merchants. Their market was located in the plaza in front of the fortress and was famous throughout Arabia for its offerings of fine jewelry. They were allies of the Khazraj and had sided with them in several of the intertribal wars of the previous decades. Their warriors had more than once saved the day for Abdullah Ubayy, the polytheist leader of the Khazraj. When Muhammad delivered his ultimatum, the Jewish leaders came out of the fortress in an attempt to reason with him. They pointed out that his Torah claims were without merit: Their holy books said nothing about him. He was not even a Jew, so how could he be their prophet? They reminded him that a nonaggression pact existed between them; the fact of not accepting his religion did not violate the pact.[13] One of the Jewish leaders was defiant: "Don't delude yourself just because you did battle with those who lacked knowledge of warfare and so you could take advantage of them. If you fight against us, you'll find us to be real men!"[14]

THE MURDER OF ASMA, the daughter of Marwan. Muhammad wanted her dead because of a poem she composed criticizing the tribes of Yathrib for failing to retaliate against him after he assassinated an elderly sheikh who had composed satirical verses about him. The assassin Muhammad recruited at the mosque broke into her home late at night and plunged his sword into her while she slept with her five children, including a newborn. Only the infant is depicted here.

Muhammad was a stickler for adhering to agreements when they benefited him, but discarded them when they were no longer useful. His solution to the nonaggression pact was to compose a Koran verse that allowed him to repudiate a treaty if he feared treachery from the other party. To this end he had God say, "And if thou fearest treachery from any folk, then throw back to them (their treaty) fairly. Lo! Allah loveth not the treacherous."[15]

With this, all he needed to do to nullify the pact with the Qaynuqa Jews was to allege feeling fear of them. He got the pretext he needed from a prankish incident at the Qaynuqa market. A young Bedouin woman who was married to a Yathrib convert had taken a trinket to sell to a goldsmith at one of the Qaynuqa artisan booths. While she sat with him haggling over its value, a Jew came up from behind and pinned her skirt in such a way that when she stood up her buttocks were exposed. Everyone broke out in laughter at her embarrassment. One of Muhammad's followers saw what happened and killed the perpetrator. In reprisal, a group of Jews surrounded him and slew him. That was all Muhammad needed to declare, "I fear the Banu Qaynuqa."[16,17]

That same day he assembled several hundred followers to lay siege to the Qaynuqa fortress. The Jews barricaded themselves inside and prayed their allies would come to their rescue, but help never came. Over the next few days, Muhammad used the promise of booty to encourage even more people to join the siege. The number of volunteers ended up formidable enough to dissuade anyone from helping the Qaynuqas. Not even the other Jewish tribes sent help. Their closest non-Jewish ally was Abdullah Ubayy, but his power was in decline relative to Muhammad's, and he decided it was not in his interest to intervene.

The Jews held out for two weeks, but despairing of outside help, they finally threw themselves at Muhammad's mercy. He was the wrong man to go to for mercy. He hated them for rejecting him and wanted to exterminate them. Perhaps anticipating the need for it, he composed a verse at Badr in which he gave himself God's blessing to commit mass murder: "It is not for any Prophet to have captives until he hath made slaughter in the land."[18]

As the surrendering Jews came out of the fortress, they were shackled, and word spread through the valley that Muhammad intended to behead them all. Though Abdullah Ubayy had not come to their rescue militarily, he rushed to the scene and demanded that Muhammad treat them properly. When Muhammad ignored him, the burly Khazraj chieftain grabbed him by his tunic and screamed in his face to leave them alone. Muhammad turned red with rage and shouted, "Damn you, let me go!" Abdullah said, "No, by God, I will not let you go until you treat my (allies) well. Four hundred men without armor and three hundred with coats of mail, who defended me from the Arab and the non-Arab alike, and you would mow them down in a single morning? By God, I do not feel safe and am afraid of what the future may have in store." Muhammad finally yielded and said in effect, "Have it your way then, damn you."[19]

Muhammad expelled the Qaynuqas and seized their property, including their fortresses, blockhouses, businesses, artisan tools, and a huge cache of armor and weapons. All that he left to them were their camels and personal possessions. He gave them a few days to pack up and leave the land that had been theirs for nearly a thousand years. On the day of departure, Muhammad ordered one of his men to escort them out of town. When they had gone beyond the limits of the valley, the man told them to keep going, the farther the better, and never to come back. Some of them went to Khaybar, others to the Jewish oasis of Wadi al-Qura. Most of them eventually migrated to Syria where they settled in Jewish communities.

Muhammad, meanwhile, had the booty transported to the mosque courtyard where he divvied it up. He gave himself first pick of the weapons as a part of his fifth, selecting for himself swords, spears, and armor that had acquired such fame in battles they were given names. The balance he distributed among his companions. As he made the distribution, he said to the faithful, "Those who take God and His apostle and the believers as friends, they are of God's party, they are the victorious."[20]

Following the expulsion of the Qaynuqa Jews, the assassination of poet-critics continued.

At the top of Muhammad's hit list was Kab Ashraf. He was a wealthy perfume merchant, half-Jewish through his mother, who was of the Nadir tribe. Before the battle of Badr, he had insulted Muhammad repeatedly in aggressive poetry that expressed the theme taken up by the other critics, essentially that Muhammad was an outsider who had disrupted the life of the valley and should be ousted. After the Meccan defeat at Badr, a distraught Ashraf went to Mecca to urge them to take revenge against their mutual enemy. He flattered them by telling them their religion was better than Muhammad's. "You are more righteous and better guided," he said. From Mecca, Ashraf composed poems that praised the Meccans, lamented the death of their people, and called for action against Muhammad.

When Muhammad learned of his poems, he undertook a smear campaign not only against Ashraf, but also against Meccans who harbored him. Hassan Thabit, Muhammad's hired poet, branded Ashraf's hosts as "slaves of deceit" and "schooled monkeys." Volleys of insulting poems were fired in each direction, but Muhammad's invective eventually won out. Even though Ashraf espoused their cause, the notoriety resulting from Thabit's barbs led the Meccans to end their hospitality, forcing Ashraf to leave.

By the time he returned to Yathrib, Abu Afak and Asma had been murdered, and Ashraf feared for his life. When Muhammad learned of his return, he recruited an assassin during a mosque assembly. The volunteer this time was a man named Muhammad Maslama, a Badr veteran who jumped at the opportunity to curry favor with Muhammad by killing someone for him. But he worried that he was presented with a technical challenge the previous assassins had not faced. Whereas their victims were relatively easy to reach, Ashraf lived in a fortified blockhouse built atop a low hill. Given that he knew his life was in danger, Ashraf did not readily venture beyond the walls of his stronghold. He would have to be lured out, but Maslama was concerned the use of deceit would offend God. When Muhammad told him to do whatever was necessary to get the job done, Maslama enlisted the help of four other zealots, one of them a foster brother of Ashraf nicknamed Abu Naila. The foster brother was able to earn Ashraf's trust by claiming during a visit with Ashraf that he was dissatisfied with Muhammad. He was bringing ruin to his followers through taxes, and it was getting so tough they did not have enough money left over for food. He and several other men badly needed an emergency loan to buy food for their families. Would he please help them out? As security for the loan, they were willing to turn over their weapons and armor to him.

Abu Naila knew the lure was working when Ashraf said, "So, by God, you too are tired of him!"[21]

On the night of the murder, the conspirators met with Muhammad at the mosque to inform him of their plan. He escorted them as far as a cemetery and said, "Go in Allah's name." The lure worked as planned. While the other men hid in the darkness, Abu Naila, with Maslama at his side, called to Ashraf from the road to meet with them to exchange their weapons for the loan money. He came out with the money reeking of perfumed hair. He had just gotten in bed with his wife and they were bedaubed with the expensive perfume Ashraf dealt in. Abu Naila complimented him on the perfume and ran his fingers through his scented hair as if to show appreciation, then grabbed hold and pulled Ashraf's head back—the signal for the other men to rush in. Shouting "Kill the enemy of Allah!" Maslama shoved a knife into Ashraf's abdomen and ripped it downward so that his intestines spilled out. In some versions of the story, they cut his head off, either by sawing it off with the knife or with the slash of a sword.[22] Fearful the Jews would send out search parties, they made their way back to the mosque through the outlying lava fields, taking Ashraf's head with them. By the time they got to the mosque it was nearing dawn and Muhammad was at prayer. When he greeted them they dropped Ashraf's head at his feet.[23] Muhammad gave praise to God for the death of his enemy and complimented them for their good work in the cause of God and his messenger.

The literature does not state what was done with the head; possibly it was impaled on a spear for everyone to see. What is known is that following dawn prayers, Muhammad incited his followers against all the Jews: "Whoever of the Jews falls into your hands, kill him!"[24]

The Jews locked themselves in their strongholds, fearful they would soon be subjected to a siege, but the only known victim of the murder directive at that time was a Jewish merchant named Sunayna. He was slain when one of his business associates, a convert named Muhayyisa, lured him out of his home and stabbed him to death. The killer's older brother, who was not a convert, beat him savagely for it. "Did you kill him when much of the fat on your belly comes from his wealth?" Muhayyisa revealed the depth of his zealotry when he replied, "Had the one who ordered me to kill him ordered me to kill you I would have cut your head off." The literature states that the brother saw the light. He exclaimed, "By God, a religion which can bring you to this is indeed a marvel." He soon signed up.[25]

When some Jews and polytheists complained that Ashraf had not committed any crimes that merited death, Muhammad warned that anyone insulting him in the future "shall be put to the sword."[26]

The murders spread terror throughout Yathrib and beyond and brought many of the polytheists into the fold, if only nominally to protect themselves and their property from Muhammad's growing corps of zealots. Even Asma Marwan's extended family joined because they "saw the power" of Muhammad's religion.[27] Fearing for his life, Abdullah Ubayy, the Khazraj chieftain and would-be king of Yathrib, also converted.

During his years of proselytizing in Mecca, Muhammad had gained only a hundred or so core believers. The string of assassinations and the expulsion of the Qaynuqa Jews took place over a period of months and brought about a rapid expansion to his religion so that it now included much of the non-Jewish population of Yathrib.

Terror, it turned out, was a convincing missionary.

CHAPTER 17

Reversal of Fortune

Following the battle at Badr, three important weddings and a funeral took place in Yathrib in quick succession. The funeral was for Muhammad's daughter Ruqaya. She had fallen ill before he left with his small army for Badr, and her husband, the future caliph Uthman Affan, stayed in Yathrib to care for her. She died while Muhammad was on the way back from the battle, and her grave had just been smoothed over when Zayd rode into Lower Yathrib to bring the news of victory. The literature does not indicate what she died from, but it is known that she was in her twenties and was without any surviving children. She had borne a male child in Mecca, but it is said the boy died after his eyes were pecked out by a predatory bird. Muhammad grieved over Ruqaya's grave and said prayers. A few months later, Uthman married Ruqaya's sister, Umm Kulthum.

A second marriage took place shortly after between Muhammad, now fifty-four years old, and Umar's daughter Hafsa, then twenty and a widow. She and her husband Khunais were among the émigrés to Abyssinia and joined Muhammad after his flight to Yathrib. Khunais died shortly after Badr, either from battle wounds or disease. Muhammad married Hafsa several months later and moved her into one of the small rooms built alongside the mosque, thereby joining the still small harem consisting of Sauda and Aisha, who was at that time nearly twelve years old.

The third marriage was between Ali and Muhammad's youngest daughter Fatima. Ali was about twenty-four years old while she was three or four years younger. Ali had asked Muhammad's permission to marry her just before Badr, but at the time he was a man without means and had nothing to give Fatima as a dowry. Muhammad told him it would be sufficient if not quite romantic to give her his suit of chain-mail, worth about four dirhams. It was the intention that counted. The chain-mail was not much to look at. It was a cheap Hutami suit that consisted of thirty-five pounds of unalloyed iron links fashioned into a garment that included a hood. It had to be oiled to keep from rusting, but even oiled it still left rust stains on his garments when it got wet. He gave it to Fatima, but presumably borrowed it back when he mounted up for the attack on Abu Sufyan's caravan.

After returning from Badr, Ali began the marriage preparations. His sword now had more than twenty notches, and he had booty to boast for his battlefield exploits: two camels and some weapons and armor. The preparations for the happy event ran into a bump, however, when Muhammad's uncle Hamza literally devoured Ali's booty. Ali intended to raise money for the wedding feast by gathering sweet-smelling rushes from the swampy lowlands of Yathrib to sell to Qaynuqa artisans.[1] He had hobbled his two booty camels outside the home of the one of the Yathrib converts who was throwing a victory party for Hamza, but when he went to fetch the camels to go gather the rushes, he found the camels dead. Not only were they dead, they were butchered. Their humps had been cut off and their livers removed. Suspecting Hamza, Ali ran to Muhammad to denounce the perpetrator. Nobody else but Hamza could have done it, he was sure of it! How was he going to raise money now for his wedding?

Muhammad, followed by Ali and Zayd, marched to the party house and found Hamza totally hammered on wine, a pretty slave girl at his side. It turned out the young lady had whispered in his ear that nothing would please a girl more than roast camel hump, whereupon Hamza stumbled outside and butchered the closest camels at hand. Quite likely he killed them knowing they were Ali's and slew them out of a simmering jealousy that had been uncorked by the wine. It was a fact and everyone knew it that Ali had scored four times more kills at Badr than he, yet Hamza was the one known as "The Lion." He may have been a lion, but Ali was now the lion king.

THE MURDER OF KAB ASHRAF. A wealthy Jewish perfume merchant, Ashraf was one of several poets Muhammad assassinated for
composing poems critical of him. Ashraf lived in a fortified compound
and had to be lured out. One of the killers Muhammad sent was Ashraf's
foster brother, Abu Naila. He was able to trick Ashraf into coming out
of his compound on the pretext of borrowing money to buy food.

His eyes bloodshot, Hamza was unrepentant. At the sight
of Muhammad glaring down at him, he belched and said to
his prophet-nephew, "You are nothing but my father's slave."
Perhaps knowing what Hamza was capable of while drunk,
Muhammad gingerly backed out the door.[2] The marriage
proceeded despite the setback. As wedding gifts, Muhammad
gave Fatima a soft gown, a water skin, and a leather pillow stuffed
with sweet-smelling rushes, and he ensured there was a goat to
roast for the marriage feast. The literature does not record that
Hamza was among the wedding guests.

Ali and Fatima had two children, Hasan and Hussein. Along
with their father they would eventually play an important role in
the expanding religion and would become catalysts for its split
into Sunni and Shia factions.

These three marriages and Muhammad's earlier marriage to Aisha cemented the family relationships between Muhammad and his top people: Abu Bakr, Ali, Umar, and Uthman. Each of them would eventually take over leadership of the religion, and with the exception of Abu Bakr all would end up assassinated.

The defeat at Badr did more than strip the Meccans of experienced leadership. Their traditional trade route to Syria through the tribal territories west of Yathrib was now cut off, threatening a major part of their livelihood. The Meccans had longstanding treaties with coastal tribes that allowed safe passage of their caravans. Muhammad undermined some of these vital relationships by promising tribal leaders a share in the spoils if they alerted him to Meccan caravans. It was an informant from one of these groups who tipped him off about Abu Sufyan's caravan while it was heading north, and one of the tribes sheltered Muhammad's spies while they waited for the caravan's return. With his stunning victory over the Meccans at Badr Muhammad was now able to get his way with the remaining tribes whose territories lay between Yathrib and the coast, effectively sealing off the Red Sea route to Meccan commerce.

For their part, the Meccans launched a diplomatic campaign to incite the major nomadic tribes of the desert plateau east of Yathrib against Muhammad and to open a secure caravan route through their territories. They painted Muhammad as a danger not only to Mecca but to all Arabia. With Abu Sufyan's successful punitive raid, the Meccans were able to stir up interest with some of the eastern tribes to mount raids on Yathrib. Muhammad took a preemptive stance. Whenever he learned of such preparations, he would assemble an attack force and launch a strike. These were smash-and-grab operations intended to kill as many people as possible, steal precious livestock, and spread fear.

On one of these expeditions, as these raids were later tagged, Muhammad thundered out of Yathrib at the head of two hundred men after he learned Sulaym Bedouins sixty miles to the south of Yathrib were planning a raid against him. The Bedouins scattered before he got to them, leaving behind five hundred camels under the care of a shepherd boy. Muhammad seized the camels and the shepherd. The rustlers herded the animals back to Yathrib and divided the booty just outside of town. Muhammad kept one hundred camels as his share, and his raid companions each got two. Muhammad offered the shepherd the choice between converting or losing his head. He chose to convert.

A similar raid four months after the Badr victory targeted the Ghatafan nomads northeast of Yathrib. On this raid, Muhammad left Yathrib with a force of four hundred and fifty men, but returned empty-handed eleven days later. The story goes the Ghatafan ran for the mountains with their livestock before his arrival and hid until he left.

The most spectacular of the raids resulted in the capture of a small Meccan caravan that had attempted passage along the new eastern route six months after Badr. The Meccans sent the caravan under the command of Safwan, the son of Umayya Khalaf, carrying merchandise valued at one hundred thousand dirhams. Silver coins supposedly were part of the cargo, but it was more likely crudely smelted silver from regional mines cast into bars that the Meccans intended to sell to refiners in Syria.[3] Safwan hired a guide to lead them through the unfamiliar territory. The caravan would have made it to Syria were it not for the loose lips of a Meccan merchant who talked about it while on a visit to Yathrib. The Meccan spent an evening at the highland fortress of Kinana Rabi, one of the rabbi-leaders of the Nadir tribe, and made the mistake of talking about the Meccan caravan and the wealth it carried while feasting with Kinana and some guests. Kinana was a man worthy of confidence, but one of the guests was not. He ran to the mosque to inform Muhammad, who immediately assembled an attack force of one hundred men and put it under the command of his adopted son Zayd.

Zayd intercepted the caravan. Except for the guide, the caravan members escaped, but all the pack camels and their cargo fell to the attackers. Zayd brought the loot back to Yathrib, and an exulting Muhammad divvied it up in the mosque courtyard. It was often Muhammad's practice to auction miscellaneous booty to merchants and then distribute the proceeds of silver and gold coins among the people who had a stake. In this heist, it was likely the method he used, as his fifth was said to consist of twenty thousand dirhams. As he had done with the shepherd captured during an earlier raid, Muhammad offered the guide the choice between converting or dying. The guide chose to convert as well.

It was clear that another battle between the Meccans and Muhammad was coming, and all Arabia knew it. Muhammad's blockade and his attacks on Meccan caravans were taking a toll. They needed to buy grains and other foodstuffs, and that could only be paid for through the profits from their trade missions. With their northern trade cut off many of the merchants now found themselves spending their capital for food. The economic danger they faced became undeniable when Muhammad seized Safwan's caravan. But more than their economic life was at stake. Their status among the Arabs had been shaken, and their way of life as the center of Arabia's polytheist culture was threatened.

Preparations for a new war had begun the moment Abu Sufyan's caravan returned to Mecca after the Badr defeat. The Meccans agreed to set aside the profits from that venture to equip an army. These preparations took place over the course of the next twelve months so that by March of the following year they were ready to mount an attack on Yathrib under the leadership of Abu Sufyan. It was a mightier army than the one sent to Badr: three thousand men packing power in the form of freshly sharpened swords and javelins, sturdy hardwood bows, an abundance of arrows with razor-sharp brass arrowheads, and small arms in the form of daggers and slings. The cavalry and front-line fighters brought along suits of chainmail and assorted leather armor with metal plates stitched in. The force was made up of Meccans and their regional allies. The Thaqif of Taif supplied three hundred warriors, various Bedouin tribes surrounding Mecca supplied hundreds more, and a contingent of Abyssinian mercenaries rounded out the count. Dozens of slaves, whose role was to set up and break down camps and perform other menial chores, accompanied the force.

One of the slaves was an Abyssinian named Wahshi, famed for his skill with the javelin. Jubayr Mutim, the son of the Meccan leader who gave Muhammad protection after he was run out of Taif, offered Wahshi his freedom if he killed Hamza. At Badr, Hamza had slain Jubayr's uncle Tuayma, and he wanted vengeance. Abu Sufyan's wife Hind seconded his offer. "Go to it, Abu Dasma, avenge us and help yourself too!"[4]

When the army departed, the entire population poured out to cheer them on. Some of the fighters carried idols such as al-Uzza and Hubal on poles, shouting "Glory to al-Uzza! Glory to

Hubal!" as they marched out. Others carried the war banners of the tribes and clans. Accompanying the army in swaying howdahs were two dozen women—the wives, mothers, and daughters of some of the warriors. As the army left town, the women beat tambourines and sang victory songs.

Muhammad learned of the army's departure from his uncle Abbas, his eyes and ears in Mecca. After his capture at Badr, Abbas declared himself a true believer, but he went back to Mecca. He was too connected to Mecca financially to drop everything. The fact that he paid the costliest of the ransoms led the Meccans to believe he was loyal to them, whereas in fact he began informing Muhammad about their activities in general and their war preparations in particular. Just before the Meccan army marched out of town, Abbas paid a Bedouin a handsome sum to rush a secret letter to Muhammad that gave the details about the army's strength and leadership. The Bedouin hand-delivered it to Muhammad at the highland mosque of Quba where one of the literate believers read it to him. Muhammad commanded silence about it until he could decide what to do, but the news got out even before he returned to the main mosque in the center of Yathrib.

A debate then raged about how to confront the Meccans. One of the first to offer advice was Abdullah Ubayy, the burly Khazraj chieftain who talked Muhammad out of mass murdering the Qaynuqa Jews the year before. Ubayy showed up at a mosque assembly, and after Muhammad gave him the floor, he stood up to advise defensive warfare: Yathrib should not allow itself to be drawn out to a field of battle. He pointed out that in the wars of the distant and not-so-distant past the Yathribites lost whenever drawn into pitched battles. The successful wars had been defensive. Walls were built to connect buildings so that Yathrib became like a fortress in every direction. The enemy fighters who broke through were taken out by marksmen shooting down from rooftops or were finished off in the streets by swordsmen. Ubayy argued they should follow the example of their ancestors.

Muhammad agreed, chiefly because he had a dream that told him his skin was on the line, and a pitched battle would not be favorable to him. Umar and others of his inner circle also agreed, but the rank and file did not. Several people jumped to their feet to argue they would be perceived as weak and cowardly if they hid behind walls. The Meccans would plunder the outlying areas, burn their palm groves and fields, and they would be encouraged to attack again in the future. Better to go out and confront them as a united force. Others begged Muhammad for an opportunity to fight in a pitched battle because it would give them a chance to achieve martyrdom and the Paradise reward Muhammad promised them.

Muhammad announced his decision symbolically. Accompanied by Abu Bakr and Umar, he retreated to the room behind the preacher platform, and with their assistance he donned his armor. When he came back out to the prayer area, he was all warrior, and it signified they were going out to meet the Meccans on the battlefield. Some of the followers who had urged such action now regretted it because they saw they were thrusting their beloved leader into danger. They urged him to remain behind, but Muhammad replied, "It is not fitting that a prophet who has put on his armor should lay it aside until he has fought."[5]

It took the Meccan army ten days to reach Yathrib. Muhammad sent spies to track their movements, and two of them were able to infiltrate the Meccan ranks. The spies accompanied the Meccans as far as the final encampment at the foot of Mount Uhud, a mountain that straddled the north end of the Yathrib valley. Abu Sufyan had no choice but to enter from the north as the valley was impregnable from any other direction. Mountains and lava fields formed natural barriers along much of the perimeter, while the thick patchwork of buildings, orchards, and date groves created obstacles in the interior. Abu Sufyan therefore led his force along the caravan trails that cut through the lava fields on the west side of the valley until reaching a plain at the foot of Mount Uhud, the main entrance to the valley of Yathrib.

Muhammad was able to put together a force of only seven hundred men. Another three hundred warriors were under the command of Abdullah Ubayy. The two forces assembled separately, but joined up at the north end of the valley. Muhammad still did not have a plan. The last settlement of the north was a fortress called Shaykhayn with high twin towers. From one of the towers, Muhammad was able to observe the surroundings and the open terrain leading up to Mount Uhud. Beyond the fortress the ground was flat and barren. A dry riverbed cut across it. Unlike Badr, the terrain was devoid of rocks, which meant the Meccans would have full use of their cavalry. He knew from Abbas's letter and from his spies that the Meccans brought two hundred horses with them. Forming his battle lines at the Shaykhayn settlement was not an option. It was at the sparsely populated fringe of Yathrib, and it was surrounded by open land. By staying there, he would risk encirclement. The only defensible position appeared to be at the foot of Mount Uhud, about half a mile across the plain. Directly north of Shaykhayn, Uhud curved sharply inward like a coastal inlet with rocky headlands on each side. Muhammad saw it as the perfect fighting position. If he could form a tight line across the inlet, he would have the mountain to his back and security against flank attacks by the Meccan cavalry.

Just as he prepared to march, Muhammad suffered a serious setback when Abdullah Ubayy pulled out, taking with him his three hundred men. Ubayy offered Muhammad a lawyer's explanation: His original agreement with Muhammad, struck shortly after Muhammad arrived in Yathrib, called for mutual protection if Yathrib was attacked, but the moment Muhammad went beyond Shaykhayn, he was no longer in Yathrib. He and his fighters were not obligated to engage in war beyond Yathrib's boundary because it would then become offensive. His advice to fight defensively had been rejected, and he saw no reason why he and his men should die because his good advice had been ignored. Muhammad shrugged and said in effect, "We can do without you."

As with Badr, Muhammad ended up shaping the battlefield to his advantage. The Meccans, who were encamped less than a mile to the west of the Shaykhayn fortress, had kept a close watch on his movements, but had not yet marched out to confront him. It did not take his army long to reach the inlet. He quickly formed tight battle ranks with straight rows, but found that he did not have enough men to cover his left flank, leaving him vulnerable to a cavalry charge. He therefore sent fifty archers to a hill that extended out from the mountain and gave them strict orders to stay in place. "Remain at your post and guard our rear. If you see us collecting booty do not join us, and if you see us being slain, do not help us."[6]

The Meccans soon arrived in force and arrayed themselves opposite Muhammad's lines. Abu Sufyan's troops outnumbered Muhammad's four to one and presented a formidable wall of men on foot and on horseback. Adding to the menace, Hind and the other Meccan women pounded war drums and cried for vengeance for their kinfolk slain at Badr.

The only equalizer was the zealotry of Muhammad's followers. None of the Meccans desired death, but the most fanaticized of the believers were eager for it and were even more eager to slay as many unbelievers as possible before dying themselves. Muhammad's war cry that day was "Kill! Kill!"[7] and he made no bones about it. To encourage slaughter, he handed a bifurcated slasher sword, a trophy acquired at Badr, to one of his men and said, "Strike their faces until it breaks." After taking the sword, the man wrapped a red turban around his helmet—the "turban of death" as it came to be known—and strutted up and down in front of the Muhammadan lines, taunting the Meccans with insults about their gods.[8]

As at Badr, the battle began with duels and skirmishes, and as at Badr, Ali and Hamza slew the Meccans who stepped out to face them in individual combat. With each death, Muhammad shouted "*Allahu Akbar,*" a cry that was repeated by his entire army. Volleys of arrows soon followed as the opposing lines advanced toward one another. When they met, the fighting broke out into the general confusion of hand-to-hand combat. As the infantry battle raged, the Meccan cavalry under the command of Khalid, the son of the Meccan leader Walid, attacked Muhammad's exposed left flank, but the charge was repelled by the hilltop archers who brought down some of the horses and their riders.

Muhammad targeted the enemy banners. They were rallying points, and as long as they were aloft they offered assurance the battle was not lost. Early in the fray, Zubayr leaped onto the camel of one of the Meccan standard bearers, threw him to the ground, then jumped off the camel and hacked him to death. Muhammad, who could not have been more than fifty yards away, witnessed the exploit and shouted loud enough to be heard above the din of battle, "Every prophet has his disciple, and my disciple is Zubayr!"[9]

Hamza was in the thick of the fighting and did not realize he was being stalked. Wahshi, the Abyssinian slave recruited by Jubayr Mutim to slay him, was hunting him like he would a lion, crouched with his javelin ready to throw. He closed in on his prey just as Hamza drove his sword into a Meccan. When Hamza turned toward him, the Abyssinian threw the javelin. It cut through Hamza's abdomen and came out of his lower back like a tail. Hamza took several steps toward Wahshi, but then fell on his side and died in great pain. Mission accomplished, Wahshi reported his success to Hind and left the battlefield a free man.[10]

Muhammad's men kept up attacks on the Meccan standard bearers. In all, nine were slain. The last was a slave who kept the banner aloft until his forearms were cut off. His death occurred about the time a group of Muhammad's most ferocious fighters punched through the Meccan lines and raced toward the Meccan camp, scattering the women. Abu Sufyan's wife Hind and the other Meccan women ran for the mountain, pulling up the hems of their skirts to enable them to run faster.

When they saw their lines had been breached and their flag had fallen, the Meccans panicked and fled the battlefield. Instead of chasing them, the less committed among Muhammad's followers raced toward the Meccan camp to grab booty. Muhammad's archers had a commanding view of the action, and when they saw their own people going for plunder, all but ten of the archers abandoned their position and scurried down the hill to join in the grab before someone else beat them to it. This turned out to be a fatal mistake. Khalid, in command of a hundred horsemen, and Ikrima, the son of Abul Hakam who was in command of another hundred cavalrymen, charged the hilltop. They killed the remaining archers and attacked Muhammad's army from behind.

The ferocious cavalry charge reversed the battle. Muhammad's people were felled by the lances and swords of the cavalry and by Meccan foot soldiers who swarmed back to the battlefield. It was now the turn of the believers to run, most of them fleeing south toward Yathrib. Zubayr's mother Safiya was one of the few who refused to retreat. She tried to reverse the stampede by grabbing a spear and shaking it at everyone who fled. When Zubayr ran up to her and said, "Mother! Get back! Get back!" she brandished the spear at him and said, "Get away from me! You have no mother!"[10]

The failure of the archers to hold their position nearly cost Muhammad his life. He and a small band of zealots were cut off by the surge of Meccans. Fearing for his life, he cried out for people to defend him. "Is there anyone who offers himself for the hereafter?"[12] Many of the fleeing men were in the grip of panic and ignored him as they rushed by to get to the security of a nearby ravine. Others, however, rallied around him and fought to the death, giving him cover to run toward the mountain. Before he reached mountain, however, Ubayy Khalaf, the brother of the slain Meccan leader Umayya Khalaf, galloped straight at him, his sword raised. His son had been one of the Badr captives, and when he went to Yathrib to pay his son's ransom, he warned Muhammad the day would come when he would kill him. Muhammad replied, "No, it is I who will kill you."[13] As Ubayy closed in, several of Muhammad's people blocked his horse. While the Meccan fought them from horseback, Muhammad thrust a spear into his neck, causing him to fall from the horse. Muhammad would likely have cut off his head if it were not for Meccan soldiers closing in. He and a small group scrambled up the ravine and fired arrows from behind boulders while some of his followers fought holding actions to keep the Meccans from pursuing them. Muhammad encouraged them by shouting, "Whoever will repel them from us will be my companion in Paradise!"[14]

Some of the Meccans were armed with slings and pelted the small group with stones. One of the projectiles hit Muhammad on the chain mail hood that covered the side of his face, driving iron links deeply into his cheek. The blow knocked him to the ground where he struck his face against a rock, breaking a lower tooth and splitting his lip open. Meccan soldiers continued to rush at him, and one of them got close enough to land a sword blow on his helmet. This crushed the helmet into his scalp, causing profuse bleeding. With all the blood, the Meccan was certain he had split his head open. The joyous cry went up, "Muhammad has been slain!"

Believing their primary objective had been accomplished, the Meccans pulled back. When they were out of sight, Muhammad, as bloodied as his entourage, climbed farther up the ravine in search of a hideout. Another group of his people that included Abu Bakr, Umar, and other leaders, had found refuge near a cave. Not recognizing Muhammad, one of the men aimed an arrow at him, but Muhammad shouted in effect, "Don't shoot! It's me, the Messenger of God!"[15]

Abu Bakr and Umar were ecstatic. They had heard the triumphant shouts that he had been slain and were in despair. Before he showed up, they were discussing the idea of sending someone to Abdullah Ubayy to get him to arrange a truce with Abu Sufyan. Now they shouted with joy that their leader was alive, but Muhammad told them to quiet down. The area was still crawling with Meccans, and he did not want to alert them. He ordered them to attend to the other wounded men and seethed about his own wounds. "The wrath of God is great toward those who did this," he said, pointing to his broken tooth.[16] His men gave him aid, which consisted first of removing the iron links embedded in his cheek. One of the zealots was Abu Ubayda, the man who slew his father at Badr. He pried the links from Muhammad's cheek with his teeth, breaking a front tooth in the process. Then he proceeded to lick the blood off of Muhammad's face, lapping it up as if it were divine elixir. Muhammad did not object: "Whoever has had his own blood touch mine will not be touched by hellfire," he said.[17]

Down below, the battlefield was strewn with bodies. The official count put the number of Meccans killed at twenty-two, while more than seventy of Muhammad's followers were slain. The Meccans stripped the dead of their weapons and armor and mutilated the most loathed of the Meccan converts by cutting off their ears and noses. Hind, who had vowed vengeance against Hamza, sliced open his abdomen and cut out his liver. It is said that she bit into it and chewed it, and then spat it out to show her hatred for the man who had slain so many of her family members.

Abu Sufyan searched for Muhammad's body, but when he could not find it, he began to doubt he was dead. The man who claimed to have killed him described what occurred and led Abu Sufyan to the ravine where there were a number of bodies, but Muhammad was not among them. He wondered if the survivors had carried off his body

Still in hiding on the mountainside, Muhammad was in a quandary. He feared the Meccans would now attack Yathrib, but he was stuck on the mountain and could do nothing to organize a resistance. A half-mile of open terrain separated Uhud from the

northernmost settlements of Yathrib, and crossing that terrain
with the heavy Meccan presence would be suicidal. But Abu Sufyan
decided against attacking Yathrib, in part because of the danger
of house-to-house combat, but primarily because he believed
his battle was with Muhammad, not the people of Yathrib. After
burying their fallen tribesmen, the Meccans strapped their tents
and gear onto baggage camels and prepared to leave.

Before departing, Abu Sufyan trotted his horse to the ravine
where the last contact with Muhammad had occurred. He shouted
toward the mountain that Hubal had been victorious and called
out, "And where is Abu Kabsha's son? And where is Abu Quhafa's son? Where is al-Khattab's son?"[18] he said, referring to
Muhammad, Abu Bakr, and Umar. He shouted it several times.
Hidden behind boulders, Muhammad kept Umar and Abu Bakr
from answering, fearing the Meccans would come up after them
if they were discovered, but when Abu Sufyan yelled out, "Well,
these men have been killed; if they were alive, they would have
responded," Umar could not restrain himself. "You lie, you enemy
of Allah! May Allah give you lasting torment!"[19] The Meccan
merchant-leader taunted him that it was Hubal who was the victor, not the god of Muhammad. Prompted by Muhammad, Umar
shouted, "Our dead are in Paradise, and your dead are in Hell."[20]

The theological back-and-forth ended when Abu Sufyan
pointed out that it was only Umar's belief and demanded to know
if Muhammad was alive. Umar said, "He hears your words." At
that, Abu Sufyan informed Muhammad about the mutilations.
"This was not from a decision of our leadership. However, if we
had deliberated the matter, we might well not have decided against
it!"[21] He challenged Muhammad to a rematch at the valley of
Badr the following year. Umar turned to Muhammad to see what
he wanted to do. When Muhammad nodded, Umar shouted in
effect, "We will meet you there."

After the Meccans departed, Muhammad ordered Ali and
others to follow them to see where they were going. "If they lead
their horses and ride their camels, then they will be heading for
Mecca," he said. "If they ride the horses and lead the camels, they
will be heading for Yathrib." He vowed that if they were heading
for Yathrib, he would fight them until they were annihilated.[22]
Ali brought back encouraging news: The Meccans were riding
their camels, and they were going south along the caravan trail.

When he was certain it was safe, Muhammad came down from Uhud and led the people who had been with him on the mountain in prayer. In pain from his wounds, he dispensed with the prostration routine, but sat cross-legged while reciting verses. When the praying was done, he searched for Hamza's body. Hamza was barely recognizable. His nose and ears had been cut off, and his intestines were spilled out. His liver had been cut out and was laying on the ground beside his body with a deep bite mark in it. Muhammad told Zubayr to keep Safiya back so that she would not see her brother in this condition, but she came anyway and wept over him. Muhammad learned it was Hind who had cut out Hamza's liver and taken a bite out of it. The thought horrified him that she might have swallowed or absorbed some of it. On the Day of Judgment, Hind would surely be consigned to the eternal furnace for having rejected God and his messenger. What tormented Muhammad was the thought that the atoms of Hamza's body that had become part of her body would experience the indignity of perpetual fire.[23]

Many of the grieving families came out of Yathrib to collect the bodies and take them home for burial, but a dozen or so were buried at the battlefield. Hamza was laid to rest in a single grave. The other bodies were buried two or three to a grave after they were briefly placed next to him as a blessing. As dirt was shoveled over them, Muhammad announced they would all rise up on the Day of Resurrection with their wounds exposed. Their wounds would smell of exquisite perfume and would be evidence of their devotion to God.

Some of the parents of slain Yathrib converts were furious over the deaths of their children and charged they had been duped into getting themselves killed. A young man named Yazid was one of the casualties. Mortally wounded, he was carried to the home of his father Hatib and laid on a carpet where he died. The men who had brought him sat around the body with the grieving father and mouthed pieties about martyrdom and Paradise and the reward of black-eyed virgins. Like many in Yathrib, Hatib had become a nominal member of the religion in order to escape persecution, and at some point he could not take it any longer. He blew up at them: "By God, you did this to him! You seduced him from himself until he came out and was killed. Then you told him something else: You promised him that he will enter

Paradise. Paradise is a delusion!" He ordered them out of his house. As they left, they called him a hypocrite and said, "May God destroy you!"[24]

On the way back to his mosque-residence, Muhammad, his face bandaged, stopped by the fortress of Sad Muadh's Aws clan. The clan had lost twelve men including Sad's brother Amr, and another thirty men had sustained wounds of varying degrees of severity. Remaining on his horse, Muhammad announced he had good news for the wounded: Their wounds were pleasing to God. They would be resurrected with their wounds oozing "deep red, the color of blood." For the families of the dead he offered a prayer: "O God, remove the sadness from their hearts and restore them from their misery." He also promised the slain would be heavenly representatives for their loved ones. "Rejoice," he said, "and inform the families that their dead have risen in Paradise together—they are twelve men—and they will intercede for their families."[25]

Given the grueling events of the day and the extent of his injuries, Muhammad displayed remarkable will power by keeping upright on his horse. His army had suffered a demoralizing defeat; he needed to project strength, but by the time he got to the mosque he was about ready to fall off his mount. He handed his sword to his daughter Fatima. "Wash the blood off this, my child. I swear by God, it was true to me today!"[26] Several of his men helped him dismount and carried him to one of the rooms where his wives busied themselves removing his armor and cleaning his wounds. When Bilal made the call to evening prayer, Muhammad, leaning on Sad Muadh, came out to the prayer area. He led the prayers, sitting throughout, and went to bed. He slept soundly until before dawn when he was awakened by the shrieks of wailing women. He looked out from his room to see what it was about. It turned out Abdullah Rawaha, thinking it would be pleasing to Muhammad, had recruited women from various clans to mourn Hamza by wailing, shrieking, and throwing themselves on the ground. This came about because he heard Muhammad remark during the return trip from Uhud that there were not any women to mourn Hamza's death except for his sister Safiya. To Rawaha it sounded like an implied command, but Muhammad got angry about it. For one thing, it was phony, like paying professional mourners to make sounds of grief. Not a single one of

these women cared about Hamza. More importantly, he loathed
the sound of wailing. It was physically repugnant; it drilled into
his brain, as did music and dog barking and hand clapping and
other sharp sounds that threatened to spark neural explosions
deep in his brain. He came out of his room and ordered them to
stop. He thanked them for the good thought behind the wailing, but
he could not help snarling, "I don't like wailing!"[27] From then on, he
forbade wailing, regardless of whether it was done as an expression
of sincere grief or the for-hire kind of the professional mourners.
He permitted weeping, however, as long as it was silent.

Muhammad was an astute leader. He knew he could not allow his followers the luxury of thinking about the implications
of their defeat. They would ask obvious questions: Where was
God? Why did God allow them to lose to the polytheists? What
had they done to earn God's displeasure? Such questions could
lead to doubt. Muhammad would give God the opportunity to
explain himself in the Koran, but it would take time to create
the verses to say what had to be said. In the meantime, action
was needed. He decided to pursue the Meccans to show them
he was still a power to be reckoned with. Just after the prayers
of the first light, Muhammad sent heralds to the various clans
ordering them to form an army, but only those who fought
at Uhud would be allowed to go. The heralds were the clan
leaders. A group of them had slept in the mosque courtyard
to guard Muhammad, and they fanned out to their various
territories to roust fighters. To people who tried to beg off
because of their wounds, Muhammad pointed to his own. After
assembling as many men as possible, he followed the trail of
fresh horse and camel dung of Abu Sufyan's army to a place
called Hamra al-Asad—Red Lion—about eight miles south of
Yathrib and pitched camp.

The Meccans had encamped there the night before and had
moved on, but the army halted when quarrels broke out among
the commanders over Abu Sufyan's leadership. Ever since leaving
Uhud, he had been under harsh criticism for failing to follow
up on his victory. He had Muhammad in his hands, trapped on a
mountainside, yet he failed to pursue him. What's more, he had
refused to attack Yathrib and deal a crushing blow to Muhammad's
followers. He had played by old rules of Arabian chivalry
in a situation where the old rules no longer applied. "You

MUHAMMAD WAS WOUNDED during the battle of Uhud when one of the Meccans brought his sword down on his helmet and another got close enough to sling a stone that hit him in the side of his face, causing the chain mail of his hood to embed in his cheek. The Meccans thought he had been killed, but later learned he was hiding with some of his men on Mount Uhud.

have accomplished nothing," said one of Abu Sufyan's critics. "You damaged their leadership and their elite, but then you left them without finishing them off. They still have leaders left who will gather men against you."[28] Many of them wanted to go back and finish what they had set out to do. Abu Sufyan finally agreed.

Muhammad learned of their plans from a traveling merchant, a leader of one of the southern coastal tribes who knew how to play both sides. Abu Sufyan paid him to take a message to Muhammad that the Meccans were on their way and would not leave until he was dead and his followers exterminated. Muhammad sent the merchant back to tell the Meccans he would greet them with an army much more formidable than theirs. His force could not have numbered more than five hundred, but he understood the value of psychological warfare. What counted in such a situation was not so much strength as the appearance of strength. Announcing that "war is deception," he had his men light hundreds of campfires in the surrounding hills that night so they could be seen for miles, giving the impression of a huge army. The bluff worked. The Meccans turned around and headed back to Mecca.

Before setting out in pursuit of the Meccans, Muhammad sent two spies ahead to gather intelligence about them, but they were captured, and their bodies were left for him to find. Muhammad, in turn, captured a Meccan straggler named Abul Azza, a member of Umayya Khalaf's Jumah tribe. He had overslept, and the Meccans departed Red Lion without him. He happened to be a poet who was among the Badr captives. At the time, he begged Muhammad to spare his life because he was poor and had many daughters to care for. Muhammad let him go without paying ransom on the promise he would never again take up arms against him, but he had broken his promise by accompanying the Meccans to Uhud. He again begged for his life, but Muhammad refused to spare him. "You're not going to stroke your beard in Mecca and say, 'I've twice deceived Muhammad!'"[29] The literature is divided as to the executioner. Some sources claim it was Muhammad's cousin Zubayr; others say it was Asim Thabit, the man who beheaded Uqbah Muayt at Badr. Following the execution of Abul Azza, Muhammad's small army returned to Yathrib.

A similar fate befell a Meccan who had run from the battlefield when Muhammad had the upper hand and fled to Yathrib to the home of Uthman Affan, a first cousin, to seek his protection. Muhammad wanted to kill him, but at Uthman's insistence he gave the man three days to leave Yathrib. When Muhammad returned from the Red Lion expedition five days later, he learned the man had only just left. He sent his adopted son Zayd and another man to track him down. They captured him outside of Yathrib, tied him to a tree, and used him for target practice. After retrieving their arrows, they left the corpse for the vultures.[30]

The battle of Uhud made it into the Koran in convoluted verses wherein Muhammad, in his God voice, chastised the archers for disobeying him. They had abandoned their position despite his strict orders, and disaster was the result. The verses also noted that others had run by him in their panic and ignored his pleas to defend him in his moment of mortal danger. Yet Muhammad praised his people because they were on the right track. They had given proof of their surrender to God by accepting the guidance of his chosen messenger; they proved they had love in their hearts for him and for God by fighting in the cause of God. It just had not been sufficient for them at the moment of testing—a lapse. God had tested their firmness as believers against their thirst for booty. They were entitled to the spoils of the people they killed, but they were not patient. They desired the immediate gratification of the world, not the delayed sort when the messenger would distribute shares from the booty. They were to blame for this, but God had allowed the lapse to give some of them the opportunity to attain the martyrdom they desired. For the ones who survived, it served as a lesson in the importance of obedience to God and his messenger, and because it was intended as a lesson, God was forgiving of them for their lapse.[31]

There was still one final act to the Uhud episode. Muhammad learned that during the battle one of the believers, a man named Harith, killed another believer to settle an old score, hoping to hide the murder in the confusion of battle. But he was seen, and the murder was reported to Muhammad. It was a vengeance killing stemming from the previous conflicts between the Aws and the Khazraj. The man that Harith slew had murdered his father ten years before, sparking a tribal war. For ten years he had harbored hatred for his father's killer and had waited for an opportunity to slay him in vengeance.

After he returned from the Red Lion raid, Muhammad mounted a donkey and rode to the village of Quba where the killer lived. Muhammad had the habit of going to Quba once a week to lead prayers and preach at the mosque, the first that had been built in the valley of Yathrib. This was not the usual day, and the people at the mosque were surprised when he showed up. Harith arrived for the prayer session just as Muhammad was arranging people in straight rows. When he saw Harith joining the ranks, he ordered him to stand and accused him of murder. After reciting the particulars, he ordered him seized. The man admitted to the killing, but begged for his life. He would do anything if God and his messenger forgave him.

He would pay blood money, fast for two months, free a slave, and feed the poor. Muhammad was unmoved. He sentenced him to death by beheading. Harith was taken outside to the mosque entrance and forced to his knees. The swift slash of a sword brought an end to his life.[32]

The man had failed to grasp that it was a new world. The conflicts between the Aws and the Khazraj belonged to the old world. Muhammad had replaced these tribes with a new tribe, the tribe of believers. All the old relationships had been dissolved by the new relationship that was created by being a member of the new tribe. It was permitted for believers to fight and kill anyone who was not a member of the new tribe. Indeed, it was an obligation to do so, but it was forbidden for them to fight and kill one another.

By this execution, Muhammad demonstrated that the defeat at Uhud had not diminished his authority. He could still take a life with impunity—the ultimate power. Nobody from the new tribe would dare challenge him. The man's family would not seek vengeance against him, nor would they demand blood money. They were believers too, and they had to play by the new rules—by Muhammad's rules.

CHAPTER 18

What's Yours is Mine Too

Fear drove many people to join Muhammad's religion. The idol-smashing campaigns, the midnight murders, the assassination of foreign tribal leaders, the ousting of an entire tribe of Jews—all these resulted in harvests of converts. Terrified he would do to them what he had done to others, they flocked to his mosque to grasp his hand and make the declaration of faith—the *shahada*: There is but one God and Muhammad is his messenger! The religion grew, but Muhammad's use of terror had a downside in that it created an entirely new class of opponents, people who feigned belief but plotted against him. These were people who adopted the appearance of faith by mouthing the Koran and publicly carrying out the ritual requirements, but behind the façade they strove to undermine him.

In the early years in Yathrib, Muhammad had difficulty understanding insincerity or that his recruitment through fear was the cause of it. He was so mesmerized by his verses and his belief in a divine mandate that he could not see it when others were not equally mesmerized. He believed it was sufficient to recite verses to nonbelievers to convert them. The spirit of the verses would enter into them, their souls would fill up with luminance, and they would become believers on the spot. But then he discovered the ranks were full of fakes. They were as against him as they were before they made the declaration of faith, but now they used his religion as a shield. These were people like the half-dozen Jews who had feigned belief in order to spy on him at the mosque. It became an obsession of Muhammad to identify such people and deal with them. He branded them as hypocrites and composed numerous verses decrying them and warning of eternal tortures awaiting them.

Once he became aware of the problem, Muhammad began to spot hypocrisy everywhere, and over time he turned the words hypocrite and hypocrisy into all-purpose labels to cover not only fake believers and subversives, but also people who were half-hearted or harbored doubts about him. Hypocrites were people who skipped prayers, spoke badly about other believers, sided with nonbelievers in arguments, befriended infidels, or criticized him behind his back. A hypocrite could be someone who refused to volunteer to fight for the cause, or who fought only to gain booty and not out of love of God and his apostle. The label equally applied to people who heard Muhammad's verses recited to them but refused to convert and people who had converted and then reverted to disbelief but hid it from everyone. By the time he was done, he had labeled as hypocrisy any and every thought, word, or deed that did not conform to his teachings.

Muhammad often resorted to group pressure and humiliation to deal with offenders. The story is told of the time he singled out several such people during one of the packed congregational prayer sessions. He had learned that they said something in private that signaled them as hypocrites. What they said that earned them the label is not stated in the literature, only what he did to them: During the assembly he announced from the pulpit that there were hypocrites present. Yes, hypocrites! He revealed what he had heard, then without naming names he asked several times for the offenders to stand up, demanding they voluntarily acknowledge their hypocrisy and seek God's forgiveness. When nobody stood up he threatened to reveal their names, but insisted he much preferred for them to acknowledge their sin themselves by standing up and begging him to intercede with God on their behalf for forgiveness. When still no one stood up, he named them and ordered them to their feet for everyone to see. "They rose, disgraced, and covering their faces," reported the historian Ibn Sad.[1]

As for unmasking hypocrites, Uhud was a watershed. The moment Abdullah Ubayy pulled away from him at Shaykhayn, taking with him three hundred men, Muhammad knew he had a bad one on his hands. The graybeard Khazraj patriarch had left him to fend for himself against the superior Meccan army, and it could have ended fatally for Muhammad—very likely the reason Abdullah pulled back his force. Had Muhammad been killed, he would have been free to pick up where he had left off and seek to unify Yathrib under his leadership.

Abdullah's treachery must have shocked Muhammad and hurt him deeply. The Khazraj chieftain had pledged to him personally, with seeming sincerity. He joined the religion not long after the expulsion of the Qaynuqa Jews, and he did so because of the murder of poets that was taking place at the time. Abdullah feared it would only be a matter of time before he was a target. Rather than challenging Muhammad militarily, the Khazraj leader opted for safety. He knew how to read people, and in Muhammad he saw a man who craved adoration. All you had to do to gain his good graces was to flatter him, and all that was needed to flatter him was to make him believe that you believed God talked to him. Abdullah played the game with flair, beginning with the day he took Muhammad's hand to make a showy declaration of faith. After that, he would arrive at the mosque for the Friday sermon and take a place reserved for him at the front. When Muhammad made his entrance from Aisha's room and sat in the pulpit-throne, Abdullah would jump to his feet and declare, "People, this is the Messenger of God before you. God has given you honor and glory through him. Give him aid and support, and listen and obey."[2]

But then Abdullah blew it at Uhud. To Muhammad he was now the vilest of hypocrites. Even after the battle, he kept at it with his hypocrisy. When word of the defeat spread throughout Yathrib—and this was even before the wounded and demoralized fighters trudged back to their clans—Abdullah went public with criticism of Muhammad's leadership: Muhammad had not listened to him; he had rejected good advice, and look what happened. If they had stayed in Yathrib as he advised, the dead would still be alive, and Yathrib would not be mourning its tragedy. They had followed bad advice, and by implication, a bad leader.

If he had indeed wagered on Muhammad getting killed, he lost. Sensing where this could go, Abdullah tried to patch things up. When Muhammad formed an army to pursue the Meccans, he showed up at the mosque and offered to accompany him and bring his men too, but Muhammad brushed him off. Only those who participated in the battle could go. Those who had gone to Uhud were guided by God and followed the true path. Those who had not gone were hypocrites, and they would suffer the penalties imposed by God.

After he returned from Red Lion, Muhammad considered how to deal with the Khazraj chieftain and others who had proven to be hypocrites. Always eager to chop off heads, Umar offered to kill them all. They only converted "to take refuge from the sword," not from sincere belief, he argued. They were hypocrites from the start.[3] Muhammad, however, understood that killing such people would be a disastrous policy, for it would undermine the security of the faithful. No one would feel safe any longer, not even those possessing the deepest faith. The protection of the *shahada* had to be inviolable. Muhammad ruled that killing a believer could be justified in only three instances: adultery, apostasy, and the murder of a believer by a believer.

Instead of unleashing Umar on Abdullah, Muhammad set the Khazraj nobleman up for a humiliating fall. This came about when Abdullah stood up at the next Friday sermon to pronounce his usual words of praise for Muhammad. A number of people suddenly shouted, "Sit, O enemy of God!" As if on cue, Abu Ayyub, the man who lodged Muhammad during the construction of the mosque, grabbed Abdullah by his beard and dragged him across the packed courtyard to the mosque entrance. Shoving him into the street, Abu Ayyub shouted, "You are not good enough for this place!" Several of Abdullah's clansmen happened to be going into the mosque at that moment. They urged him to return and beg Muhammad to seek God's forgiveness for him. Abdullah replied, "By God, I do not desire that he seek forgiveness for me."[4]

Muhammad later slammed him even more with a Koran entry: "And when it is said to them, 'Come, the Messenger of Allah will pray for your forgiveness,' they turn aside their heads, and thou wouldst see them turning away their faces in arrogance. It is equal to them whether thou pray for their forgiveness or not. Allah will not forgive them. Truly Allah guides not rebellious transgressors."[5]

The rough eviction brought Abdullah low. Hundreds of people had witnessed his humiliation, including his son, a convert who had been wounded at Uhud. He was in one of the back rows and averted his eyes as his father was dragged out. Word of the humiliation spread throughout the big valley. Abdullah was a man of noble accomplishment, a brave warrior in the early battles between the tribes, and a conciliator who brought about peace. He was the owner of a fortress, productive fields, and date groves and was noted for his generosity, hospitality, and wise counsel. But from then on what people had in mind when they thought of him was the image of him being dragged by his beard and thrown into the street.

Abdullah's humiliation and the publication of a set of Koran verses about hypocrisy set in motion a witch hunt to identify the insincere ones. Fear of being branded a hypocrite brought about feverish conformity to the point that both sincere and insincere believers went to great lengths to avoid the tag. In public and private, they would declare to one another their love for God and his messenger, particularly for his messenger. People would perform extra sets of prayers. Some would bang their head on the ground so vigorously while praying they ended up with permanent bruises on their foreheads—the badge of true piety. Sick people who would normally be excused would have themselves carried to the mosque for the mandatory prayers. Others would march to their death in battle.

The label was a sword, and it hung over them all.

Outside of Yathrib, Muhammad staged a number of raids aimed at thwarting military action against him. As he had done before, whenever he received word some tribe was planning to attack, even if only to raid his livestock, he immediately sent out a force to deal a crushing blow. These new raids began soon after Uhud. The first was to the north near Khaybar against a group of Bedouins who were supposedly plotting against him. This raid was led by Abu Salama, a first cousin of Muhammad who had been wounded at Uhud. The Bedouins scattered without a fight, but the raiders returned to Yathrib with a large haul of livestock. Shortly after Abu Salama returned, he died from an infection to the wound. He had been hit by an arrow in his upper arm, and it became inflamed while he was on the raid. Four months later, Muhammad married his widow, Umm Salama,[6] who moved into one of the rooms at the mosque, thereby becoming a next-door neighbor to Sauda, Aisha, and Hafsa.

About the same time Abu Salama returned from his raid, Muhammad received intelligence that yet another group of Bedouins was planning an attack. These were desert people from a region far south of Yathrib who were allies of the Meccans. They fought against him in the battle at Uhud, and he feared they were forming a coalition of Bedouin tribes for another attack. As they were too far out of range to risk a large force, Muhammad recruited an experienced assassin to kill their leader, Khalid Sufyan. The assassin returned to Yathrib with Khalid's head as proof of mission accomplished. Terrorized by the slaying of their leader, the Bedouins backed off.[7]

Khalid's assassination, however, led to a spiraling of violence. Muhammad intended the murder to deter aggression, but a tribe with family ties to the slain leader retaliated by luring Muhammad's missionaries to their territory to kill them. They accomplished the lure by sending people to Muhammad to praise his religion and ask for instruction in it. Not suspecting a trap, he sent a group of preachers—some say it was six, others ten—to instruct them in the prayer routines and teach them the Koran. But as soon as they were in the territory of the conspirators, the preachers were attacked, and all but two were killed.

The two who survived, a man named Khubayb and the other Dathinna, were sold to the Meccans for fifty camels each. The Meccans killed both of them, one by beheading and the other by crucifixion. Safwan, the son of Umayya Khalaf, personally beheaded Dathinna because he was said to have been one of the men who slew his father and brother at Badr after their surrender. Khubayb was killed because he was one of Muhammad's people. He was tied either to a cross planted in the ground or he was strapped to a crossbar that was fastened to a tree trunk. The Meccans took turns jabbing him with spears until he died. His last words were: "O God, reckon them by number and kill them one by one, let none of them escape."[8]

Before Khubayb was put to death, Abu Sufyan, by now the leader of the Meccans, took the bold and for him uncharacteristic step of recruiting someone to kill Muhammad. A Bedouin took him up on it, but in Yathrib he was captured and confessed that Abu Sufyan sent him. In reprisal, Muhammad recruited an assassin to kill Abu Sufyan, but the hitman proved as inept as Abu Sufyan's Bedouin and was nearly captured. Though he missed Abu Sufyan, Muhammad's recruit left a trail of blood all the way back to Yathrib, wantonly murdering several "infidels" on the way.

Muhammad soon suffered an even greater setback when seventy of his preachers were slaughtered after he sent them to proselytize a seemingly receptive tribe to the southeast of Yathrib. Because of what happened to Khubayb and his companions, Muhammad was reluctant to send out any more preachers, but the aging tribal leader who invited them offered an ironclad guarantee of protection. After they arrived in the tribal territory and pitched their tents, however, the preachers were surrounded by a coalition of clans and massacred.[9] The preachers were experienced fighters and were armed to the teeth, and their enemies did not dare to take them on frontally. They killed most with volleys of arrows shot from a distance, then moved in to finish off the wounded and slay the few who escaped the arrows. Only one of Muhammad's men survived the attack, which came to be known as the Mauna's Well incident from the location.

These massacres were a sign of the depth of hatred for Muhammad and the growing Arab determination to resist him. The message was not lost on him. He was shaken to the core and drew back temporarily from external aggression to focus on expanding his control over Yathrib.[10]

This internal focus began when he attacked and expelled another of the Jewish tribes, the Nadirs. The motive was a combination of hatred and greed. Muhammad hated them because they rejected him, but he also wanted what was theirs. The Nadirs owned numerous date plantations and farms and were among the most prosperous tribes of the Hijaz. He needed plunder to ensure continuing loyalty among his followers and to finance his operations. To justify the attack, he used the same pretext that he used to assault the Qaynuqa Jews a year earlier: He accused the Nadirs of creating a situation that caused him to "fear treachery." Because they brought about in him a fear of treachery, God permitted him to repudiate whatever treaty he had with them and attack them.[11]

The incident that caused him to fear treachery occurred at the gate of the Nadir fortress. Accompanied by his top people including Umar, Abu Bakr, and Ali, Muhammad went to the fortress ostensibly to demand blood money from the Jews over two murders that the sole survivor of the Mauna's Well massacre had committed.[12] The Jews had nothing to do with the murders, but the literature explains that they had an obligation to pay a share of the blood money for the slain men due to tribal alliances. The Jews would not allow Muhammad inside, but kept him and his group at the gate while they discussed the matter. While they were waiting, Muhammad suddenly left and never came back. Umar and the others at first thought he had wandered off somewhere to urinate. They eventually tired of waiting for him and went to search for him at the mosque. They found him there in a state of anger and excitement. He was angry because the Angel Gabriel had informed him while he was with them at the gate that the Jews were plotting to drop a millstone on him from the battlement. That was why he left. He feared their treachery. Yet he was excited because he now had a reason for attacking them. By their vile plotting they themselves had voided whatever treaties and agreements they had with him. He was no longer bound by them.[13]

Muhammad ordered a siege of the Nadirs. With the scent of booty in the air, he had no trouble raising an army. Hundreds of the faithful strapped on their armor and swords and flocked to the cause of despoiling the Jews. Before laying siege to their fortress, however, Muhammad gave the Jews the opportunity to leave their homes and their lands of a thousand years voluntarily. He sent Maslama, the man who orchestrated the murder of the Nadir poet Kab Ashraf the year before, with the message: "Leave from my land. I have granted you a period of ten days. Whoever is seen after that, his head will be cut off."[14] There could be no question Muhammad intended to carry through on his threat if he sent someone like Maslama. The Jews knew he was involved in Kab Ashraf's murder so that sending Maslama was like sending Ashraf's head as a calling card. Nevertheless they refused to leave. Their ally Abdullah Ubayy had gotten word to them he would back them up with warriors. Another promise of support came from the Qurayza Jews.

Before the siege could be mounted, the Nadirs, who lived scattered among the villages of their territory, flocked to the main fortress for protection. It was the role of large fortresses to serve as places of refuge during times of danger. They were typically stocked with food and weapons, and within the thick walls was a deep well capable of supplying the needs of an entire tribe. Muhammad surrounded the Nadir fortress on all sides. To taunt the Jews, he and his men performed prayer routines within sight of the warriors manning the battlements, but out of reach of their arrows. He ordered his red tent erected in one of the courtyards of the Khatma tribe of Asma Marwan, one of the poets he assassinated the year before, to serve as a command post, but he was forced to move it when a Jewish marksman named Azwak hit the tent with an arrow. Azwak was captured and beheaded soon after. Under cover of darkness, he and a small group of warriors slipped out of the fortress for a commando raid, but Ali captured him and brought his head to Muhammad. After leaving the head with Muhammad, Ali hunted down the rest of the commandos and returned with more heads. Muhammad ordered them thrown down a well belonging to the Khatmas.

As the Jewish resistance continued, Muhammad resorted to the extreme measure of cutting down or burning the date palms surrounding the fortress. He did this to demoralize the Jews. Date palms had high value for the fruit they produced, and it took years of care after planting to bring such trees into production. The Jews agonized at the sight of their beloved trees thus destroyed. From the battlement, a herald complained to Muhammad about the wanton destruction. Muhammad laughed and said it was God's way of humiliating and harming the Jews. He did not desist until pressured by some of his followers, who saw their eventual booty going up in smoke. He relented, but justified the destruction of the trees with a Koran verse.[15]

Anticipating support from their allies, the Jews held out for two weeks, but help never came. As had happened with the Qaynuqa Jews, Abdullah Ubayy failed to deliver on his promise. He was weak then, but he was weaker now because of the humiliating treatment Muhammad dealt him at the mosque, and he may not have been able to raise a sufficient force. Another obstacle was his son Abdullah, a convert who was among the people besieging the fortress. If the disgraced Khazraj leader went to the defense of the Jews, he would end up fighting his own son.

The Nadirs finally gave up, but only after securing a promise from Muhammad to allow them to leave. He permitted them to take with them whatever they could load onto their camels, the only exception being their weapons. He required them to surrender all their arms and military gear. The Jews spent three days strapping their belongings onto camels. Some tore down their homes to retrieve valuable lintels and beams, which they also loaded onto camels. They formed an enormous caravan of six hundred camels. On the day they left, the rabbi-leaders Sallam Huqayq, Kinana Rabi, and Huyayy Akhtab rode at the head of the caravan on horseback. Women and children were mounted on camels while the men walked at their side. They made an attempt at retaining their dignity by appearing joyful rather than dejected. Walking behind the camels and horses, boys drummed tambourines and played flutes while girls sang joyful songs. They made a show of their wealth as a way of taunting the people who lined the roads to cheer their departure: The women and children, riding in tasseled howdahs, sported bracelets and necklaces of gold and pearl. The women were dressed in their finest silk gowns and held up goblets of gold and silver. Their gold and silver dinnerware was so famous the Meccans sometimes borrowed it for festive occasions. Muhammad became so infuriated by the showy departure that he whipped some of the horses to move them along faster.[16] Some of the Nadir families went on to join the Qaynuqa Jews in Syria, but most settled in Khaybar ninety miles north where they owned property and once again devoted themselves to cultivating dates.

For Muhammad, the take was enormous. It included all the fortresses, blockhouses, date plantations, and farms of the Nadir tribe. There were seven major farm-plantation complexes and a number of smaller farms. The real estate encompassed the entire territory of the Nadirs, measurable in square miles in one of the most fertile regions of Yathrib. The booty was also impressive. It included fifty suits of armor, fifty helmets, and three hundred and forty swords. The literature does not give a count of the number of believers who took part in the siege, but it was likely close to a thousand. Each eagerly anticipated a share, but Muhammad had a different idea about the distribution: Everything was going to the Meccan émigrés. The Yathrib converts, who were far more numerous than the Meccan expatriates, were cut out.

Muhammad broke the news with sweet talk and flattery. It was God's will, he explained to his Yathrib supporters. God had communicated to him through the Angel Gabriel that in cases where infidels gave up without fighting, he would be awarded everything, and it would be up to him to dispose of the booty as he saw fit.[17] He now saw fit to give everything to the Meccans. This was because the converts of Yathrib had displayed great generosity in hosting the Meccan refugees. They had taken them in, had brothered with them, and had done more for them than was ever asked of them. For three years they had extended such hospitality, but it was clearly a financial challenge, a strain that was greater for some than for others. The booty distribution arrangement, Muhammad went on, would relieve them of the burden. The Meccans would now be able to stand on their own feet and would no longer be a burden to their brothers. He brought God into it with a Koran verse: "So take what the Messenger assigns to you, and deny yourselves that which he withholds from you. And fear Allah; for Allah is strict in Punishment."[18] It is not recorded that any of the Aws or Khazraj converts protested. If it was God's will, who were they to object? If they were truly upset, they kept it to themselves. They knew that if they protested they ran the risk of being branded as hypocrites.

Following his practice of giving himself a fifth of the take, Muhammad selected the largest of the farm-plantations for himself and appointed one of his servants as foreman. Other major properties he gave to Abu Bakr, Umar, and Zubayr, and another went to Abdul Rahman, a Meccan merchant who was one of the earliest converts. Other properties he divided into smaller shares and apportioned them among the remaining Meccans. Even his former Abyssinian slave Baraka, who was married to Zayd and was the mother of Osama, got a section of date palms. Of the Yathrib converts, only two ended up receiving real estate, and this only after complaining of indigence despite all their services to God's cause at Badr and Uhud. Muhammad gave the men joint ownership of a small farm. To the ever-faithful Aws leader Sad Muadh Muhammad awarded the famed sword of the Nadir leader Sallam Huqayq.

The literature reports that two of the Nadir Jews converted in exchange for keeping their farms and their families. They slipped out of the fortress before the surrender and made the oath of fealty. One of them was named Yamin Umayr. Muhammad tasked him with proving his loyalty by murdering his brother-in-law, a

Nadir Jew named Amr Jahash. It appears that the offense Jahash committed was entering into Muhammad's imagination at the wrong time. When Muhammad imagined that someone was about to drop a millstone on his head, it was the face of Jahash that came into his head. To please Muhammad, Yamin paid someone ten gold coins to do the deed. The murder occurred after the surrender of the Nadir Jews, but before their departure. The literature records that when Yamin informed Muhammad that the mission had been accomplished, "the Prophet was pleased."[19]

The fate of the Nadir Jews was the inspiration for a short Koran chapter entitled "Banishment." The verses recap the action and give convoluted rationalizations for the expulsion of the Jews and the confiscation their property. The first few verses read: "God is the one who got those among the people of the scripture who scoffed out of their homes for the first gathering: you didn't think they would get out, while they thought their fortresses would defend themselves against God. But God came to them from where they weren't expecting, and cast terror into their hearts, so they demolished their homes with their own hands, and by the hands of the believers. So let those with eyes take warning: for if God had not decreed banishments for them, God would have punished them in this world; and in the hereafter they would have the agony of the fire. That is because they opposed God and the messenger of God, and if anyone opposes God, then God is severe in punishment."[20]

Several of the verses were intended as jabs at Abdullah Ubayy. One of them reads: "Haven't you seen the hypocrites saying to their brethren who scoff among the people of scripture, 'If you are driven out, we will leave with you, and we will never obey anyone in regard to you.' But God testifies that they are liars."[21,22]

With the murder of his critics, the expulsion of the Jewish tribes, and the theft of their property, Muhammad turned Yathrib into a Twilight Zone where the moral compass no longer worked. He had given the needle a vigorous spin, and when it stopped evil was good and good, evil.

CHAPTER 19

Fear and Loathing
in Prophet City

Repent! The end is at hand! So fervently did Muhammad believe the end of time was just around the corner that he could stand in for the caricature of the white-bearded codger carrying a sign with the warning of doom. He shouted the message to his Arab contemporaries: The portents are upon us, the Day of Doom approaches, the guardians of Hell have thrown open the gates! If ye but believe in God and his messenger and repent thy sins, ye will be spared the eternal flames!

Muhammad believed he was not just the announcer of doom, the hoary sign bearer of the message of the Last Hour; he was the final messenger to bring these warnings. He was the ultimate of a long line of God's messengers because the end was fast approaching. The angel was already reaching for the trumpet. There would never be need for another messenger to sound the alarm.

He told this to everyone, and he prophesied about the time frame. He was certain it would occur not long after his death. That is when the harbingers of the end would begin. Some Bedouins once came to visit him at his mosque to question him about it. After they were seated cross-legged on the frond mats of the prayer area, they said, "O Messenger of Allah when will the Last Hour come about?" Muhammad pointed to a child who was with them and said, "If this young boy lives, he may not grow very old till he would see the Last Hour coming to you."[1]

Muhammad was an intuitively brilliant manipulator. He knew from his insights into human nature and from the laboratory of his early experience in Mecca that creating fear was the first step in controlling people. It worked back then with a small corps of followers, and it was working now with larger groups. It worked because he believed his own fantasies, and he had the eloquence and imagination to convince people they were not just private nightmares.

To bring about fear and the control that came with it, he sometimes held marathon fear sessions whose topic was the end of time, the portents of its coming, and the hellfire awaiting people who did not believe him. The objective of these events was to instill dread of the future. He would follow up with marathon hope sessions that provided the path out of the fear he had created in them—step number two for gaining control over people. It was the good old one-two of the supersalesman: Whip them up with fear, then give them the prescription for relief.

Whenever he held a fear session, it would last all day and night and would push his followers to the brink of emotional and physical exhaustion. One such session recorded in the literature began with the feeble first light of day.[2] After leading the congregation in rounds of prayer, he ensconced himself in the pulpit-throne, and from there he harangued the faithful about what lay gestating in "the womb of the future." He kept at it, inviting questions now and then until Bilal's call for the next obligatory prayer at noon. At that prayer-prompt, he stepped down from the platform, led the faithful in more rounds of his anxiety-suppression routines, reciting whatever verses were fit for the occasion, then resumed his commanding position in the pulpit. He kept it going throughout the entire day, stepping down to lead the believers in prayer in the afternoon, before it got dark, and then again after it got dark.

Throughout these grueling sessions, Muhammad was like a preacher in a sweaty Southern revivalist tent whipping up his congregation with fear of God's punishment. He would describe the sadistic torments awaiting the damned and challenge people to ask him about their fate. "Ask me questions about it," he demanded. "Ask me!" On one occasion a man jumped to his feet. "Where will my entrance be, O Messenger of God?" "Hellfire!" thundered Muhammad to him and others who asked where they would end up. "Ask me! Ask me!" he kept shouting. When no one else dared to speak, he roared, "Paradise and Hell were displayed before me across this wall while I prayed." He pointed to one of the mosque walls and growled, "I never saw such good and evil as I saw today." He kept at them, asking which they were destined for, Heaven or Hell. "Ask me! Ask me!" He was able to make them smell not just the smell of burning flesh, but the smell of their own flesh burning. He was able to make them hear not just the screams of the tormented, but the screams of torment ripping from their own throats. He had people so terrified they would roll on the ground and weep uncontrollably. Even the fearsome Umar was nearly frightened out of his mind. He dropped to his knees and wept and said the words that guaranteed Heaven: "We accept Allah as our Lord and Islam as our religion and Muhammad as our messenger!"[3]

However draining these events, the believers had the satisfaction of knowing they were privileged to sit face to face with the Messenger of God, the man who had been summoned before the throne of God Almighty. They were certain everything they heard from him came from God. It was for their benefit, for their moral uplifting, to keep them from burning in the bowels of Hell. When they were finally released from one of these marathons, they would slog home for a brief respite of sleep until reveille early the following morning that would call them for the next round of prayer.

Muhammad was the first and firmest believer in his End Time stories, and they ruled his mind. He fixated so much on the Day of Doom that he even had nightmares about it. One night when his bedmate happened to be Zaynab bint Jahsh,[4] the former wife of his adopted son Zayd, he woke up agitated, his face flushed red. He jumped to his feet and shouted to the startled woman, "There is destruction in store for Arabia because of turmoil which is at hand, the barrier of Gog and Magog has been opened."[5] This declaration was an allusion to his belief in a myth about ferocious tribes that had been sealed behind an iron wall by Alexander the Great somewhere far off in the East in a land of ice. Their escape would be one of the portents of the end. In his dream, the wall had been breached and hordes of barbarians were rampaging in their direction. He made a large "O" by joining his thumb and index finger to show Zaynab how the breach looked. It would not be long before these emissaries of Hell were thundering across the Arabian desert. Dreams do not lie, he said, and his dream was clear evidence the End Time was at hand.

When his sermons turned on doom and damnation he would often burst out with anger. On one occasion he screamed "I have warned you of the Fire!" so loudly he could be heard at the market more than a block away from the mosque. His body shook so forcefully on another occasion that an upper garment pinned to his shoulder fell to the ground.[6] His voice trembling with urgency, he would warn what awaited the damned: "Hellfire will be a man who will have two sandals whose straps will be made of fire that will cause his brain to boil just as a cauldron boils. Yet he will not think that anyone is receiving a torment more severe than him, even though he will be receiving the lightest punishment of them."[7]

When Muhammad was on stage during one of these marathons, he was all performer. He would pace back and forth, jabbing his forefinger in the air and scowling at his audience. His marathon sermons would begin with ecstatic shouts to the faithful about the coming of the minor signs of approaching doom: There will be wars of great slaughter and crushing oppression; tremendous natural catastrophes such as earthquakes will shake everything to the ground; great fires will blacken mountains and plains. Just when things seem to get worse, they will get better, but then another round of events will ensue so horrific the living will envy the dead. Believers will fight believers, pilgrims will be robbed and murdered, fighting will occur on the holy mounts, order will give way to chaos. Adding to the turmoil, the Euphrates will suddenly uncover a mountain of gold, unleashing savage greed that will lead to the demise of all but one out of a hundred of the gold seekers. Such conditions will signal the emergence of the Imam Mahdi—the Guided One, a blood descendant of Muhammad who will bear a striking resemblance to him. His coming out will be in Yathrib when he is forty years old, and he will be the hope of Islam.[8]

The Mahdi's first challenge, Muhammad continues, will be to deal with a descendant of Abu Sufyan[9] who will spread corruption and mischief from his base in Damascus, a man so vile he will kill children and rip open the bellies of pregnant women. This Sufyani, as he will be called, will learn of the Mahdi's appearance and will send an army to slay him, but his forces will be swallowed up by the desert. About this time there will also be wars of succession to the caliphate. The Mahdi will be a reluctant ruler; he will flee to Mecca prior to this Sufyani invasion, and in Mecca his admirers will draft him for the role of caliph by dragging him from his home to the Kabah where they will pledge their loyalty to him in front of the Black Stone. The Guided One, as he will be called, will accept their pledges. He will form alliances and lead true believers in wars against apostates and Christians.

Muhammad reveals these predictions during the morning session. The believers are seated cross-legged—row after row of them all the way to the back of the covered prayer area, and they spill out into the huge courtyard. At the call to noon prayer, he jumps down into the mosh pit to lead the congregation, giving them as always his example of perfect prayer prostrations and precisely intoned verses. Then he is back on stage, and he is just warming up. His turban is tightly wrapped on his head with the trailing edge tossed over his shoulder. He sits in his pulpit-throne and closes his eyes to let visions of the future enter his head. Like all gifted preachers, he has a flair for drama. As he gives words to the images that come into his mind, he pounds the arms of the pulpit with his fists for emphasis; he points upward at unseen forces; he raises both hands in supplication to God; he thumps the wood floor with the butt of his staff. At times he gets so worked up he jumps to his feet. Hands on his hips, he bends forward and hurls questions at the congregation, only to answer them himself, or he struts back and forth, speaking with trembling fervor toward the heavens. The faithful listen with their mouths and eyes frozen wide open.

In the near future world, Muhammad tells them, the rule of the Mahdi will be one of the first major signs that The Hour is approaching. The Guided One will reign for seven years and will be harbinger of the Second Coming of Jesus the son of Mary and also of the Antichrist—the Dajjal, who is known as the Great Deceiver, a powerful but false prophet. Rumors of Dajjal's appearance in the world will spread after the Mahdi leads an army of believers against the Christians of Syria and Byzantium. Though a third of his warriors will be slain and another third will desert, the Mahdi will be victorious over a massive Syrian army, and then he will turn his forces on Constantinople. There, his troops will yell in unison: "Allahu Akbar!" and the walls of Constantinople will come tumbling down. The Mahdi will not get to enjoy his victory, however, for at that moment word will come that the evil Dajjal has appeared in Syria and is seducing people to his false religion through sorcery and eloquent words.

Muhammad's End Time scenario at this point is like a script for a Hollywood epic with a huge cast and startling special effects: Dajjal, blind in his left eye and with thick hair all over his body, will come out of Persia followed by seventy thousand Jews dressed in silk and carrying double-edged swords. The Evil One will have crooked legs, and branded on his forehead will be the three Arabic letters for the word "*kafir*"—infidel. He will travel at great speeds on a gigantic mule, one mightier than the winged Buraq that had once carried Muhammad from Mecca to Jerusalem. In Dajjal's hands fire will be water and water fire. He will have with him musical instruments and he will make beautiful music to seduce music lovers. He will bring more people to follow him through his ability to perform magic tricks so clever they appear to be miracles. In one of these stage tricks, he will slice a man in half and then bring him back to life. In another, he will restore life to a deceased father and his brother, but in fact they will be devils who have taken their form. No magic there, only deceit! And the worst of deceit because it leads to Hell! Dajjal will then cause drought in the land of the true believers of Muhammad's religion, but the Evil One will give a horn of plenty to his own followers. Inflated by the power he acquires, he will then attack Yathrib and Mecca, but he will not be able to get beyond its angelic guardians led by the angel Malaika. Frustrated by the angelic power, Dajjal will lead his forces north for a showdown with the Imam Mahdi in Syria.

Muhammad takes another prayer break, this one for afternoon prayer. After again leading the faithful from the mosh pit with his perfect prayer prostrations and exquisitely intoned verses, he climbs back onto the stage to tell them about the return of Jesus. He was not killed on the cross as the Christians claimed, but was taken up into Heaven at the time of the Last Supper through a hole in the roof. The role of the son of Mary is to defeat Dajjal, who is now marching on Syria to attack the Imam Mahdi. Wearing garments lightly dyed with saffron, Jesus will descend from Heaven. He will come down either on a cloud or with his hands resting on the shoulders of two angels. If he descends with angels, they will let him down gently near a mosque in Damascus where the Imam Mahdi is about to lead twelve hundred true believers—eight hundred men and four hundred women—in dawn prayer. Jesus will enter the sacred mosque moments before the Mahdi has commenced praying, and the faithful will turn to look at the newcomer when they hear a voice in their minds saying, "The one who listens to your pleas has come!" Jesus will introduce himself, and the Mahdi will invite him to lead the prayers, but Jesus will gracefully decline and ask the Guided One to proceed. Following the prayers, Jesus will announce that Dajjal, who has just reached the gates of Damascus, is as good as dead. All it will take is for Jesus to breathe out and every infidel his breath reaches will drop dead—as far as the eye can see. Jesus goes to the gates of Damascus. The effects of his breath provide a tactical opening for hordes of true believers to come screaming down from distant mountains where they have been holed up, and they destroy the army of Dajjal. Dressed in armor and wielding two swords and a shield, Jesus stalks Dajjal on the battlefield. He slays him in the grand finale in front of one of the gates of the city and leaves the field of battle with his shield splattered with the blood of the Evil One.

Eventually all the followers of Dajjal will be annihilated, and Jesus will then set about to kill all the swine of the world, loathsome animals because they eat their own excrement. He will also destroy the cross of the false religion that had been created about him, that had wrongly declared he died on the cross and was resurrected whereas in truth it was a disciple who had volunteered to die in his place. Jesus will make it clear he is merely mortal, a messenger of God whose truth the Jews denied. Shortly after the slaying of Dajjal, Imam Mahdi will die and Jesus will then assume the role of caliph—the Commander of the Faithful. Jesus will visit the grave of Muhammad where he will pay homage to the last and final Messenger of God.

But despite the death of Dajjal, the worst is not over. God will continue to throw challenges at Jesus. At one point God will inform him that he is releasing the inhabitants of Gog and Magog from their distant iron prison, and they will surge forth in all their fury. They will scorch their way across the land with an army so huge that just one half of its warriors will able to drink all the water from the lake of Tiberias. It will become a dry lakebed. They will arrive in Jerusalem and proclaim, "We have conquered the people of the earth, now we will annihilate those in the sky." By then, Jesus and his followers will have fled to Mount Sinai, and they will suffer hunger and hardship. Jesus will pray to God for relief. God will honor his prayer by causing sores to appear on the necks of the soldiers of the armies of Gog and Magog. They will all die quick but painful deaths. Jesus and his followers will then descend from the safety of Sinai, and they will find an ocean of rotting bodies that lets off a horrendous odor of putrefaction. Upon this, Jesus will offer a prayer of supplication to God to rid the world of these corpses, and God will send huge birds with necks as thick as the necks of camels, and they grab the bodies in their beaks and dump them in the faraway sea.

From then on the reign of Jesus will be utopian. He will be a just ruler and a fair judge who will preach the teachings of Muhammad and his *sunna*—the details of Muhammad's exemplary life as the last and final messenger of God. The *sharia* that Muhammad brought to the world will regulate the lives of believers. All the disbelievers will convert or will die, leaving only the faithful so there will no longer be any need for holy war or the taxation of subjugated infidels. Peace will reign throughout the world, and even wild animals and snakes and scorpions will become inoffensive; the lamb will lie down with the lion. Wealth will be so abundant that no one will lack for anything. The earth will become a cornucopia. Pomegranates will grow so huge that a single one will feed an entire community and its peel will be used for shade in the hot sun. Every family will have a camel and a goat to supply their needs. As a result of the guidance of such a righteous ruler as Jesus, people will acquire a love for the prostrations of Muhammad's prayer routines more than they love anything else in life, and they will gladly perform their prayers five times daily. Jesus will remain on earth for forty years and will marry when he has nineteen more years to go and will have children. When he dies, he will be buried next to the grave of Muhammad.

The fear marathon continues even though it is now getting dark. Another round of prayers is performed. Torches are lit, casting wicked flickers of light. When he gets back on stage, Muhammad, his hands on his hips, listens to a question. "O Messenger of God, are the believers not then in Paradise? What you describe is Paradise."

"No!" Muhammad roars, gesturing towards the heavens. "Have I not yet informed you of the end signs, about the smoke and the day the sun will rise from the West, about the Beast of the Earth and the destruction of the Kabah? Have I not yet spoken to you of the Trumpet?"

His congregation is running on fumes, but Muhammad is as full of energy as when he started twelve hours earlier. He continues dumping the torments of his imagination on his congregation by telling them that after the death of Jesus, other rulers will follow, and once again corruption and decadence will slowly set in. At some point God will cause a thick fog or smoke to envelop the skies and it will last for forty days. This smoke will cause the believers to be sick, and those who have fallen into disbelief will lapse into unconsciousness. This will end when night lasts for three days, followed by a disturbing celestial phenomenon: The sun will rise from the West, and its rays will be extremely dull. At midday it will turn on itself and then set down where it normally sets. This is the event horizon of redemption or damnation. The moment the sun turns on its path will mark the time when it is too late for believers to repent their sins or for disbelievers—due to the shock and awe of the stellar spectacle—to now declare their belief in God. People will be sealed by their deeds prior to this event.

And then will come the Great Marking: An earthquake will split the earth near the Kabah, and an enormous beast that speaks Arabic will emerge from the fissure. After dusting the sand off its head, it will head towards the Kabah, and people who do not flee will have their faces illuminated like shining stars. From the Kabah the beast will travel across the world at enormous speed. It will be tasked by God to make the faces of believers glitter, but will blacken the faces of infidels. Once all humanity has been thus differentiated the beast will disappear. A fragrant breeze from the south will then blow across the world, and all the people with illuminated faces will die, leaving only the blackened ones—the wicked disbelievers in God and his Messenger. The forces of darkness will destroy the Kabah. The inglorious and unimaginable will follow: The words of the Koran will disappear from their pages, and no one will fear God or obey the commands that he had transmitted through his Apostle Muhammad. People will therefore stoop to the lowest level of behavior possible, perpetrating the worst acts of immorality, corruption, and evil. Tyrants will inflict the cruelest punishment upon their subjects and the masses of unenlightened humanity will indulge in bloodshed and anarchy. There will be such ignorance that not a single man, woman, or child will utter the name of God. This will mark the moment when a great fire breaks out in Yemen and proceeds north. People will flee from it, driving them towards Syria, and when they are all assembled in Syria, the fire will end. This is the final sign of the Hour, Muhammad declares, the moment when the angel Israfil will blow the trumpet to announce the end has arrived. At first no one will take notice, but it will grow louder than thunder, and people will be overtaken by panic because it will become the sound of the final destruction of creation. The seas will burst against the mountains, the mountains will break up, the skies will rip apart, and the stars, the moon, and the sun will crumble and be no more. This will mark the beginning of the Resurrection. All people who ever existed will at that time rise from the dead. They will be resurrected in the flesh. Trembling, they will await the determination of their fate from God.

Muhammad brings the fear marathon to a close by reciting some of his Koran verses. Indeed, he peppered the entire marathon with quotes from his Koran. He ends with the words: "On that day man shall cry, 'Where is there a place to flee to?' But in vain—there is no refuge. With thy Lord on that day shall be the sole refuge."[10]

Such fear seminars would leave some of his followers emotionally traumatized, and occasionally he had to counsel them after they became gripped by paranoia. Everywhere they looked they saw signs of the end. After one of these marathons, several of his followers came to him to tell him they were certain they had spotted the Dajjal among the palm trees of a date grove. Their faces were in a state of meltdown. Muhammad told them not to fear. "If he comes forth while I am among you, I shall contend with him on your behalf."[11] However, if the Dajjal came after his death, God could be relied upon to take care of the Evil One. He advised his distraught followers that if the day ever came that they actually encountered the Evil One, they should recite the opening verses of one of the Koran chapters, and that would give them protection from his evil. He advised them that Chapter 18, called "The Cave," was the best for such a situation, and he recited it as a way of refreshing their memory.

Muhammad was not sure about the timing of Dajjal's appearance. He could already be born into the world, but he would not make his presence known until years after Muhammad's death. This prediction was confirmed the day he was presented with news that Dajjal had been spotted on an island. The information came from a recent convert from Gaza named Tamim Dari,[12] who told Muhammad he had personally seen Dajjal on the island, and he provided details that convinced Muhammad he was not lying.

Excited by the news, Muhammad dispatched heralds to call the faithful to the mosque for a special announcement. By the hundreds, the faithful dropped whatever they were doing and assembled before him. After leading them in prayer, Muhammad took his usual place in the pulpit-throne, an eager smile on his face. "Do you know why I asked you to assemble?" he said. Several of the believers gave the obligatory reply: "God and his Messenger know best." Muhammad then said, "By God, I have not made you assemble for an exhortation or for a warning, but I have detained you here because Tamim Dari, a Christian who came and accepted Islam, told me something which agrees with what I was telling you about the Dajjal."[13]

Muhammad repeated word for word what he heard from the convert: Tamim was on a merchant ship with thirty other men when the vessel became lost at sea in a storm and was blown towards an island. They lowered boats and rowed to shore where they came across a huge beast covered with so much hair that it did not look any different from the front or the back. They said, "Woe to you, who can you be?" The creature said, "I am Jurassa." They tried to find out more about him, Muhammad related, but the creature pumped them for information and told them they would find out about him in due time. Meanwhile they should look for a person at a monastery nearby who was eagerly waiting to find out about them. The stranded seamen proceeded with fear that they were going to run into a devil, but instead they found a man whose hands were chained behind his neck and whose feet were in iron fetters. They said, "Woe be upon you, who are you?" The man pulled violently on his chains and warned, "You will soon come to know about me, but tell me who are you." After learning they were from Arabia, the captive asked them a series of questions, one of them having to do with Lake Tiberias. "What do you want to know about it?" they said. The man in chains asked, "Is there water in it?" They informed him there was an abundance of water in it, but he replied ominously, "I think it will soon become dry." He then asked them to tell him about the unlettered prophet, and they replied that he had gone from Mecca to Yathrib and had overcome many of his opponents, who now submitted to him. At that, the chained man revealed his identity. "I am Dajjal." He predicted he would soon be free of his chains and would ravage the land and not spare any town except for Mecca and Yathrib. These were the only places prohibited to him. If he approached them, angels armed with swords would block his path.

In retelling the story he had heard from Tamim, Muhammad was in a state of manic excitement. The dryness of the Lake Tiberias—this could only be emptied by the thirsty hordes of Gog and Magog! And rows of angels blocking Dajjal's path to Mecca and Medina! This was confirmation of his predictions. "Have I not told you an account like this?"[14] But he disagreed with the implication that Dajjal was somewhere to the west or northwest of Yathrib, as he would necessarily be if he were held captive on an island. That would place him somewhere in the Mediterranean Sea or the Red Sea. He was convinced the Dajjal and his army would advance from the east—from Persia. Bursting with excitement, Muhammad banged the floor with his staff and pointed with it to the east. That is where the evil Dajjal will come from!

Judging from the weirdness of the story, Tamim, a well traveled wine merchant, may have known about Muhammad's end-of-time accounts and invented the island story in the hope of ingratiating himself with him. As a merchant, he had journeyed to Mecca and Yathrib on business for years, and it would have been easy to for him learn about Muhammad's take on the subject just by listening to caravan companions. There were all kinds of stories floating around inspired by the Christian beliefs in the tribulation and the Antichrist. As a Christian, Tamim would have heard some of them, and it was simply a matter of tailoring this particular tale to fit the occasion. Tamim was an astute man, an opportunist who had done his due diligence before showing up at the mosque and making his declaration of faith to Muhammad. Tamim told him exactly what he wanted to hear, and he swallowed it whole. Tamim eventually became one of Muhammad's advisers, and under later caliphs he was granted a fiefdom in a region that is now in Jordan.

Muhammad's end-of-time obsession increasingly became the obsession of his spooked followers, and they looked everywhere for clues about Dajjal. He was around every corner; he was ensconced behind ever rock; he was hiding up in the fronds of every palm tree. It was inevitable that somebody would eventually be identified as the Evil One. That ended up being a skinny twelve-year-old seer from a minor Jewish village that had so far escaped Muhammad's fury. He was nicknamed Saf and was the son of a man named Sayyad. From an early age the boy had displayed a gift of foreknowledge, and people came to him for advice or to learn about the future. After the Dajjal hysteria spread, Saf became suspect number one. Rumors circulated that he was making claims he was a messenger of God, something the Great Deceiver would surely do. Muhammad caught wind of it, and one day he went to investigate accompanied by Umar and others. They found the boy playing with other children. The son of Sayyad did not realize he had visitors until Muhammad slapped him on the back and said, "Ibn Sayyad, do you bear witness that I am the Messenger of Allah?"

Though the men towered over him, particularly Umar who was the tallest and burliest of the group, the boy was anything but a pushover. He said, "I bear witness to the fact that you are the Messenger of the unlettered," he said, meaning that Muhammad was the prophet of the Arabs, who were illiterate, not the Jews, who were literate. The youngster challenged him. "Do you bear witness to the fact that I am the messenger of Allah?"[15]

By that time, few people talked back to Muhammad. He grabbed the boy by his narrow shoulders and said, "What visions do you have?"

Saf's answer was cryptic. "One who speaks the truth and one who lies comes to me."

Muhammad told him he was confused and challenged him to prove his powers by telling him what he was thinking. If the boy really was the Great Deceiver, he would know the thought Muhammad had in mind. It was a line from one of the chapters he composed back in Mecca having to do with the end of time called "Smoke." "Then wait you for the Day (of Doom) when the sky will bring forth a visible smoke."[16]

"What am I thinking?"

Saf picked up on the word "smoke," but not the end of time context of it. "Smoke" was his response.

Muhammad exulted. It was a gotcha moment. The kid was good, really good, but his abilities did not rise above the level of a *kahin*—a soothsayer. Yes, he had an ability to hear what was not given to others to hear, but Muhammad believed that such people got their knowledge from the lowly *jinn*, not from the high source he was connected to. A *jinn* had picked up on the word "smoke" from Muhammad's mind and transmitted it to the mind of Ibn Sayyad. The *jinn* were malicious tattletales who were able to pick out things from one person's mind and pass it on to another, but they were deficient transmitters and could be counted on to garble a message. Muhammad was therefore reasonably certain, though not convinced beyond all doubt, that Saf ibn Sayyad was not the fearsome Dajjal. He said dismissively, "You cannot get farther than your rank," meaning that the son of Sayyad had nothing more than a soothsayer's ability.

Umar was furious that the boy had talked to Muhammad with such insolence. Seeing that Muhammad was done with him, he reached for his sword. "Shall I cut off his head, Muhammad?"

Muhammad stayed his hand. "If he is the Dajjal who would appear near the Last Hour, you would not be able to overpower him, and if he is not there is no good for you to kill him." In one of the versions of the story, Muhammad stated that only Jesus would be able to slay Dajjal.

Muhammad had a continuing interest in the son of Sayyad. He was not fully convinced he was not the Dajjal. Perhaps he hoped that he was, for that would mean the Day of Doom was indeed at hand. Later, he made another attempt to get to the bottom of it, this time accompanied by one of his scribes in

"SHALL I CUT OFF HIS HEAD, MUHAMMAD?" Umar draws his sword to kill a young seer whom Muhammad suspected was the fearsome Dajjal—the Antichrist. Muhammad firmly believed the Day of Doom was approaching and that one of the signs would be the appearance of Dajjal. The boy was a gifted seer whose ability to speak about hidden things brought people to fear him. Here, Muhammad tests him and concludes he was nothing more than a *kahin*—a soothsayer.

order to record evidence of the encounter. The boy's home backed up against a palm grove. On this particular day, Saf was napping under the shade of one of the palms. Muhammad crept through the grove, the scribe with him, and hid behind the tree, hoping to catch the boy talking in his sleep. This would undoubtedly indicate he was conversing with Satan himself. But Saf's mother spotted him and roused her son to warn him Muhammad was hiding behind the tree. The boy jumped to his feet and glared at him. A frustrated Muhammad later told his companions, "If she had just left him alone he would have made things clear."[17]

The son of Sayyad was never able to shake off suspicion that he was the Grand Deceiver. Wherever he went, people pointed at him. He eventually joined Muhammad's religion, but it made little difference; people still considered him the Dajjal. A decade after the death of Muhammad, he was on a pilgrimage to Mecca and ended up encamped with a veteran of many of Muhammad's battles. The veteran became frightened at the sight of him and told him to move away from him. Deeply hurt, Saf tried to soften him by offering him fresh goat milk. He nearly broke into tears as he told the man how he wanted to hang himself because of the rejection he got from everyone. It was enough to drive a man to suicide.

One of the chief sources for the traditions about Ibn Sayyad was Abdullah, the son of Umar. He heard everything from his father about Saf, including the attempts Muhammad made to determine if he was Dajjal, and he remained convinced throughout his life that Ibn Sayyad was indeed the Grand Deceiver. The traditions report Abdullah declaring, "I swear by Allah that I do not doubt that the Antichrist is Ibn Sayyad."[18]

Years later, when middle-aged, Saf had a chance meeting with Abdullah on some road. At the time of the encounter, the son of Sayyad was suffering from an infected eye, and it was swollen. He must have looked like the Evil One, as Muhammad told his followers Dajjal would be one-eyed, with the bad eye bulging like a grape. Saf's swollen eye definitely looked like a bulging grape.

Abdullah said to him, "What happened to your eye?"

"I do not know."

"This is in your head, and you do not know about it?"

The long-suffering Saf exploded. He pointed to a staff Abdullah was carrying. "If Allah so wills He can create an eye in your staff." He began braying like a donkey at Abdullah and kept braying until it seemed he had lost his mind. Perhaps it was his way of telling Abdullah, the son of the man who once wanted to cut off his head for back-talking Muhammad, what he really thought of the whole lot of them.

The experience unnerved Abdullah, by then a man of importance in the expanding religion. He went to see his sister Hafsa, one of Muhammad's widows. When he told her about the chance encounter with Ibn Sayyad, she scolded him for being so stupid as to get him angry. "Why did you incite Ibn Sayyad in spite of the fact that you know it would be extreme anger that would make Dajjal appear in the world?"[19]

CHAPTER 20

Father and Son

Not long after the expulsion of the Nadir Jews, Muhammad shocked even true believers by marrying the wife of his adopted son Zayd, breaking an Arab taboo and giving the "hypocrites"—his enemies within the fold—ammunition to discredit him. The matter quieted down only after he threatened to strip his critics of the protection of the *shahada* and kill them.

The official story goes as follows:

It was a warm afternoon and Muhammad was in a dreamy state when he knocked on the door of his adopted son Zayd, paying him a family visit. It was more than the usual wait, but when the door finally opened, it was as if Allah had just parted the gates of Heaven to grant him a vision of one of the dark-eyed damsels of Paradise. Standing before him was Zayd's wife Zaynab, the daughter of Jahsh, and she was scantily clad. A diaphanous robe clung to her, revealing hips and cleavage to die for. Her lips pursed, as if inviting him to more than entry into the home: "O Messenger of Allah, what could it be that bringest thee to our humble abode?" Though he was an eloquent man in a land of eloquent men, he could hardly get out a word. He stammered, "I have, ah, come to see, ah, Zayd."

Zaynab batted her eyelashes. "He is not at home, O Messenger of Allah. Shall I tell him that you came inquiring about him?"

"Yes, yes, of course." He made dizzied steps away from this temptress and muttered something that sounded like "Praise be to Allah who disposes the hearts!"

The literature holds that when Zayd returned home, she told him about Muhammad's visit, and he said, "You asked him to come in, didn't you?"

"I bade him to, but he refused."

"Did you hear him say anything?"

"When he turned away, I heard him say something that I could hardly understand. I heard him say, 'Praise be to Allah who disposes the hearts.'"

Zayd went to Muhammad at the mosque and said, 'O Messenger of God, I learned that you came to my house. Did you come in?" When Muhammad told him that he had not, Zayd suspected it was because he had become enamored of his wife, and if that was the case, he would be happy to part with her. "O Messenger of Allah, my father and mother are your ransom. Perhaps you liked Zaynab. I can leave her."

Muhammad said, "Hold on to your wife."

"O Messenger of Allah, I will leave her."

"Keep your wife."

In the usual rendering of the story, they tussled back and forth over the matter. The upshot was that Zayd divorced her, and after a waiting period of four months to ensure she was not pregnant, Muhammad sent Zayd to her to convey his desire to marry her, which she happily accepted. There was a wedding feast. All Muhammad's other wives were joyful, Muhammad and Zaynab were joyful, and Zayd was joyful that they were joyful.[1]

This tale of hand-clasped joy over Muhammad's latest marriage obscures the real story of cruel betrayal and emotional abuse of a father to his son. Zayd was more than just a loyal follower. He was Muhammad's adopted son, his only son. For thirty years Zayd looked up to him as his father. His story is well known: Khadija's nephew Hakim Hizam bought him at the Ukaz slave market and gave him to her as a present; she in turn gave him to Muhammad as his personal slave. When years later his real father came looking for him in Mecca, Zayd chose to stay with Muhammad, who rewarded his loyalty by adopting him and announcing this father-son relationship at the temple. Thereafter he was known as Zayd ibn Muhammad—Zayd, the son of Muhammad. Along with Khadija and Ali, Zayd was the first to believe in him when he became convinced that God had anointed him for a special purpose. Muhammad later married Zayd to Baraka, the Abyssinian slave he inherited from his mother, and they had a son named Osama: Osama, the son of Zayd, the son of Muhammad. Zayd was proud of his relationship with Muhammad. When he introduced himself, he would puff out his chest and say, "I am Zayd, the son of the Muhammad!" And wherever he went, people would point to him and say, "That is Zayd, the son of Muhammad!" Later, along with Ali, Zubayr, Hamza, and other close relatives, Zayd could always be counted on to fight in the cause of his adoptive father. While he was never able to rack up the kill scores of Ali and Zubayr, he was reliably cold-blooded when necessary, such as after the disastrous Uhud battle when he tied a Meccan straggler to a tree and used him for target practice. A year after that battle, when Zayd was touching forty years old, Muhammad arranged for him to take another wife—this one being Zaynab.

She was the daughter of Muhammad's aunt Umayma, one of possibly a hundred paternal first cousins who had descended from Muhammad's grandfather, Abdul Muttalib.[2] Zaynab and her first husband were early converts and were among the group to emigrate to Abyssinia to escape Meccan persecution, but her husband died in Abyssinia. After Muhammad fled for his life from Mecca, Zaynab left Abyssinia to join him in Yathrib. Other than being noted as an enthusiastic supporter of Muhammad during his rise to power in Yathrib, not much is known about her prior to her marriage to Zayd. It is said she objected to the marriage because he was a former slave while she was of the noble line of Abdul Muttalib, but the marriage was Muhammad's idea, and she finally accepted after he gave her a generous dowry on Zayd's behalf.[3] At the time of the marriage, she was thirty-four years old.

In the official story line, it is suggested that the real reason she agreed to the marriage with Zayd was to be close to Muhammad. She would have preferred being married to him rather than to his former slave, and she must have made it known. Within a year, the marriage deteriorated, and Zayd's jealousy was likely a factor. Her eyes would light up when she looked at Muhammad, but would dim when she looked at the short, dark, round-faced, flat-nosed, and otherwise nondescript former slave she had married. Whenever Muhammad came to visit, she came on strong to him. It could not have escaped Zayd's notice. Muhammad picked up on her interest, perhaps prompting his visit to the home timed when Zayd would not be there. His lust had been aroused by those wandering eyes, and he needed to verify the truth of his desire. When Zaynab answered the door, he was certain it was the real deal. He wanted her so badly he pushed his adopted son to clear the path by divorcing her. "Praise be to Allah who disposes the hearts!"

Even accepting that Zayd truly believed God talked to Muhammad and an angel regularly visited him to give him the latest verses, it is a stretch to think he eagerly relinquished his wife. It was likely an emotionally distraught Zayd who questioned Muhammad about the visit to his home. He was caught in a trap between loyalty and suspicion. He demanded to know what was going on: "I learned you came to my house. Did you come in?" It was more an accusation than a question.

Muhammad did not go public with his desire to take Zaynab as a wife until months later, once it was certain she was not pregnant. Then one morning, while in bed with Aisha, he fell into a swoon, and when recovered he was smiling ear to ear. He was excited, and it was clear he had something important to reveal, but he waited to speak about it. It was a quirk of Muhammad to form an expression on his face—be it joy, anger, or whatever—and then wait for someone to ask the meaning of it before revealing what was on his mind, so he said nothing until Aisha finally inquired, "What is it that makes you so pleased, O Messenger of God?" Muhammad could hardly contain himself: God had just made it permissible for him to marry Zaynab! Praise the Lord! He recited the freshly confected communiqué: "O Prophet! surely We have made lawful to you your wives whom you have given their dowries, and those whom your right hand possesses[4] out of those whom Allah has given to you as prisoners of war, and the daughters of your paternal uncles and the daughters of your paternal aunts, and the daughters of your maternal uncles and the daughters of your maternal aunts who fled with you; and a believing woman if she gave herself to the Prophet, if the Prophet desired to marry her—specially for you, not for the (rest of) believers."[5,6]

Aisha, then a precocious thirteen-year-old, saw through it. Hurt by his indifference to her feelings and jealous that yet

MUHAMMAD ENAMORED. Like King David when he saw Bathsheba bathing, Muhammad lusted after the wife of his adopted son Zayd when he visited their home one day, and she answered the door in a skimpy dress. He got his adopted son to divorce her and married her, adding her to his growing harem. He blunted criticism by abolishing the practice of adoption so that Zayd could no longer be recognized as his son.

another rival for his attention was coming into her life, she said, "I see that your Lord hastens to confirm your desires."[7]

Muhammad had several ways of promulgating his verses. The chief method was to wrap sermons around them. Ensconced in the pulpit while his congregation sat cross-legged on palm mats, he would recite his work like a poet at a poetry reading and explain the meaning of the new verses—"revelations" he called them—and link them to whatever situation had given rise to them. "God has informed me that . . ." or "The angel has come to me with God's statement that . . ." were formulas for introducing new verses. Another method was to have acolytes memorize the latest batch and send them out to the various communities to repeat them publicly. However the verses were disseminated, believers were expected to memorize them and recite them during their prayer performances. Before long the faithful were intoning, "O Prophet! We have made permissible to you your spouses . . . ."

Zaynab learned from a go-between about Muhammad's proposal. In one of the versions, Muhammad sent a slave woman to bring her the glad tidings, but the most usual account is that Muhammad sent her now ex-husband Zayd. "Go and make mention of me to her," he told him. Zayd obediently went to Zaynab. He entered without knocking. Zaynab's back was to him, and she did not realize he was there. She was kneading dough, just as she used to do when they were together. Her black hair, clasped at the neck, cascaded down the back of her dress, the same one she used to wear when they were together. She was wearing the same sandals and the same beguiling anklets. When she turned to see who was there, her face dimmed, just as it used to dim when they were together. "O Zaynab, rejoice!" he is said to have said while his heart is said to have spilled over with happiness for her. "The Messenger of Allah has sent me to propose marriage to you on his behalf."[8]

A wedding feast was held at the mosque apartments, in the very room Zaynab would thenceforth occupy—next to the rooms of the other wives. While the other wives remained cloistered in their quarters, a flow of guests came to congratulate the newlyweds and partake of the feast, a dish of coarse bread and the meat of a freshly slaughtered goat. The feast dragged on, and when the visitors finally dwindled Muhammad stood up to signal it was over.

What happened next made it into the Koran: Most of the remaining people got the message and left, but three men were in deep conversation and seemed oblivious that everyone else had gone except for Muhammad and Zaynab. Muhammad was said to be shy about asserting himself in such situations, and so he was reluctant to raise his voice and throw the dawdlers out. Instead, he paid visits to his various wives in their separate rooms. Between each visit he would glance into the banquet bedroom, and there they still were! Now that four months of formalities were out of the way, he badly wanted to sleep with Zaynab, but these inconsiderate laggards were the last remaining obstacle. He became sulky and suspected that the real reason they stayed was to ogle his bride. They finally left, but Muhammad stewed about it to the point that he brought God into the matter. He had God issue rules of etiquette regarding such festivities, perhaps in anticipation of future love conquests and therefore more weddings and wedding feasts. God took time out from upholding the universe to say: "O you who believe! Do not enter the houses of the Prophet unless permission is given to you for a meal, not waiting for its cooking being finished—but when you are invited, enter, and when you have taken the food, then disperse—not seeking to listen to talk; surely this gives the Prophet trouble, but he forbears from you, and Allah does not forbear from the truth."[9]

Public reaction to the marriage was split. Though shaken by his action, true believers were convinced Muhammad could do no wrong. How could he if God himself authorized the marriage? Even if in the darkest corners of their minds they suspected there was something fishy and that the verses came across as self-serving, they kept it to themselves. To criticize Muhammad for behavior God permitted would be tantamount to hypocrisy, punishable by hellfire. The nominals, those who had embraced Muhammad's religion out of fear for their lives, were not so reticent. Led by the irrepressible Abdullah Ubayy who was always looking for a way to discredit Muhammad, they denounced him for immorality. Until the arrival of Muhammad, the Arabs had always been easygoing about sex, but taking the spouse of one's son, adopted or natural, was a strict taboo because it set sons against fathers and destroyed families. Now Muhammad had violated the taboo.

Muhammad responded to the critics in the only way he could: He took the extraordinary measure of threatening to strip them of the shield of the *shahada*. In his God voice, he threatened bloody murder: "If the hypocrites and those in whose hearts is a disease and the agitators in the city do not desist, We shall most certainly set you over them, then they shall not be your neighbors in it but for a little while; Cursed: wherever they are found they shall be seized and murdered, a (horrible) murdering."[10]

Instead of killing his critics, he killed the reason for their criticism. Like a president signing an executive order, he abolished the age-old Arabian practice of adoption and the rights of inheritance that went with it. Not only did he forbid it, he made it retroactive. There were no longer any grounds to attack him because Zayd was no longer his adopted son. Nor had he ever been. Muhammad declared in his God voice that God was not the creator nor supporter of adoptions; it was a human invention, and the practice of giving your own name to someone who was not your own was displeasing to God. "Assert their relationship to their fathers; this is more equitable with Allah; but if you do not know their fathers, then they are your brethren in faith and your friends."[11]

Zayd was the first casualty of the edict. Not only was Muhammad now sleeping with the woman who had been his wife, his father of thirty years had rejected his loyal son. He was no longer Zayd, the son of Muhammad, but Zayd, the son of Haritha, Haritha being the name of his real father, the distraught man who had come searching for his lost son decades earlier in Mecca. Zayd's emotional devastation was compounded by humiliation. Everyone knew what happened: He had been emasculated.

From then on he was a man in rage. He volunteered to lead raids and carried them out with unsparing ferocity. During one of the plunder missions, this one against a Bedouin tribe along the northern caravan route, he was wounded and some of his men were killed. After recuperating he returned at the head of a punitive force. The raiders slew everyone they could get their hands on and captured the wife of the tribal leader, Umm Qirfa, and her daughter. Zayd had Umm Qirfa killed in a manner that had never been done before: She was tied between two camels and ripped apart. It was a cruel death. She died slowly, in the midst of agonizing pain as her rent body was dragged through the desert behind one of the camels. Normally, it was only men who were slain while women and children were taken as slaves. Muhammad had issued a general order about it. Did Zayd do to the Bedouin woman what he wanted to do to his former wife? If so, what in his heart did he really want to do to Muhammad?

Zayd brought Umm Qirfa's daughter to Muhammad, perhaps as an act of contempt that only Zayd would have understood: He was now the purveyor of women to his former father. She was a beautiful desert woman, young, strong, and proud, but now a slave. At first Muhammad wanted her, but one of his maternal uncles came to him and requested her. The uncle had seen her, was pleased by her looks, and wanted to take her as a concubine. After hesitating for a few days, Muhammad turned the woman over to him.

Muhammad was David who sent the Hittite to die in battle so he could have his wife Bathsheba to himself. Following his marriage to Zaynab, Muhammad kept Zayd busy with raids, hoping to keep his seething former adopted son out of Yathrib as much as possible. Two years later Zayd met the Hittite fate—killed by a swarming enemy far from the land where his former father was sleeping with his former wife.[12,13]

CHAPTER 21

Terms of Endearment

Six months after marrying the wife of his adopted son, Muhammad acquired yet another wife, this one being Juwayriya after he subjugated her tribe in a preemptive raid.

The Mustaliq raid, as it came to be known, occurred several months after the murder of Umm Qirfa. Muhammad received word that a coalition of nomads to the southwest of Yathrib near the Red Sea was organizing an attack on him. They were marshaling under the banner of al-Harith, an important leader of the Mustaliq tribe. As he had done before to discourage military strikes against him, Muhammad attacked first. Leading a force of seven hundred men, he marched on the nomad encampment at a watering hole a four-day journey from Yathrib. Before leaving Yathrib, he dispatched a spy who returned with a report about their strength. The Mustaliqs in turn sent a spy to monitor Muhammad's movements, but he was captured and dragged before Muhammad, who offered to spare his life if he accepted the new religion. The man made the mistake of refusing unless his entire tribe embraced it. With a shrug, Muhammad ordered him beheaded.

Word of the beheading reached the nomads. Fearful it augured their own fate if they fought Muhammad, the Bedouin partners abandoned their Mustaliq allies, leaving them alone to confront the approaching enemy. Muhammad soon arrived with his chilling battle cry of "O Conqueror, kill, kill!"[1] The Mustaliqs bravely stood their ground, but they were outnumbered and quickly overwhelmed. In some of the accounts, the fight was not a pitched battle, but a surprise attack that Muhammad launched at dawn. It is recorded that ten of the Mustaliq warriors were killed, but only one of Muhammad's followers died, a man of Meccan origin. His death came about from friendly fire: One of the believers mistook him for a Mustaliq tribesman and felled him with an arrow.

In terms of booty, the raid was a smashing success. In addition to the tents and their contents there were two thousand camels and five thousand sheep and goats. Six hundred people were captured and were now slaves.[2] Before leaving, Muhammad appointed an overseer to distribute the booty, and it was the responsibility of each warrior to transport his plunder back to Yathrib. The captives were booty and were divided up. By then Muhammad had decreed that the marriages of infidel women were dissolved upon their capture and so they were fair game.[3] Thus, the women and girls were separated from their husbands, fathers, uncles, brothers, and children and were divided up among Muhammad's men. Once in their possession of their assigned owners, the women and girls were dragged off to tents and raped. "Celibacy was very hard on us," one of Muhammad's people said later.[4]

Before the women were in their hands, however, the captors became concerned about a dilemma they faced: What if they got the women pregnant? Should they ejaculate outside of the woman to prevent that? This was a worry because the women could eventually be ransomed and returned to their tribe, but getting them pregnant would reduce their ransom value. They went to Muhammad for a ruling on the matter. After mulling it over, he told them not to worry. If the women got pregnant, it was destined to be. It was God's will.[5]

Among the captives was Juwayriya, the daughter of the chief of the Mustaliqs. She was awarded to one of the attackers, but Muhammad eventually proposed marriage to her and she accepted. Two versions of the story are told: In one, she worked out an agreement with the man who owned her to buy her freedom for nine ounces of gold. Not possessing such money, she went to Muhammad's tent to ask him for help in arranging her freedom, citing the fact that she was the daughter of the chief. Muhammad had brought two of his wives with him—Aisha and Umm Salama—and Aisha happened to be with him when Juwayriya stood at the entrance of his tent and asked permission to speak to him. When she saw Juwayriya, Aisha, who was then about thirteen years old, was gripped with jealousy. Yet another rival for Muhammad's attention had just shown up. Her fear was realized when he proposed to the woman. "Would you prefer better?" he asked. "What would that be, O Messenger of God?" she asked. "I will take responsibility for your deed myself and marry you." According to the literature, she accepted then and there.[6]

Another version, most likely the real story, is that the proposal took place more than a month later in Yathrib, and part of the deal was for Muhammad to free all her relatives. She sacrificed herself for her clan. By then some of the Mustaliq captives had already been ransomed. Women and children were being redeemed for six camels each. Juwayriya's father had come to Yathrib with a set of camels to offer as ransom for her in lieu of the gold that had first been agreed upon. She asked to be taken to Muhammad regarding the deal. She was brought before him while he was with Aisha in her room at the mosque, and that is when he proposed to her. Aisha later recalled the incident: "She was a sweet, beautiful woman who captivated anyone who looked at her. She came to the Messenger of God seeking his help in the matter of her contract. By God, as soon as I saw her at the door of my chamber, I took a dislike to her, and I knew that he would see in her what I saw."[7] Juwayriya married Muhammad provided he free all her relatives who had not yet been ransomed. The raped women were restored to their husbands and the violated girls returned to their families. Juwayriya was the only one who stayed behind. That she had sacrificed herself for her people is suggested in later reports that she did not let Muhammad touch her. She would fall into a pretense of prayer whenever he came to her room as a way of avoiding him. He would tap on the door, she would drop to the ground in prostration before the door opened and mumble Koran verses, and Muhammad would leave, closing the door behind him. If he came back hours later, he would find her still apparently engrossed in prayer.

The Mustaliq raid turned out beset with unanticipated problems, among them a vengeance killing. While the booty distribution was going on, a man named Miqyas—the brother of the believer who was killed in the friendly-fire incident—arrived

THE MURDER OF UMM QIRFA. She was a prominent woman of a Bedouin tribe that had fought off Muhammad's marauders, killing or wounding some of them. In reprisal Muhammad sent Zayd to lead a punitive raid against her tribe. She was captured and Zayd ordered her death by dismemberment. She was tied between two camels and ripped apart when the camels were made to run in opposite directions.

from Mecca claiming to be a follower of Muhammad's religion. He demanded blood money as compensation for the wrongful death of his brother. After Muhammad gave him money, Miqyas lingered at the camp for a couple of days until the true purpose of his visit surfaced. At an opportune moment, he slit the throat of the man who killed his brother and fled back to Mecca.[8]

 Another problem arose when a fight broke out between Meccan and Yathrib converts over water. The water level of the Mustaliq well was running low and competition for what was left was running high. The fight started after men from each group lowered buckets into the well and they became entangled. They were only able to bring one of the buckets back up, and the men began shoving each other over it. One of the Meccan expatriates gave one of the Yathrib men a bloody nose. Each side called for reinforcements, and soon the two groups—Meccan emigrants and Yathrib converts—were facing off with swords drawn. Leaders from each tribe intervened and reminded everyone they were brothers in the new religion and bonded together through their mutual love of God and his messenger.

The fight brought about a serious complication when Abdullah Ubayy made snarky remarks about the Meccans. He and a dozen of his Khazraj friends had watched the whole thing from a distance and saw that it was the Meccans who started it. They were vulgar louts and bullies, Abdullah said, always ready to get into a fight. He derided them as "*jalabibs*," the word for the distinctive, coarsely woven long shirts the Meccans wore, but it was understood to mean "rags." The people of Yathrib were stupid to let these rags into their valley. Now the rags were eating them out of house and home; they were pushing them around and taking over. The Yathribites were being used as fodder in rag wars, and because of it their population was diminishing while the rags were growing in number. Abdullah Ubayy turned to his tribesmen and said: "This is what you have done to yourselves! You allowed them to settle in your lands and divided your wealth with them. Had you kept from them what you had, by God they would have moved to lands other than yours." He finished off by saying it was time to turn the table on them as soon as they got back to Yathrib. "Those who are stronger will drive out the weaker from it."[9]

With the Khazraj group was a teenager named Zayd Arqam, a committed believer. He heard every word and ran to tell his uncle. The uncle in turn went to Muhammad, who summoned the boy to hear it directly from him. At first, Muhammad did not believe him and questioned whether he had heard right, but the boy swore he was telling the truth and hoped God would affirm as much to Muhammad. His was a serious accusation, for Abdullah Ubayy had essentially made a call for insurrection. Moreover, if the boy was truthful it proved beyond dispute that Abdullah was a fake believer—a hypocrite. Ever since he was dragged out of the mosque by his beard, Abdullah tried to convince everybody of his sincerity. He became scrupulous in prayer observance and exacting in ritual performance; he gave long speeches praising Muhammad. But his remarks about the Meccans showed that the "disease" of hypocrisy was in his heart. Muhammad's top people, mostly of Meccan extraction, were prepared to believe the worst about Abdullah, particularly since he had insulted them by referring to them as rags. Umar offered to chop off his head. If it had been someone with less influence, Muhammad might have given Umar the go-ahead, but Abdullah Ubayy had an important following. Killing him could risk a rebellion, and they were way out in the desert where Muhammad could not count on any backup. Moreover, they were surrounded by hostile tribes that would be eager to jump into a fray against him. Some of the Khazraj converts urged him to show restraint. The boy may have thought he heard what he heard, they pointed out, but he heard incorrectly. And even if true, the Messenger of God should take into consideration the special circumstances surrounding Abdullah. Yathrib had been preparing to crown him king, but Muhammad came with his new religion and rose above him. It was natural for him to be resentful.

Abdullah soon learned that the Arqam boy had informed on him and that there was talk of killing him. He had not realized the boy, who was his personal attendant and the son of a member of the same clan as Abdullah, was such an ardent believer and a snitch; otherwise, he might have tempered his words. He hastened to Muhammad's tent and denied saying what had been attributed to him. There was a fight at the well, the Meccan emigrants started it, and he got upset when they punched one of the Yathrib believers, and as a result he made some ill-tempered remarks that the boy misconstrued, that was all.

Muhammad put a clamp on the affair by ordering the army to break camp and head back to Yathrib, hoping the activity would divert attention from the problem. People were stirred up, and he was afraid someone might take it upon himself to kill Abdullah, and then there could really be trouble. Breaking camp was always busy work. Tents had to be taken down and loaded onto baggage camels. The spoils had to be secured onto camels along with food and water. The male captives had to be roped together and the captured livestock rounded up. To keep the pressure on, Muhammad ordered the departure during the broiling heat of midday, right after noon prayers. It was an unusual time to head out into the desert and showed how concerned he was about the situation with Abdullah. He kept the long column on the march through the night until the following morning when, exhausted, they stopped to catch up on sleep.

During the punishing march, the Abdullah affair was still alive in Muhammad's mind. As the army headed out of Mustaliq territory—with captives and seized livestock in tow—he fell into a meditative state facilitated by the rhythmic sway of his camel. He was riding his favorite mount, a white camel named al-Qaswa. Words to express what he wanted to say about the whole thing came into his head, swirling around, combining, breaking apart, combining again. At some point it all coalesced into a set of eleven verses. The theme of it had to do with phony believers, and it recapped the Abdullah incident. Without naming him, it was an indictment against Abdullah. He was a pretend believer, a hypocrite. The curse of Allah was upon him!

It so happened that the Arqam boy was riding slightly behind Muhammad. He had observed Muhammad fall into a meditative state and wondered if he was witnessing one of those marvelous moments when God talked to his messenger. He soon found out, because after Muhammad was satisfied with his composition and came out of his contemplative state, he turned in his saddle and motioned for the Arqam boy to trot forward. As soon as the boy was up next to him, Muhammad leaned over and grabbed him by the ear so hard he lifted him from his saddle. "Your ear is perfect, lad," he said, "God confirms your news!"[10] Still holding the boy's ear, Muhammad turned to the riders surrounding him to inform them that the kid was telling the truth after all. God had just confirmed it! As his camel plodded along, Muhammad recited the entire set of verses loudly enough for everyone around him to hear.[11]

The new chapter, which eventually acquired the title "Hypocrites," circulated among the rank and file and everyone then knew with certainty that God considered Abdullah Ubayy a hypocrite, a liar who did the devil's work against God and his messenger. While inspired by Abdullah, the verses were intended to make a general statement about fake belief and phony believers, but they ended up adding fuel to the hatred that had been stirred up against Abdullah. This became evident the following morning after the army stopped to rest. Muhammad was getting a back massage from a young black slave under the shade of a tree when Umar came to him and offered again to kill Abdullah. Umar said that if

God's messenger did not want him to do the deed, he could always order Maslama to kill him, or Abbad ibn Bishr, or one of the other experienced assassins, but Muhammad turned him down. "Umar, how will it be if people start saying that Muhammad kills his companions?"[12]

Umar was not the only volunteer. Abdullah Ubayy's son, Abdullah Jr., also offered to kill him. His logic was convoluted and only makes sense in the upside-down world created by Muhammad: He was afraid that if someone else killed his father, he would feel compelled to kill the killer, but then he knew he would surely suffer in Hell for killing another believer. To avoid going to Hell, he had to be the one to slay his father. "If you must do it, then order me to do it and I will bring you his head." Muhammad again put his foot down. "Let us deal kindly with him and make much of his companionship, while he is with us."[13]

Instead of killing his father, Abdullah humiliated him by blocking his entry into Yathrib. His father was at the head of the long column as it approached the valley. The son stood his camel in his path and said, "By God, you will not enter until the Messenger of God gives you permission to do so!"[14] The son forced the Khazraj chieftain to wait for Muhammad, who was at the rear of the column, to reach them. With a nod, Muhammad allowed him to proceed.

Muhammad faced an even more serious problem during the return trip when Aisha disappeared. Whenever he went on a raid, he would bring along a wife or two. They rode in tasseled, curtained howdahs, and their role was to keep Muhammad sexually satisfied and take care of chores such as preparing food and keeping the tent neat and tidy. But when they were still a day away from Yathrib, after the long column had stopped for rest, it was discovered that Aisha was not in her howdah, nor was she anywhere else in the long column. Vanished! Everything came to a halt while Muhammad considered what to do. He questioned the men who had lifted her howdah onto the camel. It was fastened to poles underneath, and four men would each grab an end and lift it onto the camel while it was kneeling. The whole contraption was secured with ropes and straps. They thought she was inside it, but it was curtained so they had no way to know for sure; they simply assumed her to be inside, and besides, she was a young girl and did not weigh much. Muhammad considered the angles. She could not have run away. Who would run away in the middle of the desert? And why would she run away? The only explanation was that somehow she got left behind. He would have to send out a search party.

It proved unnecessary. While he was assigning people to the task, a camel appeared in the distance, and as it came closer they could see a smallish veiled figure sitting on top and a man on foot leading the camel by a rope. It took a while for these solitary figures to reach the army, and when they did everyone could see it was Aisha on the camel, and it was led by a young man named Safwan. An embarrassed Aisha explained to Muhammad what happened: She had gotten left behind the evening before. Muhammad had given the order to move out after the sun went down, and she hastened out into the surrounding desert to relieve herself before the journey commenced. On the way back she realized that the prized Zafar necklace her mother gave her as a wedding present had fallen from her neck. She went back in search of it, but by the time she found it, the army had departed. She did the only thing that was possible to do under such circumstances, which was to sit down, wrap herself up, and hope and pray they would soon discover the empty howdah and return for her. At some point Safwan, a young convert from one of the southern Bedouin tribes who had fallen behind the army after it departed from the Mustaliq territory, came riding up on his camel. When she saw him she covered her face because by then Muhammad had already commanded the full-face cover. Safwan gallantly knelt his camel, helped her to climb onto the saddle, and without a word led the camel in the direction the army had taken. But it was not until the following morning that they were able to catch up. When the army resumed the trip that evening, Aisha took her place in the howdah, and they were back in Yathrib the following day.

Aisha did not give any more thought to the incident until a couple of weeks later when an aunt told her that gossip was swirling around that she had had a fling with Safwan. She had known nothing about the gossip until that moment. Upon returning to Yathrib, she had fallen ill and was at first confined to her room, but then she went to stay with her parents so that her mother could nurse her. Strange things were happening that she could not explain: People had become cool to her, even Muhammad. In the past he was always there to comfort her when she fell ill; now he merely stuck his head in the door and asked whoever was attending her, "How is she doing?" When she asked him if she could stay with her parents while she was ill, his answer was a curt "Do what you like." Even her parents were unusually quiet around her and looked down at her with sorrow, as if she was on her death bed. Then one day she went out with her auntie to relieve herself. Then as now, women went to the ladies room together, only then the ladies room was a field with bushes and trees to hide behind or was in one of the gullies carved into the lava field. On the way back, the auntie stumbled and nearly fell to the ground. She cursed one of their close relatives for it, a man named Mista, leading Aisha to ask her why she had cursed that particular person, especially since he had status as one of the Badr veterans. The auntie said, "Innocent woman, have you not heard what he said?"[15]

That is when it all came out: Mista and others were accusing her of an illicit affair, a forbidden act, a grave sin against God and his messenger, and it was the conclusion of many that she deserved to be stoned. She and Safwan had been seen talking together in the past, before the veil was imposed and even after, so what other conclusion could be drawn from the fact she had been missing the entire night and showed up the next morning with him? Perhaps hoping to divert attention from himself, Abdullah Ubayy started these rumors even before they got back to Yathrib. But now others were spreading gossip about it, particularly Mista, a ne'er do-well relative who relied on handouts from Abu Bakr to survive. Hamna, a sister of Muhammad's wife Zaynab, also had a hand in spreading the gossip. Muhammad's poet Hassan Thabit made things worse by composing some inflammatory lines about Safwan.

After learning what was being said about her, Aisha cried so hard she "almost burst her liver," as she would later say. What defense did she have when appearances were so damning and gossip so vicious? Even before she became aware of the situation, Muhammad began a quiet investigation to determine if he should divorce her. He called in Ali and Osama, Zayd's young son, to ask their opinion about her. Ali was ready to throw her under a camel. "Women are plentiful and you can easily change one for another," he said, but he could not come up with anything damaging about her.[16,17] Osama stood up for her. They called in various people to solicit opinions. One of them was a slave woman named Burayra who attended upon Aisha. When she was brought before Muhammad, Ali beat her and told her to "speak the truth to the Messenger of God." Thus loosened up, the slave woman said, "I never found fault with Aisha at all, except that when I knead dough and ask her to watch over it she may fall asleep, and the pet lamb comes and eats it!"[18]

Whatever the truth, the malicious gossip circulating about her was making Muhammad look weak and vulnerable: the Messenger of God cuckolded by his thirteen-year-old wife! He needed to put an end to it. As far as he could tell, Abdullah Ubayy was the one who had started the slander mess, but he was in the same quandary about him now as he had been out in the desert when Abdullah had talked insurrection. Though diminished in power, he still had influence, and he could not be eliminated without serious consequences. Was it worth the risk? Muhammad took to the pulpit before a packed assembly to test the water. If there was broad support for a killing, or at least no real resistance, then the *shahada* be damned, Abdullah was history. From the pulpit, he first defended Aisha by saying he found nothing in her but goodness. He even had supportive words for Safwan, whom he called "a thoroughly pious person." Then he issued a call for a volunteer to take care of the situation—just as he had done after Badr to get rid of critics who mocked him with their poetry: "Who would exonerate me from imputations of that person who has troubled (me) in regard to my family?"[19] Muhammad did not mention Abdullah by name, but everyone understood he was alluding to the Khazraj chieftain and was calling for his death.

The response started off on a positive note. Sad Muadh, Muhammad's chief follower among the Aws and one of the major Aws clan leaders, got to his feet and declared his tribe would support striking off the head of the culprit no matter which tribe he belonged to—Aws or Khazraj. He said in effect, "You order, we obey." But then it started to go south. Sad Ubada, one of the important Khazraj leaders and a long time friend and ally of Abdullah, jumped to his feet. He was practically foaming at the mouth. An Aws would never be allowed to kill a Khazraj, he shouted. The Khazraj would protect him. Ubada shook his fist at Muadh and said, "By God, you said these words only because you know that he is from the Khazraj. If he were from the Aws you would not have spoken thus."[20] Then another of the Aws, a first cousin of Sad Muadh, joined in and said they would indeed carry out an order to kill him. "You are a hypocrite," he said to Sad Ubada, "and so you argue in defense of the hypocrites."[21]

Those were fighting words. Everyone in the prayer area and out in the courtyard jumped up. It was getting explosive—right along tribal lines just as Muhammad had feared. Tempers reached such a point that if they had had swords with them—weapons were forbidden in the mosque—they would surely have drawn them, and the ground would have quickly gone red. Muhammad stood up in the pulpit and yelled at everyone to stop, but he had to descend into the crowd and mix among the people before they finally settled down.

The matter clearly needed resolution and the sooner the better. By then, Aisha had moved from her parent's home in the highlands back to her room directly behind the preacher platform. She was at the center of the storm that had just raged outside in the prayer area, and she must have heard every word. After the congregation dispersed, Muhammad pushed aside the curtain separating the room from the platform and went in. Aisha's father, mother, and a young friend were with her. She and her friend were crying. Muhammad seated himself, praised God, and said, "Aisha, as you know, people have been saying things. Fear God, and if you have committed an evil deed such as people say, repent to God, for God accepts repentance from his servants."[22]

It was the question he had been dreading to ask. If she admitted guilt, she would be forgiven by God, but she would still face the earthly penalty. Adulterers were to be stoned. He had established the precedent several years earlier when two Jews caught in adultery were brought before him. This happened before Badr when he and the Jews were still talking. It is likely the culprits belonged to a minor clan over which Muhammad claimed jurisdiction, otherwise they would have been judged in a Jewish court.[23] He asked Jewish rabbis how they dealt with such situations. They explained that in the days of the harsh prophets, adulterers were stoned to death, but then it happened the daughter of a king was found in adultery. The king could not bring himself to stone her, and so the penalty was reduced to humiliation. The guilty were flogged, their faces were blackened with ash, and they were mounted back to back on a donkey and paraded through town. That should be the penalty for the man and the woman, the rabbis told Muhammad. He demanded to see their scriptures. They brought their Torah scroll to him, and he made one of them read from it. As he read, the rabbi slid his hand over the important passage, the one regarding the penalty imposed by the harsh prophets, but another Jew, a scholar who had defected to Muhammad's religion, forced him to uncover the words and read them aloud. The penalty was stoning, and so Muhammad ordered the execution of the adulterers. They were taken outside the main gate of the mosque, and a crowd smashed their heads with stones until they were dead. The same penalty would have to apply to Aisha.

Muhammad had been under tremendous stress over Aisha in fear of this moment of truth. The near riot outside in the prayer area had ramped up the tension. He was beginning to feel the slight dizziness and anxiety that often preceded a fit, along with a buildup of pressure in his head. He looked at her face, now reddened with tears, and the thought that her pretty young face would end up smashed to a pulp the way those Jewish faces had been smashed caused the dizziness and anxiety to worsen. She had been in his life for thirteen years. He was the first to congratulate her parents after her birth and was among the first to hold the swaddled infant. There were so many precious memories, cute little things like the way she used to footrace in the mosque courtyard with him, and to everyone's amusement she would win. She was playful, like when he prayed extra prayers in bed in the middle of the night. She used to lie crossways, and he once had to shove her out of the way to make her understand not to block him when he performed the precise motions of prayer. She ended up making a game of it: Thereafter she would lean her back against the wall and with a giggle pull her knees to her chin when he did the prayer prostrations, then let her legs stretch out again after he went back to standing and kneeling, and then pull her knees up to her chin again when he prepared for another prostration. Many of the Koran verses had come to him while he was in bed with her. He would have been hard pressed to put a number on it, but it was certainly more than when he was with his other wives combined.

The symptoms that a fit was approaching grew as Muhammad waited for Aisha to answer. She seemed to be dodging him, adding to his pressure in his head. She appealed to her parents to say something in her defense, but her mother said, "By God, we do not know what to reply to him." Finally, Aisha said, "I'll never repent to God for what you refer to. I swear, I well know that if I were to affirm what people say while God knew me to be innocent of it, I would be affirming what had not happened. And if I were to deny what they say, you would not believe me!"[24]

Muhammad was never above faking a fit whenever it was convenient, as he had done when he announced to Aisha—in that very room and on that very same bed only a few months before—that Allah had permitted him to marry Zaynab, but this time it was not faked. The earlier feelings of uneasiness and the pressure in his head had progressed first into a feeling of dread followed by flashes of ecstatic joy that made him so certain he was in touch with the divine. Then came the trembling of his body as he submitted to the might of the temporal-lobe experience. Abu Bakr and his wife and Aisha recognized the symptoms. To them, God was once again communicating with Muhammad. They were thrilled at the privilege of being there as witnesses to a sublime event. Aisha had never thought herself to be significant enough for God to speak about her, but it was part of the family lore that God had once done so with Abu Bakr when he designated him as Muhammad's companion during his flight from Mecca. That honor had so melted Abu Bakr that he had broken into tears. Now God was communicating with his messenger about her! She put her faith in God. There could be but one verdict.

Muhammad was stretched out on Aisha's bed. They slid a leather cushion under his head and covered him with his garment. It is not recorded how long the seizure lasted, but when he came out of it he sat up. Wiping beads of sweat from his forehead, he smiled and said: "Rejoice, Aisha! God has revealed your innocence."[25] He repeated verses that had come to him, very likely lines that had been kicking around in his head for days. He followed it up with verses that condemned the slanderers for harming Aisha, and these were accompanied by more general verses that forbade rumor mongering and false testimony, sins that required a severe punishment—eighty lashes. When he was back on his feet, he called for an assembly of the faithful, and from the pulpit he recited God's communiqués. Among them was a divine tongue lashing: "Why did not the believing men and the believing women, when you heard it, think well of their own people, and say: 'This is an evident falsehood?'"[26] He finished by ordering the flogging of Mista, Hamna, and Hassan, but still fearful of a Khazraj backlash, he spared Abdullah Ubayy.

To patch things up between the Aws and the Khazraj, Muhammad arranged two private intertribal dinners. For the first of these, he took the Aws leader Sad Muadh by the hand and led him to the residence of Sad Ubada, who was with a group of Khazrajis. Before long Ubada motioned for food to be brought, and the group made peace over dishes of stewed meat. A few days later, Muhammad reversed the procedure by taking Ubada by the hand and led him to the clan compound of Sad Muadh, who was with a group of his people. Again food was served.

Despite Muhammad's best efforts to resolve the matter, yet another complication to an already complex situation occurred when Safwan attempted to kill Hassan. He was deeply offended by verses Hassan composed that ridiculed him and was not satisfied that he had been flogged. Safwan had defended himself all along by noting that he arrived with Aisha on his camel in broad daylight in full view of the entire army and of Muhammad himself. If they had truly done what they were accused of, would they have been so obvious about it? But his defense had not impressed Hassan, who unleashed cutting words about him. Safwan tracked him down at a Khazraj tribal meeting, but he only got in one sword slash before people disarmed him. As he swung at Hassan, Safwan shouted, "Here's the edge of my sword for you! When you lampoon a man like me you don't get a poem in return!"[27] Hassan was seriously wounded. When Muhammad learned about it, he had both Safwan and Hassan brought before him at the mosque. After hearing both sides, he said, "Imprison Safwan, and if Hassan dies kill him."[28]

The Khazraj tribe had had enough trouble over the Aisha incident and put pressure on Hassan to drop his right to retaliate against Safwan and resolve the matter peacefully. Muhammad agreed. "Be nice about your injury," he said to Hassan.[29] He sweetened it up for his poet by awarding him one of the fortresses and a plantation that had been taken from the Nadir Jews. It had originally been awarded to someone else as booty, but he had turned it over to Muhammad to use for charitable purposes.

Many decades later, Aisha was able to get in the final word: "Enquiries were made about Ibn al-Muattal (Safwan) and he was found to be impotent; he did not approach women. Thereafter he was martyred. May God be pleased with him."[30]

CHAPTER 22

Trench Warfare

The raids and assassinations continued. On one of the raids, Muhammad led four hundred men against the powerful Ghatafan tribe of the northeastern plateau, the first of a series of attacks he would launch against them, and after a skirmish he made off with a number of their women. The Ghatafans, whose combined population matched that of Yathrib, were scattered across a wide region to the east and north of Yathrib. The clans and subclans roamed separately and pitched their tents wherever water and forage could be found for their livestock. The attack came about after a traveler informed Muhammad he had seen the Ghatafans assembling fighters for a harrying attack on Yathrib. The details of the raid are sketchy, but the literature reports the capture of women. In the sequel, one of the bereft husbands went after the raiders with the intention of killing Muhammad and recovering his wife, but he only got close enough to shoot one of the guards with an arrow.[1] The fate of the husband and his wife and the other captive women is not recorded, but for the women there were only three possible outcomes: They were turned into sex slaves, sold on the slave market, or held for ransom.

During this period, Muhammad led a bold raid on Duma, an ancient caravan town on the east-west trade route that linked the Red Sea to the Persian Gulf. It was a sunbeaten, sandstone Christian town five hundred miles north of Yathrib on the southern fringe of the Byzantine Empire. It was home to an important regional market and featured the ruins of ancient pagan temples.

This was the first time Muhammad personally led a force that far north, and he did so in part with the intention of intimidating the Christians to keep them from joining Jews and polytheists in attacking him, in part to score plunder. At the time the region was infested with highwaymen who waylaid merchants and their cargoes, so he knew there was plenty of booty to be had just by robbing the robbers. A guide led his army of one thousand to a valley where bandits were grazing stolen livestock, and Muhammad fell on them without warning. "The Messenger of God attacked whomever he attacked," the literature reports. "Those who escaped fled in every direction."[2] From there Muhammad and his marauders marched on Duma, but by the time they got there everyone—townspeople, Bedouins, and traders—had fled. After looting the town, Muhammad headed back to Yathrib and reached home after being gone an entire month.

By then a year had gone by since the battle of Uhud, and it was time for Muhammad to take up Abu Sufyan's challenge to meet the Meccans at Badr for a rematch. But faced with a draught that made forage scarce throughout the region, Abu Sufyan backed down at the last minute. This gave Muhammad an easy public relations coup: Knowing ahead of time Abu Sufyan would stay in Mecca, he led an army to Badr and crowed victory when the Meccans failed to show. Abu Sufyan, however, spent the next year preparing for a large-scale attack on Yathrib with the intention of finishing Muhammad off once and for all. Meccan envoys were sent to Bedouin tribes that were hostile to Muhammad to persuade them to join a coalition under Meccan leadership to attack Yathrib. They found an eagerness throughout much of Arabia, as Muhammad's drive to impose his religion by force had caused harm in every direction.

Chief among Muhammad's enemies were the Nadir Jews, now in Khaybar where they had settled after Muhammad drove them out of Yathrib. A half dozen Nadir leaders led by Sallam Huqayq, who was known by the nickname Abu Rafi, went to Mecca and offered to make common cause with the Meccans. When they arrived, Abu Sufyan embraced them with open arms. They were feted throughout the town for assuring the Meccans their religion was better than Muhammad's and that they were closer to the truth.[3] In a show of solidarity the Jews accompanied the Meccan leaders to the temple where Meccans and Jews alike touched the temple cover to their hearts and pledged to fight Muhammad until he was destroyed.[4] From Mecca, the Jews left for the Ghatafan territories northeast of Yathrib to invite the tribes and clans to join them against Muhammad.

But the solidarity did not last. Muhammad learned of the Jewish visit to his enemies. To strike fear into the Jews, he recruited a team of killers to slay Abu Rafi in his fortress in Khaybar. The hitmen were led by Abdullah Atik, a Khazraj zealot who spoke Hebrew, and included Abdullah Unays, the believer whom Muhammad recruited eighteen months earlier to assassinate the Hudhayli chieftain Sufyan Khalid. Khaybar was situated in a narrow valley between ancient lava fields and consisted of a string of large fortresses overlooking vast date palm plantations. Abu Rafi's fortress was one of the largest and had a commanding view of the valley. Due to his fluency in Hebrew, Atik and his hit team were able to get into the fortress at night, and they murdered Abu Rafi in his bedroom. The killers eluded searchers by hiding in an irrigation ditch and made their way back to Yathrib to report their success to Muhammad.[5] When the coalition attack on Yathrib finally came, the Khaybar Jews backed out. This was one of the consequences of the assassination of Abu Rafi, but it was also due to pressure from the Qurayza Jews, the last remaining Jewish tribe in Yathrib. They feared that if the coalition attack were unsuccessful, Muhammad would use the involvement of the Khaybar Jews as a pretext for doing to them what he had done to the Qaynuqa and Nadir tribes. While putting pressure on Khaybar to stay away, the Qurayzas also sent word to Muhammad reaffirming a nonaggression agreement they had made with him when he first came to Yathrib.

The coalition attack came in late February of A.D. 627, about four and a half years after Muhammad fled for his life from Mecca. Under the command of Abu Sufyan the Meccan army departed with four thousand men. His troops included Abyssinian mercenaries and forces supplied by allies from neighboring Bedouin tribes and the more distant Taif. As the army advanced north it was augmented by warriors from sundry Bedouin tribes that had had conflicts with Muhammad or that joined at the prospect of plunder. By the time the coalition army reached Yathrib, it had swollen to ten thousand men. The Ghatafans, meanwhile, marched on Yathrib from the north with two thousand warriors.

News that a large army was heading for Yathrib reached Muhammad only after it was underway, giving him little time to prepare a defense. As usual, his informant was his uncle Abbas who had remained embedded with the Meccans, but the message reached Muhammad only six days before the army arrived. A Persian convert named Salman suggested digging a trench around the exposed parts of the valley, which was what the Persians would do in such a situation to neutralize cavalry and create a death trap for troops foolish enough to attempt crossing the trench. Muhammad put together a work force of three thousand men, essentially every able-bodied man remaining in Yathrib with the exception of the Qurayza Jews. The Qurayzas loaned picks and shovels to show goodwill, but ignored Muhammad's request to join the work force. To rally his people, Muhammad pitched his command tent near the dig. He grabbed a shovel and worked alongside the faithful. The resulting trench was more than three miles long. It zigzagged along the south side of the valley, went up the west end where it connected to a mount, and continued across the northern region as far as the lava fields to the east, linking buildings, walls, and hills. Muhammad counted on the rugged lava fields on the east side to serve as a natural barrier along with the network of walled plantations, fortresses, and villages of the settled areas. The excavation was enormous: The trench was at least six feet deep and was wide enough in most places to keep cavalry from leaping over it. The dirt was piled along the inner rim to form a protective rampart for the defenders. When the enemy army neared the valley, Muhammad ordered everyone who lived outside the entrenched area to move inside, bringing livestock and everything of value with them. While the men took up positions along the dirt ramparts, women, children, and the elderly were sent into the fortresses.

As a result of feverish work day and night, the trench was completed just as the invaders poured into the valley from the northwest entrance at the foot of Mount Uhud. The Meccans and their allies pitched camp in the shadow of the mountain and prepared to assault Yathrib, believing an easy victory lay before them. Their forces would smash through Muhammad's defenses and attack the settled areas; Muhammad would be slain along with the other Meccan turncoats; his mosque would be torched and razed; his religion would perish. But they did not know about the trench until they got to it. When the cavalry and the masses of foot soldiers reached it, they were greeted by volleys of arrows and sling stones fired at them from behind the ramparts, and they had no choice but to back off. What had been intended as a crushing invasion turned into a frustrating standoff.

The siege lasted about three weeks. There were occasional skirmishes, but the fighting consisted mostly of people shooting at each other across the ditch. Given all the arrows flying back and forth, there must have been numerous wounded on both sides, but the literature reports only ten deaths. Two of the slain were Meccan cavalrymen, part of a small group of horsemen who leaped their mounts over the trench at a narrow spot. One of the horsemen was a famed Meccan warrior name Amr who dismounted once on the other side and challenged Muhammad's people to a duel, but when Ali stepped forward, Amr asked for someone else. "Your father was my friend. I don't want to kill you." Ali replied, "But I desire to kill you."[6] They faced off, and when it was over Amr lay dead. It is said that one of the other horsemen was killed after he fell with his horse into the trench during the retreat. A strap of his saddle had been severed by a sword blow, and he slipped from his mount, taking the horse into the trench with him. Muhammad's people threw stones at him until he begged them to kill him more honorably. "A death better than this, I pray you, fellow Arabs!" Some sources say Ali—others insist it was Zubayr—jumped into the trench and hacked him to death.[7] Several more deaths, the equivalent of friendly fire, occurred late one night when two of Muhammad's patrols met coming from opposite directions. They battled one another in the darkness before realizing they were on the same side. Yet another killing was attributed to Zubayr's mother Safiya. From the tower of the fortress where she had taken refuge, she spotted a man she believed to be a Jew climbing over a wall to get into the compound. She rushed down with a club and beat him to death. Among the wounded was the Aws leader Sad Muadh, one of Muhammad's closest people. An arrow struck him above the wrist, and he died several weeks later from an infection.

The Meccans and their allies were unprepared for a lengthy siege and soon had to worry about supplies—food for themselves and fodder for their animals. They opened up a supply line from Khaybar with the help of Huyayy Akhtab, who had become the leader of the Nadir Jews after the assassination of Abu Rafi. Several small caravans made it to Yathrib from Khaybar, but the supply effort ended when Muhammad's people captured one of the convoys. The Meccan leaders were in a quandary. They could not see how to overcome the obstacle of the trenches. They feared the slaughter of their people should they attempt to storm across. Abu Sufyan concluded that their only hope for breaking the stalemate was to convince the Qurayza Jews to attack from the rear. That would divert Muhammad's people from the trenches and create an opening for the alliance to cross in force.

Huyayy was dispatched to secure Qurayza support. Their territory was in the southeast region of the highlands and abutted the lava fields, and the only way to get to their fortress from outside the valley was through the rugged lava beds. The roundabout journey took Huyayy more than half a day. He pleaded with the Qurayza leaders to join the offensive, but the reception was anything but warm. The Qurayzas were convinced that maintaining neutrality gave them their only hope of survival. Huyayy finally won them over by pointing to the size of the coalition. The numbers were overwhelming. How could they not be victorious if they were able to break through the trench defense? With Muhammad finally dead, the Jews would no longer have to fear for their safety. The Qurayzas could help bring about Muhammad's destruction by attacking him from behind. They could field seven hundred warriors. Muhammad would have to pull fighters from the trench line to repel them, creating an opening for the coalition troops. Huyayy offered to send in warriors through the lava fields to augment the Qurayza forces.

Kab Asad, the Qurayza rabbi-leader, finally agreed, but reluctantly. "O Huyayy, I have entered into what you want detesting it, and I fear that Muhammad will not be killed, the Quraysh will leave for their land, and you will return to your people, while I remain in the center of my land, and I and those who are with me will be killed."[8] Huyayy pledged that if that was the outcome, he would join them in their fate.

Muhammad had eyes and ears everywhere, and a rumor that the Qurayzas had broken their neutrality quickly reached him. He sent Zubayr to determine if they were making preparations to fight. From a distance he saw they were herding women, children, and livestock into their main fortress, and the men were going about armed. After Zubayr reported his observations, Muhammad then sent the Aws chieftain Sad Muadh and several other men to question the Qurayza leaders. A tall, robust man in his late thirties, Sad was a former ally of the Qurayzas. The fortresses and plantations of Sad's Ashal clan, a branch of the Aws tribe, were less than two miles north of the Qurayza territory. They had supported one another in the intertribal wars a decade earlier, fighting side by side against the Khazraj and their allies. Sad was admitted into Kab Asad's fortress and grilled the Jewish leader about the rumor that he had broken his agreement with "the Messenger of God." Kab bristled and denied there had ever been an agreement with Muhammad. "Who is this 'Messenger of God'? We have no pact with Muhammad."[9] Sad warned them they were setting themselves up for a disaster if the Meccans and their allies left in defeat. The Qurayzas were not powerful enough to fight Muhammad on their own, but Kab reminded him it was the Qurayzas who had prevented the defeat of his Ashal clan by the Khazrajis ten years earlier. It was the Qurayzas warriors who were to be feared, he said. The meeting degenerated into mutual insults and threats. A furious Sad reported what he had learned to Muhammad.

Muhammad's forces were in dire condition. The invasion had come at the end of winter, and his fighters were cold, hungry, and on the verge of exhaustion. They were increasingly frightened by the harrying of the enemy, and the sight of their huge numbers across the trenches drained their confidence. News of the Qurayza defection spread, and the defenders now feared a surprise attack from the rear. These tensions brought out the Machiavellian in Muhammad, and he came up with desperate stratagems to divide his enemy. His first effort was to send word to the Ghatafans that he had a deal for them if they made peace and went back to their tribal lands: He would give them one-third of the year's date crop. He sent an envoy to them, but the offer fell flat. The Nadir Jews had already promised the Ghatafans an entire year's worth of Khaybar dates for their participation in the offensive. In their northern oasis, the Jews produced dates on an industrial scale, and Yathrib was no match for their output. Additionally, Muhammad's people balked at turning over their dates to Bedouin polytheists. Though the negotiations went nowhere, word that their northern allies were talking to Muhammad reached the Meccans and caused them to question their loyalty.

More astutely, Muhammad sent a disinformation agent to stir up mutual suspicions among his enemies. This was a man named Nuaym who had come with the invasion force but who secretly met with Muhammad to tell him he had converted and said he could create mistrust between the Meccans and the Qurayzas by spreading false information. He was a merchant who ingratiated himself wherever he went, and he knew everybody, including the Meccan leaders, the Qurayza rabbis, and the sheikhs of the various tribes of the coalition. No one knew of his conversion so that he was still trusted.

Nuaym first went to the Qurayza leaders and raised questions about the trustworthiness of the Meccans and Ghatafans. He claimed to be privy to information that they could not be relied upon to continue the fight to the end. If they returned to their lands without finishing off Muhammad, it would leave the Qurayzas dangerously exposed. For their own security, the Qurayzas should therefore demand hostages from the Meccans and the Ghatafans as insurance against abandonment. Nuaym then went to Abu Sufyan and told him to beware of the Qurayza Jews. He had come into possession of confidential information that the Qurayzas now regretted taking sides with the coalition, and they hoped to mend their relationship with Muhammad by demanding hostages from the Meccans and Ghatafans. They would then turn the hostages over to Muhammad in exchange for immunity for their treason. Nuaym went to the Ghatafans with the same story.

The Meccans fell victim to the ploy when they and their allies sent Ikrima, the son of Abul Hakam, and several other men to the Qurayza leaders to work out an attack plan. It was a Friday night, and the Meccans wanted to start the attack the following day. But instead of enthusiasm, the envoys were greeted with suspicion. The Qurayzas would not lift a finger until the Meccans and their Ghatafan allies handed over some of their important people, preferably honored elders, as security so that they would not be left in the lurch. The Jewish leaders were polite but firm, believing the request was reasonable and that the Meccans would act upon it. Additionally, they stipulated that the attack would have to take place on Sunday, not Saturday, as Saturday was the Sabbath. A frustrated Ikrima returned to his camp to inform Abu Sufyan of this development. Recalling Nuaym's warnings, the Meccan leader concluded they were being set up by the Qurayzas. "If they asked me for a goat I would not pledge it," Abu Sufyan fumed. "I will not pledge the elders of my companions so that they hand them to Muhammad to be killed."[10]

The Nadir leader Huyayy Akhtab tried to repair the damage. He urged the Meccans to delay the assault for another day and to give him time to work things out with the Qurayzas, but the Meccans told him the assault could not wait until the Sabbath was over. The situation of the coalition forces was rapidly deteriorating: Some of their horses and camels were dying for lack of fodder; their own food was dwindling; they were cold and exhausted; they could no longer trust the Ghatafans. Moreover, the weather was turning bad.

Following his meeting with the Meccans, Huyayy went to the Qurayza Jews and pleaded with them to drop their demands for hostages and to agree to fight on the Sabbath, given what was at stake, but they refused. Huyayy returned to the Meccan camp to bring Abu Sufyan the news, then returned to the Qurayzas to inform them that the Meccans now demanded hostages from the Qurayzas. The round trips through the lava fields and across the plain to the foot of Mount Uhud were time consuming, and when Huyayy returned to the Qurayzas with Abu Sufyan's demand for hostages, it was already the morning of the Sabbath. The Qurayzas refused to commit themselves to a hostage exchange, and they again insisted on waiting until the holy day was over to attack Muhammad.

It was the Sabbath evening when Huyayy returned to the Meccan camp with the Qurayza response. When Abu Sufyan learned of it, he pronounced it proof they were indeed bent on treachery. By that time, the weather had turned nasty and so had the mood of the Uhud encampment. The coalition forces were huddled around hundreds of campfires. Freezing rain began to fall and picked up in intensity. A frigid wind that had been sweeping through the valley the entire day now picked up force. By late night it turned into a gale. In unrelenting blasts, the winds extinguished the campfires, turned over cooking pots, and upended tents. The men wrapped themselves as best they could to keep warm and crouched next to their hobbled camels.

In a meeting with the coalition leaders, Abu Sufyan denounced the Qurayzas as traitors. Demoralized by their intransigence and by the devastation the wind was causing, he made a fateful decision to end the invasion and return home. He said to the tribal leaders, "Leave, for indeed I am leaving."[11] In a fury, he mounted his camel and kicked it to get to its feet, but in his anger he had forgotten that it was still hobbled and had to dismount to free it. He rode through the camp, ordering the Meccans to load up their tents and follow him home.

Muhammad's cunning was the victor. When it became light out, he and his followers were relieved when they looked across the trench and saw the huge army had vanished.

As usual, Muhammad drew inspiration from the experience. He composed a set of verses about the battle that became part of a Koran chapter called "The Confederates." It included these lines: "O ye who believe! Remember the Grace of Allah, (bestowed) on you, when there came down on you hosts (to overwhelm you): But We sent against them a hurricane and forces that ye saw not: but Allah sees (clearly) all that ye do. Behold! They came on you from above you and from below you, and behold, the eyes became dim and the hearts gaped up to the throats, and ye imagined various (vain) thoughts about Allah! In that situation were the Believers tried: they were shaken as by a tremendous shaking."[12]

While Muhammad worked on his Recital, Huyayy Akhtab, true to his word, joined the Qurayzas in their fortress and awaited his fate.

CHAPTER 23

The Final Solution

The literature informs us that the Angel Gabriel appeared to Muhammad after the coalition forces left and commanded him to attack the Qurayza Jews. The angel happened to look remarkably like a handsome young man named Dihya, the son of Khalifa of the Kalb tribe. Wearing an embroidered turban, the dapper angel trotted into the mosque courtyard on a donkey, and Muhammad went out to talk to him. The angel was soon gone, but Umm Salama, one of Muhammad's wives, saw them talking and was certain it was none other than the real Dihya—all the women of Yathrib could recognize the delectable Dihya.[1] Muhammad set the record straight: That was not the real Dihya, but the Angel Gabriel who looked so much like the real Dihya that it was easy to mistake one for the other. In sermons and in private conversations, Muhammad often compared the appearance of the prophets and the angels to certain members of his congregation. It was to flatter the faithful, but also to give them a way to visualize these creatures of his imagination.

Muhammad went on to elaborate about his meeting with the Dihya of the donkey who was in reality the Angel Gabriel: The angelic version of Dihya informed him he had just returned from pursuing the Meccans as far south as Red Lion. He was the commander of an army of angels, and he scolded Muhammad for having removed his armor while the angelic hosts were still garbed in their battle gear. Their mission now was to assist Muhammad in making war on the Jews. The angel said, "God commands you,

Muhammad, to go against Banu Qurayza. I myself am heading for them and am going to shake them up!"[2]

Muhammad's weary men had already dispersed to their clan compounds and villages. They groaned when he sent heralds to them with orders to put their armor back on and head for Qurayza territory. He also ordered them to delay the obligatory afternoon prayers until they were facing the Jewish fortress.

The literature assures us that Umm Salama was privileged to be able to see the Angel Gabriel, for ordinarily he manifested himself in such a way that only Muhammad could see him. It was not only Umm Salama who had a privileged vision of him that day, but also warriors from a nearby Najjar village. Someone who looked exactly like Dihya told them to put their battle gear back on and wait for further instructions from Muhammad, who would arrive shortly.[3] By the time Muhammad, riding a horse and accompanied by a guard of cavalrymen, got to the village, all the able-bodied men were gathered. He stopped his horse in front of them and said, "Did anyone pass by you?" They said, "Yes, Dihya al-Kalbi passed on a mule with a saddle." Muhammad stunned them with the truth: "That was Gabriel; he has been sent to Banu Qurayza to shake them up, and to cast terror into them."[4,5] He ordered the Najjar warriors to march to the Qurayza territory.

Muhammad and his cavalry went ahead at a gallop. He was accompanied by three dozen of his closest people,[6] an all-star team that included the four future caliphs: Abu Bakr, Umar, Uthman, and Ali; the Aws leader Sad Muadh, who went along despite the arrow wound he had suffered to his forearm; Muhammad's first cousins Zubayr and Sad Waqqas, both made men of Allah many times over; Maslama, the man who carried out the assassination of the Jewish poet Kab Ashraf; Abu Naila, one of the members of the hit team that murdered Ashraf; Talha Ubaydullah,[7] the early Meccan convert and cousin of Abu Bakr who lost several fingers defending Muhammad at Uhud; Abu Ubayda, the Meccan convert who licked the blood off Muhammad's face at Uhud and lost a tooth extracting chain mail links embedded in Muhammad's cheek; Abdullah, the son of the disgraced Khazraj leader Abdullah Ubayy; Abu Hudhayfa, the son of Utba Rabia, the Meccan leader slain at Badr; and another twenty or so notables, all of them veterans of Badr and Uhud. Riding powerful horses and carrying swords, shields, and spears, they formed a praetorian guard around Muhammad.

Muhammad sent Ali and a detachment of the guard ahead to take charge of arriving forces. As soon as he arrived, Ali planted the war banner at a well not far from the Jewish stronghold. When they saw him from the battlement, the Qurayzas knew a siege was about to begin and shouted insults and threats. They threw in insults about Muhammad and his wives as well. One of the believers shouted back, "O enemies of God! We will not leave your fortress until you die of starvation."[8] Over the next few hours, Muhammad's forces arrived by the hundreds and soon totaled three thousand fighters, armed to the teeth with the accoutrements of war. When Muhammad and his mounted guard arrived, Jewish marksmen took aim at him, but he was too far away for their arrows. He pitched his red command tent at the well so that he was within view of the Qurayza stronghold, but beyond the reach of arrows. When Ali informed him of the Jewish insults, Muhammad approached within shouting distance and yelled, "O brothers of monkeys and pigs and worshipers of evil, did you insult me?"[9] The Jews shouted back denials.

Before taking position around the fortress, Muhammad's troops assembled for showy rounds of prayer prostrations with recitations of Koran verses. When it was over he sent fifty archers forward to fire barrages of arrows. The Jews fired back. The shooting continued until dark. By then a shipment of dates sent by one of the Khazraji plantation owners arrived, and Muhammad's people spent the night eating them. The siege resumed the next morning and continued for three weeks.

The Jews were in a hopeless situation: They were not well provisioned, they were outnumbered, and it was a matter of time before they would have to give up or starve to death. After the twentieth day of the siege, seeing they could not last much longer, they sent Nabbash, one of their noblemen, with an offer to surrender provided Muhammad allow them to leave as he had the Qaynuqa and Nadir tribes. Muhammad turned him down. When Nabbash returned to the fortress with the bad news, Kab Asad and the other leaders considered their options. One was to seek protection from the sword by accepting Muhammad's religion and declaring him to be their prophet, but that idea was rejected: They would prefer to die faithful to the Torah and the religion of their ancestors than to accept what Muhammad claimed about himself. Another idea showed the depth of their desperation: Kab Asad suggested they do as the Jewish rebel holdouts at the mountaintop fortress of Masada had done following the destruction of Jerusalem. The rebels chose mass suicide to deprive their enemy of the satisfaction of butchering them one by one. Kab said, "Let us kill our children and our women and then go forth to Muhammad and his companions with our swords drawn; that way we will not leave any responsibilities behind us, and God will decide between us and Muhammad. If we perish, we perish; but we won't be leaving behind any children to worry about. And if we are victorious, we'll certainly acquire other women and children." But the other Jewish leaders found the idea revolting. "Shall we kill these unfortunates? What good would there be in living on after them?"[10]

Word of these discussions spread throughout the fortress; even the bravest of the men trembled and the women and children wept. The leaders finally decided that the only recourse was to throw themselves at the mercy of Muhammad, but it would be best to do so through a trusted intermediary who could intercede on their behalf. They sent word to Muhammad that they wished to speak to Abdul Mundhir, a former ally and friend from the Aws tribe who went by the nickname Abu Lubaba. Muhammad allowed him to go, and when he entered the fortress the Jewish leaders jumped to their feet to greet him. Women and children crowded around him and broke into tears. He was their only hope. He was deeply moved, but he knew there was nothing he could do for them. When the Jews asked him if they should submit to Muhammad's judgment, he said they should do so. The only alternative was for all of them to suffer the painful death of starvation. Muhammad had supply lines and could wait them out, but they were cut off and their provisions would soon run out. When they pressed him about what to expect from Muhammad, he drew his finger across his throat.

The literature reports that no sooner had Abu Lubaba made the gesture than he became gripped with fear and remorse. Muhammad had evidently made it clear what he planned to do to the Jews, and with the throat gesture Abu Lubaba had divulged Muhammad's intention. It was like passing on a state secret to a foreign enemy. He was certain he had betrayed Muhammad,

"O BROTHERS OF MONKEYS AND PIGS!" Muhammad began the siege of the fortress of the Jewish tribe by repeating derogatory names he had called them when they refused to join his religion and accept him as their prophet. The siege lasted three weeks and ended when they surrendered. They begged him to let them leave Yathrib, but he beheaded all of the men and adolescent boys.

and he was now fearful he might suffer the same fate. Instead of reporting back to Muhammad, he fled in panic to the main mosque where he had someone tie him to one the pillars. He made it known that he would not seek release until God forgave him for his vile betrayal.[11]

Hoping for the best, but expecting the worst, the Jews gave up the following day. As the men filed out of the fortress, their hands were bound, and they were forced stand in the hot sun. At a meeting inside Muhammad's tent, some of the Aws leaders begged him to treat their former allies with lenience. They argued that the Qurayzas regretted taking sides against him, having been persuaded against their better judgment by the Nadir leader Huyayy Akhtab. Muhammad had been merciful with the

Qaynuqas and the Nadirs, so he should be equally merciful to the Qurayzas. Banish them from Yathrib as he did with the other tribes. The pressure was such that Muhammad sought a way to shift responsibility for the decision from himself, yet still obtain the outcome he desired. He therefore proposed letting one of the Aws decide the fate of the Qurayzas. When they agreed, he selected Sad Muadh.

By then, Sad was dying from the arrow wound he received during the Battle of the Trench, as the coalition attack came to be known. The arrow hit him in the forearm just above his wrist, and Muhammad personally cauterized the wound with a heated iron rod, a standard treatment for sword and arrow wounds. It appeared to be healing and Sad was among the horsemen who accompanied Muhammad to the Qurayza assault, but during the siege his forearm became swollen to the point that he became incapacitated. He was a tall, stout man who previously had the strength of a bull. When it was clear the infection was spreading and he would die from it, Muhammad sent him to the main mosque to be cared for. A woman named Rufayda had set up a tent in the courtyard to nurse the wounded during the coalition attack and now received the wounded from the Qurayza assault. When Muhammad named Sad as judge over the Qurayzas, his clansmen had to fetch him from the mosque. They mounted him on a donkey and led him across the valley. By then he was feverish and could barely hold himself upright. When he arrived, his tribesmen stood up and formed two rows for him to pass between. Muhammad stood at the end to greet him.

The Aws leader was one of the truest of the true believers. He was among the first of the Yathrib converts, and as clan leader he had brought his people into the fold. He was a Badr veteran who had urged Muhammad to fight the overwhelming Meccan force; he had guarded Muhammad the night of the Uhud defeat by sleeping at his door. He was steady and reliable—an anti-pagan agitator when anti-pagan agitation was needed, a good counselor when good counsel was sought, a guard when guarding was required, a warrior when war was afoot, and a volunteer to cut throats if throat cutting was ordered. Before Muhammad came on the scene, he had been a neighbor and trusted ally of the Qurayzas. He knew their rabbis and had always been welcome among them. But these Jews had refused to accept Muhammad as their prophet, and they had insulted him personally when he sought to dissuade them from joining with the coalition against Muhammad. They were the enemies of God and his messenger and were destined for hellfire. "There is not a people I would like to fight more than those who refused to believe in the Messenger of God," he once said.[12] Sad therefore knew exactly what Muhammad wanted of him, and what Muhammad wanted he wanted.

While Sad was on the way, his clansmen pleaded with him to decide on the side of mercy. "Deal kindly with your friends, for the apostle has made you umpire for that very purpose," said one of them.[13] But Sad was as immovable as the stone idols of the old days. Propped up by men of his tribe inside the crowded command tent, he asked various people including Muhammad if his decision would be binding on them. When the various sheikhs of the Khazraj and Aws—and finally Muhammad—said, "Yes," Sad declared, "I therefore decree that the men among them shall be executed." He also ordered the women and children to be sold into slavery and all the property of the Qurayzas seized and distributed as booty.[14] A beaming Muhammad congratulated him for his decision. "Surely you judge with the judgment of God above the seven heavens."[15]

The Qurayza prisoners were roped together and marched to a fortress near the center of Yathrib. The women and children, about a thousand in all, were taken to another compound near the mosque. The contents of the Jewish fortress and the other properties of their territory were inventoried for future distribution as booty. In the main fortress they found fifteen hundred swords, three hundred suits of armor, a thousand lances, and fifteen hundred shields. In the lodgings fine furniture and silver utensils were discovered. The conquerors also uncovered amphoras containing wine. The contents were spilled out and the huge jars were retained as booty. Of even greater value was the real estate of the Qurayza territory: the blockhouses and villages, the barley fields and date plantations—the accumulated wealth of generations.

When he was back at the mosque, Muhammad ordered a trench dug in the main marketplace of the Najjars that would be long enough, deep enough, and wide enough to accommodate the bodies of all the condemned men. The work began after he had breakfast in one of the food stalls of the marketplace.[16] It took until the early afternoon for the trench to be completed. Surrounded by the usual inner circle—the "distinguished among his companions," as Waqidi phrases it—Muhammad ordered the captives to be brought out from the imprisonment compound for execution. The Qurayzas had spent the night praying, reciting the Torah, and encouraging one another to find strength in their faith. When the time for their deaths arrived, Muhammad's companions took them out five or six at a time. Hands bound, they were marched to the marketplace and beheaded by either Ali or Zubayr.[17]

The Nadir leader Huyayy Akhtab was among the first to die. He was wearing an expensive red garment that he had ripped in many places so that it would have no value as booty. He was brought before Muhammad, who taunted him that God had granted him the victory, not the Jews, which meant he was guided by the truth, not the Jews. Huyayy replied, "I do not blame myself for opposing you."[18] Muhammad signaled for him to be taken away. He was led to the edge of the trench, forced to his knees, and his head was cut off.

When the Qurayza leader Kab Asad was brought before him, Muhammad taunted him that he had had a chance to accept him as the true prophet and join his religion, but now it was too late. The Qurayza leader replied: "If the Jews did not reproach me about fearing the sword I would have followed you. But to me is the religion of the Jew." Muhammad then gave the order for his execution: "Send him forward and cut off his head."[19]

Nabbash, the Jewish leader who was unable to secure a favorable surrender agreement from Muhammad, struggled with his captors as he was being hauled to the trench and ended up with a bloodied face. Muhammad scolded the guard for hitting him. The guard replied that his prisoner tried to get away, but Nabbash said, "By the Torah he is lying. If he released me I would not delay from the place where my people are to be killed until I am as one of them." Muhammad ordered the guards to be good to the captives. "Let them rest; quench their thirst until they are cool. Then, kill those who remain."[20]

Few of the Qurayzas were spared. Prior to the surrender, several Jews and their families escaped death by fleeing the fortress and announcing their conversion. The day of the executions, one of Muhammad's maternal aunts begged him to spare the life of one of the Jews who was like a family member. She wanted him to come under her protection and promised she would eventually bring him to convert. "He is for you," Muhammad declared. Another whom Muhammad agreed to spare was an old, half-blind rabbi who chose instead to die with his people. He had saved the life of one of the Aws converts more than a decade earlier during the intertribal wars. The convert was indebted to the Jew for this and petitioned Muhammad to allow him to come under his protection, but the old man begged him instead to take his wife and son and their property under his protection rather than him. He would rather die with the rest of the Jews provided his son could live. When Muhammad accepted, the old man went up to Zubayr, sank to his knees, and Zubayr struck off his head.

A young Qurayza woman was also beheaded. During the siege, one of the Submitters was killed by a millstone someone dropped from the battlement. After the surrender, it became known that the woman did it. Her name was called out. As she was dragged to the trench, she laughed hysterically.[21] Boys were killed too if they had reached puberty. If there was any question about their age, they were checked for pubic hair. If so, they were sent to the trench. Men with clothes worth preserving were forced to remove them, so that some of them died naked.

Though it is not mentioned in the literature, it is likely that Muhammad had the pulpit moved from the mosque to the marketplace. One of the early depictions of the massacre shows him presiding over the event while seated in his pulpit. He would have had it transported to the killing site in part to project his authority, but also for comfort, as the beheadings lasted well into the night.

It was a massive undertaking. The numbers reported in the literature range from four hundred to nine hundred men and boys. At a rate of one beheading per minute, it would have taken about seven hours to kill four hundred and more than double that to slay nine hundred.[22] Muhammad's companions performed their tasks as efficiently as assembly-line workers, hustling the men out the prison compound every five minutes in lots of five or six and escorting them to the marketplace.

Once they were knelt at the edge of the trench, Ali and Zubayr quickly lopped off their heads. Assistants swung the torsos into the trench in such a way that it was filled evenly. Down in the trench, torsos, legs, and arms were sprawled in every which way, and sandwiched between the torsos were the heads—face up, face down, sideway, all with severed necks exposed. Though the men were at the height of terror at the moment of death, the severing of their necks relaxed the muscles and gave their faces the appearance of repose, as if they had gone to sleep.

It is likely that Ali and Zubayr advised their victims to make it easy on themselves by bending their necks forward. This would have been more for their own benefit than their victims, as they did not want to have to make multiple swings to get a head off. If they did not do it right the first time, they would end up with a Jew who had fallen on his side shrieking and writhing from pain. They would then have to either get him back onto his knees to get the job done or hack his head off while he lay on his side, potentially dulling or chipping the sword because it would slam into the ground after cutting through the neck. There were too many people to kill to waste time.

Nowhere in the literature is there a report of any of the Jews crying, begging for their lives, or fainting, but it is conceivable some of them lost control of their bowels while they waited for the sword to slash down on them. As they knelt at the edge of the trench and gazed down at what was left of their fathers, cousins, sons, brothers, and uncles, many of them must have wept with grief while others slipped into a semiconscious state of shock and denial.

It is not clear if Muhammad presided over the entire event. In the Waqidi account, he ordered Sad Muadh to take over so that he could attend to other business. Sad was close to death and had to be carried on a litter from the nursing tent in the mosque courtyard to the slaughter site where he was propped up so as to be able to watch the beheadings. If Muhammad did in fact leave, he returned toward the end of the slaughter. By then it was late at night. The marketplace was lit up with torches, and amber light flickered on a dozen Jews who remained to be killed. Early into the executions Muhammad noted that the Khazraj seemed to enjoy watching Jewish heads being cut off whereas the Aws, their former allies, showed signs of disapproval. He therefore

GENOCIDE OF THE QURAYZA JEWS. Muhammad presided over the beheading of four to nine hundred men and boys. According to the literature, they were brought out in batches and forced to kneel next to a trench in the marketplace near Muhammad's mosque. The beheadings lasted from early afternoon until late at night—one every minute for seven to fifteen hours. Muhammad's first cousins Ali and Zubayr did most of the beheading.

decided to force their participation in the slaughter. Teaming up two Aws for each of the twelve remaining Jews, he ordered them do the beheading instead of Ali and Zubayr. Some were eager, most were not, but fearing accusations of hypocrisy if they did not comply, they slew the last of the Jews.[23]

The trench was filled the following morning. The dirt was heaped higher than the ground level, mounded like a fresh grave in a cemetery, and it eventually subsided with the decomposition of the bodies. The stench of death must have persisted for a long time. Given the timeframe for digging the trench, it could not have had great depth, and methane and other gasses of putrefaction would have seeped through the earth and spread over the marketplace like ground fog.

WOMEN AND CHILDREN witness the beheading of their loved ones. Some, perhaps even all, of the women and children were forced to watch. A young woman was also executed for having killed one of Muhammad's men during the siege of the Qurayza fortress. When the slaughter was finished, Muhammad sold the women and children into slavery and used the proceeds to buy weapons and horses.

In most reports, Sad Muadh died soon after the slaughter. Several versions are given, each with variations in detail, but all agreeing that he died in the nursing tent in the mosque court-yard. In one of the mythologized versions, Muhammad learned about his death during the night from the Angel Gabriel, who woke him to give him the news. Muhammad then rushed to the tent and found his comrade dead. In another account, Muhammad was at his bedside when he died. It happened quickly: Sad's swollen arm burst like a balloon, splashing Muhammad's face and beard with blood, and Sad bled to death. In a third and more likely version, Muhammad was informed by someone other than an angel of Sad's death. The nursing tent had been pitched in a corner of the mosque courtyard close by his living quarters, so it did not take long for him to reach the tent. He tugged on Sad's shirt to see if he was dead, and when it was clear he had expired, Muhammad ordered his funeral. The body was wrapped in the usual burial shrouds, and it was carried on a litter to a nearby cemetery reserved for the faithful. There, Sad's body was lowered into the grave, and Muhammad said prayers over him.[24]

No sooner had the mass grave been filled in than Muhammad turned his attention to the tricky task of distributing the Qurayza booty in a way that satisfied everybody. The plunder of real estate, livestock, weapons, and human beings formed the biggest take yet, far outmatching the Nadir and Qaynuqa plunders because there were now a thousand women and children included in the booty. Muhammad retained a portion of the real estate for himself, and the rest he evenly divided among the clans of the Aws and Khazraj as communal property. Everything else was put up for auction and the proceeds—minus Muhammad's cut—were distributed among the fighters, who numbered three thousand.

The disposition of the women and children involved complex transactions. They could not be carved up and distributed in parts to the three thousand men. Rather, most were sold and the proceeds were turned over to a paymaster to distribute. Muhammad divided the captives into five portions of two hundred each and kept two hundred for himself. The literature indicates he gave many away as presents or to settle outstanding debts. He freed some who agreed to adopt his religion, and he retained others as servants. Of the remaining eight hundred, two of his chief people—future caliph Uthman Affan and the early Meccan convert Abdul Rahman—had the wherewithal to buy entire portions, or two hundred slaves each. Uthman opted for older women because they had a higher value than younger women and children. Both men were astute businessmen and made a substantial profit over time through the resale of their slaves. The money they initially paid for them was handed over to the paymaster, who then distributed it in equal shares to the participating warriors.

There were still another four hundred women and children to dispose of. Muhammad had them taken under armed guard to slave markets in northern Arabia and Syria. The money obtained from their sale was used to buy weapons and horses, but in order for the men who took part in the Qurayza attack to get their fair share, the horses and weapons had to be resold in Yathrib. The money from these sales was then turned over to the paymaster. The horses fetched high prices. They were seen as good investments because fighting in Muhammad's cause was far more lucrative on horseback than on foot, as it was now the policy that a horseman received three shares of the booty whereas the foot soldier got only one.

One of the captives who fell to Muhammad was a beautiful woman, very likely a teenager at the time, named Rayhana, whose husband was among the beheaded. After the Qurayzas surrendered and came out of their fortress, the female captives were paraded before Muhammad. As messenger of God and commander of the faithful, he had first pick of the booty, and Rayhana was his pick from among the women shown to him. When he saw her, he became enamored of her beauty, and he offered her freedom if she married him and joined his religion, but she refused. Rather, she made it clear that she had no choice in the matter of his ownership of her, but that his religion was repugnant to her, and she would remain Jewish. She therefore became his sex slave and was given a room in the wives' quarters. It is said that he kept aloof from her, but it is more likely she kept aloof from him. Only hundreds of yards away from the mosque was the mass grave where her husband and everyone she had loved were buried, and it was a perpetual reminder of the horror he had inflicted upon them.

The literature relates that one day a servant informed Muhammad that Rayhana had accepted his religion, and this "gave him pleasure."[25] She died four years after the massacre, a year before Muhammad's death. The cause of her death is not given, but it cannot be ruled out that it was the consequence of a prolonged depression from being forced to live with the killer of all that she had cherished. Her spirit died first, then her body.

Muhammad gloated about the massacre of the Jews and his confiscation of their property in two Koran verses: "And those of the people of the book who aided them (the Meccans) - Allah took them down from their strongholds and cast terror into their hearts, (so that) some you slew, and some you made prisoners. And he made you heir of their lands, their houses, and their goods, and of land which you had not frequented (before). And Allah has power over all things."[26]

CHAPTER 24

All Rise!

Religion was law and Muhammad was the lawgiver. He
fancied himself Moses coming down from the flashing
mountain with the commands of the Lord inscribed on stone
tablets, but he was Moses with a much broader mandate.
Whereas the Jewish patriarch brought the commandments to
his own people, Muhammad saw himself as messenger of the
Lord to the entire world. His grandiose idea of himself expanded to the point he believed he was chosen to transmit the
law even to the invisible *jinn* as a comprehensive set of rules
that defined the narrow path leading to Paradise.

His role as lawgiver and rule maker started out as an arbiter. After he settled in Yathrib, people came to him to resolve
their disputes. He was an outsider who was seen as impartial
in a valley where no one was impartial. At first, he arbitrated
civil matters and brought people together to work out mutu-
ally agreeable solutions. One of the first cases he was asked to
resolve had to do with a dispute over water, a frequent problem
in a valley where agriculture was the dominant activity. Some
property owners had dammed riverbeds to retain water during
the dry season, but in so doing they deprived agriculturalists
downstream. The ones who were harmed sought out Muhammad. How he reconciled the matter is not known, only that he
brought all parties to a resolution.[1]

He was also sought out to arbitrate claims dating back to
the intertribal wars that had ended years earlier with the battle
of Buath. The Khazraj still had complaints against the Aws,

the Aws against the Khazraj, and the several Jewish tribes also had claims stemming from their alliances with the polytheist tribes. Most of these matters had to do with blood money, but also with seized property. He brought people into agreement as to who had the right to what. People also came to him about family matters, inheritance issues, contract disputes, and more.

After he established his *al-qaeda* with the construction of the mosque, Muhammad dropped the role of arbiter and began to impose solutions. He held court at the mosque, and he became the judge and jury of matters big and small. He backed himself up with the authority of commands that he issued in the form of Koran verses, giving them the appearance of divine decree. These verses, spread over numerous chapters and frequently repeated with nuances, gave the general idea of his law; his handling of cases became the precedents for their application.[2]

Civil matters were often heard in private, as people were reluctant to have their affairs aired publicly. These were generally held in Aisha's room. People were ushered in through the curtain that separated the room from the preacher platform, and they sat cross-legged facing Muhammad. The demand for private hearings became so heavy that at one point he charged a fee in the form of charitable donations, though for people without means he substituted additional prayers.

Anecdotes abound about civil matters he ruled on, some amusing, some not so amusing. One of the amusing ones concerns a woman who demanded a divorce from her second husband because of his penis size. "His sexual organ is minute like a string," she complained. She pulled a thread from her garment and held it up to show Muhammad how small it was. Her situation was complicated. She wanted to return to her former husband who had divorced her, but he now wanted her back. Under the divorce rules Muhammad established, however, she first had to remarry and consummate the marriage. If the second marriage did not work out, then she could obtain a divorce and remarry her first husband. But penis size got in the way of her reuniting with her former love, as she had not been able to have sex with the second husband. The second husband did not contest the divorce, therefore Muhammad granted it to her, but he ruled she could not return to her previous husband due to the lack sex in the second union.[3]

This bizarre twist came about as a result of Muhammad's effort to make divorce harder for men. Previously, it was a matter of saying "I divorce you," but men frequently changed their minds and wanted the wife back, but then in a fit of anger would divorce her again. Muhammad came up with a three-strikes rule to make men think about divorcing: After the third time, he could only get his wife back if she remarried and later divorced.[4] This rule did not have its intended effect, however, as a man who wanted his former wife back would sometimes hire someone to marry her, sleep with her, and then divorce her. Muhammad railed against the practice and threatened hellfire, but it was difficult to punish offenders because it was hard to come up with witnesses.

Another amusing incident involved a woman named Khuwaylah whose husband divorced her using a pagan divorce pronouncement that compared having sex with her like having sex with his mother. Not long after the pronouncement, the husband changed his mind because he wanted to resume having sex with her, but she refused to let him touch her and went to Muhammad about it. "O Allah's Messenger," she wailed. "He spent my wealth, exhausted my youth, and my womb bore abundantly for him. When I became old, unable to bear children, he pronounced the Zihar on me!"[5] After she gave him the story of her marital woes, Muhammad fell into a showy swoon, and when he came out of it he said, "O Khuwaylah! Allah has revealed something about you and your spouse." He informed her that if her husband really wanted her back, he would have to expiate his insulting language by freeing a slave. Khuwaylah, however, replied that her husband did not own any slaves. Muhammad then gave an alternative: The husband had to fast for two months, but Khuwaylah shook her head. That would not work because he was an old man; he would not survive a fast of that length. "Then have him donate a camel load of dates to the poor," Muhammad continued. "But we are poor," she lamented. He burned had through the money she had when they got married. Muhammad ended up giving her a bushel of dates and told her to match it and distribute the dates to the poor, then her husband would once again have a right to her. Khuwaylah was thrilled, not so much that she was returning to her husband, but that she believed she had witnessed

Muhammad in communication with God! For the rest of her life she boasted that her marital dispute had caused God to reveal the opening verses of a Koran chapter that came to be known as "The Pleading Woman," meaning her.[6]

Muhammad's rulings on matters big and small were beyond appeal, as one man found out the hard way. The story is told that the man became upset with Muhammad's ruling in a civil dispute. The nature of the case is not given, only that the man who lost did not agree with it and appealed to Abu Bakr, who replied that Muhammad's word was God's word and it was final. Still not satisfied, he went to Umar's home to complain about it to him. Umar became enraged. How dare he question God's messenger? Muhammad was God's representative on earth. To question his rulings was to question God Almighty. Umar rendered a swift appellate decision. He rushed into his house and raced back out with a sword. Within seconds the complainer's head was lying on the ground.[7]

Muhammad was a prohibitionist at heart, and he used the authority he gave himself through his Koran compositions to regulate and then crush popular activities such as drinking and gambling. Wine was the favored drink and could be readily purchased by the cup in wine shops or bought by the amphora from merchants. People also drank crude beer made from a mash of millet and barley. A beverage derived from fermented dates was also popular as was fermented honey. To what extent alcohol abuse was a social problem is not known, though there are stories of at least one tribe where alcoholism was rampant. At first, Muhammad expressed only disapproval of alcohol, as when he glared at Hamza for getting drunk and slaughtering Ali's booty camels. After Uhud, he scolded his warriors when he learned some of them drank wine before the battle to quell their fear. At first, his chief concern about alcohol was that it clouded the mind and kept people from the contemplation of God, but he shifted from condemnation to outright prohibition as a result of pressure from Umar. Umar's father Khattab was a violent drunk and had often beat him savagely so that Umar grew up hating alcohol and alcoholics. He himself used to get drunk and stagger home from wine taverns, but he ceased drinking after adopting Muhammad's religion. That he petitioned Muhammad to prohibit alcohol and also gambling is clear from the literature, which relates that Muhammad summoned him to the mosque one day to recite a missive from God regarding the matter: "They ask you about intoxicants and games of chance. SAY: In both of them there is a great sin and means of profit for men, and their sin is greater than their profit.'"[8] This condemnation was too weak for Umar. He wanted God to come down hard and ban alcohol altogether. It is recorded that he said, "O Allah! Give us a clear ruling regarding intoxicants."[9] Wanting to please Umar, Muhammad summoned him at a later date to recite another celestial tweet: "O you who believe! Do not go near prayer when you are intoxicated until you know (well) what you say."[10] Muhammad believed that the verse was as clear as it could get and sent a herald out to announce the new law, but Umar was still dissatisfied. He again cried out to the Lord for a clear ruling. Umar finally got what he wanted. Muhammad called him a third time to recite a sweeping prohibition that went beyond alcohol: "O you who believe! Strong drink and games of chance and idols and divining arrows are only an infamy of Satan's handiwork. Leave it aside in order that you may succeed. Satan seeks only to cast among you enmity and hatred by means of strong drink and games of chance, and to turn you from remembrance of Allah and from (His) worship. Will you not then abstain?"[11]

It was a command, not a suggestion. From then on, anyone caught drinking alcohol was dealt with harshly. On orders from Muhammad or anyone else with judicial authority, they were turned over to crowds for punishment. In the early days, they were punched, slapped, beaten with sandals, and hit with the stalks of palm fronds. Eventually, they were publicly whipped by an enforcer, forty lashes being the prescribed punishment. Muhammad's court in such matters could be wherever he happened to be when a violator was brought before him. One frequently told story recalls the time he was visiting someone's home when a drunk was hauled in. He ordered all the men in the house to beat him.[12] Though the pain and humiliation of a beating was considered sufficient punishment, in one instance Muhammad threatened death to a repeat drinker. "If he does it again a fourth time, kill him."[13]

Theft he dealt with more severely. A hand was cut off above the wrist, depriving the offender of the instrument that committed the crime. Amputation for theft was practiced in Arabia previously, but Muhammad codified it and applied the punishment unsparingly. Though at one point he warned that amputation was the penalty even for the theft of an egg, the punishment was generally inflicted for the theft of anything having a value greater than a quarter of a gold coin, or three silver coins, an amount that could buy a shield or body armor. Amputation was carried out as an exemplary punishment: It served as a warning to others because amputees could not hide their missing hand.[14]

When he came down from the flashing mountain, Muhammad was lugging a staggering pile of rules, regulations, prohibitions, and promises regarding sex. He came down with rules concerning who could marry whom, imposed celibacy on the unmarried, prescribed purification rituals following sex, and forbade praying until they were carried out. He forced the segregation of the sexes, imposed the veil on women, and regulated the movement of women outside the home. For adultery he imposed the death penalty, and for sex outside of marriage a severe flogging. Yet, as an incentive to get men to fight for him, he allowed them to take captive women as sex slaves, and he promised unending sex in Paradise to men who died fighting for his cause.

He upended old practices, sometimes on a whim as when he imposed the veil on women. Prior to Muhammad's rule making, the men and women of Arabia were not particularly self-conscious about nudity. If they could not afford ritual clothing, both stripped to the buff to perform the orbits around the Meccan temple. Young women would sometimes sashay through village or town dressed only from the waist down, with their long hair cascading over firm breasts. They decked themselves out with earrings, bangles, and ankle bracelets, and they wore saucy perfumes that trailed far behind them.[15] Even Muhammad liked to ogle pretty women. But for him there was blowback when his harem grew to include a share of young beauties. His own people—believers in the oneness of Allah who feared the punishment of the fire!—were taking to ogling his women. How could they not? Like rows of motel rooms, the doors of their abodes opened on the mosque courtyard, and their coming and going was there for all to see.

The veil was an innovation Muhammad came up with at the time he married Zaynab, his former adopted son's former wife, as a way of shutting out these gawkers. The last straw came when several male guests lingered behind in Zaynab's room following the wedding feast, and Muhammad suspected the real reason was that they desired her as much as he did. Her looks intoxicated them. As with wine and liquor, he put an end to the intoxicant by requiring all believing women from then on to wear the veil. And not just a veil over their face, but also full body cover. Let the lust of no one be aroused by the curvature of those breasts and hips! God called down to Muhammad from the top of the mount: "O Prophet! Tell thy wives and thy daughters and the women of the believers to draw their cloaks close round them (when they go abroad). That will be better, so that they may be recognized and not annoyed. Allah is ever Forgiving, Merciful."[16]

As with everything, Muhammad took it to an extreme. He defined who was permitted to see women without full body cover even when they were at home. Thus women were allowed to wear normal clothes in the presence of blood relatives and in-laws, but if anyone else came to the home, they had to stay behind a screen and speak if spoken to from behind it. They could only come out from behind the screen if they dressed up in full garb. All of Muhammad's wives came under this invisibility rule, including when he took them with him on raids. They were required to ride inside stuffy howdahs, curtains drawn. When encamped, they stayed behind a curtain inside Muhammad's tent to keep from the gaze of men who came in to consult with him about campaign matters.

Muhammad's overturning of old sexual mores was hard on men as well. Previously Arab males enjoyed a robust sexuality, the only complications being paternity. The story is told of a beautiful courtesan in Mecca who had a son who became a famous poet. Meccans by the dozens claimed paternity. Such matters were typically disposed of by tribal councils with a wink and a nod. Men and women indulged in temporary marriages, short-term contractual arrangements that required a dowry, but at the end of the stipulated period, both parties walked. Sexual jealousy had to have been one of the complications of the freewheeling, but there is not any record of blood being spilled because of it. Under the new regime, men who were not married were now required to remain celibate, an inducement to marriage, but many did not have the means to pay for the dowry that was required for marriage. Thus they were eager to participate in raids in order to make money from booty, or even better, score themselves a sex slave. Any unmarried man or woman caught engaging in "illicit sex," as Muhammad branded sex outside of wedlock, suffered a penalty of one hundred lashes and banishment for a year. Adulterers were taken to an execution spot outside the main gate of the mosque and were stoned to death. Before their execution, they were made to suffer one hundred lashes.

Flogging itself was regulated. The punishment had to be inflicted with a knotless, medium length leather whip with a single tip. Men had to be stripped of clothing because clothing could create a barrier to pain, and they were to be whipped all over their body. For women the lashes fell only on the back and shoulders. The lashes could not be so severe as to cut the skin or threaten the life of the victim, but not so weak that they did not inflict severe pain.

Because of the consequences, Muhammad set a high evidentiary bar for adultery. Four pious, upright witnesses were required, and anyone making a false accusation or even accusations that could not be proven would face the whip. "Give me the evidence, or the punishment will be on your back," Muhammad warned accusers.[17] The witness rule was inspired by the rumors of infidelity that had circulated about Aisha. There were not any witnesses; it was all circumstantial. She was left behind on the return trip from the Mustaliq raid; Safwan rescued her and brought her back in full view of the army, yet malicious tongues wagged. Muhammad punished the men and women who spread the rumors, setting the precedent for what would happen to anyone who made false accusations or accusations that could not be proven.

The requirement for witnesses had a downside, however. One man who caught his wife *in flagrante* complained to Muhammad that he did not have enough time to round up witnesses. When Muhammad threatened him with the whip, the man raised his hands heavenward and appealed to God for help. His back was spared when Muhammad came up with several verses to deal with such situations.[18] The solution involved an oath: He had the woman in this particular matter brought before him and made the husband state the accusation to her face four times and then take an oath to God as to its veracity. Then the woman, who knew she would die by stoning if she confessed, swore vehemently four times that her husband was a liar and made an oath in God's name as to her truthfulness. Thus Muhammad washed his hands of it: God would punish the one who lied in the next life.[19]

It was not only the whip and the stone that encouraged compliance to the new law, but also the threat of hellfire. Muhammad equated sex outside of marriage with sin, an offense against God, and God was wrathful with sinners. God would throw the wicked into the pits of Hell and slam the furnace doors shut forever. With sadistic detail, Muhammad used to describe tortures awaiting the damned. The scenes were so gruesome the faithful would sometimes openly weep. Punishment in this life was purification, he told them, and it was less severe than the punishment of the next life. If they accepted punishment in this life with repentance, God would forgive them in the next.

What Muhammad accomplished by equating adultery and fornication with evil was to create sexual guilt and hysteria where it had not previously existed. This can be seen in anecdotes where people confessed their sexual sins to Muhammad, hoping to obtain from him the purification of punishment in this life to avoid the eternal fire in the next. The story is told of a man named Maiz who came before Muhammad to confess to adultery. "I earnestly desire that you should purify me," he said.[20] At first, Muhammad turned away from him, perhaps not wanting to let it go any further, but each time he turned away the man moved so that he stood in front of him and repeated his self-accusation. After he did it for the fourth time, Muhammad said, "Are you insane?" When he replied that he was not, Muhammad sent people to make inquiries about him. Once it was determined he was mentally competent, Muhammad ordered his death. It is said they took him out to the execution site where a crowd hurled stones at him, but he became frightened and broke free. The frenzied crowd chased him to the lava fields on the west side of the valley. "I was among the ones who participated in stoning him," reported Jabir Abdullah, a prominent believer. "When the stones troubled him, he fled, but we overtook him at the lava field and stoned him to death."[21]

A similar case involved a woman. She was a married woman who confessed to an affair, but Muhammad at first rebuffed her. She returned one day and said she was pregnant, proof of her sin, and asked to be purified through punishment. "If you insist," Muhammad said. The execution was delayed until she delivered, but even then Muhammad gave her another two years to nurse the child. When it was weaned, she came before him carrying the child, who was holding a piece of bread. Muhammad turned the child over to someone and ordered her death. Her execution was done differently: She was buried up to her chest so that she could not run away. The crowd hurled stones at her head until life was gone from her.[22]

Much of Muhammad's law was a restatement of Arab practices regarding equal retaliation—an eye for an eye and a tooth for a tooth. These matters involved crimes of violence or accidental injury. People had the option of vengeance or settling through the payment of blood money. Much of his caseload involved determining settlements for loss of life or limb, and he fashioned many Koran verses to deal with such matters. In cases of deliberate violence, he encouraged forgiveness as an option, but did not stand in the way of vengeance, as with a murder incident in which a woman beat another woman to death with a rolling pin. The woman who died was pregnant, and the fetus died with her. Muhammad ordered compensation of a camel for the death of the fetus and turned the woman over to the victim's family for them to impose the penalty. The family beat her to death, presumably with a rolling pin.

Accidental killings or mutilations had to be resolved through the payment of blood money, and Muhammad established the values: Townspeople had to pay four hundred gold coins or the equivalent in silver for the loss of a life. Bedouins paid in livestock: two hundred camels or two thousand goats. A full penalty of one hundred camels was due to someone whose nose got cut off, but if it was only the tip of the nose, half was to be paid. For the loss of a hand or a foot, fifty camels. For lesser injuries, lesser amounts were due. When it came to loss

"STONE THEM!" was Muhammad's command for adulterers. Within a year of his arrival in Yathrib, he ordered the stoning of two Jews caught in adultery. They evidently were converts who belonged to one of the Arab tribes that Muhammad claimed jurisdiction over. Rabbis argued for mercy, but to no avail. They were taken outside of Muhammad's mosque and a crowd stoned them to death. It is said that the man bent over the woman to protect her from the stones.

of fingers or teeth, ten camels were to be paid for each finger, and five for each tooth.

Muhammad resolved some of the cases brought before him by laughing them out of court, as when a man who had lost a front tooth when he bit someone during a fight demanded a tooth in return or five camels. "Were you trying to eat his flesh?" Muhammad said. He gave a thumbs-down ruling and dismissed the plaintiff.[23]

One crime Muhammad never forgave was the killing of a believer, particularly by another believer. He gave a precedent for this after the battle of Uhud when he ordered the beheading of a man who had killed another believer during the battle for having murdered his father a decade earlier. Another believer-on-believer murder came about during one of the military campaigns. A man named Muhallim had been sent with others on a mission, and en route they came across someone whom Muhallim hated because of problems between them that occurred before they embraced Muhammad's religion. Though the man gave the formulaic greeting indicating he was a Submitter, Muhallim killed him with an arrow and stole his camel and belongings. The murderer was dragged before Muhammad, who was sitting in the shade of an acacia tree. The desert became the courtroom, and numerous Bedouins from the affected tribes sat cross-legged in rows in front of Muhammad to watch the proceedings. Witnesses stood up to relate what they knew. Members of Muhallim's tribe spoke about his virtues and begged forgiveness; members of the victim's tribe demanded the death penalty. One of Muhallim's tribesmen threatened to bring fifty people to swear the dead man was not a true believer, that he had never prayed—in short, that he was a hypocrite, in which case the death penalty would not apply because believers could not be killed for killing infidels, no matter what the circumstances. Muhammad offered the victim's family blood compensation: fifty camels up front, another fifty when they returned home, but the victim's family demanded blood. The accused sat in the back until he was summoned to stand before Muhammad. He was young and tall and had tears in his eyes. He acknowledged his crime, but asked for forgiveness. Muhammad's ruling came when he raised his hands to the heavens and said loudly enough for everyone to hear, "May God not forgive you!" He repeated it three times. It was a death sentence, and there was no appeal. The condemned was thrown off a cliff and buried under a pile of rocks.[24]

Unless they repented and swore fidelity to him, Muhammad also killed people for mocking or criticizing him, beginning with the poets he assassinated following the battle of Badr. He also approved when his followers killed such people on their own initiative. The story is told of a blind man who killed his Jewish concubine for railing against Muhammad. She had often criticized Muhammad, but one night she kept berating him even though the husband ordered her to stop. He ended up stabbing her to death. Word of this circulated, and the next day at a mosque assembly Muhammad demanded that the perpetrator stand up and give an accounting. The blind man got to his feet and said, "Apostle of Allah! I am her master; she used to abuse you and disparage you. I forbade her, but she did not stop, and I rebuked her, but she did not leave the habit. I have two sons like pearls from her, and she was my companion. Last night she began to abuse and disparage you. So I took a dagger, put it on her belly and pressed till I killed her." Muhammad accepted the explanation. He said to the congregation, "Be witness. No retaliation is payable for her blood," thus making it legal that people who criticized him may be killed.[25,26]

Before he died, Muhammad ended up formulating rules that regulated nearly every aspect of life as it was then lived in the frontier region of Arabia: real estate, money lending, inheritance, sharecropping, the buying and selling of dates, date trees, and animals—all were matters he concerned himself with. He ruled on how to defecate, how to wash, how to dress, how to address people, what to eat, and what not to eat. The rituals surrounding marriages, births, and funerals all had the stamp of his rules. He forbade music, singing, and dancing as idle activities that took people from the path of God. He devoted attention to ruling on the minutiae of the prayer rituals, pilgrimages, and the sacrificing of animals, all of it ending up as formulas for the faithful. What became Muhammad's law was a combination of Koran verses and his *sunna*—his "legal ways," essentially meaning whatever he himself did in every situation, whether it was a formal pronouncement or merely the example of his behavior. This amalgamation was called then, and it is still called today, the *sharia*, from the word for path. Walk along the path paved with the flagstones of Muhammad's verses and his example, and surely you will attain Paradise.

Throughout much of this, Muhammad employed scribes to capture the hot flashes of his poetic Muse. He was semiliterate, and it is likely dyslexia associated with epilepsy that kept him from ever learning to read or write properly, but many of his followers were literate, and he made use of their skills. "Take it down, take it down!" he would cry out from his bed when emerging from the alpha state or while pacing back and forth. Then out came the stylus and parchment as the scribe faithfully captured his words. Compared to the snappy and occasionally brilliant lines he came up with in Mecca, however, many of the

Yathrib verses are windy and legalistic, as in this verse having to do with breaking oaths: "Allah will not call you to account for what is futile in your oaths, but He will call you to account for your deliberate oaths: for expiation, feed ten indigent persons, on a scale of the average for the food of your families; or clothe them; or give a slave his freedom. If that is beyond your means, fast for three days. That is the expiation for the oaths you have sworn. But keep to your oaths. Thus does Allah make clear to you His signs, that you may be grateful."[27]

One of his scribes, seeing how the sausage was made, apostatized and fled. This was a man whose full name was Abdullah ibn Sad ibn Abi Sahr—Abdullah Sahr for short. He was from Mecca and was an early convert who fled with Muhammad to Yathrib. Because he was intelligent and knew how to read and write, he became one of Muhammad's favorite aides. His skills were used to transcribe contracts, letters, even treaties. When it was Koran composition time, Muhammad kept him close by. It is said that during the course of taking down Muhammad's flashes, Abdullah sometimes suggested slight changes in the wording. On one occasion, when Muhammad ended a verse with "And Allah is mighty and wise," Abdullah suggested "knowing and wise," possibly as a matter of logic or because of a poetic demand for alliteration. Muhammad did not object to his suggestions, and at some point it occurred to Abdullah that the words of a mere scribe were being attributed to God. Being physically close to Muhammad during these moments, Abdullah was able to observe "revelation" moments, and it reminded him of how the poets he knew in Mecca struggled with their Muse to bring forth the best expression of their ideas. He concluded that the Koran did not come from God, but from Muhammad. His faith shattered, he fled back to Mecca, and to the delight of the Meccans, he discredited Muhammad's claim that God talked to him. "Muhammad does not know what he says! Indeed I wrote for him what I wished. This, which I wrote, was revealed to me just as it was revealed to Muhammad."[28]

Muhammad did more than consign Abdullah to the eternal fire. When he conquered Mecca years later, he carried with him a list of people he wanted killed on sight. At the top of the list was Abdullah ibn Sad ibn Abi Sahr.

CHAPTER 25

The Way, the Truth,
and the Life

Muhammad's violence against opponents inside and outside of Yathrib was dictated at first not so much by his desire to spread his religion as by his desire to stay alive. The expansion of his religion was the byproduct of the logic of his violence: The more he attacked and plundered and murdered, the more he made enemies who were motivated to strike back at him; the more they struck at him, the more he needed to strike out at them. He pushed back at these enemies of his own creation through proactive and exemplary violence. Being more motivated through his delusion that God talked to him, he was more ferocious than any of his opponents. He overwhelmed them until his very name caused fear. Though his enemies were able to inflict occasional setbacks on him, they ultimately saw the embrace of his religion as the only refuge from the pain and misery he was able to inflict. The more people sought to shield themselves from him by joining him, the safer he became. Thus his religion grew.

Following the Qurayza massacre, Muhammad had little to worry about any longer in Yathrib. The population, once around twenty thousand, had been reduced to half that number due to the purge of the Jews, but was in regrowth as new converts and an assortment of opportunists lured by the prospect of booty arrived from various Bedouin tribes. The Aws and the Khazraj now formed the bulk of the native population and had almost entirely converted, if only nominally to avoid persecution. From this secured base—all Yathrib now being his *al-qaeda*—Muhammad began raids on enemies to the north, south, east, and west, launching more that a dozen attacks over the course of the next year. As before, he placed great emphasis on plunder, and it was the outcome of most of the raids. The spoils from brigand-age and pillage were his chief sources of revenue and were the superglue that bound his followers to him. Without the bribe of plunder it is unlikely he would have gotten far based only on what he claimed about himself. As historian Muir put it, the prospect of enrichment fanned a "zeal for active service"[1] among people who might have otherwise ignored his call to fight.

The need for such revenues kept raiding parties on the road. Not long after the last shovels of dirt were thrown over the bodies of the Qurayza Jews, Muhammad put Maslama, the man who had murdered the Jewish poet Kab Ashraf, in charge of a plunder raid targeting a Bedouin clan that roamed the desert highlands sixty miles east of Yathrib and was known to possess numerous livestock. Maslama set out with thirty men, and it took them several days to reach their destination and position them-selves for an attack. Muhammad had instituted a policy of early morning surprise attacks, ostensibly to allow for the possibility the targets were converts. If they were, they would make the call to prayer at dawn. The absence of the call meant their targets were *kuffars*, disbelievers—fair game for Muhammad's marauders who were then free to kill and pillage at will. Following this policy, Maslama and his men surrounded the Bedouin encamp-ment before dawn, and when they did not hear the prayer call, they swooped down with cries of "Kill, kill," catching the desert people unprepared. Maslama and his men hacked them to death as they ran out of their tents to defend themselves. The rest of the Bedouins fled, leaving behind one hundred and fifty camels, three thousand goats, and all their tents and personal belongings. The raiders grabbed everything that was transportable and herded the livestock back to Yathrib where Muhammad divvied up the loot, keeping twenty percent for himself.[2]

Around the same time, Muhammad launched a raid on a Meccan caravan that was attempting to sneak through his blockade of the Red Sea route. Given their desperate need for revenue, the Meccans began sending out small caravans along the coast to Syria or across the burning desert to Iraq, hoping to avoid detection by traveling at night. Muhammad learned of one of these caravans on its return from Syria. He sent his now former adopted son Zayd at the head of one hundred and seventy men to attack it. They caught up with it at Al-Is, a coastal village south of Yathrib between Yanbu and Rabigh. Swooping down on the caravan, they slaughtered the men who resisted and confiscated the camels and cargo, which turned out to include sacks of silver coins—profits from the venture. Some of the Meccans escaped, but others were captured and were brought back to Yathrib where they were held for ransom.

Aisha was given a role when Muhammad ordered her to watch over one of the captives. His hands were tied behind his head, but he was able to free himself and slip away while she was chatting with someone. Muhammad was furious. "May God cut off your hand!" he screamed at her before rushing out to organize a search for the escapee. When he returned, Aisha, who had only recently witnessed him cut off the heads of hundreds of Jews, was at the verge of tears. She stuck out her arm to show she was prepared to lose her hand, but Muhammad had already forgotten his outburst. "What is the matter with you?" he said. When she reminded him of his words, he raised his hands to the heavens in exasperation and said, "O God, surely I am a man. I get angry and I regret it just as any other man would. Whichever one of the believing men or women I pray against, transform my prayer into a blessing."[3]

A few months later, a raid against a Bedouin tribe in the region surrounding Fadak, a Jewish oasis north of Khaybar, netted an impressive plunder of five hundred camels and a thousand goats. This raid came about after Muhammad received word the Bedouins were plotting to help the Jews of Khaybar against him in exchange for some of the Khaybar date harvest. Muhammad sent Ali with one hundred men to inflict a punishing blow that would discourage them from joining in plots against him. By the time Ali reached the nomad encampment, however, the desert dwellers had already fled for their lives, leaving behind their livestock and camp gear. Ali returned to Yathrib with the booty, and Muhammad divided it up among the raiders after taking his usual fifth.[4]

The only subjugation raid of this period was directed at the largely Christian town of Duma, which bordered on Syria five hundred miles north of Yathrib and was an important trade center along the east-west caravan route. Muhammad himself had briefly occupied the town six months before the Meccan coalition marched on Yathrib. That raid was launched to smash a suspected buildup of forces he feared could join a Meccan assault on Yathrib. Now a new northern coalition appeared to be forming that included Jews, Christians, and Arab polytheists. By conquering Duma, Muhammad hoped to keep the Christians from joining his enemies. He put Abdul Rahman at the head of seven hundred men and instructed him to wage pure *jihad* against Duma: "Fight everyone in the way of God and kill those who disbelieve in God."[5] Before attacking, Abdul was to invite the people to join Muhammad's religion, warning them of the consequences if they refused. After surrounding the town, Rahman sent word to the Christian ruler that they had three days to convert or they would all be put to the sword. Knowing that Muhammad had slaughtered the Qurayza Jews earlier that year, the Christians took the threat seriously. However, instead of converting, they proposed paying a subjugation tax. Abdul Rahman dispatched a courier to Yathrib with the proposal, and Muhammad sent back an order for Abdul Rahman to seal the deal by marrying the ruler's daughter. He returned to Yathrib with his bride, along with the first installment of the tax.

During this period, Muhammad personally led a raid against the southern Lihyan tribe to avenge the murder of ten of his preachers two years earlier. The Lihyans had lured them on the pretext of wanting to learn about the new religion, but it was a trap to avenge Muhammad's assassination of the chieftain of one of their allies, Khalid Sufyan. If it had not been for the major battles that intervened, Muhammad would likely have undertaken the raid sooner, as he placed great importance on avenging the deaths of his followers. So eager was he to crush the Lihyans that he took extraordinary measures to take them by surprise. They were a branch of the Hudhayl tribe that roamed a wide area northeast of Mecca. But instead of heading south out of Yathrib, he led a force of two hundred seasoned fighters in the opposite direction for more than a day before cutting west to the Red Sea. After traveling south along the coast, he headed inland toward the Lihyan encampment. This roundabout maneuver, taken out of fear of leaks, must have added an additional two hundred miles to the trip, but it turned out to be of no avail. The Lihyans somehow learned of his approach and fled to the mountains, taking their flocks and possessions with them. Muhammad sent out squads to locate them, but they came back empty handed. Seeking to get some benefit from the raid, he led his men farther south to the village of Usfan, about a day's journey from Mecca. This he did with the intention of projecting his power and intimidating the Meccans, but they sent a force of horsemen under the command of Khalid,[6] the cavalry leader who smashed Muhammad's lines at Uhud, to challenge him. This confrontation resulted in a standoff as neither Muhammad nor Khalid had sufficient confidence of prevailing in a pitched battle. Both forces backed off and Muhammad returned home, unavenged and without any booty to spread around. The only casualty of the raid was the reputation of the Lihyans, who were tagged by one of Muhammad's hired poets as "mere weasels" for running away from a fight.[7]

During all of this Muhammad had to deal with rustling attacks on his livestock. Though he returned empty handed from the Lihyan raid, stolen livestock continued to flow into Yathrib, and the scores from recent raids were impressive: fifteen hundred animals here, five thousand there, another two thousand from yet another raid. As a result of these successes, Yathrib became livestock rich, but pasturage poor. Additional grazing land was needed, which created a dilemma: The only source of fresh pasturage was outside of Yathrib, particularly to the east, but at a distance that made protecting flocks from rustlers difficult. Muhammad secured grazing rights with nomads that controlled these areas and sent out shepherds to tend to his personal flocks. He relied on his reputation for ferocious retaliation to keep rustlers at a distance, but it was not always a sufficient deterrent.

Only a few days after he returned from the Lihyan raid, he got word that a Bedouin raiding party had just stolen twenty of his booty camels from a grazing area about a half-day's journey from Yathrib. They killed the shepherd and made off with his wife along with the camels. These camels included one of Muhammad's favorites, al-Abda, a famous racing camel that Muhammad acquired as booty from a recent raid. Upon learning of the attack, Muhammad sent horsemen to chase the raiders and hastily assembled an army of five hundred men to join in the pursuit. The man who sounded the alarm was Salama, son of al-Akwa, a young zealot who was always looking for ways to please Muhammad.

He was on the way to the grazing area either to check up on things or to fetch the day's dairy production—most of these were milk camels that provided a supply that was taken back to Yathrib every day—when he saw the attack from a distance. Forty raiders had come down from the mountains that separated the grazing area from Ghatafan territory to the northeast, and they were already heading back into the mountains with Muhammad's livestock and the shepherd's wife. Salama had come on horseback accompanied by a slave. He sent the slave back on the horse to alert Muhammad. Armed only with a bow, he chased the raiders on foot. They were slowed by the narrow trail of the mountain pass, allowing Salama to catch up with them and shoot at them from behind the sparse trees of the slopes. With each arrow he cried out, "I am Salama, the son of al-Akwa. Today the wicked will die!"[8] His relentless assaults slowed the raiders down to the point that a squad of horsemen Muhammad dispatched caught up and engaged the rear guard in running skirmishes. One of Muhammad's men was killed along with four or five of the raiders. Half of Muhammad's now twice-stolen camels were recovered, but not al-Abda.

It turned out the chief of the Bedouin raiders was none other than Uyayna, the Ghatafan leader who was part of the Meccan coalition that attacked Yathrib only months earlier. He was the man Muhammad attempted to buy off with an offer of a third of the Yathrib date harvest. Uyayna was the chief of a branch of the Ghatafan tribe that roamed a large region to the north and northeast of Yathrib. His importance can be seen in the fact that he was able to bring two thousand fighters into the Meccan coalition. It was perhaps this strength that led him to believe he could get away with rustling Muhammad's camels. Muhammad decided against pursuing Uyayna over the mountain, as the Ghatafan leader would then be in his own territory and would be able to pull together a significant force to counter him.

Instead of continuing the pursuit, Muhammad had some of the recovered camels slaughtered for his men to feast on and sat back at a campfire to enjoy war stories about the skirmishes, relishing the fact that one of Uyayna's sons was among the dead. When Salama told him about shooting arrows at the marauders and shouting, "I am Salama, the son of al-Akwa, and the wicked will die today," Muhammad threw his head back in a hearty, open-mouth laugh and declared Salama the hero of the day. On the return trip to Yathrib, Muhammad honored him by allowing him to ride with him. For the young zealot, this was like being in Seventh Heaven. The mood throughout the ranks was joyful. The troops amused themselves by coming up with extemporaneous verses about their exploits. When they approached Yathrib, someone proposed a camel race into Yathrib. Thanks to his new status, Salama was given a fast camel. The starting gate was a line in the sand. His head still swirling with joy at having earned Muhammad's special favor, Salama jockeyed his mount to a smashing victory.

The captive shepherd's wife, meanwhile, was able to escape and fled during the night on al-Abda, knowing that the camel was accustomed to riders and was swift. She vowed that if she made it to Yathrib alive she would sacrifice it as a way of thanking God. She arrived safe and sound in Yathrib two days after Muhammad's return. He was pleased to get one of his favorite camels back, but when the woman informed him of her vow to slaughter it as a sacrifice to God, he scolded her: "No vow in disobedience to God is valid, nor is one relating to what one does not own," he said, evidently oblivious to the fact that the camel she vowed to sacrifice was one of his first picks of recent plunder.[9]

As if the Bedouin attack on his livestock were not enough, Muhammad also had to deal with thieves from within his ranks. The story is told of eight men from the southern Urayna tribe who came to Yathrib to pledge fealty to him, but at the first opportunity they made off with his camels. They were from healthy open country of the south where the mountains were their walls and the sky their ceiling, and they succumbed to illnesses that were always a problem in stuffy and insalubrious Yathrib, especially during the hot months when flies and mosquitoes spread disease. To help them get better, Muhammad sent them out of town to live with a freed slave he had recruited to tend his milk camels in the same area the Ghatafans had previously raided. He instructed the men to drink plenty of milk to regain their strength, but also camel urine, as he considered it the best medicine. After they put meat back on their bones and felt well again, the Bedouins killed the shepherd and made off with Muhammad's camels. According to the literature, they tortured the herdsman before killing him by cutting off his hands and legs and sticking thorns through his tongue and eyes. Muhammad soon learned of their treachery and sent a former camel rustler named Kurz to hunt them down. Six years earlier, Kurz had successfully stolen some of Muhammad's livestock, but he later converted and gained a reputation as a dependable fighter. Leading twenty men, he captured the thieves and brought them back to Yathrib. As punishment, Muhammad ordered their arms and legs cut off and their eyes gouged out. In one account, he had their eyes seared with branding irons, then ordered them dumped in the lava fields to die of thirst. It is said they died begging for water.[10]

The event inspired Muhammad to compose verses that later became part of Chapter 5 of the Koran. One of the verses gave the penalty for theft: "As to the thief, male or female, cut off his or her hands: a punishment by way of example, from Allah, for their crime: and Allah is Exalted in power."[11] For heinous crimes such as the one committed by the eight Bedouins, he prescribed a harsher penalty: "The punishment of those who wage war against Allah and His Messenger, and strive with might and main for mischief through the land is: execution, or crucifixion, or the cutting off of hands and feet from opposite sides, or exile from the land: that is their disgrace in this world, and a heavy punishment is theirs in the Hereafter."[12]

CHAPTER 26

Peace for Our Time

To Muhammad's inventive mind, the humble cubic temple in humble dusty Mecca became the center of creation. He closed his eyes, and in his mind he saw the resplendent throne of God in the firmament directly above the temple. It hardly mattered to him that two centuries before his time, during the era of Qusay, the temple was merely a rectangular wall of stacked stones so low a goat could jump over it, or that two centuries or so before Qusay that Mecca was nothing more than an uninhabited valley overgrown with scrubby thorn trees, or that two centuries after Qusay, at the time of Muhammad's birth, that the temple was merely a high rectangular stone wall without a roof. To his imagination the Kabah became the original temple of God. It had existed in one form or another since the beginning of creation when it was sent down from Heaven as a brilliant jewel that was transformed by Adam into a place of worship. But now it was fallen. It was in hands hostile to God, and it needed to be liberated and returned to those who worshipped none but the one God.

A year after facing the might of the Meccans across the trench, Muhammad undertook a daring pilgrimage to Mecca. It was a bold move to claim the temple for his God concept, if only symbolically, by doing the seven orbits while his enemies looked on, helpless to do anything about it. Dressed in the white garb of the pilgrim, he set out in the first month of the sacred months accompanied by a force of fifteen hundred men and a herd of sacrificial camels, and he dared the Meccans to do something about it.

The literature relates that Muhammad's inspiration for the pilgrimage came in a dream. He saw himself enter the temple with his head shaved and holding the key to the "House," as the temple was often called. If he did indeed have such a dream, it was a reflection of what he had been contemplating ever since the Meccans abandoned the Yathrib offensive. He was convinced he now had the upper hand and could get away with a journey to Mecca and its temple by using the religious customs of the Arabs as a shield. Would the Meccans dare attack him during the holy months while he and his people were garbed in the white garments of ritual purity? Would they dare to slay him while he was performing rites that they allowed all other Arabs?

Though he counted on the traditional protection of the holy months, Muhammad did not take any chances. His followers were heavily armed and brought along cavalry horses. As they proceeded south, he attempted to beef up his numbers by inviting various Bedouin tribes, believers and nonbelievers alike, to join him in the pilgrimage, but most of them turned him down. Given the harm he had caused the Meccans, they thought him foolish and did not believe he was going to make it back alive. Some declined out of fear his intention was to use them as fodder.

At some point in the journey, Muhammad's men followed his lead by donning the white pilgrim garments. He had dressed so before leaving Yathrib, but traditionally this was carried out at one of the stage stops of the journey between Yathrib and Mecca. Most of the men waited until they reached the demarcation point. "Assuming" the role of pilgrim meant not just wrapping themselves in two white sheets, the upper one being wound or clasped over the right shoulder while the other shoulder is left bare, but refraining from sex and wearing a turban, and foregoing grooming, including hair cutting and nail clipping.

These demands of ritual purity were traditional among polytheistic pilgrims, but during the trip Muhammad could not refrain from coming up with additional rules and regulations. Spinning rules was fundamental to his controlling nature, and he never passed up an opportunity to create laws about matters as they arose, no matter how trivial. On the journey to Mecca, for instance, he forbade hunting for food since it involved killing, and killing was forbidden for pilgrims except for the slaughter of the sacrificial animals when the pilgrimage ended. He decreed, however, an exception for varmints. It was allowable to kill rats, vultures, scorpions, and rabid dogs at any time because they were harmful.

The stricture against hunting, however, gave rise to confusing situations that forced believers to seek clarification. At one of the overnight stops, some desert dwellers who were not part of the pilgrimage came into the Muhammadan camp with three big lizards, intending to cook them for dinner over a campfire while enjoying the conviviality of the pilgrims. They roasted the lizards, offering to share the meat with some of the people in white, but the latter refused to touch it until Muhammad consulted with God. "Eat," Muhammad declared after pondering the matter, "for all that has not been hunted for you is permitted when you are in *ihram* (state of ritual purity). But you must avoid what you hunt or what is hunted for you."[1] A similar situation occurred when one of the believers, a man who had not yet donned pilgrim clothes, came into camp with the carcass of a wild donkey. Unaware of the new regulation, he had gone hunting. When he brought his kill into camp, he found that no one would partake of the meat until they had consulted Muhammad. As with the lizards, Muhammad finessed it with an exemption: The hunter still had not assumed pilgrim status, he ruled, and none of the pilgrims had ordered him to hunt the donkey, therefore the meat was legal to consume. To assure the believers they would not fry in Hell for eating the meat, Muhammad reserved a cut of shoulder for himself and feasted on it.

Then there was a lice situation that arose at al-Abwa, the village south of Yathrib where Muhammad's mother was buried, that also needed regulation. One of the believers, a man named Kab Ujra who had donned the pilgrim garb early in the journey, was blowing on the embers underneath a cooking pot when Muhammad noticed his head was crawling with lice. Even though it was the rule not to shave or cut hair until the pilgrimage was over, Muhammad created an exception for lice infestation and ordered Kab to shave his head, but required him to fast or give something in charity. This ruling soon became part of a Koran verse, and for the remainder of his days Kab boasted that God Almighty himself had taken note of his itchy scalp.[2] Since God stated in his missive that he should give something for the relief from

lice, Kab purchased a sheep from a Bedouin, then branded it
and decked it out with garlands of colored knotted ropes—the
marks of a beast destined for sacrifice.

Muhammad reveled in the roles of legislator, teacher, and
role model. In his mind, his rules, regulations, verses, and the
example of his behavior were shining beacons that showed
the way for anyone who hoped to succeed in reaching the ultimate
destination of Paradise, and he was not shy about proclaiming it.
At one of the rest stops on the way south he ordered his people
to sweep the cool ground underneath an acacia tree so that he
could sit in its shade while giving a sermon. After a large group
of pilgrims crowded around him, he made a statement that was
stunning for its grandiosity: "O People, indeed I exist for you as
a reward. I leave with you, in your hands, what will not lead you
astray, the book of God and its practices," referring to his verses
and his *sunna*, his example.[3]

When the Meccans learned of Muhammad's approach, they were
not sure what to make of it. He was already famous for his declaration that war was deception. Was this a trick? They had the
collective memory of their forefather Qusay and the coup he
staged by sneaking hundreds of foreign warriors into Mecca in the
guise of pilgrims. Thus he and his Quraysh tribe took over control
of the sacred territory and the rites of the temple pilgrimage from
the Khuzas, the tribe that had previously been in control. Qusay
had proven himself to be a master of deception. Did Muhammad
intend to repeat Qusay's ploy?

The Meccan leaders were determined to block him from entering the sacred territory, the boundary of which was roughly
ten miles in every direction from Mecca. They posted spies on
mountaintops to monitor his movements and sent a force of two
hundred cavalry under the command of Walid's son Khalid to
block his path and engage him in a battle if necessary. Additionally, the Meccans threw together a defensive force at home and
sent word to regional allies to come to Mecca's aid in the event
of a fight. Muhammad learned of Khalid's cavalry from a spy who
returned with news of Mecca's defensive actions. Hoping to avoid a
clash, Muhammad hired a local Bedouin to guide his force over
a rugged mountain pass that led to the plain of Hudaybiyya,
which was to the west of Mecca just outside the boundary of

the sacred territory. Despite the maneuver, he and his people were easy to spot. Dressed as pilgrims, they stood out in the distance as an elongated mass of white that flowed down the mountain pass into the brown desert plain below. But Khalid left Muhammad alone. It is said that he refrained from a confrontation because at that time he was contemplating switching sides. Rather than attacking Muhammad, he returned to Mecca to report his movements.

Muhammad set up camp next to a watering hole at Hudaybiyya and waited to see what developed. Before long, a group of Khuza tribesmen, descendants of the tribe Qusay ousted from Mecca two centuries before, showed up in front of Muhammad's tent. The various tribes of the Khuzas had become cooperative after Muhammad crushed and subjugated the Mustaliq tribe, a branch of the Khuzas, eighteen months earlier. They were now Muhammad's eyes and ears in the desert region northwest of Mecca all the way to the Red Sea. Given their history with the Meccans, the Khuzas were favorable to Muhammad even without being terrorized. The leader of the visitors was a forthright man named Budayl Waraqa, who asked Muhammad why he had come. Muhammad explained he had no hostile intentions. They only came with a desire to perform the rites of the minor pilgrimage. This was different from the annual major pilgrimage that began the following month and drew people from all over Arabia. Muhammad pointed out that the minor pilgrimage could be performed at any time of the year, and the rites were limited to making the seven circuits of the temple, kissing the Black Stone, and performing another seven rounds between the mounts of Safa and Marwa—followed by the shaving of the head and the sacrifice of the animals. These were the rites that had developed centuries before out of the belief the Black Stone was a gift of the moon god Hubal. That was all they came for, Muhammad told Budayl, to perform the traditional rites of the Meccan temple, but in the name of the one God. If the Meccans wanted to fight, then so be it. He would fight them.

Budayl took Muhammad's explanation to the Meccans, but knowing the Khuzas had come under Muhammad's sway, they questioned Budayl's truthfulness. The Meccans, therefore, dispatched an ally from one of the outlying tribes to Hudaybiyya, and after questioning Muhammad, he returned to Mecca with the same report they had received from Budayl. Still not satisfied, they sent Hulays Alqama, the Bedouin commander of their Abyssinian mercenaries. When Muhammad, who knew the Bedouin to be a devout polytheist, learned he was approaching, he ordered the herd of sacrificial camels placed in his path so that he would see the neck decorations and the brandings that marked them for sacrifice. It is said that when Hulays saw the animals, he turned back without bothering to talk to Muhammad, convinced they were indeed performing the pilgrimage. He reported his observations to the Meccan leaders at the meeting platform of the temple, but it was not what the Meccans wanted to hear. After listening to his report, one of the Meccan leaders insulted him. "You're only a Bedouin, without any sense!" Hulays retorted, "Shall someone who has come to venerate God's house be barred from it?"[4]

The Meccans were furious. It was clear Muhammad was using their customs to gain an advantage over them. He was hiding behind the security of the sacred months even though he himself had little respect for the tradition. Neither did he have any respect for their tolerance. He was exploiting their openness: The temple was for everybody to worship whatever they wished, but Muhammad tolerated only his own idea of the one God. They again faced the dilemma they had always faced with him: To tolerate Muhammad was to tolerate his intolerance. One of the leaders said, "He shall never come in here against our will, nor shall the Arabs ever say that we have allowed it."[5]

They dispatched Urwa Masud, a citizen of Taif whose mother was Meccan, to relay their decision. He was the son of one of the Taif leaders who ran Muhammad out of town ten years earlier. A self-confident man, Urwa was not intimidated by Muhammad. Once he was seated cross-legged next to him, he firmly stated the Meccan position and noted that they were already gearing up for battle. Muhammad would have to fight his way through to get to Mecca, and the outcome would not necessarily be favorable to him. Looking around at the mix of people in Muhammad's tent, Urwa questioned whether they would stand by him if it came to a confrontation. "By God, I'll wager these people will abandon you tomorrow!" he declared. This angered Abu Bakr more than Muhammad. Knowing that Urwa was from Taif, Abu Bakr shouted, "Go suck al-Lat's tits! Us abandon him, indeed!"[6]

Urwa persisted. He hoped to persuade Muhammad to go back to Yathrib, but Muhammad was unyielding: He and his people came to perform the rites at the temple, and they wanted to do so peacefully. They would fight if attacked. However, to make it worth their while to resolve the matter peacefully, he was prepared to offer the Meccans a truce that would allow them to resume their commerce with Syria without fear of attack.

Urwa was an astute observer. While he was with Muhammad he noted the reverence people had for him. When his followers talked to him, they spoke in a low, respectful voice and did not look at him directly. Any command he issued, it was immediately obeyed. When Muhammad at one point washed his hands in a bowl of water, people took what was left and daubed themselves with it or drank it. The same any time he spat: Someone would stick his hand out so that Muhammad could spit into it, then the recipient would smear the spittle on his skin and share it with others. Urwa was also startled to find that Muhammad had attracted an exceptionally dangerous desperado to his religion—Urwa's own nephew Mughira, the son of his brother Shuba. While palavering with Muhammad, Urwa had leaned close and stroked Muhammad's beard, an Arab custom intended to show trust. As he did so, a warrior wearing a steel helmet that covered everything but his mouth and eyes tapped his hand with the flat of his sword and said, "Remove your hand from the face of the Messenger of God, or you'll never get it back!"[7] When Urwa, who thought the voice sounded familiar, asked about the man behind the helmet, Muhammad seemed extremely pleased to inform him that it was none other than his nephew Mughira.

Urwa was stunned. His nephew was a fugitive mass murderer. He and a confederate robbed and murdered some people in the vicinity of Taif, causing a serious blood feud between the two major tribes of Taif, then he went to Egypt with a group of thirteen Taif traders. On the way back to Arabia, he murdered all thirteen of his companions while they slept and stole their possessions. Urwa only now learned the sequel: Mughira ended up in Yathrib where he swore allegiance to Muhammad and his religion, and Muhammad now used him as an errand boy and bodyguard. When Urwa went back to Mecca to report what he had seen, he advised the Meccans to work out some kind of a deal with Muhammad. "I have seen people who would never abandon him for any reason. So draw your own conclusions."[8]

The Meccans, however, did not give Muhammad a response. When he did not hear back from them, he sent a Bedouin from the Khuza tribe to repeat the message that he had given to Urwa, that he desired only to perform the rites at the temple. But the Meccans assaulted the Bedouin before he could speak. It is said that Ikrima, the son of Abul Hakam, slashed the foreleg of the envoy's camel, and all that saved the Bedouin from death was the intervention of the commander of the Abyssinian troops, who was upset at the rude treatment the Meccans had given him. He and some of his soldiers surrounded the Bedouin and escorted him out of town. After the hapless envoy reported his failed mission, Muhammad decided to send Uthman, one of the most important of his inner circle, because he was from one of the prominent families of Mecca. The Meccans were likely to listen to him. He sent him accompanied by a guard of Meccan expatriates who wanted to visit their families. As Uthman approached town, he met an acquaintance who gave him his personal protection by allowing him to ride behind him on his camel. He took Uthman to the temple platform where Abu Sufyan and Safwan, the son of Umayya Khalaf, and other notables were assembled. After Uthman relayed Muhammad's message, Abu Sufyan informed him that the Meccan position remained as before—no entry would be allowed for Muhammad. But they would extend to Uthman the courtesy of allowing him to perform the temple orbits. Uthman declined. "I could never circumambulate it before the Messenger of God did so."[9]

About that time, the tense situation worsened when Ikrima, acting on his own initiative, led a troop of seventy cavalrymen to harass Muhammad and take hostages, but some of the Meccans were captured instead. Ikrima had gone off with his cavalry after he attacked the Khuza envoy Muhammad had sent, and the Meccan leaders only learned of his action and of their captured compatriots while Uthman was speaking with them at the temple. The Meccans promptly arrested Uthman and the people who accompanied him and held them hostage. A rumor quickly reached Muhammad's camp that Uthman and his companions had been killed. Muhammad vowed to fight, but perhaps remembering Urwa's prediction that his men would abandon him if it came to a battle, he demanded a pledge from the each of the pilgrims to stand their ground and fight to the death if necessary. A herald went through the camp announcing that the "holy spirit" had descended upon Muhammad, who now commanded them to come out of their tents and go to him to make a pledge "in the name of God" to fight the Meccans.[10] For this pledge, Muhammad was seated in the shade of an acacia tree. Over the course of several hours, the pilgrims fell to their knees before him, and one by one they grabbed his hand and swore not to flee if it came to combat. They would defend him and his cause with their lives.

The pledge turned out to be unnecessary. Muhammad realized that the rumor of Uthman's death was false when Suhayl Amr rode into the camp. The Meccans would not send one of their prominent men to him if Uthman had been killed. Suhayl was the former brother-in-law of Muhammad's wife Sauda. He was captured at Badr and held prisoner for a time in Sauda's room at the mosque. Muhammad knew him to be a reasonable man, so if the Meccans sent him it meant they wanted to negotiate. He was now certain he had the upper hand: The Meccans had been weakened by the deaths of so many of their leaders, and they were financially drained by the enormous cost of sending out armies. Their economy had also been shattered due to his interdiction of their vital trade with Syria.

When Suhayl was brought to his tent, Muhammad was surrounded by his closest people, all of them seated cross-legged. Standing behind Muhammad were the usual warriors wearing helmets with face masks. The guards forced Suhayl to kneel before the group, and one of them warned him not to raise his voice when speaking to "the Prophet." Suhayl apologized for the harassment of the Meccans against Muhammad's camp, saying it had been undertaken by people who had no standing in Mecca and whose opinions were of no account. Muhammad agreed to Suhayl's offer for a prisoner swap—Uthman and his companions in exchange for the Meccans he had captured.

Once the exchange of prisoners was accomplished, Suhayl and Muhammad worked out what came to be known as the treaty of Hudaybiyya. Under its terms, Muhammad would be not be allowed entry into Mecca that year, but could return the following year. The Meccans would permit him to undertake the pilgrimage the same month of the following year, but he would be limited to a three-day stay, and he and his followers would be allowed to enter with sheathed swords only. No other weapons would be permitted. Furthermore, both parties agreed to a ten-year cessation of hostilities, a truce that would allow the Meccans to resume their commerce to Syria. Additionally, the agreement forbade secret treaties and alliances among the tribes of the region. Tribes could align themselves with whomever they pleased, but it had to be done openly.[11]

Of lesser importance was an agreement to return young people from Mecca who joined Muhammad in Yathrib without the permission of their father or guardian. The Meccans, however, would not be obligated to return anyone from Yathrib who sought refuge in Mecca. This clause came about because more of Mecca's youth were converting to Muhammad's religion, including Suhayl's son Abu Jandal, and the Meccans struggled with how to deal with them. It was a problem they had faced ever since Muhammad began proselytizing nearly two decades earlier. As had other Meccans with rebellious children, Suhayl imprisoned his son when he refused to renounce the religion.

After they came to terms, Muhammad dictated the agreement to Ali, who wrote it down on parchment. But Suhayl disagreed with the opening language: "By the Name of God, the most Beneficent, the most Merciful. This is the peace treaty which Muhammad, God's Apostle, has concluded." Suhayl said, "If we knew that you are God's Apostle we would not prevent you from visiting the temple and would not fight with you." He told Muhammad to identify himself instead as Muhammad, the son of Abdullah. Muhammad said, "By God! I am the Apostle of God even if you people do not believe me," but Suhayl's wording prevailed.[12]

Muhammad's followers were unhappy with the agreement, particularly Umar. They had come all that way believing they would perform the rites of pilgrimage only now to be told they must return to Yathrib, yet it was Muhammad's dream of entering the temple that triggered the pilgrimage. Umar complained about it to Muhammad and to Abu Bakr, decrying it as an agreement that benefited the polytheists, but diminished their religion. He was vehement when he said in essence, "Are we not believers and are they not infidels? Aren't our dead in Paradise and theirs

in Hell? How can we make a treaty with people we should kill?"
Muhammad shrugged it off. While it may have appeared to
be of more benefit to the Meccans, he saw it as a resounding
victory. He had gotten much more out of the trip than he had
hoped for. He was facing an ever-increasing threat from Jewish tribes to the north of Yathrib and polytheistic tribes to the
east and north. He had received intelligence that the Jews of
Khaybar were forging alliances with the Jews of Fadak, Wadi
al-Qura, and other northern Jewish settlements. The powerful
Ghatafans and other nomadic tribes were also entering into
alliances against him. If they ever combined their forces, they
had the potential to crush him. A truce with the Meccans would
free him to concentrate on his northern enemies. He had the
big picture, Umar did not.

The pilgrims were also unhappy and balked when he ordered
them to finish the rites of the pilgrimage then and there at Hudaybiyya. What was left of the pilgrimage involved shaving or
trimming their hair, slaughtering the sacrificial animals, then
putting their usual clothes back on and heading home. The
opposition vanished after Muhammad initiated the slaughter.
After shaving his head, he cried out, "In the name of God most
great,"[13,14] and slit the throat of his sacrificial camel with a
spear. Following his example, the pilgrims slaughtered the
other sacrificial camels, and they spent the day feasting on
roasted and stewed meat.

On the return trip, Umar became gripped by panic for having argued with Muhammad over the treaty, fearing he had
condemned himself to eternal hellfire. Though hot-tempered,
he was unusually timid in the presence of Muhammad and spoke
to him in a voice that was at times so low that Muhammad
had to tell him to speak louder. When the details of the treaty
became clear, however, he lost his timidity and the real Umar
came through. He had been loud and obnoxious, but not with
just anybody; he had been rude to the most perfect man in the
world, the man whom God had chosen as his messenger! Now
he was in fear that God would "send down" verses branding
him a hypocrite, a phony believer, sealing his fate for eternity.
Umar's worrying took place while the long column of pilgrims
plodded northward, mounted on camels with their horses in
tow. His fears about his future became heightened when, after

trotting his camel up close to Muhammad, he called to him timidly, but Muhammad ignored him. This happened three times, throwing Umar into a panic. It felt like the contents of his stomach were rising to his throat. "Your mother has lost you, O Umar!" he said to himself.[15] He spurred his camel to get to the head of the column so that he would at least be out of hearing range when the divine condemnation came. Before long he heard a herald cry out his name, summoning him to Muhammad. He said the Arabic equivalent of "Oh, crap!" and turned his camel around. But when he reached Muhammad, he realized he had let his imagination get away from him. Muhammad had not even heard his greetings because he had been communing with God! He now greeted Umar cheerfully and said, "O Umar, a verse has been revealed to me that is dearer to me than what the sun rises over."[16] He recited the first verse of a new chapter he had composed since leaving Hudaybiyya. It began, "Verily, We have given you a manifest victory."[17] God, he went on, had just given him glad tidings of forgiveness and the perfection of his goodness and help, and he had given assurances of the greatness of those who obeyed God and his messenger.

Word raced through the entire column that a "Koran" had just been revealed and that Muhammad was about to recite it. People hobbled their camels and rushed forward to listen. Much of Muhammad's recital was standard fare: The faithful would earn a place in eternal gardens beneath which rivers flow, while hypocrites and polytheists and anybody who refused God and his messenger were destined for eternal fire. He recapped the major events of the pilgrimage; he criticized people who refused to join the pilgrimage and ridiculed their excuses; he praised the people at Hudaybiyya who pledged to die for him; he assured them that God kept them back from warring on Mecca only because innocent, secret believers in the town might have been slain: "If they had been apart, We certainly would have punished the Unbelievers among them with a grievous punishment."[18] He finished the recital by assuring the faithful that his dream of entering the sacred temple of Mecca would be fulfilled at some future time—God willing, of course.

What was strikingly new in this Koran chapter was his declaration that *jihad* was now obligatory. Previously, fighting for the cause had been voluntary and many avoided it. Thenceforward the only excuses would be blindness, lameness, and illness. Mu-hammad backed up the mandate with divine carrots and sticks: Paradise awaited those who obeyed the command to fight; hellfire would be the reward for those who disobeyed. He also held out the promise of imminent booty to everyone who had taken the pledge at Hudaybiyya, repeating it several times. "God will soon grant him a great reward,"[19] and, "Many gains will they acquire,"[20] and, "Allah has promised you many gains that you shall soon acquire."[21]

It was perhaps the finest performance he had ever given. He was sitting in the high saddle on al-Qaswa, his favorite she-camel. He spoke in the pleasing cadences that he learned from Halima, and his strong voice carried far. Of the fifteen hundred people present, perhaps half were true believers. The rest were a mix of fence sitters who neither wholly believed nor wholly disbelieved, the nominals who thought it was in their best interest to pretend, and the outright opportunists who could smell good moneymaking prospects from miles away. For the true believers, it was a magical moment. Most had never before witnessed their beloved prophet communing with God, but here it was unfolding before their eyes: God intersecting with man through Muhammad and revealing his divine will! The more imaginative among them could visualize light streaming down from the heavens and hosts of angels in the sky. It is difficult to believe they did not feel a thrill everywhere a thrill could be felt—particularly when Muhammad came to the verses that promised booty.

The treaty with the Meccans was soon put to the test when a young Meccan convert named Abu Basir showed up at the Yathrib mosque and asked Muhammad for asylum. The Mec-cans had been holding him against his will, but he escaped and made the journey to Yathrib on foot. The Meccans sent a bounty hunter with a letter that asked Muhammad for the return of Abu Basir and reminded him of the Hudaybiyya treaty. Muhammad had no choice but to hand the defector over. The bounty hunter had come with a freed slave to help him keep watch over the man, but barely ten miles out of Yathrib, Abu Basir made a grab for the bounty hunter's sword and killed him. The freed slave fled for his life. Abu Basir chased him, but the freed slave made it to the mosque and threw himself at the mercy of Muhammad. The killer showed up not long after riding the bounty hunter's camel with his victim's belongings in tow on another. He told Muhammad he had behaved like a man true to his faith and offered Muhammad a fifth of the booty, but Muhammad declined. "If I take a fifth, they will think that I have not fulfilled my contract with them."[22] When the terrified freed slave refused to have anything more to do with repatriating Abu Basir, Muhammad banished the Meccan defector from Yathrib. Now an outcast, he went to the Red Sea coast where he quickly earned a reputation for banditry. He was soon joined by seventy other young Meccan defectors, including Suhayl's son Abu Jandal. They appointed Abu Basir as their leader, prayed together five times a day, attacked Meccan caravans, and killed every infidel they could get their hands on. The situation became so desperate that the Meccans ended up begging Muhammad to take them—all of them—regardless of the treaty. He took them in.[23]

Another test came when a female convert from Mecca fled to Yathrib and asked for asylum. She was the daughter of Uqbah Muayt, the man who had once slopped camel entrails onto Muhammad's back while he prayed and whom Muhammad executed after the battle of Badr. Two of her brothers soon came to Yathrib to demand her return, but she played the damsel-in-distress card: "O Messenger of God, indeed I fled with my religion to you, so keep me and do not return me to them, they will prevent me from leaving and hurt me. I have no patience with pain. I am a woman and women are weak, as you know."[24]

After doing some thinking on the idea of returning a faithful woman to a den of polytheists, Muhammad unilaterally changed the terms of the Hudaybiyya treaty to exclude the forced repatriation of women. He backed it up with a new Koran chapter that came to be known as "The Woman to Be Examined." "O you who believe," Muhammad said in his God voice, "When there come to you believing women refugees, examine (and test) them. Allah knows best as to their faith. If you ascertain that they are Believers, then do not send them back to the Unbelievers."[25] After publicizing the new verses at the mosque, Muhammad informed her brothers that he was sorry, but he was obligated to obey the law of God and keep them in Yathrib. In another verse of the same chapter, however, he allowed the Meccans to keep married women who fled to them from Yathrib provided they reimburse a deserted husband for her dowry. This verse was inspired by the flight of two of Umar's wives. Evidently fed up with him and Muhammad's religion, they escaped to Mecca and refused to go back. Umar divorced them, and one of them later married Muawiya, a son of Abu Sufyan. According to the traditions, Umar was never reimbursed for his dowry.

CHAPTER 27

God's Mercy to Mankind

"And we have not sent you except as a
mercy to mankind."—Koran, 21:107

The "many gains" Muhammad promised his disappointed followers at Hudaybiyya was the wealth of the Jews of Khaybar. The truce neutralized the Meccans as a threat, clearing the way for him to attack the Khaybar Jews and seize everything that belonged to them, just as he had done to the Jews of Yathrib. For several months, he kept his intentions to himself, then one day he ordered the mobilization of the people who had accompanied him to Hudaybiyya. When the word spread the target was Khaybar, many others stepped forward to sign up, but Muhammad rejected them because they had not been a part of the pilgrimage. He accused them of volunteering only out of a desire for plunder, not from a desire to advance his religion. They could join, but only for the sake of the cause; they would not be awarded booty. It was his way of teaching them a lesson, but by cutting them out of the spoils of war he ended up with a relatively small fighting force of fifteen hundred men.

The Khaybar oasis was one of the richest regions of western Arabia. It was a narrow, serpentine, fertile valley that had been carved between ancient lava beds. It was famed as the date farm of the Hijaz and was also noted for its vegetables, grains, silk garments, metal tools, and instruments of war. A half-dozen clans tied together by blood and religion lived in fortresses and surrounding villages, each with its own plantations and fields. Some of the plantations were industrial in size. One boasted of forty thousand palm trees, another twelve thousand. With so much produce and merchandise to trade with the outside world, the

Khaybar Jews enjoyed a standard of living that made them the envy of the less industrious.

Apart from the prospect of booty, Muhammad's motivation for the attack was his prophet conceit. As had the Jews of Yathrib, the Khaybar Jews refused to adopt his religion and accept him as their spiritual master. Instead of embracing him, they were plotting against him. On more than one occasion he had received intelligence of Khaybar Jews offering the Ghatafans a share of their date harvest to help them against him. He interpreted this as proof of a conspiracy to attack him, but it appears the Jewish intention was defensive rather than offensive. His war machinery was growing, and they sought the help of the more numerous Ghatafans to protect their oasis in the event of an attack. Thus when rumors reached them of Muhammad's pending assault, Kinana, one of the Nadir leaders who settled in Khaybar after being driven from Yathrib, made a hurried trip to the Ghatafan leaders to arrange for military assistance.

Hoping to launch a surprise attack, Muhammad made a lightning journey north, covering the distance between Yathrib and Khaybar in only three days. He also sent agents in advance to spread rumors an army was heading for the exposed Ghatafan encampments, which were located on the desert plateau that began where the vast lava plains ended. The stratagem worked. Ghatafan reinforcements had already reached Khaybar or were on the way, but rushed back to their territory when they heard rumors that their own people were endangered. Upon nearing Khaybar, Muhammad placed his army, which included from one to two hundred cavalrymen, at a strategic mountain pass to block the Ghatafans should they return, thus securing his rear.

The camp was about six miles from Khaybar, and served as the base for the initial phase of the attack. That began at dawn. Under cover of darkness, the assault force moved to the edge of the lava crags overlooking the valley. Following his policy, Muhammad waited to hear if there was a dawn call to prayer, always music to his ears, before initiating the attack. It appears absurd that he should wait for such a prayer call from a Jewish community that was implacably hostile to him, but it followed the pattern he had set: Everything he did was his *sunna*, the example of his behavior that advanced "God's" cause. Believers were required to follow the instructions of his Koran, but also his *sunna*. He therefore took care to be consistent and waited for the prayer call even though he knew it would not be forthcoming. It is said that he prayed while waiting for the call by petitioning God to grant him the "good" of the Khaybar valley, meaning booty and prisoners. The final words of the prayer represent a textbook example of psychological projection: "And we seek refuge in You from its evil, from the evil of its people, and the evil of what it contains!"[1]

The Jewish fortresses were numerous, arranged in three major clusters that were spread through the long valley, imposing stone structures amid the lush green of the date plantations. The major clan fortresses were built either at the top of the lava fields overlooking the valley, or they were constructed on rocky prominences within the valley. The most formidable was a castle built atop a mount that stood more than a hundred feet above the level of the tree tops. It had a secret water supply— spring water diverted into a hidden tunnel carved through the rock that was accessible from the castle high above. The Jews were early risers, and as it grew light the attackers saw them leaving the protection of their compounds with hoes, shovels, and other agricultural tools to begin the day's work. The Jews had anticipated an attack, but did not realize it was imminent. Muhammad gave the attack signal by shouting, "*Allahu Akbar!* God is most Great! Khaybar is ruined!"[2] On horseback and swift camels, they poured into the valley shouting, "O Conqueror, kill, kill!"[3] Everywhere the Jews raised the bandit alarm: "Muhammad is coming! Muhammad is coming!"

Instead of bringing their warriors together into a single army to take on the invaders, the Jews chose instead to lock themselves into their separate fortresses, hoping to outlast the attack. Each of the compounds was provisioned with food and weapons and had access to water. This defensive strategy proved to be a mistake, as Muhammad ended up taking the fortresses one at a time. The siege began with the first cluster of strongholds called Nata, whose central fortress belonged to a Jewish warrior named Marhab. Muhammad laid siege to Marhab's castle for more than a week without being able to break through its heavy main gate. Each evening, his fighters returned to the security of the distant camp out of fear of night attacks if they remained in the valley. For the first few days, Muhammad was immobilized by a severe migraine headache that kept him laid up in camp. He gave the leadership to a succession of commanders, but they were unable to break into Marhab's fort and returned to camp each night with their wounded and dead. One of the first casualties among Muhammad's men was Maslama's brother Mahmud. Someone dropped a heavy stone on him from the castle battlement, crushing his head. He was brought back to the camp and died three days later. Frustrated by the lack of progress, Muhammad ordered date palms within view of the castle to be cut down as a way of inflicting suffering on the Jews, for he knew that each tree was as dear to them as a firstborn son. Four hundred trees were felled before Abu Bakr appealed to him to put an end to the wanton destruction. They were too valuable as eventual plunder.

Near the end of the first week, Jewish warriors came out of the fortress to challenge Muhammad's people to duels. The first was Marhab, the lord of the castle, a tall, strong, and heavily armored warrior celebrated for fierce bravery. The literature gives several versions of the duel, which ended in Marhab's death. In one, Ali took up the challenge and killed him with a ferocious blow that sliced through Marhab's helmet. In another version, Maslama asked Muhammad for permission to fight Marhab in reprisal for the death of his brother. After exchanging numerous sword blows with Marhab, Maslama cut off one or both of his legs and left him to bleed to death, but Ali stepped in to cut his head off and stripped the body of weapons and armor, leading to a dispute over who had the right to the booty. Muhammad decided in favor of Maslama. It is said that Marhab's brothers came out one after another to duel with Muhammad's people, and they too were killed.

The big break for the attackers came when a Jew either defected or was captured and persuaded to cooperate. Muhammad learned from him that the Jews were terrified and had moved their women and children from Marhab's castle to other fortresses farther down the valley. The Jew told Muhammad of siege weapons hidden in the castle—a catapult and two battering rams with roofs that protected the carriers from arrows and from rocks dropped from above. He also offered to show them how to get in through a secret passage, but the literature also raises the possibility he was allowed to return to the castle and opened the gates from the inside. Most of the Jewish fighters escaped over the walls and fled to neighboring strongholds. Those who put up a resistance were overpowered and killed. Some attempted to hide, but when they were discovered they were forced to their knees and beheaded.

The taking of Marhab's castle was an important victory because it gave Muhammad a foothold in the valley. He moved the camp from the highlands to the castle where they were secure against counterattack. His troops, however, complained that after all their efforts, they still did not have much booty to their credit. Furthermore, there was a shortage of food. They had left Yathrib with only enough provisions for the trip to Khaybar and they expected to live off the fat of the land from then on. Not much that was edible was found in Marhab's castle, and now food was running short. Many of them had their last meal the day before conquering the fortress, and this came about because of the showy heroics of one of the fighters. Some sheep had gotten out of the Jewish compound, but they were close to the castle walls, within range of arrows. Muhammad asked for a volunteer to grab the sheep by saying, "Which man will feed us from these sheep?" A man who was famed for his goofy gait said, "I will, Messenger of God!" Dodging arrows, he grabbed an ewe under each arm and ran back toward his lines, his eyes bulging and his head thrown back like a fear-crazed ostrich. Muhammad was thrilled by the performance and gave him the equivalent of a standing ovation. "O God, let us enjoy him long!" he exclaimed.[4]

But two sheep divided among fifteen hundred men hardly amounted to more than a mouthful for each, if even that. In desperation, some of the troops rounded up a number of donkeys and slaughtered them. Pots were already stewing the meat and the fighters were getting ready to chow down when Muhammad found out about it. He declared that eating the meat of donkeys was forbidden. Like pigs, donkeys were known to eat excrement, so they were unclean. He gave an order for all the cooking pots to be overturned. The famished fighters grudgingly complied.

Muhammad was in a rule making mood that day and came up with a list of new injunctions. One even worse than the ban on donkey meat was a ban on sex with captive women, at least at the time of capture. That was a tough one because such sex was one of the perks and was as much a motivator to fight for the cause as was booty. Muhammad had never had a problem with it before. Captured women had always been fair game for rape, but no longer: It turned out it was displeasing to God. Muhammad stood among his men in the courtyard of Marhab's castle and listed the new restrictions, beginning with the one regarding captive females: "It is not permissible for a man who believes in God and the last day to mingle his sperm with that of others."[5] He clarified it so that even the dullest among them would understand: That meant they had to let enough time elapse to ensure she had not been impregnated by her husband. She had to have her period, and then they could have all the sex with her they wanted. If it turned out she was pregnant, they could not touch her until she delivered. He also ruled out the practice of short-term marriages—pleasure marriages as they were called, the equivalent of one-night stands. This practice had been taken up by believers to get around his earlier rulings against sex outside of marriage, which was punishable by a severe flogging of the unmarried and a painful death by stoning if adultery was involved.

The other injunctions had to do with the theft of booty. Pilfering of plunder had become a serious problem. In earlier raids and battles, people had taken things from the booty piles before they had been apportioned to the rightful people. Believers would grab a horse or a camel, ride it until it was exhausted, and then return it. Or they would take clothing, only to return it in tatters. Or they would take things and not return them at all. Muhammad informed them this was displeasing to God. Even if he never found out about it, it was impossible to hide such things from God because God knew everything. They could not even hide their thoughts from God, let alone their petty thefts from the booty piles. Thieves be warned: A stolen garment would become a garment of fire that God would wrap around the thief; a stolen pair of sandals would turn into flaming footwear that would fry crooked feet forevermore.

Overturning the pots of donkey meat was a brilliant motivational move for Muhammad. Hungry warriors were ferocious warriors, particularly once informed that the next castle on the hit list was heavily stocked with food. The turncoat Jew had informed Muhammad that one of the fortresses of Nata belonged to a Jew named Sab and was one of the best provisioned of the valley. The next day Muhammad's men quickly breached its doors with one of the battering rams confiscated from Marhab's castle and poured into the fortress. As had occurred with Marhab's castle, most of the Jewish warriors fled over the walls and those who were unable to escape died. The army feasted on the stashes of food found inside. Among the provisions were enormous amphoras of wine. Muhammad ordered the jars to be overturned or smashed and warned against imbibing, but one of the believers—Abdullah the Alcoholic he was called—could not resist and ended up slobberingly drunk. Muhammad beat him with his sandal and turned him over to his companions for further pounding, but he was so far gone he did not feel any pain. With a dopey smile, he sat down cross-legged with everyone when food was brought out, and the men watched him wobble in place while they ate.[6]

The last of the major Nata strongholds was called Zubayr's castle, a seemingly impregnable fortress built atop a sheer rocky mount that towered above the plantations. Many of the warriors from the conquered castles had fallen back to Zubayr's fortress. It required an exhausting climb along a steep path just to get to the castle gate, ruling out the use of siege machines. It was supplied water through a secret tunnel that allowed spring water to pool inside the mountain as in a cavern. A turncoat named Ghazzal led Muhammad to the tunnel, and Muhammad diverted the water. Though well-provisioned with food, the occupants of the soaring fort could not survive long without water. After a three-day siege a number of Jewish warriors came down for a pitched battle with Muhammad's people. Ten of the Jews were slain. It was apparently a diversionary tactic. While the fighting was going on, the remaining warriors escaped to the next major plantation region, which was known as Shiqq.

After mopping up the Nata area, Muhammad marched his army to Shiqq and began the siege of the major strongholds there. The first fell within a few days, beginning with sword fights between Jewish and Muhammadan champions and ending when Muhammad's forces smashed through the heavy gate. They found plenty of food and livestock inside. Most of the Jewish warriors were able to fall back to another Shiqq fortress called Nizar, one of the largest castle in the entire valley. With an outer wall that surrounded the castle, it was considered the strongest and most defensible of all the fortresses, so much so that the Jews moved two thousand of their women and children there. The defenses were strengthened by the men who fled from the defeated strongholds. Muhammad used the catapult seized from Marhab's castle against the Nizar walls. The catapult was a clumsy device that was difficult to aim, but it hurled heavy rocks. With incessant pounding, one of the walls was eventually breached, and Muhammad's forces took control of the castle.

One of the captives was Safiya, the seventeen year-old wife of the Nadir chieftain Kinana. She was the daughter of Huyayy Akhtab, the Nadir rabbi whom Muhammad beheaded along with the Qurayza Jews fifteen months earlier. Kinana was the nephew of Abu Rafi, the Jewish leader who was murdered months earlier by Muhammad's squad of assassins. Kinana had sent his wife to the Nizar castle along with the other women and children of his clan thinking they would be safe within the sturdy walls.

After cleaning out the pockets of resistance at Shiqq, Muhammad moved on to the final region of Khaybar called Katiba where the Nadir castle and two other imposing forts were located. The strongest of these was called Qamus, the fortress that had belonged to Kinana's family for generations along with the properties in Yathrib that Muhammad seized three years earlier. When he learned Muhammad was marching on Katiba, Kinana and his warriors formed a battle line in front of the fort with the intention of fighting a pitched battle, but when they saw the size of the army they retreated inside and rained down arrows on the attackers. The siege ended when Muhammad positioned the catapult and prepared to pummel the fortress. With two-thirds of Khaybar already in Muhammad's hands, Kinana realized that further resistance was useless and sent word he wanted to talk peace. After Muhammad guaranteed his safety, Kinana arrived with other leaders from his tribe and worked out an arrangement similar to the one granted to the Nadirites three years earlier when they were driven from Yathrib. Muhammad agreed to spare their lives in exchange for their weapons, fortresses, and plantations, but this time they would also have to surrender of their wealth in gold, silver, and jewelry. They could leave Khaybar with as many personal belongings as they could pack onto their camels, but nothing more. The two remaining fortresses of Katiba also surrendered under the same terms. Soon, all the Khaybar Jews begged for similar treatment.

The confiscation of Jewish wealth began with their weapons. In Kinana's castle alone a hundred coats of chain mail, four hundred swords, a thousand spears, and five hundred bows with their quivers were found, but none of the gold and silver the tribe was known for was uncovered. Hoping to have something to start over with if they were exiled, Kinana had buried the tribal treasures in the ruins of an older part of the Qamus fort. This wealth consisted of gold necklaces and bracelets, and gold and silver dinnerware such as goblets and serving dishes, all family heirlooms. He hid these treasures while the siege of Shiqq was ongoing, believing it was only a matter of time before Katiba also fell to Muhammad.

Hiding these objects turned out to be Kinana's undoing because Muhammad knew beforehand of their existence. To mock him, the Nadirs made a showy display of their gold, silver, and jewelry when he drove them from Yathrib, but the existence of these treasures had been common knowledge even before then as the Nadirs used to loan them to rich Meccans for weddings and other celebrations. Muhammad demanded that Kinana turn all of it over to him, but he denied having the treasure any longer. He had to sell everything, he told Muhammad, to raise money for weapons and provisions. "We saved it for such a day as this. The war and provisions for the warriors left nothing behind."[7] Muhammad warned him against lying: "Do you know that if we find you have it I shall kill you?"[8]

It is said Muhammad learned where Kinana hid some of the treasured possessions by grilling his cousin Thalaba, a son of the assassinated Abu Rafi. He revealed that he had seen Kinana pottering around in some ruins next to the Qamus fort at night. Muhammad sent his cousin Zubayr with Thalaba to the ruins and they came back with a bulky leather sack containing bracelets, bangles, anklets, necklaces, earrings of gold, and other valuable adornments.[9]

Muhammad demanded to know where the goblets and trays and utensils of gold and silver were hidden. When Kinana refused to speak, Muhammad had Zubayr torture him. According to the literature, Zubayr either seared Kinana's chest with a red-hot branding iron, or he kindled a fire on his chest and kept stoking it until the Nadir leader was close to death.[10] Given his interest in the gold and silver dinnerware, it is likely Muhammad

conducted the interrogation. Despite the torture, Kinana did not
give up the remaining treasure. Muhammad turned him over to
Maslama, who took him to the edge of a date plantation and cut
off his head as vengeance for the death of his brother Mahmud
in the earlier Nata battles. The same fate befell one of Kinana's
brothers, who was also tortured, interrogated, and beheaded.
The bodies and heads were left next to a trail that cut through
the Nadir date plantation.

Following these beheadings, all the Khaybar prisoners were
assembled, and Muhammad allowed his men to stake claims on
the females. Dihya Kalbi, the handsome Submitter and Angel
Gabriel look-alike, rushed to Muhammad to ask for first pick
of the women taken from the Nizar fortress, and Muhammad
told him to go select one. He chose Kinana's wife Safiya, but
after his choice became known, one of the believers went to
Muhammad and told him that the beauty of the young woman
Dihya had chosen made her more worthy of him than Dihya.
Muhammad wanted to get a look at her: "Call him along with
her." When Muhammad saw her he said to Dihya, "Take another slave girl from the captives."[11]

The story is told that Bilal, the freed slave who performed
the prayer calls, brought Safiya to Muhammad from the Shiqq
castle, but deliberately led her along the path where the bodies of
Kinana and his brother had been left so that she would see what
was had been done to them. With Safiya was her sister-in-law.
Safiya was numbed at the sight of the bodies, but the sister-in-law
shrieked and clawed at her hair and face. She was still hysterical
when they were brought before Muhammad. Muhammad, whose
temporal lobe could not tolerate the high-pitched cries of grief,
shouted, "Take this she-devil away from me!"[12] He scolded Bilal
for insensitivity for letting the women see what was left of the men
he had just butchered. "Had you no compassion, Bilal, when you
brought two women past their dead husbands?"[13] Bilal replied,
"O Messenger of God, I did not think that you would hate that.
I wanted her to see the destruction of her people."[14]

Muhammad turned sweet with Safiya and kept her under
protective guard until it was time to head back to Yathrib. It is
said that he proposed marriage to her before leaving Khaybar. He
gave her a choice of accepting his religion and marrying him, or
she could remain in her religion but she would then be his slave,

his concubine. Were she to accept the former, her promised her that her freedom would be her dowry. It is said that she chose to join his religion.

Before the army left Khaybar, Muhammad's fighters specu-lated about his plans for the beautiful young woman. It was the talk of the encampment. Would he marry her? Muhammad always kept his intentions to himself, but they would know his plans if he made her wear a veil. That would indicate a marriage was in the works. As the army prepared to depart, the people watched intently as Muhammad helped Safiya onto his camel. He gallantly knelt on one knee so that she could use his thigh as a step to climb onto the double saddle. When she was mounted, Muhammad threw a cloak over her. It was like raising a flag. The mantle was the veil! The news swept through the ranks of a coming marriage, and the warriors winked at one another and broke into smiles.

A stickler for rules, Muhammad had to obey his own edict and wait before sleeping with his captive to ensure she was not pregnant, but he did not have to wait long. Safiya's period began before they left Khaybar and ended while they were on the road. The marriage took place at a stage stop midway between Khaybar and Yathrib. Muhammad's aunt Safiya was among the women who accompanied the Khaybar attack, and they joined in preparing the bride for the marriage. They bathed her, anointed her with perfumed oil, and dressed her in one of the gowns taken from Khaybar. The wedding feast was a simple affair: Dates, stew, but-ter, and other dishes were served on leather dining mats spread out on the ground. The first guests were the elite of Muhammad's companions including Ali, Abu Bakr, Umar, and Uthman. When they were done, others were invited to partake of the meal. Mu-hammad spent the night with Safiya in his tent. During the night, Abu Ayyub, the man who hosted Muhammad in his home while the mosque was under construction, served as a self-appointed bodyguard by stationing himself outside armed with a sword. In the morning, Muhammad was disturbed to find him there and wondered if there was something peculiar about him, but Abu Ayyub explained his behavior: "I was afraid for you with this young lady. You had killed her father, her husband, and many of her relatives, and till recently she was an unbeliever. I was really afraid for you on her account."[15]

Safiya is portrayed in the literature as seemingly indifferent to the fate of her people because she joined Muhammad's religion just after he slaughtered them and took their land and wealth, but Muhammadan literature is not known for psychological realism. In the real world, she would have been severely traumatized; her mind would have shut down to protect herself from the horror of it all. She would have been in a state of shock the moment she saw what had been done to her husband and others of her family. She had not even begun to grieve when she was claimed as a sex slave by their killer, a man forty years older than her who desired to possess her because of her youth and beauty. It was the same man who had driven her and her tribe from Yathrib three years earlier and beheaded her father, Huyayy Akhtab, the following year during the mass murder of the Qurayza Jews. Numbed and cheerless, she would have yielded to anything her dangerous captor wanted.

Much later—long after Muhammad was dead—she admitted to her real feelings. She told the early gatherers of tradition: "I thought of the Messenger of God as the most hateful of men for killing my father and husband."[16] She went on that Muhammad used to rationalize his behavior to her. Her father had "incited" the Arabs against him and was in part responsible for the attack of the coalition forces on Yathrib. He deserved what he got. The literature does not indicate if Safiya pointed out the obvious to him, but it is likely she reminded him that her father had rallied people against him because he had taken everything in Yathrib that belonged to him and his Nadir tribe—fields, plantations, fortresses, weapons. To this Muhammad would have had a ready response: The Nadirs had plotted to kill him, didn't she know? He had gone to their fortress regarding a matter of blood money, and while he was standing at the fortress gate they plotted to drop a heavy stone on him from the battlement to kill him. Her father was the chief of those plotters. Muhammad knew of it with absolute certainty because the Angel Gabriel had warned him of their evil intention. That is why he drove her Nadir tribe out of Yathrib and confiscated their property. Their scheming was at the root of it. They rejected the guidance that God had given him; they refused to accept him as the anointed of God; they were jealous because prophethood had passed from the Jews to the Arabs,

MUHAMMAD INTERROGATES KINANA, the leader of the Nadir Jews of Khaybar, while one of his men pours lamp oil onto a fire that was started on his chest. Muhammad tortured him so that he would reveal the whereabouts of tribal treasures he had withheld that included gold and silver dinnerware, precious stones, and other valuables. Despite the torture, Kinana refused to reveal their location, and Muhammad had his head cut off.

and so they resorted to plotting against him. Safiya let him drone on. "Eventually all that left my mind," she said.[17]

The official death count from the fighting at Khaybar is put at ninety-three Jews and fifteen of Muhammad's followers. There were likely many more victims who did not enter into the count, such as people who were summarily killed after surrendering and the male members of Kinana's extended family who were put to the sword.[18]

Shortly after the victory, Muhammad came close to joining the death count. This occurred at a dinner where he was fed poisoned meat. In his hubris as conqueror, he could not imagine that anyone would dare to cause him harm and so accepted a food offering from a Jewish woman—an entrée of roast mutton that she had seasoned with poison. The woman was Zaynab, the daughter of the chieftain of the Nata region and niece of Marhab, whose fortress was the first to fall to Muhammad. Her husband was Sallam Mishkam, one of the Nadir rabbis who used to debate theological questions with Muhammad during his first year in Yathrib, but later openly mocked him. Sallam was killed at the siege of Marhab's castle where he had gone to join in the defense, but had fallen gravely ill and was killed on his sickbed after Muhammad's forces stormed the castle. Zaynab had lost everyone: her father, her uncles, her brothers, and her husband, and she hoped for vengeance by poisoning Muhammad. Once presented with cuts of the seasoned leg and shoulder, Muhammad and several of his men bit into the meat, but he spat it out without swallowing and warned, "Stop! It is poisoned!"[19] The only one who had swallowed any of the meat was Bishr al-Bara, the believer who was said to have participated in the torture and beheading of Kinana's brother. Bishr died from the poison. Sallam's widow was dragged before Muhammad. She admitted to poisoning the meat, but gave a clever explanation: "I wanted to find out if you are a prophet. Because if so, God would make you aware of it. And if you were an impostor, I'd be ridding people of you."[20] The literature is inconsistent about her fate. Some sources say Muhammad spared her, others that he ordered her execution and she was either beheaded or crucified.

The plunder from Khaybar was staggering, more valuable than all the booty from the raids and attacks of the previous six years combined. Muhammad ended up devoting more time sorting out the plunder than he had spent conquering Khaybar. Apart from the real estate, the wealth to be distributed was a cornucopia that included the most recent Jewish agricultural output of dates, date products, oil, honey, and barley. It included ample flocks of sheep and goats, and herds of camels and horses. Additionally, there were household furnishings galore, either locally manufactured or imported; tools of the various trades such as blacksmith hammers, anvils, and bellows; stocks of imported textiles that included bolts of velvet, silk, and cotton; arsenals of weapons including swords, spears, armor, lances, maces, shields, bows, arrows, quivers, and siege machines. Beyond that were large caches of gold and silver coins, jeweled adornments, and gold and silver dinnerware. After seeing what Muhammad did to Kinana

MUHAMMAD TAKES SAFIYA as his wife. Following the torture and beheading of Kinana, Muhammad forced his benumbed seventeen-year-old widow into marriage. He was told of her beauty and had her brought before him. He proposed to her while the headless body of her husband lay in a palm grove nearby, promising her freedom if she married him and adopted his religion.

and his family for hiding their treasures, none of the Jews dared to hide any of their wealth from him.

Muhammad reduced the complexities of the plunder distribution with sweeping edicts. Everything taken from Nata and Shiqq would go to the troops; everything from the Katiba region was his. He divided Nata and Shiqq into one thousand eight hundred shares—one share for each foot soldier and three for each horseman. He appointed an administrator to oversee the distribution. One of the administrative tasks was to assess the value of seized goods such as bulky furniture so that it could be auctioned. It was easier to distribute money than bulky goods. With the news of the fall of Khaybar, merchants flocked to the oasis to make offers. The story is told of a recent convert, a Meccan merchant named Hajjaj Ilat, who was eager to turn a profit, but it happened that all of his money was tied up in Mecca. He hastened to Mecca to collect what was owed to him. The Meccans were eager to hear news about Khaybar. Thus far, they only knew that Muhammad had laid siege to it, and they were rooting for the Jews. Many had placed bets on the outcome. Hajjaj thought up a ruse that would ensure he could quickly collect what was owed to him: When he arrived in Mecca, he breathlessly announced that Muhammad had been defeated; many of his men had been killed. Muhammad was now a captive, and the Jews intended to turn him over to the Meccans. Hajjaj explained that he needed to get his money quickly so that he could rush to Khaybar and bid on what had been seized from Muhammad and his people. The Meccans were so overjoyed that they were almost dancing in the streets, and they fantasized about what they would do to Muhammad once they got their hands on him. The ruse worked. Hajjaj was able to get his money and get out of town before the Meccans learned the truth.

As a matter of pragmatism, Muhammad decided that the surviving Jews should remain as sharecroppers. At first he wanted to drive them out as he had done to the Nadir Jews of Yathrib, but he realized from his experience with the seized plantations that it would be a mistake to get rid of them. Under the new owners, the Yathrib palm groves had suffered a steep decline in productivity. He had given these properties to his Meccan followers who had no knowledge of horticulture or the complex irrigation techniques needed to keep the trees alive and flourishing. The purging of the Jews had led to a shortage of skilled labor, and the new owners were men who had become habituated to making a living through plunder rather than hard work. Due to these considerations, Muhammad offered to let the Khaybar Jews work the plantations and fields they had formerly owned, but they had to turn over half the annual yield to him. Muhammad retained the right to exile them at any time.

The estimated crop yield for the Katiba region alone shows the productivity of the Jews. That region produced eight thousand *wasqs*—camel loads—per year of dates, a camel load weighing approximately four hundred and twenty-five pounds. This works out to seventeen hundred tons of dates per year. Additionally, the region produced three thousand camel loads of barley annually. Muhammad awarded everyone in his immediate family and all his Meccan clansmen and clanswomen who had been loyal to him annuities in the form of camel loads of dates and barley for them to sell or give away as they wished—every year until their deaths. Each of his wives was awarded eighty *wasqs* of dates and twenty of barley. Loyalists such as Abu Bakr were allotted a hundred *wasqs* each. Muhammad's ever-faithful aunt Safiya got forty *wasqs* of dates. Oddly, Osama, the son of Muhammad's ousted adopted son Zayd, is on record as receiving one hundred and fifty *wasqs* of dates, yet none were reported for his father. Muhammad used what was left as he saw fit. Some of it went to feed new converts and the less fortunate among his followers.[21] The remainder was sold to raise money for war.

The wealth continued to roll in when Fadak, another Jewish oasis a day's journey to the northeast of Khaybar, capitulated without an arrow being fired. Fadak was similar to Khaybar, but on a smaller scale with fortresses, date plantations, and crop fields in two shallow valleys amidst the lava plain. When the Fadak leaders learned of the terms the defeated Khaybar Jews had obtained, they sent word to Muhammad not to attack: They would submit to him under a similar sharecropper arrangement. Muhammad sent representatives to work out the deal, and Fadak was turned over to him. Since it had been conquered without fighting, he claimed the oasis for himself, and from then on he received half of its agricultural production. He used this flow of wealth to purchase horses and weapons to expand his growing army and extend his reach.

On the return trip to Yathrib, Muhammad made a detour to the northwest to attack the Jewish oasis of Wadi al-Qura, a valley in a region that had been the target of previous raids. He sent word ahead of the arrival of his army that if the Jews converted he would spare their lives and allow them to continue living in the valley, but they rejected the offer. The valley consisted of a string of villages that did not have the fortifications of Khaybar and Fadak, easy pickings for Muhammad's seasoned fighters. The Jews made a show of bravery: About a dozen of their champions stepped out from their battle lines to duel with Muhammad's warriors, but all were slain. The Jews surrendered before the day was out, and Muhammad spent four days taking everything that was not nailed down. As with Khaybar and Fadak, he left the Jews to work the land as sharecroppers.

After the conquest, the Jews of Khaybar cheerlessly continued to work the fields and plantations their ancestors had labored over centuries to create. They turned over half of the fruits of their labor to Muhammad, but now serfs in their own land they were filled with resentment. The castles, plantations, and fields now belonged to the elite of Muhammad's companions, and they occasionally came on lordly visits to make sure everything was being run to their satisfaction.

They were walking targets. During one of these visits, one of Muhammad's people ventured out alone and was not seen again until his body was discovered in a well. The Jews denied killing him. Muhammad ended up paying blood money for the death, but demanded repayment from the Jews. When it was not forthcoming, he devised a scheme to punish them and serve as a warning against any further murders. He sent thirty men under the command of Abdullah Rawaha, the man who oversaw the collection of the annual harvest, to lure one of the prominent Jews to Yathrib, ostensibly to work out an arrangement that would give him formal leadership over the Khaybar Jews. This was Yusayr Razim, who had been one of the Jewish military commanders before the fall of Khaybar. Muhammad made it clear to Rawaha that he did not want Yusayr to make it to Yathrib, meaning he was to be killed en route.[22] Rawaha persuaded Yusayr to accompany him to Yathrib to meet with Muhammad. Despite warnings from other Jews not to trust Muhammad, Yusayr left for Yathrib on a camel accompanied by thirty other Khaybar Jews—one for each of Rawaha's men. Having been completely disarmed after the conquest, none of the Jews carried weapons whereas Rawaha's men were armed with swords. When they were a half-day's journey outside of Khaybar, Yusayr became suspicious of a trap. He made a grab for Rawaha's sword, but Rawaha got to it first. It turned into a massacre. Only one of the Jews escaped.[23]

Twenty years after the death of Muhammad, Umar expelled the Khaybar Jews from their land. By then there was sufficient skilled Muhammadan labor to replace the Jews, but Umar needed a pretext to get rid of them. That came when Umar's son Abdullah, Muhammad's cousin Zubayr, and another of the elite of the new religion went to Khaybar to inspect their properties. During the night Abdullah was assaulted while he was asleep in his castle, and one of his wrists was injured. It was not a serious injury, but when Umar learned of it he ordered the expulsion of the Jews, as it occurred not long after the murder of one of the planta- tion usurpers named Muzahhir Rafi. He had come from Syria with ten Christian slaves to work the Khaybar property that Muhammad had given him. The Khaybar Jews, the literature alleges, encouraged the slaves to kill Muzahhir, then helped them flee back to Syria.

Muhammad proved that hell existed, but it was the hell of his creation in this world. Like the Qaynuqa and Nadir Jews of Yathrib before them, the Jews of Khaybar packed their belongings onto camels, and with profound sorrow they left their ancestral lands, never to return.

CHAPTER 28

The Station of Abraham

The treaty of Hudaybiyya freed Muhammad to conquer Khaybar. That task accomplished, he turned his attention back to Mecca by making the pilgrimage allowed to him by the agreement. Though it was brief, the visit represented a symbolic conquest of the center of Arabian polytheism, for during his short stay Muhammad transformed some of the polytheist rites into the practices of his religion.

The pilgrimage took place during the same month as the aborted pilgrimage of the previous year. Under the terms of the agreement, Muhammad was allowed three days to perform the rites of the minor pilgrimage only—the off-season pilgrimage whose rituals were limited to Mecca. One of the important stipulations required him to leave his war instruments behind. He and his followers would only be allowed to carry their swords while in Mecca provided they were kept sheathed.

He left Yathrib with two thousand of his men dressed in the simple white wraps of the pilgrim, but fearful of assassination, he sent military equipment ahead with a cavalry of one hundred warriors under the command of Maslama, who was ordered to secure a staging area just outside the sacred territory. Muhammad and his pilgrim-warriors followed a day later on camels, driving sacrificial animals ahead of them. The staging area was close enough to the sacred territory that the stone idols marking the border were visible. By the time Muhammad reached the boundary, the Meccans had learned that his men were heavily armed. Fearing an invasion, they sent envoys to remind him of the terms

373

of the treaty. Muhammad replied that he intended to abide by it. The arms, he informed them, were security in the event they broke the agreement.[1]

After the envoys returned to Mecca to convey assurances that his intentions were peaceful, Muhammad left a military detachment of two hundred men at the camp and led the bulk of his followers, all clad in white, into the vale of Mecca. The pilgrims came through one of the northern passes that went by the cemetery where Muhammad's wife Khadija, his firstborn son Qasim, and his grandfather Abdul Muttalib were buried. This was the first time he had set foot in Mecca since running for his life seven years earlier. Looming over the valley was Mount Hira, the scene of his shattering epileptic experiences twenty years earlier. Once he cleared the pass, he saw the cubic temple that he helped build standing quietly in the center of town next to the dry riverbed that cut through the valley and separated the mounts of Safa and Marwa.

As they entered town, his followers formed a tight human shield around him, and when they neared the temple they formed lines for him to pass between on his she-camel al-Qaswa. Leading Muhammad's camel by the halter was Abdullah Rawaha. He loudly recited a poem that revealed Muhammad's influence over him:

> Get out of his way, you unbelievers, make way.
> Every good thing goes with His apostle.
> O Lord I believe in his word,
> I know God's truth in accepting it.
> We will fight you about its interpretation
> As we have fought you about its revelation
> With strokes that will remove heads from shoulders
> And make friend unmindful of friend.[2]

In some accounts, Muhammad remained on his camel while he made the seven orbits; in others, he did the circuits on foot, touching the Black Stone with his staff or kissing it as he made each round. Everything he did his followers did. With these rituals he staked his claim: It was no longer the temple of tolerance of the Meccans, the temple that opened its doors to any and all pagan deities and even allowed Christian and Jewish images; it was now the temple of Muhammad's god concept, the mono-theistic abstraction upon which he had grafted the furious demons of his mind. When he was done with the temple, Muhammad made the runs between the mounts of Safa and Marwa. These were the two rocky mounts the Meccans devoted to Isaf and Naila, the luckless lovers who were turned into stone for having sex inside the low temple walls of yore. Now the mounts belonged to God, and Muhammad gave the polytheist custom of running between them a new meaning: The running was to be done in remembrance of his revamped Hagar story, in which she frantically runs between them in search of water after Abraham dumped her and Ishmael in the arid valley. The semicircular stone platform at one end of the temple, the meeting site of the Meccan nobles, was now the burial site of Ishmael.

When these redefined rituals were completed, Muhammad shaved his head to mark the end of the pilgrimage and began the slaughter the sacrificial animals. They had to be killed exclusively in the name of God, or God would reject the blood offering. Following the sacrifices, Muhammad sent two hundred of his people to relieve the men who had stayed behind to guard the camp and its weapons so that they could proceed to Mecca to carry out the rites.

Muhammad took one more action to mark his symbolic takeover of the temple. Over the protests of the Meccans he went inside the temple with Bilal and ordered the former slave to climb a ladder to the roof to make the call to prayer. The Meccans were outraged, particularly at the sight of Umayya Khalaf's former slave "braying" from the top of their beloved temple,[3] but they could do nothing about it. Even though such an action was not in their agreement, Muhammad was in control. He came out of the temple and took position in front of rows of pilgrims who had assembled for prayer. At Bilal's prayer call from the roof, the pilgrims followed Muhammad in the precise routines of his prayer rituals, repeating the Koran verses that he recited.

It is likely it was during this pilgrimage that Muhammad pointed out the *Maqam Ibrahim*—the Station of Abraham—to Umar, as it was the first opportunity for him to do so. As noted earlier,[4] Muhammad invented the Abraham-Meccan temple sto-ryline after he changed the prayer direction to Mecca, marking his break with the Yathrib Jews. The Station of Abraham was a fanciful addition to his Abraham story. We can still hear the ferocious Umar, in the timid voice he used when he talked to Muhammad, asking, "Is this the *Maqam* (station) of our father (Abraham)?" And in the mind's eye we can still see Muhammad nodding to Umar that it was indeed the stone that Abraham had stood upon to hand up rocks to Ishmael for the construction of the temple. We can still hear Umar's timid follow-up question, "Should we take it (as) a place of prayer?"[5,6] Fourteen hundred years later, we can still discern the untimid voice of Umar boasting that these prayers came about because God had taken note of his question and "sent down" a verse to Muhammad commanding such prayer.[7,8]

During this brief stay in Mecca, Muhammad acquired yet another wife. This was Maymuna, the half-sister of Zaynab, the daughter of Khuzayma, who died shortly after marrying Muhammad many years before. Maymuna was also the sister of the wife of Muhammad's uncle Abbas, who gave her away in a marriage ceremony held at the end of his stay in Mecca. Other than the fact that he had a penchant for collecting wives, no clear explanation has been given for the marriage, though it is possible Muhammad hoped to bring the wealthy Abbas more tightly into his circle through this union.

Maymuna was the second wife he acquired during the previous six months. The other was Ramlah, a daughter of Abu Sufyan. She was an early convert who had migrated with her husband to Abyssinia. Her husband died there, and Muhammad proposed to her through an intermediary. As she was the daughter of one of his chief enemies, this was more a political than romantic affair. It is said that the Abyssinian ruler, who had allowed a number of Muhammad's followers to emigrate to his kingdom, arranged a proxy marriage and then sent her and other émigrés to Muhammad in Yathrib. This included Ali's older brother Jafar. They arrived while Muhammad was laying siege to Khaybar.

Because of the marriage to Maymuna, Muhammad ended up overstaying his time limit. Several Meccans approached him while he was sitting with some of the Khazraj and Aws leaders outside his tent, which had been pitched in an open area near the temple, to tell him he had to leave. It is said that one of them was Suhayl, the man who had negotiated the treaty of Hudaybiyya with him the year before. The Meccans were in a testy mood and said, "Your time is up, so get out from us." Muhammad answered, "How would it harm you if you were to let me stay and I gave a wedding feast among you and we prepared food and you came too?" The Meccans replied, "We don't need your food, so get out."[9]

An agreement was an agreement. Muhammad left Mecca peacefully and returned to Yathrib.

CHAPTER 29

Jihad! Jihad! Jihad!

Imagine the scene at Muhammad's mosque on the eve of a raid: Muhammad is sitting in the pulpit of the preacher platform. He is angry and shakes his fist at the crowds in the prayer area and courtyard. Fighting in the cause of Allah is an obligation for Submitters, he tells them, but many of the faithful are resisting going to war and have been coming to him with excuses. He reminds them of their duty by reciting a Koran verse: "Fighting is enjoined on you, and it is an object of dislike to you; and it may be that you dislike a thing while it is good for you, and it may be that you love a thing while it is evil for you, and Allah knows, while you do not know."[1]

The rewards are great for the faithful who fight in the cause of God and his messenger. Muhammad reminds them of the black shepherd of Khaybar, a story by then famous because the shepherd was the only man to have gained Paradise without ever once praying. He was an Abyssinian slave who took care of a herd for one of the Khaybar lords. During the siege of Marhab's castle he went to Muhammad to ask him what was required of his religion. "I invite you to bear witness that there is no god but God, that I am the Messenger of God, and that you will not worship any other than God."[2] The slave asked, "What will I get if I bear witness to that and believe in God?" Muhammad replied, "Paradise, if you die believing that." That was all it took. The shepherd grabbed Muhammad's hand to make the pledge of fealty and rushed out to fight. This new believer was killed in battle that same day without having had even a moment to pray.

Muhammad assures the congregation the black shepherd was taken into Paradise and was immediately rewarded. And what a reward! Muhammad had a vision of it: "I saw his two wives, *houris*, competing to take off his gown; they were entering the space between his skin and his gown."[3]

A new expedition in the cause of God is at hand, and it needs people to do what they do not like. Muhammad offers the usual bribes of heavenly sex or terrestrial booty, but the best persuader is the hellfire threat: God gives them an opportunity to fight for him as a test of their worthiness. It is a test of their faith. If they fail the test by finding excuses not to go to war when they are asked to go, then they are hypocrites—fake believers—and the fake believers are destined for hellfire, for God hates hypocrites. They must prove their worthiness, prove their faith, prove their love for God and his messenger by doing what they may not like, such as sallying forth into battle and perhaps dying. It is good for them. "Allah knows while you do not know!"

From the pulpit, Muhammad surveys the congregation, a mass of faces looking up at him with rapt attention. He has them where he wants them, trapped between Heaven and Hell. He jumps to his feet and shouts down at them, "Could it be that you desire hellfire?"

"No!" they cry.

"What do you desire then?"

"Paradise, O Messenger of God. Paradise! Give us the chance for Paradise!"

"What must you do to gain Paradise?"

"*Jihad!*"

"I can't hear you!"

"*JIHAD!*"

"Say it again so that God can hear you!"

"*JIHAD, JIHAD, JIHAD!*"

They still need more rousing to pump them up for action. They need to smell blood, taste blood, think blood. He raises trembling hands to the heavens as if to plead to God for mercy upon these miserable souls, then shouts down at them: "What is the cry in battle that is most pleasing to God?"

"Kill, kill!"

"I can't hear you!"

"KILL, KILL!"

379

"Say it again so that God can hear you!"

"KILL, KILL, KILL, KILL!" they shout as they leap to their feet and thrust their fists in the air.

And off they go on another raid, thirty of them, or three hundred, and soon three thousand and eventually thirty thousand and more, to attack at dawn and kill and plunder and subjugate and ultimately to enslave with what has enslaved them.[4]

Over the course of the year that followed the attack on Khaybar Muhammad sent out more than a dozen raiding parties. As always, the raids served multiple ends: proactive attacks on enemies, real or imagined; forcing conversions; fundraising through plunder; and spreading fear—terror. He had a policy of peacefully inviting people to join his religion and accept him as their prophet. If they refused, he proclaimed them guilty of turning their back on truth. They were then subject to God's punishment; attacking them was rendering divine justice.

Some of the raids that year were primarily smash-and-grab operations intended to capture women and children and make off with livestock. Shortly after returning from Khaybar, Muhammad sent Umar on such a mission against one of the Hawazin clans in their territory northeast of Taif. The Hawazins were a confederation of nomadic tribes to which Muhammad's foster mother Halima belonged and were spread over a large area. They had rejected Muhammad's calls to join his religion, leading to an attack that he hoped would bring in revenue, but Umar returned empty-handed. The Hawazins learned he was coming and scattered to nearby mountains with their women, children, and livestock.[5]

Abu Bakr had better luck on a raid against one of the Fazarah clans in the desert plateau several hundred miles northeast of Yathrib. After performing dawn prayers and waiting to see if there was a prayer call coming from the Bedouin encampment, he and his band launched a surprise attack. Shouting "Kill, kill," they blitzed in, slaughtering many of the men and rounding up women, children, and livestock. This attack was made memorable by Salama al-Akwa—the man who boasted he had single-handedly fought the Ghatafans after they stole Muhammad's herd of camels. In a story attributed to him, he boasted of slaughtering men from seven families and capturing the women and children before they could flee to the mountains. One of the women was young and exceptionally beautiful. Abu Bakr awarded her to Salama as part of his share of booty, but once back in Yathrib Muhammad asked him for her. Eager to sleep with her once it was certain she was not pregnant, Al-Akwa reluctantly parted with her, and Muhammad exchanged her for some recent converts the Meccans had imprisoned.[6]

One of these attacks could be tagged the "dowry raid." A Yathrib believer named Hadrad wanted to marry a Najjar woman and promised her a dowry of two hundred silver coins. The problem was that he did not have any money to pay for the wedding feast, let alone the dowry. He asked Muhammad for a loan, but Muhammad joked with him about such a large amount for a woman. He did not have that kind of money on hand, Muhammad informed the destitute lover, but he offered him a moneymaking opportunity: Reports had reached Muhammad that a Bedouin named Rifa Qays was plotting to steal his camels. Rumor had it that he was encamped near the valley where Muhammad grazed his booty camels, the same pasturing area that had already been the target of rustlers. Muhammad dispatched Hadrad and some other men to deal with the threat. The literature gives only a sketchy account of the raid, but it turned out Hadrad got the money he needed to get married. He later boasted about killing Rifa in a surprise attack: "I jumped out at him and cut off his head, then raced towards their camp, shouting *Allahu Akbar!* My companions did the same. I swear, they fled in disorder, taking with them their women, children, and those possessions they could. We drove off large numbers of their camels and livestock that we took back to the Messenger of God. I went to him carrying the man's head. He gave me thirteen baggage camels from those we captured as my dowry. So I concluded my marriage."[7]

The raids did not always end favorably, as resistance to Muhammad's predatory practices was growing. Not long after the fall of Khaybar, he sent fifty cavalrymen under the command of a man named Awja against Bedouins of a region to the northeast of Mecca who were related to the Hawazins. Muhammad chose Awja as leader because he came from that tribe and would have a better chance at bringing them into the religion through persuasion. He instructed him first to "invite" his fellow tribesmen to join the religion. If they refused, then he was to attack. Awja made the mistake of entrusting the scouting to a fellow tribesman, believing that he too was a committed convert, but the scout turned out to be loyal to his tribe and alerted them to the coming attack. The raiders fell into a trap. When they reached the Bedouin territory, Awja did as Muhammad had instructed by inviting his tribesmen to join up or face the consequences. When the tribal leader replied, "We don't need what you're offering,"[8] Awja and his warriors attacked, but it ended like the charge of the light brigade through the valley of death. Bedouin marksmen hidden in adjacent hills fired volleys of arrows down at them, decimating their ranks. Bedouin cavalry finished them off. Only a few of the raiders made it back to Yathrib.

A second disaster occurred when another Bedouin tribe Muhammad targeted up near Fadak overwhelmed a raiding party of thirty warriors and killed all but one. This took place after the raiders stole their livestock and were heading back to Yathrib. A large force of Bedouins caught up with them, and only Bashir, the commander, escaped. In reprisal, Muhammad sent two hundred men under the leadership of a more experienced fighter named Ghalib. The force included Zayd's son Osama, who was then in his mid teens. Ghalib was able to mount a crushing surprise attack at dawn. With cries of "Kill, kill,"[9] the attackers poured into the Bedouin encampment and slaughtered all the men they could get their hands on. The raiders returned to Yathrib with prisoners and herds of camels and goats.

During this vengeance raid, Osama, itching to slay infidels, committed the equivalent of a mortal sin when he butchered a man just after he declared himself a believer. During the fighting, the man taunted him by promising to send him into the arms of the dark-eyed beauties of Paradise. Osama chased him and killed him even though at the last second he made the declaration of belief. Such taunting about the *houris* of Heaven was a common occurrence during fights, as were desperation conversions. Bedouins learned of some of the more bizarre ideas of Muhammad's religion by word of mouth and discussed them while sitting around campfires, more often than not to make fun of them, particularly the idea of heavenly females with looks to die for awarded to men who died for Muhammad. They also learned of the trick of uttering the magic words as a last resort to keep from being killed—the shield of the *shahada*. All you had to do was to say, "There is but one God and Muhammad is his messenger," and you would be spared. The downside was that you were stuck with the religion for life, for if you renounced it later you were subject to the death penalty for apostasy. The Bedouin Osama chased was evidently aware of the magic formula, for when Osama caught up with him and was about to kill him the Bedouin cried out, "There is but one God and Muhammad is his messenger!" Still steaming over the earlier taunts about the dark-eyed beauties, Osama killed him anyway. Muhammad blew up at him when he found out about it. Osama protested: "But Messenger of God, he only said it to avoid being killed."[10]

In a rant, Muhammad explained the theory and practice of terror to him: The raids, the attacks, the killings, they were all intended to frighten people into either joining the religion or paying a subjugation tax. You were victorious the moment you got people to submit. That was what it was all about—submission, even if it was to keep from being killed. If they made a declaration of faith, that meant they submitted, and they then had the protection of the *shahada* and were not to be slain. When Muhammad's anger finally subsided, a sheepish Osama promised never to kill anybody like that again.

What distinguishes the period following the conquest of Khaybar is Muhammad's bold expansionism. The wealth of Khaybar and revenues from tithes and subjugation taxes allowed him to go on a spending spree for weapons and horses. His policy of terror combined with the incentive of heavenly reward and threats of hellish punishment was paying off in the form of increased recruitment. People were coming to him from all over to pledge allegiance. Some tribes submitted in their entirety either by joining his religion or agreeing to pay the submission tax in lieu of conversion. Because of the influx of manpower, battle losses were becoming easier to replace. Muhammad was also emboldened by important defections from Mecca. Two of its prominent military leaders—Khalid, the son of Walid,[11] the man who had led the successful cavalry charge against Muhammad's lines at Uhud, and Amr al-As,[12] also an emerging Meccan military leader—journeyed to Yathrib in secret and pledged fealty to him. Their defection came about not long after fall of Khaybar. The literature casts the defections as sincere conversions: God allowed the light of

Muhammad's religion to enter their hearts, but their pledge was more likely the result of cold calculation. They saw it was only a matter of time before Mecca ended up like Khaybar and decided it was in their interest to switch sides.

Encouraged by such successes, Muhammad now envisioned spreading his religion beyond Arabia. With astounding grandiosity he proclaimed that God had ordained his religion for the entire world. He repeated an earlier claim: "Every prophet used to be sent to his nation exclusively, but I have been sent to all mankind."[13]

In line with this belief about himself, he dispatched messengers to all the potentates of the region to invite them to join his religion—to the rulers of the Byzantines, Persians, Egyptians, Abyssinians, and Ghassanids. With the exception of Persia, these were Christian powers. As he handed letters written on parchment to his envoys, he told them, "I have been sent as a mercy and for all. Therefore, convey this message from me, and God shall have mercy on you."[14]

As he was only semiliterate, Muhammad dictated the missives to his scribes, tailoring the contents for each of the rulers. To the emperor of Persia, he wrote: "In the name of Allah, the Compassionate, the Merciful. From Muhammad, the Prophet of Allah, to Kisra, the ruler of Fars (Persia). May peace be on him who follows the guidance, believes in Allah and His Prophet. I testify that there is none worthy of worship but Allah, who is alone and without an associate and Muhammad is His servant and Prophet. Allah has made me a Prophet and sent me for the entire world, in order that I may infuse the fear of Allah in every living person. Accept Islam and be secure. If you refuse, the sins of all the Zoroastrians shall be your responsibility—Allah's Prophet Muhammad."[15] To give these letters an official look, Muhammad had a signet ring made with the words "Messenger of Allah" engraved and used the ring to stamp the wax that sealed the letters.

Most of the rulers had never heard of Muhammad and concluded the messages were delusional nonsense, but they were incited to find out about the impudence behind them. The Persian emperor was so infuriated that he tore up the letter and sent an order to the governor of Yemen, a vassal state of the Persians, to arrest Muhammad and bring him before him, but the emperor was assassinated in a coup before the order could be carried out. When Heraclius, the Byzantine emperor whose seat was in Constantinople, read the letter, he stuffed it in his crotch to show what he thought about it and sent guards to round up Arabs from the Hijaz to question them about Muhammad. They detained thirty men, among them Abu Sufyan, who happened to be in Gaza on a caravan venture. The Meccan leader told Heraclius what he knew, but in cautious language in case word got back to Muhammad of the conversation. He had undertaken the caravan trip under the terms of the Hudaybiyya truce, and he did not want to jeopardize Mecca's renewed commerce with the lands of the north by angering Muhammad.

Aside from the Abyssinian king who had a longstanding friendly relationship with Muhammad, the only ruler to respond positively was the governor of Egypt, an appointee of Heraclius. From his seat in Alexandria, he sent what amounted to a thank you note: gifts of two young female Coptic slaves named Maria and Shirin, a black eunuch named Mabur,[16] and a white female mule. The governor's friendliness was likely influenced by the Abyssinians, who believed Muhammad's religion to be a persecuted Christian offshoot. Muhammad kept Maria as a concubine and gave Shirin to his poet-spokesman Hassan Thabit.

The Ghassanid ruler, al-Harith, the son of Shimr, whose court was in Damascus, responded to Muhammad's missive with open contempt. The Ghassanids were a major Christianized Arab tribe that occupied a large part of what is today Jordan. Vassals of the Byzantines, their territory served as a buffer against Bedouin raids, and they supplied manpower for the endless fighting between the Byzantine and Persian empires. It is possible the letter that reached Heraclius came to him indirectly through the "King of the Christian Arabs," as al-Harith was known. Al-Harith received Muhammad's letter from the hands of either Dihya Khalifa—the Angel Gabriel look-alike—or a warrior named Shuja. It is said that after reading it, he threw it to the ground and said, "Whoever disputes with me about my country I shall march against him even though he be in Yemen and shall send men to bring him to me." He dismissed the envoy by saying, "Convey to your master what you have seen."[17]

Muhammad sent a second envoy to Syria. The details are sketchy, but it is possible he did so because he did not receive a

DARK-EYED BEAUTIES OF PARADISE. Muhammad motivated people to die for his cause by promising them the reward of eternal sex and the never-ending delights of wine in Paradise. "Verily for the Righteous there will be a fulfillment of (the heart's) desires; Gardens enclosed, and grapevines; And voluptuous women of equal age; And a cup full (to the brim). No vanity shall they hear therein, nor Untruth."[18]

response from the Byzantine emperor, who had limited himself to gathering intelligence about Muhammad. It so happened that around this time Heraclius was on a pilgrimage to Jerusalem to commemorate the recent victory of the Byzantines over the Persians for control of the Levant and to restore the True Cross to Jerusalem that had been recovered from the Persians.[19] It is possible Muhammad hoped his envoy could reach the emperor en route to hand-deliver the message, but the envoy never made it. He was intercepted at a place called Mutah east of the Dead Sea, and Shurahbil, the Ghassanid governor of the region, put him to death.[20] Muhammad reacted to the death by assembling his largest army to date—three thousand men—to strike back at Shurahbil. He put his former adopted son Zayd in command and named his cousin Jafar, one of Ali's older brothers, and the always reliable Rawaha, as second and third in command. The force consisted not only of Meccan expatriates and Yathrib converts, but also of recent Bedouin converts. They assembled at a staging ground north of Yathrib where Muhammad gave last minute instructions and a Paradise pep talk before sending them off.

It cannot be ruled out that the Byzantines deliberately killed the envoy in the hope of luring Muhammad, now a self-announced enemy of the Byzantines, out of Yathrib so that he could be eliminated. As governor, Shurahbil would not have killed the envoy without consulting the Ghassanid king, who would in turn have sought permission from his overlord Heraclius. Giving support to this idea is the fact that a large army led by Theodore, the brother of Heraclius, lay in wait near Mutah. This came as a shock to Zayd. When his force was about a day's march from Mutah, scouts reported the huge Byzantine army to him and a rumor that it was led by Heraclius himself. Zayd debated with his subordinates about sending word to Muhammad for reinforcements and awaiting further instructions, but some of them, particularly Rawaha, longed for martyrdom and wanted to proceed. Rawaha, who was noted for his poetry, had composed some lines before leaving Yathrib that revealed a death wish.[21,22] He gave a forceful martyrdom speech to his comrades that echoed Muhammad's indoctrination: "What you dislike is that which you have come out in search of—martyrdom. We are not fighting the enemy with numbers, or strength or multitude, but we are confronting them with this religion with which God has honored us. So come on! Both prospects are fine: victory or martyrdom."[23] And so they proceeded north to confront an enormous enemy.

Compared to earlier battles, details of the Mutah battle are remarkably thin, perhaps because it turned into a disaster for Muhammad's army. The clash with the Byzantines took place at Mutah. Zayd, Jafar, and Rawaha were killed. The literature gives the gory details for Jafar, who died holding the battle flag: First one of his forearms was cut off, then the other arm was chopped off, and he hugged the flag to his chest between the stumps of his arms until the death blow came. In the Rawaha death account, he was wounded and left the battlefield, but then recited poetry to encourage himself to go to his death, his sure ticket to Paradise and Muhammad's promised reward of divine damsels. The literature recounts that someone handed Rawaha a chunk of meat to chew on for energy, but he tossed it aside and said about himself: "And you are still living?"[24] He threw himself at the Byzantines, who cut him to pieces. All that saved the army from annihilation was the quick thinking of Khalid, the recent Meccan convert and military leader, who took command and organized a retreat. Again, no details are given, but one can imagine the main force fleeing through a narrow mountain pass while a sacrificial rear guard held off an overwhelming enemy, like the Spartans at Thermopylae.

The literature plays down the humiliation of defeat by claiming the Byzantine army consisted of two hundred thousand fighters, a mix of fair-skinned Byzantine regiments and swarthy Christianized Arabs formations drawn from regional tribes. Only eight of the Muhammad's followers are officially listed as dead. Some scholars suggest the size of the Byzantine army was only two or three times larger than Muhammad's force, and it was better equipped, its soldiers battle-hardened from years of war with the Persians.[25] Muhammad's losses were possibly in the hundreds— mostly fresh converts or Bedouin opportunists since their names were never included in the literature.

Muhammad shed appropriate tears for the slain, particularly for his cousin Jafar, and rendered verdicts about their reward. They were all in Paradise, but some had attained greater distinction than others. From the pulpit-throne, he proclaimed he had a vision about them: "I saw Jafar as an angel, flying in Paradise, his foremost feathers stained with blood. And I saw Zayd below him, and I said, 'I did not think that Zayd was less than Jafar.' Then Gabriel came to him and said, 'Indeed, Zayd is not less than Jafar. But we prefer Jafar because of his relationship to you.'"[26] The believers ate up the story and from then on referred to Jafar as "the Flyer."[27]

As to the death-desiring Rawaha, Muhammad was at first stingy in his praise. He proclaimed that Rawaha was only allowed into Paradise through a side entrance instead of the pearly gate. His fellow Khazrajis were upset when they heard this. Had he not died in the cause of God and his messenger? Muhammad explained that when wounded, Rawaha hesitated to go to his death. Because he wavered, he was granted only side entrance to Paradise, but even so, he was indeed in Paradise. "When he suffered wounds, he drew back. But he criticized himself, regained his courage, was martyred, and entered Paradise," Muhammad explained.

Ibn Kathir reports that Rawaha's fellow tribesmen were "much relieved" to hear this.[28]

CHAPTER 30

Capitulation

The pilgrimage that was allowed under the treaty of Huday-biyya gave Muhammad the opportunity for a symbolic conquest of Mecca, but only months after the pilgrimage a bloody fight stemming from an insult about him gave him the pretext to nullify the pact and conquer Mecca militarily.

The bloodletting was rooted in the new tribal alignment that had formed after the treaty of Hudaybiyya, which allowed Muhammad to forge alliances with whomever he wished, even with tribes within Mecca's traditional sphere of influence. Most of the Bedouins who had previously supported the Meccans remained in their camp, but others who harbored grievances shifted allegiance to Muhammad. Some of them converted. What unsettled the truce occurred a year and a half after the Hudaybiyya agreement was signed when a young Bedouin from one of Mecca's allies said something insulting about Muhammad to one of the recent converts and was savagely beaten. This resulted in a cycle of violence that led some of the Meccans to aid their Bedouin friends with weapons, horses, and a few warriors. In the end, a number of people were killed, all of them of the Bedouin tribe allied with Muhammad.[1]

The Meccans realized their involvement in the affair, however limited, had been a serious mistake when they learned that leaders of the losing tribe went to Yathrib to complain to Muhammad about the deaths and implicate the Meccans. Worried that Muhammad could use the incident as a pretext to attack them, the Meccans sent Abu Sufyan to Yathrib to deny involvement and argue for a continuation of the truce. Muhammad listened to him, but when he did not give any assurances the truce would continue, Abu Sufyan sought out people who were the closest to him, hoping to convince them to use their influence to ensure a continuation. Abu Sufyan began with his daughter Ramlah, who had been living at the wives' quarters of the mosque since the conquest of Khaybar, but she made it clear she would not help him. His very presence irritated her. When he was about to sit on a mat that served as a bed, she barked at him to stay off it. "You are a dirty polytheist!"[2] She ridiculed his religion and informed him that any further involvement with him would be contingent upon his conversion. He pleaded with her, but it was no use. He visited other influential people such as Abu Bakr, Umar, Uthman, Ali and his wife Fatima, and others in the hope of getting their help, again to no avail. Umar was openly hostile: "Me intercede for you with the Messenger of God!" he said. "I swear, if ants were all I had to fight you with, I'd do it!"[3]

Once he was back home, the Meccans gave Abu Sufyan a rough reception for returning empty-handed. They questioned his leadership, and he ended up having to defend himself against suspicions he had secretly converted. Rumors about this started because he had been gone longer than he should have given the mission he was sent on. Had Muhammad imprisoned him and threatened to kill him if did not convert? Was he now secretly plotting with Muhammad against them? Even his wife Hind was upset with him. When they were in bed after his return, he tried to explain what happened in Yathrib, but she jumped to her feet and stomped on his chest. He only regained Mecca's confidence when he shaved his head, slaughtered animals on the altars of Isaf and Naila, and publicly proclaimed he would die in the religion of his forefathers.

Muhammad, meanwhile, prepared to attack Mecca. The incident between the Bedouins gave him the excuse he needed to drop the pretense of peace. He was now in a position of strength, and he did not intend to wait for the expiration of the armistice—another eight years—before adding Mecca to his conquests. Mecca was too important both symbolically and strategically. He understood human nature, and he understood the Arabs: They gravitated towards power. Once Mecca was under his control, they would flock to him to declare fealty to him and his religion.

In order not to give the Meccans the opportunity to prepare a defense, Muhammad carried out the invasion preparations quietly. Only a few people were trusted with the plan, and they were sworn to secrecy. As an additional security measure, he posted guards at all the exits from Yathrib with instructions to intercept anyone leaving. The precaution paid off when a woman was caught carrying a hidden letter from someone in Yathrib who had learned of the invasion plans and wanted to alert the Meccans. Behind this secrecy screen, Muhammad assembled a force of ten thousand men. Seven hundred were Meccan expatriates and four thousand were Yathrib converts or recent settlers, and they possessed among them eight hundred horses. The rest were Bedouin converts whom he brought to Yathrib using a ruse: He ordered them to come to the valley for the now mandatory month-long Ramadan fast. It was only after they arrived that they learned they were to be part of a major expedition, but they were not told the objective. While he was still preparing the invasion, he created a diversion by sending a force to attack a tribe far to the north of Yathrib. If the Meccans had picked up any rumors of his military preparations, they would then conclude they were not the target.

It was still Ramadan when the army left Yathrib, but due to the hardships of travel, Muhammad ended up granting the soldiers a dispensation from fasting. News traveled faster than armies, and by the time Muhammad was a day away from Mecca, the Meccans, the people of Taif, and the nomadic Hawazins were on the alert. Since his army was descending along a route that would take it to the east of Mecca, it was unclear if he intended to attack the Hawazins and their confederates in Taif or the Meccans. A spy the Hawazins sent was captured and brought before Muhammad. In exchange for a promise his life would be spared, the spy told Muhammad the Hawazins and Thaqifs were assembling a large joint force, but he was not clear if their intentions were defensive or offensive. He also had intelligence about Mecca. He had been there the day before and learned the Meccans were exasperated with their chieftain Abu Sufyan because he had become "fearful and apprehensive." This was good news for Muhammad: It meant the will of the Meccans to resist him was weakening.

That night he ordered his people to light campfires, one for each man, so that the combined glow could be seen from a great distance and give the impression of an army greater than he possessed. He also sent his uncle Abbas to the Meccans to inform them of his presence and to convey to them his intentions and that their best course of action would be to surrender. Before Abbas had gone far, however, he came across Abu Sufyan and Hakim Hizam, Khadija's nephew. They had gone out towards Muhammad's camp to gather intelligence, but Abbas warned that if they continued on their own, they would be killed. He offered them his protection and escorted them to Muhammad's tent. It is said that before they reached the tent, Umar recognized Abu Sufyan and rushed into the tent behind them. Umar said to Muhammad, "O Messenger of God, this is Abu Sufyan, the enemy of God," and offered to cut off his head. But Abbas intervened and said the Meccan leader was under his protection.

Muhammad said to Abu Sufyan, "Isn't it time for you to know that I am the messenger of God?"[4] He ordered Abbas to keep Abu Sufyan with him overnight and bring him back in the morning. Abbas spent the night trying to convince the Meccan leader that resistance was futile. If Muhammad attacked Mecca he would kill everyone who resisted and enslave the women and children. The dead would be thrown into mass graves and the women and children auctioned off at slave markets. His conversion and the conversion of all Meccans was the only option. The next morning, Abbas escorted him to Muhammad's tent. Muhammad repeated his question from the night before: "Is it not time for you to know that I am the Messenger of God?" Abu Sufyan said, "I'm still having some trouble with that." His response angered Abbas: "Woe on you, accept Islam! Bear witness that there is no god but God and that Muhammad is the Messenger of God, before your head is cut off!"[5]

Abu Sufyan hesitated. There can be little doubt that he hated Muhammad more than he had ever hated anyone. Muhammad had torn Mecca apart. He had pitted brother against brother, son against father, cousin against cousin, nephew against uncle. The Meccans had erred in tolerating him. They had only done so to avoid a civil war with the Hashimites, but if they had slain him while they still had the chance, none of the subsequent events would have come about: Badr, Uhud, the Trench, and now this huge army just outside of Mecca. His firstborn son Hanzala would still be alive; his brothers-in-law Utba and Shayba

393

Rabia would still be with them as well as his friends and business partners Umayya Khalaf, Uqbah Muayt, Abul Hakam, and so many others. The Meccans and all the peoples of the Hijaz would continue to practice the religion of their forefathers without fear. Muhammad had not prevailed because of what he believed about himself, but only because of the violence he was now threatening him with. *"Bear witness that there is no god but God and that Muhammad is the Messenger of God, before your head is cut off!"*

Abu Sufyan could see from Muhammad's eyes that he did not have much time left to make up his mind. It was the face of a man who had presided over the beheading of an entire tribe of Jews. Abu Sufyan heard about how Muhammad sat there while Ali and Zubayr beheaded the men, young and old, and threw the bodies into a pit. All it would take was a signal from Muhammad, and he would be dragged outside and killed. Umar would be only too happy to force him to his knees and chop off his head, and it would no more bother Muhammad than had the killing of the Jews or the beheading of Uqbah Muayt and Nader al-Harith following their capture at Badr. The fear of death gripped him. He reached out and grabbed Muhammad's hand. "I accept that there is but one God and that you are his messenger."

Muhammad broke into a smile. He knew Abu Sufyan was insincere, but it did not matter. The declaration of faith in God and in his messenger was an inviolable contract; reneging on it meant death. Now that he had obtained the submission of the most important man of Mecca, he ordered Abbas to take him to the mountain pass at the far end of the valley that led to Mecca. They were to stand there while Muhammad paraded his army before them. He wanted to impress Abu Sufyan with his might and then release him so that he would return to Mecca before his army reached it and convince the Meccans to surrender.

The army units, arranged by tribes, first passed in review before Muhammad, then proceeded toward the mountain pass. Riding camels and horses, warriors bristling with weapons and carrying black or white war banners marched forward to where Abu Sufyan and Abbas were standing. A thousand Sulaym warriors with Khalid in command were the first to pass in front of them. Abu Sufyan did not recognized Khalid at first, but then realized it was the son of Walid. Then came Muhammad's first cousin Zubayr at the head of five hundred warriors, a mix of

Meccan expatriates and Bedouins. Following him were various tribes with three or four or eight hundred warriors each. As each group passed in front of Abu Sufyan, they cried out *"Allahu Akbar"* three times. In the rear was the largest group of about four thousand warriors, most of them from the Aws and Khazraj tribes of Yathrib and the remainder Meccan converts. This group was led by Muhammad, who stopped in front of Abu Sufyan and told him that what was about to happen to Mecca was happening because they had rejected him when all he had done was to bring them truth. "It is you and your people who have done this; these people believed me when you called me a liar. They assisted me when you exiled me."[6]

As he watched the parade of power, Abu Sufyan realized there was more to Muhammad's success than violence. The night before and then again that very morning he had witnessed people scrambling for the leftover water that he had washed with before engaging in prayer. It was disgusting to see grown men daub themselves with it or drink it, but it said something about the man. He himself had once led a force of ten thousand warriors, and he knew with certainty he could never have gotten any of them to drink water that he had washed in. There was indeed something remarkable about Muhammad. The more he thought about it, the more he understood. It was not that Muhammad brought truth, but that he brought the ability to convince people he had the truth. It was his fluency, his gift of speech. Even before he began claiming angels talked to him way back when he was still just the neighbor next door who suffered from the falling sickness, he had the tongue of a sorcerer; he was more eloquent than any Meccan had ever been except perhaps for Qusay. He had to hand it to Muhammad. He had hit upon the magic formula for getting people to do what he wanted. With silken tongue he had gotten them to believe God talked to him and revealed a book to him. He had gotten them to believe in those Christian notions of an afterlife of Heaven and Hell. He had filled them with dread of burning in hellfire. Then he had gotten them to fight for him by promising sex in Paradise to people who died for him and booty if they survived. It was the magic formula that had given him the power to conquer Yathrib and then Khaybar and take over the great wealth of the Jews. His sorcerer's tongue had unleashed a dark force that was unstoppable.

Abu Sufyan rushed back to Mecca and arrived only hours ahead of Muhammad's army. Muhammad had promised him to spare all who locked themselves in their homes. Abu Sufyan therefore ran through town warning people to stay in their homes if they wanted to be safe. At the temple, a large crowd formed to hear him speak and became angry when he warned that Muhammad's army was too strong to resist. The Meccans jeered him. They demanded to know why they had not learned about his army in time prepare a defense. Had he been in league with Muhammad ever since his visit to Yathrib? They called him a coward and a traitor. Even his wife turned against him. She grabbed him by his moustache and shouted, "Kill this overweight bag of fat! He is too disgraceful to lead our people!"[7] But Abu Sufyan pushed her away and warned that Muhammad intended to kill anyone who resisted him. His army was huge, with more horses, weapons, and armor than he had ever seen before. "I saw what you did not see! I saw the men, the quivers, and the weapons."[8]

Most of the people took Abu Sufyan's advice and locked themselves in their homes, but others prepared to fight. Safwan, Ikrima, and Suhayl gathered a group of men in battle gear and waited for the enemy to arrive. Not long after Abu Sufyan sounded the warning, Muhammad began his entry and was pleased to see the streets were nearly empty. The army entered from the north, but branched into five divisions to secure different sections of the valley. Khalid, in command of a thousand Bedouins, descended to the south end and then looped north again where his troops clashed with the band of defenders, but given their small number they were easily defeated. Some of the sources say a dozen were killed, another puts the number at close to thirty. Ikrima, Khalid's former comrade in arms, fled for his life as did the remainder of the defenders.

Muhammad's servants pitched his red command tent at the north end of the valley not far from the grave of Khadija. He gave orders to his commanders before entering the valley to fight only those who resisted, but he also gave out the names of ten people he wanted dead. These were people Muhammad hated for offenses they had committed against him. They were to be killed on sight, and whoever killed them would be free of blame. Six men and four women were on the list, including Hind, the wife of Abu Sufyan, for her role in the death and mutilation of Muhammad's uncle Hamza at Uhud. The manhunt began immediately. One of the first to be slain was Miqyas, the man who had come from Mecca following the Mustaliq raid to slay the fighter who had accidentally killed his brother. His offense was that he had feigned conversion in order to get close to the man, then fled back to Mecca after killing him. It is said that Miqyas knew he was a target even before his name was announced and got drunk on wine while waiting for his death. He was slain either at his mother's house or while staggering across the riverbed near Mount Safa. Another who was killed was Abdullah Khatal. He had committed the offense of converting, but then reverting to polytheism after killing a believer. He was a professional entertainer and used to have two of his singing girls sing verses that mocked Muhammad. When Muhammad learned Khatal was hiding behind the drapes of the temple, he said, "Kill him!"[9] The singing girls were also on the list. One of them was caught and beheaded, the other hid until things cooled down and declared herself a believer, thereby gaining the protection of the *shahada*.

Two of the men on the list, Habbar Aswad and Huwayrith Nuqaydh, were condemned for causing Muhammad's daughter Zaynab to miscarry. They had attempted to prevent her from going to Yathrib following the battle of Badr, causing her to fall from her camel. She was pregnant at the time and the fall caused her to miscarry. Ali caught Huwayrith outside the man's home and cut off his head. Habbar was able to keep out of sight for several days and went before Muhammad to declare he had become "impregnated" by the new religion. He made the pledge of allegiance, thereby coming under the shield of the *shahada*.

Several others also escaped death by converting. A woman named Sara had made it onto the hit list for repeatedly insulting Muhammad. The literature does not indicate the nature of the insults, only that she had offended him while he was still in Mecca. It is said that she escaped the death squads and converted, but she was later killed when someone trampled her under a horse. Abu Sufyan's wife Hind survived by remaining locked in her house under the protection of her husband and was spared when she converted. Ikrima was also on the list. Following the skirmish with Khalid, he fled Mecca and was preparing to cross the Red Sea to Abyssinia when he got word that Muhammad was willing to forgive him if he converted.

Another on the kill list who survived was one of Muham-mad's former scribes, Abdullah Sahr. Of all the people marked for death, he had committed the most serious offense by calling Muhammad's claim of divine inspiration a lie. He was one of the early Meccan converts who had gone with Muhammad to Yathrib, and because he knew how to write, Muhammad made use of his ability by dictating Koran verses to him. But Abdullah began to doubt Muhammad's claim to divine inspiration after he proposed some minor changes to various verses, and they became part of the Koran, memorized and repeated by the faithful. He ended up fleeing back to Mecca where he denounced Muham-mad as a fraud. On the day of the invasion, someone warned him Muhammad had ordered his death. He fled to Uthman Affan and begged his protection based on the fact they were foster brothers. At Uthman's urging, Muhammad took his erstwhile scribe back into the fold after he apologized for his behavior and reaffirmed his faith, but Muhammad accepted him reluctantly. The story is told that he refused to acknowledge Abdullah's pledge three times, hoping one of his people would get the hint he did not truly want him back and cut off his head. After Abdullah left Muhammad said, "Is there no wise man among you who could have got up and killed him when you saw I was remaining silent?" They replied, "But Messenger of God, could you not have given us some signal?" He replied, "Prophets do not kill by making signals."[10]

While the manhunt was still underway, Muhammad went into his tent to take a bath and rest. He scrubbed himself in a low bronze tub while his daughter Fatima held up his garment as a screen. Before he finished, his cousin Umm Hani showed up. Ten years earlier, it was while he stayed overnight at her house that he claimed he was transported to Jerusalem on a winged mule and was taken up to Paradise to stand before the throne of God, but she knew for a fact that he had never left his bed and begged him not to tell anyone about his delusion. Knowing what she knew about him, she never converted. Nevertheless, he was pleased to see her, but made her wait until he dressed and performed eight rounds of his elaborate prayer routines. Only then did he attend to her and learn she wanted protection for two of her brothers-in-law. Though they were not on the kill list, they had fought Khalid and then sought refuge in her home. Her brother Ali, wearing a full helmet that covered everything except his eyes, barged in intending to kill them, but Umm Hani stood in his path and told him he would have to kill her first. Muhammad granted her request: "We give protection to those you protect and immunity to those to whom you extend it. We will not execute them."[11]

Once Mecca was under complete control, Muhammad called for his camel to be brought. After donning his helmet and strapping on his sword, he mounted the camel. Accompanied by Abu Bakr and other elite followers, he rode at a processional pace to the temple. It was his day of victory, the day when the idols were to be destroyed and the temple rededicated exclusively to his idea of God. It was the day he had longed for ever since he first condemned the Meccans for their beliefs. On the way to the temple, he recited the entire "Victory" chapter he composed at the time of Hudaybiyya "in a vibrant, quivering tone," recalled a man who was with the group.[12] Still riding the camel, Muhammad orbited the temple, touching the Black Stone with his staff on each round. According to the literature, thunderous outbursts of *Allahu Akbars* spread throughout the valley and continued until Muhammad signaled for it to stop.

The temple area bristled with idols. Surrounding the Cube were the idols of the three goddesses and of Isaf and Naila and also the lesser idols of tribes, clans, and families. Inside the temple was the large onyx statue of the moon god Hubal, showing him holding divining arrows. He was on a pedestal and dominated the interior. Another statue of Hubal, the one that was used as a sacrificial altar, was outside facing the temple entrance, while yet another was on the roof.

Muhammad undertook the destruction of the idols outside the temple first. Those of stone were broken up; those of wood burned. In the mythologized versions of the event, Muhammad had such power that all he had to do to destroy an idol was to point his staff at it, recite a Koran verse, and it would topple to the ground. After finishing up outside the temple, he went inside and was enraged to discover a graffiti of Abraham on one of the walls. It showed Abraham casting divining arrows and was perhaps hastily sketched prior to his arrival as a way of mocking him. "May God kill them!" he shouted, cursing the perpetrators. The literature reports that someone ran into the temple with a wet rag to wipe it away.[13,14]

After the idols were destroyed, Muhammad performed two rounds of prayer prostrations inside the temple, then summoned the Meccans to announce that a new day had arrived. He gave a rambling speech: The era of worship of anyone or anything in the place of God was over. The Cube was now exclusively the House of God. Mecca was God's sanctuary and would remain so until the Day of Judgment. From the moment he created Heaven and earth, God had made Mecca sacrosanct, and no killing had ever been permitted within the sanctuary, but God had granted him an exception for one hour in order to hunt down and kill Khatal, Miqyas, and others who had offended God and his messenger. Thenceforward, the only permissible killings within the sacred territory would come as a result of a legal judgment for a violation of God's law. He announced that the Meccans were now subject to God's law, meaning all the rules and regulations he had incorporated in the Koran and the example of his precedents in implementing them. He enumerated many of them. They were the laws that God conveyed through his messenger and must be obeyed. He announced that since the Meccans had surrendered to him instead of fighting, all Mecca and its people were now his personal property. The Meccans were his legal slaves and their property his booty, but he made them a deal: He would grant them their freedom provided they convert; if not, they would forfeit their lives and property. He gave some of the Meccan leaders a month or two to think about it. He was offering them membership in a new tribe, he said, in the community of Submitters to God. He explained the value of membership in the new tribe: "The Submitter is the brother of the Submitter. The Submitters are brethren and are as one hand against those who oppose them. Their blood is equal. The strong among the Submitters will protect the weak among them, and the active will help the incapable."[15]

Following the speech, Muhammad climbed Mount Safa. From there he had a clear view of the temple. Thousands of people—Meccans, Yathribites, and Bedouins—were swirling around it in dizzying counterclockwise motion in worship of his singular God concept. At the foot of Mount Safa, hundreds of his Yathrib followers who had already completed the temple orbits were waiting to see what he would do next. As they watched, he raised his arms heavenward and pronounced words of praise for God, but at that moment he suffered an epileptic fit. After twenty years of struggle, the euphoria of his victory must have been too much for his brain to handle, and an electrical storm arose in his temporal lobe. It was as if the universe were playing a joke on him: At the very moment of his success his brain stripped the victory away by showing his inspiration had not come from the heavens above, but from down below, from the electric explosions of his malformed brain. As the cosmos laughed, he fell to the ground, his face flushed red and beads of sweat pearling on his forehead. The cosmic humor was lost on the believers. They averted their eyes. For them, Muhammad was receiving a revelation from the heavens, and they did not deem themselves worthy to look upon their master while he was communing with God.[16]

The literature does not inform us how long the seizure lasted, but when it was over the people surrounding him were perplexed to see that he was angry. "What is it that angers you, O messenger of God?" He laid into them. Just before the seizure felled him he had heard some of the Yathrib converts speculate that he was now going to remain in Mecca with his Quraysh tribe, meaning that he would turn his back on the people who had believed in him and taken him in. It was tantamount to calling him a traitor. He repeated verbatim what he had heard people say just before the fit engulfed him. He scolded them: "I am God's servant and his messenger. I migrated to God and to you. It is with you I shall live and with you I shall die."[17] They were mortified that they had offended him. With tears in their eyes they said, "We only said what we did because of our passion for God and his messenger." Muhammad finally softened and said, "God and his messenger believe you and forgive you."[18]

One of Muhammad's first acts was to implement his laws. People brought cases to him at his tent for adjudication, primarily custody matters. One of them was a dispute involving a relative of his wife Sauda. With these cases he gave common sense rulings. In more serious matters his rendering of punishment was swift and inflexible. The story is told that on the very day of the conquest, not long after the epileptic seizure that felled him on Mount Safa, he was walking through the crowd toward Khalid's tent when an inebriated man was brought before him. The man had gotten drunk on wine, and the people who dragged him to Muhammad asked what should be done with him. Muhammad said, "Beat him!" Surrounding the man, a crowd set about to punch, slap, and hit him with sandals, sticks, and whips. Muhammad grabbed a handful of dirt and threw it in his face.[19]

Another serious matter involved a woman accused of theft. Before she was brought before Muhammad, one of her relatives had gone to Osama to beg him to intercede with him, hoping to obtain mercy. When Osama pleaded on her behalf, however, Muhammad became enraged. "Do you intercede with me in a matter involving one of the legal punishments prescribed by Allah?" After determining her guilt, he went outside where people were assembled and gave a speech. "The nations prior to you were destroyed because if a noble amongst them stole, they used to excuse him, and if a poor person amongst them stole, they would apply legal punishment to him. By Him in Whose hand is Muhammad's soul, if Fatima, the daughter of Muhammad stole, I would cut off her hand." He then announced the punishment of amputation. The woman was taken away, and one of her hands was chopped off above the wrist.

For several days following the conquest, Meccans lined up to take the oath of fealty. For these pledges, Muhammad seated himself on a rock near the top of Mount Safa. One by one people knelt and pronounced the irrevocable oath: "I testify that there is but one God and Muhammad is his slave and messenger."[20] In the past, Muhammad would clasp the hands of each convert, but given the numbers, he delegated the hand clasping to Umar, who sat on a rock below him. He also accepted pledges at his tent. The story is told of ten highborn women, including the wives of Abu Sufyan, Ikrima, and Safwan, who went to Muhammad's tent for the pledge. Along with their husbands, they had been among his foremost enemies, particularly Hind, who lost her son, her father, her brother, and her uncle at Badr. For their formal act of submission, the women had donned the full dress and veil. Hind, who was still on Muhammad's kill list, kept her face tightly covered. She had been living in terror for days, fearing Muhammad's people would break into her home and cut off her head. From behind the veil, she oozed flattery: "O Messenger of God, praise God who makes distinct the religion which He chose for Himself, let your grace touch me, O Muhammad. Indeed I am a believing woman attesting before God."[21] Hoping her words had given her the protection of the *shahada*, she identified

herself. Muhammad was startled, but he must have been relieved to see she had come on board: He no longer had to fear
that the atoms of his uncle Hamza that had become part of her
body when she took a bite out of his liver would fry in Hell with
her. She would be spared the flames as long as she lived by the
new law. He told the women it was now forbidden for them
to commit adultery, spread slander, or kill their children.
"And you must not disobey me." Hind could not help but
bristle at his statement about killing their children and said
in essence, "You are the only one who has been killing our children."[22] Muhammad took the formal oath from them, but refused
to touch their hands. This was forbidden; flesh-to-flesh contact
with a woman could incite lust. Instead, he dipped his hand into
a bowl of water. The women sealed their oaths by dipping their
hands into it after him.[23]

Some of the Meccans who had fled after the skirmish with
Khalid returned when they were informed Muhammad would
forgive them provided they convert. One of them was Zibara, a
poet who had composed numerous satires about Muhammad. He
came out of hiding and groveled before him: "Peace upon you
who are the Messenger of God! I testify that there is no God but
Allah and that you are His servant and messenger. Praise God
who guided me to the religion of Submission to Allah." Muhammad was pleased. He said, "Praise be to God who guided you to
Submission. Indeed the religion of Submission to God cancels
what was before!"[24]

Safwan, the son of Umayya Khalaf and one of the most prominent of the Meccan merchants who opposed Muhammad, had
gone into hiding on the seacoast and made it known he would
sooner kill himself than fall into Muhammad's hands. One of the
recent Meccan converts, a merchant with whom Safwan had business dealings, tracked him down and told him it was safe for
him to return provided he adopt the religion, that Muhammad
guaranteed his protection. Safwan demanded proof. The man returned with one of Muhammad's turbans and a personal message:
Muhammad would grant him immunity for two months to give him
time to make up his mind about converting. Back in Mecca in the
company of his merchant friend, Safwan stood before Muhammad
and asked if the grant of two months was true. Muhammad, eager
to obtain the support of his erstwhile enemy, said that not only was

it true, he would now extend it to four months.[25] With similar promises of immunity, he reeled in Abul Hakam's son Ikrima, Sauda's former brother-in-law Suhayl, and other influential Meccans who would be more useful to him alive than dead.

Muhammad stayed in Mecca for nearly three weeks. During that time he imposed the new order. He had a narrow understanding of governance. For him, there were the rules and regulations that he declared were from God, and there were the obligatory prayers and prayer routines in worship of God. Governance amounted to enforcement of both.

By then, he had formulated rules and regulations that covered almost every aspect of life as it was experienced at that time in the Hijaz. He appointed preachers to take on the labor of teaching the prayer routines to the Meccans and instructing them about these rules and regulations. He also appointed judges. Their role was to apply punishment to anyone who stepped out of line.

Part III

Darkness at Noon

CHAPTER 31

Death to the Gods

Living in his red tent in upper Mecca, Muhammad spent much of the time implanting the rule of his religion over Mecca, but he also dispatched raiding parties to destroy pagan sanctuaries and sent out forces to bring the holdout Bedouin tribes of the region under his control.

Al-Uzza, the goddess Muhammad and Khadija had once worshipped, was the first idol to fall. Muhammad sent Khalid with thirty men to destroy her sanctuary at Nakhla, a day's journey east of Mecca. Khalid was no stranger to the temple, which was on a mountainside under ancient acacia trees. His father Walid used to make pilgrimages there to sacrifice camels and goats at the altar of al-Uzza, and Khalid and his brothers and sisters had often participated. When Khalid arrived with his raiders, all but one of the people at the sanctuary fled up the mountain. An Abyssinian woman, either a devotee or a priestess, ran out screaming at him. Khalid attacked her with his sword and "cut her in two," the literature states. He and his men destroyed the temple, cut down the trees, and returned to Mecca with everything they plundered from the sanctuary. When Muhammad learned about the woman, he said, "That was al-Uzza."[1]

While Khalid was en route to Nakhla, Amr al-As, the former Meccan military commander, was dispatched to demolish the sanctuary of Manat, the goddess the Aws and Khazraj had worshipped during their polytheist days, near the Red Sea south of Yanbu. Muhammad also sent forces to destroy the sanctuaries of lesser tribal gods in the region surrounding Mecca. In Mecca, he sent heralds through the streets and alleys ordering people to bring all the idols out of their homes and destroy them. The cry, "Whoever believes in God and His messenger does not leave an idol in his house but breaks it or burns it," was heard in every neighborhood.[2] Whenever Ali learned of holdouts, he would force his way into the home and destroy the idols himself.

Muhammad also kept hundreds of his warriors busy with attacks against outlying tribes that had not yet converted. The literature mentions three such raids: one involving two hundred men that attacked desert Arabs in the direction of Yalamlam to the southwest of Mecca and another involving three hundred men sent against Bedouins near Urana, a day's journey north of Mecca. The literature does not report the results of these two raids but goes into great detail about the third. On that raid Khalid, fresh from his return from Nakhla, led three hundred and fifty men against the Jadhima tribe near the Red Sea in order to "invite" them to join the religion. This raid turned into a savage massacre when he used his power to avenge the murder of one of his uncles that the Jadhima tribesmen had committed years before. By all accounts he ended up beheading nearly thirty men after they surrendered their weapons to him. Before giving them up, the tribesmen said they had recently converted and believed they had the protection of the *shahada*. Khalid killed them anyway. When Muhammad learned about the massacre, he was furious and absolved himself of any blame for the deed.[3] As he had done earlier with Osama for slaying a man after he declared belief, Muhammad gave Khalid a severe tongue lashing regarding the inviolability of the *shahada*. He sent Ali to pay the tribe blood money for their losses.

Meanwhile, a new battle was looming, one that in numbers of combatants would surpass all the previous conflicts. The spy who was captured while Muhammad was on the march to Mecca had alerted him that the Hawazins and Thaqifs had formed an alliance against him. The latest intelligence, brought to him at his tent headquarters, indicated they had assembled a huge army and were about to set out on an offensive against him, evidently with the intention of attacking him in Mecca. While consolidating his hold on Mecca, Muhammad prepared

MUHAMMAD DESTROYS THE IDOLS inside and around the temple of Mecca. It is said that the temple and temple grounds held three hundred and sixty idols, representing major deities such as Hubal and al-Uzza, and included minor tribal and family idols. After the conquest of Mecca, Muhammad ordered the stone idols broken up and the wooden ones burned. He left the Black Stone untouched.

to confront them. It is likely the attacks he ordered against outlying tribes were intended to keep them from joining with the numerous Hawazins.

Hawazin territory straddled the caravan route leading to the Persian Gulf, and it overlapped the region of the walled agricultural town of Taif. As were the people of Taif, the Hawazins were committed to their polytheist beliefs and were shaken by the capitulation of Mecca. When they learned of Muhammad's systematic destruction of pagan sanctuaries, they feared they would soon be targeted and decided to attack him before he could attack them.

They united under the leadership of Malik Awf, chieftain of one of the Hawazin clans. Though only thirty years old, he was a renowned warrior and an eloquent speaker. He persuaded the two major clans of Taif to join with his tribe in an offensive against Muhammad. Against the advice of older sheikhs, Malik put the fortune of the entire tribe on the line by bringing along all the women and children and all the tribal possessions including vast herds of camels and goats. Malik intended to keep the women and children and the herds in the rear of the army to give the warriors motivation to fight to the death if necessary. Not only would they be fighting against their hated enemy, they would also be fighting to protect their loved ones.

Muhammad, meanwhile, assembled an army that included the ten thousand men who had accompanied him to Mecca and two thousand Meccans who had sworn allegiance to him following the capitulation. He ensured his army had the best equipment available to the point of borrowing an arsenal of weapons and armor from Safwan, his former enemy. Safwan, Suhayl, and other Meccans to whom Muhammad had given time to think about joining his religion accompanied the army. He appointed Abu Sufyan to lead the Meccan contingent.

Instead of waiting for the enemy to attack him in Mecca, Muhammad went on the offensive. The two forces clashed at the entrance to a rugged, uninhabited valley called Hunayn. The exact location of the valley is unknown today, but it was likely closer to Mecca than to Taif. Each side sent out scouts and knew of the advance of their enemy. When he learned of Muhammad's approach, Malik prepared a clever trap. As bait, he positioned the masses of women, children, the elderly, and the vast herds of his tribe behind lines of cavalry and foot soldiers at the bottom of the valley. The women and children were mounted on camels so that from a distance the formation appeared to be a formidable mass of fighters. The only approach for Muhammad's forces was down a wide, dry riverbed that descended between mountains into the valley and was flanked by numerous ravines whose depths were not visible from the riverbed. Malik placed hundreds of horsemen and archers on each side within the folds of the ravines, anticipating that Muhammad's troops would march down the riverbed toward his formal battle lines, exposing them to a surprise attack.

From his scouts, Muhammad knew of Malik's battle formation, but he did not learn of the ambush. It is clear from a Koran verse that he had become overconfident due to the size of his army and that he anticipated an easy victory over the Hawazins.[4] As his army descended towards the Hawazin position, Muhammad, dressed in battle gear and riding the white mule the ruler of Egypt had given him, rode in and out of the numerous formations and shouted encouragement for them to fight. Booty or Paradise! When Malik gave the signal for the surprise attack, Muhammad had just returned to the rear of the army and joined a group of early converts and close family members. Suddenly, hundreds of marksmen popped up from hiding and showered Muhammad's lead troops with arrows while hundreds of horsemen surged from the ravines. The attack was so swift and furious that his army broke in panic and stampeded back up the riverbed. It was such a surge of blind fear that the panicked army pushed Muhammad and his small group against the mountainside. By then, the Hawazin and Thaqif cavalry and foot soldiers who had been positioned in front of the women and children rushed forward to join in the fight.

This was the only battle where Muhammad had to prove himself a valiant warrior. Previously he had stayed behind the lines and directed fighting from a safe distance surrounded by a security force. At Uhud, after spearing an attacker in the neck, he had fled up the mountain while his followers fought to the death to allow his escape. Now, seeing that all was lost if he did not give an example of bravery, he drew his sword and spurred the white donkey toward the surging enemy. He was cut off from his army, with only a hundred of his people with him, among them his uncle Abbas. Abbas, a big man who was known for his stentorian voice, bellowed at the top of his lungs for the army to return and called out the names of tribes and their leaders. He kept it up until various commanders such as Khalid regained control of their troops and returned to the fight. Once regrouped, they launched a ferocious counterattack, leading Muhammad to exult, "The fires of war are really hot now!"[5]

His forces soon beat back the army of the polytheists. Few details are given, but it is presumed that once they reorganized, Muhammad's troops moved as a solid body against the Hawazins and their Taif allies. While Muhammad was still in Mecca, Malik had spread the word that he disposed of twenty thousand "swords," but it was likely only a third that number, or half the troop strength that Muhammad possessed. Overwhelmed by a superior force, Malik's soldiers broke and ran, leaving the women, children, and livestock without protection. Muhammad's army captured six thousand women and children. The take in Hawazin livestock was enormous: twenty-four thousand camels and forty thousand goats.[6]

All the men who were captured or surrendered were executed on Muhammad's orders.[7] The women, children, and livestock were taken to a valley called Jirana ten miles from Mecca to be held until he could dispose of them. Muhammad sent Khalid in pursuit of Malik, but after a skirmish Malik and the Thaqifs fled to the safety of their walled town while the Hawazins scattered into the mountains. Muhammad pushed on to Taif, intending to attack the town. He marched his army through the mountains surrounding Taif, which was at an elevation of three thousand feet, destroying a couple of fortified haciendas on the way. His rapid advance was stopped by the walls of Taif. The town had started as a colony of the ancient caravan kingdoms of the Yemenis, who were masters at building stone fortifications, and the walls were famous for their thickness, height, and the precision of the masonry.

Muhammad besieged Taif for nearly a month, but gave up after the town turned out to be impregnable even to his large force. The Thaqifs were expert bowmen and controlled the surroundings from the heights of the battlements. Muhammad lost a number of people to their arrows. It is recorded that he made use of siege machines, primarily catapults and covered battering rams,[8] but the catapults turned out to be ineffective against the superior strength of the walls. Abandoning the catapults, Muhammad sent in a battering ram to smash through the huge double door of the main gate. He must have derived great pleasure in watching the device pound the gate because it was through that same entrance that he was run out of Taif a decade earlier. The battering ram also proved useless. While his troops, hiding from arrows under the protective covering of the device, rammed the gate, the defenders dropped red hot iron spikes onto them, setting the roof on fire. Archers picked off Muhammad's men as they ran from the flames. Furious over the lack of progress, he ordered the destruction of vineyards and only stopped when someone reminded him that he was destroying what would be his if he conquered Taif. His only success came after his heralds shouted to the town that Muhammad would set free any slave who escaped. By the time his army left, more than twenty slaves had made it over the walls.

Unhappy about leaving without getting their hands on the wealth of the town, not to mention taking its women as slaves, Muhammad's men balked at abandoning the siege. One of the Bedouin chieftains spoke of how he dreamed of having a Thaqif woman for breeding, as they were intelligent and bore intelligent children. Relenting to such pressures, Muhammad let his army have another try at breaking through the gate, but this resulted in more casualties. It is said that he laughed at the tribal leaders when they ended up agreeing that it was time to pack up and leave. To spur them, he reminded them that plentiful booty was already awaiting them at the valley of Jirana where the Hawazin women and children had been taken along with the enormous herds.

By the time Muhammad reached Jirana, more than a month had gone by, and during the entire time the six thousand captives had been living out in the open. It was like a refugee camp. During that time their captors had taken care of providing food, as dead slaves were of no use to anyone. At least sixty goats and camels had to be slaughtered each day to provide for them, drawing down on the captured livestock. Muhammad found the captives in tatters and remedied their plight by sending people to Mecca with bags of silver that he had plundered from the Hawazins to buy clothes for them.

When it came to distributing the booty, Muhammad gave the fence-sitting Meccans priority, eager to bring them more tightly to his side. It was one thing to force someone to convert, another to get them to do so enthusiastically. He wanted their enthusiasm. He wanted especially the enthusiasm of Abu Sufyan, Safwan, Suhayl, Hakim Hizam, Jubayr Mutim, and a dozen other notables. They were therefore the first to benefit from his largesse. He gave a hundred camels to Abu Sufyan and a hundred more to each of his sons, Yazid[9] and Muawiya.[10] Each of the notables also received a hundred camels, including the brother of Nader al-Harith, one of the men Muhammad beheaded at Badr. Abu Sufyan and his sons were also given a generous portion of the plundered silver. As for Safwan, Muhammad took him on a tour of the valley to inspect the enormous Hawazin herds that were being held in makeshift pens set up in ravines. As they stopped at one of the ravines, Muhammad asked Safwan what he thought of all the animals penned in there. When his former enemy nodded approvingly, Muhammad said, "It is yours with everything in it."[11] Safwan, whose father Umayya Khalaf and his brother Abdullah had been hacked to death at Bilal's instigation seven years earlier at Badr, oozed with delight at Muhammad's generosity and pledged loyalty to him and his religion on the spot.

Muhammad handed out sex slaves as well—the comeliest of the Hawazin women—to some of the Meccan leaders such as Safwan and to each of his closest people. Ali, Uthman, Umar, Abdul Rahman, Talha, Zubayr, Sad Waqqas, and other prominent believers each got a slave girl. Umar gave his to his son Abdullah, who sent her to an uncle in Mecca to hold until it was certain she was not pregnant. "She was a slave girl, pure and admirable," the literature informs us.[12]

Disposing of such an enormous amount of booty was a time-consuming process. Ten thousand men demanded compensation from Muhammad for all their efforts on behalf of the cause. His favoritism toward the Meccans and his lieutenants grated on them, and some of the Bedouins got rough with him when days went by and they still had not received anything. The story is told that a group of Bedouins, clamoring for their share of the booty, crowded Muhammad into a thorn tree and in their aggressiveness either tore his upper garment or pulled it off. Another Bedouin boldly came into his tent and said he was sick and tired of hearing Muhammad tell everyone to "rejoice," yet what did they have to rejoice about when they had not yet been given what was due to them? Muhammad got instant vengeance by cutting the Bedouin out from partaking in a bowl of ablution water: Turning his back on the man, Muhammad made a showy wash of his face and hands and spat into the water. He gave the bowl to Bilal and another man to drink and daub themselves, saying to them, "Gladden yourselves." Muhammad's wife Umm Salama, hiding behind a curtain that screened her from outsiders, joined in the farce by saying in effect, "Hey, save some for me!"[13] The Bedouin was ignored, and he ended up leaving the tent humiliated.

When an even more impudent Bedouin told Muhammad he was being unjust, Muhammad blew up at him: "Confound you," he cried, "who will be just if not me?" Umar was angered to the point of drawing his sword. "Messenger of God, will you give me permission to behead him?" Muhammad branded the Bedouin a hypocrite and let it go at that.[14] When it finally came to giving the desert Arabs their due, Muhammad ordered a head count and determined that each should get a choice of four camels or forty sheep. Horsemen were to be awarded twelve camels or a hundred and twenty sheep.

One of the thorniest matters involved awarding personal plunder. The general rule Muhammad enunciated before battles was that whoever killed an enemy got to keep the dead man's possessions, generally meaning his weapons and armor, but it could also include a horse and saddle if the slain was a cavalryman. Sometimes heated disputes arose when two people claimed the same kill. Muhammad held long sessions to straighten these matters out, resolving them by demanding the testimony of witnesses. If the matter could not be proven, the booty was added to the general plunder.

As if these complexities were not enough, Muhammad ended up throwing the entire booty situation into disarray when he made an about-face and freed all the captives, including the slaves he had already handed over to family, friends, and people he wanted to influence. This sudden turnaround happened after he got visits from relatives and descendants of his foster mother Halima, whose clan belonged to the Hawazins. First came a group of clansmen led by a man named Abu Surad who claimed to be Muhammad's foster uncle. He gave a flattering speech in which he reminded Muhammad of his foster relationship with the clan, and by extension, to the entire Hawazin nation. The man said, "I saw you suckling and I did not see one better than you; I saw you weaned, and I did not see one weaned better than you. Then I saw you as a youth, and I did not see a better youth. In you the characteristics of goodness were perfected."[15,16] The visitor identified women among the captives who had a foster relationship with him, as they were descendants of Halima who had long before passed away. He begged Muhammad to take this relationship into consideration and show mercy to them by freeing them, promising him they would convert.

What clinched the deal was a visit from Muhammad's foster sister Shaymi, the biological daughter of Halima. She was among the captives and was brought before him after she told her captors of her special relationship with him. She was now seventy years old, ten years older than Muhammad, and hardly recognizable, but she showed him the permanent scar on her upper arm from a severe bite he had inflicted on her while she was carrying him on her hip.

Muhammad immediately restored freedom to the captives from Halima's clan, but because everything that had belonged to them had already been distributed to the Bedouins, he gave them compensation from his fifth of the booty. He took this further by freeing all the Hawazin women and children, a decision that was complicated by the fact he had already apportioned them as slaves to the various tribes as part of their pay for services rendered. Muhammad agreed to this when representatives of the defeated Hawazins accepted to convert en masse and to be satisfied with only the return of their women and children. After the Hawazins signed a document stating the terms of the agreement, Muhammad ordered a meeting of all the tribal and clan leaders of his followers and appealed to them to release the women and children. They had the right to the slaves that had been awarded to them, but he promised them God's special consideration should they restore them to the Hawazins. After much grumbling, the women and children were returned and the families were reunited. Even the comely ones who had been given to the Meccans and to Muhammad's family and friends were returned, several of them now pregnant.

The complications stemming from the Hawazin plunder did not end there, however. By the time it came to satisfying the numerous Yathrib contingent, nothing was left. There were four thousand men from Yathrib, and they were angry, particularly the younger ones. What really irked them was Muhammad's generosity to the Meccans leaders. They had not done any of the fighting, "whereas our swords are still dripping with blood,"[17] one of them said. Sad Ubada, one of the Khazraj chieftains, came to Muhammad to report the discontent. In diplomatic language to keep Umar from reaching for his sword, he added that he could not bring himself to disagree with them. They had followed Muhammad faithfully to Mecca and had not hesitated to join him in battle against the Hawazins and Thaqifs. They deserved compensation.

Muhammad was miffed. He issued a call for all the Ansars—Helpers, as the Yathrib converts were called—to gather before him. The meeting was in an enclosed area, and only Yathrib converts and the original Meccan émigrés were allowed in. When they were fully assembled, Muhammad launched into a harangue. The selfishness of the Helpers was the theme of it: Look what he had done for them! Had he not come to them in Yathrib when they were immersed in ignorance about God? Had he not guided them to God? Had they forgotten that they had been warring against one another, and he had brought them together? Had he not brought prosperity to them through previous plunder? He shook his head in disbelief that they were angry with him over this matter of his generosity with the Meccans. Could they not trust in the judgment of the Messenger of God? He was generous with the Meccans because their faith was newly acquired, meaning it was still weak, whereas the faith of the Helpers was now deeply rooted. The Meccans were in need of this kind of outreach until they could become more secure in their faith.[18]

When he was done with the guilt trip, Muhammad turned to promises and flattery: He would conquer Bahrain for them, and only they and not the Meccans would get anything out of it. If they liked, he would write up a contract about this with them so they could hold him to his word. He loved them more than anyone, he told them. How could he not? He was disbelieved in Mecca, but they trusted him; when he was alone, they helped him; when he was an outcast, they gave him refuge; when he was in distress, they comforted him. By God, there was no one else he would rather be with! The Meccans may have gotten some plunder, but it was the messenger of God who was returning with his beloved people to Yathrib!

Then he really poured it on: In the next life, after everyone is resurrected but prior to the final judgment before God, the Helpers will meet him at the Great Pond, a body of water so extensive it equals the distance between Sana and Oman. They will be the first and the foremost of his companions as they go before the thone of God for judgment, and Muhammad will intercede in their favor for all that they had done in the cause of God. The Helpers, and the children of the Helpers, and the children of the children of the Helpers, would be the greatest before God. It is said that Muhammad's eloquence was so moving that before he was finished men were crying until their beards became soaked with tears.[19]

Muhammad was triumphant. Everyone was yielding to him. In less than two months, he had conquered and converted Mecca and its environs and had subdued and converted the entire Hawazin nation. He had wiped away the vestiges of idolatry in much of the region. People who had scattered out of fear for their lives started drifting back to seek forgiveness from him for past enmity in exchange for converting. He was in such a hearty mood that he was generous to everyone who came to him. If they wanted something, he gave it to them from his fifth of the plunder. The literature gives the example of an elderly woman who came to him saying she was a sister of Halima's husband. She reminded him of incidents that proved her claim. She came with an offering of a case of cheese, heartwarming stories of Halima's final days, and a desire to convert. She made the pledge of faith directly to him, but he took her pledge in the manner he did with women, which was to dip his hand in a bowl of water first, then pass it to her to dip her hand. Before she left she told him a sad story that her family had fallen on hard times and were in need of assistance. She was as good at evoking tears as he was, and Muhammad ended up giving her bundles of clothes, a camel with a howdah, and two hundred gold coins. As she was leaving she said, "You were the best foster child as a baby, and you are the best of men as an adult. You are a great blessing."[20]

Turning to diplomacy, Muhammad sent word to the Hawazin leader Malik, who was still in hiding in Taif, that he would forgive him and return his family to him provided he convert. He would throw in a hundred camels to make it even more enticing. Malik took him up on it, and in exchange Muhammad gave him command over the Hawazins and sent him to steal Thaqif livestock.

After the last of the Hawazin booty was distributed, after streams of people had been forgiven, and after leadership positions had been doled out, Muhammad performed a minor pilgrimage to Mecca. Prior to leaving for the pilgrimage, however, he suffered another epileptic attack. The attack happened in the open, and Umar and others held a blanket over him to shield him from the sun until it was over.[21] Following the fit, he led the entire army on the pilgrimage. When it was completed, the Bedouins returned to their tribal territories while he and the Aws and Khazraj went back to Yathrib, leaving preachers, administrators, and judges in charge of Mecca.

Within a year Taif capitulated. The mountain town was surrounded by the rising sea of Muhammad's religion and had become as isolated as an island. With the constant attacks by their former Hawazin friends and allies, converting became a matter of survival. The decision was precipitated by the defection of Urwa Masud, the son of one of the Taif sheikhs who had run Muhammad out of town ten years earlier and was now an influential leader. He was one of the men the Meccans sent to talk to Muhammad at Hudaybiyya, trusted by the Meccans because his mother was from Mecca and was a relative of Abu Sufyan. He was among the first in Taif to recognize that Muhammad's dominion was inevitable. He went to Yathrib to make a declaration of faith, then returned to Taif, but no sooner had he gone public about his conversion than he was assassinated, shot in the chest with an arrow fired by an irate townsman.

His death led to a citywide debate about Taif's precarious situation, and in the end the town sent a delegation to Muhammad to explore their options. The delegates asked Muhammad for one condition, that if they converted they be allowed to keep their beloved al-Lat for a period of three years. Muhammad refused. The sanctuary of al-Lat, her temple, and all personal idols of the Thaqifs had to be destroyed. The delegates returned to Taif and persuaded the town to capitulate through conversion. If they did not, Muhammad would surely return and subjugate them as he had done to the Hawazins and so many others. In the end, the people acknowledged they were afraid of what Muhammad would do to them and agreed to convert. They "chose security over fear," the literature notes.[22]

Before leaving Yathrib, the delegates advised Muhammad that the people of Taif would balk at destroying the temple of al-Lat with their own hands, so Muhammad dispatched Mughira ibn Shuba, Urwa Masud's nephew, with a small force to destroy it for them. It is likely Muhammad selected Mughira to show his contempt for the town that had run him out a decade earlier.

Mughira was a fugitive and desperado in the eyes of the people of Taif for murdering thirteen of his tribesmen and stealing their merchandise. What better man to send to destroy what they most cherished than he? Muhammad also sent Abu Sufyan due to his family connections to Taif, but fearing for his life if he went into Taif with Mughira, Abu Sufyan parted company at the outskirts of town.

Mughira entered through the main gate with ten heavily armed men and took over the temple. No one dared to challenge them. The idol of al-Lat, carved of white stone with inscriptions, was inside the temple behind curtains.[23] Using pickaxes and sledgehammers, Mughira and his men smashed the idol to pieces, then leveled the temple. They kept all the gold, silver, perfume, fabrics, and everything else of value they found.

The townspeople stood nearby, weeping as the goddess of fertility that had reigned over their mountain town for centuries, their beloved Lady of Taif, was turned into a pile of rubble. A mosque was eventually built over the ruins.[24]

CHAPTER 32

Ménage à Quatorze

Officially, Muhammad had thirteen wives and concubines, beginning with Khadija, his wealthy wife of twenty-five years who died three years before he fled Mecca to Yathrib. Then came Sauda, the stout, matronly woman he married several months after Khadija's death as a caretaker for his children; Aisha, Abu Bakr's daughter whom he married shortly after he arrived in Yathrib when she was nine years old; Umar's daughter Hafsa, a twenty-year-old widow when he married her; Zaynab Khuzayma, who died eight months after the marriage; Umm Salama, an early convert and widow of one of Muhammad's first cousins; Zaynab the daughter of Jahsh, a maternal first cousin previously married to Muhammad's adopted son Zayd; Juwayriya, the Bedouin princess taken as booty after he conquered her Mustaliq tribe; Ramlah, the daughter of Muhammad's foremost Meccan enemy Abu Sufyan; Rayhana, a Jewish woman enslaved after the massacre of the Qurayza Jews; Safiya, a seventeen-year-old Jewish girl taken as booty during the conquest of Khaybar; Maria the Copt, given to him as a slave by the ruler of Egypt along with her sister, a eunuch, and a mule; and Maymuna, the thirty-six-year-old half-sister of Zaynab Khuzayma.

These were the established wives whose involvement with Muhammad is given detailed attention in the early histories and biographies. A deep search of the literature, however, reveals Muhammad acquired or attempted to acquire many other women during his years in Yathrib, particularly during the several years leading up to his death—at least another twenty, but perhaps many more. He offered dowries of gold, the fame of being married to the man God talked to, and an assured place in Paradise, but none of these relationships worked out. Some were brief marriages that ended in divorce due to conflicts or disenchantment; some were marriages performed at a distance by proxy, but which also ended in divorce when the bride saw Muhammad or Muhammad got a gander at the bride. In several cases, the established wives conspired to undermine new or emerging rivals. To his embarrassment, several women to whom he proposed flatly rejected his advance.

His endless womanizing confounds unless seen as yet another compulsion, like the elaborate and exhausting prayer rituals he performed day and night, each a fleeting fix for deep emotional problems. We read of unions with Fatima, the daughter of Shuray, and Saba, the daughter of Asma, and Sharaf, the sister of the Angel Gabriel look-alike Dihya, and Amra, the daughter of Zayd of the Kilab tribe who had been previously married to Muhammad's first cousin Fadl, the son of Abbas. We learn that two of the women he married by proxy died on the way to join him in Yathrib: Khawla the daughter of Hudhayl, a famous tribal chieftain in Syria, and Sana, who was also known as Nashat, a Yemeni woman. These women and many others are hardly more than names. There is more detail about Amra, the daughter of Yazid: When she was brought to Muhammad and he disrobed her, he discovered she had leprosy and sent her back to her tribe. And we know something about Duba, the daughter of Amr, famed for her beauty and Rapunzel hair. Eager for a marital connection to Muhammad, her clan had played up her beauty to entice him into an engagement, but he backed out when he learned she was in fact old, her looks faded.

Several of the established wives made a sport of scuttling the prospects of some of the more promising upstarts, as they did to Asma, the daughter of a leading sheikh of the Kindah tribe. After converting, the sheikh offered Muhammad his daughter, touting her as the most beautiful among Arab widows. He explained that her husband had only recently died, and now her heart inclined to the Messenger of God. Muhammad offered him twelve gold coins for Asma and held firm when the man plied him for more. News of her beauty reached the established wives before she got to the mosque. Once there, she was taken to the wives' quarters where Aisha and Hafsa, mischief in their hearts, prepared her for Muhammad's bed. One of them said to her, "The Prophet likes a woman brought before him to say, 'I seek Allah's protection from you.'" So, when she entered his room and he locked the door, let down the curtain, and reached out to her, the woman said, "I seek Allah's protection from you." Muhammad, who had worked himself up in anticipation of the finale, was taken aback. It was a formulaic petition he himself had invented, and it meant she did not want him to touch her. Deeply offended, he divorced the hapless women and sent her back to her tribe despite protestations that she had been duped.[1]

With similar guile, Aisha removed a young woman named Mulayka as a rival. She was the daughter of a Bedouin leader who was killed during the skirmish with Khalid's forces the day Muhammad conquered Mecca. Muhammad was aroused by accounts of Mulayka's youth and beauty and contracted marriage with her from a distance. She would likely have become a permanent fixture at the mosque, but when she arrived in Yathrib, Aisha said to her, "Are you not ashamed to marry the man who killed your father?" Mulayka, devastated by the rebuke, ended up uttering the same words to Muhammad as Asma: "I take refuge with Allah from you." She was sent packing as well.[2]

Tattling wives did in a couple of others. A woman named Shanba of the Ghifari tribe kept aloof from him despite their marriage, a situation he hoped would resolve itself with time. But as he waited for her to become receptive to him, a child that had been born to Maria the Copt died, Muhammad's only offspring other than his children with Khadija. Shanba was heard to remark, "If he were a prophet, his son would not have died!" One of the established wives reported her comment to Muhammad, and he divorced her.[3] Another victim of the tattlers had a habit of peeking through the cracks of the door to her room at the young bucks going to and from the prayer area or hanging around the mosque courtyard. It is unknown how long she and Muhammad had been married, but it was long enough for her to have a room of her own. When Muhammad learned of her behavior, he spied on her and divorced her after catching her in the act.[4] Muhammad's reputation as a skirt chaser scuttled another. We read of Layla, a Khazraj girl who came up behind him at the mosque one day and startled him by smacking him on the back. When he turned around, she said, "I am the daughter of him who feeds the birds and outpaces the wind. I am Layla, daughter of al-Khatim. I have come to you to present myself to you. Will you marry me?" He liked what he saw and said, "Consider it done!" She went back to her people to announce the marriage, but her relatives said, "What a bad thing you have done! You are a self-respecting woman, but the Prophet is a womanizer. Seek an annulment from him." She returned to Muhammad to request an annulment, and he complied.[5,6]

Muhammad's appearance doomed other unions. During the last few years of his life, he put on weight to the point of corpulence. His face became fleshy; he walked with a lurch that left unnaturally wide footprints; when he was seated cross-legged, it looked like he could never get up again without help. He had taken to applying henna to his beard so that it went from salt and pepper to blazing orange. People who saw him for the first time sometimes remarked, "*That* is your prophet?"[7]

The only thing he had going for him was his reputation for getting what he wanted and his claim that God talked to him, but even that did not impress some of the ladies. When the chieftain of a powerful Yemeni tribe paid a visit to him to swear allegiance, he brought his daughter Umayma as an offering in marriage. It was arranged for Muhammad to meet with her in a garden. Various accounts are given, but in all of them it appears the woman found him repugnant. "Can a princess give herself in marriage to an ordinary man?" she said. When he reached out to touch her, she told him to keep his hands off of her and appealed for God's protection against him. He became furious and only calmed down when the go-between, a nephew of her father, said, "Don't let that bother you, Messenger of God. I have someone more beautiful for you." He arranged for Muhammad to marry his sister Qatila. She turned out to be the last of the would-be wives, because he died while she was en route to join him in Yathrib.[8]

Perhaps the rejection that hurt him most deeply came from his first love, Umm Hani, one of Abu Talib's daughters. They had been raised together under Abu Talib's roof and Muhammad had one day asked his uncle for her hand, but his uncle turned him down and married her instead to a Meccan nobleman named Hubayra. Neither Umm Hani nor Hubayra believed in Muhammad's claims about himself, particularly Umm Hani, who knew from their early life together of Muhammad's maladies. Better than anyone, she knew that his delusion of being taken up into Heaven from her home one night was the product of his illnesses. She had attempted to stop him from talking about it, without success. Her husband was a poet, and until the day of the conquest of Mecca he had never ceased to ridicule Muhammad in verse. After the conquest, Umm Hani joined the rest of the Meccans in converting to avoid the death penalty, while Hubayra fled for his life to Najran where he died a disbeliever. According to Muhammad's rules, conversion annulled a prior marriage if the spouse remained an unbeliever, so that Umm Hani's conversion cleared the way for him to propose to her. But she turned him down with lame excuses, such as the fact she had young children and she did not want them bothering him. She also pointed to one of the self-serving verses he composed several years earlier to justify his marriage to Zayd's former wife, which stated that the only Meccan women allowed to him for marriage were those who had emigrated with him.[9] "So I became unlawful to him because I did not emigrate with him. I was one of those who were converted to Islam against their will," she later told an interviewer.[10]

The net result of these misadventures was that Muhammad ended his life with an official harem count of only thirteen women. Three of them died before him: Khadija, Zaynab Khuzayma, and Rayhana. That left ten women with whom he was cohabitating in his latter years. He rotated among them, spending a night with each in turn when he was in town, taking one or two of them with him when he was on the warpath. Though there were ups and downs among the established wives and occasionally acute tensions, the majority of his wives did not make too much of a fuss over the fact they were but one of many. They benefited from their status as wives of Muhammad and enjoyed honorific titles such as "Mother of the Believers" and "Consort of Purity." Though they sometimes accused him of stinginess, Muhammad was a reliable provider and made certain they had what they needed—food, clothing, spending money, all paid for from his share of the spoils of war. After the conquest of Khaybar and Fadak and the seizure of the Jewish date plantations and crop fields, Muhammad awarded each of his established wives an annuity of camel loads of dates and barley.

Apart from the two Jewish wives who had been traumatized by his mass murder of their loved ones, the only wife who appears to have suffered deep psychological damage from Muhammad was Aisha, whom he married when she was but a child. Throughout her marriage, she continually experienced severe jealousy as new women came onto the scene to compete for Muhammad's affection, transforming her into an angry and disruptive presence at the mosque. Stories are told of her smashing dishes of food sent by other wives to her room when Muhammad was with her and of catfights and loud arguments with other wives.[11]

Her relationship with Muhammad was psychologically complex. As a girl she needed devoted love to thrive emotionally, yet to Muhammad she was merely a favorite among his other wives because of her youth. He had sex with her for the first time when she was nine years old, and she later said that she did not understand what was happening to her the first time he penetrated her. Back then, the only other spouse was Sauda, and she was more like a mother to Aisha than a rival for Muhammad's affection. Muhammad began accumulating more wives two years after marrying Aisha with his marriage to Umar's daughter Hafsa, who was twenty years old at the time.

Seeing Muhammad shift his affection away from her to Hafsa gave Aisha the first stab of jealousy. It became so severe that on one occasion she wished for death. This occurred when he took both of them on a raid. On the way, Hafsa rode her camel next to his, and they chatted amiably while Aisha trailed behind, in anguish over being forgotten and ignored. When they made a rest stop, she wandered barefoot into a grassy area and begged God for a scorpion or snake to bite her and put an end to her misery.[12]

Wittingly or unwittingly, Muhammad fanned her jealousy by often praising his first wife to her face. Whenever he slaughtered an animal, he would praise the memory of Khadija and send choice cuts to her sister Hala and other women who had been close to her. Khadija was the best wife he had ever had, Muhammad would often tell Aisha. Khadija had believed in him when no one else did and was the first to embrace his religion. She was so great a wife that God had instructed him to tell her before she died that that she would have a palace in Paradise made of precious stones and pearls. Aisha countered that Khadija had been nothing more than a talkative, meddlesome old woman with inflamed gums in the place of teeth. "Allah has given you somebody better than her," she would say, referring to herself.[13]

What compounded her anguish was that Muhammad was not so much indifferent to her feelings as completely oblivious. He continuously violated her heart, as when he gleefully informed her while in bed with her that God had just granted him permission to marry Zaynab, his former daughter-in-law, or when he proposed to the comely Juwayriya while in Aisha's presence. She had no recourse, as he was incapable of seeing the impact of his behavior on her. Again and again he tried to convince her that her jealousy had nothing to do with him; it came from a devil that possessed her. She should cheerfully accept what almighty God, in his mercy and kindness, allowed his prophet. His reasoning was of no avail. In the grip of her devil, she spied on him, peeping through cracks in the door when he was with a new wife. On one occasion he beat her after she followed him. He had gone out from her room late one night, and suspicious he was heading for an amorous rendezvous, she tailed him. It turned out he had only gone to a nearby cemetery to perform sets of his prayer routines and offer prayers for the dead. He realized she had been following him after he returned to her room and saw she was out of breath. When she admitted to having followed him, he hit her. In one account of the incident, he slapped her hard; in another, he punched her in the chest.[14]

Instead of exorcising her devil, the chastisement pushed her into aggressiveness. She subverted Muhammad's new love interests whenever she could, as she did with Mulayka and Asma and others. She was quick to anger with other wives. On one occasion she punched and kicked Sauda for a perceived slight. Having witnessed the mass beheading of the Qurayza Jews, she absorbed Muhammad's hatred for Jews and was merciless with Safiya after he brought her from Khaybar as a new wife. She became a prankster as well. On one occasion she and Hafsa convinced the slow-witted Sauda that the fearsome Dajjal was on the way to Yathrib at the head of hordes of blood-dripping monsters that had broken free of Gog and Magog. Sauda became so frightened that she hid in a shed and only came out after Muhammad found out about the cruel prank and coaxed her out of hiding. She pulled some pranks on Muhammad as well, once convincing him that he emitted an offensive body odor every time he ate honey given to him by one of the wives Aisha was jealous of. For that prank, she recruited Sauda, who took part in it because she was afraid of

Aisha, to repeat to Muhammad about his body odor whenever he ate the honey. He had a horror of body odor to the point that he constantly bathed and brushed his teeth. He even banned garlic and onions for people joining in congregational prayer or who had appointments to see him. Having heard that he stank from two of his wives, he refused to eat any more of the honey.

Her behavior turned cruel when she raised doubts about Muhammad's paternity of Ibrahim, the child he had with Maria the Copt. Maria was a fair-skinned Egyptian with wavy hair. Everyone raved about her beauty, particularly Muhammad. He began spending more time with her than anyone else, moving her to one of the Nadir properties he had seized several years earlier to keep her apart from the rest of the wives. This became a necessity after she became pregnant. With the announcement she was expecting, all the other wives became hostile to her. Unfortunately for Muhammad, Aisha knew everything about him, including his self-doubts about the pregnancy. Most of his wives were of childbearing age; none had ever become pregnant, yet now the Egyptian slave girl was swelling up. Muhammad had suspicions about her from the start after the slave Mabur was seen going into her quarters. The slave was spared only when it became clear he was a eunuch. After she became pregnant, his suspicions about her fidelity resurfaced. The literature informs us that it took a visitation of the Angel Gabriel to assure him that he was truly the father.[15] After the child was born Muhammad made a five-mile round trip every day to visit Maria and the baby. Some time after the birth, he came back to the mosque with the swaddled Ibrahim to show him around. Aisha was quick with a cruel dig: "Neither I nor others see a resemblance."[16]

Then Umar's daughter Hafsa turned hostile on him. He had no one to blame but himself over this: She returned to her room from a visit to relatives one day to find him in her bed on top of the Christian slave girl. She screamed hysterically: "In my room, on my day, and on my own bed!"[17] Like any husband caught in the act, Muhammad was red faced and was eager to hush it up. It was not exactly adultery, but it upset the rotation schedule, the *modus vivendi* that he had established among his wives—one night with each in turn. He swore he would not have anything more to do with Maria and begged Hafsa not to say anything about it to anyone, but she told Aisha and soon everyone knew.

Muhammad's apology was not enough for Hafsa. Following the example of Aisha, she began to talk back to him and joined with Aisha in plotting ways to upset him. Her father Umar found out about it as a result of a heated argument with his wife. When he rebuked her that it was not the place of a woman to argue with a man, she said that Hafsa argued with Muhammad all the time to the point that he would be upset for an entire day. If Hafsa could argue with Muhammad, she could argue with Umar. Umar was shaken. This was surely the influence of Yathrib women. In Mecca, men dominated their women, but Yathrib women ran roughshod over their men. Aisha had taken up the bad habits of Yathrib women, and now she had infected his daughter. He stormed into Hafsa's room at the mosque. Hulking over her, he scolded her and warned her she was on the path to ruin for upsetting "God's Apostle." If she kept at it Muhammad would likely divorce her. He blamed Aisha and warned Hafsa against her influence. Then he sought out Aisha and Umm Salama and gave them a tongue lashing as well. They were all on the road to ruin, he warned. If they earned Muhammad's anger they earned God's anger, and if they earned God's anger they were doomed to burn forever in Hell. Aisha told Umar to mind his own business; so did Umm Salama.

Even without the back-talking of Aisha and Hafsa Muhammad was losing patience with his wives. Their bickering over everything had become nightmarish. Not just one or two wives, but now all them began hammering him. For a time it was about Maria. Lately, the wives were complaining to him about Aisha. She was his favorite, and because of that whenever anyone brought gifts for him, they would always leave them with Aisha. It was not right. People with gifts should have the courtesy to bring them to the woman whose day it was to be with him. Then there was the intractable problem of Zaynab. Zaynab acted like a snotty princess. She considered herself superior to all the other wives because she was the only one among them whom God Almighty had authorized Muhammad to marry. She knew the verses he had come up with when he was in bed with Aisha, and she happily recited them to anyone foolish enough to challenge her about it. That was a tough one for Muhammad to deal with: God said to him what he said while he was in bed with Aisha, and there was no way to change what God said. He let them fight it out.

Following the conquest of Mecca and the battles of Hunayn and Taif, Aisha and Hafsa teamed up to cause Muhammad yet another harem headache by organizing the wives to pressure him for a greater monthly allowance. They got him to meet with them as a group to discuss their demands, but it did not go favorably for them. Possibly arranged ahead of time, Umar and Abu Bakr showed up as muscle. Umar listened to the wifely complaints for a while, then stood up to tell a story of what happened when one of his wives, the daughter of his Yathrib "brother," pestered him for money. "I wish you had seen it," he said to Muhammad. "I got up and slapped her." Muhammad laughed and said in essence, "That was only one woman. Take a look around, they all want more money out of me." At that, Umar and Abu Bakr grabbed their daughters by the hair and beat them, a lesson to all the wives. "You ask Allah's Messenger for what he does not possess," Umar and Abu Bakr shouted as they slapped away, but Aisha and Hafsa held firm. "By Allah, we do not ask Allah's Messenger for anything he does not possess."[18]

Muhammad blew up at this. It is said that he became so upset that he stormed out of the room and declared himself on strike from his wives. He had had enough! He was furious about their bickering and their demands for more money, and he was still fuming at Hafsa for telling Aisha he had had sex with Maria in her room. That had caused him no end of embarrassment. He announced he intended to boycott them for an entire month. He climbed a ladder to a loft at the back of the residential quarters and posted a muscular Abyssinian slave at the foot of it to keep people away. For twenty-nine days, he never came down. Food was brought to the slave, who climbed the ladder to hand it off to him.

The boycott was ill-timed. While he was hiding out, reports reached Yathrib that the Ghassanids of Syria were preparing to make war on him. They were Christianized Arabs who controlled a large swath of what is now southern Syria and Jordan and had helped the Byzantines in their recent victory over the Persian Empire. They were well equipped, battle-hardened, and fearsome. Spurred by Muhammad's recent incursions into Syria and encouraged by Heraclius, the Ghassanids were preparing to make war on Muhammad, or such were the reports reaching Yathrib. The believers were in a fright. They were leaderless in a time of mortal danger. Muhammad was not even leading them in prayer any longer, nor was it he on the preacher platform giving them the guidance of God. Muhammad must have known about the geopolitical developments, but he remained cloistered, tossing around verses in his head to deal with the situation caused by his wives.

Toward the end of his boycott, a rumor coursed through the valley like a flash flood that Muhammad had decided to divorce them all. Umar learned about it from a friend who kept him informed of developments. The man pounded on his door early one morning shouting, "Open, open!" In a fright, Umar rushed to the door. "Are the Ghassanids coming?" "No," the man said. "It's even greater and more horrifying than that. Allah's Apostle has divorced his wives!"[19]

Such was not the case, but the rumor was fanned by a verse Muhammad had crafted that sported with the idea of divorce: "Maybe his Lord, if he divorces you, will give him in your place wives better than you." The verse went on to define the characteristics of the ideal wife: A widow or a virgin, it mattered not as long as she was submissive, believing, pious, penitent, devout, and inclined to fasting.[20] Muhammad had recited these new verses to someone, very likely the Abyssinian slave, with instructions to repeat them in the mosque. Once they were thus publicized, the divorce rumor was born.

After learning the horrifying news, Umar ran to find Hafsa. She was in her room weeping. A scowling Umar said, "Did I not warn you about that? Did the Prophet divorce all of you?" Tears streaming down her face, she wailed, "I don't know."[21] He called her a loser and went to the loft, but he could not get by the slave. The slave announced his presence three times, but Muhammad did not acknowledge him. Frustrated, Umar said in a loud voice so that Muhammad could hear that he had not come to seek any favors for Hafsa. Quite the contrary. "By Allah, if Allah's Messenger would command me to strike her neck, I would certainly do it."[22] Those were magic words. Muhammad let him climb up. Umar found him laying on his side on a palm mat, his head propped up on one arm. He had welts on his skin from the palm fronds, and the sight caused Umar to weep that his beloved prophet was living like a pauper. Other than the simple bed, there was little in the loft: leather water bags hanging from a rafter, a modest stock of dates, a chamber pot. Once he got a grip on himself, Umar brought Muhammad up to date about the Ghassanid threat and finally asked him point blank if he had divorced his wives. He let out a sigh of relief when Muhammad shook his head. When Umar first climbed into the loft, Muhammad was in a foul mood, but after hearing Umar's stories about his arguments with his wife and his thoughts about the differences between Meccan and Yathrib women, he softened up and even smiled. Umar advised him to take a hard line with his wives.

After a long chat, they climbed down the ladder and went to the wives' quarters. It was day twenty-nine of Muhammad's rebellion against his wives, and he had thoroughly shaken up the entire Submitter community, particularly his wives. They were guilt-ridden wrecks, so that when he gave them the choice of divorce and the freedom to pursue the wealth of the world or staying with him subject to his restrictions and modest lifestyle, they gladly accepted to remain with him.

The boycott of his wives over, Muhammad prepared to make war on the Ghassanids.

CHAPTER 33

Terror Has Made
Me Victorious

The rumor that the Byzantines were equipping an army to attack Yathrib was started by Nabataean traders from the region of Petra who had arrived in Yathrib about the time Muhammad was hiding from his wives in the loft. It was only a rumor, but it stirred up fear. The Byzantines and their Christian Arab allies formed the most powerful empire of the age. Heraclius had only recently defeated the Persian Empire and was now free to attack the upstart prophet, or so was the talk that swirled around Yathrib. The rumor snowballed: Heraclius had advanced his troops a year's salary in anticipation of the campaign. Worse yet, the Ghassanids, the Judhamis, the Lakhmids, and other Christianized Arabs were "flocking around the Roman eagles, and the vanguard was already at Balqa" near Mutah where Jabir, Rawaha, and Zayd met their end a year earlier.[1]

After he came down from the loft, Muhammad wasted no time in putting together the largest army he had ever assembled. He wanted to bring war to the Byzantines, not wait for them in Yathrib. He issued a general call to arms, ordering even the recently conquered Meccans to send forces. Muhammad proclaimed it was the command of God that all able-bodied men must fight for the cause or face the punishment of God and his messenger. He confected fresh *jihad* verses to back up the threats.[2] He called his top people and demanded contributions from all of them. Uthman provided several hundred baggage camels along with a thousand gold coins. Abu Bakr handed over sacks of silver coins; women donated gold bracelets and anklets; others brought camel-loads of grains and dates. The obligatory charity tax became a war tax and was collected from every tribe Muhammad had subjugated.

Despite the threats of divine punishment for failure to obey the call to arms, Muhammad faced resistance. Many in Yathrib did not want to go to war. Among their objections was the fact that it was midsummer and the heat was set on broil, yet it was Muhammad's intention to march four hundred miles north across the burning sands to Syria. From the pulpit, Muhammad fumed that such resisters were hypocrites. He crafted yet another round of verses about pretend believers who unmasked themselves by refusing to obey.[3]

At one point he went beyond threatening oratory by employing a tactic he had recently used to get people to attend the dawn and late night prayers, which was to torch the houses of people who did not show up, occupants still inside.[4] Thus when he learned that a group of dissidents had assembled in the home of a Jewish convert to organize resistance to the expedition, he sent a squad of zealots to burn the house down. Only the Jewish convert was said to have died in the flames, but others suffered broken bones leaping from the roof.[5] Despite the strong-arm tactics, people still came to him begging for an exemption, alleging illness, poverty, family complications, and a host of other excuses. The most original came from a man who said he would be tempted into sin at the sight of Byzantine women, who were famed like Muhammad's concubine Maria for their fair beauty and beguiling eyes. Muhammad gave them the exemption they asked for, but he compiled a mental list for later action against them.

Because of the timing and the unquestionable might of the Byzantines, the expedition against the Yellow Skins, as the fair Byzantines were called, makes sense only if seen as a desperation move by Muhammad, who feared that his control over Yathrib was slipping.[6] Disenchantment over his rule was on the rise. This took root among many of the Yathrib converts following the conquests of Mecca and Hunayn. They had done the fighting, yet Muhammad had given the Meccans the choicest part of the booty and had returned much of the remainder to the Hawazins to secure their support, leaving the Yathrib converts with leftovers. He had promised to conquer Bahrayn for them and give them exclusive right to the plunder, but after they returned to Yathrib they heard no further talk about it. Additionally, his successes had led to the flooding of Yathrib with indigent converts at a time of declining agricultural output. As previously noted, he had driven out or slaughtered the most productive people of the valley—the Jews—and had turned over their fields and plantations to his Meccan compatriots, men who had no prior experience in agriculture and were disdainful of physical labor. As a result, there was less food to go around. On top of that was Muhammad's perennial problem of "hypocrites" hiding behind the shield of the *shahada*. Under the leadership of the Khazraj chieftain Abdullah Ubayy, they were gaining ground and were eager to take advantage of any misstep. By attacking the Byzantines, Muhammad hoped to score a major victory that would boost morale and give him sufficient plunder to keep his people happy.

His fears about losing control over Yathrib were heightened when the army left for Syria. The assembly area was at a mountain pass just north of Yathrib called Farewell Pass. Abdullah Ubayy had camped his people there in preparation for the expedition, but on the day Muhammad left at the head of the army, Abdullah did what he had done at Uhud: He returned to Yathrib, taking loyalists with him. Muhammad had appointed the assassin Maslama to run Yathrib in his absence, but now he sent Ali back to keep an eye on things, very likely as "a precaution against (Abdullah Ubayy's) ambitions and to suppress any revolt that broke out," noted military historian Richard Gabriel.[7]

The literature claims thirty thousand men took part in the expedition and that the rear trailed two days behind the vanguard. Latecomers straggled even farther behind. Because of the heat, the army traveled at night and sheltered itself from the sun during the day. Syria was at a distance of more than four hundred miles, but Muhammad never got any farther than the minor oasis of Tabuk about three hundred and thirty miles north of Yathrib. The literature reports that Muhammad remained in Tabuk for ten days, sent out a number of raiding parties, then returned to Yathrib without ever encountering a single Yellow Skin; not a single dinar had been acquired in plunder; not a single woman taken captive. No explanation is given for the aborted expedition, but it can be deduced from the numerous water and food miracles attributed to Muhammad during the trip that the army was running dangerously short of both.[8] To proceed on to Syria would likely have resulted in a significant loss of manpower to dehydration and defection. He may have also received intelligence that the Byzantine army was not at Balqa as he had first believed, but was much farther north and was not on a war footing.

This turn of events made Muhammad look inept, and he now faced a new and potentially more serious foe in his discontented troops. It is unlikely that more than one in ten of Muhammad's men believed what he claimed about himself, if even that many. Apart from the threats against them if they did not participate, the motivator for the majority of them was the prospect of booty. Most had spent their own money and resources to equip themselves; they had endured the grilling heat, the hardships of travel, and the shortages of food and water. Yet they had nothing to show for it, just as they had nothing to show for their efforts in Mecca, Hunayn, and Taif. Even the true believers must have had their faith tested. Muhammad tried to dampen discontent with sermons that his religion of Abraham was the best religion, that his personal example was the best way of life, that the best account of God was the Koran, and that the noblest death was dying in God's cause.[9]

More pragmatically, he sent raiding parties in every direction to the towns and tribes of the region with a message: submit or be destroyed. He gave Christians and Jews the choice between conversion or paying a submission tax.[10] Pagans were given no such choice. For them, they had to abandon polytheism and embrace Muhammad's religion or they would be put to death.

In terms of the needed booty, the raids were unsuccessful. Christians, Jews, and polytheists surrendered to Muhammad's overwhelming force. Much of the region north of Tabuk and west to the Red Sea and the Gulf of Aqaba was Christian. Instead of suicidal resistance, the kings and bishops of various towns sent envoys to him to work out agreements to pay the submission tax in exchange for being left alone. The tax came out to one gold coin for every adult payable every year on the first month of the lunar calendar. Various towns were also made to turn over a percentage of their agricultural produce or their manufactured goods, such as the textiles and fine perfumes of the Jarba and Adruh tribes.

While Muhammad's cause prospered through these capitulations, his troops remained without pay. The discontent must have been running high because Muhammad ended up fearing for his life. He became paranoid that a plot was afoot against him, and he may have suspected some of his closest people were involved. On the return trip a real or imagined assassination attempt took place as he was descending a narrow, steep trail of a mountainside with a cliff on one side. He had given the order that no one except two of his most trusted people were to go down with him, one leading his camel by its bridle, the other following behind; the rest of the army was to take an alternate route. Despite the order, a dozen men riding camels appeared at the top of the trail. The tails of their turbans were wrapped around their faces so that only their eyes peered out. It looked to Muhammad like some of them were unfolding slings. He was certain they intended to pelt his camel into bolting over the cliff with him, or they were going to descend down the path and crowd him off the trail, pushing him and his camel into the abyss below. He shouted curses at them and sent his two trusted men, both early Meccan converts, to attack them, but the riders wheeled away before they could get close enough. Muhammad had suspicions about who they were and named them to Hudhayfa, one of the two men with him. Hudhayfa offered to have them killed, but Muhammad shook his head. He did not want to be known as a prophet who killed his companions. God would take care of it by striking them with bolts of fire to give them a foretaste of what awaited them in the eternal furnace. Not certain the riders were the men he named, he swore Hudhayfa to secrecy, though as an insurance policy against further attempts on his life he made sure everyone knew that Hudhayfa knew the names.[11]

The incident heightened Muhammad's paranoia about treacherous people hiding behind the *shahada*. He was certain of the identity of many of them such as Abdullah Ubayy, but others needed to be exposed. Before getting back to Yathrib, he decided that a mosque that had been built recently near Quba in the southwestern corner of the highlands was a nest of false believers and conspirators. It had been completed just before the army left Yathrib against the Byzantines. The builders had come to him to ask him to pray in the mosque and give it his blessing. It was not only a place of prayer but a shelter for the poor and ill, they told him. Before reaching Yathrib, however, Muhammad had a "revelation" informing him that the real purpose of the new mosque was nefarious. The evidence hit him like a bolt of lightening: The dozen men who built it were of the Aws tribe and none of them had gone north with the army. This branded them automatically as hypocrites. Moreover, upon inquiry he learned the mosque had been built as an extension of the home of Abu Amir, a Christian convert and sworn enemy of Muhammad. Abu Amir had converted to Christianity prior to Muhammad's arrival in Yathrib and had assumed an ascetic life-style that earned him the nickname The Monk. After the battle of Badr, The Monk had fled with a dozen supporters to Mecca, and they fought with the Meccans at Uhud.[12] Abu Amir later fled to Syria where he was said to have urged Heraclius to wage war against Muhammad. That clinched it for Muhammad. What else could this mosque be, therefore, than a foothold of the Byzantines in Yathrib, a place of gathering for dissenters and subversives, vile hypocrites one and all? Muhammad branded it the "mosque of dissent." As he led the returning army into Yathrib, he sent a troop of zealots to torch the mosque. "Go to this mosque whose people are evil, and demolish it and burn it!" he commanded.[13] At least one man was burned to death inside. "Even his scrotum was burned," one of the arsonists recalled.[14]

Days before he got back to the valley, Yathrib was alerted that Muhammad was in a rage. Couriers who reached Yathrib in advance of the army spread the news that "hypocrites" had attempted to kill him and that he intended to deal with phony believers once he got back. The news caused panic. Even before the "mosque of dissidence" was a smoldering ruin, seven men who had not gone out with the army tied themselves to columns inside Muhammad's mosque and proclaimed they would remain tied up until forgiven by God and his messenger for having refusing to fight in the cause of God. They confessed to laziness. They were procrastinators, they were sinners, but in their hearts was true and sincere love of God and his messenger. When Muhammad, covered with the dust of the journey, entered the mosque courtyard and saw the row of tied-up men, he said, "I swear by God, I'll not release them, nor will I forgive them until God, the Almighty and Glorious, releases them!"[15] He let them stew a few days and then came up with a verse that commended them for doing a good deed by confessing to their sin. "They have mixed a deed that was righteous with another that was evil. Perhaps Allah will turn unto them in forgiveness. Surely, Allah is Oft-Forgiving, Most Merciful."[16] With that they were set free.

Requiring believers to go to war on behalf of his cause was Muhammad's version of a loyalty test. Going off to fight, killing or being killed, was proof of loyalty; not going was proof of disloyalty. Most of Muhammad's followers passed the test by participating in the Tabuk expedition. Those who did not were put through a course of rough reeducation by shaming and ostracism before being allowed, heads bowed and repentant, back into the fold. While the seven slackers remained tied up in the mosque, a stream of men—some eighty in all—came to him to explain their reasons for not obeying his command to go with the army. He greeted them one at a time with an angry smile and had them sit before him to explain their absence from the expedition. "What kept you back?" All but a few offered elaborate excuses. Muhammad sent them away with a warning that God would know if they were telling the truth or not. He sent his agents to investigate their claims, and they reported back that thirty-six of them had lied. On a day of a packed congregational meeting, Muhammad lowered the boom. From the pulpit he announced, "There are hypocrites among you!" He named all thirty-six men and ordered them to get to their feet so everyone could see them.[17] As their names were called out, the men reluctantly stood up, some covering their face. Muhammad denounced their sin of disobedience to the crowd and growled at the men to seek God's forgiveness. Shaken to the core at being publicly singled out as hypocrites, they admitted to their sin; some wept. Arms outstretched to Muhammad, they begged forgiveness.

The shaming of the thirty-six men was relatively mild punishment compared to the penalty he imposed on three men who had been honest about not going. When they were called before him, they confessed they had no excuse. They were guilty of disobedience to God and his messenger. Though all three were steadfast believers who had taken part in previous expeditions, Muhammad imposed an exemplary punishment. He announced that God had ordered them to be shunned, an ostracism that lasted nearly two months. Two of the men stayed in their homes, weeping most of the time. Another, a stalwart Yathrib convert named Kab Malik, continued to go out to the markets and even went to the mosque to pray, but everyone including his relatives gave him the cold shoulder. They refused to speak to him or even look at him. When he spoke to them they looked the other way. It was as if he no longer existed. He was like a ghost passing undetected through the crowd. At the mosque he would strive to catch Muhammad's attention, but if Muhammad even looked in his direction, he stared straight through him. After the fortieth day of excruciating rejection, a messenger pounded on his front door with news of even more punishment: Muhammad forbade him to have sexual relations with his wife. They were to be separated. This state of affairs continued until the fiftieth day when Kab heard someone in the distance shouting "Rejoice, Kab!" He was on the roof of his blockhouse engaged in prayer when this occurred, and he did not know what to make of it. The voice was coming from the top of Mount Sal, a small mountain near the mosque that had served as an observation post during the battle of the Ditch. Before long, someone came to his front door to announce glad tidings: God Almighty had communicated to Muhammad that Kab and the other two men were forgiven. Kab rushed to the mosque where Muhammad was seated cross-legged in the prayer area surrounded by his most prominent followers. Many of them jumped to their feet to shake Kab's hand and congratulate him. Muhammad said to him, "Rejoice at the best day you have ever had since your mother gave you birth!" God had forgiven him! Kab was so overcome with gratitude that he offered in charity everything he possessed, which consisted primarily of his share of the loot from the many raids and battles he had participated in, including Khaybar. Muhammad at first rejected the offer, but then accepted a portion. "Keep some of what you own, that will be best for you." Kab replied, "I will just keep my share of the booty from Khaybar."[18]

As usual, Muhammad left Abdullah Ubayy alone despite his having abandoned the expedition the day the army marched out of Yathrib. This was likely out of fear of his latent power. The Abdullah problem resolved itself, however, when he died, apparently of natural causes, about a month after Muhammad's return from Tabuk. At the funeral, Muhammad said prayers for him, but then kicked himself for having thus honored the arch-phony believer of Yathrib, the man who had survived by skillfully exploiting the shield of the *shahada*. Muhammad may have secretly admired Abdullah for playing the game so well, but some of the true believers questioned him about the prayers.[19] As a result, he composed a Koran verse criticizing himself and forbidding himself any further such slip-ups. "Nor do you ever pray for any of them that dies, nor stand at his grave; for they rejected Allah and his Messenger, and died in a state of perverse rebellion."[20]

While he failed in his original objective of engaging the Byzantines in battle, the Tabuk expedition enabled Muhammad to complete the conquest of northern Arabia. The conquest had begun three years earlier when he sent Abdul Rahman to subjugate the Christian caravan town of Duma. It continued with attacks on the Tamims and Tayyis, important tribes to the southeast of Duma that ended up accepting Muhammad's suzerainty. With the latest capitulations he now controlled the vast northern area stretching from the Red Sea and the Gulf of Aqaba to the Tamim and Tayyi territories of north-central Arabia. With his control came administrators, Koran teachers, and tax collectors.

His show of military strength in Tabuk accelerated the surrender of Arabia to him. Prior to marching out of Yathrib with thirty thousand men, only a dribble of representatives of tribes and clans had come to Yathrib to pay homage and either join the religion or agree to pay the subjugation tax. Now these "delegations," as the literature tags them, turned into a steady stream of men who were eager not to become the object of a Muhammad raid. Stories are told of men dismounting from their camels in the courtyard of the mosque and rushing to grab his hand and kiss it. Though he expressed a preference for people who did not shed their dignity when approaching him, Muhammad was never one to discourage fawning behavior and rarely sent any of weak-kneed tribal representatives away except with gifts of several pounds of silver, either in coin or bullion.

He was a sucker for flattery, and even former enemies knew they would score well with him if they heaped praise on him, as did the Meccan poet Kab Zuhayr who used to mock him in verse. At the time of the conquest of Mecca, Muhammad ordered him to be killed on sight. Zuhayr fled to southern Arabia, but when it became clear there would never be a long-term escape from Muhammad's reach, he joined the stream of visitors to Yathrib to ask to be forgiven for his past hostility. In front of a crowd in the mosque courtyard, he declared himself a believer and recited an effusive ode that described Muhammad as "a light-giving illumination, an unsheathed sword of God, of fine Indian steel."[21] With his pledge of fealty, Zuhayr acquired the shield of the *shahada*. With his flattering poetry, he earned himself a place in Muhammad's heart.

The southern part of the Arabian Peninsula, which until then had been largely spared Muhammad's aggression, now became the target for expansion. As he had done in the past, he used shock-and-awe terror tactics—"making slaughter in the land" was the way he termed it—to undermine the will to resist. This phase began three months before the Tabuk expedition when he sent a party of zealots on a surprise attack against a tribe in the mountainous region of what is now the Asir province of Saudi Arabia. They attacked at dawn, killing as many people as they could, and made off with one hundred and fifty camels, three thousand goats, and some women. This was followed by a raid led by Ali deep into the heart of Yemen near Sana. His cavalry clashed with a local tribe and came out the winner after slaying twenty of the tribesmen.

A few months later Muhammad struck again with an attack on Jurash, an ancient caravan town and commercial center of the Asir region. This was essentially a proxy raid, as it was carried out by a local chieftain named Surad who had gone to Yathrib to pledge allegiance to Muhammad. He was sent back to Yemen with instructions to wage war on his polytheist neighbors in Muhammad's name, but he was told that he was required to set aside one fifth of the booty for Muhammad. Once back in Yemen, Surad raised an army and besieged Jurash for an entire month. Unable to breech the walls or force the surrender of the defenders, he made a showy withdrawal of his forces, but waited in the mountains for the townspeople to come out, then attacked and slaughtered them. It so happened that the people of Jurash had sent representatives to Muhammad before they knew he had ordered an attack against them. This delegation must have been en route to Yathrib while Surad was returning home to make war preparations. While the delegates from Jurash were meeting with Muhammad, Surad was slaughtering their people.

When Muhammad informed them of this, they rushed home to find that many of their kinsmen and tribal neighbors had been put to the sword. They returned to Yathrib and embraced Muhammad's religion.[22]

About the same time, Muhammad sent another Yemeni convert to destroy the temple of Dhu Khalasa, famed as the "southern Kabah," which was also in the Jurash region. Dhu Khalasa was the male equivalent of the goddess al-Lat, and the sanctuary was the destination of the annual pilgrimage for many of the southern Arabs. The Yemeni convert was an important sheikh of the Bajila tribe that maintained the sanctuary. He succeeded in destroying the temple, but only after killing three hundred men who rushed to the defense of their beloved temple.

With these actions, Muhammad subjugated the religious and commercial centers of an entire region of Yemen, and the rest of Yemen took note. After that, Ali or Khalid usually had only to show up at the head of a cavalry force and the targeted population would surrender, as happened when Khalid stopped at the gate of the largely Christian town of Najran and cried out, "O people, accept Islam and you will be safe."[23] Najran ended up paying the subjugation tax to remain Christian, though it also had to accept an infusion of preachers, judges, and tax collectors. From then on the delegations that visited Yathrib had distinctly southern and eastern accents. The rulers of Himyar, Hadramaut, Oman, and Bahrayn came to Muhammad on bended knee. He commissioned the ones who converted to wage war on polytheists, and when they did so, he sent them letters congratulating them for killing infidels.

Whereas booty was the driving force behind the expansion of Muhammad's cult, with success came diminishing opportunities for plunder; but with conquest came taxes that became an important source of revenue. Christians and Jews who refused to convert paid a head tax in gold, silver, agricultural products, or merchandise. Converts paid what Muhammad termed a charity tax, though in reality it ended up in the general fund and much of it went to pay for the costs of war. Over time, the balance of his revenues shifted from plunder to taxes.

There were further raids into Yemen, but these were essentially mopping-up operations against holdouts. A year before his death in June of A.D. 632, Muhammad was the *de facto* ruler of the Arabian Peninsula, and his brand of monotheism had become the official religion. His crude abobe mosque and residence with its thatched roofs and large walled courtyard became the political and administrative center of his realm.

Muhammad often boasted about his success, recorded in numerous traditions: "I have been made victorious with terror (cast in the hearts of the enemy), and while I was sleeping, the keys of the treasures of the world were brought to me and put in my hand."[24]

CHAPTER 34

Intercession

Like a *generalissimo* with a chest full of medals and ribbons, Muhammad awarded himself a breathtaking sweep of titles over the course of his career as self-anointed prophet. In the earliest phase he called himself The Kind, The Truthful, The Beloved, The Chosen One, The Bearer of Good Tidings, The Light Personified, The Light-Giving Lamp, and more. These were titles he gave himself in various verses of the Koran, and hardly a chapter was without a line in praise of himself or his compositions. In the middle of his career, the self-praise turned Orwellian. Just as he was assassinating critics, mass murdering Jews, awarding the fields and plantations of his victims to his friends, and taking into his bed women whose husbands he had just butchered, he became The Perfect Man, The Best of Mankind, The Model of Conduct, God's Mercy to Mankind, and more. At the end of his career, his grandiose idea about himself leaped beyond the bounds of the planet when he became The Gatherer—the one who would be the first to be resurrected on the Day of Judgment and lead the multitudes for their adjudication before God. And on that fateful day he would be The Intercessor and The One Whose Intercession Shall Be Granted.[1,2]

It is not known exactly when he began to describe himself as The Intercessor, but it is clear from the literature that he planned it so that when he announced the new title it would not come as a surprise. This process began when he declared that God always granted his prophets and messengers a special wish regarding their followers. Previous messengers had used theirs to achieve temporal

444

ends, such as when Noah asked God to destroy his people for their disobedience to the will of the Lord, bringing about the great flood. Muhammad, however, decided his followers would most benefit if God granted him the role of intercessor on the Day of Judgment. This would allow him to have a say with God for forgiveness of their sins. He would be the barrister of the court of God and plead on their behalf.[3] It was a rank of such importance that God would award it to only one of his prophets, the one who had superiority over all the others. He announced from the pulpit that he wanted to be the one to whom God granted such an honor because he could render no greater service to his followers than to be there for them on the final day. But he needed their help. He needed the faithful to lobby God in their prayers.[4] He suggested the wording: "(O Allah) Kindly give Muhammad the highest position in Paradise and an extra degree of honor and raise him to the Station of Praise and Glory."[5]

Then one day he announced that God had honored his wish and by so doing had answered the prayers of the believers. The literature is vague about the moment of this occurrence. It is likely the first announcement came after he emerged from a swoon, either in the presence of one of his wives or one of his chief people. With the same excited nodding as when he told Aisha that God had just given him permission him to marry Zaynab, he would have said, "Rejoice! Allah has granted me the right of intercession on the Day of Judgment! Go forth and announce the glad tidings to my people." In one account, the announcement came while he was returning to Yathrib from Mecca, possibly at the time of one of the minor pilgrimages he undertook in the company of a thousand or more of his followers. As they were going through a pass of the Juhfah mountains midway between Mecca and Yathrib, Muhammad suddenly dismounted his camel. As his followers looked on in bewilderment, he raised the palms of his hands to the heavens and said prayers of supplication to God. He went through a round of the prayer ritual, ending for a long time in solemn prostration with his forehead touching the ground. As his audience watched, he performed this routine three times. When his followers finally asked him what it was about, he said, "I begged my Lord and made intercession for my people, and He gave me a third of my people, so I prostrated myself in gratitude to my Lord. Then I raised my head and begged my Lord for my people, and He gave me a third of my people, so I prostrated myself in gratitude to my Lord. Then I raised my head and begged my Lord for my people and He gave me the remaining third, so I prostrated myself in gratitude to my Lord."[6]

Muhammad's imagination went to work constructing scenes of his role on the Last Day. In sermons, at small group sessions, during dinners with his closest people, in meetings with tribal leaders who came to Yathrib to take the oath of fealty, or while on the road with nothing but conversation to break the tedium, he talked about the end times and what the faithful should expect: It will begin, Muhammad asserted, when the Angel Israfil blows a trumpet to announce the time for resurrection has arrived, a blast so powerful it will be heard throughout creation. By then the earth will be a desolate ruin where life no longer exists. But through the intervention of God, all the dead will be raised and reconstituted in the flesh, as naked as when they were born, though in appearance they will be as they were when they died. Their bodies will be reassembled at the plain of the great Pond of Abundance, an immense body of water thousands of times larger than the lake created by the fabled dam of Marib. The location of the assembly has a name: The Place of Gathering, and Muhammad is The Gatherer. He will be the first to be resurrected, and he will arrive dressed in a resplendent green garb and wearing a green turban—the only one of the resurrected to be clothed, and that will be in honor of the modesty he displayed throughout his life. He will stand atop a hill like that of Arafat, or he will enter riding a horse, proudly carrying The Banner of Praise and Glory to symbolize the honor God has bestowed upon him by raising him to the highest station in Paradise, second only to the throne of God.

Muhammad was never at a loss to add details. At a banquet he once held forth on the theme of his superiority over the other prophets and went through the prophet list from Adam to Jesus. The scene was a typical banquet setting: A huge leather sheet that served both as table and table cloth was spread out on the floor and the guests were seated cross-legged around it. They were served meat, bread, and soup while Muhammad was brought a roasted leg of mutton, his favorite dish. Holding it in his hands, he alternated between tearing at the flesh with his teeth, chewing, and talking. The subject of the Last Day had come up and guests were asking him questions about the right of intercession of the other prophets. Won't they have the right to intercede as well? While still chewing, Muhammad shook his head. "I shall be the leader of all mankind on the Day of Resurrection." Looking around at his guests, he said, "Do you know why?" When the perplexed guests said nothing, Muhammad became irked at their lack of etiquette. There were rules to follow in conversing with God's representative on earth. He said, "Why don't you say, 'How would that be, O Messenger of God'?" His compliant guests then said, "How would that be, O Messenger of God?"[7] After taking another bite of mutton, he explained that the other prophets would eagerly yield their right of intercession to him because God had granted him superiority over them, which meant that he would then intercede on behalf of *all* the children of Adam, not just his own followers. In effect, that meant all mankind, since everyone descended from Adam. Modestly, he admitted that he would not be the only intercessor; he would only be the first, and he would be allowed to intercede for the greatest number. After him, the other prophets would be permitted intercession as would angels and even humans who had gained intercession rights for their family members as a result of their good deeds in the cause of God, such as being wounded in battle or killed while fighting for the cause.

He gave a rundown of how his superiority will be acknowledged: On the Day of Resurrection, God will delay the Great Adjudication and he will do it to cause confusion among the multitudes, the generations of people going back to the time of Adam who will be waiting in anguish to learn of their fate. God will cause the sun to come close, making the people sweat as they had never sweated before. They will become nervous, thinking that the delay meant God was angry with them. This will move them to petition various prophets to intercede with God for them, starting with Adam.

Muhammad loved telling this part of the story. Mimicking the timid and anguished voice he imagined people would use in addressing Adam, he said: "O Adam, thou art the father of mankind. God created thee by His own Hand and breathed in thee of His spirit and ordered the angels to prostrate before thee. Intercede for us with thy Lord. Don't you see in what trouble we are?"

WHAT SAYEST THOU, MUHAMMAD? Muhammad preached that God had granted him the right to intercede for all of mankind following the Day of Resurrection when people must render an account of their lives and face judgment. Muhammad would be the first to be resurrected. In some of the traditions he would be seated at the right hand of God to assist him in making determinations of Paradise or damnation. Muhammad's influence with God as the last and final prophet would be important for getting sinners released from the punishments of Hell.

But Adam declines. He has his own problems with the Lord for having eaten the fruit of the forbidden tree, and he tells the people to go to Noah. But Noah begs off as well, as do Abraham and Moses. Moses claims he has issues because he once accidentally killed someone whom God had not ordered him to kill. He refers the desperate masses to Jesus, but Jesus tells them, "Go to someone else: better go to Muhammad."[8]

Muhammad continues the story: Once the other prophets have thus acknowledged his superiority, he will make his entry wearing green garments and a green turban and carrying the Banner of Praise and Glory. This is when he will arrive either on a horse or he will appear on top of a hill that is like the hill of Arafat. He will assume leadership over all the children of Adam[9] and will lead the naked hordes across Sirat, a narrow bridge over Hell.[10,11]

It could be called the Bridge of Triage, for here will occur the separation of good people from the half-good, the not-even-half-good, and the all-bad. Muhammad will cross it as swiftly as a bolt of lightning as will those earmarked for Paradise, but the bridge will be treacherous for everyone else—full of booby traps for sinners, he tells his audience. Sharp hooks will latch onto people and chop them up before throwing them into the pit of fire below. People will try to crawl on all fours to get across, hoping to slip underneath the hooks, but it will be of no avail; they will be grabbed and thrown down. Idolaters in particular will be snagged and sliced up before being thrown into the fires where they will roast for eternity, but others will be cast into Hell pending rescue through Muhammad's intercession with God.[12]

This is when the first phase of his intercession will begin, Muhammad affirms. On the Day of Judgment he will first pray for blanket forgiveness for his followers, even for those who merited Hell. He will raise his face to the Lord and cry out, "My *ummah*, O Lord! My *ummah*, O Lord!"—his *ummah* meaning his nation, the transtribal supertribe of believers. He will pray for God to spare them from the torments of the fire, even if deserved. God will accept this initial request, but only for seventy thousand, and He will give permission for them to enter Paradise through a gate specially built for them. They were the ones who made it across the bridge over Hell. They were allowed to cross because God in his foreknowledge knew they were those whom he should immediately forgive because of Muhammad's supplications. The seventy thousand, therefore, will go through the gate of Paradise without having to give God an account of their actions in life.

Then comes the main event. Muhammad will rescue many of the sinners who were pushed off the bridge. These are people who had at least a grain or even an atom of faith in God and his messengers, but whose deeds in life merited punishment, though not eternal damnation. They will be made to suffer the torments of Hell, and it will not be short term. A day in the afterlife is the equivalent of fifty thousand earth years, so even if only condemned to a day in Hell, they will suffer excruciating tortures for a thousand times the length of time they spent on earth doing the things that merited such punishment. Their bodies will be roasted to the point of charcoal, only to be regenerated so they can be roasted again. Every part of the body will be consumed by the flames, the only exception being prayer marks on the forehead. The foreheads of those who touched their heads to the ground in prayer ritual will be spared, but not all the forehead—only the part that actually touched the ground, a roundish portion about the size of a large coin. Those prostration marks will make them easy to recognize as salvageable sinners.[13]

Muhammad used to tell his audiences that when the time for intercession comes, he will throw himself in prostration before the throne of God and pray for the release of these sinners. God will say, "Raise your head, speak and you will be heard, intercede and your intercession will be accepted."[14] In some versions, Muhammad is seated in a throne next to God—the Station of Praise and Glory.[15] Despite the honor shown him, Muhammad's intercession will still not be a guarantee of rescue. God will show his mercy to whomever he pleases, and at his command the angels will pluck out of Hell whomever he pleases to pluck out. Whatever their shape or condition at that moment—charbroiled or burnt down to a skeleton—angels will bring them to the River of Life whose waters will cause them to regenerate into human form. From there, they will be allowed into Paradise, but being rescued sinners they will have to enter Paradise from the lowest gate, and they will reside in the lowest part of the celestial realm.

Muhammad always got a kick out telling the final act of the intercession story. This was his last-man-out-of-Hell story, the tale of the last mortal to be rescued from the fire. He will crawl out of the pit of Hell, and God will have some fun with him by asking if he will be satisfied merely with getting his body back and being spared any further torment. When he replies, "Yes," God will say, "Will you ask for anything more in case this favor is granted to you?" He agrees not to ask for anything more; just being spared any further blistering torment would be good enough, thank you. After the body of the last man out of Hell is restored in the River of Life, God will tease him by allowing him to go up to the gate of Paradise, but He will not allow him to enter. This will make the man's heart ache because through the pearly gate he will get a glimpse of "the life, charm, and pleasure of Paradise." He will be so torn by what he is denied he will cry out, "O my Lord! Let me enter Paradise." God will say, "O son of Adam! How treacherous you are! Haven't you made covenants and given pledges that you will not ask for anything more than what you have been given?" The last man out of Hell and God go back and forth. The man keeps asking for more. By the end of it, the man is finally allowed to enter Paradise, and God tells him he can have ten times more than he wanted as a way of showing the extent of his mercy towards even the lowliest creature. This lowly creature evidently has a big appetite for real estate, for he tells God he wants a lot of space for himself, as big as the world, and God cheerfully gives him ten times the size of the earth! This was the punch line, and Muhammad throws his head back in a hearty, open-mouthed laugh, then looks around to see if everyone got it: The lowest of the low would be allowed to enter the lowest part of Paradise, and look how enormous the lowliest part of Paradise will be for the last man out of Hell—ten times the space of the earth![16] With that, Muhammad again throws his head back and roars with laughter.

Many, perhaps even most, of the children of Adam will be doomed to eternal fire, and no amount of interceding will help them. These are the polytheists, the hypocrites, and the apostates. Muhammad did not spare any heathens from Hell, not even his mother or the kindly Abu Talib who had taken him in when he had no one to care for him and raised him like a son. He made it known that he would intercede with God to raise Abu Talib from the depths of Hell reserved for idolaters to a higher station where only his feet would burn up to his ankles. That would cause his brain to boil, but at least it would not be as painful as the torments inflicted in the lower depths.[17] As for Muhammad's mother, there was no hope. She had lived and died a polytheist.[18]

Bound for Hell too are Christians and Jews, though presumably they would benefit from the intercession of Jesus or Moses. In Muhammad's reckoning, Jesus and Moses were second in rank to him. They would also have the right to intercede with God on behalf of their faithful, but only after he finished his own labor of intercession. Unlike the others, the Jews and Christians will not be pushed into the flaming pit while crossing the bridge over Hell, but will fall over a cliff like lemmings while running toward a mirage of water in the hope of quenching their thirst. Muhammad crafted the mirage imagery to symbolize what he thought were Christian and Jewish false beliefs about the nature of God. The chief sin of the Christians was their belief that Jesus was the son of God, a form of idolatry. Muhammad never tired of explaining the illogic of the Christian belief: By virtue of being the one God, God could not have a son or a wife.[19] He also accused the Jews of worshipping one of their prophets, Uzayr, as the son of God. For this they would also be punished.[20]

Muhammad ended his storytelling with further self-aggrandizement: When the Great Adjudication is completed, when the last of the saved have been plucked out of Hell and have taken their place in Paradise, and when the eternally damned realize there will never be any hope for them, Muhammad will take up his own abode in Paradise. His quarters will be at the top of the Seventh Heaven, above all the other prophets, closer than anyone else to the throne of God.

There in praise and glory he will reside for eternity.

CHAPTER 35

Farewell Pilgrimage

Muhammad now dominated most of the Arabian Peninsula, which meant that he also controlled the pilgrimage, but he did not yet control the meaning of all its rituals. He still faced the creative challenge of converting the remainder of the rites of the polytheists into the practices of his monotheism.

This reinvention had started years earlier when he declared the Meccan temple was constructed by Abraham and Ishmael as the House of God, and it continued after the conquest of Mecca when he adapted the ritual of the running between the mounts of Safa and Marwa to fit his Abraham story. But more recasting needed to be done. The annual pilgrimage, which took place during the last month of the lunar calendar, extended beyond the vale of Mecca to Mount Arafat twelve miles to the east and to the hills and plains of Muzdalifa and Mina, pilgrim stations closer to Mecca. Mecca and its temple were devoted to moon worship; to the east the rituals had to do with the worship of the sun. These sun worship practices—the departing from pilgrim stations with the setting and rising of the sun, the slaughtering of sacrificial animals, and the stoning of pillars—now also required an Abraham rebranding.

The year after the conquest of Mecca, Muhammad prepared the way for completing the makeover by sending Abu Bakr and Ali on the pilgrimage trail to announce his pilgrim policy for Arabia. Beginning the following year, only members of Muhammad's religion, the new transtribal supertribe of believers, would be allowed to participate. Polytheists were impure and destined for hellfire and were forbidden to mingle with the pure who were striving for Paradise. From mounts at each of the pilgrim stations, therefore, Ali announced the new order of things: Polytheists would be granted a four-month period of immunity to allow them to complete the pilgrimage that year, but after the grace period they would no longer have a guarantee of security anywhere in Arabia, not even during the sacred months—unless they converted. To give the threat the imprimatur of God, Ali recited one of the Koran verses Muhammad composed to announce the new policy: "But when the forbidden months are past, then fight and slay the Pagans wherever ye find them, and seize them, beleaguer them, and lie in wait for them in every stratagem (of war); but if they repent, and establish regular prayers and practice regular charity, then open the way for them." The verse ends with the Orwellian refrain found in many of Muhammad's compositions: "For Allah is Oft-forgiving, Most Merciful."[1]

The final makeover took place in A.D. 632, a year after Muhammad publicized the pilgrimage policy. Now that it was cleansed of polytheists, he announced that he was ready to don the white garbs of the pilgrim. In the pilgrimage month of that year, therefore, he joined thousands of people on the long journey south. He was accompanied by his wives who rode in curtained howdahs, numerous relatives, and his most prominent companions and their families. Pilgrims from the entire region joined them in a valley south of Yathrib where they "assumed" the state of ritual purity by donning a two-piece white garment—one a waist wrap, the other a wrap that fit loosely around the upper body. Since turbans were banned during the pilgrimage, Muhammad had his wives braid and perfume his hair to keep out dust and lice. He brought a hundred sacrificial camels, one of them being his personal sacrificial beast, the remainder for other people. Blood sacrifice had always been an important part of the pagan ritual, but now instead of slaughtering animals in the name of the deities of the polytheists, their blood was to be spilled exclusively in the name of God and in remembrance of Abraham's willingness to shed the blood of his son in obedience to God's command. Muhammad prepared his sacrificial camel by scraping the hair off of one side of the hump until it bled, then tied sandals and other ornaments around its neck, marking its sacrificial status.[2] When Muhammad set out from the staging area, he was surrounded by throngs of people, either on foot or riding camels, all shouting the ancient pilgrim cry: "I am here at your service, Oh Lord. I am here at your service."

By the time Muhammad arrived, Mecca had been transformed into a desert metropolis. Forty thousand people had converged on it from all over Arabia. Since this was an era of new meanings and new procedures, the pilgrims followed Muhammad's lead and listened to his instructions, imitating his every action. The true believers believed his *sunna*—the example of all that he did—was the path to Paradise and was to be imitated. Muhammad's first act upon arriving in Mecca was to orbit the temple, no longer in imitation of the motion of celestial objects, but in worship of his God concept. In some accounts, he did the orbits on his camel, but in most versions he performed them on foot. He was a sight to be seen: a rotund if not corpulent man with braided hair and a blazing orange beard wearing the loose-fitting white garments of the pilgrim. He followed the old custom of exposing his right shoulder by tucking the garment under his armpit, but he broke tradition by jogging three times around the temple and walking for the remaining laps. Previously, pilgrims walked briskly or at a leisurely pace; the speed was not prescribed. Each time he passed by the Black Stone he either touched or kissed it. He finished the orbiting ritual with two sets of prostrations and Koran recitations at the hewn rock that he now called the Station of Abraham. Umar, who was tall, sturdy, and bald on top, followed in his footsteps, as did throngs of worshippers.

From there he went to the rocky outcroppings of Safa and Marwa and walked the thousand or so feet between them seven times, but quickening his pace to a jog while crossing the dry riverbed that separated the hillocks. The running between the mounts had been the custom of the polytheists, a practice that originated out of a healthy respect for nature: The valley was subject to occasional flash floods that coursed down the riverbed and carried away anyone caught in rushing water. It therefore became the pagan custom to run across the riverbed while making the seven circuits between the two mounts—this done in worship of the idols of Isaf and Naila that had been erected at the foot of the mounts—regardless of weather conditions. As previously noted, under Muhammad's religion, the running was now to be

performed in imitation of his story of Hagar rushing in desperation to find water for her son. Thus Muhammad quickened to a
Hagar pace while crossing the riverbed, making it the rule for
his followers. To cap the ritual, he climbed each hill and prayed
in the direction of the temple, the roof of which was about the
same height as the hillocks.

Prior to setting out on the journey to Mecca, Muhammad commissioned new drapes to replace the previous temple
coverings, which were intended to dress up the plainness of the
structure and give it an air of dignity.[3] The new ones, made of
Yemeni fabric, were ready by the time he arrived. Once they
were installed, Muhammad went up the stairs of the entrance,
took off his sandals, and entered accompanied by Bilal, Osama,
and a third man. Inside, Hubal and other idols were no more.
Other than the columns supporting the roof, the interior was
empty, filled now only with Muhammad's monotheistic idea.
Muhammad performed two rounds of prayer prostrations to
this idea, but when finished he told Bilal and Osama that
he had made an error in entering the building. Now it would be
considered *sunna* and everyone would want to go inside
to pray.[4] He therefore made an announcement from the stairs
that it was not God's policy for people to pray inside, but to
worship from the outside of the building.

These pilgrim days were filled with mass movements of
people from one place to another and with mass prayer sessions—rows upon rows of people touching their foreheads to the
ground in synchronized performance. Wherever they were when
the piercing call to prayer was heard—first at the break of dawn,
then at noon, then in the late afternoon, then before sunset and
finally after darkness brought out the stars—people did their ritual
purification routines and formed ranks and rows.

Muhammad was at the center of the swirl, sometimes mobbed
by people who had never seen him before. His blazing orange
beard would be spotted, people would shout, "This is Muhammad, this is Muhammad!"[5] Very quickly he would be surrounded
by men and women, young and old, their arms outstretched and
their faces glowing with joy at being in the presence of God's
messenger. Some would touch him, but if not close enough to
reach him, they would be satisfied by touching his camel. At
times he would break away, whipping his camel to push through

the crowd; at other times he would remain in place. The press of people trying to get near him then was crushing. He had created catchy myths about himself that marked him as a living legend: the prophet to whom a mighty angel appeared at the cave of nearby Mount Hira; the chosen one who was taken into the highest levels of Heaven and brought before the throne of God; the mercy to mankind who would intercede on their behalf on the Day of Judgment. He was the nexus between God and man, and if they were able to get close enough to him people would grab hold of his hand and rub their face with it in the hope of connecting to God through him.[6] He allowed it, just as he allowed people to drink his ablution water and rub his spittle on their skin.

Arafat was the next pilgrim station, a two hundred foot high rocky mount where pilgrims had previously stood in worship of the sun. For the sun worshipping polytheists, the pilgrimage used to begin on the slopes and surrounding plain of Mount Arafat and then proceed west toward Mecca, ending at Mina. That was because it followed the arc of the sun from east to west. The polytheist pilgrimage to the Meccan temple was a separate pilgrimage carried out in homage to the moon and the mysteries of star motion, hence it was limited to orbiting the temple and running between the two adjacent mounts of Safa and Marwa. Muhammad now combined them into a single pilgrimage in worship of his idea of God, the first station of his rebranded pilgrimage being Mecca, the second Arafat.

Arafat was an important station. For the polytheists, it was known as the Place of Standing because they would begin the pilgrimage rites by standing on the hill or the dusty plain from midday until sunset in homage to the sun. With Muhammad, Arafat became the Place of Gathering. The Angel Gabriel, he proclaimed, had taken Abraham to Arafat to reveal to him that it was symbolic of the gathering place at the time of resurrection so that standing on Arafat was a dress rehearsal for what will come when Israfil blows the fateful trumpet.

On the way to Arafat, Bilal walked and sometimes trotted beside Muhammad's camel carrying a parasol on a long pole to shade him from the pounding sun. When he climbed to the top of Arafat, he was surrounded by the masses of pilgrims in white garb. It was surely Muhammad's most gratifying moment. Nearly twenty-three years had gone by since the hallucinatory experiences of the cave of Mount Hira—twenty-three years of struggle to impose his version of monotheism despite all manner of opposition. He had beaten all odds and crushed all opposition, and now forty thousand people were at his feet, all affirming his beliefs about himself. Looking down at the throngs, he gave a long, rambling address that was later named the Farewell Sermon due to the fact he died a few months later. It was his Sermon on the Mount, a mix of rulings, warnings, and freshly crafted Koran verses. Among other matters, he issued proclamations that outlawed interest on loans, required people to return the full amount of what was borrowed, dissolved the blood debts of homicides committed in the polytheist era, and prohibited the adding of an extra month every three years to adjust the lunar calendar to the solar.[7] And finally he defined the relationship between men and women. Speaking to the men, he said, "Treat women well, for they are like domestic animals with you and do not possess anything for themselves. You have taken them only as a trust from God."[8] He finished the sermon by saying, "Understand and listen to my words, O people. I have conveyed the Message, and have left you with something which, if you hold fast to it, you will never go astray: that is, the Book of God and the *sunna* of His Prophet."[9,10]

Following the practice of the polytheists, Muhammad waited until the sun dropped behind the mountains to release the pilgrims for the traditional rush to the fire mountain of Muzdalifa, the next station between Arafat and Mina. For the polytheists, there had always been important symbolism in the rush: The sun set in the west, in the direction of Muzdalifa; the released pilgrims went off in pursuit of the sun, but what they were to accomplish in doing so is no longer known. Perhaps it was a way of expressing good wishes to the sun for a safe journey into the netherworld, like relatives rushing down the road as a loved one departs into the night with a caravan. It was traditional since the days of Qusay to light a fire atop the rocky mount of Muzdalifa. In the light of the bonfire, the polytheists would maintain a reverent vigil throughout the dark hours and break into celebration when the first glimmer of dawn announced the return of the sun.

Muhammad was among the first to leave Arafat for Muzdalifa. As the light faded in the west, he mounted his camel and became the point man of the flow of pilgrims riding camels or on foot. Osama, then about nineteen years old, rode with him. The rushing after the sun was a custom that was hard to break. Overly eager riders pushed up close behind Muhammad, prompting him to admonish them: "Take it easy, everyone! Piety is not measured by speed!"[11] Yet he himself whipped his camel to a fast trot once he was on clear ground. When finally at the low mount of Muzdalifa, Muhammad combined the late evening and night prayer routines, performing them in the light of a bonfire. It is not noted in the literature, but it is likely he gave more sermons, issued more rules, and recited fresh Koran verses. He stayed the night along with the throngs of pilgrims, then at the break of dawn led them in performing the first round of daily prayers.

For Muhammad, Muzdalifa was no longer a celebration of the mystery of the reappearance of sun, but was about Abraham and the purity of his worship of the one God. As mentioned earlier, Muhammad had always been deeply affected by the story of a man who would slay his own son as a test of his faith in his Lord. He had fathered three sons, the last being Ibrahim with his Coptic slave Maria, each of them dying before they were two years old, so that he had experienced the suffering such deaths cause. He was also deeply affected by the outcome of the Biblical story: An angel of the Lord intervenes at the last moment, just before Abraham could cut the throat of his beloved son. Muhammad now linked the Biblical story to Muzdalifa. It was on a mountainside near Muzdalifa that the angel stayed the hand of Abraham, but in Muhammad's version it was no longer Isaac whose life was to be sacrificed.

From Muzdalifa Muhammad led the pilgrims three miles west to the station of Mina where the traditional pelting of three pillars took place. Muhammad devised an Abraham story for this station as well. To the polytheists, the pillars represented the invisible *jinn* that inhabited the deserts and skies, some of them mischievous and others plainly evil. Stoning the pillars was done to drive them away. Muhammad dressed the ritual in a makeover of a Jewish legend in which Satan tempts Abraham, Isaac, and Sarah not to go through with the sacrifice. The Jewish legend was a fanciful story that enhanced the Biblical tale of Abraham's sacrifice. In it, Satan is scolded for his interference and sent away.[12] In his revamped version,

Muhammad changed the characters from Isaac to Ishmael and Sarah to Hagar. Instead of scolding Satan, they drove him off with stones. In this way, Muhammad adapted the tradition of stoning the three pillars to his Abraham story. It was not the *jinn* being stoned any longer, but a vile Satan for attempting to get Abraham, Ishmael, and Hagar to disobey the Lord. The pillars were made of rocks stacked in the shape of columns, but they were not very high since the rocks were not cemented together. Each was now the devil tempting Abraham, or Ishmael, or Hagar, and each pillar had to be stoned seven times—just as the polytheists used to do. After each throw, Muhammad shouted "*Allahu Akbar!*—Allah is the Greatest!" When done with a pillar he raised his hands to the heavens and uttered prayers before moving on to the next. The pilgrims imitated him.

Once the stoning was completed, it became time for the slaughter of the sacrificial animals. This had always been part of a three-day festival, often referred to as "the festival of immolation" or "the days of the drying of meat," and for the polytheists it was the last stage of the sun pilgrimage. In their version, the polytheists would slaughter animals as a blood offering to the various deities to appease them and gain favor. Now with Muhammad, the slaughter became a commemoration of Abraham's willingness to sacrifice his son to God. The animals were a substitute sacrifice, like the ram of the Abraham story.

While the pilgrims were making the rounds of Arafat and Muzdalifa, the sacrificial animals were taken out to pasture. Following the stoning of the pillars, the animals were herded to an area reserved for slaughter. The one hundred camels Muhammad brought, each decorated with garlands and his particular brand to distinguish them from other sacrificial camels, were lined up and made to kneel. Their forelegs were hobbled so that they could not break away when the carnage started. One after another they were killed. It is said that Muhammad slaughtered sixty-three of them with the assistance of Ali and a knife-sharp spear.[13] Holding the shaft just below the spear head, Muhammad would position the tip of the spear at the camel's neck, whereupon Ali, who was holding the end of the spear, would thrust it forward with enough force to cut through the neck. Muhammad then sliced downward using the spear head as a butcher knife, and the animal quickly bled to death. The literature does not indicate what prayers Muhammad uttered upon each killing. Perhaps none at all given that the death-dealing was intense, absorbing, and exceedingly bloody work. Following each killing, a crew of butchers set upon the animal to strip it of its hide, gut it, and carve up the meat. Muhammad ordered a cut from each of the animals thrown into a cooking pot. Later, he and Ali feasted on the stew and drank the broth. None of the pilgrims went hungry, as most had brought a slaughter animal and there was plenty of meat to go around. The surplus was cut thin and dried in the sun to preserve for later consumption, and the hides were gathered for eventual tanning. All that was inedible was left for the vultures.

The slaughter of the animals was followed by the ritual of the shaving of the head. For the polytheists, the sun pilgrimage came to an end at that point and the festivities began. For them, the head shaving was seen as an act of humility and submission to the gods, but once the symbolic act was completed the pilgrims, now duly humbled, were out to have themselves some fun. They would begin by dumping the white wraps of ritual purity and put on their usual garments. The final three days consisted of noisy celebration where the pilgrims caught up on food, wine, sex, and merrymaking. They loved music and the talented would pull out all manner of tambourines, drums, and flutes. It was like a three-day tailgate party. But now the old days were gone. A dour puritan, Muhammad put a damper on high spirits by prohibiting sex, alcohol, and music. What little was left of fun took place between rounds of prayer prostrations and recitals of his verse.

Muhammad retained the head shaving as important to the pilgrimage and sealed it as *sunna* by calling for a barber. This resulted in a rush of people who crowded around him to grab the falling locks, some almost coming to blows for possession of even a single hair. It is said that he gave the shavings from one side of his head—the scholars are uncertain if it was the right side or the left—to Talha, the man who lost fingers protecting Muhammad from a sword blow at Uhud. Talha then distributed strands to the pilgrims.[14] Khalid, his erstwhile enemy and now one of his most devoted military commanders, begged him for an entire lock, and when he got it he pressed it against his eyes and mouth.[15]

Before he released them to return home, Muhammad required the pilgrims to perform a final set of orbits around the temple and do the running once more between Safa and Marwa as farewell gestures. Once these were completed, the pilgrims had the option of partaking in what remained of festive activities or going home. Muhammad made this farewell act official by being the first to perform the final temple orbits, then he returned to the festival site to throw more stones at the devil. With these acts he finished the labor of reinventing the entire pilgrimage.

Muhammad was a creative genius. He had the type of mind that it takes to write an epic like *War and Peace* or compose an opera worthy of an audience of powdered kings and queens. He turned himself into the hero of his own epic tale, casting himself in the lead role as interface between God and man. His creativity was not limited to the weird brilliance of the Koran, but expanded into the recasting of the rituals of the Arabs into the framework of a myth that he had taken from the Jews and transported to a valley a thousand miles south that had little going for it other than a nondescript temple. He blended the minor pilgrimage of Mecca in honor of the moon and the major pilgrimage of sun worship into a single act of monotheistic worship that now began at Mecca, at the House of his God concept, and also ended there.

The creative task completed, Muhammad returned to Yathrib, now not only the religious and political master of the Arabian Peninsula, but as master of its myths.

CHAPTER 36

Death of Muhammad

Muhammad died three months after returning to Yathrib. The literature informs us that he had a premonition of his death and warned during the pilgrimage that it could be his last. When he returned to Yathrib it was back to business as usual. One of his first acts was to order the assassination of the leader of a breakaway movement in Yemen. As before, he continued to receive delegates from tribes who came to pledge loyalty to him, and he appointed governors, preachers, and tax collectors over them.

These activities continued until he was gripped by an illness that began while an army was forming for a raid on Syria, intended as retaliation for Muhammad's defeat at the hands of the Byzantines two and a half years earlier that had resulted in the deaths of his former adopted son Zayd, Ali's brother Jafar, and the death-longing zealot Abdullah Rawaha. The illness began one night while Muhammad prayed in a cemetery in the company of one of his freed slaves. Instead of remaining cooped up in the room of one of his wives to perform extra prayers at night, Muhammad would sometimes go the cemetery to pray. The cemetery was called the Garden of Gharqad and many of Muhammad's fallen comrades were buried there along with three of his daughters—Zaynab, Ruqaya, and Umm Kulthum. Ibrahim, his son by Maria the Copt, was also buried there. Judging from the prayers attributed to him that night, he seemed world weary, weighed down by the endless strife that his war against all and sundry had engendered. He spoke out loud to the graves, saying the dead were fortunate. They were free of the challenges of the world that came one after another in seemingly endless succession, the last being even worse than those that preceded.[1]

By the time he got back to the mosque compound, Muhammad was in the grip of a raging headache. That night he was sleeping with Aisha, who was then eighteen years old. It turned out she had a raging headache as well, perhaps due to suppressed jealousy since he had once again gone out on her in the middle of the night, yet she could not follow him out of fear of a beating. Her face was a portrait of pain. When he asked what was wrong with her, she groaned, "Oh my head." Muhammad replied, "I'm the one with the headache!" In a bantering tone, he said that it would be better if she died from the headache before him, that way he could wrap her in a shroud, bury her, and pray over her. Her jealousy bled through her response: "I imagine that if you did that you would return to my room and celebrate a wedding night there with one of your wives!"[2]

Muhammad's headaches continued to the point he believed his head would explode, and to suppress the pain he wrapped his head so tightly in bandages he looked like he had been wounded in battle. Only days after he first complained of the headache he became feverish to the point that he collapsed. He was with one of his wives when this happened—some say Maymuna, others Zaynab. He asked his wives to be allowed to stay in Aisha's room, and he was taken there, his feet dragging on the ground.

Sensing that his illness was terminal, he sought forgiveness from people he had harmed and ask God to forgive whoever had harmed him. He called for a general assembly, and heralds went out ordering everyone within range to report to the mosque. Muhammad was in a high fever. Before going out to the assembly, he sat in a bronze tub belonging to Hafsa, either with his clothes on or behind a screen, and had his wives pour cold water on him. When he was finally able to stand, he emerged from behind the curtain that separated Aisha's room from the preacher platform, his head wrapped tightly in a bandage, and sat in the pulpit. The prayer area and courtyard were packed with the faithful. Muhammad began by saying, "O people, your rights are dear to me so whomever I have flogged on his back, here is my back—let him avenge."[3] He was full of goodwill: He prayed to God to forgive the archers who disobeyed him at Uhud, leading to the Meccan victory. He praised Abu Bakr as a reliable companion. He he got down from the pulpit to lead prayers, then resumed his seat in the pulpit and declared that anyone to whom he owed money should speak up. "Those of you I like best are those who will either take their due if I am in their debt or release me therefrom, that I may meet Almighty God without any injustice on anyone because of me."[4]

At that, a man jumped to his feet and demanded three dirhams he had loaned Muhammad years before. Muhammad told him to refresh his memory because he had no idea what he was talking about. "Don't you remember how once a beggar passed you and you gave me orders, so I awarded him three dirhams?" Muhammad ordered one of his cousins to give the man his money, then told him to sit down.[5] Another man confessed to having taken three dirhams, an amount that put him just below the threshold that would have cost him his hand. Muhammad ordered him to dig into his money purse and pay back the dirhams. His audience seemed obsessed by their sinfulness and many jumped to their feet in breast-beating confessions. Normally, Muhammad would have reveled in such a meeting and would have kept it going, but his fever returned. He offered a blanket prayer for everyone who was troubled by things they had done and dragged himself back to Aisha's room.

His wives forced medicine on him. It was the general opinion that he was suffering from pleurisy, a lung inflammation, and the Abyssinians were renowned for a remedy, a foul-tasting shamanic concoction of herbs and oils. In a weakened condition, he could not fight back when they opened his mouth and poured it down. Shortly after, his condition improved, either because of the medicine or as a spontaneous respite, and he took revenge by forcing his entire household, bar none, to swallow the snake oil. He blamed his illness on the poison he was fed at Khaybar by the Jewish woman whose husband and relatives he had slaughtered. "I still suffer pain from the food I ate at Khaybar," he told Aisha. "At this time I sense my aorta being severed by that poison."[6]

His illness lasted for nearly two weeks. Until his strength slipped away, he continued to lead the five daily prayers. Toward the end, he ordered the ever-faithful Abu Bakr to lead the prayer sessions, interpreted by many as a sign that he favored Abu Bakr to succeed him. Given the stressful circumstances, Aisha did not think her father was the best choice as prayer leader for he was constantly weeping about Muhammad's declining health, and he could hardly recite a single line of the Koran without bursting into tears. Nevertheless, he took up the challenge and succeeded in containing his emotions. During one prayer session, Muhammad, his strength briefly improving, went out to the prayer area propped up between two burly relatives and sat behind Abu Bakr. Abu Bakr wanted to relinquish the lead to his master, but Muhammad signaled for him to continue. Though he was too weak to perform the standings, bowings, kneelings, and prostrations, he repeated whatever Koran verses Abu Bakr recited.

He died on a Monday at noon. The day started out promising when it appeared Muhammad was regaining strength. He had been bedridden for three days straight, but at the dawn prayer that morning, he stood up and pushed the curtain aside that separated the room from the prayer area and observed the rows and ranks of the faithful as they followed Abu Bakr in prayer performance and Koran recital. Muhammad smiled and at one point laughed with delight. This caused the faithful to look up from their prayers. Abu Bakr thought he was coming out to take over the lead, but Muhammad signaled for him to continue. He let the curtain drop and lay down on the bed with Aisha.

He seemed in high spirits, and Abu Bakr believed that he might even recover. He felt so confident about it that after the prayers were over he asked Muhammad for permission to return to his home in the highlands to be with his favorite wife, the daughter of Kharija. That day was her turn and he wanted to spend time with her. Muhammad consented, and Abu Bakr rode off on a horse. But as the morning progressed Muhammad's body became racked with pain. At times he was coherent, others times he babbled. He was lying on the mattress, his head resting on Aisha's breast. Other people were in the room, but it was fluid, with people dropping in to check on him. In addition to Muhammad's top people, only close relatives such as his daughter Fatima, his uncle Abbas, Abbas's sons Fadl and Qutham, Aisha's half-brother Abdullah, the other wives, and some longstanding servants and aides were allowed entry to the small room.

In the early morning he was coherent. As he rested with Aisha, he reminded people of his eventual role as intercessor and urged them to pray for him after his death, particularly every Friday, the day of obligatory congregational prayer, because such prayers would enhance his ability to intercede with God on their behalf on the Day of Judgment. "Friday is one of the best of your days. On it Adam was created and on it he died. On it life began with a breath, and on it life will end with a thunderbolt. Pray for me often on that day, for your prayer will be made known to me." When asked how it would be possible since his body would be in a state of decay until the Day of Resurrection, he said, "God has forbidden the earth to eat the bodies of prophets," meaning that his body would be spared the indignity of decay.[7] He gave instructions for his body to be washed, but only by his closest male kinfolk "along with many angels who see you from where you do not see them," and that his shroud should consist of his ordinary clothes "or of a Yemeni cloth or a white one from Egypt."

He had a special request regarding the angels: "When you have washed me, embalmed me, wound me in a shroud, and placed me at the edge of my grave, then depart from me for a while. The first persons to pray for me shall be my two companions and friends, Gabriel and Mikail, then Israfil, then the angel of death, along with troops of angels, upon whom be peace."[8]

By late morning, his fever rose and he became incoherent, uttering whatever came into his mind between frequent lapses of consciousness. Throughout the morning, his head was propped against Aisha's bosom. At one point he opened his eyes and said, "Those persons most suffering affliction are the prophets." At another: "A man is afflicted to the degree of his faith; if firm in his faith, he will be severely afflicted." Earlier, he had made it clear he did not want a fancy grave because that could end up as a site of worship, a form of idolatry. As he was fading away, the thought entered his head that Christians and Jews turned the graves of their prophets into places of worship. At this, he became furious and shouted without looking at anyone in particular, "May God destroy the Jews and the Christians! They have adopted the graves of their prophets as mosques!"[9] The outburst exhausted him. His head fell back against Aisha, but his hatred of Jews and Christians and polytheists and all and sundry who had ever opposed him and his religion had resurfaced. In a final outburst he said, "Two religions shall not remain in the land of the Arabs!"[10]

It was the beginning of summer, and by noon the heat in the room was stifling. Someone brought a bowl of water and placed it next to him. As he dipped his fingers into it and wiped his face, he cried out, "O God, spare me the pangs of death." It so happened at that moment Aisha's brother Abdullah came into the room. He had a toothpick with him that had been either sliced from a palm trunk or was a twig from a siwak tree. Muhammad had always used such items to clean his teeth. Thinking it would please him, Aisha took the toothpick and chewed on the end to fray it into a brush and gave it to Muhammad. He rubbed his teeth with it feverishly. After that he raised his hands and said, "There is no god but God!" Then he groaned, "Death has its pangs!" After a moment, his eyes became fixed as if on some distant object. He lifted his left forefinger and said, "With the Highest Companion! With the Highest Companion!" perhaps referring to God.

Death came when he reached again for the water. Just as he touched the water, his hand went limp, and his head slumped forward, crushing his orange beard against his chest. At the moment of death, he was still leaning against Aisha. She got up and tucked a leather pillow under his head. She and the other women began beating their chests and slapping their faces in grief, but they restrained themselves from shrieking or rolling on the ground as Muhammad had forbidden such displays of grief.[11]

Word of his death spread quickly, but many people refused to believe it. Aisha sent Abdullah to inform Abu Bakr, and Fatima went to inform Ali. When Abu Bakr returned to the mosque, he rushed through the crowd and went straight for Aisha's room. "To God we belong, and to Him we return! The Messenger of God has died!" he said upon viewing the body.[12] He kissed Muhammad on the forehead and went out to the platform. Umar was in a state of denial and was ranting at the crowd from the platform: It was untrue that Muhammad was dead! Hypocrites had spread rumors about it, but it was the same lie people had spread about Moses when he disappeared for forty days and then returned! "By God, the Messenger of God will also return and cut off the hands and feet of those who allege he is dead."[13] Umar threatened to kill whoever was guilty of spreading such rumors. Abu Bakr tried to get him to quiet down, but when the ranting continued, he interrupted and took charge. He confirmed Muhammad had indeed died, and he recited a verse that said Muhammad was only a messenger of God and messengers had come and gone before and that only God was immortal.

Against the backdrop of grieving was the stirring of a power struggle. It had begun more than a week earlier when Muhammad's top people defied his order to follow Osama to Syria, dragging their feet to delay the departure. Ostensibly this was because they objected to being under the command of a nineteen-year-old son of a former slave. Muhammad criticized them over this during a mosque assembly, praising Osama and upholding his appointment. Osama's army, however, never got beyond the staging grounds north of Yathrib. Everyone knew that a struggle for power would occur if Muhammad died, and Umar and other important Meccans whom Muhammad had ordered to accompany Osama did not want to be left out. They therefore stalled the departure by failing to show up at the staging area.

By the time of Muhammad's death, three major factions had formed. The Meccans split into two camps, one backing Ali as the rightful successor since he was a blood relative and Muhammad's blood continued through his two male children, Hasan and Hussein. Zubayr was an Ali partisan, as were many of the Meccan émigrés who believed the succession should be reserved for Muhammad's Hashimite clan. Another group formed around Abu Bakr and Umar, also Meccans but from different clans, because of their importance to Muhammad and the spread of his religion. Aisha was a strong supporter of her father, in part out of devotion to him, but also out of hatred for Ali for not having backed her when she was accused of infidelity at the time of the Mustaliq raid. The third group consisted of the early Yathrib converts who also claimed a right to succession. Their demand was fueled in part by resentment toward the Meccans, who had come to their valley ten years earlier and had taken over.

Following Muhammad's death, the Yathrib converts were the first to make a power play by organizing a meeting of Aws and Khazraj leaders at the clan compound of Sad Ubada, the Khazraj chieftain, to choose a successor. When Umar and Abu Bakr learned about it, they left Muhammad's body locked in Aisha's room and hastened to the meeting along with Abu Ubayda ibn al-Jarra, the man who had distinguished himself at the battle of Badr by killing his father and at the battle of Uhud by licking the blood off Muhammad's face.

It was a highly charged meeting. At stake was not only leadership of Muhammad's religion, but also control over the Arabian Peninsula. One after another, the Yathrib men took the floor to boost the Ansars—the early Aws and Khazraj helpers and supporters of Muhammad—as the legitimate successors. The Meccans may have been the people of the prophet, the Yathrib men said, but the Ansars were the squadrons of God and were entitled to power. At a minimum they wanted to share power with the Meccans. "A leader from us and a leader from you" became their slogan.[14]

Abu Bakr stood up to speak. He agreed with the Ansars about the importance of their role, but he pointed out that the Arabs in general would only recognize the authority of Muhammad's tribe, the Quraysh. After making his arguments, he lifted the hands of Umar and Abu Ubayda and challenged the assembly to choose between them. But the Ansars continued to insist on two leaders, one from Mecca and one from Yathrib. It is not certain on how long the discussions lasted, but it is clear that all the participants understood that if a successor was not chosen then and there each side might end up appointing a leader, and that could result in a bloody conflict. Ultimately Umar persuaded the assembly to choose Abu Bakr. He argued that God had selected Abu Bakr as a special companion because it was he who had arranged the escape from Mecca. He was Muhammad's companion of the cave of Mount Thaur where they had hidden for three days from the Meccans. He was qualified because his knowledge of the Koran and the *sunna* of Muhammad was flawless. Moreover, though Muhammad had not specifically named a successor, he had indicated his preference by appointing Abu Bakr to lead the daily prayers, an honor that had gone to him exclusively. When it finally came to a vote, Abu Bakr was chosen. He extended his hand and the Ansars and Meccans came to him one by one to pledge fealty.

It was not until the next day that Abu Bakr was presented as Muhammad's successor to a large assembly of the faithful at the mosque. With the body of Muhammad still under a blanket in the room behind the platform, Abu Bakr took a seat in the pulpit. Umar stood at the edge of the platform and addressed the packed crowd. He apologized for the rant of the previous day, saying his words could not be justified either by God's book that had been given to Muhammad as guidance, or by Muhammad's *sunna*. His words had come deep from the heart in that he had hoped Muhammad would outlast all of them. Though Muhammad was dead, the Koran was alive. He pointed to Abu Bakr. "God has given responsibility for your affairs to the very best man among you," he said, repeating the arguments he had made the day before with the Ansars. "Arise and pledge allegiance to him."[15]

Abu Bakr had accepted the role reluctantly out of hope of unifying the various factions and preventing bloodshed. Following the mass pledge, he gave a conciliatory speech and promised to follow the Koran and the example of Muhammad in all things. "I have assumed authority over you, even though I am not the best of you. If I do well, then help me. If I err, then set me straight."[16] It was a long speech that he concluded by proclaiming *jihad* was obligatory. "No one from you should refrain from fighting in the cause of God, because if it is forsaken by a people, God will smite them with disgrace."[17]

Ali and his faction were conspicuously absent from the meeting. The day before, Zubayr had publicly unsheathed his sword and declared he would not put it back until Ali was recognized as Muhammad's successor. Following Abu Bakr's speech, Umar summoned Ali and his supporters to the mosque to take the pledge, but they refused. Abu Bakr and Umar therefore led a band of armed men to Ali's house and ordered everyone out. Umar shouted, "Either you come out to render the oath of allegiance to Abu Bakr, or I will set the house on fire."[19] Zubayr ran out with his sword drawn, but stumbled when someone hit him with a stone. He was quickly subdued and disarmed. The rest of the holdouts eventually submitted.

The burial of Muhammad took place either later that day or during the night of the following day. This began with the washing of the body. Though it was not the usual practice, only male relatives were allowed to wash Muhammad's body, and they performed the washing with his clothes on, also unusual. The literature claims that having only male relatives wash him was done out of respect for his wishes, but washing him in his clothes may have been due to an embarrassing situation that has been largely scrubbed from the literature. This involved a surge of blood to his penis upon death, resulting in a death erection—"angel lust," as it is often termed. Such was noted by historian Edward Gibbon who cited Abu al-Fida, an influential 14th century Muhammadan historian. Abu al-Fida wrote that when Ali saw the condition of Muhammad's body, he exclaimed with admiration, "O Prophet, without a doubt your penis reaches up to the heavens!"[19]

This detail is not found in the standard accounts and may have been edited out or left out.[20] This is supported by the strangeness and suggestiveness of the wording in the standard accounts. In one version, Ali was said to have exclaimed upon viewing the body, "How excellent you are in life and in death!"—suggestive of an allusion to Muhammad's famed sexual prowess. Tabari noted that the body "did not look like what an ordinary corpse would look like."[21]

Though in admiration, Ali and the other men were in a quandary about how to proceed, as nobody wanted to undress the corpse though such was the accepted procedure for washing prior to enshrouding. The literature relates that such was their confusion about how to proceed that all of them suddenly fell asleep, their beards pressing against their chests. They were only awakened when a voice out of nowhere commanded, "Wash the Prophet with his clothes on!"[22] Muhammad's body was therefore washed with his death garments on. Water was poured on him and Ali rubbed his skin through the wet clothing. Aisha later complained, "Had I known first what I later learned, only the wives would have washed the Messenger of God."[23]

Once Muhammad's body was enshrouded, the men argued about where to bury him. Some thought the best place would be the mosque courtyard; others that it should be the very spot where he used to lead the faithful in prayer, which was the area in front of the preacher platform. Others argued he should be buried in the Garden of Gharqad where many of his companions were interred. Abu Bakr, however, recalled that Muhammad had once stated prophets were always buried where they died. They therefore agreed to bury him in Aisha's room. A gravedigger was brought in. Throughout the digging Muhammad's body lay on the mattress, which had been pushed up against a wall. When the digging was completed, everyone left the room for an hour to allow the angelic legions to pray over him.[24] When the hour was up, people formed a line to file through the room and offer prayers. Abu Bakr and Umar led a slow procession that began with Muhammad's close relatives, his wives, and the many children of his relatives and wives. When they were done the faithful were allowed to enter in small groups.

Muhammad was buried in the middle of the night under torchlight. Four people including the sons of Abbas stood in the hole, and the body was lowered to them. The grave was filled in and some bricks were placed over the mound as markers. The following day the room was sealed. Mughira ibn Shuba, the fugitive mass murderer from Taif who had served as Muhammad's body guard and was the man he sent with Abu Sufyan to destroy the temple of al-Lat, boasted that he was the last person to have physical contact with Muhammad. Before the first shovel of dirt was thrown onto the body, he tossed his ring into the grave so that it landed squarely on Muhammad. "I dropped it there deliberately so that I would touch the Messenger of God with it and so be the last person to be with him," he used to say.[25]

No sooner was Muhammad in his grave than rebellion erupted throughout Arabia. North, south, east, and west, Bedouin tribes that had sworn allegiance to him broke away with a vengeance. The first sign of discontent had occurred in the months before Muhammad's death in the Hadramaut region of Yemen. A juggler and magician named Aswad of the Ans tribe proclaimed himself a prophet. He raised an army and drove out or killed the people Muhammad had appointed to govern the region. He was slain by an assassin Muhammad recruited, his murder taking place only days before Muhammad died. After Muhammad's death, the rebellion became widespread and was particularly ferocious with tribes Muhammad had crushed militarily, such as the Hawazins. Even Mecca stirred with revolt. Upon learning of Muhammad's death, the Meccans chased the governor he had appointed out of town, but their rebellion was cut short when Suhayl, the former Badr captive who had been lodged for a time as a prisoner in Sauda's room at the Yathrib mosque—now a committed believer—threatened to behead everyone.

The emotional Abu Bakr, so ready to weep at any happy or sad moment, seemed an unlikely leader during such a challenging time, but he proved as ruthless and determined as Muhammad. When he learned that some women in the Hadramaut had celebrated the death of Muhammad by decorating their hands with henna and singing and banging tambourines in the streets, he sent a force to deal with them. At his orders, their hands were chopped off and they were thereafter branded as the "harlots of Hadramaut" though they were from noble families. He did not waste any time getting involved in military matters. The day after Muhammad's burial, he sent Osama on the delayed vengeance raid to Syria at the head of an army of three thousand, this despite warnings that various rebellious tribes intended to attack Yathrib. Osama crushed minor revolts along the way to Syria and on the return trip. In Syria, his army was victorious against the Christianized Arabs of western Syria, a region known in the Bible as Moab. It is said that he tracked down the man who killed his father in battle nearly three years earlier and cut off his head.

The political change in Arabia following Muhammad's death was stunning. Whereas prior to his death he controlled essentially all Arabia, following his death most of Arabia turned against what he had imposed, and it was only Abu Bakr's luck and ferocity that saved Muhammad's legacy from annihilation. The turnaround happened almost overnight. Two weeks after Osama left for Syria, a coalition of Bedouin tribes that included the Hawazins and Ghatafans, itching for payback for all they had suffered from Muhammad, came within striking distance of Yathrib. Abu Bakr hastily assembled another army and named Ali, Zubayr, and Talha as commanders. They were able to mount holding actions against the furious tribes until Osama returned from the Syrian foray. Abu Bakr then fused together a larger army and named Khalid as commander. Khalid, who would eventually be called the "Sword of Allah" due to his reputation for mass slaughter, beat back the menacing tribes until he reached one of the major rebel strongholds at the walled town of Yamama in east-central Arabia. After a week-long siege, Yamama fell. During the same period, Abu Bakr sent smaller forces to crush revolts that continued to break out in Yemen and in other regions of Arabia. Though the rebels initially controlled most of Arabia, they were unable to form a unified front, and by the end of his first year as ruler Abu Bakr succeeded in extinguishing the rebellion. He lived for only another year, but during that time he began the expansion of what Muhammad created beyond the confines of Arabia. With a base now in Yamama, Khalid went on a six-month rampage in what is now western Iraq, defeating the Persians and their Christian-Arab allies in numerous clashes. These were bloody battles. If the literature is to be believed, thirty thousand Persian and Christian Arab soldiers were killed in one battle, seventy thousand in another. In the latter, thousands of captured soldiers were brought to the edge of a river where they were beheaded. Their bodies were thrown into the river, causing it to flow red for three days.[26] From Iraq Khalid turned his ferocious sword on Syria, leaving a trail of death all the way to Damascus. Every territory he conquered he plundered, and to the delight of Abu Bakr enormous wealth flowed back to Yathrib, now called Medina, the City of the Prophet, the seat of a new empire.

Abu Bakr died in August of A.D. 634 while Khalid was at the gates of Damascus. He was succeeded by Umar, who was assassinated in November of A.D. 644. He was succeeded by Uthman, who was assassinated in June of A.D. 656. He was succeeded by Ali, who was assassinated in January of A.D. 661. During those twenty-seven years, they conquered Syria, Egypt, and Persia and either compelled conversions or forced the conquered regions to pay the subjugation tax. To the north, their armies touched the shores of the Black Sea and pushed as far as the Indus River. To the west they slashed their way into what is now Tunisia. Vast wealth flowed into Arabia from the conquered lands.

The armies of what Muhammad created were successful because they applied the magic motivational formula he developed that promised believers unlimited sex in Paradise if they were slain in battle and material rewards if they survived. Indeed, Zubayr, Talha, Abdul Rahman, and others who survived were the equivalent of billionaires by the time they died.[27]

As ferocious as were the external conquests, the infighting over power was even more so. A civil war over the right of succession and control over dogma led eventually to a split into Sunni and

Shia branches, resulting in hostility between the two groups that has continued to this day.

Muhammad was a diseased genius, an epileptic psychopath with a clever tongue who believed he communed with God, a toxic mixture that transformed him over time into a mass murderer and a despot pushing a delusional cult about himself. What energized him was the power of conviction derived from his epileptic experiences that he had a special mission. He was intolerant of all and sundry who opposed him and unleashed unending warfare against them. What he called the religion of submission to God's will was in effect submission to his will, since he was the creator of the concept of a God that demanded submission. He divided the world into lands conquered and lands yet to be conquered, into lands that submitted to his delusions about himself and lands yet to submit. His successors took up where he left off. What began as a trickle of blood in Mecca when Sad Waqqas hit someone over the head with the jawbone of a camel became a river of red that has flowed for nearly fourteen centuries.

Muhammad's diseased legacy continues unabated, and it threatens to consume the world of today.

A Manual for the Future

The antidote to what Muhammad created is the aggressive, relentless, and unapologetic exposure of the truth about him, particularly through dramatization in film.

What he created is an aberration, a cult of violence centered in his delusional belief that God talked to him. On its own, based solely on what he claimed about himself, his cult would not have been able to sustain itself. It succeeded because of the terror he unleashed against people who opposed him. Thereafter it continued to succeed thanks to terror, but also because the myths he created about himself became entrenched. Myths are like lies: Repeated often enough, they are taken to be the truth.

The myths have persisted even though what Muhammad claimed about himself is breathtaking nonsense: An angel came to him with eternal truths for all mankind; a winged mule flew him to Jerusalem, and he was taken up into Heaven to negotiate with God over the number of times per day people must prostrate in worship; Moses and Jesus and other prophets prayed in rows behind him before the winged mule flew him back to Mecca. This nonsense continues with his claim that he is the last and final prophet before the Day of Doom; that he will be the first to be resurrected and will appear in green garb and turban to lead the naked masses across the bridge over Hell; that he will be the intercessor for the faithful before God and rescue them from hellfire—provided they continuously pray to God to give him the honor of intercession. And when all is said and done, he will reside forevermore in the highest place of Paradise, close to the throne of God. There is much more to this nonsense, but these are the major elements. If nothing else, Muhammad gave a new degree of meaning to the word grandiosity.

He can be seen as the world's first ideological killer. Totalitarians start out as idealists and end up as mass murderers. Muhammad was not an exception. He believed he was doing people a favor by forcing them to submit to him and follow his path because submission would give them a chance to go to Paradise. He created a utopian fantasy around the idea of doing people a favor. He brought people "light" for their own good, but when they rejected him and his ideology, he resorted to terror.

His crimes against humanity were vile and would get him hung today: his mass murder of the Jews, his assassinations of critics and enemies, his endless attacks on tribes that opposed him, his relentless theft through plunder and the takeover of real estate, his enslavement of men, women, and children, among other crimes. He was cruel and heartless in the harm he did to people who rejected him—an ideological psychopath who got away with murder.

It is now easier than ever for people to learn the truth about the man who is the inspiration behind the terrorism that is spreading across the globe. People who take the trouble to acquire this knowledge can put it to good use. Until recently the facts about him remained among the world's best kept secrets, and the general ignorance about him and the nature of what he created helped to facilitate its spread. But it is no longer possible to keep it hidden. This is in part due to the ubiquity of the Internet and the diverse social media that allow for the rapid sharing of information. It is also due to the fact that Muhammadan scholars have only recently completed the translation of all the important early literature about Muhammad into English and other languages. What was once hidden from everyone is now available to anyone: the biography of Ibn Ishaq; the collections of the traditions about Muhammad compiled by Bukhari, Muslim, Abu Dawud, and others; the voluminous history of Tabari; the chronicle of Muhammad's raids and battles by the historians Waqidi and Ibn Sad; the ten-volume Koran commentary of Ibn Kathir and his four-volume biography of Muhammad. They can all be purchased today with the swipe of a credit card. Many of the collections of traditions are available online for free. Works such as *Reliance of the Traveler* and other books about what Muhammadans consider jurisprudence are now also available in translation. Koran translations are everywhere. The scholars must certainly be thanked for their labors. They brought out these translations hoping to bring Muhammad's "light" to the world. But people who have not been brainwashed from infancy into adulthood as have these scholars can see through this "light" for the dangerous nonsense that it is.

What Muhammad created is self-discrediting, and now because of the Internet, self-destructive. Each act of terror, and there have been more than 25,000 lethal terror attacks since the destruction of the Twin Towers on Sept. 11, 2001, drives more people to understand what is behind it, and this leads to the heart of the problem, to Muhammad.[1]

It is futile to hope that what he created can ever change. It's all about Muhammad. How can what he created be changed when it's all about him? Take him out of it and there is nothing left. Since that will never happen, what he created has to be pushed back and ultimately gotten rid of, for if you do not get rid of it, sooner or later it will get rid of you and everything you believe in because that is what it aspires to do. That is the struggle, the *jihad*, to make you submit to Muhammad's "light" for your own good—or destroy you and all that you cherish if you reject this "light."

What spreads through the mind cannot be fought only by dropping bombs. You have to attack what is in the mind. You have to attack the foundation of this belief by attacking the big lie that supports it. The cult that Muhammad created about himself rests solely on his claim that God talked to him through an angel. Like an inverted pyramid, the entire edifice rests on that one claim. It has been kept from toppling through a balancing act that required the cultivation of ignorance about Muhammad's sordid history and the imposition of the mythologized Muhammad—through violence if necessary. The inverted pyramid can be brought down by the exposure of his psychopathic evil. This is already happening to some extent, but it needs acceleration. That can be done by bringing out the truth about him using every graphic means possible, especially in motion pictures. The greater the exposure, the greater the number of people who will see that what he created is not a religion, but a dangerous cult that is balanced on the pathologies of a 7th century ideological killer.

People with means who understand the need to defend against what Muhammad created should consider stepping into producer shoes and turn to filmmaking. There is certainly money to be made, for the entire world is the audience. The audience can be broken down into two groups. The first is made up of the non-believers, five billion strong. The spread of such knowledge to this vast group is still in its early stages. People around the world are certainly aware that what Muhammad created is a serious problem due to the fact that people are being slaughtered in its name everywhere. Mass murder events are becoming weekly occurences, yet most people still do not know why this is happening or what they can do about it. The rapid dissemination of the truth about Muhammad through dramatic recreation in film—in feature films and docudramas—would serve the purpose of lifting the veil for people everywhere to see the face behind it. When the truth about the cause of it all becomes universally known, spines throughout the world will stiffen with resolve to take meaningful action. Even if only one percent of those five billion people were to become activists, that would mean fifty million people who are pushing back, a formidable number indeed.

The second audience is made up of the faithful, estimated to consist of one and a half billion people worldwide. Most of these people do not know the truth about Muhammad either. They were raised with the mythologized version, and in that mythology he is a man so holy that he will assist God on the Day of Judgment in determining the fate of believers. Most of these people have never read the Koran, and many are forced to memorize it in Arabic even though not understanding a word. What it will take to destroy the grip of the mythology is the kick in the gut that can come from movies that show this "prophet" send off hitmen to kill his critics, mass murder people who refuse to join his religion, and scream "Kill! Kill! Kill!" as he and his followers attack the caravans, towns, villages, and camps of people who rejected him and his claims about himself.

Truth trumps the lie, truth dissolves the myth, and already many people raised in this cult can see the lie and are abandoning it. Plenty of prominent examples can be cited, such as that of Mona Walter, a Somali living in Sweden. She lost her faith after reading the Koran in a language she could understand, and she now devotes her life to liberating others from the cult of Muhammad.[2] Reports that six million Africans[3] and two million Indonesians[4] abandon his cult every year have circulated on the Internet. These numbers may be exaggerated, but they indicate that the grip of the Muhammad myth is loosening. Film can accelerate this process. Relatively few people read books so that their impact is at best trickle down. But everyone watches film. A group of creative people who know the facts about Muhammad's life and their connection to the Koran could easily come up with dozens of ideas for documentaries, skits, and movies in a single brainstorming session. Knowledge, talent, and money are what it takes. It is rare that all of these come together in one person, but people possessing these elements separately have always coalesced around a shared goal. This is virgin territory. It has enormous potential.

Here is a treatment of an idea for a short film like the kind they do in film school, free for the taking:

A former Submitter, call him Rashid, is in Starbuck's reading a book. Years before, he belonged to a Muhammadan student organization that attacked critics of what Muhammad created, but he has lost his faith. A woman who used to know him in his student days comes into the coffee shop. Call her Amanda, a typical American with a superficial knowledge of Muhammad and what he created. Rashid recognizes her and waves to her. They catch up on things. Amanda is surprised to learn of his apostasy and asks him about it. He confesses that he had never truly understood the religion he grew up with until he read the Koran thoroughly and studied the early documents. He forced himself to take a critical look because of all the violence that he saw his co-religionists perpetrating around the world. He was shaken to the core by what he discovered about Muhammad. His faith fractured, and before long he was crawling out of the rubble of his former belief. He began a study of different religions.

When she asks him specifically what there was about Muhammad that disturbed him, he tells her about the atrocities. He is very descriptive. He draws word pictures and puts her into the scene. We watch her face as she reacts to his stories. When he gets to the slaughter of the Qurayza Jews, Amanda is visualizing it. She is there when it is happening, at the center of the action. What she sees in her visualization is what the viewer sees: Muhammad is seated in his pulpit-throne near a trench in the marketplace. A half-dozen frightened men with their hands tied behind their backs are brought before him, and with a wave of his hand they are taken to the trench and forced to kneel. Muhammad's cousins Ali and Zubayr cut off their heads, and their bodies are thrown into the trench. Amanda is terrified and disoriented. It is like a nightmare she cannot escape from. Everything she sees is horrifying: Women and children are wailing at the sight of their beloved ones being slain; Muhammad's face shows gloating satisfaction. Though terrified she goes up to him and screams, "Stop this! Stop! How can you do this? You are supposed to be a holy man. What is holy about this?" But Muhammad ignores her. It is as if she is not there. By then, more men have been brought out and are forced to kneel at the edge of the trench. Amanda rushes up to Ali and begs him to stop. "Please, don't do this. This is not right!" But Ali brings down his sword on one of the men. Amanda's face is frozen with horror at the sight of the head dropping and the torso falling to one side.

The scene dissolves back to the coffee shop, and we see her weeping, her trembling hand covering her mouth. Rashid takes her hand to comfort her. He says, "It is not possible to change the past, Amanda. You can only have an impact on the future." Several months later, they meet again at the coffee shop. Amada is cheerful and tells Rashid that he inspired her to form a group to study about Muhammad. She invites him to talk to them about what brought him to leave his religion, apologizing that she could only promise him twelve people, fifteen at the most. Rashid smiles. "I would be delighted."

Naysayers may scoff at the idea that something as seemingly entrenched as the cult of Muhammad could be undermined and ultimately made to disappear through such exposure. Yet how many people in Athens still believe that Zeus is God and resides with a family of gods on Mount Olympus? How many people in Rome still hold that Jupiter is God and make blood sacrifices before his temple? Or in the Scandinavian countries, how many worship Thor and fear his lightning bolts? Civilizations were once held together by these myths, but eventually the light of reason penetrated them, and the myths were abandoned. The light of reason is now penetrating the Muhammad myth, and it will be abandoned, not just because it is myth but because it is a vile myth that has harmed the world for fourteen centuries. When the myth is finally exploded and the real Muhammad is there for everyone to see, people will scratch their heads in wonder that the world could have been duped for so long.

Will they not like this? Will they become violent or threaten violence? All the more reason to proceed. The fact that they—they being people brainwashed into believing what Muhammad claimed about himself; they being people who bang their foreheads to the ground in worship of his violent God concept—could cause harm over such exposure *is* the reason it needs to be done. Whatever the reaction, it will only serve to draw attention to the very thing that will eventually bring the end to what they believe.

People who think this is not of any real concern should take a lesson from the Meccans. They did not have the foresight to do what needed to be done when it would have made a difference. Muhammad had only a few dozen followers at first, then it became a hundred, then thousands. And in the end the Meccans were overwhelmed and joined Muhammad's feral enterprise to keep from being slaughtered. Ignore the threat, deny that it is real, and this machinery of enslavement will sooner or later come your way too.

Western civilization is not immune from being swallowed by Muhammad's cult. If there any doubt about this, resurrect the slaughtered Christians of Syria and Egypt, and the Zoroastrians of Persia, and the Buddhists and the Hindus farther east. Put them in chairs and stick microphones in front of them. Let them spill their guts about what happened to them and their civilizations. Ask them if they knew what was coming from Umar and Uthman and Khalid and Zubayr and others ten years before what happened to them, or five years, or even one year. They will testify that what was done to them was unimaginable before it happened, but it happened and then it was too late. Swing around to New York and resurrect those who died in the Twin Towers. Ask them about it. Could they see what was coming even a minute before it happened? Go to India, Pakistan, Bangladesh, China, Thailand, Burma, the Philippines, Israel, Syria, Iraq, Mali, Nigeria, Chad, Cameroon, Sudan, Kenya, the Central African Republic, among other Muhammad-afflicted countries. This time ask the survivors if they knew what was coming. Ask them about the Muhammad replicates who came out of nowhere with bombs, rifles, knives, and cries of *Allahu Akbar*, and slaughtered their loved ones at will. Ask them about the unimaginable and what it feels like when it happens.

When the replicates are finished with the East and with Africa and with Europe and other places, they will come your way, you can count on it, and maybe they will come even before they have finished with other places. They've already announced it. The whole planet is their unfinished business. It is in the marching orders Muhammad gave them: "Fight and kill the disbelievers wherever you find them, take them captive, harass them, lie in wait and ambush them using every stratagem of war."[5]

What Muhammad created will never burn itself out. It has to be made to burn out, and this can be brought about today because of the universality of film. It is the aggressive, relentless, and unapologetic barrage of images of Muhammad's savagery that can bring an end to what he created: potent truth bombs exploding in minds throughout the world. No one will be able to escape the truth. People who were raised in the lie will see the lie. There will be nowhere for them to hide. It will be in the air, coming from every direction. The believers in Muhammad's nonsense, men and women, young and old, will run hither and thither on this new field of battle trying to escape the graphic bomblets, but no sooner will they turn in one direction than another explodes, and another, and another, and out of each comes the shrieks and agonies of people who were slaughtered by the dark side of human nature that Muhammad unleashed. The vaunted billion and a half believers will shrivel down. What is left of diehards will die off, and the world will emit a universal sigh of relief.

And now prophecy:

The true Day of Doom is approaching. It will not be the blast of Israfil's trumpet to announce the end, but a gavel slamming down in a courtroom. Muhammad will be resurrected in film, not to lead the naked masses across the bridge over Hell to stand in judgment before the throne of God, but to stand trial in the court of Mankind. He will be in the docket of the accused along with Ali, Umar, Uthman, Abu Bakr, Zubayr, Zayd, and others, charged with assassination, mass murder, genocide, plunder, torture, enslavement, and more, all crimes against humanity.[6] The long-awaited resurrection will occur. Victim after victim will crawl from their graves to testify about what he did to them: Abu Afak, Asma, Kab Ashraf, and Umm Qirfa and Kinana too. And the Qurayza Jews, a long line of them with the dirt of the trench still on them, and the endless victims of plunder attacks and raids. All will come forth with their stories.

The defense will have its chance. And we will hear the closing arguments, and then will come the time for the jurors to go out. And when they go out we will hear drums tapping slowly. The jury is not a panel of twelve or twenty. We see faces, one after another, of men and women, young and old, of all races and nations. It is an endless stream. To the quickening drums more faces appear, faster and faster. It speeds up and there are so many flashing that it becomes a blur. The drums tap furiously to keep up, and finally we hear the powerful slam of a kettle drum and the dizzying whir stops.

The slam of the big drum is the announcement that the true Day of Judgment has arrived.

And at last humanity will render its verdict.

CHAPTER NOTES

The Koran translations of J. M. Rodwell, Abdullah Yusuf Ali, Muhammad Marmaduke Pickthall, Mohsin Khan and M. H. Shakir were quoted in this work. The translation of Thomas Cleary was also consulted.

Except for the first reference, the author's name is usually only given for the most frequently cited primary sources:

Ibn Ishaq – *The Life of Muhammad*
Ibn Kathir – *The Life of the Prophet Muhammad*
Ibn Sad – *Kitab al-Tabaqat al-Kabir (Book of the Major Classes)*
Tabari – *The History of al-Tabari*
Waqidi – *The Life of Muhammad*

CHAPTER 1 – Sanctuary

1. Hitti, Philip, *History of the Arabs*, p. 103. Hitti believes the name was derived from the Sabaean word *"makuraba,"* meaning "sanctuary." The Sabaeans dominated Yemen in the millennium before Jesus, and Sabaean emigrants ended up populating much of Arabia, influencing its language and culture.
2. Tabari, Abu Jafar Muhammad Ibn Jarir, *The History of al-Tabari*, vol. 1: *From Creation to the Flood*, p. 293, and Muhammad ibn Sad, *Kitab al-Tabaqat al-Kabir (The Book of the Major Classes)*, vol. 1, p. 26. Muhammad made extensive use of Jewish prophet legends, modifying them according to his needs. This modification began with his story that Adam founded Mecca. From Tabari: "When God cast Adam down from Heaven, Adam's feet were upon earth, while his head was in Heaven and he heard the speech and prayers of the inhabitants of Heaven. He became (too) familiar with them, and the angels were in awe of him so much that they eventually complained to God in their various prayers. God, therefore, lowered Adam down to earth (meaning, shrunk him down in size). Adam missed what he used to hear from the angels and felt lonely so much that he eventually complained about it to God in his various prayers. He was therefore sent to Mecca. [On the way, every] place where he set foot became a village, and [the interval between his steps] became a desert, until he reached Mecca. God sent down a jewel of Paradise where the House is located today. (Adam) continued to circumambulate it until God sent

down the Flood. That jewel was lifted up, until God sent his friend Abraham to (re)build the House (in its later form)."—Tabari, vol. 1, p. 293. From Ibn Sad: "Allah revealed to Adam: 'There is a sanctuary opposite My throne, so go and erect a house for me and circumambulate round it as you have seen the angels doing around My throne, and there I shall accept thy prayer and of thy sons who obey Me.' Thereupon Adam said, 'O Lord! How can I? I have no power and I have no guidance. Then Allah sent an angel who led Adam to Mecca.... And on the way wherever he halted, it became a populated place, and from where he passed on, it became a wilderness and desolate. Then the House of Allah was built with material obtained from five mountains—Sina, Zaytun, Lubnan, and Judi. Its plinth was made from Hira. When he had completed the work, the angel led him to Arafat and instructed him in all the rituals which people perform even today. He then returned to Mecca and circumambulated round the Kabah for a week. After that he returned to India and died on the mountains of Nawhd."—Ibn Sad, vol. 1, p. 26. For comparison with the Jewish story of Adam, see Genesis and Ginzberg, Louis, *The Legends of the Jews*, vol. 1: *From the Creation to Jacob*, pp. 49-102.

3. No trace of Mecca can be found in any of the records of the Romans, Byzantines, Greeks, and Persians. There is also an absence of archeological evidence, including telltale rock graffiti, dating before the fourth century A.D. None of the records of the millennial caravan commerce through western Arabia nor any of the tens of thousands of inscriptions that have been discovered on the monuments and ruins of ancient Arabia make any mention of Mecca.

4. Tabari, *History*, vol. 6: *Muhammad at Mecca*, pp. 28-9.

5. Shahid, Irfan, *Byzantium and the Arabs in the Fifth Century*, pp. 389-90.

6. Ibn Sad, vol. 1, p. 64.

7. Ibid., vol. 1, p. 67.

CHAPTER 2 – Ancestors

1. Tabari, vol. 6, p. 16.

2. Ibn Sad, vol. 1, pp. 78-9.

3. Ibid., vol. 1, p. 78.

4. Ibn Ishaq, Muhammad, *The Life of Muhammad*, p. 59.

5. Tabari, vol. 6, pp. 11-2.

6. Ibn Ishaq, p. 20.

7. Ibid., p. 23.

8. Ibid., pp. 26-7.

9. Koran, 105:1-5.

10. Tabari describes the use of divination arrows at the Meccan temple: "Beside Hubal there were seven arrows, on each of which there was writing. On one was written, 'the blood money'; when a dispute arose as to which of them was responsible for paying blood money, they cast lots with the seven arrows to settle the matter. On another arrow was written 'yes'; when they were considering some course of action, they cast lots, and if the 'yes' arrow came out they acted on it. Another arrow had 'no,' and if that came out they did not proceed with their course of action. On the other arrows was written 'of you,' 'attached,' 'not of you,' and 'Water.' When they wanted to dig for water they cast lots with the arrows, including this

last one, and wherever it fell they started digging. Whenever they wanted to circumcise a boy, arrange a marriage, or bury someone who had died, or when they were in doubt as to the descent of one of them, they took him to Hubal together with a hundred dirhams and a slaughtering-camel which they would give to the custodian who used to cast lots with the arrows. Then they would bring forward the person about whom they wished to consult the oracle and would say, 'O god of ours, this is so-and-so the son of so-and-so, about whom we wish to know such-and-such; so reveal the truth concerning him.' Then they would say to the custodian of the arrows, 'Cast!' The latter would cast them, and if 'of you' fell to the person in question, that meant that he was a fellow tribesman; if it was 'not of you,' he was a confederate; and if it was 'attached,' he remained as he was, linked to them neither by descent nor alliance. In matters other than these, when 'yes' came out they acted accordingly, and when 'no' came out they deferred the matter until the following year, when they brought it up again. This recourse to the way the arrows fell was their ultimate method of deciding their affairs."—Tabari, vol. 6, p. 3. These consultations were expensive. A dirham was a Byzantine silver coin, and one hundred of them contained about 25 ounces of silver. The oracle-priest was either a member of the clan having the hereditary gatekeeper role, or was soothsayer appointed by the clan.

11. Tabari, vol. 6, pp. 2-4.
12. Ibid., vol. 6, pp. 6-7.

CHAPTER 3 – Fits

1. Tabari, *History*, vol. 5: *The Sasanids, the Byzantines, the Lakhmids, and Yemen*, p. 271. The translator of vol. 5 of Tabari's History, C. E. Bosworth, suggests that stories of supernatural events surrounding the birth of Muhammad were influenced by legends regarding the births of earlier religious leaders such as Zoroaster, Buddha, and Krishna.—Tabari, vol. 5, p. 270, n. 645.

2. Ibn Sad, vol. 1, p. 112.

3. Korkut, Dede, M.D., *Life Alert, The Medical Case of Muhammad*, p. 41. A neurologist and psychiatrist, Korkut believes that the bright visual experiences of Amina preceding Muhammad's birth and during his birth suggest she suffered from epilepsy. He believes the evidence is overwhelming that Muhammad was afflicted with the disease, and that it is likely he inherited it from her as modern studies have shown that about thirty percent of epileptic children have a close relative who is also afflicted.

4. Halima was from the Banu Sad b. Bakr, a tribe of the Hawazin confederation, allies of Thaqifs, who were the inhabitants of the town of Taif. Halima's link to Taif is clearly established after the Battle of Hunayn, which took place near Taif in A.D. 630. Some of the captives were of Halima's tribe, and to gain favorable treatment from Muhammad, they reminded him of their connection to his foster mother.

5. Ibn Ishaq, p. 71.

6. Two of the primary sources, Ibn Ishaq, pp. 71-2, and Tabari, vol. 5, pp. 274-5, both relate the same story almost verbatim, quoting

Halima that Muhammad's hallucinatory event took place several months after she returned to her camp from the visit to Amina. This would put Muhammad's age at the time at about 2½ years. In the Ibn Sad account, vol. 1, pp. 123-4, Muhammad was four years old and was tending sheep or goats with other children when the incident occurred. Muhammad was returned to his mother not long after, but she sent him back to the countryside with Halima where he remained for another year. Aloys Sprenger, *Life of Muhammad, from Original Sources*, p. 78, n. 3, believes Muhammad spent at least five years with Halima's tribe. Sprenger argues that throughout his life Muhammad spoke with their distinctive accent, which he would not have retained if had returned to Mecca while still learning to speak.

7. Tabari gives the official version of the incident. The seed of this story may have been Muhammad's dim recollection of an epileptic experience as a four- or five-year old boy, and the story grew with the telling until it solidified into its final form. The latter part of this excerpt suggests the self-aggrandizing of a man suffering from low self esteem: "One day, I was away from the rest of my people in the bottom of a *wadi* (gully), with a group of children of my own age and we were playing at throwing between us pieces of camels' dung. Suddenly, a group of three men approached us, bearing a gold pitcher filled with snow. They took me out of the group of my friends, and the latter fled until they reached the edge of the *wadi*. Then they came back to the group of the three and they said, 'What do you

intend to do with this lad? He is not one of us but is the son of the lord of the Quraysh, and he is an orphan, for whom a wet nurse was sought among us; he has no father. What good will killing him bring you, and what will you gain from that? But if you are determined ineluctably on killing him, then choose one of us, whichever you like; let him come to you in his stead, and then kill him; but leave this lad alone; he is an orphan.' However, when the children saw the group of three men returning no answer to them, they fled at top speed back to the tribe, telling them what had happened and imploring help against the men. One of the three men came up to me and laid me gently on the ground, and then split open my body from the division of my rib cage to the end of the pubic hair, while I was watching all this but not feeling any touch at all. He then took out the viscera from my abdomen and washed them with that snow. He washed them carefully and replaced them. Then the second man stood up and said to his companion, 'Stand aside,' and he drew him away from me. He then put his hand into my insides and brought forth my heart, with me watching all the time. He split it asunder, extracted a black drop and threw the drop aside. He went on to say: In his hand, at his right side, there was as if he were holding something, and lo and behold, just by me was a seal ring in his hand, emitting light that dazzled anyone that looked at it, and by means of which he sealed my heart so that it became filled with this light of prophethood and wisdom. Then he returned it to its place. I felt the coolness of that seal ring in my heart for a long time afterward. The third man now said to his companion, 'Stand aside from me,' and he passed his hand over my body from the division of my rib cage to the end of the pubic hair, and that slit was henceforth healed together, by God's permission. He now took my hand and gently made me get up from my resting place, and said to the first man, who had slit open my body, 'Weigh him against ten of his community!' They weighed me against them, and I outweighed them. Next he said, 'Weigh him against a hundred of his community.' Then he weighed me against them and I outweighed them. Finally he said, 'Weigh him against a thousand of his community.' He then said, 'Let him be, even if you were to weigh him against the whole of his community, he would outweigh them all!'"—Tabari, vol. 5, pp. 277-8.

8. Ibn Ishaq, p. 72.

9. Korkut, p. 42.

10. Tabari, vol. 5, p. 279.

11. Ibn Sad, vol. 1, p. 124.

12. Ibid., vol. 1, p. 141.

13. Tabari, *History*, vol. 6: *Muhammad at Mecca*, p. 47.

14. Ibn Ishaq, p. 81.

15. Korkut, pp. 55-6. Muhammad had an aversion to sharp, penetrating sounds, very likely because such sounds provoked seizures. It is possible the first of these two episodes was triggered by the sound of festive music, as he reported hearing tambourines and pipes prior to blacking out. Korkut cites the case of a 62-year-old British civil servant who suffered seizures only when he was exposed to the sound of church bells "heard either in the open or over the radio." Such sounds can drill into the brain of a person suffering from temporal lobe epilepsy and set off neural explosions resulting in a seizure. Possibly because of this negative effect on him, Muhammad acquired such a repugnance for music that he banned all music. He also loathed the sound of women shrieking at funerals, particularly by hired mourners, to the point that he later prohibited wailing—real or faked—at funerals. Ibn Sad quotes Muhammad: "I prohibited from wailing and the two high pitched sounds of fools and libertines, i.e., voices raised in joyful parties with Satanic instruments and another raised in distress by scratching the face, tearing the collars, and shouting like Satan."—Ibn Sad, vol. 1, p. 156. Muhammad loathed dogs as well, very likely due to the neural disturbances the sound of barking caused him. This led him eventually to threaten his followers with loss of the value of their good works if they kept dogs. In a Bukhari tradition, Muhammad said, "Whoever keeps a dog, one *qirat* (of the reward) of his good deeds is deducted daily, unless the dog is used for guarding a farm or cattle."—Bukhari, *Sahih Al-Bukhari* (Darussalam), trad. 2322. A *qirat* is a large unit of weight.

16. Tabari, vol. 6, pp. 45-6. The Bahira story is also told by Ibn Sad, vol. 1, p. 134, and Ibn Ishaq, pp. 79-81.

17. Muir, William, *The Life of Mohammad*, p. 11.

18. Ibid., p. 14, n. 1.

19. Hoyland, Robert, *Arabia and the Arabs*, pp. 225-6, quoting Ali ibn Husayn al-Isfahani, a ninth century Muhammadan scholar.

20. Ibn Sad, vol. 1, p. 143.

CHAPTER 4 – Protectress

1. Ibn Sad, vol. 1, p. 145.
2. In his biography of Muhammad, R. V. C. Bodley describes Khadija's business practices: "Khadija's business methods were modern. She loaned money to reliable Koreishite merchants, in return for which she became a partner in the transactions which she had backed. She also invested the money of her smaller depositors in caravans. When the caravans returned from their trading expeditions, the profits were shared in proportion to the investments. Khadija also had her employees, in the town office and on the road, financially interested in her various business enterprises. They thus found themselves, at the same time, her employees, her creditors, and her shareholders. The success, therefore, of everything the firm undertook was to the interest of all, from the president and managers to the accountants and the lowliest cameleers."—Bodley, *The Messenger*, p. 41.
3. Muir, pp 25-6. See also *Shamaa-il Tirmidhi (Outer Form)*, by Tirmidhi). The *Shamaa-il* is a compendium of traditions about Muhammad describing his physical appearance, habits, and mannerisms. To this day devout believers strive to model their gestures and daily habits on Muhammad's practices as described in such traditions. Osama bin Laden was known to be obsessive about such emulation.
4. Ibid., p. 22, n. 2.
5. Ibn Sad, vol. 1, p. 147.
6. Ibid., p. 178.

7. Ibid., p. 148.
8. Tabari, vol. 6, p. 49.
9. Ibn Sad, vol. 1, p. 149.
10. It is not unanimously accepted that Muhammad had four daughters with Khadija. The Sunnis make it an article of faith, but the Shiites believe Muhammad was the biological father of Fatima only. The other daughters were either children from a previous marriage of Khadija, or were children of a deceased sister that Khadija took under her care.
11. Ibn Sad, vol. 1, pp. 125-6.
12. Ibn Ishaq, p. 114.
13. Fidai and Shaikh, *The Companions of the Holy Prophet*, pp. 5-16.
14. Ibid., pp. 319-20.
15. Ibn Ishaq, p. 84, and ibn Sad, vol. 1, pp. 164-5. Sources differ as to the motive for the temple reconstruction. Ibn Sad stated it was due to flood damage while Ibn Ishaq alleges it came about as a result of the theft of the treasures of the temple that had been facilitated by the fact the building had low walls and was roofless. Flood damage was the more plausible motive, but Ibn Ishaq's version is significant because it describes the temple up until that time as a modest affair consisting of low walls of stacked rocks without a roof. Ibn Ishaq writes, "They (the Quraysh) were planning to roof it and feared to demolish it, for it was made of loose stones above a man's height, and they wanted to raise it and roof it because men had stolen part of the treasure . . . which used to be in a well in the middle of it."
16. Tabari, vol. 6, p. 57.
17. The original temple walls were too far apart to allow a roof even with the lumber from the

salvaged ship. To accommodate a roof, the Meccans built the temple with a narrower width and depth. This is affirmed in a tradition attributed to Muhammad's wife Aisha in which he tells her that he wanted to rebuild the reconstructed temple on its original foundations, though in this account he attributes the original foundation to Abraham—*Sahih al-Bukhari*, trad. 1585.

18. Ibid., trads. 1584 and 7243.

19. That Muhammad fell unconscious is noted in a tradition attributed to Jabir ibn Abdullah, a companion of Muhammad and the source of numerous traditions. Abdullah is quoted saying that when the temple was being rebuilt, "the Prophet and Abbas went to carry stones. Abbas said to the Prophet, '(Take off and) put your waist sheet over your neck so that the stones may not hurt you.' (But as soon as he took off his waist sheet) he fell unconscious on the ground with both eyes towards the sky. When he came to his senses, he said, 'My waist sheet! My waist sheet!'"—*Sahih al-Bukhari*, trad. 3829. The Bukhari tradition does not mention that Muhammad heard a voice, but in a similar tradition recorded by Ibn Sad, a voice said to Muhammad, "Beware of your nakedness." Ibn Sad added that it was the first time Muhammad heard a voice that no one else heard.—Ibn Sad, vol. 1, p. 165. Auditory hallucinations are often a part of the epileptic experience. See Korkut, Dede, *Life Alert, the Medical Case of Muhammad*, ch. 2.

20. Ibn Sad, vol. 1, p. 179. This claim is attributed to Aisha, to whom Muhammad became betrothed following the death of Khadija. She was

nine years old when the marriage took place, and she was eighteen years old when he died.

21. Ibn Ishaq, p. 105; Tabari, vol. 6, pp. 63-4; Ibn Sad, vol. 1, p. 179.

22. Ibn Sad, vol. 1, p. 195.

CHAPTER 5 – Cave Dwellers

1. Numani, Allama Shibli, *Sirat-un-Nabi* (*Biography of the Prophet*), vol. 1, p. 129. Numani, a Sufi scholar of the late 19th and early 20th centuries, gives grudging acceptance that Muhammad's first-born son was likely named al-Uzza. He writes: "Accordingly they say the first-born child of the Prophet was named Abd al-Uzza (Uzza being the name of an idol). Even if true, it is no argument against the Prophet and does not establish his responsibility. Khadija had been an idol-worshipper before coming into the fold of Islam. She might have given her son this name, and the Prophet, not yet entrusted with his mission, might have passed over it in silence." Numani gives the source of such claims: *Tarikh Saghir* (*Short History*) of Bukhari, which is not available in English translation.

2. Ibn Sad, vol. 1, p. 185.

3. Sozomen, *Ecclesiastical History*, pp. 318-19. See also Cook, Michael, *Muhammad*, pp. 80-1.

4. Ibn Sad, p. 185.

5. Sozomen, pp. 318-19.

6. Ibn Ishaq, *The Life of Muhammad*, p. 100.

7. Koran, 17:31 and 81:8-9.

8. *Sahih al-Bukhari*, trad. 3826.

9. Ibid., trad. 3828.

10. Siddiqi, Muhammad Iqbal, *Asharah Mubash-Sharah: The Ten*

Companions of the Holy Prophet who were Promised for Paradise, p. 55.

11. Ibn Ishaq, p. 101.

12. *"A Bag of Meat": A Study of an Early Tradition.* This monograph is included in a collection of articles by M. J. Kister in *Studies in Jahiliyya and Early Islam* (Variorum Reprints, London, 1980).

13. The primary goddesses of the Meccans—al-Uzza, al-Lat, and al-Manat—are usually referred to as the "three daughters" of Allah. The literature, however, is not consistent, and this verse in Zayd's poem may reflect the idea of al-Uzza as spouse of Allah. It was the pattern in Middle Eastern pagan religions to pair the male supreme deity with a supreme consort. As such, al-Uzza was not the sister but the mother of al-Lat, an Aphrodite equivalent, and al-Manat, who represents fate, destiny.

14. Various translations of Zayd's poem can be found. The version included here is from the Guillaume translation of Ibn Ishaq, p. 100. Tisdall finds the following ideas expressed in Zayd's poem that Muhammad later expanded upon in the Koran: "Among these may be instanced: (1) the prohibition of killing infant daughters by burying them alive, according to the cruel custom of the Arabs of the time; (2) the acknowledgment of the Unity of God; (3) the rejection of idolatry and the worship of Al-Lat, Al-Uzza and the other deities of the people; (4) the promise of future happiness in Paradise or the "Garden", (5) the warning of the punishment reserved in Hell for the wicked; (6) the denunciation of God's wrath upon the Unbelievers, and (7) the application of the titles *Ar Rahman*

(the Merciful), *Ar Rabb* (the Lord), and *Al Ghafur* (the Forgiving) to God."—Tisdall, W. St. Clair, *The Original Sources of the Qur'an*, p. 271.

15. LaPlante, Eve, *Seized: Temporal Lobe Epilepsy as a Medical, Historical, and Artistic Phenomenon*, pp. 213-4. See also Korkut, Dede, *Life Alert, The Medical Case of Muhammad*, pp. 34-5.

16. Details of Muhammad's cave experience can be found throughout the literature. See Ibn Sad, *Kitab al-Tabaqat al-Kabir*, vol. 1, pp. 223-30; *The History of al-Tabari*, vol. 6, pp. 66-76; Ibn Ishaq, *The Life of Muhammad*, pp. 104-7; *Sahih Muslim*, traditions 301-307.

17. Ibn Kathir, Ishmael, *Tafsir ibn Kathir*, vol. 9, pp. 309-10. A 14th century Muhammadan historian, Ibn Kathir recorded this telling evidence of an epileptic fit, but he does not venture an opinion about why saliva was found on Muhammad's cheeks.

18. Tempkin, Owsei, *The Falling Sickness, A History of Epilepsy from the Greeks to the Beginnings of Modern Neurology*, p. 153. Tempkin quotes the *Chronographia* of Theophanes that Muhammad "had the disease of epilepsy. And when his wife noticed it, she was very much grieved that she, being of noble descent, was tied to such a man, who was not only poor but epileptic as well. Now he attempts to soothe her with the following words: 'I see a vision of an angel called Gabriel and not being able to bear the sight of him, I become weak and fall down.' But she had a certain monk for her friend who had been exiled because of his false faith and who was living

there, so she reported everything to him, including the name of the angel. And this man, wanting to reassure her, said to her, 'He has spoken the truth, for this angel is sent forth to all prophets.' And she, having received the word of the pseudo-prophet, believed him and announced to the other women of the tribe that he was a prophet."

19. Freeman, Frank R., *A Differential Diagnosis of the Inspirational Spells of Muhammad the Prophet of Islam*, published in the journal *Epilepsia*, vol. 17:423-7 (Raven Press, New York, 1976).

20. Korkut, *Life Alert*, pp. 41-2.

21. Ibid., p. 94.

CHAPTER 6 – The Amalgamated Monotheism of Mecca

1. Ibn Ishaq, *The Life of Muhammad*, p. 112.

2. Mohamed, Dr. Mamdouh N., *Salaat: The Islamic Prayer from A to Z*, pp. 33-46.

3. See the Wikipedia entry: "Obsessive-Compulsive Disorder."

4. Typical of such prayers, Muhammad would say: "I pray to You as does one who is fearful and in distress, as one who submits his neck to You, and sheds his tears before You, bending low his body before You, humiliating himself before You. O God, do not render me, O God, wretched in my prayer to You; be compassionate and merciful with me, O Best of all who receive requests, and Best of all who give." Ibn Kathir, *Life of Muhammad*, vol. 4, p. 252

5. In the standard Koran, this is the lead chapter. It contains only seven verses and is considered the

preface to the work. Koran translator J. M. Rodwell, however, placed it as Chapter 8 based on the chronology of its composition.

6. In the standard versions of the Koran, the chapters are arranged in descending order, from the longest at the beginning and the shortest at the end, an artificial ordering that obscures the chronology of Muhammad's work. This makes it difficult to connect the events of Muhammad's life to the entries in the Koran, which often read like a diary or a blog in that they frequently recap and comment on events. Rodwell corrected the problem by organizing his version chronologically, at least to the extent that scholars have been able to establish the chronology. Though not entirely accurate due to the fact that later material was sometimes fused together with earlier material, either by Muhammad or by his followers after his death, Rodwell's arrangement is reasonably accurate and is invaluable for helping the reader understand the connection between the events of Muhammad's life and his Koran compositions. A word of caution about the Rodwell editions: An authentic edition of Rodwell's work, which was first published in 1909, is the Dover edition published in 2005 as a reprint of the original. (Dover Publications, Inc., Mineola, New York, 2005). Not so with the Bantam Books version. Its 2004 publication retained Rodwell's translation, but rearranged the chapters according to the standard order—from longest to shortest. Bantam also eliminated the scholarly introduction by G. Margoliouth and Rodwell's extensive footnotes. As a chronological and

scholarly guide the Bantam edition is completely useless.

7. The Chapter 55 title varies with the translation. In the Thomas Cleary translation, it is "The Benevolent One." In the Abdullah Yusuf Ali version, it is "Most Gracious." Rodwell translates it as "The Merciful."

8. This is an amusing irony since "We" and "Us" are plural, yet Muhammad was the champion of the concept of the "Unity of God," which holds there is but one God who has no "associates" and that placing other gods with the Creator is idolatry—the greatest sin. Muhammad was in fact trapped by grammar. The use of first person singular pronouns when speaking in his God voice would have been confusing to listeners, who would think that Muhammad, as the reciter of verses allegedly coming from God, was speaking in his own voice. Hence the need for the God voice of his Koran to use rhetorical plural pronouns. Muhammad occasionally slips, and the God voice occurs in the first person singular. One of the best examples is in Koran, 5:3: "Today have I perfected your religious law for you, and have bestowed upon you the full measure of My blessings, and willed that self-surrender unto Me shall be your religion."

9. Muir, p. 38.

10. Ibn Ishaq, p. 114.

11. Sprenger, Aloys, *The Life of Muhammad from Original Sources*, p. 171.

12. Ibn Kathir, *Life of Muhammad*, vol. 1, p. 318.

13. Khalid, Khalid Muhammad, *The Men around the Messenger*, p. 172.

14. Hasan, Masudul, *Hadrat Othman Ghani*, p. 6.

15. Sprenger, p. 44.

16. Koran, 73:14.

17. Ibid., 73:11-13.

18. Ibid., 96:15-16.

19. Ibid., 74:27-29.

20. LaPlante, Eve, *Seized*, p. 116.

21. Ibid., p. 37.

22. Ibn Kathir, *Life of Muhammad*, vol. 1, p. 300.

23. Koran, 93:3-5.

CHAPTER 7 – Fire and Brimstone

1. Ibn Sad, vol. 1, p. 180.

2. Ibn Ishaq, p. 117.

3. Ibid., p. 118.

4. Ibn Kathir, *Life of Muhammad*, vol. 1 p. 331.

5. Ibid., vol. 1, p. 331.

6. Bodley, R. V. C., *The Messenger, the Life of Mohammed*, p. 68.

7. Koran, 111:1-5.

8. *Tafsir Ibn Kathir*, vol. 10, p 626.

9. Given that they lived next door to each other, Abu Sufyan's children were likely playmates of Muhammad's children and the children in his care such as Ali. Abu Sufyan's children included Muawiya, who was two years younger than Ali. Decades later, Ali would lead an army against Muawiya in a civil war for control over Muhammad's religion. Following Ali's assassination in A.D. 661, Muawiya would become the first caliph of the Umayyad dynasty.

10. Ibn Sad, vol. 1, p. 232.

11. "When the apostle openly displayed Islam as God ordered him, his people did not withdraw

or turn against him, so far as I have heard, until he spoke disparagingly of their gods. When he did that they took great offense and resolved unanimously to treat him as an enemy."—Ibn Ishaq, p. 118.

12. Ibn Kathir, vol. 1, p. 334.

13. Koran, 78:21-25.

14. Ibid., 78:41-43.

15. Ibn Ishaq, p. 119.

16. Ibid., p. 119.

17. Ibid., p. 119.

18. Ibid., pp. 119-20.

19. Koran, 74:11-15.

20. Ibid., 74:18-25.

21. Ibid., 81:22-25.

22. Ibid., 83:29-32.

23. Ibn Kathir, vol. 1, p. 323.

24. Asin, Miguel, *Islam and the Divine Comedy* (Goodword Books, 2002).

25. Hamid, Abdul Walid, *Companions of the Prophet*, vol. 1, pp. 1-6.

26. Ibn Ishaq, p. 118.

CHAPTER 8 – I will Bring You Slaughter

1. Koran, 88:21.

2. *Tafsir Ibn Kathir*, vol. 7, pp. 701-2.

3. Muhammad clearly states his belief in his role as messenger of Allah in a later verse, composed about four years after he fled Mecca for Yathrib: "Muhammad is not the father of any of your men, but he is the Apostle of Allah and the Last of the prophets; and Allah is cognizant of all things."—Koran, 33:40. "Muhammad is not the father of any of your men" means that he did not have any surviving male offspring.

4. Khalid, *Men Around the Messenger*, pp. 173-4.

5. Abu Bakr and Talha were from the same Taym clan, but neither had gotten support from their kinsmen after they came out as followers of Muhammad. Their clan, which descended from Murra, a paternal grandfather of Qusay, was an important branch of the Quraysh tribe and had close family and commercial ties with Abu Sufyan's Umayyad clan, which was among the leading Meccan families that opposed Muhammad.

6. Nawfal Khuwaylid was a half-brother of Khadija. He is noted for having rescued his nephew Zubayr from his abusive mother Safiya, who used to beat him. Nawfal, however, also beat Zubayr after he found out he had become a follower of Muhammad. Not much is recorded about Nawfal, but it can be concluded that he knew a great deal about Muhammad, including his maladies, as he was clearly unimpressed when Muhammad declared that God talked to him. A man of great physical strength, Nawfal was later slain by Muhammad's cousin Ali at the battle of Badr after he had been taken prisoner and was disarmed. Badr was the first major battle between Muhammad and the Meccans. When Muhammad learned Ali had killed Nawfal, he said, "Praise be to God who answered my prayer concerning him."—Waqidi, *The Life of Muhammad*, p. 47.

7. Hamid, *Companions of the Prophet*, vol. 2, pp. 230-1.

8. Ibn Ishaq, p. 145.

9. Ibn Kathir, vol. 1 p. 339.

10. Ibid., vol. 1, p. 340. Muhammad's curse against the Meccan leaders has alternately been translated as "kill" or "punish" or "take

away." Based on subsequent events, it is clear that he prayed for their demise. About six years later, all the men present that day would end up slain at the battle of Badr and their bodies dumped down a well.

11. Ibid., vol. 1, pp. 342-3.

12. Ibn Ishaq, p. 131.

13. Ibid., pp. 131-2. The literature is inconsistent about the age of Muhammad's uncle Hamza, an important figure in the early years of Muhammad's religion. Some sources claim he was four years older, while others say he was two years older. Yet the literature also states that Abdul Muttalib, Hamza's father and Muhammad's paternal grandfather, married a woman from the Zurah tribe at the same time Muhammad's father Abdullah married Amina, another woman of the Zurah tribe, in a double ceremony. Since Muhammad was born within a year of Abdullah's marriage to Amina, Hamza would have been the same age as he or even slightly younger. If so, then Hamza and Muhammad were in their mid-forties at the time of this incident. If Hamza was in fact older than Muhammad, then his father would have married earlier than Abdullah.

14. Ibid., pp. 132-3.

15. Koran, 41:2-4.

16. Ibid., 41:6.

17. Ibid., 41:37.

18. Ibn Ishaq, p. 133.

19. Sprenger, *Life of Muhammad*, p. 139, n. 3. This comment is also attributed to Muhammad's uncle Abu Lahab and is echoed in a later Koran verse: "We know indeed the grief which their words do cause you (Muhammad): It is not you they reject: it is the Signs of Allah, which the wicked disdain."—Koran, 6:33.

20. Ibn Ishaq, p. 134. Muhammad repeated these requests in the Koran: "They say: 'We shall not believe in thee until thou cause a spring to gush forth for us from the earth, Or (until) thou have a garden of date trees and vines, and cause rivers to gush forth in their midst, carrying abundant water; Or thou cause the sky to fall in pieces, as thou sayest (will happen), against us; or thou bring Allah and the angels before (us) face to face; Or thou have a house adorned with gold, or thou mount a ladder right into the skies. No, we shall not even believe in thy mounting until thou send down to us a book that we could read.' Say: 'Glory to my Lord! Am I aught but a man, a messenger?'"—Koran, 17:90-93.

21. Ibn Ishaq, p. 134.

22. Ibid., p. 135.

23. Ibid., pp. 136-7.

24. Koran, chap. 18.

25. Ibid., 17:85.

26. "Any one who, after accepting faith in Allah, utters Unbelief,- except under compulsion, his heart remaining firm in Faith - but such as open their breast to Unbelief, on them is Wrath from Allah, and theirs will be a dreadful Penalty."—Koran, 16:106.

27. *Sahih al-Bukhari*, trad. 3852.

CHAPTER 9 – Obey Me!

1. Koran, 20:9.

2. Ibid., 21:58-61.

3. Ibid., 37:97.

4. Tisdall, *The Original Sources of the Qur'an*, p. 92.

5. Koran, 25:5-6.

6. Ibid., 21:98.

7. Ibid., 44:45-46. The "dregs of oil" of the Rodwell translation is rendered as "molten copper" in the Yusuf Ali version and "like molten brass" in the Thomas Cleary translation.

8. Ibn Kathir, vol. 2, p. 36.

9. Ibid., vol. 2, p. 35.

10. "Christ the son of Mary was no more than a Messenger; many were the Messengers who passed away before him. His mother was a woman of truth. They had both to eat their (daily) food."—Koran, 5:75.

11. "They do blaspheme who say: 'God is Christ the son of Mary.' But Christ said: 'O Children of Israel! Worship God, my Lord and your Lord.' Whoever joins other gods with Allah, Allah will forbid him the Garden, and the Fire will be his abode. There will for the wrongdoers be no one to help. They do blaspheme who say: God is one of three in a trinity: for there is no god except one God (Allah). If they do not desist from their word (of blasphemy) verily a grievous penalty will befall the blasphemers among them."—Koran, 5:72-73.

12. Ibn Ishaq, p. 165.

13. Ibn Ishaq, pp. 165-166. The "Satanic Verses" that Muhammad recited to the Meccans were part of Chapter 53, entitled "The Star," beginning with verse 19: "Do you see Al-Lat, and Al-Uzza and Manat the third idol besides? They are the Sublime Birds and their intercession is desirable indeed!" Sublime Birds has been rendered as high-flying cranes or swans, suggesting they are flying upwards to God.

14. Ibn Sad, vol. 1, p. 237.

15. Muhammad revised the verses simply by cutting out "They are the Sublime Birds and there intercession is desirable indeed!" A few verses down he then attacks the goddesses as "mere names" that had no reality for God.

16. Ibn Kathir, vol. 2, p. 40.

17. Ibid., vol. 2, p. 41.

18. Ibid., vol. 2, p. 42.

19. Ibid., vol. 2, p. 43.

20. Ibn Ishaq, p. 151.

21. Ibn Kathir, vol. 2, p. 5.

22. Chapter 19 of the Koran is entitled "Mary." In it Muhammad reveals his belief that Jesus was born of a virgin, though for him this was a sign of divine favor rather than of divine nature.

CHAPTER 10 – Obey You? YOU?

1. Ibn Ishaq, p. 157.

2. Ibn Kathir, vol. 2, p. 24. A Sabian is one who abandons his religion.

3. Ibid., vol. 2, p. 29.

4. Ibid., vol. 2, p, 82. Ibn Ishaq words it similarly: "You know the trouble that exists between us and your nephew, so call him and let us make an agreement that he will leave us alone and we will leave him alone; let him have his religion and we will have ours."—Ibn Ishaq, p. 191.

5. Ibid., p. 192.

6. One of the traditions quotes Abu Talib's son Ali that Muhammad did not attend the funeral: "I heard Ali say, 'When my father died, I went to the Messenger of God and told him, 'Your uncle has died.' He replied, 'Go and bury him.' I said, 'He died a polytheist.' So he replied, 'Go and bury him and do not cause (a scene), then return to me.' I did so, returned to him and he told me

to wash."—Ibn Kathir, vol. 2, p. 86.

7. *Sahih Al-Bukhari*, trad. 7497.

8. Ibn Kathir, vol. 2, p. 98.

9. Ibid., vol. 2, p. 99.

10. Some of the versions state that Muhammad was accompanied by his adopted son Zayd, but most sources indicate he went alone.

11. Ibn Ishaq, p. 192.

12. In a tradition quoted by Ibn Kathir, Muhammad was bloodied from the stoning: "The people of Taif positioned themselves in two lines along his path and as he passed by every time he raised and put down a foot they threw stones at it until his feet began to bleed. His feet streaming with blood, he withdrew and made his way beneath the shade of a palm tree, completely overcome. In that garden were Utba and Shayba, the two sons of Rabia."—Ibn Kathir, vol. 2, p. 101. It is unlikely Muhammad suffered anything more than a few lumps and a bruised ego.

13. Ibn Ishaq, p. 193.

14. Koran, 72:23.

15. Ibn Sad, vol. 1, p. 245.

16. *Sahih Al-Bukhari*, trad. 3895.

17. Swarup, Ram, *Understanding the Hadiths*, p. 68n.

CHAPTER 11 – Winging it

1. Though diverging in many of the details, traditions about the "Night Journey" abound in the literature. This chapter is a synthesis of material found in Ibn Ishaq, pp. 181-187; *Sahih Al-Bukhari*, traditions 3887 and 7517; Ibn Sad, vol. 1, pp. 245-9; Ibn Kathir, vol. 2, pp. 61-75; and in *Tafsir Ibn Kathir*, vol. 5, pp. 550-574.

2. Ibn Kathir, vol. 2, p. 69.

3. Ibn Sad, vol. 1, p. 247.

4. The year of his fanciful journey to Jerusalem, a Christian church occupied the Temple Mount. It had been built over the ruins of a Roman temple that had been built over the ruins of the Second Jewish Temple. During his reign as caliph, Umar replaced the Christian church with a small mosque, later replaced by the domed al-Asqa mosque that still stands today.

5. Ibn Ishaq believes the journey to Jerusalem and the visit to Heaven occurred on different days though close together. Most sources, however, combine them as a single event.

6. *Tafsir Ibn Kathir*, vol. 5, p. 553.

7. Ibn Ishaq, p. 185.

8. Ibn Kathir, vol. 2, p. 67.

CHAPTER 12 – War on the World

1. Ibn Kathir, vol. 2, p. 68.

2. Ibn Ishaq, p. 194.

3. Ibn Kathir, vol. 2, p. 106.

4. Ibid., vol. 2, p. 106.

5. Ibid., vol. 2, p. 104.

6. Ibid., vol. 2, p. 107.

7. Ibid., vol. 2, p. 131.

8. Ibid., vol. 2, pp. 107-108.

9. Ibn Ishaq, pp. 197-8.

10. Koran, 22:39. This is considered to be the first *jihad* verse of the Koran. See *Tafsir Ibn Kathir*, vol. 6, pp. 582-583. Within two years, Muhammad would join the idea of fighting for his cause with a promise of Paradise for those killed fighting for him. "So, when you meet those who disbelieve, strike necks till when you have killed and wounded many of them, then bind a bond firmly. Thereafter either for

generosity, or ransom, until war lays down its burden. Thus, but if it had been Allah's will, He Himself would have certainly punished them. But (he lets you fight) in order to test some of you with others. But those who are killed in the way of Allah, He will never let the deeds be lost. He will guide them and set right their state. And admit them to Paradise which He has made known to them."—Koran, 47:4-6.

11. Ibn Ishaq, p. 203.

12. Ibid., pp. 203-4.

13. Ibid., p. 204. This key passage of Ibn Ishaq's *The Life of Muhammad* is widely quoted in other primary sources, but the wording of the translations vary. Whereas Guillaume translates it as "all and sundry," the version found in al-Tabari's *History*, vol. 6, p. 134, translated by W. Montgomery Watt and M. V. McDonald, reads: "In swearing allegiance to him, you are pledging yourselves to wage war against all mankind." Ibn Kathir's *The Life of the Prophet Muhammad* quotes the same passage in vol. 2, p. 136, but it is translated by Trevor L. Gassick as: "You are pledging to go to war with all kinds of people."

14. Ibn Sad, vol. 1, p. 258.

15. Ibid., vol. 1, p. 259.

16. Ibn Kathir, vol. 2, p. 143.

17. Hamid, Abdul Wahid, *The Companions of the Prophet*, vol. 1, p. 36.

18. Ibn Ishaq, p. 217.

19. Ibid., pp. 221-2.

20. Koran, 8:30.

21. Ibn Sad, vol. 1, p. 260.

22. Ibn Kathir, vol. 2, p. 59.

CHAPTER 13 – Al-Qaeda

1. See Wensinck, A. J., *Muhammad and the Jews of Medina*, for a general description of Yathrib, and Lecker, *Muslims, Jews, and Pagans*, Chapter One: *The Aliya: Orchards and Fortresses*.

2. Ibn Kathir, vol. 2, p. 165. Ibn Sad, vol. 1, p. 271, also quote the Jew: "O Banu Qayla, here is your master! He has arrived."

3. Ibn Kathir, vol. 2, pp. 178-9. Traditions about the length of Muhammad's stay in Quba vary considerably. Though biographies generally give three to four days, some sources say he remained in Quba as long as three weeks.

4. Ibid., vol. 2, p. 180.

5. Wensinck estimates the Jewish population at ten thousand. He notes that the German Orientalist Aloys Sprenger estimated the Jewish population was between seven and eight thousand and the Arab population nine thousand.

6. Ibn Ishaq, pp. 207-8.

7. Ibn Kathir, vol. 2, p. 181.

8. Ibid., vol. 2, p. 217.

9. Wensinck, pp. 51-61.

10. Ibn Kathir, vol. 2, p. 96.

11. Ibid., vol. 2, p. 224. See also Waqidi, Muhammad b. Umar, *Kitab al-Maghazi (The Book of Campaigns)*, pp. 6-7.

12. Ibid., pp. 8-11.

13. "They ask you concerning the sacred month about fighting in it. SAY: Fighting in it is a grave matter, and hindering (men) from Allah's way and denying Him, and (hindering men from) the Sacred Mosque and turning its people out of it, are still graver with Allah, and persecution is graver than slaughter; and they will not cease fighting with you until they turn you back

from your religion, if they can; and whoever of you turns back from his religion, then he dies while an unbeliever—these it is whose works shall go for nothing in this world and the hereafter, and they are the inmates of the fire; therein they shall abide."—Koran, 2:217.

CHAPTER 14 – The Jewish Question

1. These alleged Bible foretellings are discussed in "Muhammad the Paraclete (The Holy Spirit)," an article by Ibn Kammuna at http://www.faithfreedom.org/op-ed/muhammad-the-paraclete/

2. For comparisons of Jewish fables and Muhammad's Koran prophet stories, see *The Origins of the Qu'ran*, Chapter III, by W. St. Clair-Tisdall. Further comparisons were undertaken by Abraham Geiger in an essay "What did Muhammad borrow from Judaism?" which is included in *The Origins of the Koran*, pp. 165-226, and by Abraham Katsh in his book, *Judaism in Islam: Biblical and Talmudic Backgrounds of the Koran and its Commentaries.*

3. Ibn Ishaq, p. 257.

4. Koran, 2:92.

5. Ibid., 3:184.

6. Ibid., 4:153.

7. Ibn Ishaq, p. 258.

8. Ibid., p. 258.

9. "And because of their saying, 'We killed Al-Masih Isa (Jesus the Messiah), son of Maryam, the Messenger of Allah,' but they killed him not, nor crucified him, but it appeared as that to them, and those who differ therein are full of doubts. They have no (certain) knowledge, they follow nothing but conjecture. For surely, they killed him not. But Allah raised him up unto Himself. And Allah is Ever All-Powerful, All-Wise."—Koran, 4:157-8.

10. *Tafsir Ibn Kathir*, vol. 3, pp. 26-7, gives a complete account of Muhammad's version of the ascension: "They surrounded Isa (Jesus) in the house, and when he felt that they would soon enter the house or that he would sooner or later have to leave it, he said to his companions, 'Who volunteers to be made to look like me, for which he will be my companion in Paradise?' A young man volunteered, but Isa thought that he was too young. He asked the question a second and third time, each time the young man volunteering, prompting Isa to say, 'Well then, you will be that man.' Allah made the young man look exactly like Isa, while a hole opened in the roof of the house, and Isa was made to sleep and ascended to Heaven while asleep. When Isa ascended, those who were in the house came out. When those surrounding the house saw the man who looked like Isa they thought that he was Isa. So they took him at night, crucified him and placed a crown of thorns on his head. The Jews then boasted that they killed Isa and some Christians accepted their false claim, due to their ignorance and lack of reason. As for those who were in the house with Isa, they witnessed his ascension to Heaven, while the rest thought that the Jews killed Isa by crucifixion. They even said that Maryam (Mary) sat under the corpse of the crucified man and cried, and they say that the dead man spoke to her. All this was a test from Allah for His servants out of His wisdom."

11. *Musnad Hanbal*, Ahmad bin Muhammad bin Hanbal, trad. 23464, cited at http://www.answering-islam.org/Muhammad/Jews/BQurayza/had.html.

12. Koran, 2:65.

13. Ibn Ishaq, p. 247.

14. Koran verses in which Muhammad relocates Abraham to Mecca are 3:96-7, part of a lengthy chapter called "*The Family of Imran*" that Muhammad composed in Yathrib. They read in part: "Lo! the first Sanctuary appointed for mankind was that at Becca, a blessed place, a guidance to the peoples; Wherein are plain memorials (of Allah's guidance); the place where Abraham stood up to pray; and whosoever entereth it is safe." See also Koran, 2:125-127.

15. The only verse linking Abraham and Mecca that can be found in a chapter that Muhammad was known to have composed in Mecca is Koran 14:37. Here Muhammad gives Abraham the floor: "O our Lord! I have made some of my offspring to dwell in a valley without cultivation, by Your Sacred House; in order, O our Lord, that they may establish regular prayer." This verse is one of seven sequential verses (35 to 41) that appear to be insertions as they break the flow of ideas of the preceding lines. These ideas abruptly resume with verse 42. Given that the seven lines are thematically inconsistent with the chapter, they are most likely verses Muhammad composed in Yathrib after his falling out with the Jews. It can be suspected that Chapter 14 was retrofitted to give Muhammad's Abraham story the appearance of an earlier birth.

16. *Tafsir Ibn Kathir*, vol. 1, p. 373.

17. Koran, 2:125.

CHAPTER 15 – I Bring You Slaughter

1. Waqidi, *The Life of Muhammad*, p. 12.

2. Ibid., p. 21.

3. Ibn Ishaq, p. 294.

4. Earlier that day, at a watering hole called al-Rawla near Badr, Muhammad's men had questioned a Bedouin who was riding a pregnant camel about the Meccan army and Abu Sufyan's caravan, but he denied knowledge of them. When one of the Muhammad's warriors invited him to pay his respects to the "Messenger of God," the Bedouin perked up. "The Messenger of God is with you?" When he was pointed out, the Bedouin said, "Are you the Messenger of God?" Muhammad said, "Yes." The Bedouin said, "If what you say is true, tell me what is in the belly of my camel." Salama, one of the Meccan believers, interrupted and said, "You had sexual intercourse with it, and it has been impregnated by you!" It is not known what happened to the impertinent Bedouin, but Muhammad was scandalized by Salama's obscene talk and turned away from him in anger. The story goes that Muhammad did not scold him about it till later, not until after the slaughter at Badr was finished and some of the prisoners were beheaded and they were returning to Yathrib with booty and captives. Muhammad kept giving Salama the silent treatment, leading Salama to wonder what he had done to offend him. He finally said to Muhammad:

"I seek refuge from God against His anger and the anger of His Prophet. Surely, you, O Prophet of God, keep turning away from me since we were in al-Rawla." Muhammad broke his silence and scolded him. It was all about his obscene language. "As for what you said to the Bedouin— 'You fell upon your camel and it is impregnated by you'—you are shameless and you speak of what you do not know." A sheepish Salama apologized profusely, promising to follow the light of Allah scrupulously from then on, and thus he regained the good graces of Muhammad.— Waqidi, pp. 24-5 and p. 58.

5. Ibn Kathir, vol. 2. p. 264.

6. Ibid., vol. 2, p. 272.

7. Ibid., vol. 2, p. 279.

8. It is worth quoting source material here at length: "Umar ibn Uqba related to me from Shuba, the *mawla* (emancipated slave) of Ibn Abbas saying: 'I heard Ibn Abbas say: When the people stood up, the Prophet fell down in a faint for an hour. Then he was lifted from it and he proclaimed to the believers that Gabriel was with an army of angels to the right of the people, Mikael was with an army on the left of the Messenger of God, and Israfil was with another army of a thousand.'" —Waqidi, p. 36. Adding to this, Ibn Kathir reports: "The Messenger of God said, 'Rejoice, Abu Bakr! I saw Gabriel wearing a yellow turban, holding the reins of his horse, up there between Heaven and earth! When he came down to earth, I lost sight of him for a while, but then he appeared again; he was dusty all over and he was saying, 'God's aid did come to you when you prayed to Him!'"—Ibn Kathir, vol. 2, p.

284. Ibn Kathir continues: "The Messenger of God then left the shelter, dressed in chain-mail, and began urging on the men to battle. He told them of Heaven and gave them encouragement in news of the coming of the angels. The men were meanwhile still in their battle ranks, not yet having advanced against their enemy. The result was that they felt tranquility and confidence."—Ibn Kathir, vol. 2, p. 286.

9. Ibn Kathir, vol. 2, p. 281; Waqidi, pp. 34-5.

10. Ibn Kathir, vol. 2, p. 276.

11. Waqidi, p. 47.

12. Ibn Kathir, vol. 2, p. 272.

13. Ibid., vol. 2, p. 279.

14. Accounts differ as to who dealt Abul Hakam (Abu Jahl) the mortal wound, but all versions agree that Muhammad's servant Abdullah Masud found him alive and cut off his head. In most accounts, Masud brought the head to Muhammad. In one version, however, Masud led Muhammad to the place where the body lay so that he could see it for himself. All versions report Muhammad's joy that his enemy had been slain.

15. Ibn Kathir, vol. 2, p. 292.

16. Waqidi, p. 56. Waqidi earlier relates a tradition that Hudhayfa stepped out to challenge his father when Utba Rabia called for a duel, but Muhammad called him back. Other stories report he assisted in the killing of his father, but this is not supported by the majority of sources, which claim that Hamza alone killed him. See Waqidi, p 36.

17. Muhammad believed people would be physically resurrected and would suffer torment in the flesh if their destination was Hell. During

the time between their death in this world and their resurrection in the afterlife, those whose deeds destined them for hellfire would suffer the "torments of the grave" for their sins in this world, this presumably being the torment of knowing they were going to burn in Hell forever.

18. Ibn Ishaq, p. 306. Abu Jahl, roughly meaning Spawner of Madness, was the nickname Muhammad had given to Abul Hakam.

19. Waqidi, p. 40.

20. Among the numerous examples in the literature of this fantasy life was Muhammad's claim he was visited by angels after the battle of Badr to seek his permission to leave: "The Prophet prayed Asr (afternoon prayers) in al-Uthayl, and when he prayed a bowing he smiled. When he said the greeting he was asked about the smile. He explained that the Angel Mikail had appeared to him riding a female horse with knotted forelock and dust on its front teeth, saying, 'O Muhammad, my Lord sent me to you and He commanded me not to leave you until you are satisfied. Are you satisfied?' The Messenger of God replied, 'Yes.'"—Waqidi, p. 57.

21. Koran, 10:88.

22. Ibid., 8:39.

23. Ibid., 8:60.

24. Ibid., 8:69.

CHAPTER 16 – Murder, Inc.

1. Ibn Kathir, vol. 2, p. 316.

2. Ibid., vol. 2, p. 317.

3. Ibid., vol. 2, p. 320.

4. Ibid., vol. 2, p. 309. An *awqiyya* (also transliterated as *uqiyah*) was a unit of weight equivalent to the weight of forty silver dirhams, each dirham containing about 3.13 grams of pure silver. One *awqiyya*, therefore, is equivalent to 125 grams, which is equal to 4.38 troy ounces. If Abbas paid forty *awqiyyas* of gold, then he gave Muhammad a total of 175 troy ounces to secure his freedom. According to Ibn Ishaq, Abbas was made to pay one-hundred *awqiyyas*.

5. Ibn Ishaq, p. 316.

6. Waqidi, p. 62.

7. Ibn Ishaq, p. 675.

8. The literature notes that Asma's poem contained vulgar language, but the standard translations omit it. The first words of the poem are usually translated as: "I despise."

9. Ibn Ishaq, p. 676.

10. Ibid., p. 676.

11. Waqidi, p. 86.

12. Ibn Ishaq, p. 363.

13. The literature claims a treaty or agreement between Muhammad and all the tribes and clans of Medina was reached after he arrived in Yathrib. It has been tagged the Constitution of Medina, but no signatories are named. This suggests the pact was either a verbal agreement or a unilateral pronouncement on the part of Muhammad that he expected everyone to adhere to. To his mind, the articles came from God, and since they came from God, they were binding on everyone.

14. Ibn Ishaq, p. 363.

15. Koran, 8:58.

16. Tabari, vol. 7, p. 86. The word *banu* means tribe or clan. It is possible Muhammad composed Koran verse 8:58 immediately following the Qaynuqa prank, and it became part of the chapter called

"Booty." The verses of this chapter were composed over a period of several weeks.

17. The literature casts this as a dialogue between Muhammad and the Angel Gabriel: "Muhammad [b. Abdullah] related to me from al-Zuhri from Urwa, saying: 'Surely when the Prophet returned from Badr, they (the Jews) were envious and displayed deceit. Jibril (Angel Gabriel) revealed this verse to him: 'If you fear treachery from any group, throw back (their covenant) to them (so as to be) on equal terms, for God loves not the treacherous.' He said: 'When Jibril had finished, the Messenger of God said to him, 'I fear them.' The Prophet marched to them on the basis of this verse until they yielded to his judgment.' The Prophet got their possessions, and they kept their children and their women."— Waqidi, p. 89.

18. Koran, 8:67.

19. Tabari, vol. 7, p. 86.

20. Ibn Ishaq, p. 364.

21. Ibn Kathir, vol. 3, p. 5.

22. Waqidi, p. 94.

23. Ibid., p. 95.

24. Tabari, vol. 7, p. 97.

25. Ibid., pp. 97-8.

26. Waqidi, p. 96. Waqidi quotes Muhammad: "He (Kab Ashraf) hurt us (Allah and his messenger) and insulted us with poetry, and one does not do this among you (Jews and polytheists) but he shall be put to the sword." Muhammadanism is all about the precedents (*sunna*) set by Muhammad. Because of his example of killing his critics, even today the followers of his cult continue to murder people for "blaspheming" him or his cult.

27. Ibn Ishaq, p. 676.

CHAPTER 17 – Reversal of Fortune

1. This event took place in the days preceding Muhammad's siege of the Qaynuqa Jews and their expulsion from Yathrib.

2. *Sahih Al-Bukhari*, trad. 4003.

3. Some of the sources indicate silver and gold coins were part of the cargo, whereas Ibn Ishaq, p. 364, merely states the caravan was carrying "a great deal of silver, which formed the larger part of their merchandise." This likely means bars of crudely smelted silver since the Meccans had no reason to transport money to Syria. Typically, they transported merchandise for sale at various markets and used some of the profits to buy goods for resale back in Mecca. They repatriated the balance of the profits in the form of Byzantine dirhams and dinars—the currency of the region. There were silver mines in the vicinity of Mecca, but due to the scarcity of firewood it was not possible to fully extract the metal from the ore, hence their commerce with Syria would have been in the form of crudely smelted silver.

4. Ibn Kathir, vol. 3, p. 13. Abu Dasma, meaning "The Dark One," was a nickname for Wahshi.

5. Ibn Ishaq, p. 372.

6. Ibn Sad, *Kitab al-Tabaqat al-Kabir*, vol. 2, p. 46.

7. Waqidi, p. 128.

8. The sword was the two-pointed scimitar named Zulfiqar that was part of Muhammad's Badr booty. This fearsome sword eventually

became the symbol of Muhammad's cult.

9. Ibn Kathir, vol. 3, p. 27.

10. Like many people, Wahshi eventually joined Muhammad's religion to avoid being killed. At the time of his declaration of faith, Muhammad questioned him about the death of Hamza. Now that he was a believer, he could not be killed for it, but Muhammad told him he never wanted to see his face again. Wahshi participated in later battles, but he was shunned for being the killer of Muhammad's uncle. It is said that he took to drinking and died an alcoholic.

11. Ibn Sad, Muhammad, *The Women of Medina*, p. 29.

12. Waqidi, p. 119.

13. Ibn Kathir, vol. 3, p. 48.

14. Ibid., vol. 3, p. 35.

15. Ibid., vol. 3, p. 31.

16. Ibid., vol. 3, p. 40.

17. Ibid., vol. 3, p. 32.

18. Ibid., vol. 3, p. 33.

19. Ibid., vol. 3, p. 34.

20. Waqidi, p. 144.

21. Ibn Kathir, vol. 3, p. 33.

22. Ibid., vol. 3, p. 53.

23. Quoting a tradition reported by Sunni scholar Ahmad ibn Hanbal, Ibn Kathir relates: "When they searched, they found Hamza. His liver had been cut out and chewed by Hind, but she had been unable to swallow it. The Messenger of God, asked, 'Did she eat any of it?' 'No,' they told him. He commented, 'God would never have allowed any part of Hamza to enter hell-fire!'—Ibn Kathir, vol. 3, p. 56.

24. Waqidi, p. 129.

25. Ibid., p. 153.

26. Ibn Kathir, vol. 3, p. 65.

27. Ibid., vol. 3, p. 67.

28. Ibid., vol. 3, p. 67.

29. Ibid., vol. 3, p. 64.

30. Waqidi, p. 162.

31. Koran, 3:121-200. As with much of the Koran, these verses come across as blog entries wherein the author recaps events and comments on them. The Koran can be seen as a collection of such writing done over a period of twenty-three years.

32. Waqidi, pp. 147-148. Ten years earlier, a man named Mujadhdhar of the Khazraj tribe murdered Harith's father, who belonged to the Aws tribe. The killing was in cold blood and was one of the causes of a war between the two tribes that eventually led to the battle of Buath, a major battle on a plain on the outskirts of Yathrib that pitted the Aws and the Khazraj against each other. Each had Jewish allies who were obligated through treaties to join in. Thus Jews ended up fighting Jews. Harith later joined Muhammad's religion as did Mujadhdhar. Harith was unable to suppress his desire to avenge his father. During the thick of the battle, he came up behind Mujadhdhar and struck off his head.

CHAPTER 18 – What's Yours Is Mine Too

1. Ibn Sad, vol. 1, p. 202.

2. Ibn Kathir, vol. 3, p. 72.

3. Waqidi, p. 154.

4. Ibid., p. 154.

5. Koran, 63:5-6. These verses are part of a chapter called "Hypocrites" that Muhammad composed on the return trip from the Mustaliq raid. See Chapter 21: Terms of Endearment.

6. "Umm" means "mother of"

and is the counterpart of "Abu," which means "father of." Umm Salama's formal name was Hind bt. Abi Umayya (Hind, the daughter of the father of Umayya) of the Makhzum clan of Mecca. Abu Salama's given name was Abdullah ibn Abd al-Asad. His mother Barra was one of the six daughters of Abdul Muttalib, the grandfather of Muhammad. Muhammad had numerous first cousins, and some of them such as Abu Salama joined his religion and took part in raids and battles. Others cousins fought against him.

7. Muhammad recruited Abdullah Unays, one of the hitmen who murdered the Jewish poet Kab Ashraf, to carry out the assassination of Khalid Sufyan. The literature quotes the account Unays gave of the murder: "The Messenger of God called for me and said, 'I have been informed that Khalid b. Sufyan b. Nubayi al-Hudhali is gathering a force of men to attack me. He is at Urana. Go to him and kill him.'"— Ibn Kathir, vol. 3, p. 190. The story continues: "I took him by surprise, killed him, and took his head. Then I turned, leaving his women crying over him. . . . I traveled by night, and concealed myself by day until I came to Medina and found the Prophet in the mosque. He said, 'May you prosper!' and I said, 'May you prosper, O Messenger of God.' I placed Sufyan's head before him and informed him of my news."— Waqidi, p. 262. The only reward Unays got from Muhammad for his effort was a stick. At first he was disappointed, but then Muhammad informed him it was a special stick. "It is a sign between yourself and me for Judgment Day. There will

be very few that day with something to lean upon." Unays attached it to his sword, and it was always with him "until, upon his death, it was included in his winding sheet and he and it were buried together."—Ibn Kathir, vol. 3, p. 191.

8. Ibn Ishaq, p. 428.

9. As many men were killed in this incident as were killed in the battle of Uhud, but these represented a more serious loss to Muhammad, as all of them had undergone rigorous training as preachers. They had memorized what existed of the Koran up until then; they had mastered the dogmas of the religion; they knew how to perform the ablution and prayer routines to perfection. Says Waqidi of their preparation: "When it was evening they would gather on a side of Medina, studying together and praying, until it was dawn. They would gather fresh water and firewood and bring it to the rooms of the Messenger of God. Their families thought that they were in the mosque, while the people in the mosque thought that they were with their families."—Waqidi, p. 169.

10. For a month, Muhammad "invoked curses" during dawn prayers against the tribes involved in the massacre. These were prayers of hatred that were repeated in unison by the faithful.—*Sahih Muslim*, trad. 1433.

11. "And if thou fearest treachery from any folk, then throw back to them (their treaty) fairly. Lo! Allah loveth not the treacherous."—Koran, 8:58.

12. A man named Amr Umayya was the only survivor of the Mauna's Well massacre. While vultures de-

scended on the bodies of the slain preachers, Umayya made his way back to Yathrib on foot. During the return trip he murdered two men he encountered in vengeance for the deaths of his comrades. He had determined they were polytheists, meaning it was permissible to kill them, but he was unaware that they had just returned from Yathrib after arranging protection from Muhammad for their tribe and were supposed to be untouchable. The literature does not explain why the Nadir Jews would have an obligation to pay blood money to the tribe of the murdered men.

13. It is likely Muhammad believed his own paranoid fantasy, because by then he was certain that anything that came into his head came from God via the Angel Gabriel. He was gifted with a vivid imagination, and as he waited in front of the fortress gate the image would have suddenly come to him of a millstone being dropped on his head from the battlement. This paranoid fantasy frightened him so that he left abruptly, abandoning his companions without explanation.

14. Waqidi, p. 180.

15. "Whether ye cut down (O ye Muslim!) the tender palm-trees, or ye left them standing on their roots, it was by leave of Allah, and in order that He might cover with shame the rebellious transgressors."—Koran, 59:5.

16. Muhammad later boasted to Safiya, the daughter of Huyayy Akhtab, about whipping the caravan along. "You should have seen me lash the saddle of your uncle Bahri b. Amr and drive him away from here!"—Waqidi, p. 183. Most of

the Nadir Jews, including Safiya's family, settled in Khaybar, which Muhammad attacked several years later. She was taken captive and was forced to marry Muhammad after he tortured and beheaded her husband. She was brought back to Yathrib where she became part of his harem. See Chapter 26: God's Mercy to Man.

17. In his Koran commentary Ibn Kathir had this to say about these verses: "The wealth of the Banu An-Nadir was of the *fai* type (booty obtained without fighting) that Allah awarded His Messenger and for which the Muslims did not have to use cavalry or camelry. Therefore, it was for the Messenger of Allah, and he used it for the needs of his family for a year at a time, and the rest was used to buy armor and weapons used in the cause of Allah, the Exalted and Most Honored."—*Tafsir Ibn Kathir*, vol. 9, p. 555.

18. Koran, 59:7.

19. Waqidi, p. 183.

20. Koran, 59:2-4. As with may of the Koran verses, the real meaning can be extracted by substituting Muhammad for God.

21. Koran, 59:11.

22. Muir says of Muhammad's Koran compositions of this period: "... the tendency of the Coran now [was] to become the vehicle of military commands. In the Coran, victories are announced, success promised, actions recounted; failure is explained, bravery applauded, cowardice or disobedience chided; military or political movements are directed;—and all this as an immediate communication from the Deity."—Muir, *Life of Muhammad*, p. 298.

CHAPTER 19 – Fear and Loathing in Prophet City

1. *Sahih Muslim*, trad. 7051.
2. Ibid., trad. 6913.
3. *Sahih Al-Bukhari*, trad. 7294.
4. Muhammad scandalized even his followers by adding the wife of his adopted son Zayd to his harem. See Chapter 20: Father and Son.
5. *Sahih Muslim*, trads. 6881-6884.
6. *Tafsir Ibn Kathir*, vol. 10, p. 511.
7. Ibid., vol. 10, pp. 511-2.
8. Details about Muhammad's End Time predictions can be found throughout the literature. This chapter, however, is based primarily on the traditions of the Persian Sunni scholar Muslim ibn al-Hajjaj in his *Book Pertaining to the Turmoil and Portents of the Last Hour*, which is one of the numerous thematic sections of *Sahih Muslim*. See traditions 6881 to 7057.
9. The mention of Abu Sufyan and his descendants shows that details were added to Muhammad's End Time stories following his death. Abu Sufyan joined the religion at the time of the conquest of Mecca, which took place three years before Muhammad died. Three decades later his son Muawiya would become the first caliph of the Umayyad dynasty. He or one of his descendants is likely the "Sufyani" alluded to in the End Time story. Muhammad created the core of the end time stories.
10. Koran, 75:10-12. Muhammad composed Chapter 75 of the Koran in Mecca. It is called *Al-Qiyama*, which is usually translated as The Resurrection or The Rising of the Dead.
11. *Sahih Muslim*, trad. 7015.
12. According to *The Encyclopedia of Islam*, (Brill Academic Publishers, Leiden, The Netherlands) Tamim Dari, a well-traveled wine merchant before his conversion, may have been the major if not exclusive source for Muhammad's ideas for the Antichrist. The traditions cited herein, however, suggest Dari confirmed what Muhammad previously preached on the subject, but outdid him in imaginative enhancements.
13. *Sahih Muslim*, trads. 7028-7030.
14. Ibid., trad. 7028.
15. Ibid., trads. 6990-7004.
16. Koran, 44:10.
17. *Sahih Muslim*, trad. 7000.
18. Imam Abu Dawud, *Sunan Abu Dawud*, trad. 4316.
19. *Sahih Muslim*, trad. 7004.

CHAPTER 20 – Father and Son

1. Ibn Sad, Muhammad, *The Women of Medina*, pp. 72-81; *Tafsir Ibn Kathir*, vol. 7, pp. 695-9.
2. Seven of Abdul Muttalib's children—twelve male and six female—have been mentioned in this biography thus far: Abdullah (Muhammad's father), Abu Talib, Abu Lahab, Hamza, Abbas, Safiya and Umayma (Zaynab's mother). The literature records that Abdul Muttalib's daughters had among them twenty-four children. The number of children of the male offspring is not as well documented, but it is known that Abu Talib had at least nine children: Talib, Aqil, Jafar, Ali,

Tulayq, Jumana, Tayta, Fakhita, and Hind (also known as Umm Hani from whose house Muhammad claimed he went up into Heaven). Because of the high birthrate, it is likely that the number of Muhammad's paternal first cousins totaled more than one hundred. There were also numerous maternal first cousins, such as Sad Waqqas. Some of his first cousins joined his religion, others became bitter opponents. First cousins from both factions died in the battles and skirmishes between Muhammad and the Meccans.

3. *Tafsir Ibn Kathir*, vol. 7, p. 696. "For her dowry he (Muhammad) gave her ten dinars, sixty dirhams, a veil, a cloak and a shirt, fifty *mudds* of food and ten *mudds* of dates." One *mudd* is equal to a bushel.

4. "Those whom thy right hand possesses" refers to slaves, but here meaning female slaves.

5. Koran, 33:50.

6. In Koran Chapter 33, Muhammad composed a verse mentioning Zayd by name that recaps the essentials of the episode. Here is the latter half of this lengthy verse: "Then when Zayd had dissolved (his marriage) with her, with the necessary (formality), We joined her in marriage to you: in order that (in future) there may be no difficulty to the Believers in (the matter of) marriage with the wives of their adopted sons, when the latter have dissolved with the necessary (formality) (their marriage) with them. And Allah's command must be fulfilled."—Koran, 33:37, from the Yusuf Ali translation which includes the words in parenthesis. What this verse means in plain

language is that Muhammad used his fictive Allah to command himself to marry the wife of his adopted son—subject to penalties for disobedience if he did not obey himself.

7. *Tafsir Ibn Kathir*, vol. 7, p. 722.

8. Ibid., vol. 7, p. 697.

9. Koran, 33:53.

10. Ibid., 33: 60-61.

11. Ibid., 33:5.

12. Chapter 33 of the Koran is important in that it represents a concentration of evidence of Muhammad's disturbed mind. In the seventy-three verses that make up the chapter, Muhammad has God address him as "The Prophet," recaps the battle of the Trench, and excoriates men who were afraid to fight and die. He gloats about the extermination of the Qurayza Jews, the theft of their property, and the enslavement of their women and children. In this chapter, he authorizes himself to take as many wives as he likes, permits himself to marry the wife of his adopted son, forbids himself from taking any more wives after he has taken as many as he likes, but allows himself sex slaves. He imposes full body and face cover for women when outside the home, threatens people with humiliating punishment in the afterlife for annoying him, threatens to murder his critics, prohibits the practice of adoption, and dishes up images of sadistic torture in Hell awaiting people who disobey him. He also praises himself as a "lamp spreading light" and holds up his behavior as a "beautiful pattern" for people to follow if they want to score well with God. Among the verses is a celestial advisory that Muhammad

must be obeyed: "It is not fitting for a Believer, man or woman, when a matter has been decided by Allah and His Messenger to have any option about their decision: if any one disobeys Allah and His Messenger, he is indeed on a clearly wrong Path."—Koran, 33:36.

13. The belief that God dictated the Koran to Muhammad has survived fourteen centuries and finds its way today even into Wikipedia. In the Zaynab bt. Jahsh entry, we find: "The marriage was used by Munafiqs (Hypocrites) of Medina in an attempt to discredit Muhammad on two fronts, one of double standards as she was his fifth wife, while everyone else was restricted to four, and marrying his adopted son's wife. This was exactly what Muhammad feared and was initially hesitant in marrying her. *The Qur'an, however, confirmed that this marriage was valid. Thus Muhammad, confident of his faith in the Qur'an, proceeded to reject the existing Arabic norms.* When Zaynab's waiting period from her divorce was complete, Muhammad married her." (Italics added for emphasis) Wikipedia entries about Muhammad's religion are largely written by believers, as the article about Zaynab shows. The author of the Wikipedia entry seems oblivious to the idea that the Koran "confirmed that the marriage was valid" because Muhammad was the author of the Koran. (N.B. The above excerpt quotes the Wikipedia entry as it appeared at the time of publication of this book. The Zaynab entry has since been revised.)

CHAPTER 21 – Terms of Endearment

1. In Waqidi, p. 199, it reads, "O *Mansur*, kill, kill!" *Mansur* means conqueror.

2. It is useful to note how the phraseology of the literature obscures Muhammad's responsibility for his actions by attributing them to God. Regarding the Mustaliq raid, it is written: "The people advanced toward each other and fought fiercely. God put the Banu al-Mustaliq to flight and killed some of them. He gave their children, women, and property to the Messenger of God as booty—God gave them to him as spoil."—*The History of al-Tabari*, vol. 8, p. 51. Substituting Muhammad for God gives the real story.

3. This was implicit in a verse that Muhammad composed around the time of the Nadir expulsion: "Also (prohibited are) women already married, except those whom your hands possess."—Koran, 4:24.

4. Ibn Kathir, vol. 3, p. 216.

5. The traditions show that Muhammad's men were concerned about impregnating captive women, not about raping them. Typical of these anecdotes: "Narrated Ibn Muhairiz: 'I entered the Mosque and saw Abu Said Al-Khudri and sat beside him and asked him about *al-azl* (i.e. *coitus interruptus*). Abu Said said, "We went out with Allah's Apostle for the *ghazwa* (raid) of Banu Al-Mustaliq and we received captives from among the Arab captives and we desired women and celibacy became hard on us and we loved to do *coitus interruptus*. So when we intended to do *coitus interruptus*, we said, 'How can we do *coitus interruptus* before asking Allah's Apostle who is present among us?' We asked

(him) about it and he said, 'It is better for you not to do so, for if any soul (till the Day of Resurrection) is predestined to exist, it will exist.'"—*Sahih Al-Bukhari*, trad. 4138.

6. Ibn Kathir, vol. 3, p. 216.

7. Tabari, vol. 8, p. 57.

8. Muhammad never forgot the incident. Miqyas was included on a hit list Muhammad drew up before he conquered Mecca three years later. It is said that Miqyas awaited his death while getting drunk on wine at his mother's house. See Chapter 30: Capitulation.

9. Tabari, vol. 8, p. 52.

10. Waqidi, p. 205.

11. Koran Chapter 63: The chapter begins with the usual self-affirmation of his role: "When the hypocrites come to you, they say: We bear witness that you are most surely Allah's Apostle; and Allah knows that you are most surely His Apostle, and Allah bears witness that the hypocrites are surely liars."—Koran, 63:1. Alluding to Abdullah Ubayy, Muhammad continues: "When thou lookest at them, their exteriors please thee; and when they speak, thou listenest to their words. They are as (worthless as hollow) pieces of timber propped up, (unable to stand on their own). They think that every cry is against them. They are the enemies; so beware of them. The curse of Allah be on them! How are they deluded (away from the Truth)!"—Koran, 63:4. The chapter concludes that true believers should spend "something (in charity) out of the substance which We have bestowed on you."—Koran, 63:10, meaning they should give some of the stolen property that Muhammad gave them—the booty awarded to them after they attacked and killed people who were at odds with him. Seemingly lost on Muhammad were his own final words: "And Allah is well acquainted with (all) that ye do."—Koran, 63:11.

12. Tabari, vol. 8, p. 52.

13. Ibn Ishaq, p. 492.

14. Ibn Kathir, vol. 3, p. 215.

15. *Sahih Muslim*, trad. 6673.

16. Ibn Ishaq, p. 496.

17. Aisha learned of Ali's remarks and never forgot. His lack of support for her was a factor in the split decades later of Muhammad's religion into Sunni and Shia factions.

18. Ibn Kathir, vol. 3, p. 220.

19. *Sahih Muslim*, trad. 6673.

20. Waqidi, p. 211.

21. Tabari, vol. 8, p. 61.

22. Ibid., p. 62.

23. Several versions of the story can be found in the literature. Muhammad's involvement as judge in the matter can only be explained if the accused were Jewish converts from a clan or subclan of the Aws or Khazraj. The Qaynuqa and Nadir Jews did not accept Muhammad's authority and would not have turned their own people over to him, but would have decided the matter among themselves. The presence of Jewish rabbis would therefore have been as advocates to argue for the punishment they deemed appropriate for the offense, but Muhammad decided on death. Abdullah, the son of Umar, was one of the people who took part in the stoning. He said, "I saw him (the Jew) protecting her (the Jewess) with his body."—*Sahih Muslim*, trad. 4211.

24. Tabari, vol. 8, pp. 62-3.

25. Ibid., p. 63.

26. Koran, 24:12.
27. Ibn Ishaq, p. 498.
28. Waqidi, p. 214.
29. Ibn Kathir, vol. 3, p. 222.
30. Ibid., p. 222.

CHAPTER 22 – Trench Warfare

1. Waqidi, pp. 194-5.
2. Ibid., pp. 197-8.
3. Ibn Kathir, vol. 3, p. 128.
4. Presumably through his uncle Abbas, Muhammad learned of the conversation between the Nadir rabbis and Abu Sufyan, for he came out with a Koran verse that alluded to it: "Have you not seen those to whom a portion of the Book has been given? They believe in idols and false deities and say of those who disbelieve: These are better guided in the path than those who believe. Those are they whom Allah has cursed, and whomever Allah curses you shall not find any helper for him."—Koran, 4:51-2. As with many of the Koran verses, the meaning comes through more clearly by substituting Muhammad for God.
5. In most versions of this story, Muhammad awarded credit for the kill to Abdullah Unays after the assassins argued over who landed the mortal blow. In the Tabari version, vol. 7, p. 103, Muhammad settled the matter when he examined their swords and found bone nicks on Abdullah's sword. In the Waqidi version, however, Abdullah Unays is quoted as saying that it was a trace of food on his sword that proved he killed him: "We arrived before the Prophet, and he was at the pulpit. When he saw us he said, 'May your faces prosper!' We replied, 'And may your face prosper, Oh Messenger of God.' He said, 'Did you kill him?' We said, 'All of us claim to have killed him.' He said, 'Hurry and show me your swords.' So we brought our swords. Then he said, 'This killed him. This is the trace of food on the sword of Abdullah b. Unays.'"—Waqidi, p. 193.
6. This is a paraphrase. In Waqidi, Amr says: "I detest that I kill the likes of you. Your father was my friend. So return! You are a young lad. Rather I would like an older Quraysh, Abu Bakr or Umar." Ali replies: "Indeed I invite you to the duel, for I desire to kill you."— Waqidi, p. 230.
7. Ibn Kathir, vol. 3, p. 146.
8. Waqidi, p. 223.
9. Ibn Kathir, vol. 3, p. 141.
10. Waqidi, p. 236.
11. Ibid., p. 240.
12. Koran, 33:9-11.

CHAPTER 23 – The Final Solution

1. *Sahih Al-Bukhari*, trad. 4980.
2. Ibn Kathir, vol. 3, p. 158.
3. Waqidi, p. 245.
4. Ibn Kathir, vol. 3, p. 160.
5. A man named al-Haritha al-Numan was present when Muhammad told them that the man on the donkey they took to be Dihya was actually the Angel Gabriel. For the remainder of his life Haritha boasted about having seen the angel: "I saw Gabriel twice in my lifetime: on the day of al-Sawrayn (the Najjar village), and on the day of the site of the funeral when we returned from Hunayn (a later battle)."—Waqidi, p. 245. This anecdote, reported by numerous

sources, reveals the gullibility of Muhammad's followers.

6. Waqidi, pp. 244-5.

7. An early Meccan convert who was famed for having once been roped together with Abu Bakr and dragged through the streets of Mecca, Talha lost several fingers when he, Muhammad, and others were trapped on the side of Mount Uhud during the battle of Uhud. According to one account, he lost the fingers in a sword fight with Meccan soldiers who were attempting to get at Muhammad. In another account, his fingers were severed by an arrow that had been aimed at Muhammad, but was deflected by his hand.

8. Waqidi, p. 245.

9. Ibid., p. 245.

10. Ibn Kathir, vol. 3, p. 163.

11. Abu Lubaba's behavior could be taken as humorous if it did not reveal the extraordinary terror of punishment Muhammad had inculcated in his followers—punishment by Muhammad in this life and punishment in the fires of Hell in the next. Abu Lubaba remained tied to the palm trunk for twenty days. He would allow his daughter or his wife to untie him so he could perform the scheduled prayers and eat a few dates, then he had them tie him back up. "I will not leave this place until God forgives me for what I have done," he declared. Seeing a benefit in allowing him to make such a spectacle of guilt and repentance, Muhammad allowed him to remain tied up until he became delirious and there was a real chance he could die. The story goes that Muhammad was with Umm Salama in her room when a smile came over his face.

When she asked him about it, he said a revelation had just come to him that Allah had forgiven Abu Lubaba! He sent someone to tell him, but Abu Lubaba refused to allow anyone to release him until he heard it directly from the mouth of Muhammad himself. Muhammad then went out from Umm Salama's room to the prayer area and personally informed him of "Allah's mercy."—Ibn Ishaq, p. 462. In the prayer area of the so-called Mosque of the Prophet in Medina is a pillar called the "Pillar of Abu Lubaba," which commemorates him as a hero of the faith for his act of repentance.

12. Waqidi, p. 251.

13. Ibn Ishaq, p. 463.

14. Ibn Kathir, vol. 3, pp. 165-6.

15. Waqidi, p. 251.

16. Ibid., p. 252.

17. Ibid., p. 252. Waqidi alone identifies the men who beheaded the Jews as Muhammad's first cousins Ali and Zubayr. Ibn Ishaq writes that the beheadings were carried out by the Khazraj, who enjoyed the slaughter because the Qurayza Jews had sided with their enemies during the intertribal wars.—Ibn Ishaq, p. 752, n. 580.

18. Ibn Ishaq, p. 464.

19. Waqidi, p. 253.

20. Ibid., p. 252.

21. Muhammad's wife Aisha, then thirteen years old, later told an interviewer about the woman's death: "Only one of their women was killed. By Allah! She was actually with me and was talking with me and laughing immoderately as the apostle was killing her men in the market when suddenly an unseen voice called her name. 'Good heav-

ens,' I cried. 'What is the matter?' 'I am to be killed,' she replied. 'What for?' I asked. 'Because of something I did,' she answered. She was taken away and beheaded." Aisha, who evidently had a front-row seat of the slaughter, had become so numbed and desensitized by the brutality she was witnessing that she mistook the woman's hysterical and delirious reaction of fear for cheerfulness. The story continues: "I shall never forget my wonder at her good spirits and her loud laughter when all the time she knew she would be killed."—Ibn Ishaq, pp. 464-5.

22. Ibn Ishaq is the primary source for the number of Qurayza Jews executed that day. He wrote: "There were six hundred or seven hundred in all, though some put the figure as high as eight hundred or nine hundred."—Ibn Ishaq, p. 464. However, Ibn Hisham, in his revision of Ibn Ishaq's biography, includes a lengthy note based on information provided by Abu Ubayda—the man who killed his own father at Badr and at Uhud gained fame by breaking a front tooth while extracting metal links from Muhammad's cheek and licking the blood off his face—claimed that the death count of the Qurayza massacre was four hundred. (see Ibn Ishaq, p. 752, n. 580.) The upper range is the most likely as the executions began in the early afternoon after the trench digging was completed and continued until well after dark. The one-per minute rate is given here as a way of conceptualizing the magnitude of the undertaking, but the beheadings could have been accomplished at a more rapid clip. The number

that were beheaded can be roughly calculated based on the assumption of a one-to-one ratio of males to females. It is reported there were a thousand women and children taken captive. Assuming that the prepubescent boys Muhammad spared numbered a hundred and fifty, that leaves eight hundred and fifty captive females of all ages. If the one-to-one ratio holds, then it can be assumed there was a total of eight hundred and fifty males in the tribe. Subtracting the one hundred and fifty prepubescent boys from this number leaves seven hundred Qurayza males who were sent to the trench for slaughter.

23. Ibn Ishaq, p. 752, n. 580.

24. Waqidi, pp. 258-60. Both Waqidi and Ibn Kathir give lengthy, maudlin accounts of Sad's death and funeral.

25. Ibn Ishaq, p. 466.

26. Koran, 33:26-27.

CHAPTER 24 – All Rise!

1. Wensinck, A. J., *Muhammad and the Jews of Medina*, p. 15. Wensinck cites Ahmad b. Yahya al-Baladhuri, a ninth century Persian historian.

2. These precedents were recorded in the numerous traditions about Muhammad, which were compiled by "traditionists"—scholars who collected Muhammad traditions such as Bukhari, Muslim, Abu Dawud, and many others. Along with the Koran, the traditions form the basis for the various schools of Sharia law—the jurisprudence of Muhammad's religion.

3. *Tafsir Ibn Kathir*, vol. 1, p. 641.

4. Muhammad composed a verse about it: "And if he has divorced her (the third time), then she is not lawful unto him thereafter until she has married another husband. Then, if the other husband divorces her, it is no sin on both of them that they reunite, provided they feel that they can keep the limits ordained by Allah. These are the limits of Allah, which He makes plain for the people who have knowledge."—Koran, 2:230.

5. *Tafsir Ibn Kathir*, vol. 9, p. 510. "*Zihar*" refers to the words polytheists used to pronounce divorce. "You are like my mother's back," which is taken to mean, "You are unlawful for me to approach."

6. Muhammad has Allah comment about Khuwayla's predicament: "Allah indeed knows the plea of her who pleads with you about her husband and complains to Allah, and Allah knows the contentions of both of you; surely Allah is Hearing, Seeing. (As for) those of you who put away their wives by likening their backs to the backs of their mothers, they are not their mothers; their mothers are no others than those who gave them birth; and most surely they utter a hateful word and a falsehood and most surely Allah is Pardoning, Forgiving. And (as for) those who put away their wives by likening their backs to the backs of their mothers then would recall what they said, they should free a captive before they touch each other; to that you are admonished (to conform); and Allah is Aware of what you do. But whoever has not the means, let him fast for two months successively before they touch each other; then

as for him who is not able, let him feed sixty needy ones; that is in order that you may have faith in Allah and His Apostle, and these are Allah's limits, and the unbelievers shall have a painful punishment."—Koran, 58:1-4.

7. *Tafsir Ibn Kathir*, vol. 2, p. 506.

8. Koran, 2:219.

9. *Tafsir Ibn Kathir*, vol. 1, p. 604.

10. Koran, 4:43.

11. Ibid., 5:90-1.

12. *Sahih Al-Bukhari*, trads. 6774-6777.

13. *Sunan Abu Dawud*, trad. 4469.

14. "And (as for) the man who steals and the woman who steals, cut off their hands as a punishment for what they have earned, an exemplary punishment from Allah; and Allah is Mighty, Wise."—Koran, 5:38.

15. *Tafsir Ibn Kathir*, vol. 7, pp. 67-9.

16. Koran, 33:59.

17. *Tafsir Ibn Kathir*, vol. 7, p. 30.

18. "And for those who launch a charge against their spouses, and have (in support) no evidence but their own, their solitary evidence (can be received) if they bear witness four times (with an oath) by Allah that they are solemnly telling the truth; And the fifth (oath) (should be) that they solemnly invoke the curse of Allah on themselves if they tell a lie. But it would avert the punishment from the wife, if she bears witness four times (with an oath) By Allah, that (her husband) is telling a lie; And the fifth (oath) should be that she solemnly invokes the wrath of Allah on herself if (her

accuser) is telling the truth."—Koran, 24:6-9.

19. *Sunan Abu Dawud*, trad. 2248.

20. *Sahib Muslim*, trad. 4206.

21. *Sahih Al-Bukhari*, trad. 6816. The tradition continues that Muhammad "spoke well of him and offered his funeral prayer."

22. *Sahib Muslim*, trad. 4206.

23. Ibid., trads. 4145-4149.

24. Ibn Kathir, vol. 3, p. 306.

25. *Sunan Abu Dawud*, trad. 4348. A footnote to this tradition (vol. 3, p. 1215, n. 3799) contains a discussion about whether nonbelievers can be killed for insulting Muhammad: "It is unanimously agreed that if a Muslim abuses or insults the Prophet (may peace be upon him) he should be killed. There is a difference of opinion about the killing of a non-Muslim. According to al-Shaffii, he should be killed. Abu Hanifah is of opinion that he should not be killed. The sin of being a polytheist is far greater than it. Malik maintains that he should be killed except that he embraces Islam."

26. The murdered woman may have been one of the Qurayza women enslaved after the mass beheading of their men. Women were part of the booty, and many ended up as concubines—sex slaves. This would explain why she berated Muhammad.

27. Koran, 5:89.

28. Waqidi, p. 421.

CHAPTER 25 – The Way the Truth and the Life

1. Muir, p. 354.

2. Waqidi, p. 262. This attack became known as the al-Qurta or al-Qurata raid and took place fifty-five months after Muhammad arrived in Yathrib, according to Waqidi.

3. Ibid., p. 272.

4. Ibid., p. 276. Waqidi titles the raid "The Expedition of Ali b. Abi Talib to the Banu Sa'd in Fadak." It took place around the time Muhammad's ex-adopted son Zayd killed an old woman of the nearby Fazara tribe by ripping her apart between two camels.

5. Ibn Ishaq, p. 672.

6. Ibn Kathir, vol. 3, p. 110.

7. Ibid., vol. 3, p. 204.

8. Ibid., vol. 3, p. 207.

9. Ibid., vol. 3, p. 210.

10. Ibid, vol. 3 pp. 243-4.

11. Koran, 5:38.

12. Ibid., 5:33.

CHAPTER 26 – Peace in Our Time

1. Waqidi, p. 283.

2. The verse reads, "And complete the *hajj* or *umra* in the service of Allah. But if ye are prevented (from completing it), send an offering for sacrifice, such as ye may find, and do not shave your heads until the offering reaches the place of sacrifice. And if any of you is ill, or has an ailment in his scalp, (necessitating shaving), (he should) in compensation either fast, or feed the poor, or offer sacrifice; and when ye are in peaceful conditions (again), if any one wishes to continue the umra on to the *hajj*, he must make an offering, such as he can afford, but if he cannot afford it, he should fast three days during the *hajj* and seven days on his return, making ten days in all. This is for those whose household is not in (the precincts

of) the Sacred Mosque. And fear Allah, and know that Allah is strict in punishment"—Koran, 2:196. The words in parenthesis were inserted by the translator, Abdullah Yusuf Ali. The *umra* is the minor pilgrimage to Mecca only whereas the *hajj* is the major pilgrimage that begins in Mecca and follows the ancient sun worship stations beginning at Arafat. The *hajj* terminates with orbits of the temple of Mecca.

3. Waqidi, p. 284.

4. Ibn Kathir, vol. 3, p. 226.

5. Ibn Ishaq, p. 501.

6. Ibn Kathir, vol. 3, p. 226.

7. Ibid., vol. 3, p. 226.

8. Ibid., vol. 3, p. 227.

9. Ibid., vol. 3, p. 227.

10. Waqidi, p. 297.

11. Ibn Ishaq, pp. 504-505.

12. *Sahih Al-Bukhari*, traditions 2731, 2732.

13. Muhammad complained to his wife Umm Salama, the only wife who had accompanied him on the pilgrimage, that no one was listening to his order. She urged him to take the lead and everyone would follow. She is quoted saying, "The Messenger of God put on his robe leaving his right shoulder exposed, and then set out taking a spear with him to urge on the sacrificial beast. . . . Then, as I watched, he pounced with his spear on the animal, crying out, 'In the name of God most great." She added, "As soon as the people saw him slaughter, they too pounced on the animals."—Waqidi, p. 302.

14. Animal sacrifice was an ancient practice of the pagans to obtain favor from the gods. Muhammad sacrificed the animals "in the name of Allah" whereas the polytheists sacrificed theirs in the name of whatever deity they believed in. The same with prayers: Muhammad prayed to Allah for favor, whereas the pagans prayed to gods and goddesses, generally with the idea their prayers would get relayed to the supreme deity through the intermediary. Muhammad deemed their blood sacrifices and prayers invalid because they were misdirected, and that praying and sacrificing to other than Allah merited eternal punishment in Hell.

15. Waqidi, p. 304.

16. Ibid., p. 304.

17. Koran, 48:1.

18. Ibid., 48:25.

19. Ibid., 48:10.

20. Ibid., 48:19.

21. Ibid., 48:20.

22. Waqidi, p. 308.

23. Ibid., p. 309.

24. Ibid., pp 310-311.

25. Koran, 60:10.

CHAPTER 27 – God's Mercy to Mankind

1. Ibn Kathir, vol. 3, p. 248.

2. Ibid., vol. 3, p. 249.

3. Waqidi, p. 317.

4. Ibn Kathir, vol. 3, p. 264.

5. Ibid., vol. 3, p. 261.

6. Waqidi, p. 327.

7. Ibid., p. 330.

8. Ibn Ishaq, p. 515.

9. Waqidi, p. 331.

10. Ibn Ishaq quotes Muhammad giving the order to Zubayr: "Torture him until you extract what he has."—Ibn Ishaq, p. 515.

11. *Sunan Abu Dawud*, trad. 2992.

12. Ibn Ishaq, p. 515.

13. Ibid., p. 515.

14. Waqidi, p. 331.

15. Ibn Ishaq, p. 517.

16. Ibn Kathir, vol. 3, p. 271.

17. Ibid., vol. 3, p. 271.

18. Waqidi quotes one of the participants that all the elite of the Khaybar Jews were slaughtered: "As for the nobility of the Jews, and the people of affluence among them—the sons of Abu l-Huqayq, Sallam b. Mishkam, and Ibn al-Ashraf—had been killed. The remaining people had no wealth and indeed were laborers."—Waqidi, p. 351. This begs the question as to the true number of slain. In the official count, ninety-three Jews were killed, but the number may have been much higher.

19. Ibn Kathir, vol. 3, p. 284.

20. Ibid., vol. 3, p. 284.

21. Waqidi, pp. 341-4.

22. Waqidi reports that Muhammad authorized the murder: "Kharija b. al-Harith related to me from Atiyya b. Abdullah b. Unays from his father, who said: 'I was mending my bow. He said: 'When I arrived I found my companions were going to (fetch) Usayr b. Zarim (a variant of Yusayr Rizam).' The Prophet said, 'I will not see Usayr b. Zarim,' meaning, kill him."—Waqidi, p. 279.

23. The murder of Yusayr Rizam and his thirty Jewish companions is generally placed before the attack on Khaybar, but this chronology does not stand up to scrutiny. According to the literature, Yusayr and the other Jews left Khaybar unarmed, but this would not have occurred prior to the conquest of their valley as they would never have left Khaybar without the ability to defend themselves,

certainly not while traveling with Muhammad's people. After the conquest of Khaybar, however, the Jews were stripped of their weapons and would not have had any choice but to travel unarmed. Also, the lure that was used to draw them out of Khaybar was for Yusayr to meet with Muhammad about giving him leadership over Khaybar. Prior to the attack, Muhammad did not have any power over Khaybar so that the offer of a leadership role to Yusayr could only have occurred after the conquest. This mass murder only makes sense as a punitive action in retaliation for the murder of one of Muhammad's men. It was intended as a warning against rebellion.

CHAPTER 28 – The Station of Abraham

1. Waqidi, p. 361-2.

2. Ibn Ishaq, p. 531.

3. Waqidi, p. 363.

4. See Chapter 13, The Jewish Question, pp. 182-3.

5. Umar's first question to Muhammad was: "Is this the *Maqam* (station) of our father (Abraham)?" The question is devastating to the Muhammadan mythology about Abraham, for it is a smoking gun that reveals Muhammad's Abraham-Kabah stories were post-*hijra* (flight from Mecca) inventions. As noted in Chapter 14, Umar, a native of Mecca, would not have had to ask Muhammad about the stone if it had been part of the history or lore of Mecca. In his voluminous Koran commentary, Ibn Kathir attributed Umar's question to a tradition by Jabir ibn Abdullah, who was present at the pilgrimage and was a

Muhammad "companion" credited with numerous reports about him. Ibn Kathir obtained his version of the Jabir narration through the work of Ibn Abi Hatim al-Razi, a 9th century Sunni scholar who specialized in hadith (tradition) criticism. Jabir's tradition is repeated almost verbatim in Sahih Muslim, one of the two major Sunni collections of Muhammad traditions, but Umar's question is not included.—*Tafsir Ibn Kathir*, vol. 1, p. 373.

6. Jabir's lengthy tradition appears to refer to the full pilgrimage, which was traditionally undertaken during *Dhu al-Hijja* (Pilgrimage Month)—the twelfth month of the lunar year, rather than the minor pilgrimage that Muhammad had undertaken during *Dhu al-Qidah* (Truce Month)—the eleventh month of the lunar calendar. Muhammad only made one full pilgrimage, the so-called Farewell Pilgrimage, a year before his death. The placement of the Station-of-Abraham incident in this chapter is based on the assumption Muhammad invented this particular story at the time of his break with the Yathrib Jews, which was the period when he conceived the Abraham-Kabah narrative. The minor pilgrimage to Mecca in fulfillment of the Treaty of Hudaybiyya would therefore have been the first opportunity for Umar to ask Muhammad about the stone. If Umar posed his questions at the later full pilgrimage, it would mean that Muhammad invented the Maqam Ibrahim story at a later date.

7. "Remember We made the House a place of assembly for men and a place of safety; and take ye the station of Abraham as a place of prayer."—Koran, 2:125.

8. Umar used to boast that this was one of three occasions when Allah transmitted a verse to Muhammad via the Angel Gabriel that was inspired by something he had said to Muhammad. It apparently never occurred to Umar that Muhammad was merely rephrasing his words in God-speak.

9. Ibn Ishaq, p. 531.

CHAPTER 29 – *Jihad! Jihad! Jihad!*

1. Koran, 2:216.
2. Ibn Kathir, vol. 3, p. 258.
3. Ibid., vol. 3, p. 259.
4. This scene is a construction based on details from multiple sources that suggest Muhammad's sermons were often angry and manipulative, intended to get people to fight and die for him. As an example, Ibn Kathir quotes a witness of an incident at the Yathrib mosque: "I heard the Messenger of Allah giving a sermon in which he said, 'I have warned you of the Fire.' And he said it in such a voice that if a man was in the marketplace he could hear if from where I am standing now. And he said it (with such force) that the garment that was on his shoulder fell down to his feet."—*Tafsir Ibn Kathir*, vol. 10, p. 511.
5. Ibn Sad, vol. 2, p. 146.
6. *Sahih Muslim*, trad. 4345.
7. Ibn Kathir, vol. 3, p. 304.
8. Ibid., vol. 3, p. 319.
9. Waqidi, p. 356.
10. Ibn Kathir, vol. 3, p. 301.
11. Khalid, whose full name was Khalid b. al-Walid b. al-Mughira, would become known as "The

Sword of Allah" for his ruthless crushing of a rebellion following Muhammad's death in A.D. 632 and for his later defeat of the Persians in Iraq and the Byzantines in Syria. He conquered Jerusalem in A.D. 637. He was addicted to killing and preferred to annihilate his enemies. He died in A.D. 642. As noted in earlier chapters, his father Walid, who led the reconstruction of Mecca's temple in A.D. 605, was one of the chief opponents of Muhammad in Mecca.

12. Like Khalid, Amr b. al-As emerged as an important military leader after the death of Muhammad. He took part in the conquest of Jerusalem and led an army that conquered Egypt in A.D. 640, twice serving as its governor. He died in A.D. 664. Until he switched sides after the fall of Khaybar, he had been a bitter opponent of Muhammad and was one of the envoys the Meccans sent to the king of Abyssinia seeking the repatriation of the Meccan emigrées. He fought against Muhammad at Badr, Uhud, and the Battle of the Ditch.

13. *Sahih Al-Bukhari*, trad. 335. In this tradition Muhammad also states that he was the only prophet to whom Allah had ever given the right to take booty.

14. Tabari, vol. 8, p. 99.

15. Qureshi, Sultan Ahmed, *Letters of the Holy Prophet*, p. 70.

16. Ibn Kathir tells the amusing story that no one realized Mabur was a eunuch until he was spotted visiting Mariya at one of the confiscated Nadir properties where Muhammad had lodged her. Upon hearing Mabur had gone to her there, Muhammad "ordered Ali b.

Abu Talib to kill him, but Ali let him go when he found him to be a eunuch." Mabur had climbed a palm tree to get away from Ali. He either pulled up his garment to show Ali he was a castrate, or Ali was able to observe this from the ground.—Ibn Kathir, vol. 3, p. 370.

17. Ibn Sad, vol. 1, p. 308.

18. Koran, 78:31-36.

19. The Persians took the cross and other relics of the crucifixion as plunder after conquering Jerusalem in A.D. 614. The Byzantines recovered the relics after defeating the Persians in A.D. 628, and amid great fanfare Heraclius restored it to its place in Jerusalem the following year. It is said that Heraclius carried the cross on his back along the Via Dolorosa to its place in the Church of the Holy Sepulchre.—Norwich, John Julius, *A Short History of Byzantium*, p. 95.

20. The envoy was named al-Harith b. Umayr al-Azdi. His tomb is near Tafilah, Jordan, a historic town south of Mutah that dates from era of the Edomites.

21. A death wish poem attributed to Rawaha goes as follows: "But I ask the All-Merciful for forgiveness/and a large wound that bleeds profusely/Or a spear from a warrior armed with one that goes through/ my intestines and my liver./So that it will be said when people pass by my grave,/God gave him guidance as a warrior, and he behaved well."—Ibn Kathir, vol. 3, p. 327.

22. Abdullah Rawaha was an early prototype of the fanaticized believer. He was one of the first of the Khazraj to join Muhammad's religion, converting when he was in his late teens or early twenties. He

5

was one of the seventy-five people at Aqaba who pledged to give their lives for Muhammad's cause. He was an eager combatant at Badr two years later. He became of note when he proposed burning all the Badr captives alive in a forest fire. He fought at Uhud, the Battle of the Ditch, and Khaybar. Muhammad thought enough of his leadership ability to place him in charge of Yathrib when he went to Badr for a rematch with the Meccans the year after the Uhud defeat. After the conquest of Khaybar, Rawaha was put in charge of the distribution of Khaybar's date produce. It was Rawaha who lured Yusayr Rizam and thirty other Jews out of Khaybar and mass-murdered them. By the time of Mutah, he had become infatuated with the idea of dying in combat, thereby winning a place in Muhammad's Paradise.

23. Ibn Ishaq, p. 533.
24. Ibid., p. 535.
25. Glubb, *The Life and Times of Muhammad*, p. 290.
26. Waqidi, p. 375.
27. Ibn Kathir, vol. 3, p. 347.
28. Ibid., vol. 3, p. 334.

CHAPTER 30 – Capitulation

1. Waqidi, p. 385.
2. Ibn Kathir, vol. 3, p. 379.
3. Ibid., vol. 3, p. 379.
4. Ibid., vol. 3, p. 392.
5. Ibid., vol. 3, p. 392.
6. Ibid., vol. 3, p. 393.
7. Ibid., vol. 3, p. 393.
8. Waqidi, p. 405.
9. *Sahih Al-Bukhari*, trad. 4286.
10. Ibn Kathir, vol. 3, p. 402.
11. Ibid., vol. 3, p. 406.
12. *Sahih Al-Bukhari*, trad. 4281.

13. Ibn Kathir writes, "When the Messenger of God entered the Kabah the day of the conquest, he saw inside it representations of angels and others. He saw Abraham pictured holding divining arrows in his hand. He said, 'May God kill them. They have depicted our elder using divining arrows. What would Abraham have to do with divining arrows?'"—Ibn Kathir, vol. 3, p. 408.

14. Some sources attribute the drawing of Abraham to a Coptic sea captain named Baqum or Pachomios who helped the Meccans rebuilt the temple in A.D. 605 with lumber recovered from his wrecked ship. Historian F. E. Peters quotes Abu al-Walid Muhammad al-Azraqi, a 9th century historian of Mecca, that Baqum "built the roof and inside made pictures of the Prophets, including Abraham and Mary and the child Jesus."—Peters, *The Hajj*, p. 48. The conquest of Mecca, however, took place twenty-five years after the temple reconstruction. Muhammad had been part of the reconstruction crew and would have had access to the interior of the temple thereafter. Had the Abraham image with the divining arrows been in existence at that time, he would have known about it and would not have expressed the surprise and outrage attributed to him in the Ibn Kathir account noted above. The fact it only took a wet rag to erase the drawing suggests it was more recent graffiti, perhaps hastily drawn in mockery of Muhammad.

15. Waqidi, p. 412. The word "Muslim" of the Waqidi quote is

replaced here with the word "Submitter" in order to emphasize the meaning of the word "Muslim."

16. Ibn Kathir, vol. 3, p. 417.

17. Ibid., vol. 3, p. 417.

18. Ibid., vol. 3, p. 417.

19. *Sunan Abu Dawud*, trad. 4474.

20. Ibn Ishaq reports the ceremony in these words: "Then the populace gathered together in Mecca to do homage to the apostle in Islam. As I have heard, he sat (waiting) for them on al-Safa while Umar remained below him, imposing conditions on the people who paid homage to the apostle promising to hear and obey God and His apostle to the best of their ability."— Ibn Ishaq, p. 553.

21. Waqidi, p. 418.

22. Ibn Ishaq quotes her as saying: "I brought them up when they were children and you killed them on the day of Badr when they were grown up, so you are the one to know about them," meaning, about the killing of children.—Ibn Ishaq, p. 553.

23. Ibid., p. 554.

24. Waqidi, p. 417. The word "Islam" of the Waqidi quote is replaced here with the words "Submission" or "Submission to Allah" in order to emphasize the meaning of the word "Islam."

25. Ibn Kathir, vol. 3, p. 418.

CHAPTER 31 – Death to the Gods

1. Ibn Kathir, vol. 3, p. 428.

2. Waqidi, p. 428.

3. Waqidi, pp. 430-5; Ibn Kathir, vol. 3, pp. 423-7.

4. "Assuredly Allah did help you in many battlefields and on the day of Hunayn: Behold! your great numbers elated you, but they availed you naught: the land, for all that it is wide, did constrain you, and ye turned back in retreat."—Koran, 9:25.

5. Ibn Kathir, vol. 3, p. 448.

6. Ibn Sad, vol. 2, p. 188.

7. Waqidi, p. 441.

8. Muhammad had the use of a number of siege machines at Taif. Their origin is unclear. They could have been taken from one of the haciendas Muhammad destroyed prior to besieging Taif, or they could have been brought disassembled from Khaybar and reassembled for the Taif attack. It is also possible they were built on the spot from local materials as some of his followers had learned by reverse-engineering the Khaybar machines how they were constructed. Salman, the Persian convert credited with the idea of digging defensive trenches around Yathrib, was said to have knowledge of their construction.

9. Yazid became a military leader during the caliphate of Abu Bakr and took part in the conquest of Syria. He was appointed governor of Damascus in A.D. 634, then later governor of Syria. He died in A.D. 640 of the plague.

10. Like his brother Yazid, Muawiya also had a military role in various conquests. He succeeded Yazid as governor of Syria in A.D. 640 and was at the center of a later civil war against Ali, the fourth Caliph. He succeeded Ali as "Commander of the Faithful," as the caliphs were known, following Ali's assassination in A.D. 661, becoming the first caliph of the Umayyad dynasty.

11. Waqidi, p. 420.

12. Ibid., p. 462.

13. *Sahih Muslim*, trad. 6091; Ibn Kathir, vol. 3, p. 489. In the *Sahih Muslim* account, Muhammad's wife says, "Spare some water in your vessel for your mother also." Ibn Kathir renders it as, "Keep some for your mother!"—mother being part of the title "Mother of the Faithful" that Muhammad gave to his wives.

14. Ibn Kathir, vol. 3, p. 493.

15. Waqidi, p. 465.

16. The Arabs gave great importance to foster relationships due to a belief in shared atoms. A foster mother was a nursemaid, though in the case of Halima she ended up as Muhammad's substitute mother for the first four or five years of his life. Arabs considered that anyone who suckled at the breast of the same woman shared the same elements they absorbed from her. These elements became a permanent part of their bodies, and therefore they were related to anyone else who had these elements within them. As a result, foster children were also related to the biological offspring of the woman. The foster mother relationship was considered so close that Muhammad prohibited marriage between a man and a woman who had had the same wet nurse. This idea of shared atoms may explain why believers were so keen on drinking water Muhammad spat into or rinsed his mouth with or cleansed his nostrils. He had transmitted his elements to the water, and by drinking it they absorbed his elements. They may have done so as a hedge against Hell, believing God would not incinerate a body that contained elements of Muhammad.

17. *Sahih Muslim*, trad. 2303.

18. Waqidi, p. 469.

19. Ibid., p. 469.

20. Ibid., p. 428.

21. The official story about the fit holds that a Bedouin approached Muhammad to ask if it was permissible to wear perfume during a pilgrimage. Muhammad fell into a swoon, communicated with Allah about the matter, and when he came out of it he informed the man that perfume was prohibited. In several of the Bukhari traditions, Umar invited the Bedouin to get a look at Muhammad while he was in a state of communion with Allah. Umar had covered Muhammad's face with a cloth. "Come!" Umar said, "Will you be pleased to look at the Prophet while Allah is inspiring him?" When the Bedouin nodded, Umar lifted one corner of the cloth so that the man could see Muhammad. He appeared to be asleep and was snoring like a camel.—*Sahih Al-Bukhari*, trad. 1789.

22. Waqidi, p. 475.

23. *Tafsir Ibn Kathir*, vol. 9, p. 319.

24. Ibn Kathir describes Mughira ibn Shuba, one of the important companions of Muhammad, as a "much-married man." "He (Mughira) used to say, 'A man with one wife suffers menstruation along with her, and when she gets sick, so does he. And a man with (only) two wives is right between two blazing fires!' He would marry four women at once, and divorce them all together!"—Ibn Kathir, vol. 4, p. 478.

CHAPTER 32 – *Ménage à Quatorze*

1. Tabari, vol. 39, p. 190.

2. Ibid., p. 165.

3. Ibn Kathir, vol. 4, p. 416.

4. Tabari, vol. 39, p. 187.

5. Ibn Kathir, vol. 4, p. 428.

6. Another instance of such a marriage proposal occurred when a woman stood up during a mosque assembly and brazenly asked Muhammad to marry her, but she got less than she had hoped for her boldness. When Muhammad did not give an answer, a man stood up and said, "Messenger of Allah, marry her to me if you have no need of her." Muhammad grilled him about what he had to offer her as a dowry. He was a pauper and possessed nothing more than the clothes he wore, but he boasted that he had memorized a number of Koran chapters. Muhammad announced that his knowledge of the Koran was her dowry, and he pronounced them man and wife on the spot.—Malik's *Muwatta*, trad. 1069.

7. In his work, *Understanding Muhammad, a Psychobiography*, Ali Sina compiled evidence that Muhammad suffered from acromegaly, a disorder that in the last years of his life caused an abnormal enlargement of his head, fingers, hands, legs, and feet. He became barrel-chested as a result of it and walked with a lurch.

8. Ibn Kathir, vol. 4, pp. 423-4.

9. Koran, 33:50: "O Prophet! surely We have made lawful to you your wives whom you have given their dowries, and those whom your right hand possesses out of those whom Allah has given to you as prisoners of war, and the daughters of your paternal uncles and the daughters of your paternal aunts, and the daughters of your maternal uncles and the daughters of your maternal aunts who fled with you; and a believing woman if she gave herself to the Prophet, if the Prophet desired to marry her—specially for you, not for the (rest of) believers; We know what We have ordained for them concerning their wives and those whom their right hands possess in order that no blame may attach to you; and Allah is Forgiving, Merciful."

10. Tabari, vol. 39, p. 197.

11. "The Role of Aisha in the History of Islam," http://www.alhassanain.com/english/book/book/history_library/various_books the_role_of_Aisha_in_the_history _of_Islam_volume_1/005.html. The article contains traditions by the Sunni theologian Ahmad Ibn Hanbal whose work is unavailable in English except where included in translated works such as those of Ibn Kathir. He recorded numerous anecdotes about Aisha's jealous behavior, most of them citing her as the source.

12. *Sahih Muslim*, trad. 5991.

13. *Sahih Al-Bukhari*, trad. 3821.

14. "He struck me on the chest which caused me pain."—*Sahih Muslim*, trad. 2127. Another tradition found in *Sahih Muslim* does not mention the physical violence but records Muhammad's explanation for her jealousy: "Aisha, the wife of Allah's Apostle (may peace be upon him), reported that one day Allah's Messenger (may peace be upon him) came out of her (apartment) during the night and she felt jealous. Then he came and he saw me (in what agitated state of mind) I was. He said: 'Aisha, what has happened to you? Do you

feel jealous?' Thereupon she said, 'How can it be (that a woman like me) should not feel jealous in regard to a husband like you?' Thereupon Allah's Messenger (may peace be upon him) said: 'It was your devil who had come to you,' and she said: 'Allah's Messenger, is there along with me a devil?' He said: 'Yes.' I said: 'Is devil attached to everyone?' He said:. 'Yes.' I (Aisha) again said: 'Allah's Messenger, is it with you also?' He said 'Yes, but my Lord has helped me against him and as such I am absolutely safe from his mischief.'"—*Sahih Muslim*, trad. 6759.

15. Ibn Kathir related the tradition about the Angel Gabriel's intervention in the matter: "When Mariya gave birth to Ibrahim, the Messenger of God seemed almost to begin having suspicions about him. Then Gabriel came down to him and said, 'Peace be upon you, father of Ibrahim!'"—Ibn Kathir, vol. 4, p. 432.

16. Ibn Kathir, vol. 4, p. 433.

17. Swarup, Ram, *Understanding the Hadith*, p. 79.

18. *Sahih Muslim*, trad. 3506.

19. *Sahih Al-Bukhari*, trad. 5191.

20. The complete verse reads: "Maybe his Lord, if he divorce you, will give him in your place wives better than you, submissive, faithful, obedient, penitent, adorers, fasters, widows, and virgins."—Koran, 66:5.

21. *Sahih Al-Bukhari*, trad. 5191.

22. *Sahih Muslim*, trad. 3507.

CHAPTER 33 – Terror has made

me victorious

1. Muir, *Life of Muhammad*, p. 454.

2. "O ye who believe! what is the matter with you, that, when ye are asked to go forth in the cause of Allah, ye cling heavily to the earth? Do ye prefer the life of this world to the Hereafter? But little is the comfort of this life, as compared with the Hereafter. Unless ye go forth, He will punish you with a grievous penalty, and put others in your place; but Him ye would not harm in the least. For Allah hath power over all things."—Koran, 9:38-39.

3. Most of Chapter 9 of the Koran was composed around this time, and much of it is an argument for people to go to war for Muhammad's cause. In the verses cited above, he threatens divine punishment. In another verse he threatens to expose resisters in the Koran: "The hypocrites fear lest a chapter should be sent down to them telling them plainly of what is in their hearts. SAY: Go on mocking, surely Allah will bring forth what you fear."—Koran, 9:64.

4. A Bukhari tradition quotes Muhammad that he "planned" or "intended" or was "about to" torch the homes (*Sahih Al-Bukhari*, trad. 644), but the same tradition in the online version (www.searchtruth.com) leaves no doubt that he carried it out: "Certainly I decided to order the Muadhdhin (the one who makes the prayer calls) to pronounce *Iqama* (the call to begin ritual prayers) and order a man to lead the prayer and then take a fire flame to burn all those who had not left their houses so far for the prayer

along with their houses."

5. Ibn Kathir, vol. 4, p. 3.

6. Gabriel, Richard, *Muhammad, Islam's First Great General*, pp. 191-7.

7. Ibid., p. 194.

8. The most amusing of the water miracles describes Muhammad's fingers turning into spigots: "The Messenger of God called for a pot and emptied what was in the vessel of water into it. Then he placed his fingers on it and the water gushed out from between his fingers. The people approached and quenched their thirst. The water overflowed until they quenched their thirst and the horses and the riders quenched their thirst; indeed there were twelve thousand camels in the camp, and some say fifteen thousand camels. The people numbered thirty thousand, and the horses ten thousand."—Waqidi, p. 510.

9. Ibn Kathir, vol. 4, p. 16.

10. A letter Muhammad sent to the rulers of the coastal town of Aqaba reveals the bluntness of his threats to crush them if they did not submit. "In the name of the Compassionate, the Merciful, from Muhammad, Prophet of Allah, to the People of Aqaba: May peace be upon you. I praise Allah who is one and except whom there is nobody else to be worshipped." Then he goes on to notify them that he is honoring them with a forewarning before attacking them, that he is giving them the option of accepting his religion or paying a submission tax and consenting "to remain obedient to Allah, His Prophet and his messengers." He instructs them to treat his envoys well because whatever pleases them "pleases me," and he implies that the converse is also true. If they reject his offer, he will have to "wage war (to establish peace and security). Its result would be that the big ones shall be killed and the commoners shall be taken prisoners." The letter continues with Muhammad's assurance that he is indeed "a true Prophet of Allah." It concludes with the words: "If you accept obedience, may peace be upon you."—Qureshi, Sultan Ahmed, *Letters of the Holy Prophet*, pp. 106-7. The parenthetical note was added by Qureshi.

11. To his dying day nearly three decades later, Hudhayfa kept his mouth shut about the names, but many people worried they were on the list. After he became caliph, a distraught Umar, fearful that Muhammad might have considered one of his most faithful followers a traitor, begged Hudhayfa to tell him if he was among those named and was relieved to learn he was not.—Ibn Kathir, vol. 4, p. 24.

12. Abu Amir's son Hanzala had joined Muhammad's religion and was killed during the battle of Uhud. His end came just after he knocked Abu Sufyan from his horse. He was about to kill the Meccan leader when other Meccans came to the rescue and slew him.

13. Waqidi, pp. 512-3.

14. Ibid., p. 513.

15. Ibn Kathir, vol. 4, p. 34.

16. Koran, 9:102.

17. Ibn Kathir, vol. 4, p. 35.

18. Ibid., vol. 4, p. 33.

19. The true believers have always reviled Abdullah Ubayy as a "hypocrite." The title of the section of Ibn Kathir's write up about Abdullah's death is revealing: "An account of the death of Abd Allah b. Ubayy,

may God find him repulsive!"—Ibn Kathir, vol. 4, p. 45.

20. Koran, 9:84.

21. Ibn Kathir, vol. 3, p. 505.

22. Ibn Kathir, vol. 4, pp. 100-1.

23. Tabari, vol. 9, p. 83.

24. *Sahih Al-Bukhari*, trad. 2977.

CHAPTER 34 – Intercession

1. *The 99 Names of Prophet Muhammad* (Islamic Book Service, New Delhi, 2004.)

2. Evidence of Muhammad's pathological drive to aggrandize his importance—grandiosity is the word for it in psychiatry—can be found throughout the literature, as in the array of titles he gave himself. But nowhere is it more clearly shown than in a tradition attributed to Abdullah, the son of Muhammad's uncle Abbas. Abdullah reported, "I posed the following question to the Messenger of God, 'Where were you, may my parents be your ransom, when Adam was still in Paradise?' He replied, smiling so broadly all his teeth could be seen, 'I was in his loins. Then the vessel carried me into the loins of my father Noah, who cast me out into the loins of my father Abraham. My parents never once engaged in fornication. God went on transporting me from respectable loins to chaste wombs, pure and unsullied, and whenever a line split I was always in the better half. God has covenanted prophethood in me and made Islam my pact. He made mention of me in the Torah and in the Bible. All the prophets made clear my qualities; the earth brightens with my light

and the dark clouds with my face. He taught me His Book and gave me honor in His Heaven. He cut off for me one of His own names; the Enthroned One is Mahmud, while I am Muhammad and Ahmad. He promised me that He would reward me with a garden and with al-Kawthar, the river of Paradise, that He would make me the first intercessor and the first for whom there was intercession. He drew me forth, moreover, out of the best marriage for my people, and they are those who give much praise, enjoin good deeds and prohibit sin.'"—Ibn Kathir, vol. 1, p. 140. Despite the absurdity of these claims, his own unshakeable belief in these grandiose ideas about himself convinced many people that they were the truth.

3. A tradition in *Sahih Muslim* attributed to Abu Huraira states: "The Prophet of Allah (may peace be upon him) said: 'There is for every apostle a prayer which is granted, but every prophet showed haste in his prayer. I have, however, reserved my prayer for the intercession of my *Ummah* on the Day of Resurrection, and it would be granted, if Allah so willed, in case of everyone amongst my *Ummah* provided he dies without associating anything with Allah.'"—*Sahih Muslim*, trad. 389. Ummah, also spelled *umma*, is the collective word Muhammad used for his followers and can be roughly translated as his "people" or as his "nation" of believers—the transtribal supertribe of his followers.

4. In Muhammad's own words: "Then ask Allah to grant me Al-Wasilah, which is a status in Paradise to which only one of the servants of

Allah will be entitled, and I hope that I will be the one. Whoever asks Allah for Al-Wasilah for me, it will be permitted for me to intercede for him."—*Tafsir Ibn Kathir*, vol. 8, pp. 38-39. Al-Wasilah refers to Muhammad's idea of the highest station of Paradise, the Station of Glory and Honor.

5. *Sahih Al-Bukhari*, trad. 614. Muhammad later demanded that people say a prayer every time they heard his name or his title "Messenger of God." "May he be humiliated, the man in whose presence I am mentioned and he does not send Salah (prayer) upon me."—*Tafsir Ibn Kathir*, vol. 8, p. 38. This is why his followers say "May peace be upon him" at every mention of his name. This is done to build up a relationship with him to enhance the chances he will intercede for them on the Day of Judgment. "Then intercession for me will be permitted for him on the Day of Resurrection."—*Sahih Al-Bukhari*, trad. 614

6. *Sunan Abu Dawud*, trad. 2769.

7. *Sahih Muslim*, trad. 379.

8. Ibid., trad. 378.

9. In many of the accounts, Muhammad is not on a horse, but is standing on a hill that allows him to observe the multitudes. In this case he presumably leads mankind across the bridge over Hell on foot.

10. Zoroastrianism, a religion that preceded Muhammad by more than a thousand years, warned of the Chinvat Bridge—"the bridge of judgment"—in the afterlife that crosses over Hell and is the place where evil people are toppled into eternal damnation. Muhammad's

Hell bridge was evidently inspired by this teaching. It is likely he learned of the Zoroastrian belief from one of his closest followers, Salman the Persian, a Zoroastrian turned Christian turned believer of Muhammad's religion, who often spent hours with Muhammad discussing religion.

11. Muhammad's imagination knew no bounds, as this tradition about the depth of Hell reveals: "Abi Huraira reported: We were in the company of Allah's Messenger (may peace be upon him) that we heard a terrible sound. Thereupon Allah's Apostle (may peace be upon him) said: 'Do you know what (sound) is this?' We said: 'Allah and His Messenger know best.' Thereupon he said, 'That is a stone which was thrown seventy years before in Hell and it has been constantly slipping down and now it has reached its base.'"—*Sahih Muslim*, trad. 6813.

12. *Sahih Muslim*, trad. 349.

13. Ibid., trad. 349.

14. *Tafsir Ibn Kathir*, vol. 2, p. 27.

15. Muhammad is the "Enthroned One"—one of the titles he gave himself.

16. A version of the story can be found in *Sahih Muslim*: "Abdullah b. Masud reported that the Messenger of Allah (may peace he upon him) said: I know the last of the inhabitants of Fire to be taken out therefrom, and the last of the inhabitants of Paradise to enter it. A man will come out of the Fire crawling. Then Allah, the Blessed and Exalted, will say to him: Go and enter Paradise. So he would come to it and it would appear to him as if it were full. He would go back and say:

O my Lord! I found it full. Allah, the Blessed and Exalted, would say to him: Go and enter Paradise. He would come and perceive as if it were full. He would return and say: O my Lord! I found it full. Allah would say to him: Go and enter Paradise, for there is for you the like of the world and ten times like it, or for you is ten times the like of this world. He (the narrator) said: He (that man) would say: Art Thou making a fun of me? or Art Thou laughing at me, though Thou art the King? He (the narrator) said: I saw the Messenger of Allah laugh till his front teeth were visible. And it was said: That would be the lowest rank among the inhabitants of Paradise."—*Sahih Muslim*, trad. 359.

17. *Sahih Al-Bukhari*, trad. 3885.

18. Ibn Kathir, *Life of Muhammad*, vol. 1, p. 169.

19. Muhammad never admitted that he had erred in his understanding of the Christian concept of the Trinity. In his mind, Christians believed Mary the mother of Jesus was one of the persons of the Trinity. His idea about Mary as God's spouse was shaped by logic. How could God have a son without having a wife?

20. Muhammad also had a misconception about Jewish beliefs. He erroneously believed the Jews took their prophet Ezra, whom he called Uzayr, as a son of God.

CHAPTER 35 – The Farewell Pilgrimage

1. Koran, 9:5.
2. Ibn Kathir, vol. 4, p. 161.
3. Waqidi, p. 538.

4. Ibid., p. 538.
5. Ibn Kathir, vol. 4, p. 233.
6. Ibid., vol. 4, p. 242.
7. The Arabs had always counted their days in terms of lunar months consisting of twenty-eight days, but the Arabic names of the months showed that they abided by the solar cycle. Rabi I and Rabi II, the third and fourth months of the lunar calendar, mean "the first spring" and "the second spring," and Jumada I and Jumada II, the fifth and sixth months of the calendar, mean "the first month of parched land" and "the second period of parched land," clearly referring to the hot summer. A strict lunar calendar consists of only 354 days, so that an unadjusted calendar would cause a rotation of the lunar months backwards though the solar cycle so that summer and winter would become inverted every eighteen years. Jumada would occur during the freezing of winter. To avoid this rotation the Meccans reconciled the lunar cycle with the solar by adding a month every three years or so to bring them back into harmony. They would announce the intercalation during the pilgrimage. For reasons that have never been adequately explained, Muhammad prohibited intercalation.

8. Tabari, vol. 9, p. 113.
9. Ibid., vol. 9, p. 113.
10. The meaning of the word *sunna* is of great importance. *Sunna* is the word in Arabic for example, but Muhammad gave it a broader meaning by calling his behavior and his teachings his *sunna*, his "legal ways" since they were in furtherance of God's cause, that is

to say, Muhammad's cause. This is where the Sunnis get their name. They are the followers of the example of Muhammad, his "legal ways," which include his use of terror and violence against people who refused to accept him as the messenger of God and bow to his authority. This explains the plague of violence and terror caused by his followers today, not to mention the plagues of violence and terror of their predecessors for the last fourteen centuries. The Sunnis form the majority of believers today, but all the minor cults of Muhammad historically have done the same and continue to do so today and for the same reason.

11. Ibn Kathir, vol. 4, p. 255.

12. Ginzberg, Louis, *The Legends of the Jews*, vol. 1, pp. 276-8.

13. Ibn Kathir, vol. 4, p. 271.

14. Ibid., vol. 4, p. 272.

15. Waqidi, p. 542.

CHAPTER 36 – The Death of Muhammad

1. Ibn Kathir, vol. 4, p. 322.

2. Ibid., vol. 4, p. 323.

3. Tabari, vol. 9, p. 170.

4. Ibn Kathir, vol. 4, p. 332.

5. Ibid., vol. 4, p. 332.

6. Ibid., vol. 4, p. 325.

7. Ibid., vol. 4, p. 393.

8. Ibid., vol. 4, p. 363.

9. Ibid., vol. 4, p. 341. The idea of the graves of prophets being turned into places of worship had preoccupied Muhammad for months and found expression in one of the verses of Koran Chapter 9 entitled "Repentance," the last chapter he composed before his death: "They have taken as lords beside Allah their rabbis and their monks and the Messiah son of Mary, when they were bidden to worship only One Allah. There is no Allah save Him. Be He Glorified from all that they ascribe as partner (unto Him)!"— Koran, 9:31.

10. His dying words, now demanding the elimination of all Jews and Christians from the Arabian Peninsula, echoed the virulent sentiments that he had only recently expressed in Koran Chapter 9. "Fight those who believe not in Allah nor the Last Day, nor hold that forbidden which hath been forbidden by Allah and His Messenger, nor acknowledge the religion of Truth, (even if they are) of the People of the Book, until they pay the *Jizya* with willing submission, and feel themselves subdued."—Koran, 9:29. The entire chapter oozes with Muhammad's hatred of people who rejected him. It is also highly defamatory of Jews and Christians, as seen in this verse: "O ye who believe! Lo! many of the (Jewish) rabbis and the (Christian) monks devour the wealth of mankind wantonly and debar (men) from the way of Allah. They who hoard up gold and silver and spend it not in the way of Allah, unto them give tidings (O Muhammad) of a painful doom."—Koran, 9:34.

11. Tabari, vol. 9, p. 183.

12. Ibn Kathir, vol. 4, p. 346.

13. Tabari, vol. 9, p. 184.

14. Ibn Kathir, vol. 4. p. 353.

15. Ibid., vol. 4, p. 355.

16. Ibid., vol. 4, p. 355.

17. Tabari, vol. 9, p. 201.

18. Ibid., vol. 9, pp. 186-7.

19. In a footnote, Edward Gibbons quotes a Latin translation of

a work by Abu al-Fida in which Ali exclaims: "*O propheta, certa penis tuus coelum erectus est!*"—Gibbons, *The Decline and Fall of the Roman Empire*, vol. 4, p. 308. See also, "The Disgraceful and Distressing Things Ibn Hisham Omitted from Ibn Ishaq's Biography of Muhammad," by Louis Palme, http://www.islam-watch.org/authors/139-louis-palme.html

20. The original version of Ibn Ishaq's biography of Muhammad no longer exists, but was replaced with an extensive revision—recension is the word used by academics—by Abdu'l Malik b. Hisham a century after Ibn Ishaq's death. In his version, Hisham famously stated that he had left out things which were "disgraceful to discuss; matters which would distress certain people." This admission is found on the first page of his notes regarding the revision. See Ibn Ishaq, *The Life of Muhammad*, p. 691. Such omissions could be justified in terms of Muhammad's *sunna*. The biographers, historians, collectors of traditions, and Koran commentators were obligated by their belief to faithfully record all that was Muhammad's *sunna*, the example of his behavior in the furtherance of "God's" cause. This is the reason why two-thirds of Ibn Ishaq's *Life of Muhammad*, all of Waqidi's biography, and much of Tabari's History—two important sources for this book—give detailed accounts of the violence Muhammad perpetrated against people who rejected him. It was considered part of his *sunna*. Hisham could justifiably leave out mention of the priapus event, however, as it was an involuntary, post-mortem occurrence and

would not be considered *sunna*.

21. Tabari, vol. 9, p. 203.
22. Ibid., vol. 9, p. 203.
23. Ibn Kathir, vol. 4, p. 372.
24. Muhammad's great grandson Ali b. al-Husayn later repeated the mythology that evolved about these angels: "When the Messenger of God became ill, Gabriel came to him and said, 'Muhammad, God has dispatched me to you to express special honor and respect for you, to ask you about what He knows better than yourself: How are you?' 'Gabriel, I am much afflicted. Gabriel, I am in agony.' Gabriel returned to him the second day, asked him the same and the Prophet responded to him as he had on the first day. Gabriel then came to him a third day, asking as he had on the first, and the response was the same. Then he came to him accompanied by an angel named Ismail, who had charge of 100,000 angels, each angel in charge of another 100,000 angels. He asked to introduce him, and he (the Prophet) asked about him. Gabriel told him, 'This is the angel of death who asks permission to visit you, having never asked such permission of any human being before yourself, and never will of any person after you.' The Prophet responded, 'Allow him in,' and Gabriel did so. He (Ismail) entered and said, 'Muhammad, God has sent me to you. If you order me to take your soul, I will do so. If you order me to leave you alone, I will do so.' 'Would you really do that, angel of death?' he asked. 'Yes,' he replied. 'That was what I was ordered, and I was ordered to obey you.' The Prophet looked over at Gabriel and Gabriel said to him, 'Muhammad, God is longing to meet you.' The

Messenger of God then said to the angel of death, 'Proceed as you were ordered.' And he took away his soul."—Ibn Kathir, vol. 4, pp. 394-5.

25. Ibn Kathir, vol. 4, p. 386.

26. Tabari, vol. 11, pp. 24-5.

27. Zubayr, Muhammad's maternal first cousin and one of the beheaders of the Qurayza Jews, was stabbed to death in A.D. 658 when he was sixty-seven years old. At the time of his death he owned a thousand slaves and, according to Ibn Kathir, his estate was estimated to be worth 59,800,000 gold dinars—Ibn Kathir, vol. 4, p. 488. This is equivalent to approximately 2.1 million ounces of 24K gold. If Zubayr were alive today, his net worth would be more than $3 billion, assuming a gold value of $1,500 per ounce. Abdul Rahman, Talha, Sad Waqqas, and other early Meccan converts also ended up wealthy.

EPILOGUE – A Manual for the Future

1. The Religion of Peace website tracks deadly terror attacks since 9/11 and reports the numbers of dead and wounded. Visit www.thereligionofpeace.com.

2. See: https://en.wikipedia.org/wiki/Mona_Walter.

3. http://www.orthodoxytoday.org/view/six-million-african-muslims-leave-islam-per-year.

4. A video posted on YouTube laments that two million Indonesians convert from Muhammad's cult to Christianity every year. See: https://www.youtube.com/watch?v=3Mdgbnq7tTI.

5. Koran, 9:5.

6. Based on the evidence of the canonical literature, Muhammad could be charged with nearly every crime against humanity included in the definitions of such crimes in Part 2, Article 7, of the Rome Statute of the International Criminal Tribunal: 1. For the purpose of this Statute, "crime against humanity" means any of the following acts when committed as part of a widespread or systematic attack directed against any civilian population, with knowledge of the attack: (a) Murder; (b) Extermination; (c) Enslavement; (d) Deportation or forcible transfer of population; (e) Imprisonment or other severe deprivation of physical liberty in violation of fundamental rules of international law; (f) Torture; (g) Rape, sexual slavery, enforced prostitution, forced pregnancy, enforced sterilization, or any other form of sexual violence of comparable gravity; (h) Persecution against any identifiable group or collectivity on political, racial, national, ethnic, cultural, religious, gender as defined in paragraph 3, or other grounds that are universally recognized as impermissible under international law, in connection with any act referred to in this paragraph or any crime within the jurisdiction of the Court; (i) Enforced disappearance of persons; (j) The crime of apartheid; (k) Other inhumane acts of a similar character intentionally causing great suffering, or serious injury to body or to mental or physical health. See: http://www.preventgenocide.org/law/icc/statute/part-a.htm#2

BIBLIOGRAPHY

99 Names of Prophet Muhammad, Islamic Book Service (New Delhi, 2004).

Abu Dawud, *Sunan Abu Dawud*, trans. Ahmad Hasan, 3 vols. (Kitab Bhavan, New Delhi, 1990).

Arabs and Arabia on the Eve of Islam, ed. L. I. Conrad (Ashgate/Variorum, Great Britain, 1999).

As-Salabi, Ali Muhammad, *Umar ibn Khattab, His Life and Times* (International Islamic Publishing House, Riyadh, 2007).

Biography of Muhammad: The Issue of the Sources, ed. Harald Motzki (Brill, Boston, 2000).

Bodley, R.C.V., *The Messenger, the Life of Muhammad* (Doubleday & Company, Inc., Garden City, New York, 1946).

Breton, Jean-Francois, *Arabia Felix from the Time of the Queen of Sheba*, trans. Albert LaFarge (University of Notre Dame Press, Notre Dame, 1999).

Bukhari, Muhammad, *Sahih Al-Bukhari*, trans. M. M. Khan, 9 vols. (Darussalam, Riyadh, 1997).

Chelhod, Joseph, *Le sacrifice chez les arabes* (Presses Universitaires de France, Paris, 1955).

Chuvin, Pierre, *A Chronicle of the Last Pagans*, trans. B. A. Archer (Harvard University Press, Cambridge, 1990).

Cook, Michael, *Muhammad* (Oxford University Press, Oxford, 1983).

Crone, Patricia, and Cook, Michael, *Hagarism: The Making of the Islamic World* (Cambridge University Press, Cambridge, 1977).

—— *Meccan Trade and the Rise of Islam* (Georgias Press, New Jersey, 2004).

Dashti, Ali, *Twenty Three Years: A Study of the Prophetic Career of Mohammad*, trans. F. R. C. Bagley (Mazda Publishers, Costa Mesa, California, 1994).

Firestone, Reuven, *Journeys in the Holy Lands, The Evolution of the Abra-

ham-Ishmael Legends in Islamic Exegesis (State University of New York Press, Albany, 1990).

Freemon, Frank R., *A Differential Diagnosis of the Inspirational Spells of Muhammad the Prophet of Islam* (*Epilepsia*, 17:423-427, 1976).

Ginzberg, Louis, *The Legends of the Jews*, 7 vols. (The Johns-Hopkins University Press, Baltimore, 1998).

Glubb, John Bago, *The Life and Times of Muhammad* (Cooper Square Press, 2001).

Groom, Nigel, *Frankincense and Myrrh: A Study of the Arabian Incense Trade* (Longman London and New York, Libraire du Liban, 1981).

Guillaume, Alfred, *Islam* (Penguin Books, New York, 1954).

Hamid, Abdul Wahid, *Companions of the Prophet*, 2 vols. (Muslim Education & Literary Services, London, 1995).

Hamidullah, Muhammad, *The Battlefields of the Prophet* (Kitab Bhavan, New Delhi, 2003).

Hasan, Masudul, *Hadrat Othman Ghani* (Kitab Bhavan, New Delhi, 1999).

Hawting, G.R., *The Idea of Idolatry and the Emergence of Islam: From Polemic to History* (Cambridge University Press, Cambridge, 1999).

Haylamaz, Resit, *Khadija: The First Muslim and the Wife of the Prophet Muhammad*, trans. Hulya Cosar (The Light, Somerset, New Jersey, 2007).

Hitti, Philip K., *History of the Arabs* (Palgrave Macmillan, tenth edition, 1970).

Hoyland, Robert G., *Arabia and the Arabs* (Routledge, New York, 2001).

Ibn Ishaq, Muhammad, *The Life of Muhammad*, trans. A. Guillaume (Oxford University Press, 2006).

Ibn Kathir, Abu al-Fida Ismail, *The Life of the Prophet Muhammad*, trans. Trevor Le Gassick, 4 vols. (Garnett Publishing Limited, Reading, United Kingdom, first paperback edition 1998).

———— *Tafsir Ibn Kathir* (Abridged) 10 vols. (Darussalam Publishers & Distributors, Riyadh, 2000).

Ibn Sad, Abu Abd Allah Muhammad, *Kitab Al-Tabaqat Al-Kabir* (The Book of the Major Classes), trans. S. Moinul Haq, 2 vols. (Kitab Bhavan, New Delhi, 1990).

———— *The Men of Madina*, trans. Aisha Bewley 2 vols. (TaHa Publishers, London, 1997).

———— *The Women of Madina*, trans. Aisha Bewley (TaHa Publishers, London, 1995).

Ibn Warraq, ed., *The Origins of the Koran, Classic Essays on Islam's Holy Book* (Prometheus Books, Amherst, New York, 1998).

Johnson, Brian R., *The Art of Dostoevski's Falling Sickness*, a doctoral dissertation (University of Wisconsin-Madison, 2008).

Katch, Abraham I., *Judaism in Islam, Biblical and Talmudic Backgrounds of the Koran and its Commentaries* (Sepher-Hermon Press, New York, 1954).

Khalid, Khalid Muhammad, *The Men around the Messenger* (Islamic Book Trust, Kuala Lumpur, 2005).

Kister, M. J., *Studies in Jahiliyya and Early Islam* (Variorum Reprints, London, 1980).

Koran, trans. J. M. Rodwell (Dover Publications, Mineola, NY, 2005, unabridged republication of the J. M. Dent & Sons 1909 edition).

Korkut, Dede, *Life Alert: The Medical Case of Muhammad* (Winepress Publishing, Enumclaw, Washington, 2001).

Lammens, H., Islam, *Beliefs and Institutions*, trans. E. D. Ross (Routledge, New York, 2008).

—— *La cité arabe de Tàif à la veille de l'hégire* (Nabu Public Domain Reprint of the original version of Imprimerie Catholique, Beirut, 1923).

—— *Fatima et les filles de Mahomet* (University of Toronto Libraries reprint of the original version of Scripti Pontificii Instituti Biblici, Rome, 1912).

LaPlante, Eve, *Seized, Temporal Lobe Epilepsy as a Medical, Historical, and Artistic Phenomenon* (Harper Collins Publishers, New York, 1993).

Lecker, Michael, *Jews and Arabs in Pre- and Early Islamic Arabia* (Variorum, Great Britain, 1999).

The Life of Muhammad, ed. Uri Rubin (Ashgate Publishing Limited, Great Britain, 1998).

Malik, Imam, *Malik's Muwatta*, trans. Muhammad Rahimuddin (Bilal Books, Bombay, 1980).

Mohamed, Dr. Mamdouh N., *Salaat: The Islamic Prayer from A to Z* (B 200 Inc., Falls Church, Virginia, 2005).

Muir, William, *The Life of Muhammad From Original Sources* (Elibron Classic Replica Edition, 2005).

Muslim ibn al-Hajjaj, *Sahih Muslim*, trans. Abdul Hamid Siddiqi, 4 vols. (Sh. Muhammad Asraf, Lahore, Pakistan, 2001).

Newby, Gordon Darnell, *The Making of the Last Prophet: A Reconstruction of the Earliest Biography of Muhammad* (University of Southern Carolina Press, Colombia, 1989).

Norwich, John Julius, *A Short History of Byzantium* (Alfred A. Knopf, New York, 1997).

Numani, Allama Shibli, *Sirat-un-Nabi (Biography of the Prophet)*, trans. Muhammad Saeed Siddiqi and Tayyib Bakhsh Budayuni, 5 vols. (Kitab Bhavan, New Delhi, India, 2000).

Periplus Maris Erythaei, trans. L. Casson (Princeton University Press, Princeton, 1989).

Peters, F. E., *Muhammad and the Origins of Islam* (State University of New York Press, Albany, 1994).

———*The Hajj: The Muslim Pilgrimage to Mecca and the Holy Places* (Princeton University Press, Princeton, New Jersey, 1994).

O'Leary, De Lacy, *Arabia Before Muhammad* (Routledge Reprint, London, 2000).

Qureshi, Sultan Ahmed, *Letters of the Holy Prophet* (Islamic Book Service, New Dehli, 2004).

Rodison, Maxime, *Muhammad*, trans. Anne Carter (The New Press, New York, New York, 2002).

Rostovtzeff, M., *Caravan Cities*, trans. D. and T. Talbot Rice (Clarendon Press, Oxford, 1932).

Rubin, Uri, *The Eye of the Beholder: The Life of Muhammad as Viewed by the Early Muslims* (The Darwin Press, Princeton, 1995).

Ryckmans, G., *Les religions arabes préislamiques* (Publications Universitaires, Louvain, 1951).

Shahid, Irfan, *Byzantium and the Arabs in the Fourth Century* (Dumbarton Oaks Research Library and Collection, Washington D.C. 1984).

———*Byzantium and the Arabs in the Fifth Century*, (Dumbarton Oaks Research Library and Collection, Washington D.C., 1989).

Siddiqi, Muhammad Iqbal, Asharah Mubash-Sharah: *The Ten Companions of the Holy Prophet who were Promised for Paradise* (Idara, New Delhi, 2005).

Sina, Ali, *Understanding Muhammad, a Psychobiography* (Faithfreedom Publishing, Fourth Edition, 2008).

Sozomen, *Ecclesiastical History: A History of the Church in Nine Books* (Samuel Bagster & Sons, London, 1866).

Sprenger, Aloys, *Life of Mohammad: From Original Sources* (The Presbyterian Mission Press, Allahabad, 1851).

Sulaiman al-Ashqar, Umar, *The World of the Jinn and Devils*, trans. Jamaal, al-Din M. Zarabozo (Al-Basheer Company for Publications and Translations, Boulder, CO, 1998).

Swarup, Ram, *Understanding the Hadith, the Sacred Traditions of Islam* (Prometheus Books, Amherst, New York, 2002).

Tabari, Abu Jafar Muhammad b. Jarir, *The History of al-Tabari*, vol.1: *From the Creation to the Flood*, trans. F. Rosenthal (State University of New York Press, 1989).

——— vol. 5: *The Sasanids, the Byzantines, the Lakmids, and Yemen*, trans. C.E. Bosworth (State University of New York Press, Albany, 1999).

——— vol. 6: *Muhammad at Mecca*, trans. W. Montgomery Watt and M. V. McDonald (State University of New York Press, Albany, 1988).

——— vol. 7: *The Foundation of the Community*, trans. M. V. McDonald, annotated by W. Montgomery Watt (State University of New York Press, Albany, 1987).

———— vol. 8: *Victory of Islam*, trans. Michael Fishbein (State University of New York Press, Albany, 1988).

———— vol. 9: *The Last Years of the Prophet*, trans. and annotated by Ismail P. Poonawala (State University of New York Press, Albany, 1987).

———— vol. 39: *Biographies of the Prophet's Companions and Their Successors*, translated and annotated by Ella Landau-Tasseron (State University of New York Press, Albany, 1998).

Teixidor, Javier, *The Pagan God, Popular Religion in the Greco-Roman Near East* (Princeton University Press, Princeton, 1977).

Tempkin, Owsei, *The Falling Sickness, A History of Epilepsy from the Greeks to the Beginnings of Modern Neurology* (The John Hopkins University Press, Baltimore and London, 1994 edition).

Tirmidhi, Abu Isa, *Shamaa-il Tirmidhi*, trans. Muhammad bin Abdur Rahman Ebrahim (Islamic Book Service, New Delhi, India, 2002).

Tisdall, W. St. Clair, *The Original Sources of the Qur'an* (BiblioLife reprint of the 1905 original edition).

Waqidi, Abu Abdullah Ibn Omar ibn Waqid al-Aslami, *The Life of Muhammad*, trans. Rizwi Faizer, Amal Ismail, and Abdul Kader Tayob (Routledge, New York, 2011).

Watt, W. Montgomery, *Muhammad at Mecca* (Oxford University Press, 1953).

———— *Muhammad at Medina* (Oxford University Press, 1953).

———— *Introduction to the Qur'an* (Edinburgh University Press, 1970).

Wensinck, Arent Jan, *Muhammad and the Jews of Medina*, translation and editing by Wolfgang Behn (Klaus Schwartz Verlag, Freiburg im Breisgau, 1975).

Zeitlin, Irving M., *The Historical Muhammad* (Polity Press, Cambridge, Great Britain, 2001).

INDEX

Printed in September 2023
by Rotomail Italia S.p.A., Vignate (MI) - Italy